Fulton Montgomery Community College

BUS115 Quantitative Business Applications

Robert A. Brechner | George W. Bergeman |
James A. Heintz | Robert W. Parry

Dean of Academic Affairs: Diana Putnam

Business Faculty: Laurence Zuckerman CPA, MST and Charlene Dybas M.S.

CENGAGE
Learning·

Australia • Brazil • Japan • Korea • Mexico • Singapore • Spain • United Kingdom • United States

**Fulton Montgomery Community College:
BUS115 Quantitative Business Applications**

Contemporary Mathematics for Business and Consumers, Eighth Edition
Robert A. Brechner and George W. Bergeman

© 2017, 2015 Cengage Learning. All rights reserved.

College Accounting, 22nd edition, Chapters 1-27
James A. Heintz and Robert W. Parry

© 2017, 2014 Cengage Learning. All rights reserved.

For product information and technology assistance, contact us at
Cengage Learning Customer & Sales Support, 1-800-354-9706

For permission to use material from this text or product,
submit all requests online at **cengage.com/permissions**
Further permissions questions can be emailed to
permissionrequest@cengage.com

This book contains select works from existing Cengage Learning resources and was produced by Cengage Learning Custom Solutions for collegiate use. As such, those adopting and/or contributing to this work are responsible for editorial content accuracy, continuity and completeness.

Compilation © 2016 Cengage Learning

ISBN: 978-1-337-30461-0

Cengage Learning
20 Channel Center Street
Boston, MA 02210
USA

Cengage Learning is a leading provider of customized learning solutions with office locations around the globe, including Singapore, the United Kingdom, Australia, Mexico, Brazil, and Japan. Locate your local office at:
www.international.cengage.com/region.

Cengage Learning products are represented in Canada by Nelson Education, Ltd.

For your lifelong learning solutions, visit **www.cengage.com/custom.**

Visit our corporate website at **www.cengage.com.**

Brief Contents

Financial Calculator Guide and Workbook, Second Edition

Michael R. Gordon

Basic Excel Guide and Workbook

Michael R. Gordon

From:
Contemporary Mathematics for Business and Consumers, Eighth Edition
Robert A. Brechner and George W. Bergeman

From:
College Accounting, 22nd edition, Chapters 1-27
James A. Heintz and Robert W. Parry

Financial Calculator

Guide and Workbook

Second Edition

Michael R. Gordon

for

Contemporary Mathematics for Business and Consumers, Eighth Edition

Robert Brechner and George Bergeman

Table of Contents

Foreword

Instructors

The Business Calculator Workbook is designed to be used in conjunction with *Contemporary Mathematics for Business and Consumers, Eighth Edition,* by Robert Brechner and George Bergeman. It is also an additional resource for training in using a business analyst or financial calculator. The calculator selected for this workbook is the Texas Instruments *BA II Plus*™ Advanced Business Analyst, which may be purchased at most office supply stores and department stores for about $30.

Each section in this workbook shows how to use the calculator to work out solutions to problems similar to those found in selected chapters of Brechner's textbook. Most types of problems are covered. Emphasis is on the use of the financial functions of the calculator. The only assumption is that students have the identical calculator. If another model of calculator is used, it is possible, or even likely, that other keystroke sequences will be needed to achieve correct results. Some calculators will not be able to do all the types of problems demonstrated in this workbook. In particular, higher financial and business functions, such as break even analysis, may not be available on all business calculators.

The style of this workbook is similar to that used in the text-book, and students who use the textbook are accustomed to this style. Therefore students using this workbook will find each sequence of problem presentation familiar to them as they embark on gaining proficiency in the use of the calculator.

Students

A business person my often have need to solve a financial analysis or business problem while away from the office. A variety of calculators have been manufactured since 1972 that specialize in employing pre-programmed financial formulas to make the solution of such problems relatively simple. This financial calculator workbook shows how to solve a variety of problems using the Texas Instruments *BA II Plus*™ which may be purchased at most office supply stores and department stores for about $30. This is one of the most popular financial calculators available, and is capable of solving a wide variety of business and financial analysis problems. This calculator has a mode that prompts the user for entries to solve a variety of problem types. This mode is entered by pressing the 2nd function key followed by a key, above which is printed the code for the function. The calculator remains in prompted entry mode until deliberately exited. This is called the *Spreadsheet* mode.

This workbook is organized into sections that contain solution methods of selected financial problem types from *Contemporary Mathematics for Business and Consumers* by Brechner and Bergeman. Each section is named for the type of problem it explains. Each has a problem statement, calculator solution keystroke se-quence, a Try It problem and a group of practice problems to solve. Key stroke se-quences are shown with display results that appear immediately upon completion of the sequence. Entry of numbers is shown in bold, without key symbols. For example:

Emphasis is on the use of the built-in financial formulas and prompted spreadsheets provided by the calculator. Use the table of contents to guide you directly to the section that applies to the type of problem you desire to solve.

A big thank you to Robert Brechner for the many suggestions he provided for this edition of the workbook.

The manual has been extensively modified for easier use. It was rearranged to introduce all calculator modes first. The sample topics and problem sets are now arranged generally in the same sequence they are presented in the text. Text in this workbook has been edited and modified for improved meaning and clarity.

MG
May, 2011

A big thank you to Robert Brechner for the many suggestions he provided for this edition of the workbook.

The manual has been extensively modified for easier use. It was rearranged to introduce all calculator modes first. The sample topics and problem sets are now arranged generally in the same sequence they are presented in the text. Text in this workbook has been edited and modified for improved meaning and clarity.

MG
May, 2011

Calculator Modes

The Texas Instruments *BA II Plus*™ calculator has two modes: *standard* and *spreadsheet*.

Standard Mode

The *standard mode* operates as most calculators do, with the sequence of keys pressed being dependent upon the desired calculation, without any assistance to the user. Operations in the standard mode include both primary key operations and shifted key functions, using the 2nd key to access the shifted functions. Some of the example problems below will be solved using standard mode key sequences and reference the chapter in which these problems are explained.

Spreadsheet Mode

The *spreadsheet mode* includes several types of business problems involving entry of multiple values which are prompted in the display by codes of up to three letters, such as OLD. The calculator has a variety of built-in financial and business formulas that operate on the entered data to produce the desired solution. Using prompted spreadsheets usually requires the user to first enter that mode then clear all previous results. Spreadsheet mode key sequences will be shown for problems whose solutions require them.Examples that use spreadsheet mode include the clearing step.

Mode and Memory Contents at Turn-on

Turn the calculator on or off by pressing the ON/OFF button located in the upper right corner of the keyboard. The calculator will turn itself off automatically after a few minutes of non-use.

Regardless of the mode of the calculator when the user turns it off, it will not be in spreadsheet mode when it is turned on, but previously entered values will still be in memory.

Basic operations

Example: Changing the Number of Decimal Places Displayed

The *BA II Plus*™ calculator's display normally defaults to two decimal places. However, the number of decimal places the calculator displays may be changed. To change the number of decimal places displayed, proceed as follows:

1. Put the calculator into format mode:

FORMAT	
2nd ·	DEC= 2.00

2. Enter the number of decimal places (in this case, 3) to be displayed:

3 ENTER	DEC= 3.000

3. Exit format mode:

QUIT
2nd | CPT

[display: 0.000]

Storing and Recalling Constants – All Chapters

The calculator has 10 memories that retain their contents even when the calculator is turned off. The memories may be cleared individually by storing a zero, or they may all be cleared simultaneously (all 10 memories will contain zero) by using 2nd function keys. Storing a value in a memory location replaces the previous value stored there.

Example: Storing a Value

Store a six digit value for pi (π) in memory 6 of the calculator. This value is 3.14159.

Solution Strategy

1. Enter the value to be stored then select the memory in which to store it.

3.14159 STO **6**

[display: 3.14]

Note that although only two decimal places are displayed (unless a different number of display decimal places has been set), the calculator stores all digits entered. Note also that the stored value is rounded to the number of displayed decimal places.

Example: Recalling a Stored Value

Recall the value for pi stored in memory 6 of the calculator as part of a calculation:

What is the circumference of a circle, to four decimal places, whose diameter is 5.7 inches (the formula for the circumference is $C = \pi D$, where D is the diameter)?

Solution Strategy

1. Set four decimal places to be displayed.

FORMAT   QUIT
2nd | · | 4 ENTER | 2nd | CPT

[display: 0.0000]

2. Calculate the circumference using the formula and the value for pi stored in memory 6.

5.7 × RCL **6** =

[display: 17.9071]

Note that the five decimal value would be 17.90706, but because the calculator has been set to display four places, the final digit is rounded up in this case.

Example: Clearing All Ten Calculator Memories at Once

How may all memories be cleared (set to zero) simultaneously?

Solution Strategy

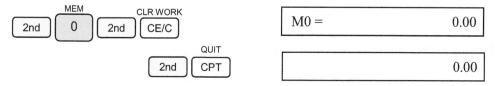

M0 =	0.00

0.00

Arithmetic – Chapters 1, 2 and 3

Problems involving addition, subtraction, multiplication and division use algebraic entry order; that is, the keys are pressed in the same sequence as you would write the arithmetic problem – left to right, with the equal sign key being pressed last.

Example: Addition

What is the sum of 3.4, 18.29 and 11.6?

Solution Strategy

3.4 [+] 8.29 [+] 11.6 [=]

33.29

Try It – a

Evaluate the following expression to two decimal places.

a. 20.44 + 6.8

Example: Subtraction

What is the difference between 134.98 and 56.12?

Solution Strategy

134.98 [–] 56.12 [=]

78.86

Try It – b

Evaluate the following expression to two decimal places.

b. 113.95 – 86.04

Example: Multiplication

What is the product of 4.22 and 34?

Solution Strategy

4.22 [×] 34 [=] | 143.48 |

Try It – c

Evaluate the following expression to two decimal places.

c. 19.99×6

Example: Division

What is the quotient of 12,855.42 divided by 1,112.67?

Solution Strategy

12855.42 [÷] 1112.67 [=] | 11.55 |

Try It – d

Evaluate the following expression to two decimal places.

d. $1,744.84 \div 15$

Example: Mixed Operators

What is the value of 25.1 + 856 − 11.83 × 3.45?

Solution Strategy

25.1 [+] 856 [−] 11.83 [×] 3.45 [=]

| 2,998.98 |

Note: expressions are evaluated from left to right as they are entered. This means that the sum and difference are calculated, then the result is multiplied by 3.45.

Try It – e

Evaluate the following expression to two decimal places.

e. $16 + 38.2 \div 9.42 - 0.87$

Example: Parentheses

When the operator uses parentheses, the *calculator* changes the order of evaluation: it evaluates the expression within the parentheses first, then it evaluates the whole expression, using the result it got for the parenthetical expression as if it were a single value.

Re-evaluate the previous example written using parentheses as follows:

$$25.1 + 856 - (11.83 \times 3.45)$$

Solution Strategy

$$\boxed{840.29}$$

Try It – f

Evaluate the following expression to two decimal places.

f. $(16 + 38.2) \div (9.42 - 0.87)$

Review Exercises

Evaluate expressions 1 through 7.

1. $1466.54 + 234.02 + 691.11$

2. $664.29 - 318.49$

3. 841×70.04

4. $115,000 \div 582.15$

5. $(59.44 - 33.76) \div (32.1 + 56.22)$

6. $1,408 - (15.6 \times 36.87)$

7. $688.43 + (1,882.64 \div 89.41)$

8. Paulo's Passionate Pizza sold two large combination pizzas and 3 medium pepperoni pizzas to a customer during half-time of a local sports broadcast. If a large combination sells for $21.35, and a medium pepperoni is priced at $9.25, and the tax rate is 7.5%, what was the total cost to the customer?

9. Fifteen employees contributed an average of $1.83 per week to the United Way campaign by method of payroll deduction. What is the total annual contribution of the employees?

10. A corporate jet has a fuel tank in each wing and a centerline tank. At 15 degrees Celcius each wing holds 4,640 pounds of fuel and the centerline tank has a capacity of 1,978 pounds. How much of the jet's weight would be fuel if all tanks were full?

Try It Solutions

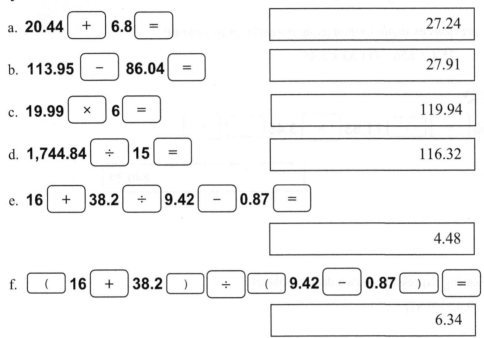

a. **20.44** + **6.8** =   27.24

b. **113.95** − **86.04** =   27.91

c. **19.99** × **6** =   119.94

d. **1,744.84** ÷ **15** =   116.32

e. **16** + **38.2** ÷ **9.42** − **0.87** =

                                                   4.48

f. (**16** + **38.2**) ÷ (**9.42** − **0.87**) =

                                                   6.34

Review Exercise Solutions

1. 2,391.67
2. 345.80
3. 58,903.64
4. 197.54
5. 0.29
6. 832.83
7. 709.49
8. $((2 \times \$21.35) + (3 \times \$9.25)) \times 1.075 = \$75.73$
9. $15 \times \$1.83 \times 52 = \$1,427.40$
10. $2 \times 4,640 + 1,978 = 11,258.00$ pounds

6

Converting Fractions to Decimals – Chapter 3

Although the calculator has no fraction mode arithmetic, a fraction can still be converted to a decimal by entering the fraction as a division problem.

Example: Convert a Fraction to a Decimal

Convert $\frac{3}{8}$ to a decimal.

Solution Strategy

Divide 3 by 8 as follows:

3 ÷ 8 =

0.38

The actual value is 0.375, which the calculator maintains internally. To see this, set the calculator to display three decimal places and do the problem again.

Try It – a-c

Convert the following fractions to decimal expressions to *four* decimal places.

a. $\frac{5}{11}$

b. $\frac{7}{4}$

c. $\frac{1}{6}$

Example: Convert a Mixed Number to a Decimal

Calculate the decimal value of 1¼.

Solution Strategy

First calculate the fraction part, then add the whole number part as follows:

1 ÷ 4 + 1 =

1.25

Try It – d-e

Convert the following mixed numbers to decimal expressions to *four* decimal places.

d. $3\frac{1}{2}$

e. $7\frac{3}{8}$

Review Exercises

Set the calculator to display five decimal places and convert the following fractions and mixed numbers to decimals.

1. $\frac{15}{4}$

2. $\frac{3}{9}$

3. $5\frac{23}{100}$

4. $\frac{5}{6}$

5. $17\frac{4}{10}$

6. $10\frac{19}{30}$

7. $25\frac{2}{9}$

8. $\frac{73}{18}$

9. $9\frac{20}{32}$

10. $7\frac{3}{4}$

11. $\frac{355}{113}$ (When it's converted, does this number look familiar?)

Try It Solutions

First set the calculator to display four decimal places.

FORMAT QUIT

| 2nd | · | 4 ENTER | 2nd | CPT |

Display: 0.0000

Next, convert the fractions.

a. 5 ÷ 11 =   0.4545

b. 7 ÷ 4 =   1.7500

c. 1 ÷ 6 =   0.2917

d. 1 ÷ 2 + 3 =   3.5000

e. 3 ÷ 8 + 7 =   7.3750

Review Exercise Solutions

1. 3.75000
2. 0.33333
3. 5.23000
4. 0.83333
5. 17.40000
6. 10.63333
7. 25.22222
8. 4.05556
9. 9.62500
10. 7.75000
11. 3.14159 (It's π to five decimal places)

Delta Percent (Δ%) – Chapter 6

In business the rate of increase or decrease over time, expressed as a percent, is often useful. A change expressed in this way is often referred to as delta percent (Δ%) after the Greek letter delta, which is used in mathematics to represent change. Delta percent could, for example, represent the change in inventory over two consecutive quarters, or the change in customer complaints across a time span of several months. By knowing the percent change, the business manager can infer a possible trend. Should the trend be undesirable (increasing customer complaints, for example) then corrective measures may be applied in attempt to change the trend.

Example: Delta Percent

If a business measure increases from 48 to 56, what is the percent change?

Solution Strategy

By observation, you can see that the number is increasing, and so you would expect a positive delta percent. Using the calculator in one of its spreadsheet modes:

1. Put the calculator into Percent Change/Compound Interest mode:

2. Clear any previous values that may have been entered:

OLD=	0.00

3. Enter the old value:

OLD=	48.00

4. Advance to the new value by pressing the down arrow key and enter the new value:

NEW=	56.00

5. Advance to the Percent Change display by pressing the down arrow key and calculate the delta percent value by pressing the compute key:

%CH=	16.67

Try It

Customer complaints are down this quarter to 34 from last quarter's count of 47. What is the percent of decrease in customer complaints?

Review Exercises

1. To improve fuel efficiency, Blue Sky Air has decided to remove the paint from their planes to make them lighter. What is the percent change in weight of a 57,300 pound plane if the weight of the paint removed is 186 pounds?

2. Thirty-seven winter coats were sold last month. Management has set a sales goal of 52 coats this month. What percent change does this represent?

3. The National Institute of Science and Technology has created a new type of atomic clock that can be packaged in a 6 inch case. If the previous clock model had a 30 inch case, what is the percent of size reduction?

4. A new model clock has a maximum error of four seconds in 300 years, but an older model is accurate to within one second in 300 years. How does the error of the new model compared to that of the old, expressed as a percent?

5. Last year in March the snow pack in the mountains measured 40 feet. This year the same measurement shows only 36 feet of snow at the same spot. What percent of reduction is this?

6. Ready Crunch Cereal Company has decided to stop marketing 10 ounce boxes and start marketing 13 ounce boxes. What percent change in box capacity does this represent?

7. In a class of 180 students, 16 received a grade of *A* last quarter. This quarter 21 students out of 180 are getting an *A*. What percent of students this quarter are receiving *A*'s compared to last quarter in the class?

8. Nine out of 40 grocery customers made spot purchases on Saturday. On Monday, only six customers in 40 made spot purchases. What is the trend in spot purchase sales from Saturday to Monday?

9. Lily White Paper Company sold 742 cases of 20 pound white laser printer paper during its first quarter of the fiscal year. It sold 836 cases of the same paper during its second quarter. What is the measure of the more recent sales, expressed as a percent increase over last quarter's sales?

Try It Solution

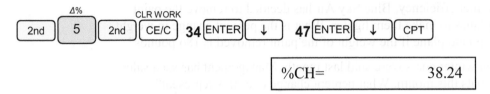

2nd	Δ% / 5	2nd	CLR WORK / CE/C	34 ENTER	↓	47 ENTER	↓	CPT		

%CH=	38.24

Review Exercise Solutions

11. Weight after paint removal is 57,300 – 186 = 57,114. Delta is -0.32%

12. 40.54% increased sales of coats

13. 80.00% reduction in size (-80.00%)

14. 300.00% greater error

15. 10.00% reduction in snow pack (-10.00%)

16. 30.00% increase

17. 31.25%

18. 33.33% reduction in spot purchases (-33.33%)

19. 12.67% increase

Percent and Trade Discount– Chapters 6 and 7

Calculations that include use of the percent key can find a percent of a given value, single and multiple trade discounts and add-on value.

Example: Percent of a Value

How much is 86.3% of 34,877?

Solution Strategy

34877	×	86.3	%	=

30,098.85

Try It – a

a. What is 18% of 74?

Example: Percent Discount

Mercheson's High Fashion, a locally owned dress shop, is having a sale. All merchandise purchased during the sale will be discounted 20 percent. Nora Schwartz has selected a dress marked $59.95. What will be the sale price of the dress?

Solution Strategy

59.95 [−] **20** [%] [=] | 47.96

Try It – b

b. How much is 25% off of $28.53?

Example: Percent Ratio

What percent of 208 is 142?

Solution Strategy

142 [÷] **208** [%] [=] | 68.27

Note: read this result at 68.27%.

Try It – c

c. 43 is what percent of 86?

Example: Percent Add-on

The sales tax rate on the dress that Nora Schwartz purchased in the above example is 7.5%. What is the final amount she must pay, including the tax?

Solution Strategy

47.96 [+] **7.5** [%] [=] | 51.56

Try It – d

d. A certain hat costs $5.82. The store has a 120% markup on all its hats. What should the retail price be?

Example: Multiple Trade Discounts

To promote aging stock, HD Supply Co., an commercial sprinkler and pipe fixture business, is offering trade discounts of 22/14/6 on selected items. If a 6" five-way hydro-indexing valve retails for $386.35, what would the net price be after all discounts are taken?

Solution Strategy

[−] [%] [−] [%] [−] [%] [=]

386.35 22 14 6

Try It – e

e. After taking trade discounts of 30/12/2, what should the net price be for an item that retails for $684.98?

Review Exercises

1. How much is 81% of $\frac{11}{4}$, expressed as a decimal number to four decimal places?

2. A recent movie runs 19% longer than the "average" movie time of 94 minutes. How many minutes does it take to show the movie?

3. A calculator that retails for $29.85 is on sale for 15% off. A sign at the display says the discount will be taken at the checkout register. What is the effective sale price of the calculator?

4. With full fuel tanks, a small airplane can fly 450 miles. The pilot must plan to land with a 20% fuel reserve. What is the maximum range she can plan to fly before landing to refuel?

5. Gil Aguirre had his automotive technician add an aftermarket chip to the engine computer in his BMW. The manufacturer of this chip advertises it will improve fuel economy 14%. This car's EPA fuel economy rating for highway driving is 25.6 miles per gallon. What highway driving fuel economy figure should Gil expect with the aftermarket chip installed?

6. Brecke Millwork Supply, a forest products wholesaler, is offering their retail customers a promotional discount on ¾ inch CDX Douglass Fir plywood. If the normal discount is 38% and the promotion allows a 12% discount on top of that, what would be the price to the retailer of a 4 x 8 foot sheet that retails for $21.39?

7. Three weeks ago an open barrel (without a top) full of water weighed 586 pounds. Since then 12% of the water has evaporated. What is the weight of the barrel and water now if the empty barrel weighs 56 pounds?

8. Paula Erickson receives an employee discount of 20% on the price of all merchandise she buys at company stores, on top of any promotional discounts that may be offered. If a Cuisinart countertop mixer that retails for $124.99 is on sale for 25% off, what out-the-door price will Paula pay if state sales tax is 8.5%?

Try It Solutions

a. **18** % **×** **74** =   13.32

b. **28.53** − **25** % =   21.40

c. **43** ÷ **86** % =   50.00

d. **5.82** + **120** % =   12.80

e. **684.98** − **30** % **12** − % **2** − % =

    413.51

Review Exercise Solutions

1. 2.2275

2. 111.86 minutes

3. $25.37

4. 360 miles

5. 29.2 miles per gallon

6. $11.67

7. 586 − 56 − 12% + 56 = 522.4 pounds (The weight of the barrel doesn't change. Only the water weight is reduced)

8. $81.37

Profit Margin – Chapter 8

A business that sells goods or services must make a profit to stay in business. This means that the cost of producing services or purchasing goods must be less than the price for which they are sold to the consumer. Cost of goods sold is a major factor in determining the retail price. So are overhead expenses such as wages, insurance, facilities lease, power and heat. Combined, all cost factors should total less than the selling price for there to be a profit, however overhead is usually apportioned. So a percentage of overhead is applied to all products and services based upon an assumed sales volume, and the retail price is determined by a *percentage markup*, or *gross profit margin*, applied to the purchase cost. **Gross profit margin** is defined as the difference between the selling price and the cost, expressed as a percentage of the selling price. **Markup** is the difference between selling price and cost, expressed as a percentage of the cost. This section deals *only* with gross profit margin.

The calculator has a profit margin worksheet, entered by pressing the two keys:

keys:

In this problem set, three variables are employed: CST (**cost**), SEL (**sel**ling price) and MAR (gross profit **mar**gin). Values for any two of these may be entered, and then the value for the third one computed.

Example: Cost

The selling price of a calculator is $32.48 and its gross profit margin is 45%. What is its cost?

Solution Strategy

1. Enter the profit margin worksheet:

CST=	0.00

   Note: if the display does not say zero, then clear the worksheet:

2. Enter the selling price:

   [↓] **32.48** [ENTER]

SEL=	32.48

3. Enter the gross profit margin:

   [↓] **45** [ENTER]

MAR=	45.00

4. Compute the cost:

   [↓] [CPT]

CST=	17.86

Try It – a

a. What would the cost for an in-dash AM/FM stereo/CD player be if it sells for $286.98 and the gross profit margin is 35%?

Example: Selling Price

What should the selling price be for a hydrotherapy tub that costs $633.58 and has a gross profit margin of 60%?

Solution Strategy

1. Enter the profit margin worksheet:

PROFIT

CST=	0.00

Note: if the display does not say zero, then clear the worksheet:

CLR WORK

2. Enter the cost:

633.58 ENTER

CST=	633.58

3. Enter the gross profit margin:

↑ **60** ENTER

MAR=	60.00

4. Compute the selling price:

↑ CPT

SEL=	1,583.95

Try It – b

b. What should the selling price of a three pound hammer that cost $18.72 if the gross profit margin is 40%?

Example: Markup Percentage

What is the gross profit margin of a suit that costs $95.31 and sells for $175.00?

Solution Strategy

1. Enter the profit margin worksheet:

PROFIT

CST=	0.00

Note: if the display does not say zero, then clear the worksheet:

CLR WORK

2. Enter the cost:

95.31 ENTER

CST=	95.31

3. Enter the selling price:

↓ **175** ENTER

SEL=	175.00

4. Compute the gross profit margin:

    | ↓ | CPT |

    | MAR= | 45.54 |

Try It – c

c. What is the gross profit margin of a saddle costing $846 and selling for $1449.99?

Review Exercises

1. An MP3 player sells for $49.95 and its gross profit margin is 32%. What is its cost?

2. Contractor's wheelbarrows sell for $79.95 and have a gross profit margin of 47.5%. How much do they cost the dealer?

3. A gross profit margin of 44% is applied to an item costing $18.44. What should the selling price be?

4. How much should a coat sell for if it cost $58.27 and the gross profit margin is 55%?

5. What is the gross profit margin of a table saw that costs $214.58 and sells for $324.99?

6. A storage shed that retails for $449.95 costs $275. What is the gross profit margin?

Try It Solutions

a.
                PROFIT   CLR WORK
    | 2nd | | 3 | | 2nd | | CE/C | | CST= | 0.00 |

    | ↓ | **286.98** | ENTER | | SEL= | 286.98 |

    | ↓ | **35** | ENTER | | MAR= | 35.00 |

    | ↓ | CPT | | CST= | 186.54 |

b.
                PROFIT   CLR WORK
    | 2nd | | 3 | | 2nd | | CE/C | | CST= | 0.00 |

    18.72 | ENTER | | CST= | 18.72 |

    | ↑ | **40** | ENTER | | MAR= | 40.00 |

    | ↑ | CPT | | SEL= | 31.20 |

c.

Key presses	Display
[2nd] [3 (PROFIT)] [2nd] [CE/C (CLR WORK)]	CST= 0.00
846 [ENTER]	CST= 846.00
[↓] 1449.99 [ENTER]	SEL= 1449.99
[↓] [CPT]	MAR= 41.65

Review Exercise Solutions

1. $33.97
2. $41.97
3. $32.93
4. $129.49
5. 33.97%
6. 38.88%

Simple Interest – Chapter 10

Interest

Simple interest may be calculated by using the formula,

$$I = PRT,$$

where I is the amount of interest obtained from the principal, P, multiplied by the annual interest rate, R, multiplied by the time, T. Time is expressed in terms of years or fraction of years. Typically, simple interest is used for short term (less than one year) financial paper, such as notes and bonds, but may also be used for long term debt or time deposits. As mentioned in Chapter 10, the number of days used for a year may be either 360 for **ordinary** interest, or 365 for **exact** interest.

Example: Interest

How much interest will a deposit of $3,635 earn in four years if it earns 6.5% simple interest?

Solution Strategy

Multiply the principal times the rate times the time:

3635 ⊠ 6.5 % ⊠ 4 = | 945.10

Example: Simple Note – Interest

What is the interest on a 102 day note for $512 at 8% ordinary interest?

Solution Strategy

Use the simple interest formula, with the time represented by a fraction of a year, $\frac{102}{360}$.

512 ⊠ 8 % ⊠ 102 ÷ 360 =

| 11.61

Try It – a-c

a. How much interest does a time $58,000 deposit earn in 3 ½ years at 5.5% simple interest?

b. A deposit of $648 earns 10.8% ordinary interest. How much interest is paid at 284 days if the deposit account is closed?

c. The Wayne State Federal Credit Union provides short term notes at 4.675% exact interest. How much interest would be owed on a 170 day $862 note?

Maturity Value

The **maturity value** of a simple interest note is the interest it earns plus the principal. Maturity value may be obtained by either of two formulas:

$$MV = P + I \quad \text{or} \quad MV = P(1+RT)$$

The decision of which formula to use will depend upon the information available.

Example: Maturity Value

A deposit of $832.88 will earn $54.11 interest at maturity. What is the deposit's maturity value?

Solution Strategy

Use the formula for maturity value that adds principal and interest:

+ | = | 886.99

Example: Simple Note – Maturity Value

A simple note for $5,000 matures in 6 years and earns 3.875% annually. What is the note's maturity value?

Solution Strategy

Use the formula for maturity value that adds 1 to the product of the interest and the time, then multiplies the result times the principal:

6 ⎡ × ⎤ **3.875** ⎡ % ⎤ ⎡ + ⎤ **1** ⎡ × ⎤ **5000** ⎡ = ⎤

6,162.50

Try It – d-e

   d. What is the maturity value of a 4% simple interest note for $8,600 for 3 months?

   e. A principal of $328.89 has earned $34.22. What is the maturity value?

Review Exercises

1. Calculate the interest on an 8% simple interest loan for $17,580 for five years.

2. What is the maturity value of a $1,940, 6 year loan at 7.75% simple interest?

3. A principal of $694 earned $61.56 simple interest. What was the maturity value?

4. A 270 day, 5% ordinary interest note for $3,250 has what value at maturity?

5. How much interest will be owed on an $86,450 loan at 6.125% exact interest at the end of 86 days?

6. If Jim borrows $500 at 5.5% simple interest for 180 days, how much will he owe when the loan matures?

7. How much interest will $392 earn in an 8.5% savings account in 3 years?

8. What is the maturity value of a 300 day 6.75% exact interest note for $810?

Try It Solutions

   a. **58000** ⎡ × ⎤ **3.5** ⎡ × ⎤ **5.5** ⎡ % ⎤ ⎡ = ⎤

11,165.00

   b. **648** ⎡ × ⎤ **10.8** ⎡ % ⎤ ⎡ × ⎤ **284** ⎡ ÷ ⎤ **360** ⎡ = ⎤

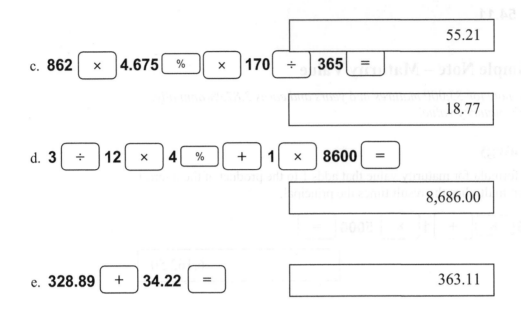

c. **862** $\boxed{\times}$ **4.675** $\boxed{\%}$ $\boxed{\times}$ **170** $\boxed{\div}$ **365** $\boxed{=}$

| | 55.21 |

| | 18.77 |

d. **3** $\boxed{\div}$ **12** $\boxed{\times}$ **4** $\boxed{\%}$ $\boxed{+}$ **1** $\boxed{\times}$ **8600** $\boxed{=}$

| | 8,686.00 |

e. **328.89** $\boxed{+}$ **34.22** $\boxed{=}$

| | 363.11 |

Review Exercise Solutions

1. $7,032.00
2. $2,842.10
3. $755.56
4. $3,371.88
5. $1,246.88
6. $513.75
7. $99.96
8. $854.94

Y^x key: Universal Power and Time Value of Money – Chapters 11 and 12

Formulas in Chapters 11 and 12 provide direct ways of computing the future value of money, present value of money, and various numerical aspects of sinking funds, annuities and debt amortization. The calculator has special functions in the prompted spreadsheet mode for solving these problems, but if the user wants to use a formula, then the universal power key, y^x, may be used.

Example: Raising a Number to a Power

What is the value of 1.05125 raised to the 16th power, expressed to 5 decimal places?

Solution Strategy

First, set the calculator to display five decimal places:

Next, enter the base and raise it to the 16th power.

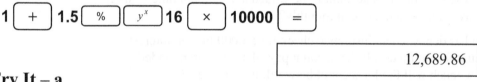

Example: Future Value

What is the future value of $10,000 in four years compounded quarterly at 5%, expressed to two decimal places?

Solution Strategy

Use the future value of money formula, $A = P(1 + i)^n$, where P is the principle ($10,000), n is the number of compounding periods – in this case, 16 (four quarters per year multiplied by four years), and i is the single period rate. The single period rate is the annual rate, 5%, divided by 4, which is 1.5%. Calculate the value inside the parentheses. Raise that value to the 16th power, then multiply by P.

$$1 \boxed{+} 1.5 \boxed{\%} \boxed{y^x} 16 \boxed{\times} 10000 \boxed{=}$$

$$\boxed{12{,}689.86}$$

Try It – a

a. What is the value in 18 years of $150.00 deposited now into an account that pays 7.375% compounded monthly?

Example: Present Value

How much money must be deposited now in an account that pays 6% compounded semiannually for the account value to be $8,450 at the end of seven years?

Solution Strategy

Use the present value of money formula, $P = \dfrac{A}{(1+i)^n}$, where A is the accumulated amount ($8,450), n is the number of compounding periods – in this case, 14 (two periods per year multiplied by seven years), and i is the single period rate. Calculate the single period rate first, 6% divided by 2, which is 3%. Then add one and raise the sum to the 14th power. Finally invert the intermediate result and multiply by A.

23

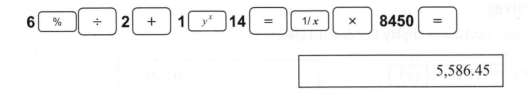

$$5,586.45$$

Try It – b

    b. How much must be deposited now into a credit union that pays 5.125% compounded quarterly if the goal is to have $22,500 in five years?

Review Exercises

Set the calculator display for two decimal places.

1. What is the value of 3.744 multiplied by itself 13 times?

2. A Gigabyte is 2^{30} bytes. How many bytes is that?

3. How many bytes are in a Megabyte (2^{20} bytes)?

4. How many Megabytes are in one Gigabyte? Hint: divide 10^{30} by (10^{20}).

5. What is the future value of $450 compounded annually for 11 years at 4.5%?

6. What is the present value of an account to be valued at $2,300 in nine years if the account pays 3.75% compounded monthly?

7. Fred Dolman has deposited an insurance check for $6,000 into an interest bearing account for future use. If the account pays 4.125% compounded quarterly, how much will Fred's account be worth in four years?

8. Mary Anne Johnson will need $58,000 in 17 years when her baby starts college to pay for the first year of tuition and books. What amount should she deposit now into a 9.2% savings certificate that compounds annually so she will have the money she needs when her child starts college?

9. Barbara Shoblad overpaid her state college tuition by $3,459 because she did not carry a full load of classes. The college has had her money for five years. The state requires public debt be repaid with interest compounded monthly at 4.5% annual interest. How much is Barbara owed?

Try It Solutions

    a. The periodic rate is 7.375% divided by 12, which is approximately .61458%. This rate should be calculated as part of the computation because the calculator will retain all digits of accuracy internally, even though the display is set for two decimal places. The number of periods, n, is 18 times 12. This can also be incorporated into the computation. Using the future value formula and the information given, calculate as follows:

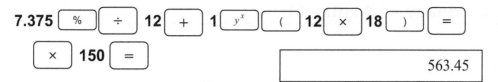

7.375 | % | ÷ | 12 | + | 1 | y^x | (| 12 | × | 18 |) | =

| × | 150 | =

$$563.45$$

b. Five years compounded quarterly gives 20 periods (5 times 4). Use the calculator to compute the quarterly interest rate by dividing the annual rate by 4. To find the present value, we invert the exponentiated quantity before multiplying by the future value to calculate the present value.

5.125 | % | ÷ | 4 | + | 1 | y^x | 20 | = | 1/x | × | 22500 | =

$$17{,}442.21$$

Review Exercise Solutions

1. 28,403,111.64

2. 1,073,741,824 bytes

3. 1,048,576.00 bytes

4. 1,024.00 – Several methods may produce this answer:

   - Divide the answer to problem 2 by the answer to problem 3.

   - First store the answers to problems 2 and 3 in different memories, then recall | RCL | the value stored for the answer to problem 2 and divide it by the recalled value stored for the answer to problem 3.

   - Calculate the result directly using the | y^x | key twice. Use of parentheses is required to produce the correct result if you use this method: $2^{30} \div (2^{20}) =$.

5. $730.28

6. $1,642.03

7. $7,070.38

8. $12,991.02

9. $4,329.96

Time Value of Money – Chapter 11

Future Value

In business the value of money invested today at compound interest increases over time. Given an amount of money invested today, the annual interest rate, the length of a compounding period, and the duration of the investment, a manager can calculate the value of that investment at maturity several months or years in the future.

Example: Future Value

$4,650 is invested at 3.25% compounded annually. What is the value of the investment in 15 years?

Solution Strategy

1. Reset all variables to their default values:

RST	0.00

2. Enter the number of compounding period in one year. For this case it is one (1).

P/Y=	1.00

3. Return to calculator mode:

	0.00

4. Enter the total number of compounding periods, N (number of compounding periods in one year multiplied by the total number of years):

15 [N]

N=	15.00

5. Enter the percent rate of interest per year:

3.25 [I/Y]

I/Y=	3.25

6. Enter the deposit amount as a negative value:

4650 [+/-] [PV]

PV=	-4650.00

7. Compute the future value of the investment:

[CPT] [FV]

FV=	7512.84

Try It

Sue Sanders can get 3.65% annual interest rate, compounded quarterly, on 18 month certificates of deposit at her credit union. If Sue buys a $3,000 certificate, what will be its value at the end of the 18 months?

Review Exercises

1. What is the future value of $18,000 invested for six years at 4.75% compounded annually?

2. How much will be in a savings account in seven years if the original deposit was $9,800? The account has an interest rate of 1.83% and the balance is compounded semiannually.

3. Monthly compounding of $1,000 invested at 6.125% will be worth how much in four years?

4. Hilbert Building Co., will need $185,000 in three years to finance a project. The company now has $168,000 it can invest at 4.18%, compounded bi-monthly (six times a year). Will this account grow to the amount needed in three years? By how much will the account fall short of or exceed the goal?

5. Van Nguyen plans to invest money in an interest bearing account. He can choose 3.00% compounded quarterly, or 3.25% compounded annually. Which option provides faster growth of his investment?

6. Linda Briggs has inherited $5600 she has decided to save for future need. Her bank offers an account compounded monthly at 4.25% annual rate. What would her nest egg be worth in three and a half years if she accepts the offer?

7. Eddie Mott plans to go into the apple juice business. Eddie needs $8,460 to buy a fruit press. He plans to offer a four year note at 4.5% compounded quarterly to finance the purchase of the press. What amount will Eddie owe on the due date four years in the future?

8. Planning to buy a water ski boat and trailer three years from now, Eric Smith deposits $16,500 into a three year Certificate of Deposit at 3.825% compounded annually. How much will his CD be worth when he is ready to buy?

Try It Solution

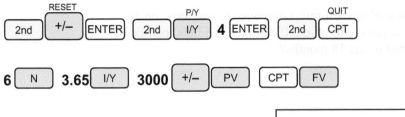

FV =	3168.04

Review Exercise Solutions

1. $23,779.17

2. $11,132.85

3. $1,276.83

4. Yes, it will grow to $190,362.32, exceeding the goal by $5,362.32

5. In the first year Juan would earn $30.34 on $1000 invested at 3.00% compounded quarterly. He would earn $32.50 on $1000 invested at 3.25% compounded annually. His investment grows faster at 3.25% compound annually.

6. $6,496.44

7. $10,118.29

8. $18,466.72

Present Value

Often a business will need money in the future to fund a planned purchase. If the future value of the purchase is known, along with the annual interest rate, the number of compounding periods a year, the total number of periods, and the duration of the investment, a manager can calculate the present value of an amount to be invested now so it will grow to the needed value by the time of the purchase.

Example: Present Value

$7450 will be needed in three years to purchase a replacement copy machine. How much should be invested now at 2.85% compounded semiannually to meet that goal?

Solution Strategy

1. Reset all variables to their default values:

RST	0.00

2. Enter the number of compounding period in one year. For this case it is two.

P/Y

| 2nd | I/Y | 2 ENTER |

P/Y=   2.00

3. Return to calculator mode:

QUIT

| 2nd | CPT |

0.00

4. Enter the total number of compounding periods, N (number of compounding periods in one year multiplied by the total number of years):

6 N

N=   6.00

5. Enter the percent rate of interest per year:

2.85 I/Y

I/Y=   2.85

6. Enter the future value:

7450 +/− FV

FV=   7450.00

7. Compute the present value of the investment:

CPT PV

PV=   -6843.62

$6,843.62 needs to be invested now to grow to $7,450.00 in three years.

Try It

John and Marsha plan to sell an antique farm tractor to help finance the first year of their baby's college education 17 years from now. Predictions say that by that time an average year of college will cost $24,800 at a public university. If they can invest the proceeds at 4.6% compounded quarterly, for what price should they sell their tractor to meet this goal?

Review Exercises

1. Reagor Metal Salvage Co. will need to replace a flatbed truck in four years. If a new truck will cost $68,400, and Raider can get 7.24% compounded monthly, how much must be invested now so Reagor can pay cash for the truck when the time comes?

2. What is the present value of $35,000 eight years in the future if investments are compounded quarterly at 4.75%?

3. Sharon wants to have $28,400 to buy a new car five years from now. If she can get 3.15% compounded monthly from her credit union on a Certificate of Deposit, how much should she put into the CD so she has enough money to pay cash for the car?

4. Suremix Flour Mills will need to buy a new packaging machine in six years when the current one reaches the end of its useful life. A new machine is projected to cost $261,000 at that time. How much does Suremix need to invest now at 3.5% compounded semiannually to have the money needed to buy the machine?

5. Drucker Consulting plans office technology upgrades on a three year cycle. Drucker's purchasing specialist projects that each of 21 computers and its software will cost $1,148, the two laser printers will cost $1,985 each, and the server with its software will cost $11,368. How much does the company need to invest today at 5.5% compounded annually to be able to pay cash for the equipment three years from now? (hint: the sum of the cost of all items should be used for this calculation.)

6. Now much would you deposit today at 4.45% compounded monthly to have $6,750 in 54 months?

7. Lassiter Construction Company has to buy a bulldozer in 18 months to clear and grade the site of a new shopping mall that is in the planning and permit stage now. If the bulldozer will cost $62,900, how much should the company invest at 8.25% compounded semiannually to be able to buy the bulldozer with cash?

8. With a goal of having $10,000 in five years, Douglas Franklin has a choice of putting money in a Certificate of Deposit (CD) that compounds quarterly at 2.35% or into another CD that offers 2.5% compounded annually. Which CD should he buy if he wants to minimize his investment outlay?

Try It Solution

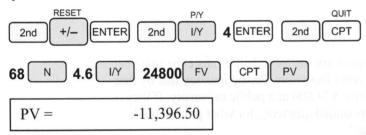

They need to get $11,396.50 for the tractor to be able to meet their investment goal.

Review Exercise Solutions

1. $51,246.28

2. $19,859.96

3. $24,266.47

4. $211,947.11

5. $33,592.75

6. $5,527.10

7. $55,716.73

8. $8,894.46 is the outlay needed for the 2.35% CD compounded quarterly. He only needs $8,838.54 if he buys the 2.5% CD compounded annually. He should buy the 2.5% CD.

Amortization – Chapter 12

A business owner or manager may need to borrow money to finance a purchase or an operation. Knowing how much the monthly payment will be can help the loan seeker in negotiating the best deal with the lending institution. The loan payment amount may be easily calculated.

Example: Loan Payment

You are considering buying a small building from which to operate your business. You believe you can buy it for $345,000 on a 30 year mortgage at 6.375%. What would the monthly payment be (principle and interest)?

Solution Strategy

1. Reset all variables to their default values:

RST	0.00

This will reset several internal variables, including the number of payments per year, P/Y, to 12.

2. Enter the number of years of the mortgage and use the payment multiplier keys to calculate the total number of payments:

N =	360.00

3. Enter the annual interest rate:

6.375 [I/Y]

I/Y =	6.375

4. Enter the amount of the loan:

345000 [PV]

PV =	345,000.00

5. Compute the payment amount (shown as a negative amount because it is owed):

[CPT] [PMT]

PMT =	-2,152.35

Try It

Susan is planning to accept a 3.9%, five year loan offered by the dealer from whom she is buying a car costing $17,003.48. What will her monthly payment be if she makes no down payment?

Review Exercises

1. To borrow $22,300 for a wedding, Kristi's parents get a 4.8% loan from their credit union. The monthly payments will be made for four years. What will their payment be?

2. Dick Schleister decides to borrow money to buy a new chainsaw. He can get a 5.5% loan for two years. If the saw retails for $489.99, what will his monthly payment be?

3. Michael McCusker is buying a small airplane that costs $184,000. If he pays $35,000 down and finances the balance with a 6%, 15-year loan, how much must he pay monthly?

4. To purchase a boat, motor and trailer, Bob King agrees to a 10-year loan at 4.75%. If the purchase price totals $28,384, and he pays $2,000 down, how much are his payments?

5. Sally and Paul are buying a new $310,000 home. They can get a 15% down, 30-year fixed mortgage at 5.375%. How much will their monthly house payment (PI) be if they can make the down payment?

Try It Solution

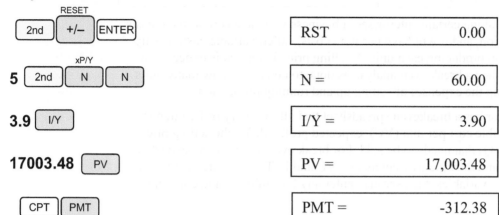

RST	0.00
N =	60.00
I/Y =	3.90
PV =	17,003.48
PMT =	-312.38

Review Exercise Solutions

1. $511.54
2. $21.61
3. $1,257.35 (The amount financed is $184,000 - $35,000 = $149,000)
4. $276.25 (The amount of the loan is $28,384 - $2,000 = $26,384)
5. $1,475.52 (The amount borrowed is $310,000 - 15% = $263,500)

Break Even Analysis

When undertaking certain enterprises, a business will have certain fixed costs in setting up production, and it will have per-item costs, called variable cost, usually materials and labor, in producing each unit. A selling price is set that is expected to be competitive, and then a break even analysis is done to determine how many units must be sold to recoup the expenses of setting up and running production.

The calculator has a breakeven spreadsheet that allows entry of five items: fixed cost (FC), variable cost per unit (VC), expected profit (PFT), the selling price (P) and the quantity (Q) that needs to be sold. For break even analysis, the expected profit is left at zero, and then the user enters FC, VC and P. The final step is to compute Q. For these five variables, the user may enter any four of them and compute the fifth.

Example: Break Even Quantity

The cost to set up a manufacturing line to produce a new model of sports shoe is expected to be $4,850. The cost of producing each pair of shoes will be $23.03. If a pair will be retailed for $49.99, how many pairs need be made and sold in order to break even?

Solution Strategy

1. Enter the Break Even mode and clear the quantities.

FC =	0.00

2. Enter the fixed cost to set up the production line.

4850 ENTER

FC =	4,850.00

3. Arrow down to the variable cost prompt and enter the value.

↓ **23.03** ENTER

VC =	23.03

4. Arrow down to the selling price prompt and enter the value.

↓ **49.99** ENTER

P =	49.99

5. Arrow down twice, leaving the profit zero, and compute the break even quantity.

↓ ↓ CPT

Q =	179.90

The company would have to produce and sell 180 pairs of shoes to break even.

Try It – a-b

a. How many bearing journal boxes would a foundry need to produce before it begins to make a profit? It will cost $176 to make the molds for casting the boxes. Steel will cost $1.85 per journal box, and labor will be $1.23. The journal boxes will sell for $3.66 each?

b. To make a profit of $8,480 on a new line of shoes, how many pairs must be sold if fixed cost to set up production is $2,344, and the variable cost is $31.38. A pair of shoes will sell for $49.95.

Review Exercises

1. A piecework factory produces dresses at a variable cost of $17.34. If set-up expenses are $326, and a dress will sell for $24.75, how many dresses must be sold before starting to make a profit?

2. To set up the production line for a certain model truck, production managers at NUMI project expenses of $684,932 will be incurred. Labor and materials to produce each truck will be $12,408. How many trucks must be sold for $16,488.34 before the model becomes profitable?

3. To set up a production line to manufacture dining tables, Able Wood Products, Inc. projects it will incur $838 in expenses. Each table will require $84.50 in materials, and the labor will cost $39.20. If a table is to be sold for $160, how many do they have to make and sell before the line becomes profitable?

4. A line to produce a new model of high security padlock will take $4,882 to set up. Each lock will cost $14.28 to make. If a lock will sell for $22.85, how many will have to be sold to break even?

5. Setup cost to establish a production line for a 17-inch flat screen monitor is going to be $45,867. Production variable cost will total $208.17 for each monitor. If the company wants to break even after selling 800 monitors, for what price should each monitor be sold?

6. The production line for the 17-inch monitors above can be modified to produce and 18-inch monitor for $18,644. The manufacturer wants to sell them for $339.99 and expects to sell a minimum of 265 units. What is the limit on the variable cost to produce the 18-inch monitors if the line is to break even?

Try It Solutions

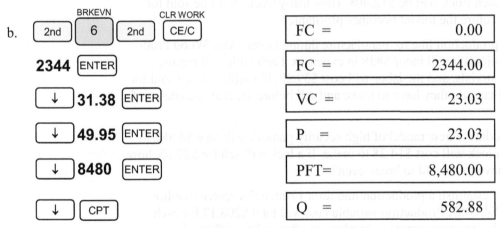

a.

Key sequence	Display
2nd [BRKEVN 6] **2nd** [CLR WORK CE/C]	FC = 0.00
176 ENTER	FC = 176.00
[↓] **1.85** [+] **1.23** [=] ENTER	VC = 3.08
[↓] **3.66** ENTER	P = 3.66
[↓] [↓] CPT	Q = 303.45

They must sell at least 304 journal boxes to break even.

b.

Key sequence	Display
2nd [BRKEVN 6] **2nd** [CLR WORK CE/C]	FC = 0.00
2344 ENTER	FC = 2344.00
[↓] **31.38** ENTER	VC = 23.03
[↓] **49.95** ENTER	P = 23.03
[↓] **8480** ENTER	PFT= 8,480.00
[↓] CPT	Q = 582.88

The number of pairs sold must exceed 582 to realize an $8,480 profit.

Review Exercise Solutions

1. 44 dresses

2. 168 trucks

3. 24 tables

4. 570 locks

5. 266 monitors

6. $269.64

Depreciation – Chapter 17

Capital assets, purchased new at cost (CST), lose value as they age for a number of years until their useful life (LIF) has ended and they are sold for salvage (SAL). Various methods have been devised to depreciate them for accounting and tax purposes. Depreciation methods discussed in Chapter 17 include straight line (SL), sum-of-the-years-digits (SYD), and declining balance (DB). For DB the rate defaults to 200%, but the user may enter any value as an option. The depreciation worksheet mode of the calculator can perform calculations to provide the depreciation (DEP) for the year, the remaining book value (RBV) at the end of the year, and the remaining depreciable value (RDV). It can do this for successive years with a few simple keystrokes so the user can obtain figures for a depreciation table. It can do this for any of the three depreciation methods mentioned. To use the calculator for depreciation problems, there are three sets of steps.

- Select the depreciation mode (SL, SYD or DB). If you select DB, key in the percentage if you are not going to use double declining balance (200% – the default value). Note: the calculator will remain in the selected depreciation mode until another mode is selected, or else the calculator is reset.

- Enter the depreciation data: the life, cost, and salvage value of the asset, and the year of service for which you want the depreciation calculated.

- Display the values for depreciation, remaining book value, and remaining depreciable value for the year you entered. These may be repeated for successive years until the RDV is zero.

Example: Choose Straight Line Depreciation

Set the calculator to do straight line depreciation, and then clear the worksheet of any previously stored values.

Solution Strategy

1. Select the depreciation worksheet.

SL

2. Clear the worksheet.

SL

Example: Choose Sum-of-the-Years-Digits Depreciation

Set the calculator to do sum-of-the-years-digits depreciation.

Solution Strategy

SYD

Example: Choose Declining Balance Depreciation

*Set the calculator to do declining balance depreciation, and set the rate to
150%.*

Solution Strategy

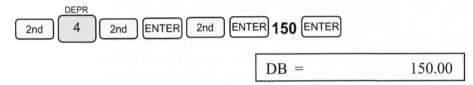

DB =	150.00

Example: Entering and Calculating Depreciation Data

*Set the calculator to do straight line depreciation for a well drilling machine
that cost $280,000. The machine is expected to be in service for five years and have a
$22,500 salvage value. What is the first year depreciation, the remaining book value
and the remaining depreciable value of the machine?*

Solution Strategy

1. Reset the calculator, select the depreciation worksheet and clear the data.

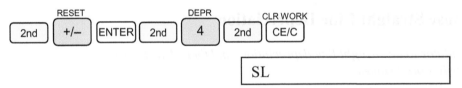

SL	

2. Enter the data asked for.

    ↓ 5 ENTER

LIF=	5.00

    ↓ ↓ 280000 ENTER

CST=	280,000.00

    ↓ 22500 ENTER

SAL=	22,500.00

    ↓

YR =	1.00

3. Display the first year depreciation data. At this point, the calculator has al-
    ready calculated this data for the first year. The remaining steps cause the
    values to be displayed.

    ↓

DEP=	51,500.00

    ↓

RBV=	228,500.00

    ↓

RDV =	206,000.00

Example: Remaining Book Value for Any Year

In the previous example, what is the remaining book value of the well drilling machine at the end of the third year?

Solution Strategy

1. Continue from the previous solution keystroke sequence, and perform the third year computations.

   | ↓ | 3 | ENTER | | YR = 3.00 |

2. Arrow down to the RBV display and read the third year remaining book value.

   | ↓ | ↓ | | RBV= 125,500.00 |

   NOTE: if a year is entered that is greater than the year when salvage value is reached, the RBV will be the same as the salvage value.

Try It

Use the double declining balance method to calculate the annual depreciation and remaining book value at the end of the *second* year for a 5-axis automated milling machine that cost $178,489 new. The machine has a salvage value of $28,400, and a useful life of five years.

Review Exercises

1. How much is the first year depreciation on a boat and motor whose combined cost when they were new was $19,229? They have an $8,450 combined salvage value at the end of 3 years and will be depreciated using sum-of-the-years digits.

2. A tower crane has a useful life of eight years and costs $471,000 new. If it is to be depreciated using straight line, and its salvage value is $65,350. What is the book value remaining at the end of year five?

3. A commercial washing machine has a salvage value of $99. It costs $486 new and will be depreciated using 150% declining balance over a four year period. What is the amount of the first year depreciation?

4. The brick liner of a boiler firebox is worn out and must be replaced at a cost of $3,200. The new liner is expected to last 10 years and will be depreciated on the books using straight line depreciation. There is no salvage value. What is the liner's remaining depreciable value after the sixth year of service?

5. A certain company has a policy of annually replacing one third of its information technology assets with current technology hardware and software. A machine being replaced has a salvage value that averages one-sixth of its cost

new. Using straight line depreciation, calculate the book value of a laser printer at the end of its second year of service. The printer cost $1,248 when it was new.

6. A new car costing $18,539 remains in the fleet of a delivery service for at least 125,000 miles and is then sold. The fleet average annual miles per vehicle is 26,400. The car when sold is expected to be worth $1,250. If the company accountant uses sum-of-the-years digits method for depreciating rolling assets, what is the remaining depreciable value of the car after the second year of service? (*Hint: calculate the number of years of service based upon the mileage.*)

Try It Solution

1. Set up the calculator for double declining balance depreciation.

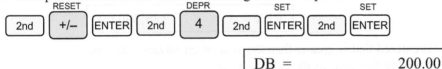

DB =	200.00

2. Enter the expected life of the machine.

↓	5	ENTER

LIF=	5.00

3. Enter the cost of the machine.

↓	↓	178489	ENTER

CST=	178,489.00

4. Enter the salvage value.

↓	28400	ENTER

SAL=	28,400.00

5. Calculate second year values.

↓	2	ENTER

YR =	2.00

6. Read out the annual depreciation and the remaining book value.

↓

DEP=	42,837.36

↓

RBV=	64,256.04

Review Exercise Solutions

1. $5,389.50

2. $217,468.75

3. $182.25

4. $1,280.00

5. $554.66

6. $6,915.60

Bonds – Chapter 20

The bond worksheet of the calculator will either calculate the price (PRI) of a bond or its percent yield (YLD). It will also calculate the bond's accrued interest (AI). Once in the bond worksheet mode, the calculator will default to the actual day-count method for calculating. An optional day count method may be selected that assumes all months have 30 days, and a year has 360 days.

The user will enter bond information, and then obtain computed results from the calculator. Information to be entered includes the date the bond is purchased, called the *settlement date* in the calculator guide, to be thought of as the *start date* (SDT) for computing purposes. The U.S. order of date notation, using the MM.DDYY format, is the calculator's default date entry mode, where MM is the number of the month, DD is the number of the day, and YY are the year's final two digits. A leading zero is not required for the month, but it is required for entry of the day. The user must enter a decimal point to separate the month from the day. The calculator assumes year 50 is 1950 and year 49 is 2049. The default coupon payment method is twice per year (2/Y). The coupon rate (CPN) is entered as a percent. Another date to be entered is the redemption date (RDT). The calculator assumes the redemption date coincides with a coupon date. If the bond is redeemed at maturity, then the redemption value (RV) is entered as 100 percent, but if the bond is called, enter the call value percent. Enter either the bond's yield as a percent to compute the price, or else enter the price to compute the yield. Accrued interest is automatically computed, compounded semiannually at the stated rate. This means the bond holder is not clipping coupons, but is allowing all payments to accrue.

Clearing the calculator, using 2ⁿᵈ [RESET], sets the following values.
- Redemption Value to $100 (per $100 of par value)
- Coupon Rate to 0%
- Yield to 0%
- Price to zero dollars
- Start Date and Redemption Date to 12-31-1990
- Day-count method to actual
- Coupon frequency to twice per year

Clearing the bond worksheet using 2ⁿᵈ [CLR Work], sets the same values for the first four bullets, but does not reset the dates, day-count method or coupon frequency.

An error will be displayed when pressing the up and down arrow keys to move through the worksheet if needed information has not been entered.

Example: Bond Data Entry

Reset all values, enter the bond worksheet, and enter the following values: Start Date – March 31, 2005; Coupon Rate – 7.5%; Redemption Date – March 31, 2015; Redemption Value -- $100.

Solution Strategy

1. Clear the values and key for the bond worksheet.

	RESET				BOND		
2nd	+/−	ENTER	2nd	9	STD=	12 – 31 – 1990	

2. Enter the start date.

3.3105 ENTER   STD=   3 – 31 – 2005

3. Enter the coupon rate.

↓ **7.5** ENTER   CPN=   7.50

4. Enter the redemption date.

↓ **3.3115** ENTER   RDT=   3 – 31 – 2015

The redemption value is already at $100 as a result of the reset in step 1.

Try it – a

a. Reset all values, enter the bond worksheet, and enter the following values: Start Date – July 15, 2006; Coupon Rate – 5.25%; Redemption Date – July 15, 2026; Redemption Value -- $98.35.

Example: Bond Price

A bond is purchased on April 17, 2003 that will mature on April 17, 2013. The coupon payments are twice per year, and the coupon rate is 5.25%. For a 6% yield to maturity, find the price of the bond if it will be redeemed at 100% of its par value.

Solution Strategy

1. Reset the calculator and enter the bond worksheet.

	RESET				BOND		
2nd	+/−	ENTER	2nd	9	STD=	12 – 31 – 1990	

2. Enter the start date, coupon rate, redemption date, and redemption value.

4.1703 [ENTER] [↓] **5.25** [ENTER] [↓] **4.1713** [ENTER] [↓]

RV =	100.00

3. Down arrow three times, leaving the defaults of actual day count and twice per year coupon payment. Enter the yield value.

[↓] [↓] [↓] **6** [ENTER]

YLD=	6.00

4. Calculate the price.

[↓] [CPT]

PRI=	94.42

The price of the bond should be $94.42 per $100 of maturity value.

Try It – b

b. A 17 year bond is purchased on October 21, 2006. The coupon payments are twice per year, and the coupon rate is 6.75%. For a 7.2% yield to maturity, what is the bond price if it will be redeemed at 100% of its par value?

Example: Bond Yield to Redemption

Susan Kollmar bought a 14 year bond on January 31, 2006. The coupon rate is twice a year, and the day-count method used is actual. If she paid $94.38 per $100 for the bond, and the coupon rate is 5.75%, what will be the bond's yield to maturity?

Solution Strategy

1. Reset the calculator and enter the bond worksheet.

[2nd] [+/-]RESET [ENTER] [2nd] [9]BOND

STD=	12 – 31 – 1990

2. Enter the start date, coupon rate, redemption date, and redemption value.

1.3106 [ENTER] [↓] **5.75** [ENTER] [↓] **1.3120** [ENTER] [↓]

RV =	100.00

3. Down arrow four times, leaving the defaults of actual day count and twice per year coupon payment. Bypass the yield value and enter the price.

[↓] [↓] [↓] [↓] **94.38** [ENTER]

PRI=	94.38

4. Up arrow and enter to compute the yield.

$$\boxed{\uparrow} \quad \boxed{\text{CPT}} \qquad\qquad \boxed{\text{YLD}= \qquad\qquad 6.36}$$

The bond yield will be 6.36 percent.

Try It – c

c. On July 29, 2005, Julie Roediger plans to redeem an eight-year bond she has kept in a safe deposit box since it was issued. The coupon rate has been twice per year, and actual day-count applies to the bond. If the coupon rate is 7.25% and price was $97.06 per $100, what is the bond's yield at maturity?

Review Exercises

1. A bond is purchased on August 18, 2004 that will mature on August, 18, 2015. The coupon payments are twice per year, and the coupon rate is 6.25%. For a 7% yield to maturity, find the price of the bond if it will be redeemed at 100% of its par value.

2. A 27 year bond was purchased on October 21, 1992. The coupon payments are twice per year, and the coupon rate is 5.75%. For a 6.4% yield to maturity, what is the bond price if it will be redeemed at 100% of its par value?

3. Bob Snellman bought a 6 year bond on January 31, 2003. The coupons are paid twice a year, and the day-count method used is actual. If he paid $95.88 per $100 for the bond, and the coupon rate is 4.75%, what will be the bond's yield to maturity?

4. On December 11, 2006, Jim McCusker plans to redeem an eighteen-year bond he has kept in a safe deposit box since it was issued. The coupon rate has been twice per year, and actual day-count applies to the bond. If the coupon rate is 8.25% and yield to maturity is 8.875%, for what price was the bond bought?

Try It Solutions

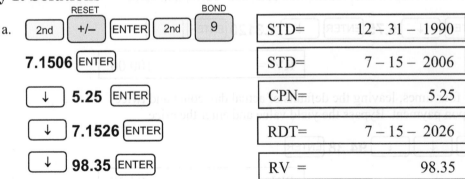

44

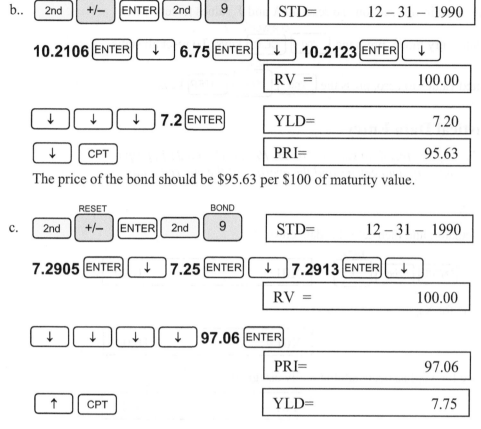

b.. The price of the bond should be \$95.63 per \$100 of maturity value.

c. The bond yield will be 7.75 percent.

Review Exercise Solutions

1. \$94.36
2. \$91.70
3. \$5.57
4. \$94.43

Statistics – Chapter 21

The calculator supports the entry of data, including histogram data. It can then calculate the data's average value and other statistics on the data. Data may be entered for up to 50 histogram pairs (the X value and its frequency count, entered as the Y value). Data may be entered in any order.

Data entry mode is different than the statistics calculation mode. Pressing the 2nd **7** (DATA) keys puts the calculator into data entry mode. Pressing the 2nd **8** (STAT) keys puts the calculator into statistics method selection and computation mode. There are two types of statistics: *single variable* and *two-variable*. Only single variable problems will be explained in this section. To reset all X and Y values to zero when the calculator is in data entry mode, press the [2nd] [CE/C] keys. (CLR WORK) To reset all statistics data and calculated values to zero, press the [2nd] [+/–] [ENTER] keys. (RESET)

Example: Statistical Data Entry

Enter the following distinct data values: 16, 23, 19, 20, 18 and 21 in preparation for finding the number of data entries and the average of the entered data.

Solution Strategy

1. Clear the calculator, and then set it for data entry.

[2nd] [+/–] (RESET) [ENTER] [2nd] [7] (DATA) | X01   0.00 |

2. Enter the value for X_{01}.

16 [ENTER] | X01=   16.00 |

3. Note the value for Y_{01} has been automatically assigned.

[↓] | Y01=   1.00 |

4. Enter the values for the remaining five numbers as X_{02} through X_{06}. Use the down arrow key to bypass the Y values. They are automatically assigned a value of one as soon as an X value is entered.

[↓] **23** [ENTER] | X02=   23.00 |

[↓] [↓] **19** [ENTER] | X03=   19.00 |

[↓] [↓] **20** [ENTER] | X04=   20.00 |

[↓] [↓] **18** [ENTER] | X05=   18.00 |

[↓] [↓] **21** [ENTER] | X06=   21.00 |

The data is now available for statistical calculation.

NOTE: if there are multiple occurrences of a value, X_{nn}, in a data set, the frequency count, Y_{nn}, should be entered also, rather than leaving the value as one. For example, if the value 38 occurs four times in a set of data and is the third value entered. Enter 38 for X_{03} and enter 4 for Y_{03}.

Example: Statistics Calculation

How many data items were entered in the previous example and what is their average value?

Solution Strategy

1. Select Statistics mode.

 LIN

2. Select one-variable statistics.

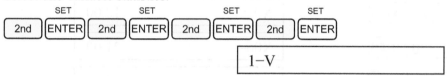

1−V

3. Display the number, *n*, of X values that were entered.

| ↓ | | n = | 6.00 |

4. Display the average value, $\bar{x}$, of the six data entries, X_{01} through X_{06}.

$\bar{x}$ = 19.50

Try It

Enter the following numbers as single-variable data. Display the number of data items entered and their average value.

36 29 33 37 27 30 32 34 35

Review Exercises

1. What is the average of 346.2, 356.8, 351.0 and 349.3?

2. A class of 15 students received the following scores on a recent exam:

   86 91 82 77 45 88 93 69 62 75 89 80 97 96 84

   What was the average test score?

3. A sampling of a certain model of production oven tested the bake temperature of five ovens after 15 minutes of operation. The measured internal temperatures were 346°, 356°, 351°, 358° and 345°. What was the average temperature measured?

4. How many numbers are there in the sequence 17, 18, 19, ... , 42, 43? What is their average value?

Try It Solution

Keys	Display
2nd [+/−] RESET ENTER 2nd [7] DATA	
36 ENTER	X01= 36.00
[↓] [↓] **29** ENTER	X02= 23.00
[↓] [↓] **33** ENTER	X03= 19.00
[↓] [↓] **37** ENTER	X04= 20.00
[↓] [↓] **27** ENTER	X05= 18.00
[↓] [↓] **30** ENTER	X06= 21.00
[↓] [↓] **32** ENTER	X07= 32.00
[↓] [↓] **34** ENTER	X08= 34.00
[↓] [↓] **35** ENTER	X09= 35.00
2nd [8] STAT 2nd ENTER SET 2nd ENTER SET 2nd ENTER SET 2nd ENTER SET	1−V
[↓]	n = 9.00
[↓]	$\overline{x}$ = 32.56

Review Exercise Solutions

1. 350.83
2. 80.93 was the average score.
3. 351.20° was the average temperature.
4. There are 27 entries. Their average value is 30.00.

Basic Excel

Guide and Workbook

Michael R. Gordon

A supplement to:

Contemporary Mathematics
for Business and Consumers, Eighth Edition

Robert A. Brechner and George Bergeman

Table of Contents

Foreword

This workbook has been created to give the student a *very* brief introduction to Microsoft Excel and its use in solving the same type of problems that may be done on a financial calculator. Excel on a personal computer is often the preferred tool of choice in an office environment where multiple and repeat calculations are the norm. Advantages of using Excel are that the results in a spreadsheet may be printed or exported to a file, emailed to a branch office or client, or copied to a new file, then revised into a similar spreadsheet for a related financial calculation. A few example problems and solutions using Excel are given.

Basic Excel Guide and Workbook

When a set of calculations is frequently repeated it is often more productive to set up a spreadsheet on a personal computer rather than to use a calculator each time the calculation is to be done. Microsoft Excel is the tool of choice for a majority of businesses for this situation. The following introduction will give you an overview of the basic concepts of Microsoft Excel.

Spreadsheet Layout

When the program is first opened, it presents a blank workbook that has three spreadsheets, labeled at their bottoms on tabs as Sheet1, Sheet2 and Sheet3. Sheet1 is the default sheet. Sheet3 is shown selected in the below figure. A sheet may be renamed by double clicking on its name, then entering the desired name followed by the Enter key. Each sheet's name must be different from the names of all other sheets in a workbook.

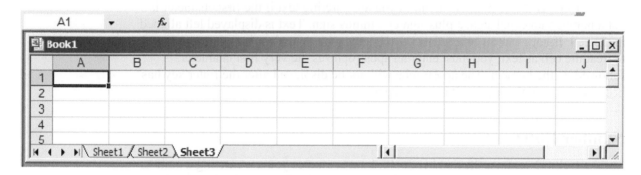

Each sheet is comprise of cells arranged in rows and columns. Each row is labeled at its left end with a number, and each column at its top with a letter or letter pair. The numbers increase going down the spreadsheet, with the highest number being 65536. The column letters go to the right from A to Z, then AA to AZ, etc. until the last column which is IV.

Cell Reference and Selection

Each cell is named (referenced) by its column letter (or letters) followed by its row number. In the above figure, the selected cell is A1. Its name appears in the Name Box, which is just above where its says Book1. Any cell may be selected by pointing to it with the mouse cursor and clicking on it. The selected cell will have a heavy border around it and a small black square in its lower right corner.

Cell Contents

Cells may remain empty, or they may contain one of three types of entries: text, numbers or formulas. The following figure illustrates all three types.

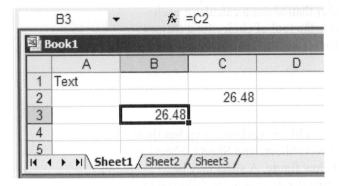

Text Entry

Cell A1 has text. Excel assumes you are entering text if the first character is not a number, an equal sign, a plus sign or a minus sign. Text is displayed left aligned in the cell. If you want to enter a label that begins with a number, but you want Excel to treat the cell as text, you must enter an apostrophe as the very first character, followed by the number. The apostrophe will not be displayed after the Enter key has been pressed and the label will be left aligned.

Number Entry

Cell C2 contains the number 26.48. Excel assumes you are entering a number when the first character entered is a number or a sign. Numbers are displayed right aligned by default.

Formula Entry

In the above figure, cell B3 is selected as can be discerned by its heavy border, and also by its name in the Name Box. It looks like it contains a number, but in the Formula Bar located just to the right of the fx in the top of the figure, you see that it actually has a formula, =C2. This means that cell B3 will evaluate cell C2 and display the result. When you enter an equal sign as the first character in a cell, Excel assumes you are entering a formula.

Internal Values and Displayed Values

Cells may be formatted to display a specified number of decimal places, or to be aligned in the center of the cell, or to display the result as currency. These are only three examples of the many choices the creator of the spreadsheet may use. Numeric values always have their full accuracy retained internally even when the displayed value has a limited number of decimal positions specified. Note that a number is rounded for display purposes. This means that 3.785 will be displayed to two decimal places as 3.79.

Correcting Errors

Often a mistake is made when typing numbers or text into a cell. If the error is detected while still making the entry, you may backspace the error out and retype. If the error is not found until after the Enter key has been pressed, the cell may be selected using the mouse, then edit the contents in the formula bar, or else simply press the Delete key to wipe it out and start over.

Change Column Width

Situation: when a text entry is too long to fit in a cell it will spill over into the adjacent cell to the right so long as that cell is empty. But if the cell on the right already contains something, then the display of the text you are entering will be cut off at the right border of the cell, although the system still accepts all of it internally.

Another situation that occurs sometimes is when instead of an expected number, the displayed value in a cell is a row of pound signs. This is Excel telling you the cell isn't wide enough to display the entire number.

For either of the above situations, you may wish to widen the column so the text or number will display correctly and completely. This may be done in one of two ways: automatically or manually. For either method begin by placing the mouse cursor over the right edge of the cell of the column letter or letters at the top of the column. The cursor will change to a black cross having arrowheads at the ends of the crossbar:

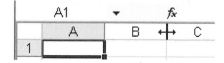

To automatically widen the column, double click the left mouse button. The column width will increase or decrease to accommodate the widest data in any cell in the column. To manually widen the column, press and hold the left mouse button then drag the border to the right as far as you need to, then release the mouse button. Columns may be made narrower manually by dragging the border to the left instead of to the right.

The height of a row may be changed in a similar manner by pointing to the cell border below the number of the row whose height you wish to change, then either double click or click and drag.

Displayed Number of Decimal Places

Excel will by default display all the decimal places needed by the number. You may decrease the number of places displayed by selecting the desired cell, then clicking on the Decrease Decimal tool $^{.00}_{\to.0}$ once for each place by which you want to reduce the displayed value. To increase the number of displayed places, select the cell then click the Increase Decimal tool $^{+.0}_{.00}$ once for each place to be added to the displayed decimal.

Try It: Change Displayed Decimal Places

Select an empty cell, then type **3.785** and press the Enter key. Next press the Up Arrow key to reselect the cell. Now locate the Increase Decimal and the Decrease Decimal tools on the toolbar (Excel 2003) or in the tool cluster (Excel 2007). Click the following sequence and observe the effect on the displayed number after each click:

Decrease Decimal, Decrease Decimal, Increase Decimal, Increase Decimal, Increase Decimal.

What value is displayed when you have finished with the sequence?

Try It Solution

Here is the appearance of the cell after you type in the number and press the Enter key (cell C2 was selected for the data entry):

	A	B	C	D
1				
2			3.785	
3				

◄◄ ◄ ► ►◄ \ **Sheet1** / Sheet2 / Sheet3 /

And after the Up Arrow key:

	A	B	C	D
1				
2			3.785	
3				

◄◄ ◄ ► ►◄ \ **Sheet1** / Sheet2 / Sheet3 /

And as the displayed decimal places change sequence progresses:

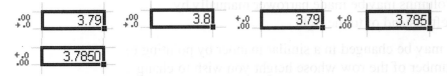

Notice the displayed value is rounded as the number is reduced, and the value is restored as the number increases. The end of sequence displayed value is 3.7850.

Arithmetic Operators

The operators in formulas for typical arithmetic are +, -, *, / and ^. They are respectively for addition, subtraction, multiplication, division and exponentiation. Parentheses may also be used to denote subexpressions. Note that in Excel you must use the multiplication symbol between a value and the subexpression surrounded by parentheses it multiplies. There is no implicit multiplication in Excel as there is in algebraic notation.

Arithmetic Operators in Formulas

In a blank spreadsheet, use cell A2 to evaluate $3^3 + 3 \times 3$ all together divided by 6, then reduced by 2.

Solution Strategy

In cell A2 enter **=(3^3+3*3)/6-2** followed by the Enter key. Notice that this formula uses all five arithmetic operators and has a parenthetical expression. Excel will begin evaluation inside the parentheses with the exponentiation operator, followed by the multiplication, then the addition. Using the calculated value for the parenthetical expression, it then does the division, and finally the subtraction.

Formulas That Reference Cells

On the same spreadsheet you used for the previous example, enter 2 in cell C1 and 3 in cell D1, then create a formula in cell C2 that again finds the result of $3^3 + 3 \times 3$ all together divided by 6, then reduced by 2. Your formula should only reference cells C1 and D1.

Solution Strategy

In the Formula Bar is the formula that was entered in cell C2.

In this formula, **=(D1^D1+D1*D1)/(C1*D1)-C1**, note that the contents of cells C1 and D1 are multiplied together to get the divisor 6, and that they are enclosed in their own parentheses. You may remove those parentheses to see what happens when they are not there: With cell C2 selected, edit the formula in the Formula Bar by deleting ONLY the second pair of parentheses, then press the Enter key and look at the value in cell C2. (Answer: 52)

Try It: Simple Interest

Set up a spreadsheet to determine the simple interest on $400 after 5 years at 3.5%.

Try It: Simple Interest Excel Solution

The Applicable formula from Chapter 10 is I=PRT. This is done in Excel as follows:

Enter the labels in column A, cells 1 through 4. Enter **400** in cell B1. Enter **3.5%** in cell B2. Enter **5** in cell B3. Finally, enter **=B1*B2*B3** in cell B4. Note that cells B1 and B4 have been formatted as currency, and so they display two decimal places and a dollar sign. Currency formatting is done by selecting the cell, then clicking on the $ tool. You may format a cell either before or after you enter a value in it. Because you entered a percent sign as part of the value in cell B2, Excel displays two decimal places there, too.

	B4		f_x =B1*B2*B3	
Book1				
	A	B	C	D
1	Principal	$ 400.00		
2	Rate	3.50%		
3	Time	5		
4	Interest	$ 70.00		
5				

Sheet1 / Sheet2 / Sheet3 /

Notice that B4 is the selected cell in this figure, and it contains the formula (see the formula bar), but it displays the result of evaluating the formula. The formula references cells B1, B2 and B3, multiplying their values together. The advantage of referencing cells, rather than copying their actual values into a formula, is that you can change a number in a cell and the formula will immediately provide the answer using the newly entered value. For example, if you wanted to know what the accrued interest would be after only 3 years, select cell B3 and enter **3**. The formula in cell B4 recalculates as soon as the new value is entered and provides the new answer: **$42.00**.

Try it: Compound Interest

Use a spreadsheet to find the value after four years of $3,600 at 6% compounded quarterly.

Try it: Compound Interest Excel Solution

The applicable formula from Chapter 11 is $A=P(1+r)^n$ where r is the periodic rate and n is the number of periods. Rather than calculate r or n, let's have Excel do it for us. Set up a spreadsheet as follows: Enter the labels in column A. Format cell B1 as currency, then enter 3600. Enter 6% in cell B2. Enter 4 in cells B3 and B4. In cell

B5 enter the formula =B3*B4. In cell B6 enter the formula =B2/B4. In cell B7 enter the formula =B1*(1+B6)^B5. Format cell B7 as currency. The completed sheet looks like this:

| B7 | ▼ | | *fx* =B1*(1+B6)^B5 | | | |

Book1

	A	B	C	D	E	F
1	Principal	$3,600.00				
2	Annual Rate	6%				
3	Years	4				
4	Pmts per year	4				
5	n	16				
6	Periodic rate	0.015				
7	Amount	$4,568.35				
8						
9						

◄ ◄ ► ►◄ \ Sheet1 \ **Sheet2** / Sheet3 / | ◄ |

In the above solution, the spreadsheet has both dependent and independent formulas. The dependent formula is in cell B7, because it depends upon the results from the formulas in cells B5 and B6. They are independent because they only reference cells that have numbers in them, not formulas. So Excel uses an evaluation sequence that evaluates the independent formulas first, then evaluates the dependent formula using the results of the independent formulas. This is similar to an expression that has a parenthetical subexpression: the value inside the parentheses must be determined first. So it is with independent formulas. Dependencies in complex spreadsheets may have to chain through several dependent formulas before reaching the independent ones.

Review Exercises

Use Excel to find the desired value.

1. Simple interest on $655 at 1.8% for five and one-half years.

2. The maturity value of a simple $2,300 note at 2.3% for three years.

3. The value in eight years of $1,000 at 2.5% compounded monthly.

4. The value in two years of $46,000 at 3.5% compounded semiannually.

5. The amount that must be deposited now into an account that is compounded quarterly at 4.44% annual rate to be worth $26,500 after five years.

6. By how much will the initial deposit in problem 5 grow?

Review Exercises Solutions

1.

B4		f_x =B1*B2*B3	
	A	B	C
1	Principal	$ 655.00	
2	Rate	1.80%	
3	Time	5.5	
4	Interest	$ 64.85	
5			

2.

B5		f_x =B1+B4	
	A	B	C
1	Principal	$2,300.00	
2	Rate	2.30%	
3	Time	3	
4	Interest	$ 158.70	
5	MV	$2,458.70	

3.

B5		f_x =B3*B4	
	A	B	C
1	Principal	$1,000.00	
2	Rate	2.5%	
3	Time	8	
4	Periods/Yr	12	
5	n	96	
6	Periodic rate	0.0020833	
7	Amount	$1,221.15	

B6		f_x =B2/B4	
	A	B	C
1	Principal	$1,000.00	
2	Rate	2.5%	
3	Time	8	
4	Periods/Yr	12	
5	n	96	
6	Periodic rate	0.0020833	
7	Amount	$1,221.15	

B7		f_x =B1*(1+B6)^B5	
	A	B	C
1	Principal	$1,000.00	
2	Rate	2.5%	
3	Time	8	
4	Periods/Yr	12	
5	n	96	
6	Periodic rate	0.0020833	
7	Amount	$1,221.15	

4. From the previous spreadsheet you only need to change the values in cells B1, B2, B3 and B4:

	A	B
1	Principal	$46,000.00
2	Rate	3.5%
3	Time	2
4	Periods/Yr	2
5	n	4
6	Periodic rate	0.0175
7	Amount	$49,305.52

5. Here you change the label in cell A1, plug the applicable numbers into cells B2, B3, B4 and B7, then enter the Present Value formula from Chapter 11 into cell B1.

B1　　▼　　f_x =B7/(1+B6)^B5

	A	B	C
1	Present Value	$21,250.23	
2	Rate	4.4%	
3	Time	5	
4	Periods/Yr	4	
5	n	20	
6	Periodic rate	0.0111	
7	Amount	$26,500.00	

6. Add to the previous spreadsheet a label in cell A8 and a formula in cell B8.

B8　　▼　　f_x =B7-B1

	A	B	
1	Present Value	$21,250.23	
2	Rate	4.4%	
3	Time	5	
4	Periods/Yr	4	
5	n	20	
6	Periodic rate	0.0111	
7	Amount	$26,500.00	
8	Growth	$ 5,249.77	

Invoices

Spreadsheets are ideal for creating invoices. Once an empty invoice is set up with all the formulas, it remains to fill in the numbers, let the formulas calculate the extensions, tax and totals, and print the invoice.

Suppose we want to have a line in an invoice that may either be blank or else have an order item entered. If the line is blank, then the extension should also be blank, but if there is an entry on the line, then the extension should show the amount for that line and be included in the total. Excel has a useful function that can help us set up such an invoice.

The IF() Function

The IF() function has three expressions that are entered between the parentheses, separated by commas. The first expression is a relation to be tested, with an expected result of TRUE or FALSE. A relation usually compares one value with another using an equal sign, greater than sign (>), less than sign (<), and such.

An example of a relation for the first expression might be **B3>0**. If the result is TRUE; that is, if the contents of cell B3 is greater than 0, the second expression is used as the result of the function and gets displayed in the cell. If the first expression is FALSE (cell B3 evaluates to zero or a negative number), then the third expression is used to determine what gets displayed. Put all together, a sample IF() function would be

$$=IF(B3>0,B2+B3,"").$$

This says that if B3 is greater than zero, then the value of cells B2 and B3 (the second expression) are to be added together and displayed, but if B3 is zero or less, then the cell containing the IF() function is to be blank, as indicated by the pair of quotation marks having nothing between them (the third expression).

Function Nesting

A function may appear within another function as one of the expressions in the outer function. The following example shows how to set up a spreadsheet to illustrate the IF() function, and it uses an inner IF() function as one of the expressions in the outer IF() function.

Demonstration Sheet

Build the following spreadsheet on Sheet1. In cell D2 enter a SUM() function to add the contents of cells A2, B2 and C2 like this: **=SUM(A2:C2)**. The expression in the parentheses means all the cells within the range A2 through C2. A range may be several contiguous cells in a row or column, or all the cells in a rectangle. For a rectangle range, list its upper left cell and its lower right cell. In cell C1 type the text **The sum is**. In cell D1 enter the nested IF() function

$$=IF(D2>0,"positive",IF(D2<0,"negative","zero")).$$

Here is the setup spreadsheet showing the functions entered in the Formula Bar:

D1	▼	*fx* =IF(D2>0,"positive",IF(D2<0,"negative","zero"))				
	A	B	C	D	E	F	G
1			The sum is	zero			
2				0			

D2	▼	*fx* =SUM(A2:C2)	
	A	B	C	D
1			The sum is	zero
2				0

Now you need to test your spreadsheet by entering various numbers in cells A2, B2 and C2. Try both negative and positive numbers, observing what appears in cell D1 each time you change one of the numbers. Here are three possibilities:

D2		fx	=SUM(A2:C2)
	A	B	C	D
1			The sum is	positive
2	1	1	0	2

D2		fx	=SUM(A2:C2)
	A	B	C	D
1			The sum is	zero
2	1	1	-2	0

D2		fx	=SUM(A2:C2)
	A	B	C	D
1			The sum is	negative
2	0	1	-2	-1

You probably noticed that the nested IF() functions in cell D1 provide different words when the sum in cell D2 is positive, zero or negative. We are now ready to construct a useful invoice spreadsheet.

Try It: Invoice Using Excel

Set up the Organic Grain Cereal Co. invoice shown in Chapter 7, page 194 in the 6th edition of the text, providing a dozen lines for order items, although only three products are shown on the invoice. The total for each ordered product should be calculated by a formula that includes the IF() function. The total cell should either display the extended price when an item appears on the line, or else it should be blank (not zero) when there is no ordered item on the line.

Try It Solution: Excel Invoice

First, erase all the cells in your test sheet by clicking on the empty cell that is immediately below the left end of the Name Box. This empty cell is above the row 1 label and to the left of the column A label. Clicking it selects every cell in the sheet.

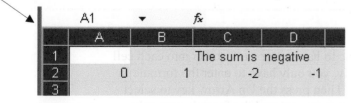

A1		fx	
	A	B	C	D
1			The sum is	negative
2	0	1	-2	-1
3				

With all the cells selected, press the Delete key. All the cells are now empty. Next rename Sheet1 by double clicking its name on the tab at the bottom of the sheet and typing in the name **Invoice** followed by the Enter key.

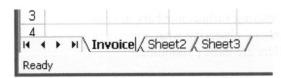

The first several rows of an invoice will contain text and dates. Copy the example from Chapter 7, page 194 in the 6th edition, adjusting column widths, using upper case and bold type where shown, and adjusting the alignment of text in cells as needed:

	A	B	C	D	E	F	G	H	I	J
1						INVOICE				
2										
3		Organic Grain Cereal Co.					INVOICE DATE			
4		697 Canyon Road							August 19, 20xx	
5		Boulder, CO 80304					CUSTOMER'S			
6							ORDER NO.		B-1623	
7										
8	SOLD TO:							SHIP TO:		
9		KROEGER MARKETS							DISTRIBUTION CENTER	
10		565 North Avenue							1424 Peachtree Road	
11		Atlanta, Georgia 30348							Atlanta, Georgia 30341	
12										
13	SALESMAN		SHIPPED VIA			TERMS		F.O.B.		
14		H. L. Mager	Terminal Transport			Net - 45 Days		Boulder, CO		
15										
16		Qty Ordered		Qty Shipped		DESCRIPTION			Unit Price	AMOUNT

Starting on row 17 enter the line items of the invoice. Formulas will be entered in column J. There are a dozen rows into which line items may be entered. Each column J of those rows (17 through 28) will contain a formula to calculate its row amount, but do not enter the formulas yet. Note that the quantities in columns B and D are entered as pure numbers in a separate column from their unit type, cs. in this example. This is because if numbers are to be used in a formula they may not have text in the same cell with them. That is why the kind of unit is listed in a separate cell.

J17   ▼ f_x =IF(D17>0,D17*I17,"")

	A	B	C	D	E	F	G	H	I	J
14	H. L. Mager		Terminal Transport			Net - 45 Days		Boulder, CO		
15										
16		Qty Ordered		Qty Shipped		DESCRIPTION			Unit Price	AMOUNT
17		55	cs.	55	cs.	Corn Crunchies 24 oz.			22.19	1220.45
18		28	cs.	28	cs.	Fruit and Nut Flakes 24 oz.			19.34	541.52
19		41	cs.	22	cs.	Rice & Wheat Flakes 16 oz.			21.14	465.08
20										

Propagating a Formula

It would be tiresome and error prone to have to type a formula into each cell in J column, rows 17 through 28. Fortunately, you only have to enter the formula in cell J17 and press the Enter key. Do it now. Then press the Up Arrow key to select cell J17. Look at the Formula Bar to make sure you entered the formula correctly before you go on. Next, move the mouse cursor over the little black square, called the *fill handle*, in the lower right corner of the cell. As the cursor gets there it changes into a black cross. Now press and hold the left mouse button and drag the cursor down the column, stopping after you pass far enough into cell J28 so that the heavy black border includes that cell. Now release the mouse button. This copies the J17 formula into all the cells you passed down through, and Excel automatically adjusted the row numbers as it propagated the formula into each cell.

At the bottom of the sheet, starting on row 29, is the summary and total area. First enter the labels in column H.

	Qty Ordered	Qty Shipped	DESCRIPTION	Unit Price	AMOUNT
16	Qty Ordered	Qty Shipped	DESCRIPTION	Unit Price	AMOUNT
17	55 cs.	55 cs.	Corn Crunchies 24 oz.	22.19	1220.45
18	28 cs.	28 cs.	Fruit and Nut Flakes 24 oz.	19.34	541.52
19	41 cs.	22 cs.	Rice & Wheat Flakes 16 oz.	21.14	465.08
20					
21					
22					
23					
24					
25					
26					
27					
28					
29			INVOICE SUBTOTAL		2227.05
30			FREIGHT CHARGES		67.45
31			INSURANCE		33.00
32			INVOICE TOTAL		$2,327.50

In cell J29 enter the function **=SUM(J17:J28)**. Enter the numbers into cells J30 and J31. Type the function **=SUM(J29:J31)** into cell J32.

Review Exercises

Use the Try It spreadsheet you created to do the following exercises.

1. Change the name of the sheet from **Invoice** to **Kroeger Order**

2. Put an additional order item on line 20: 38 cartons of Oatmeal Almond Crunch 22 ounce. Only 35 cartons were shipped. Cost is $15.58 per carton.

3. Change the Insurance from a number to a formula that calculates it: $11 plus $1 per whole hundred dollars of the Invoice Subtotal. (Hint: use the INT() function to get the whole number portion of the Invoice Subtotal divided by 100.)

4. (Challenge) A company memo has been issued stating that freight charges will be 1.8 cents per ton-mile, effective immediately. Your boss wants you to modify the invoice spreadsheet:

   a) Use column A to display the weight in ounces of a box of cereal on its order line.

   b) Show the distance in miles to be shipped on the same line as the freight charges appear. The distance from the cereal factory in Boulder to the Kroeger distribution center in Atlanta is 1425 miles.

   c) Use a formula or formulas to calculate the freight charges. A case has 32 boxes of cereal in it, whereas a carton only has 24 boxes in it.

Review Exercise Solutions

1. Double click the label tab, type in **Kroeger Order** and press the Enter Key

   ▸ ▸\ **Kroeger Order** ⟋ Sheet2 ⟋ Sheet3 ⟋

2. In row 20 enter the data in cells B through F, and cell I20, as shown below.

	41 cs.	22 cs.	Rice & Wheat Flakes 16 oz.	21.14	455.00
20	38 ctn.	35 ctn.	Oatmeal Almond Crunch 22 oz.	15.58	545.30

3. The formula for cell J31 is shown in the Formula Bar.

   J31 ▾ *fx* =11+INT(J29/100)

	A	B	C	D	E	F	G	H	I	J
28										
29								INVOICE SUBTOTAL		2772.35
30								FREIGHT CHARGES		67.45
31								INSURANCE		38.00
								INVOICE TOTAL		$2,877.80

4a. Enter a label in A16 to identify the numbers below it. Copy the number of ounces from the description.

   A20 ▾ *fx* 22

	A	B	C
15			
16	Oz. per Box	Qty Ordered	
17	24	55 cs.	
18	24	28 cs.	
19	16	41 cs.	
20	22	38 ctn.	

4b. The number of miles in cell G30 has been aligned left to be closer to its label.

E	F	G	H	I	J
			INVOICE SUBTOTAL		2772.35
SHIPPING MILES		1425	FREIGHT CHARGES		74.94
			INSURANCE		38.00
			INVOICE TOTAL		$2,885.29

4c. For each order line, the ounces per box must be multiplied by the quantity shipped, then by the number of boxes per carton or case, as applicable. To convert to pounds, divide the total of the above products by 16, then divide by 2000 to convert to tons. Finally, multiply by the miles and by the ton-mile rate. Note the Formula Bar has a long, complicated formula that only applies to this precise invoice as it has been filled in with only four items ordered. Is this a good way to set up the invoice? What if additional items are ordered? Will you need to change the formula?

	J30	▼		_fx_	=((A17*D17+A18*D18+A19*D19)*32+A20*D20*24)/16/2000*G30*0.018					
	A	B	C	D	E	F	G	H	I	J
16	Oz. per Box	Qty Ordered		Qty Shipped		DESCRIPTION			Unit Price	AMOUNT
17	24	55	cs.	55	cs.	Corn Crunchies 24 oz.			22.19	1220.45
18	24	28	cs.	28	cs.	Fruit and Nut Flakes 24 oz.			19.34	541.52
19	16	41	cs.	22	cs.	Rice & Wheat Flakes 16 oz.			21.14	465.08
20	22	38	ctn.	35	ctn.	Oatmeal Almond Crunch 22 oz.			15.58	545.30
21										
22										
23										
24										
25										
26										
27										
28										
29								INVOICE SUBTOTAL		2772.35
30					SHIPPING MILES 1425			FREIGHT CHARGES		74.94
31								INSURANCE		38.00
32								INVOICE TOTAL		$2,885.29

Better Invoice Design

Yes, you will need to change the formula if more items are ordered. A more general purpose sheet would have a cell for each order item that calculates the weight in pounds, say in column K. It could use the IF() function to select a multiplier for the number of boxes per shipping unit. Assume that cases and cartons are the only kinks of units shipped shipped by Organic Cereal Co. The row 17 formula for this might be **=A17*D17*IF(E17="cs.",32,24)/16**. Then it could be propagated down through cell K28 by using the fill handle. But using this formula on lines without an order item would result in a zero being displayed. So a better formula would provide a blank in the K cell for blank item lines: **=IF(D17=0,"",A17*D17*IF(E17="cs.",32, 24)/16)**. With this formula in column K of the order lines, then the formula in J30 would only have to convert the sum of the pounds to ton-mile-dollars. Notice in the figure below that the selected cell, K21, is blank, but has a formula in it as shown in the Formula Bar.

	K21	▼		_fx_	=IF(D21=0,"",A21*D21*IF(E21="cs.",32,24)/16)						
	A	B	C	D	E	F	G	H	I	J	K
16	Oz. per Box	Qty Ordered		Qty Shipped		DESCRIPTION			Unit Price	AMOUNT	Pounds
17	24	55	cs.	55	cs.	Corn Crunchies 24 oz.			22.19	1220.45	2640
18	24	28	cs.	28	cs.	Fruit and Nut Flakes 24 oz.			19.34	541.52	1344
19	16	41	cs.	22	cs.	Rice & Wheat Flakes 16 oz.			21.14	465.08	704
20	22	38	ctn.	35	ctn.	Oatmeal Almond Crunch 22 oz.			15.58	545.30	1155
21											

Here is the FREIGHT CHARGES cell, J30, showing the new formula that sums the pounds in column K and calculates the charge:

=SUM(K17:K28)/2000*G30*.018.

	J30	▼		f_x	=SUM(K17:K28)/2000*G30*0.018				
	A	B	C	D	E	F	G	H	I	J
28										
29								INVOICE SUBTOTAL		2772.35
30					SHIPPING MILES	1425	FREIGHT CHARGES		74.94
31								INSURANCE		38.00
32								INVOICE TOTAL		$2,885.29

This invoice sheet is now more general purpose than if the longer, more complicated formula was used that was specific just to the four items ordered. The latter set up will work for up to 12 items that may be entered on the sheet, because the insurance and freight charges will automatically be calculated no matter if the number of items on the invoice is one, a dozen, or any number in between.

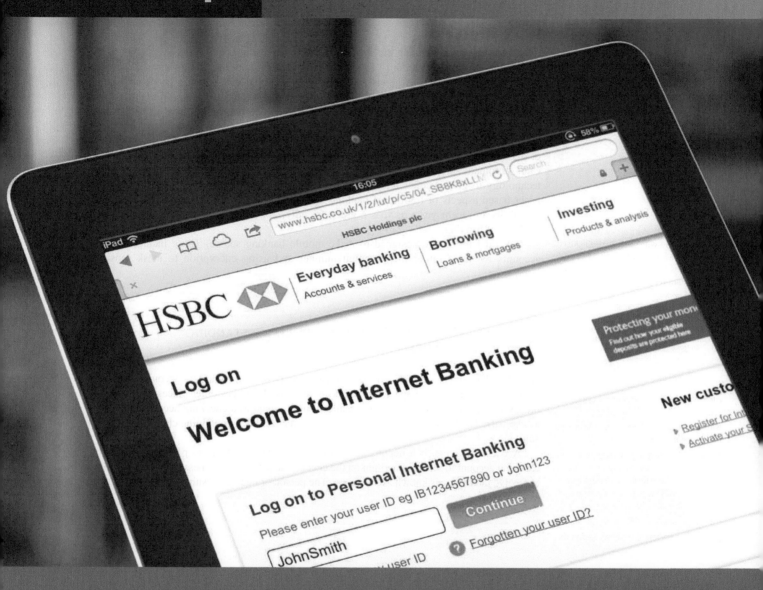

Ian Dagnall/Alamy

PERFORMANCE OBJECTIVES

The percentage of internet users who banked online was 12% in 1998. Just fifteen years later it reached 61%, and it continues to rise rapidly each year. (Pew Research Center)

Checking accounts are among the most useful and common banking services available today. They provide a detailed record of monetary transactions and are used by most businesses and individuals to purchase goods and services and to pay bills. When a checking account is opened, banks often require an initial minimum deposit of $50 or $100. Certain types of accounts require a minimum *average monthly balance* in the account. If the balance falls below the minimum, the bank may charge a fee.

Checking account transactions are processed in our banking system using a combination of paper checks and electronic options such as automated teller machines (ATMs), debit cards, automatic bill paying, and electronic funds transfer (EFT). Online banking uses today's technology to give account holders the option of bypassing some of the time-consuming paper-based aspects of traditional banking (Exhibit 4-1), Online banking has increased in popularity in recent years as it is a green-friendly, convenient alternative to paper-based methods of banking.

Several features are designed to make mobile banking secure. These include viewing accounts by name rather than account number and using encryption to mask sensitive information.

4-1 OPENING A CHECKING ACCOUNT AND UNDERSTANDING HOW VARIOUS FORMS ARE USED

deposits Funds added to a checking account.

depositor A person who deposits money in a checking account.

check, or **draft** A written order to a bank by a depositor to pay the amount specified on the check from funds on deposit in a checking account.

payee The person or business named on the check to receive the money.

payor The person or business issuing the check.

After you have chosen a bank, the account is usually opened by a new accounts officer or a clerk. After the initial paperwork has been completed, the customer places an amount of money in the account as an opening balance. Funds added to a checking account are known as **deposits**. The bank will then give the **depositor** a checkbook containing checks and deposit slips.

A **check**, or **draft**, is a negotiable instrument ordering the bank to pay money from the checking account to the name written on the check. The person or business named on the check to receive the money is known as the **payee**. The person or business issuing the check is known as the **payor**.

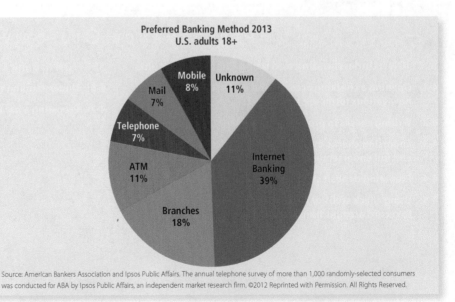

EXHIBIT 4-1
Preferred Banking Method—2013

Preferred Banking Method 2013
U.S. adults 18+

- Mobile 8%
- Unknown 11%
- Mail 7%
- Telephone 7%
- ATM 11%
- Internet Banking 39%
- Branches 18%

Source: American Bankers Association and Ipsos Public Affairs. The annual telephone survey of more than 1,000 randomly-selected consumers was conducted for ABA by Ipsos Public Affairs, an independent market research firm. ©2012 Reprinted with Permission. All Rights Reserved.

Checks are available in many sizes, colors, and designs; however, they all contain the same fundamental elements. Exhibit 4-2 shows a check with the major parts labeled. Look at the illustration carefully and familiarize yourself with the various parts of the check.

Deposit slips, or deposit tickets, are printed forms with the depositor's name, address, account number, and space for the details of the deposit. Deposit slips are used to record money, both cash and checks, being *added* to the checking account. They are presented to the bank teller along with the items to be deposited. When a deposit is completed, the depositor receives a copy of the deposit slip as a receipt, or proof of the transaction. The deposit should also be recorded by the depositor on the current check stub or in the check register. Exhibit 4-3 is an example of a deposit slip.

Either **check stubs** or a **check register** can be used to keep track of the checks written, the deposits added, and the current account balance. It is very important to keep these records accurate and up to date. This will prevent the embarrassing error of writing checks with insufficient funds in the account.

Check stubs, with checks attached by perforation, are usually a bound part of the checkbook. A sample check stub with a check is shown in Exhibit 4-4. Note that the check number is preprinted on both the check and the attached stub. Each stub is used to record the issuing of its corresponding check and any deposits made on that date.

Check registers are the alternative method for keeping track of checking account activity. They are a separate booklet of forms rather than stubs attached to each check. A sample check register is shown in Exhibit 4-5. Note that space is provided for all the pertinent information required to keep an accurate and up-to-date running balance of the account.

deposit slips Printed forms with the depositor's name, address, account number, and space for the details of the deposit. Used to record money, both cash and checks, being added to the checking account.

check stubs A bound part of the checkbook attached by perforation to checks. Used to keep track of the checks written, deposits, and current account balance of a checking account.

check register A separate booklet of blank forms used to keep track of all checking account activity. An alternative to the check stub.

EXHIBIT 4-2 Check

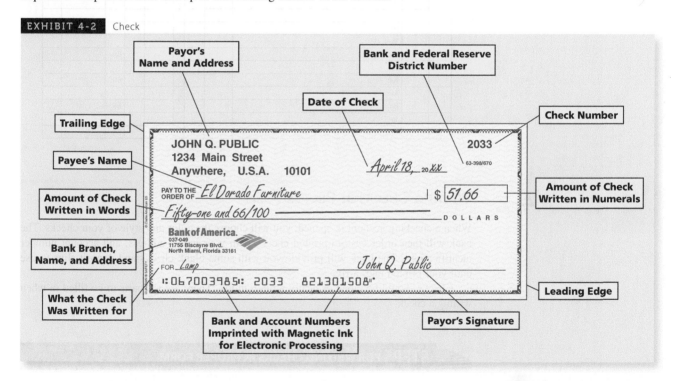

EXHIBIT 4-3

Deposit Slip

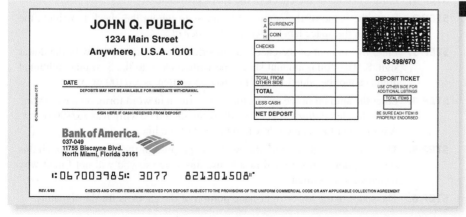

Check Stub with Check

IF TAX DEDUCTIBLE CHECK HERE ☐	$
3078	
	20___
TO	
FOR	
BAL. FWD.	DOLLARS	CENTS
DEPOSIT		
DEPOSIT		
TOTAL		
THIS ITEM		
SUB-TOTAL		
OTHER DEDUCT. (IF ANY)		
BAL. FWD.		

JOHN Q. PUBLIC   3078
1234 Main Street
Anywhere, U.S.A. 10101   _____ 20___   63-398/670

PAY TO THE
ORDER OF _____ $ _____

_____ D O L L A R S

Bank of America.
037-049
11755 Biscayne Blvd.
North Miami, Florida 33161

FOR _____

⑆067003985⑆ 3078 821301508⑇

Check Register

PLEASE BE SURE TO **DEDUCT** ANY BANK CHARGES THAT APPLY TO YOUR ACCOUNT.

CHECK NUMBER	DATE	DESCRIPTION OF TRANSACTION	AMOUNT OF PAYMENT OR WITHDRAWAL (-)	✔	AMOUNT OF DEPOSIT OR INTEREST (+)	BALANCE FORWARD	
		To					
		For				Bal.	
		To					
		For				Bal.	
		To					
		For				Bal.	
		To					
		For				Bal.	
		To					
		For				Bal.	
		To					
		For				Bal.	

4-2 WRITING CHECKS IN PROPER FORM

When a checking account is opened, you will choose the color and style of your checks. The bank will then order custom-printed checks with your name, address, and account number identifications. The bank will provide you with some blank checks and deposit slips to use until your printed ones arrive.

Checks should be typed or neatly written in ink. There are six parts to be filled in when writing a check.

IN THE Business World

When there is a discrepancy between the numerical and written word amount of a check, banks consider the *written word amount* as official.

STEPS FOR WRITING CHECKS IN PROPER FORM

STEP 1. Enter the *date* of the check in the space provided.

STEP 2. Enter the name of the person or business to whom the check is written, the payee, in the space labeled *pay to the order of.*

STEP 3. Enter the amount of the check in numerical form in the space with the dollar sign, $. The dollar amount should be written close to the $ so that additional digits cannot be added. The cents may be written as xx/100 or .xx.

STEP 4. Enter the amount of the check, this time written in word form, on the next line down, labeled *dollars.* As before, the cents should be written as xx/100 or .xx. A horizontal line is then drawn to the end of the line.

STEP 5. The space labeled *for* is used to write the purpose of the check. Although this step is optional, it's a good idea to use this space so you will not forget why the check was written.

STEP 6. The space in the lower right-hand portion of the check is for the signature.

EXAMPLE 1 WRITING A CHECK

Write a check for Walter Anderson to the Falcon Tire Center for a front-end alignment in the amount of $83.73 on June 7, 20xx.

►SOLUTIONSTRATEGY

Here is the check for Walter Anderson written in proper form. Note that the amount, $83.73, is written $83 and 73/100 and the name is signed as it is printed on the check.

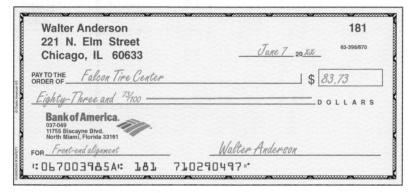

Walter Anderson
221 N. Elm Street
Chicago, IL 60633

181

63-398/670

June 7 20 *xx*

PAY TO THE ORDER OF __*Falcon Tire Center*__ $ *83.73*

Eighty-Three and 73/100 —————— DOLLARS

Bank of America.
037-049
11755 Biscayne Blvd.
North Miami, Florida 33161

FOR *Front-end alignment*   *Walter Anderson*

⑆067003985A⑆ 181 710290497⑈

►TRYITEXERCISE 1

1. Use the following blank to write a check for Natalie Eldridge to Whole Foods for a party platter in the amount of $41.88 on April 27.

Natalie Eldridge
1585 S. W. 6 Avenue
Tallahassee, FL 32399

206

63-398/670

20 _____

PAY TO THE ORDER OF _____ $

——————— DOLLARS

Bank of America.
037-049
11755 Biscayne Blvd.
North Miami, Florida 33161

FOR _____

⑆067003985⑆ 206 821451902⑈

CHECK YOUR ANSWER WITH THE SOLUTION ON PAGE 115.

ENDORSING CHECKS BY USING BLANK, RESTRICTIVE, AND FULL ENDORSEMENTS

4-3

When you receive a check, you may cash it, deposit it in your account, or transfer it to another party. The **endorsement** on the back of the check instructs the bank on what to do. Federal regulations require that specific areas of the reverse side of checks be designated for the payee and bank endorsements. Your endorsement should be written within the $1\frac{1}{2}$-inch space at the trailing edge of the check, as shown in Exhibit 4-6. The space is usually labeled "ENDORSE HERE."

There are three types of endorsements with which you should become familiar: blank endorsements, restrictive endorsements, and full endorsements, which are shown in Exhibits 4-7, 4-8, and 4-9, respectively.

endorsement The signature and instructions on the back of a check instructing the bank on what to do with that check.

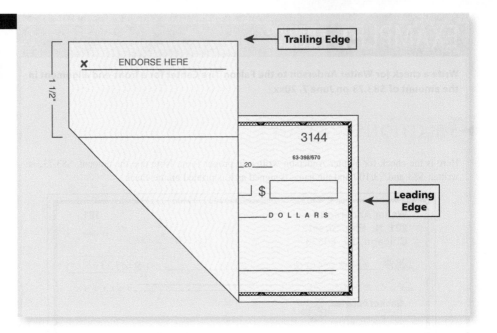

EXHIBIT 4-6
Endorsement Space

John Q. Public
82-1301-508

EXHIBIT 4-7
Blank Endorsement

for deposit only
John Q. Public
82-1301-508

EXHIBIT 4-8
Restrictive Endorsement

pay to the order of
Cindy J. Citizen
John Q. Public
82-1301-508

EXHIBIT 4-9
Full Endorsement

blank endorsement An endorsement used when the payee wants to cash a check.

restrictive endorsement An endorsement used when the payee wants to deposit a check in his or her account.

full endorsement An endorsement used when the payee wants to transfer a check to another party.

A **blank endorsement** is used when you want to cash the check. You, as the payee, simply sign your name exactly as it appears on the front of the check and write your account number. Once you have endorsed a check in this manner, anyone who has possession of the check can cash it. For this reason, you should use blank endorsements cautiously.

A **restrictive endorsement** is used when you want to deposit the check in your account. In this case, you endorse the check "for deposit only," sign your name as it appears on the front, and write your account number.

A **full endorsement** is used when you want to transfer the check to another party. In this case, you endorse the check "pay to the order of," write the name of the person or business to whom the check is being transferred, sign your name, and write your account number.

EXAMPLE2   ENDORSING A CHECK

You have just received a check. Your account number is #2922-22-33-4. Write the following endorsements and identify what type they are.

a. Allowing you to cash the check.

b. Allowing you to deposit the check in your checking account.

c. Allowing the check to be transferred to your partner Sam Johnson.

► SOLUTIONSTRATEGY

a.

Blank Endorsement
Your Signature
2922-22-33-4

b.

Restrictive Endorsement
for deposit only
Your Signature
2922-22-33-4

c.

Full Endorsement
pay to the order
of Sam Johnson
Your Signature
2922-22-33-4

► TRYITEXERCISE 2

You have just received a check. Your account number is #696-339-1028. Write the following endorsements in the space provided and identify what type they are.

a. Allowing the check to be transferred to your friend Roz Reitman.

b. Allowing you to cash the check.

c. Allowing you to deposit the check in your checking account.

a.

b.

c.

CHECK YOUR ANSWERS WITH THE SOLUTIONS ON PAGE 116.

PREPARING DEPOSIT SLIPS IN PROPER FORM

4-4

Deposit slips are filled out and presented to the bank along with the funds being deposited. They are dated and list the currency, coins, individual checks, and total amount of the deposit. Note on the sample deposit slip, Exhibit 4-10, that John Q. Public took $100 in cash out of the deposit, which required him to sign the deposit slip.

JOHN Q. PUBLIC
1234 Main Street
Anywhere, U.S.A. 10101

DATE *April 18,* 20 XX
DEPOSITS MAY NOT BE AVAILABLE FOR IMMEDIATE WITHDRAWAL

John Q. Public
SIGN HERE IF CASH RECEIVED FROM DEPOSIT

Bank of America.
037-049
11755 Biscayne Blvd.
North Miami, Florida 33161

⑆067003985⑆   821301508⑈

REV. 6/88   CHECKS AND OTHER ITEMS ARE RECEIVED FOR DEPOSIT SUBJECT TO THE PROVISIONS OF THE UNIFORM COMMERCIAL CODE OR ANY APPLICABLE COLLECTION AGREEMENT

CASH	CURRENCY	121	00
	COIN	16	10
CHECKS		237	55
		500	00
TOTAL FROM OTHER SIDE			
TOTAL		874	65
LESS CASH		100	00
NET DEPOSIT		774	65

63-398/670

DEPOSIT TICKET
USE OTHER SIDE FOR
ADDITIONAL LISTINGS

TOTAL ITEMS

BE SURE EACH ITEM IS
PROPERLY ENDORSED

Mobile Deposit Many banks now allow checks to be deposited by using a smartphone app. Part of the process involves sending photos of both sides of the check after it has been endorsed.

EXAMPLE3   PREPARING A DEPOSIT SLIP

Prepare a deposit slip for Jamie McCallon based on the following information.

a. Date: June 4, 20xx.

b. $127 in currency.

c. $3.47 in coins.

d. A check for $358.89 and a check for $121.68.

SOLUTIONSTRATEGY

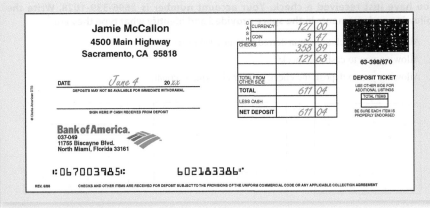

TRYITEXERCISE 3

Fill out the deposit slip for Hi-Volt Electronics based on the following information.

a. Date: November 11, 20xx.

b. $3,549 in currency.

c. 67 quarters, 22 dimes, and 14 nickels.

d. A check for $411.92 and a check for $2,119.56.

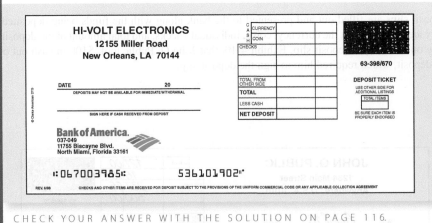

CHECK YOUR ANSWER WITH THE SOLUTION ON PAGE 116.

4-5   USING CHECK STUBS OR CHECKBOOK REGISTERS TO RECORD ACCOUNT TRANSACTIONS

In Performance Objective 4-1, we learned that some people use check stubs to keep records and some use check registers. Exhibit 4-11 shows a check and its corresponding stub properly filled out. Note that the check number is printed on the stub. The stub is used to record the amount of the check, the date, the payee, and the purpose of the check. In addition, the stub also records the balance forwarded from the last stub, deposits made since the previous check, and the new balance of the account after the current check and any other charges are deducted.

Check registers record the same information as the stub but in a different format. Exhibit 4-12 shows a check register properly filled out. The starting balance is located in the upper right-hand corner. In keeping a check register, it is your option to write it single spaced or double spaced. Remember, in reality, you would use *either* the check stub or the checkbook register.

EXHIBIT 4-11 Check with Filled-Out Stub

EXHIBIT 4-12
Filled-Out Check Register

PLEASE BE SURE TO **DEDUCT** ANY BANK CHARGES THAT APPLY TO YOUR ACCOUNT.

CHECK NUMBER	DATE	DESCRIPTION OF TRANSACTION	AMOUNT OF PAYMENT OR WITHDRAWAL (−)	✓	AMOUNT OF DEPOSIT OR INTEREST (+)	BALANCE FORWARD	
						560	00
450	1/6	To MasterCard / For	34	60			
						Bal. 525	40
451	1/8	To Allstate Insurance / For	166	25			
						Bal. 359	15
	1/12	To Electronic Payroll Deposit / For			340 00		
						Bal. 699	15
452	1/13	To CVS Pharmacy / For	15	50			
						Bal. 683	65
	1/15	To Deposit / For			88 62		
						Bal. 772	27
	1/17	To ATM—Withdrawal / For	100	00			
						Bal. 672	27
	1/21	To Debit Card—AMC Theater / For	24	15			
						Bal. 648	12

EXAMPLE4   RECORDING ACCOUNT TRANSACTIONS

From the following information, complete the two check stubs and the check register in proper form.

a. Starting balance $1,454.21.

b. January 14, 20xx, check #056 in the amount of $69.97 issued to Paints & Pails Hardware for a ladder.

c. January 19, 20xx, deposit of $345.00.

d. February 1, 20xx, check #057 in the amount of $171.55 issued to Northern Power & Light for electricity bill.

e. February 1, 20xx, debit card purchase—groceries, $77.00.

►SOLUTIONSTRATEGY

Below are the properly completed stubs and register. Note that the checks were subtracted from the balance and that the deposits were added to the balance.

IF TAX DEDUCTIBLE CHECK HERE ☐	$ 69.97
056	
Jan. 14 20 xx	
TO _Paints & Pails_	
FOR _ladder_	

	DOLLARS	CENTS
BAL. FWD.	1,454	21
DEPOSIT		
DEPOSIT		
TOTAL	1,454	21
THIS ITEM	69	97
SUB-TOTAL	1,384	24
OTHER DEDUCT. (IF ANY)		
BAL. FWD.	1,384	24

IF TAX DEDUCTIBLE CHECK HERE ☐	$ 171.55
057	
Feb. 1 20 xx	
TO _Northern P & L_	
FOR _electricity bill_	

	DOLLARS	CENTS
BAL. FWD.	1,384	24
DEPOSIT 1/19	345	00
DEPOSIT		
TOTAL	1,729	24
THIS ITEM	171	55
SUB-TOTAL	1,557	69
OTHER DEDUCT. (IF ANY)	77	00
BAL. FWD.	1,480	69

PLEASE BE SURE TO **DEDUCT** ANY BANK CHARGES THAT APPLY TO YOUR ACCOUNT.

CHECK NUMBER	DATE	DESCRIPTION OF TRANSACTION	AMOUNT OF PAYMENT OR WITHDRAWAL (−)	✔	AMOUNT OF DEPOSIT OR INTEREST (+)		BALANCE FORWARD	
							1,454	21
056	1/14	To _Paints & Pails Hardware_	69 97					
		For					Bal. 1,384	24
	1/19	To _Deposit_			345 00			
		For					Bal. 1,729	24
057	2/1	To _Northern Power & Light_	171 55					
		For					Bal. 1,557	69
	2/1	To _Debit Card—Groceries, $77._	77 00					
		For					Bal. 1,480	69

► TRYITEXERCISE 4

From the following information, complete the two check stubs and the check register in proper form.

a. Starting balance $887.45.

b. March 12, 20xx, check #137 issued to Nathan & David Hair Stylists for a permanent and manicure in the amount of $55.75.

c. March 16, 20xx, deposits of $125.40 and $221.35.

d. March 19, 20xx, check #138 issued to Complete Auto Service for car repairs in the amount of $459.88.

e. March 20, 20xx, debit card purchase—post office, $53.00.

IF TAX DEDUCTIBLE CHECK HERE ☐	$_____
137	
_____ 20 ___	
TO _____	
FOR _____	

	DOLLARS	CENTS
BAL. FWD.		
DEPOSIT		
DEPOSIT		
TOTAL		
THIS ITEM		
SUB-TOTAL		
OTHER DEDUCT. (IF ANY)		
BAL. FWD.		

IF TAX DEDUCTIBLE CHECK HERE ☐	$_____
138	
_____ 20 ___	
TO _____	
FOR _____	

	DOLLARS	CENTS
BAL. FWD.		
DEPOSIT		
DEPOSIT		
TOTAL		
THIS ITEM		
SUB-TOTAL		
OTHER DEDUCT. (IF ANY)		
BAL. FWD.		

PLEASE BE SURE TO **DEDUCT** ANY BANK CHARGES THAT APPLY TO YOUR ACCOUNT.

CHECK NUMBER	DATE	DESCRIPTION OF TRANSACTION	AMOUNT OF PAYMENT OR WITHDRAWAL (−)	✔	AMOUNT OF DEPOSIT OR INTEREST (+)		BALANCE FORWARD	
		To						
		For					Bal.	
		To						
		For					Bal.	
		To						
		For					Bal.	
		To						
		For					Bal.	
		To						
		For					Bal.	
		To						
		For					Bal.	

CHECK YOUR ANSWERS WITH THE SOLUTION ON PAGE 116.

REVIEW EXERCISES

4 SECTION I

You are the owner of the Busy Bee Launderette. Using the blanks provided, write out the following checks in proper form.

1. Check #2550, September 14, 20xx, in the amount of $345.54 to the Silky Soap Company for 300 gallons of liquid soap.

JUMP START WWW

BUSY BEE LAUNDERETTE
214 Collings Blvd.
Durham, NC 27704
2550
Sept. 14 20 xx
63-398/670
PAY TO THE ORDER OF Silky Soap Company $ 345.54
Three Hundred Forty-Five and 54/100 DOLLARS
Bank of America.
037-049
11755 Biscayne Blvd.
North Miami, Florida 33161
FOR 300 gals. Soap
Your Signature
⑆067003985⑆ 2550 821301508⑈

2. Check #2551, September 20, 20xx, in the amount of $68.95 to the Tidy Towel Service for six dozen wash rags.

BUSY BEE LAUNDERETTE
214 Collings Blvd.
Durham, NC 27704
2551
20
63-398/670
PAY TO THE ORDER OF $
DOLLARS
Bank of America.
037-049
11755 Biscayne Blvd.
North Miami, Florida 33161
FOR
⑆067003985⑆ 2551 821301508⑈

Dollars AND Sense

The Federal Deposit Insurance Corporation (FDIC) insures every depositor for at least $250,000 at each insured bank. People with more than $250,000 can split their cash among insured banks to remain fully protected. The FDIC insures more than 8,000 banks nationwide.

You have just received a check. Your account number is #099-506-8. Write the following endorsements in the space provided below and identify what type they are.

3. Allowing you to deposit the check in your account.
4. Allowing you to cash the check.
5. Allowing you to transfer the check to your friend David Sporn.

3.

4.

5.

6. Properly fill out the deposit slip for The Star Vista Corp. based on the following information:
   a. Date: July 9, 20xx.
   b. $1,680 in currency.
   c. $62.25 in coins.
   d. Checks in the amount of $2,455.94, $4,338.79, and $1,461.69.

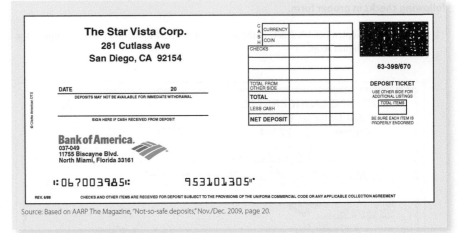

Source: Based on AARP The Magazine, "Not-so-safe deposits," Nov./Dec. 2009, page 20.

7. Properly fill out the deposit slip for Howard Lockwood based on the following information:
   a. Date: December 18, 20xx.
   b. A check for $651.03.
   c. $150 cash withdrawal.

Dollars AND Sense

Safe-deposit boxes are a type of safe usually located inside a bank vault or in the back of a bank or post office. These boxes are typically used to store things such as valuable gemstones, precious metals, currency, or important documents. In the typical arrangement, a renter pays the bank a fee for the use of the box, which can be opened only with the assigned key, the bank's key, the proper signature, or perhaps a code of some sort.

The contents of the safe-deposit boxes are not insured unless you cover them in your homeowner's or renter's insurance policy.

A "cyber backup" is a good way to protect your important documents. Banks and online vendors offer "virtual safe-deposit boxes," where digital copies of documents can be stored.

Source: *AARP The Magazine*, "Not-so-safe deposits," Nov./Dec. 2009, page 20.

8. From the following information, complete the three check stubs on page 103 in proper form.
   a. Starting balance $265.73.
   b. February 12, 20xx, check #439 in the amount of $175.05 to The Fidelity Bank for a car payment.
   c. February 15, deposit of $377.10.
   d. February 18, check #440 in the amount of $149.88 to Apex Fitness Equipment for a set of dumbbells.
   e. February 22, deposit of $570.00.
   f. February 27, check #441 in the amount of $23.40 to Royalty Cleaners for dry cleaning.
   g. March 3, debit card purchase—tires, $225.10.

IF TAX DEDUCTIBLE CHECK HERE ☐ $ _____ **439**		
_____ 20 _____		
TO _____		
FOR		
BAL. FWD.	DOLLARS	CENTS
DEPOSIT		
DEPOSIT		
TOTAL		
THIS ITEM		
SUB-TOTAL		
OTHER DEDUCT. (IF ANY)		
BAL. FWD.		

IF TAX DEDUCTIBLE CHECK HERE ☐ $ _____ **440**		
_____ 20 _____		
TO _____		
FOR		
BAL. FWD.	DOLLARS	CENTS
DEPOSIT		
DEPOSIT		
TOTAL		
THIS ITEM		
SUB-TOTAL		
OTHER DEDUCT. (IF ANY)		
BAL. FWD.		

IF TAX DEDUCTIBLE CHECK HERE ☐ $ _____ **441**		
_____ 20 _____		
TO _____		
FOR		
BAL. FWD.	DOLLARS	CENTS
DEPOSIT		
DEPOSIT		
TOTAL		
THIS ITEM		
SUB-TOTAL		
OTHER DEDUCT. (IF ANY)		
BAL. FWD.		

9. From the following information, complete the checkbook register:

a. Starting balance $479.20.

b. April 7, 20xx, deposit of $766.90.

c. April 14, 20xx, debit card purchase in the amount of $45.65 to Mario's Market for groceries.

d. April 16, ATM withdrawal, $125.00.

e. April 17, check #1208 in the amount of $870.00 to Banyan Properties, Inc., for rent.

f. April 21, 20xx, electronic payroll deposit of $1,350.00.

g. April 27, check #1209 in the amount of $864.40 to Elegant Decor for a dining room set.

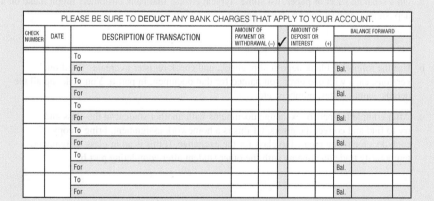

		PLEASE BE SURE TO **DEDUCT** ANY BANK CHARGES THAT APPLY TO YOUR ACCOUNT.					BALANCE FORWARD	
CHECK NUMBER	DATE	DESCRIPTION OF TRANSACTION	AMOUNT OF PAYMENT OR WITHDRAWAL (–)	✓	AMOUNT OF DEPOSIT OR INTEREST (+)			
		To						
		For				Bal.		
		To						
		For				Bal.		
		To						
		For				Bal.		
		To						
		For				Bal.		
		To						
		For				Bal.		
		To						
		For				Bal.		

10. From the following information, complete the checkbook register on page 104 through October 10.

Cheryl Roberts' account balance on September 26 was $1,196.19. On October 1, she received $3,023.11 by electronic payroll deposit. Also on October 1, she wrote check #1804 to pay her rent in the amount of $1,175.00. Cheryl used her debit card to make purchases on September 28 for $37.79, on October 2 for $311.86, and on October 3 for $164.26. On October 8, she paid her electricity bill, gas bill, and phone bill using her bank's online bill-paying service. Her electricity bill was $142.87. Gas was $18.46, and phone amounted to $38.52. On October 9, she deposited a rebate check for $50.

PLEASE BE SURE TO DEDUCT ANY BANK CHARGES THAT APPLY TO YOUR ACCOUNT.

CHECK NUMBER	DATE	DESCRIPTION OF TRANSACTION	AMOUNT OF PAYMENT OR WITHDRAWAL (−)	✓	AMOUNT OF DEPOSIT OR INTEREST (+)	BALANCE FORWARD	
		To					
		For				Bal.	
		To					
		For				Bal.	
		To					
		For				Bal.	
		To					
		For				Bal.	
		To					
		For				Bal.	
		To					
		For				Bal.	
		To					
		For				Bal.	
		To					
		For				Bal.	
		To					
		For				Bal.	
		To					
		For				Bal.	

BUSINESS DECISION: TELLER TRAINING

11. You are the training director for tellers at a large local bank. As part of a new training program that you are developing, you have decided to give teller trainees a "sample" deposit slip, check, and check register with common errors on them. The trainees must find and correct the errors. Your task is to create the three documents.

   a. On a separate sheet of paper, list some "typical errors" that bank customers might make on a deposit slip, a check, and a check register.

   b. Use the following blank deposit slip, check, and check register to create "filled-out" versions, each with one error you named for that document in part **a**. You make up all the details: names, dates, numbers, etc.

   c. After completing part **b**, exchange documents with another student in the class and try to find and correct the errors. (If this is a homework assignment, bring a copy of each document you created to class for the exchange. If this is an in-class assignment, temporarily trade documents with the other student after completing part **b**.)

Bank Teller According to the U.S. Department of Labor, bank tellers make up 28% of bank employees and conduct most of a bank's routine transactions.

In hiring tellers, banks seek people who enjoy public contact and have good numerical, clerical, and communication skills. Banks prefer applicants who have had courses in mathematics, accounting, bookkeeping, economics, and public speaking.

Stockbyte/Getty Images

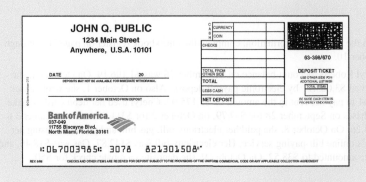

PLEASE BE SURE TO DEDUCT ANY BANK CHARGES THAT APPLY TO YOUR ACCOUNT.

CHECK NUMBER	DATE	DESCRIPTION OF TRANSACTION	AMOUNT OF PAYMENT OR WITHDRAWAL (−)	✓	AMOUNT OF DEPOSIT OR INTEREST (+)	BALANCE FORWARD	
		To					
		For				Bal.	
		To					
		For				Bal.	
		To					
		For				Bal.	
		To					
		For				Bal.	
		To					
		For				Bal.	
		To					
		For				Bal.	

BANK STATEMENT RECONCILIATION

4 SECTION II

Your monthly **bank statement** gives you a detailed review of the activity in your account for a specific period of time. It's your best opportunity to make sure your records match the bank's records. Be prepared to "match up" every activity (credits and debits) on the statement with your checkbook.

It is important that you review the bank statement in a timely fashion. If you find any discrepancies in ATM, debit card, or other electronic transactions, you must report them to the bank within 60 days of the date of the statement or the bank has no obligation to conduct an investigation. Another important reason to reconcile your checkbook with the statement is to look for debits you didn't make that might indicate that someone has access to your account.

bank statement A monthly summary of the activities in a checking account, including debits, credits, and beginning and ending balance. Sent by the bank to the account holder.

UNDERSTANDING THE BANK STATEMENT

4-6

Bank statements vary widely in style from bank to bank; however, most contain essentially the same information. Exhibit 4-13 illustrates typical online and printed bank statements. Note that it shows the balance brought forward from the last statement, the deposits and credits that have been added to the account during the month, the checks and debits that have been subtracted from the account during the month, any service charges assessed to the account, and the current or ending balance.

Credits are additions to the account, such as interest earned, notes collected, and electronic funds transfers of direct deposit payroll checks. **Debits** are subtractions from the account, such as ATM withdrawals, debit card transactions, monthly service charges, check printing charges, nonsufficient fund (NSF) fees, and returned items. A **nonsufficient fund (NSF) fee** is a fee charged by the bank when a check is written without sufficient funds in the account to cover the amount of that check. **Returned items** are checks from others that you deposited in your account but were returned to your bank unpaid because the person or business issuing the check had insufficient funds in its account to cover the check. Banks usually charge a returned item fee when this occurs.

credits Additions to a checking account, such as deposits and interest earned.

debits Subtractions from a checking account, such as service charges.

nonsufficient fund (NSF) fee A fee charged by the bank when a check is written without sufficient funds in the account to cover the amount of that check.

returned items Checks that you deposited but were returned to your bank unpaid because the person or business issuing the checks had insufficient funds to cover them.

EXHIBIT 4-13 Paper and Electronic Bank Statements

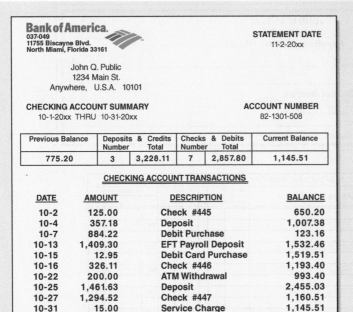

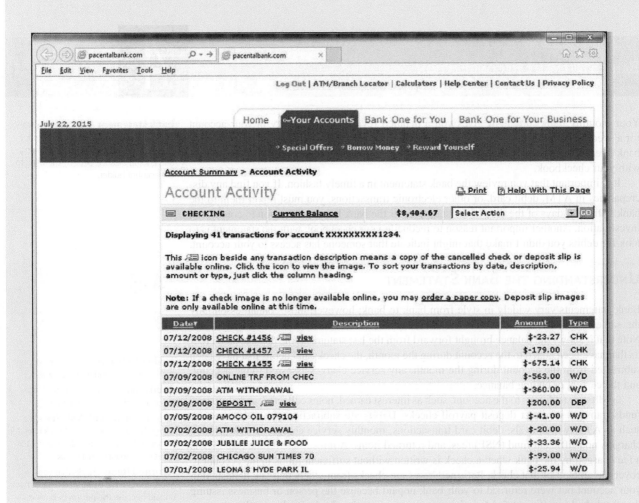

PREPARING A BANK STATEMENT RECONCILIATION

4-7

When the statement arrives from the bank each month, the depositor must compare the bank balance with the balance shown in the checkbook. Usually, the balances are not the same because during the month, some account activity has taken place without being recorded by the bank and other activities have occurred without being recorded in the checkbook. The process of adjusting the bank and checkbook balances to reflect the actual current balance is known as **bank statement reconciliation**. When we use the word *checkbook* in this chapter, we are actually referring to the records kept by the depositor on the check stubs or in the checkbook register.

Before a statement can be reconciled, you must identify and total all the checks that have been written but have not yet reached the bank. These are known as **outstanding checks**. Outstanding checks are found by comparing and checking off each check in the checkbook with those shown on the statement. Any checks not appearing on the statement are outstanding checks.

Sometimes deposits are made close to the statement date or by mail and do not clear the bank in time to appear on the current statement. These are known as **deposits in transit**. Just like outstanding checks, deposits in transit must be identified and totaled. Once again, this is done by comparing and checking off the checkbook records with the deposits shown on the bank statement.

A bank statement is reconciled when the **adjusted checkbook balance** is equal to the **adjusted bank balance**. Most bank statements have a form on the back to use in reconciling the account. Exhibit 4-14 is an example of such a form and is used in this chapter.

bank statement reconciliation The process of adjusting the bank and checkbook balances to reflect the actual current balance of the checking account.

outstanding checks Checks that have been written but have not yet reached the bank and therefore do not appear on the current bank statement.

deposits in transit Deposits made close to the statement date or by mail that do not clear in time to appear on the current bank statement.

adjusted checkbook balance The checkbook balance minus service charges and other debits plus interest earned and other credits.

adjusted bank balance The bank balance minus outstanding checks plus deposits in transit.

STEPS FOR PREPARING A BANK STATEMENT RECONCILIATION

STEP 1. Calculate the adjusted checkbook balance:
   a. Look over the bank statement and find any credits not recorded in the checkbook, such as interest earned or notes collected, and *add* them to the checkbook balance to get a subtotal.
   b. From the bank statement, locate any charges or debits such as service charges, NSF fees, or returned items that have not been recorded in the checkbook and *subtract* them from the subtotal from Step 1a.

STEP 2. Calculate the adjusted bank balance:
   a. Locate all of the deposits in transit and *add* them to the statement balance to get a subtotal.
   b. Locate and total all outstanding checks and *subtract* them from the subtotal from Step 2a.

STEP 3. Compare the adjusted balances:
   a. If they are equal, the statement has been reconciled.
   b. If they are not equal, an error exists that must be found and corrected. The error is either in the checkbook or on the bank statement.

EXHIBIT 4-14 Bank Statement Reconciliation Form

Checks Outstanding		
No.	Amount	
Total		

CHECKBOOK BALANCE	$	**STATEMENT BALANCE**	$
Add: Interest Earned & Other Credits		**Add:** Deposits in Transit	
SUBTOTAL		**SUBTOTAL**	
Deduct: Service Charges & Other Debits		**Deduct:** Outstanding Checks	
ADJUSTED CHECKBOOK BALANCE		**ADJUSTED STATEMENT BALANCE**	

Reconciled Balances

EXAMPLE5   RECONCILING A BANK STATEMENT

Prepare a bank reconciliation for Anita Gomberg from the bank statement and checkbook records below.

Grove Isle Bank

STATEMENT DATE
8-2-20xx

ANITA GOMBERG
8834 Kimberly Avenue
Surfside, FL 33154

CHECKING ACCOUNT SUMMARY
7-1-20xx THRU 7-31-20xx

ACCOUNT NUMBER
82-1301-508

Previous Balance	Deposits & Credits Number	Deposits & Credits Total	Checks & Debits Number	Checks & Debits Total	Current Balance
1,233.40	3	2,445.80	7	2,158.92	1,520.28

CHECKING ACCOUNT TRANSACTIONS

DATE	AMOUNT	DESCRIPTION	BALANCE
7-3	450.30	Check #1209	783.10
7-6	500.00	Deposit	1,283.10
7-10	47.75	Check #1210	1,235.35
7-13	1,300.00	EFT Payroll Deposit	2,535.35
7-15	312.79	Check #1212	2,222.56
7-17	547.22	Check #1214	1,675.34
7-22	350.00	ATM Withdrawal	1,325.34
7-24	645.80	Deposit	1,971.14
7-28	430.86	Debit Card Purchase	1,540.28
7-30	20.00	Service Charge	1,520.28

PLEASE BE SURE TO **DEDUCT** ANY BANK CHARGES THAT APPLY TO YOUR ACCOUNT

CHECK NUMBER	DATE	DESCRIPTION OF TRANSACTION	AMOUNT OF PAYMENT OR WITHDRAWAL (−)	✓	AMOUNT OF DEPOSIT OR INTEREST (+)		BALANCE FORWARD
							1,233 40
1209	7/1	To Home Shopping Network	450 30				
		For				Bal.	783 10
	7/6	To Deposit			500 00		
		For				Bal.	1,283 10
1210	7/8	To Food Spot	47 75				
		For				Bal.	1,235 35
1211	7/10	To Delta Air Lines	342 10				
		For				Bal.	893 25
	7/13	To Payroll Deposit			1,300 00		
		For				Bal.	2,193 25
1212	7/13	To Hyatt Hotel	312 79				
		For				Bal.	1,880 46
1213	7/15	To Wall Street Journal	75 00				
		For				Bal.	1,805 46
1214	7/15	To Fashionista	547 22				
		For				Bal.	1,258 24
	7/21	To ATM Withdrawal	350 00				
		For				Bal.	908 24
	7/24	To Deposit			645 80		
		For				Bal.	1,554 04
	7/28	To J. Crew — Debit Card	430 86				
		For				Bal.	1,123 18
	7/31	To Deposit			550 00		
		For				Bal.	1,673 18

►SOLUTIONSTRATEGY

The properly completed reconciliation form is on page 109. Note that the adjusted checkbook balance equals the adjusted bank statement balance. The balances are now reconciled. After some practice, the format will become familiar to you and you should no longer need the form.

CHECKBOOK BALANCE	$ 1,673.18	STATEMENT BALANCE	$ 1,520.28
Add: Interest Earned & Other Credits		Add: Deposits in Transit	550.00
SUBTOTAL	1,673.18	SUBTOTAL	2,070.28
Deduct: Service Charges & Other Debits	20.00	Deduct: Outstanding Checks	417.10
ADJUSTED CHECKBOOK BALANCE	1,653.18	ADJUSTED STATEMENT BALANCE	1,653.18

Reconciled Balances

Checks Outstanding

No.	Amount	
1211	342	10
1213	75	00
Total	417	10

►TRYITEXERCISE 5

Using the form provided, reconcile the following bank statement and checkbook records for Max Mangones.

North Star Bank

STATEMENT DATE
4-3-20xx

MAX MANGONES
4121 Pinetree Rd.
Bangor, Maine 04401

CHECKING ACCOUNT SUMMARY
3-1-20xx THRU 3-31-20xx

ACCOUNT NUMBER
097440

Previous Balance	Deposits & Credits Number	Total	Checks & Debits Number	Total	Current Balance
625.40	3	1,790.00	8	690.00	1,725.40

CHECKING ACCOUNT TRANSACTIONS

DATE	AMOUNT	DESCRIPTION	BALANCE
3-2	34.77	Debit Card Purchase	590.63
3-6	750.00	Payroll-EFT Deposit	1,340.63
3-10	247.05	Check #340	1,093.58
3-13	390.00	Deposit	1,483.58
3-15	66.30	Check #342	1,417.28
3-17	112.18	Check #343	1,305.10
3-22	150.00	ATM Withdrawal	1,155.10
3-24	650.00	Deposit	1,805.10
3-28	50.00	Check #345	1,755.10
3-30	17.70	Check Printing Charge	1,737.40
3-31	12.00	Service Charge	1,725.40

IN THE Business World

How Banks Process Transactions
According to the FDIC, large banks are more likely to clear checks from large to small dollar amounts, often resulting in more overdraft fees.

For example, let's say someone has $100 in his or her checking account and writes four checks: $20, $30, $40, and $110. If that person's bank clears the checks from small to large, it would charge one overdraft fee. However, if the bank clears the checks from large to small, it would be able to charge four overdraft fees!

PLEASE BE SURE TO **DEDUCT** ANY BANK CHARGES THAT APPLY TO YOUR ACCOUNT.

CHECK NUMBER	DATE	DESCRIPTION OF TRANSACTION	AMOUNT OF PAYMENT OR WITHDRAWAL (–)	✓	AMOUNT OF DEPOSIT OR INTEREST (+)	BALANCE FORWARD
						625	40
	3/2	To Naples Pet Shop — Debit Card	34	77				
		For					Bal.	590	63
	3/5	To Electronic Payroll Deposit				750	00		
		For					Bal.	1,340	63
339	3/5	To Alison Company	19	83				
		For					Bal.	1,320	80
340	3/9	To Tennis Warehouse	247	05				
		For					Bal.	1,073	75
	3/12	To Deposit				390	00		
		For					Bal.	1,463	75
341	3/12	To The Book Shelf	57	50				
		For					Bal.	1,406	25
342	3/13	To Walmart	66	30				
		For					Bal.	1,339	95
343	3/15	To Sports Authority	112	18				
		For					Bal.	1,227	77
	3/22	To ATM Withdrawal	150	00				
		For					Bal.	1,077	77
	3/24	To Deposit				650	00		
		For					Bal.	1,727	77
344	3/24	To Foot Locker	119	32				
		For					Bal.	1,608	45
345	3/28	To Cablevision, Inc.	50	00				
		For					Bal.	1,558	45
	3/30	To Deposit				240	23		
		For					Bal.	1,798	68

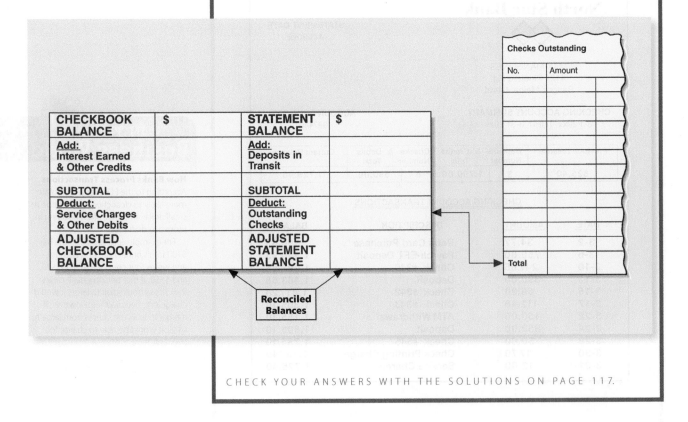

CHECKBOOK BALANCE	$	STATEMENT BALANCE	$
Add: Interest Earned & Other Credits		Add: Deposits in Transit	
SUBTOTAL		SUBTOTAL	
Deduct: Service Charges & Other Debits		Deduct: Outstanding Checks	
ADJUSTED CHECKBOOK BALANCE		ADJUSTED STATEMENT BALANCE	

Reconciled Balances

Checks Outstanding		
No.	Amount	
Total		

CHECK YOUR ANSWERS WITH THE SOLUTIONS ON PAGE 117.

REVIEW EXERCISES

1. On April 3, Erin Gardner received her bank statement showing a balance of $2,087.93. Her checkbook showed a balance of $1,493.90. Outstanding checks were $224.15, $327.80, $88.10, $122.42, and $202.67. There was an $8.00 service charge, and the deposits in transit amounted to $813.11. There was an electronic payroll deposit of $450.00. Use the form below to reconcile Erin's account.

CHECKBOOK BALANCE	$	STATEMENT BALANCE	$
Add: Interest Earned & Other Credits		Add: Deposits in Transit	
SUBTOTAL		SUBTOTAL	
Deduct: Service Charges & Other Debits		Deduct: Outstanding Checks	
ADJUSTED CHECKBOOK BALANCE		ADJUSTED STATEMENT BALANCE	

Reconciled Balances

Checks Outstanding

No.	Amount	
Total		

2. Bob Albrecht received his bank statement on July 5 showing a balance of $2,663.31. His checkbook had a balance of $1,931.83. The statement showed a service charge of $15.80 and an electronic payroll deposit of $200.00. The deposits in transit totaled $314.12, and the outstanding checks were for $182.00, $261.40, and $418.00. Use the form below to reconcile Bob's account.

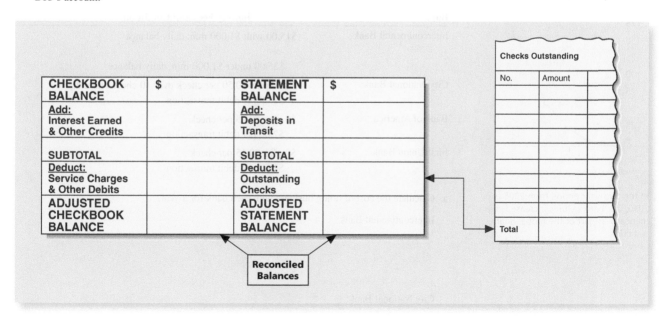

CHECKBOOK BALANCE	$	STATEMENT BALANCE	$
Add: Interest Earned & Other Credits		Add: Deposits in Transit	
SUBTOTAL		SUBTOTAL	
Deduct: Service Charges & Other Debits		Deduct: Outstanding Checks	
ADJUSTED CHECKBOOK BALANCE		ADJUSTED STATEMENT BALANCE	

Reconciled Balances

Checks Outstanding

No.	Amount	
Total		

3. On December 2, John Leahy received his bank statement showing a balance of $358.97. His checkbook showed a balance of $479.39. There was a check printing charge of $13.95, and interest earned was $6.40. The outstanding checks were for $22.97, $80.36, $19.80, and $4.50. The deposits in transit totaled $240.50. Use the form below to reconcile John's account.

Checks Outstanding		
No.	Amount	
Total		

CHECKBOOK BALANCE	$	STATEMENT BALANCE	$
Add: Interest Earned & Other Credits		Add: Deposits in Transit	
SUBTOTAL		SUBTOTAL	
Deduct: Service Charges & Other Debits		Deduct: Outstanding Checks	
ADJUSTED CHECKBOOK BALANCE		ADJUSTED STATEMENT BALANCE	

Reconciled Balances

BUSINESS DECISION: CHOOSING A BANK

4. You are looking for a bank in which to open a checking account for your new part-time business. You estimate that in the first year, you will be writing 30 checks per month and will make three debit transactions per month. Your average daily balance is estimated to be $900 for the first six months and $2,400 for the next six months.

Use the following information to solve the problem.

Bank	Monthly Fees and Conditions
Intercontinental Bank	$15.00 with $1,000 min. daily balance -or- $25.00 under $1,000 min. daily balance
City National Bank	$4.50 plus $0.50 per check over 10 checks monthly $1.00 per debit transaction
Bank of America	$6 plus $0.25 per check $2.00 per debit transaction
First Union Bank	$9 plus $0.15 per check $1.50 per debit transaction

a. Calculate the cost of doing business with each bank for a year.

Intercontinental Bank:

City National Bank:

Taking a Toll

175
150
125
100
75
50
25
0

2008   2009   2010

Source: FDIC

In the two-year period from 2008 to 2010, U.S. bank failures increased dramatically as part of the global financial crisis.

Bank of America:

First Union Bank:

b. Which bank should you choose for your checking account?

CHAPTER SUMMARY

Section I: Understanding and Using Checking Accounts

Topic	Important Concepts	Illustrative Examples
Checks **Performance Objectives 4-1 and 4-2, Pages 92–95**	Checks, or drafts, are negotiable instruments ordering the bank to pay money from the checking account to the name written on the check. The person or business named on the check to receive the money is known as the payee. The person or business issuing the check is known as the payor.	See Check with Parts Labeled, Exhibit 4-2, p. 93
Deposit Slips **Performance Objective 4-1, Page 92** **Performance Objective 4-4, Page 97**	Deposit slips, or deposit tickets, are printed forms with the depositor's name, address, account number, and space for the details of the deposit. Deposit slips are used to record money, both cash and checks, being added to the checking account. They are presented to the bank teller along with the items to be deposited. When a deposit is completed, the depositor receives a copy of the deposit slip as a receipt or proof of the transaction.	See Deposit Slip, Exhibit 4-3, p. 93 See Completed Deposit Slip, Exhibit 4-10, p. 97
Check Stubs **Performance Objective 4-1, Page 92** **Performance Objective 4-5, Page 98**	Check stubs, with checks attached by perforation, are a bound part of the checkbook. The check number is preprinted on both the check and the attached stub. Each stub is used to record the issuing of its corresponding check and any deposits made on that date.	See Check Stub with Check, Exhibit 4-4, p. 94

Section I (continued)

Topic	Important Concepts	Illustrative Examples
Check Registers **Performance Objective 4-1, Page 92** **Performance Objective 4-5, Page 98**	Check registers are the alternative method for keeping track of checking account activities. They are a separate booklet of forms rather than stubs attached to each check. Space is provided for all the pertinent information required to keep an accurate and up-to-date running balance of the account.	See Check Register, Exhibit 4-5, p. 94
Endorsements **Performance Objective 4-3, Page 95**	When you receive a check, you may cash it, deposit it in your account, or transfer it to another party. The endorsement on the back of the check tells the bank what to do. Your endorsement should be written within the $1\frac{1}{2}$-inch space at the trailing edge of the check.	See Endorsement Space, Exhibit 4-6, p. 96
Blank Endorsement **Performance Objective 4-3, Page 95**	A blank endorsement is used when you want to cash the check. You, as the payee, simply sign your name exactly as it appears on the front of the check and write your account number. Once you have endorsed a check in this manner, anyone who has possession of the check can cash it.	See Blank Endorsement, Exhibit 4-7, p. 96 John Q. Public 82-1301-508
Restrictive Endorsement **Performance Objective 4-3, Page 95**	A restrictive endorsement is used when you want to deposit the check in your account. In this case, you endorse the check "for deposit only," sign your name as it appears on the front, and write your account number.	See Restrictive Endorsement, Exhibit 4-8, p. 96 for deposit only John Q. Public 82-1301-508
Full Endorsement **Performance Objective 4-3, Page 95**	A full endorsement is used when you want to transfer the check to another party. In this case, you endorse the check "pay to the order of," write the name of the person or business to whom the check is being transferred, sign your name, and write your account number.	See Full Endorsement, Exhibit 4-9, p. 96 pay to the order of Cindy J. Citizen John Q. Public 82-1301-508

Section II: Bank Statement Reconciliation

Topic	Important Concepts	Illustrative Examples
Bank Statements **Performance Objective 4-6, Page 105**	Bank statements are a recap of the checking account activity for the month. They show the balance brought forward from the last statement, the deposits and credits that have been added to the account during the month, the checks and debits that have been subtracted from the account during the month, service charges assessed to the account, and the current or ending balance.	See Paper Bank Statement, Exhibit 4-13, p. 106

Bank Statement Reconciliation
 	
Performance Objective 4-7, Page 107
	1. Calculate the adjusted checkbook balance:
	  a. Locate any credits on the statement not recorded in the checkbook, such as interest earned or notes collected, and add them to the checkbook balance to get a subtotal.
	  b. Subtract any debits or charges such as service charges, NSF fees, or returned items from the subtotal above.
	2. Calculate the adjusted bank balance:
	  a. Locate all the deposits in transit and add them to the bank statement balance to get a subtotal.
	  b. Locate all outstanding checks and subtract them from the subtotal above.
	3. Compare the adjusted balances:
	  a. If they are equal, the statement has been reconciled.
	  b. If they are *not* equal, an error exists that must be found and corrected. The error is either in the checkbook or on the bank statement.
		See Bank Statement Reconciliation Form, Exhibit 4-14, p. 107

TRY IT: EXERCISE SOLUTIONS FOR CHAPTER 4

1.

CHAPTER 4

2. a.

Pay to the order of
Roz Reitman
Your Signature
696-339-1028

Full Endorsement

b.

Your Signature
696-339-1028

Blank Endorsement

c.

for deposit only
Your Signature
696-339-1028

Restrictive Endorsement

3.

HI-VOLT ELECTRONICS
12155 Miller Road
New Orleans, LA 70144

DATE *November 11* 20 XX
DEPOSITS MAY NOT BE AVAILABLE FOR IMMEDIATE WITHDRAWAL

SIGN HERE IF CASH RECEIVED FROM DEPOSIT

Bank of America.
037-049
11755 Biscayne Blvd.
North Miami, Florida 33161

⑆067003985⑆   536101902⑈

REV. 6/98   CHECKS AND OTHER ITEMS ARE RECEIVED FOR DEPOSIT SUBJECT TO THE PROVISIONS OF THE UNIFORM COMMERCIAL CODE OR ANY APPLICABLE COLLECTION AGREEMENT

C A S H	CURRENCY	3,549 00
	COIN	19 65
	CHECKS	411 92
		2,119 56
TOTAL FROM OTHER SIDE		
TOTAL		6,100 13
LESS CASH		
NET DEPOSIT		6,100 13

63-398/670

DEPOSIT TICKET
USE OTHER SIDE FOR
ADDITIONAL LISTINGS

TOTAL ITEMS

BE SURE EACH ITEM IS
PROPERLY ENDORSED

4.

IF TAX DEDUCTIBLE CHECK HERE ☐	$ 55.75

137
March 12 20 XX
TO *Nathan & David*
FOR *perm & manicure*

	DOLLARS	CENTS
BAL. FWD.	887	45
DEPOSIT		
DEPOSIT		
TOTAL	887	45
THIS ITEM	55	75
SUB-TOTAL	831	70
OTHER DEDUCT. (IF ANY)		
BAL. FWD.	831	70

IF TAX DEDUCTIBLE CHECK HERE ☐	$ 459.88

138
March 19 20 XX
TO *Complete Auto Service*
FOR *Car repairs*

	DOLLARS	CENTS
BAL. FWD.	831	70
DEPOSIT 3/16	125	40
DEPOSIT 3/16	221	35
TOTAL	1,178	45
THIS ITEM	459	88
SUB-TOTAL	718	57
OTHER DEDUCT. (IF ANY)	53	00
BAL. FWD.	665	57

PLEASE BE SURE TO **DEDUCT** ANY BANK CHARGES THAT APPLY TO YOUR ACCOUNT.

CHECK NUMBER	DATE	DESCRIPTION OF TRANSACTION	AMOUNT OF PAYMENT OR WITHDRAWAL (–)	✓	AMOUNT OF DEPOSIT OR INTEREST (+)	BALANCE FORWARD	
						887	45
137	3/12	To *Nathan & David Hair Stylists*	55 75				
		For				Bal. 831	70
	3/16	To *Deposit*			125 40		
		For				Bal. 957	10
	3/16	To *Deposit*			221 35		
		For				Bal. 1,178	45
138	3/19	To *Complete Auto Service*	459 88				
		For				Bal. 718	57
	3/20	To *Debit Card — Post Office*	53 00				
		For				Bal. 665	57

5.

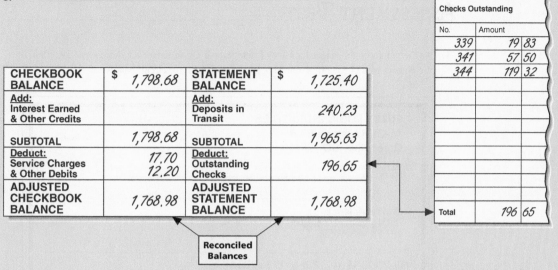

	Checks Outstanding	
No.	Amount	
339	19	83
341	57	50
344	119	32
Total	196	65

CHAPTER
4

CHECKBOOK BALANCE	$ 1,798.68	STATEMENT BALANCE	$ 1,725.40
Add: Interest Earned & Other Credits		Add: Deposits in Transit	240.23
SUBTOTAL	1,798.68	SUBTOTAL	1,965.63
Deduct: Service Charges & Other Debits	17.70 12.20	Deduct: Outstanding Checks	196.65
ADJUSTED CHECKBOOK BALANCE	1,768.98	ADJUSTED STATEMENT BALANCE	1,768.98

Reconciled
Balances

CONCEPT REVIEW

1. A(n) _____ is a written order to a bank by a depositor to pay the amount specified from funds on deposit in a checking account. (4-1)

2. On a check, the _____ is the person or business issuing the check; the _____ is the person or business named on the check to receive the money. (4-1)

3. When a(n) _____ card is used, the amount of the transaction is deducted electronically from the checking account. (4-1)

4. Write the word form of $52.45 as it would appear on a check. (4-2)

5. The signature and instructions on the back of a check are known as the _____. (4-3)

6. There are three types of endorsements used on checks: the blank, the restrictive, and the _____ endorsement. (4-3)

7. The form used to record money being added to the checking account is a called a(n) _____. (4-4)

8. When cash is being withdrawn at the time of a deposit, a(n) _____ is required on the deposit slip. (4-4)

9. Attached by perforation to checks, check _____ are one method of tracking checking account activity. (4-5)

10. A check _____ is a separate booklet used to keep track of checking account activity. (4-5)

11. A bank _____ is a monthly summary of activities in a checking account. (4-6)

12. Additions to a checking account are called _____; subtractions from a checking account are called _____. (4-6)

13. A bank statement is reconciled when the adjusted checkbook balance _____ the adjusted bank balance. (4-7)

14. Checks that have not yet reached the bank are called _____ checks. Deposits that have not reached the bank are called deposits in _____. (4-7)

CHAPTER
4

ASSESSMENT TEST

1. As the purchasing manager for Fuzzy Logic Industries, write a check dated April 29, 20xx, in the amount of $24,556.00, to Outback Electronics, Inc., for circuit boards.

2. You have just received a check. Your account number is #9299-144-006. Write the following endorsements in the space provided below and identify what type they are.

   a. Allowing the check to be transferred to Expo, Inc.

   b. Allowing you to cash the check.

   c. Allowing you to deposit the check in your account.

   a.   b.   c.

3. As cashier for Cellini's Pizza, it is your responsibility to make the daily deposits. Complete the deposit slip below based on the following information.

   a. Date: January 20, 20xx.

   b. Checks totaling $344.20.

   c. Currency of $547.00.

   d. Coins: 125 quarters, 67 dimes, 88 nickels, and 224 pennies.

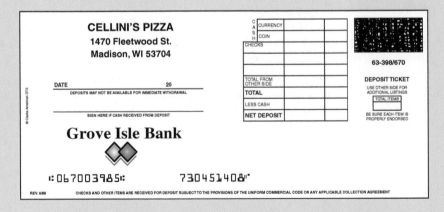

4. Simon Fitzrowdy checked his checking account online on Tuesday morning, and it showed a balance of $1,472.38. During a morning shopping trip, he used his debit card to buy gasoline for $48.92, groceries for $77.10, and a shirt for $34.98. He used his smartphone and his mobile-banking app to deposit a check for $150. What will his balance be the next morning?

5. From the following information, complete the two check stubs and the check register below.

   a. Starting balance: $463.30.
   b. April 15, 20xx, check #450 issued to the Keystone Market for groceries in the amount of $67.78.
   c. April 17, debit card purchase of $250.
   d. April 19, deposit of $125.45.
   e. April 20, deposit of $320.00.
   f. April 27, check #451 in the amount of $123.10 to Ace Appliance, Inc., for refrigerator repair.

Dollars AND Sense

Rewards Checking

Recently, a new type of checking account has been offered by banks and credit unions. These accounts, known as rewards checking, promise to pay high interest rates and are without any fees. Rewards checking accounts typically require that you use your debit card at least 10 times per month and that you give up paper bank statements in favor of online ones.

You can research various checking account offers at such sites as:

- www.bankrate.com
- www.bankdeals.com
- www.bankingmyway.com

IF TAX DEDUCTIBLE CHECK HERE ☐	$_____
450	
_____ 20____	
TO _____	
FOR _____	
BAL. FWD.	DOLLARS	CENTS
DEPOSIT		
DEPOSIT		
TOTAL		
THIS ITEM		
SUB-TOTAL		
OTHER DEDUCT. (IF ANY)		
BAL. FWD.		

IF TAX DEDUCTIBLE CHECK HERE ☐	$_____
451	
_____ 20____	
TO _____	
FOR _____	
BAL. FWD.	DOLLARS	CENTS
DEPOSIT		
DEPOSIT		
TOTAL		
THIS ITEM		
SUB-TOTAL		
OTHER DEDUCT. (IF ANY)		
BAL. FWD.		

PLEASE BE SURE TO **DEDUCT** ANY BANK CHARGES THAT APPLY TO YOUR ACCOUNT.

CHECK NUMBER	DATE	DESCRIPTION OF TRANSACTION	AMOUNT OF PAYMENT OR WITHDRAWAL (–)	✔	AMOUNT OF DEPOSIT OR INTEREST (+)	BALANCE FORWARD	
		To					
		For				Bal.	
		To					
		For				Bal.	
		To					
		For				Bal.	
		To					
		For				Bal.	
		To					
		For				Bal.	
		To					
		For				Bal.	

6. On October 1, Jessica Clay received her bank statement showing a balance of $374.52. Her checkbook records indicate a balance of $338.97. There was a service charge for the month of $4.40 on the statement. The outstanding checks were for $47.10, $110.15, $19.80, and $64.10. The deposits in transit totaled $125.50. There was a $75.70 debit for automatic payment of her telephone bill. Use the following form to reconcile Jessica's checking account.

CHAPTER 4

CHECKBOOK BALANCE	$	STATEMENT BALANCE	$
Add: Interest Earned & Other Credits		**Add:** Deposits in Transit	
SUBTOTAL		**SUBTOTAL**	
Deduct: Service Charges & Other Debits		**Deduct:** Outstanding Checks	
ADJUSTED CHECKBOOK BALANCE		**ADJUSTED STATEMENT BALANCE**	

Reconciled Balances

Checks Outstanding

No.	Amount	
Total		

 EXCEL 3

7. Using the form on page 121, prepare a bank reconciliation for Kali Loi from the following checkbook records and bank statement.

PLEASE BE SURE TO **DEDUCT** ANY BANK CHARGES THAT APPLY TO YOUR ACCOUNT.

CHECK NUMBER	DATE	DESCRIPTION OF TRANSACTION	AMOUNT OF PAYMENT OR WITHDRAWAL (–)	✓	AMOUNT OF DEPOSIT OR INTEREST (+)	BALANCE FORWARD
						879 36
801	10/1	To H & H Jewelers	236 77			
		For				Bal. 642 59
	10/6	To Deposit			450 75	
		For				Bal. 1,093 34
802	10/8	To L.L. Bean	47 20			
		For				Bal. 1,046 14
803	10/10	To Cashé	75 89			
		For				Bal. 970 25
	10/13	To Deposit			880 34	
		For				Bal. 1,850 59
804	10/13	To Four Seasons Hotel	109 00			
		For				Bal. 1,741 59
805	10/15	To American Express	507 82			
		For				Bal. 1,233 77
	10/20	To ATM Withdrawal	120 00			
		For				Bal. 1,113 77
	10/24	To Deposit			623 50	
		For				Bal. 1,737 27
	10/27	To Deposit			208 40	
		For				Bal. 1,945 67
	10/28	To Home Depot — Debit Card	48 25			
		For				Bal. 1,897 42

Aloha Bank

STATEMENT DATE
11-2-20xx

Kali Loi
1127 Pineapple Place
Honolulu, HI 96825

CHECKING ACCOUNT SUMMARY
10-1-20xx THRU 10-31-20xx

ACCOUNT NUMBER
449-56-7792

Previous Balance	Deposits & Credits Number	Total	Checks & Debits Number	Total	Current Balance
879.36	3	1,954.59	7	1,347.83	1,486.12

CHECKING ACCOUNT TRANSACTIONS

DATE	AMOUNT	DESCRIPTION	BALANCE
10-3	236.77	Check #801	642.59
10-6	450.75	Deposit	1,093.34
10-10	324.70	Returned Item	768.64
10-13	880.34	EFT Payroll Deposit	1,648.98
10-15	75.89	Check #803	1,573.09
10-17	507.82	Check #805	1,065.27
10-22	120.00	ATM Withdrawal	945.27
10-24	623.50	Deposit	1,568.77
10-28	48.25	Debit Card Purchase	1,520.52
10-30	34.40	Check Printing Charge	1,486.12

Checks Outstanding		
No.	Amount	
Total		

CHECKBOOK BALANCE	$	STATEMENT BALANCE	$
Add: Interest Earned & Other Credits		Add: Deposits in Transit	
SUBTOTAL		SUBTOTAL	
Deduct: Service Charges & Other Debits		Deduct: Outstanding Checks	
ADJUSTED CHECKBOOK BALANCE		ADJUSTED STATEMENT BALANCE	

Reconciled Balances

Dollars AND Sense

Opportunity cost is the sacrifice of benefits from the next-best alternative when you make a financial or economic decision. To fully evaluate how much a checking account with a required minimum balance costs, calculate the opportunity cost.

Consider a bank that requires an average monthly balance of $1,500. If you can earn 3% a year in interest on an investment maintaining this checking account means giving up $45 in potential interest income.

BUSINESS DECISION: CHOOSING A BANK WITH INTEREST

8. Sometimes banks offer checking accounts that earn interest on the average daily balance of the account each month. This interest is calculated using a formula known as the simple interest formula. The formula is written as:

$$\text{Interest} = \text{Principal} \times \text{Rate} \times \text{Time} \quad I = PRT$$

The formula states that the amount of **interest** earned on the account is equal to the **principal** (average daily balance) multiplied by the **rate** (interest rate per year—expressed as a decimal) multiplied by the **time** (expressed in years—use $\frac{1}{12}$ to represent one month of a year).

a. If you have not already done so, complete the Business Decision, Choosing a Bank on page **112**.

b. Use the simple interest formula to calculate the amount of interest you would earn per month if the Intercontinental Bank was offering 1.5% (.015) interest per year on checking accounts. (Note that your average daily balance changes from $900 to $2,400 in the last six months of the year.) Round monthly amounts to the nearest cent when necessary. How much interest would you earn for the year?

c. How much interest would you earn per month at Bank of America if it were offering 1% (.01) interest per year on checking accounts? How much interest would you earn for the year?

Largest U.S. Banks by Assets ($ billions)	
JPMorgan Chase & Co. (JPM)	2,312.23
Bank of America Corp. (BAC)	2,181.45
Citigroup Inc. (C)	1,944.42
Wells Fargo & Co (WFC)	1,333.80
U.S. Bancorp (USB)	340.76
Capital One Financial Corp. (COF)	322.68
Bank of New York Mellon Corp. (BK)	300.17
HSBC North America Holdings Inc.	298.14
PNC Financial Services Group Inc. (PNC)	295.88
TD Bank US Holding Co.	204.31

d. Recalculate the cost of doing business with Intercontinental Bank and Bank of America for a year.

e. Based on this new information, which of the four banks should you choose for your checking account?

COLLABORATIVE LEARNING ACTIVITY

Choosing a Checking Account

Have each team member research a local bank, a credit union, or another financial institution offering checking accounts to find the types of checking accounts they have and other banking services they offer. As a team, look over the material and answer the following:

a. How do the accounts compare regarding monthly service charges, interest paid, account minimums, debit and ATM charges, and other rules and regulations?

b. Do the banks offer any incentives such as a no-fee Visa or MasterCard, bounce-proof checking, or a line of credit?

c. Based on your team's research, which bank would you recommend for each of the following:
- College student. Why?
- Small business. Why?
- Family with three teenagers. Why?

d. Because many banks have failed in recent years, check your bank's health by looking up its "star rating" at www.bauerfinancial.com or www.bankrate.com. Also look over your bank's financial statements filed quarterly with the government at www.fdic.gov. What can you conclude from your findings?

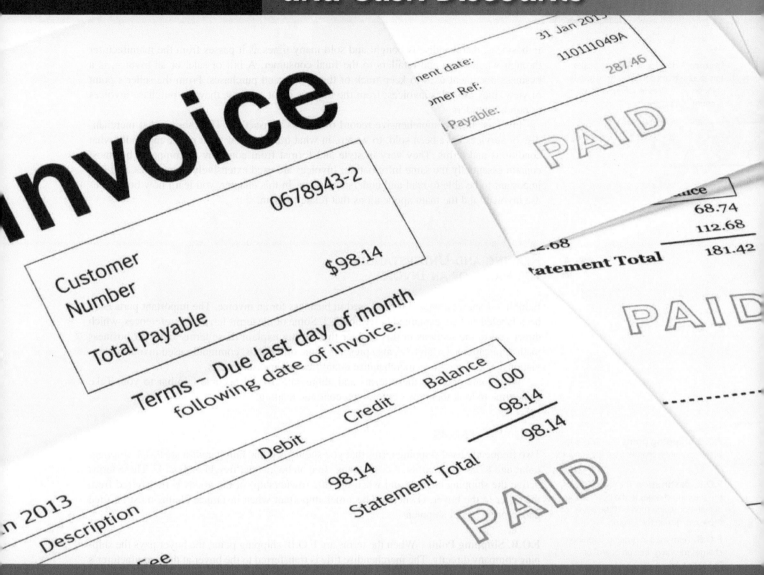

CHAPTER 7

Invoices, Trade Discounts, and Cash Discounts

invoice A document detailing a sales transaction that contains a list of goods shipped or services rendered with an account of all costs.

In business, merchandise is bought and sold many times as it passes from the manufacturer through wholesalers and retailers to the final consumer. A bill of sale, or an **invoice**, is a business document used to keep track of these sales and purchases. From the seller's point of view, they are sales invoices; from the buyer's point of view, they are purchase invoices or purchase orders.

Invoices are a comprehensive record of a sales transaction. They show what merchandise or services have been sold, to whom, in what quantities, at what price, and under what conditions and terms. They vary in style and format from company to company, but most contain essentially the same information. Invoices are used extensively in business, and it is important to be able to read and understand them. In this chapter, you learn how businesses use invoices and the math applications that relate to them.

7-1 READING AND UNDERSTANDING THE PARTS OF AN INVOICE

Exhibit 7-1 shows a typical format used in business for an invoice. The important parts have been labeled and are explained in Exhibit 7-2. Some of the terms have page references, which direct you to the sections in this chapter that further explain those terms and their business math applications. Exhibit 7-2 also presents some of the most commonly used invoice abbreviations. These pertain to merchandise quantities and measurements.

With some practice, these terms and abbreviations will become familiar to you. Take some time to look them over before you continue reading.

SHIPPING TERMS

F.O.B. shipping point The buyer pays all transportation charges from the vendor's location.

F.O.B. destination The seller pays all the shipping charges to the buyer's store or warehouse and then bills the buyer for these charges on the invoice.

F.O.B. Term used in quoting shipping charges meaning "free on board" or "freight on board."

Two frequently used shipping terms that you should become familiar with are **F.O.B. shipping point** and **F.O.B. destination**. **F.O.B.** means "free on board" or "freight on board." These terms define the shipping charges and when the title (ownership) of the goods is transferred from the seller to the buyer. Ownership becomes important when insurance claims must be filed due to problems in shipment.

F.O.B. Shipping Point   When the terms are F.O.B. shipping point, the buyer pays the shipping company directly. The merchandise title is transferred to the buyer at the manufacturer's factory or at a shipping point such as a railroad freight yard or air freight terminal. From this point, the buyer is responsible for the merchandise. It is common for the seller to prepay the freight and add the amount to the invoice.

F.O.B. Destination   When the shipping terms are F.O.B. destination, the seller is responsible for prepaying the shipping charges to the destination. The destination is usually the buyer's store or warehouse. Unless prices are quoted as "delivered," the seller then bills the buyer on the invoice for the shipping charges.

Sometimes the freight terms are stated as F.O.B. with the name of a city. For example, if the seller is in Fort Worth and the buyer is in New York, F.O.B. Fort Worth means the title is transferred in Fort Worth and the buyer pays the shipping charges from Fort Worth to New York. If the terms are F.O.B. New York, the seller pays the shipping charges to New York and then bills the buyer for those charges on the invoice. Exhibit 7-3, Shipping Terms, on page 193, illustrates these transactions.

When companies ship and receive merchandise, invoices and purchase orders are used to record the details of the transaction.

© Franck Boston/Shutterstock.com

EXHIBIT 7-1 Typical Invoice Format

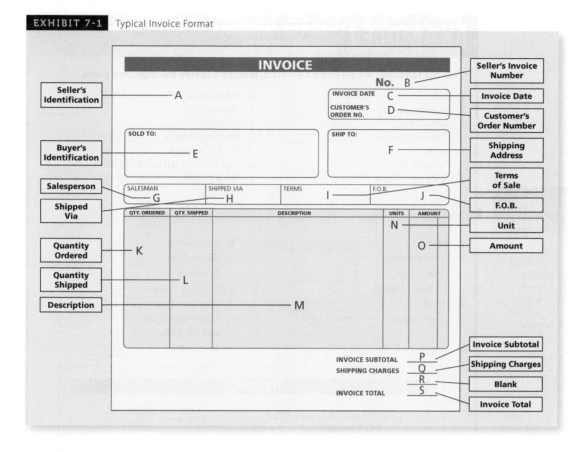

EXHIBIT 7-2 Invoice Terminology and Abbreviations

Invoice Terminology

A **Seller's Identification—** Name, address, and logo or corporate symbol of the seller

B **Seller's Invoice Number—** Seller's identification number of the transaction

C **Invoice Date—**Date the invoice was written

D **Customer's Order Number—** Buyer's identification number of the transaction

E **Buyer's Identification—**Name and mailing address of the buyer

F **Shipping Address—**Address where merchandise will be shipped

G **Salesperson—**Name of salesperson credited with the sale

H **Shipped Via—**Name of shipping company handling the shipment

I **Terms—**Terms of sale— Section detailing date of payment and cash discount

J **F.O.B.—**"Free on board"— Section detailing who pays the shipping company and when title is transferred

K **Quantity Ordered—**Number of units ordered

L **Quantity Shipped—**Number of units shipped

M **Description—**Detailed description of the merchandise, including model numbers

N **Unit—**Price per unit of merchandise

O **Amount—**Extended total—Quantity in units times the unit price for each line

P **Invoice Subtotal—**Total of the Amount column— Merchandise total

Q **Shipping Charges—**Cost to physically transport the merchandise from the seller to the buyer

R **Blank Line—**Line used for other charges such as insurance or handling

S **Invoice Total—**Total amount of the invoice—Includes merchandise plus all other charges

Invoice Abbreviations

ea	each	pr	pair	in.	inch	oz	ounce
dz or doz	dozen	dm or drm	drum	ft	foot	g or gr	gram
gr or gro	gross	bbl	barrel	yd	yard	kg	kilogram
bx	box	sk	sack	mm	millimeter	pt	pint
cs	case	@	at	cm	centimeter	qt	quart
ct or crt	crate	C	100 items	m	meter	gal	gallon
ctn or cart	carton	M	1,000 items	lb	pound	cwt	hundred weight

EXAMPLE1 — IDENTIFYING PARTS OF AN INVOICE

From the following Whole Grain Cereal Co. invoice, identify the indicated parts.

a. Seller _____
b. Invoice number _____
c. Invoice date _____
d. Customer order # _____
e. Buyer _____
f. Terms of sale _____
g. Shipping address

h. Salesperson _____
i. Shipped via _____
j. Insurance _____
k. Shipping charges _____
l. Invoice subtotal _____
m. Unit price—Fruit and Nut Flakes _____
n. Invoice total

SOLUTIONSTRATEGY

a. Seller — Organic Grain Cereal Co.
b. Invoice number — 2112
c. Invoice date — August 19, 20XX
d. Customer order # — B-1623
e. Buyer — Kroger Supermarkets
f. Terms of sale — Net - 45 days
g. Shipping address — 1424 Peachtree Rd

h. Salesperson — H. L. Mager
i. Shipped via — Terminal Transport
j. Insurance — $33.00
k. Shipping charges — $67.45
l. Invoice subtotal — $2,227.05
m. Unit price—Fruit and Nut Flakes — $19.34
n. Invoice total — $2,327.50

INVOICE

No. 2112

Organic Grain Cereal Co.
697 Canyon Road
Boulder, CO 80304

INVOICE DATE: August 19, 20XX
CUSTOMER'S ORDER NO.: B-1623

SOLD TO:
KROGER SUPERMARKETS
565 North Avenue
Atlanta, Georgia 30348

SHIP TO:
DISTRIBUTION CENTER
1424 Peachtree Road
Atlanta, Georgia 30341

SALESMAN	SHIPPED VIA	TERMS	F.O.B.
H. L. Mager	Terminal Transport	Net - 45 Days	Boulder, CO

QTY. ORDERED	QTY. SHIPPED	DESCRIPTION		UNIT	AMOUNT
55 cs.	55 cs.	Corn Crunchies	24 ounce	$22.19	$1220 45
28 cs.	28 cs.	Fruit and Nut Flakes	24 ounce	19.34	541 52
41 cs.	22 cs.	Rice and Wheat Flakes	16 ounce	21.14	465 08

INVOICE SUBTOTAL	2,227.05
SHIPPING CHARGES	67.45
INSURANCE	33.00
INVOICE TOTAL	$2,327.50

▶ TRYITEXERCISE 1

From the following FotoFair invoice, identify the indicated parts.

a. Buyer _____
b. Invoice number _____
c. Invoice date _____
d. Amount—Pocket Pro 55 _____
e. Seller _____
f. Terms of sale _____
g. Shipping address _____

h. Salesperson _____
i. Shipped via _____
j. F.O.B. _____
k. Shipping charges _____
l. Invoice subtotal _____
m. Unit price—Pocket Pro 75 _____
n. Invoice total _____

CHECK YOUR ANSWERS WITH THE SOLUTIONS ON PAGE 223.

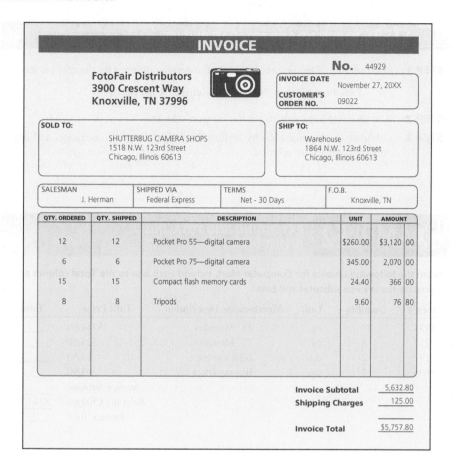

INVOICE

FotoFair Distributors
3900 Crescent Way
Knoxville, TN 37996

No. 44929

INVOICE DATE	November 27, 20XX
CUSTOMER'S ORDER NO.	09022

SOLD TO:
SHUTTERBUG CAMERA SHOPS
1518 N.W. 123rd Street
Chicago, Illinois 60613

SHIP TO:
Warehouse
1864 N.W. 123rd Street
Chicago, Illinois 60613

SALESMAN	SHIPPED VIA	TERMS	F.O.B.
J. Herman	Federal Express	Net - 30 Days	Knoxville, TN

QTY. ORDERED	QTY. SHIPPED	DESCRIPTION	UNIT	AMOUNT
12	12	Pocket Pro 55—digital camera	$260.00	$3,120 00
6	6	Pocket Pro 75—digital camera	345.00	2,070 00
15	15	Compact flash memory cards	24.40	366 00
8	8	Tripods	9.60	76 80

Invoice Subtotal	5,632.80
Shipping Charges	125.00
Invoice Total	$5,757.80

EXTENDING AND TOTALING AN INVOICE

7-2

Extending an invoice is the process of computing the value in the Total or Amount column for each line of the invoice. This number represents the total dollar amount of each type of merchandise or service being purchased. The **invoice subtotal** is the amount of all items on the invoice before shipping and handling charges; insurance; and other adjustments such as discounts, returns, and credits. The **invoice total** is the final amount due from the buyer to the seller.

invoice subtotal The amount of all merchandise or services on the invoice before adjustments.

invoice total The final amount due from the buyer to the seller.

EXHIBIT 7-3 Shipping Terms

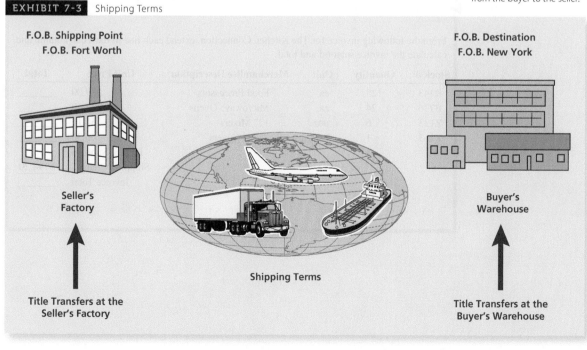

F.O.B. Shipping Point
F.O.B. Fort Worth

F.O.B. Destination
F.O.B. New York

Seller's Factory

Buyer's Warehouse

Shipping Terms

Title Transfers at the Seller's Factory

Title Transfers at the Buyer's Warehouse

STEPS TO EXTEND AND TOTAL AN INVOICE

STEP 1. For each line of the invoice, multiply the number of items by the cost per item.

Extended total = Number of items × Cost per item

STEP 2. Add all extended totals to get the invoice subtotal.

STEP 3. Calculate the invoice total by adding the freight charges, insurance, and any other charges to the subtotal.

EXAMPLE2   EXTENDING AND TOTALING AN INVOICE

From the following invoice for Computer Mart, extend each line to the Total column and calculate the invoice subtotal and total.

Stock #	Quantity	Unit	Merchandise Description	Unit Price	Total
4334	17	ea.	13" Monitors	$244.00	_____
1217	8	ea.	17" Monitors	525.80	_____
2192	2	doz.	USB Cables	24.50	_____
5606	1	bx.	Blu-ray Discs	365.90	_____
				Invoice Subtotal	
				Shipping Charges	$244.75
				Invoice Total	_____

►SOLUTIONSTRATEGY

						Total
13" Monitors	17	×	$244.00	=		$4,148.00
17" Monitors	8	×	525.80	=		4,206.40
USB Cables	2	×	24.50	=		49.00
Blu-ray Discs	1	×	365.90	=		365.90
			Invoice Subtotal			$8,769.30
			Shipping Charges		+	244.75
			Invoice Total			$9,014.05

►TRYITEXERCISE 2

From the following invoice for The Kitchen Connection, extend each line to the Total column and calculate the invoice subtotal and total.

Stock #	Quantity	Unit	Merchandise Description	Unit Price	Total
R443	125	ea.	Food Processors	$89.00	_____
B776	24	ea.	Microwave Ovens	225.40	_____
Z133	6	doz.	12" Mixers	54.12	_____
Z163	1	bx.	Mixer Covers	166.30	_____
				Invoice Subtotal	
				Shipping Charges	$194.20
				Invoice Total	_____

CHECK YOUR ANSWERS WITH THE SOLUTIONS ON PAGE 223.

REVIEW EXERCISES

7

What word is represented by each of the following abbreviations?

1. bx.   Box   2. pt _____   3. drm. _____   4. kg _____
5. gro.   _Gross_   6. oz _____   7. M. _____   8. cwt _____

Using the Panorama Products invoice below, extend each line to the Amount column and calculate the subtotal and total. Then answer Questions 9–22. (*Note:* Although 26 boxes of 2" reflective tape were ordered, only 11 boxes were shipped. Charge only for the boxes shipped.)

9. Seller	Panorama Products	10. Invoice number	R-7431
11. Invoice date	_____	12. Cust. order #	_____
13. Buyer	_____	14. Terms of sale	_____
15. Shipping address	_____	16. Salesperson	_____
17. Shipped via	_____	18. Insurance	_____
19. Shipping charges	_____	20. Unit price—2" Tape	_____
21. Invoice subtotal	_____	22. Invoice total	_____

INVOICE

No. R-7431

Panorama Products
486 5th Avenue
Eureka, CA 95501

INVOICE DATE June 16, 20XX

CUSTOMER'S ORDER NO. 12144

SOLD TO:
J. M. Hardware Supply
2051 West Adams Blvd.
Lansing, MI 48901

SHIP TO:
SAME

SALESMAN	SHIPPED VIA	TERMS	F.O.B.
H. Marshall	Gilbert Trucking	Net 30 Days	Effingham, IL

QTY. ORDERED	QTY. SHIPPED	DESCRIPTION	UNIT	AMOUNT
16 cases	16 cases	Masking Tape ½" Standard	$21.90	_____
12 cases	12 cases	Masking Tape 1½" Standard	26.79	_____
26 boxes	11 boxes	2" Reflective Tape	88.56	_____
37 cases	37 cases	Sandpaper Assorted	74.84	_____

INVOICE SUBTOTAL _____
SHIPPING CHARGES $61.45
INVOICE TOTAL _____

IN THE Business World

Frequently, merchandise that is ordered from vendors is "out of stock" and goes into back-order status.

As a general rule, companies charge only for the merchandise that is shipped.

BUSINESS DECISION: MANAGING MERCHANDISE

23. You are the store manager for The Bedding Warehouse. The invoice below is due for payment to one of your vendors, Hamilton Mills.

   a. Check the invoice for errors and correct any you find.

   b. Your warehouse manager reports that there were three king-size sheets and five queen-size sheets returned, along with four packages of queen pillow cases. Calculate the revised total due.

   c. The vendor has offered a 4% early payment discount that applies only to the merchandise, not the shipping or insurance. What is the amount of the discount?

   d. What is the new balance due after the discount?

Retail store managers manage stores that specialize in selling a specific line of merchandise, such as groceries, meat, liquor, apparel, furniture, automobile parts, electronic items, or household appliances.

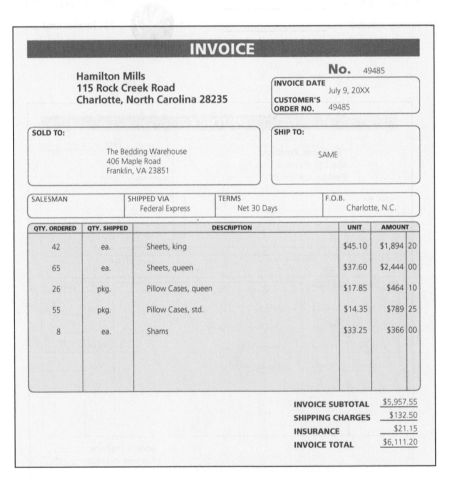

INVOICE

No. 49485

Hamilton Mills
115 Rock Creek Road
Charlotte, North Carolina 28235

| INVOICE DATE | July 9, 20XX |
| CUSTOMER'S ORDER NO. | 49485 |

SOLD TO:
The Bedding Warehouse
406 Maple Road
Franklin, VA 23851

SHIP TO:
SAME

SALESMAN	SHIPPED VIA	TERMS	F.O.B.
	Federal Express	Net 30 Days	Charlotte, N.C.

QTY. ORDERED	QTY. SHIPPED	DESCRIPTION	UNIT	AMOUNT
42	ea.	Sheets, king	$45.10	$1,894 20
65	ea.	Sheets, queen	$37.60	$2,444 00
26	pkg.	Pillow Cases, queen	$17.85	$464 10
55	pkg.	Pillow Cases, std.	$14.35	$789 25
8	ea.	Shams	$33.25	$366 00

INVOICE SUBTOTAL	$5,957.55
SHIPPING CHARGES	$132.50
INSURANCE	$21.15
INVOICE TOTAL	$6,111.20

TRADE DISCOUNTS—SINGLE

The path merchandise travels as it moves from the manufacturer through wholesalers and retailers to the ultimate consumer is known as a channel of distribution or trade channel. The businesses that form these channels are said to be "in the trade." In today's complex economy, a number of different trade channels are used to move goods and services efficiently.

Trade discounts are reductions from the manufacturer's suggested **list price**. They are given to businesses at various levels of the trade channel for the performance of marketing functions. These functions may include activities such as selling, advertising, storage, service, and display.

Manufacturers print catalogs showcasing their merchandise. Often these catalogs contain the manufacturer's suggested list or retail prices. Businesses in the trade receive price sheets from the manufacturer listing the trade discounts in percent form associated with each item in the catalog. By issuing updated price sheets of trade discounts, manufacturers have the flexibility of changing the prices of their merchandise without the expense of reprinting the entire catalog.

Trade discounts are sometimes quoted as a single discount and sometimes as a series or chain of discounts. The number of discounts is dependent on the extent of the marketing services performed by the channel member.

trade discounts Reductions from the manufacturer's list price given to businesses that are "in the trade" for performance of marketing functions.

list price Suggested retail selling price of an item set by the manufacturer or supplier. The original price from which discounts are taken.

CALCULATING THE AMOUNT OF A SINGLE TRADE DISCOUNT

7-3

The amount of a single trade discount is calculated by multiplying the list price by the trade discount rate.

Trade discount = List price × Trade discount rate

EXAMPLE3 — CALCULATING THE AMOUNT OF A SINGLE TRADE DISCOUNT

What is the amount of the trade discount on merchandise with a list price of $2,800 and a trade discount rate of 45%?

▶**SOLUTIONSTRATEGY**

Trade discount = List price × Trade discount rate
Trade discount = 2,800 × .45 = $1,260

▶**TRYITEXERCISE 3**

Gifts Galore, a retail gift shop, buys merchandise with a list price of $7,600 from a wholesaler of novelty items and toys. The wholesaler extends a 30% trade discount rate to the retailer. What is the amount of the trade discount?

CHECK YOUR ANSWER WITH THE SOLUTION ON PAGE 223.

CALCULATING NET PRICE BY USING THE NET PRICE FACTOR, COMPLEMENT METHOD

7-4

The **net price** is the amount a business actually pays for the merchandise after the discount has been deducted. It may be calculated by subtracting the amount of the trade discount from the list price.

net price The amount a business actually pays for the merchandise after the discount has been deducted.

Net price = List price − Trade discount

Frequently, merchants are more interested in knowing the net price of an item than the amount of the trade discount. In that case, the net price can be calculated directly from the list price without first finding the amount of the discount.

The list price of an item is considered to be 100%. If, for example, the trade discount on an item is 40% of the list price, the net price will be 60% because the two must equal 100%. This 60%, the complement of the trade discount rate (100% − 40%), is the portion of the list price that *is* paid. Known as the **net price factor**, it is usually written in decimal form.

net price factor The percent of the list price a business pays for merchandise. It is the multiplier used to calculate the net price.

Learning Tip

Complements are two numbers that add up to 100%. The trade discount rate and the net price factor are complements of each other. This means that if we know one of them, the other can be found by subtracting from 100%.

STEPS TO CALCULATE NET PRICE BY USING THE NET PRICE FACTOR

STEP 1. Calculate the net price factor, complement of the trade discount rate.

$$\text{Net price factor} = 100\% - \text{Trade discount rate}$$

STEP 2. Calculate the net price.

$$\text{Net price} = \text{List price} \times \text{Net price factor}$$

Note: This procedure can be combined into one step by the formula.

$$\text{Net price} = \text{List price}\,(100\% - \text{Trade discount rate})$$

EXAMPLE4 CALCULATING THE NET PRICE

Calculate the net price of merchandise at Astana Imports listing for $900 less a trade discount rate of 45%.

SOLUTIONSTRATEGY

$$\text{Net price} = \text{List price}\,(100\% - \text{Trade discount rate})$$
$$\text{Net price} = 900\,(100\% - 45\%)$$
$$\text{Net price} = 900\,(.55) = \underline{\$495}$$

TRYITEXERCISE 4

Central Hardware Store bought paint supplies listing for $2,100 with a single trade discount rate of 35%. What is the net price of the order?

CHECK YOUR ANSWER WITH THE SOLUTION ON PAGE 223.

7-5 CALCULATING TRADE DISCOUNT RATE WHEN LIST PRICE AND NET PRICE ARE KNOWN

The trade discount rate can be calculated by using the now-familiar percentage formula Rate = Portion ÷ Base. For this application, the amount of the trade discount is the portion, or numerator, and the list price is the base, or denominator.

$$\text{Trade discount rate} = \frac{\text{Trade discount}}{\text{List price}}$$

STEPS FOR CALCULATING TRADE DISCOUNT RATE

STEP 1. Calculate the amount of the trade discount.

$$\text{Trade discount} = \text{List price} - \text{Net price}$$

STEP 2. Calculate the trade discount rate.

$$\text{Trade discount rate} = \frac{\text{Trade discount}}{\text{List price}}$$

EXAMPLE5 CALCULATING THE SINGLE TRADE DISCOUNT AND RATE

Sterling Manufacturing sells tools to American Garden Supply. In a recent transaction, the list price of an order was $47,750 and the net price of the order was $32,100. Calculate the amount of the trade discount. What was the trade discount rate? Round your answer to the nearest tenth percent.

►SOLUTIONSTRATEGY

Trade discount = List price − Net price
Trade discount = 47,750 − 32,100 = $15,650

$$\text{Trade discount rate} = \frac{\text{Trade discount}}{\text{List price}}$$

$$\text{Trade discount rate} = \frac{15,650}{47,750} = .3277 = 32.8\%$$

►TRYITEXERCISE 5

Wilson Sporting Goods recently sold tennis rackets listing for $109,500 to The Sports Authority. The net price of the order was $63,300. What was the amount of the trade discount? What was the trade discount rate? Round your answer to the nearest tenth percent.

CHECK YOUR ANSWERS WITH THE SOLUTION ON PAGE 223.

REVIEW EXERCISES

7

SECTION II

Calculate the following trade discounts. Round all answers to the nearest cent.

	List Price	Trade Discount Rate	Trade Discount
1.	$860.00	30%	$258.00
	Trade discount = 860.00 × .30 = $258.00		
2.	125.50	12%	_____
3.	41.75	19%	_____
4.	395.00	7%	_____
5.	88.25	50%	_____

Calculate the following trade discounts and net prices to the nearest cent.

	List Price	Trade Discount Rate	Trade Discount	Net Price
6.	$286.00	25%	$71.50	$214.50
7.	134.79	40%	_____	_____
8.	21.29	18%	_____	_____
9.	1,250.00	45%	_____	_____

Calculate the following net price factors and net prices by using the complement method. Round all answers to the nearest cent.

	List Price	Trade Discount Rate	Net Price Factor	Net Price
10.	$3,499.00	37%	63%	$2,204.37
11.	565.33	24%	_____	_____
12.	1,244.25	45.8%	_____	_____
13.	4.60	$12\frac{3}{4}\%$	_____	_____

Calculate the following trade discounts and trade discount rates. Round answers to the nearest tenth of a percent.

	List Price	Trade Discount	Trade Discount Rate	Net Price
14.	$4,500.00	$935.00	20.8%	$3,565.00
15.	345.50	_____	_____	$225.00
16.	2.89	_____	_____	$2.15

17. Find the amount of a trade discount of 30% on a television set that has a list price of $799.95.

18. Find the amount of a trade discount of 55% on a set of fine china that lists for $345.70.

19. What is the amount of a trade discount of 45% on a dining room table that lists for $395.50?

20. Whole Foods Market ordered 12 cases of organic vegetable soup with a list price of $18.90 per case and 8 cases of organic baked beans with a list price of $33.50 per case. The wholesaler offered Whole Foods a 39% trade discount.

   a. What is the total extended list price of the order?

   b. What is the total amount of the trade discount on this order?

   c. What is the total net amount Whole Foods owes the wholesaler for the order?

21. La Bella, a chain of clothing boutiques, purchased merchandise with a total list price of $25,450 from Sandy Sport, a manufacturer. The order has a trade discount of 34%.

   a. What is the amount of the trade discount?

   b. What is the net amount LaBella owes Sandy Sport for the merchandise?

22. An item with a trade discount of 41% has a list price of $289.50. What is the net price?

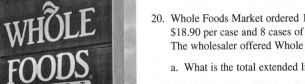

A number of supermarkets now make supporting local growers and producers a priority. Whole Foods, one such store, opened in 1980 and four years later began expanding rapidly.

Today, there are more than 310 stores in North America and the United Kingdom, and Whole Foods has acquired more than 10 natural food store chains. It is the world's leading supermarket emphasizing natural and organic foods and America's first national "Certified Organic" grocer.

23. Nathan and David Beauty Salon places an order for beauty supplies from a wholesaler. The list price of the order is $2,800. If the vendor offers a trade discount of 46%, what is the net price of the order?

24. A watch has a list price of $889 and can be bought by Sterling Jewelers for a net price of $545.75.

    a. What is the amount of the trade discount?

    b. What is the trade discount rate?

25. Nutrition Central pays $11.90 net price for a bottle of 60 multivitamins. The price represents a 30% trade discount from the manufacturer. What is the list price of the vitamins?

26. You are the buyer for the housewares department of the Galleria Department Store. A number of vendors in your area carry similar lines of merchandise. On sets of microwavable serving bowls, Kitchen Magic offers a list price of $400 per dozen less a 38% trade discount. Pro-Chef offers a similar set for a list price of $425 less a 45% trade discount.

    a. Which vendor is offering the lower net price?

    b. If you order 500 dozen sets of the bowls, how much money will be saved by using the lower-priced vendor?

General Nutrition Centers, Inc., a wholly owned subsidiary of GNC Corporation, consists of a worldwide network of over 6,600 locations and the www.gnc.com website. GNC, Inc., is the largest global specialty retailer of health and wellness products, including vitamins, minerals and herbal supplements, sports nutrition products, and diet products.

The GNC website, www.gnc.com, provides an online library where consumers may research health-related topics.

BUSINESS DECISION: QUANTITY DISCOUNT

27. You are the purchasing manager for Tiger Electronics, a company that manufactures scanners and other computer peripherals. Your vendor for scanner motors, Enfield Industries, is now offering "quantity discounts" in the form of instant rebates and lower shipping charges as follows:

Quantity	Net Price	Rebate	Shipping
1–500 motors	$16	none	$1.30
501–1,000 motors	16	$1.20	.90
1,001–2,000 motors	16	1.80	.60

    a. Calculate the cost of the motors, including shipping charges, for each category.

    b. If you usually purchase 400 motors per month, what percent would be saved per motor by ordering 800 every two months? Round to the nearest tenth of a percent.

    c. What percent would be saved per motor by ordering 1,200 every three months? Round to the nearest tenth of a percent.

d. How much money can be saved in a year by purchasing the motors every three months instead of every month?

e. (Optional) What other factors besides price should be considered before changing your purchasing procedures?

SECTION III   7   TRADE DISCOUNTS—SERIES

chain or **series trade discounts** Term used when a vendor offers a buyer more than one trade discount.

Trade discounts are frequently offered by manufacturers to wholesalers and retailers in a series of two or more, known as **chain** or **series trade discounts**. For example, a series of 25% and 10% is verbally stated as "25 and 10." It is written 25/10. A three-discount series is written 25/10/5. Multiple discounts are given for many reasons. Some of the more common ones follow.

Position or Level in the Channel of Distribution   A manufacturer might sell to a retailer at a 30% trade discount, whereas a wholesaler in the same channel might be quoted a 30% and a 15% trade discount.

Volume Buying   Many manufacturers and wholesalers grant an extra discount for buying a large volume of merchandise. For example, any purchase more than 5,000 units at one time may earn an extra 7% trade discount. Retailers with many stores or those with large storage capacity can enjoy a considerable savings (additional trade discounts) by purchasing in large quantities.

Advertising and Display   Additional discounts are often given to retailers and wholesalers who heavily advertise and aggressively promote a manufacturer's line of merchandise.

Competition   Competitive pressures often cause extra trade discounts to be offered. In certain industries such as household products and consumer electronics, price wars are not an uncommon occurrence.

Learning Tip

Remember, when calculating the net price by using a series of trade discounts, you *cannot* simply add the trade discounts together. Each discount must be applied to a successively lower base.

7-6 CALCULATING NET PRICE AND THE AMOUNT OF A TRADE DISCOUNT BY USING A SERIES OF TRADE DISCOUNTS

Finding net price with a series of trade discounts is accomplished by taking each trade discount, one at a time, from the previous net price until all discounts have been deducted. Note that you *cannot* simply add the trade discounts together. They must be calculated individually unless the net price factor method—a handy shortcut—is used. Trade discounts can be taken in any order, although they are usually listed and calculated in descending order.

For illustrative purposes, let's begin with an example of how to calculate a series of trade discounts one at a time; then we will try the shortcut method.

Dollars AND Sense

An **industry trade group**, also known as a **trade association**, is an organization founded and funded by businesses that operate in a specific industry. An industry trade association participates in public relations activities such as advertising, education, political donations, lobbying, and publishing, but its main focus is collaboration between companies, or standardization.

Associations may offer other services, such as sponsoring conferences, providing networking, hosting charitable events, or offering classes or educational materials.

A directory of trade associations may be found at http://dir.yahoo.com/Business_and_Economy/organizations/trade_associations

---

EXAMPLE6   CALCULATING NET PRICE AND THE AMOUNT OF A TRADE DISCOUNT

Calculate the net price and trade discount for merchandise with a list price of $2,000 less trade discounts of 30/20/15.

▶SOLUTIONSTRATEGY

$2,000	$2,000	$1,400	$1,400	$1,120	$1,120
× .30	− 600	× .20	− 280	× .15	− 168
$600	$1,400	$280	$1,120	$168	$952 = Net price

▶TRYITEXERCISE 6

Northwest Publishers sold an order of books to The Bookworm, Inc., a chain of bookstores. The list price of the order was $25,000. The Bookworm buys in volume from Northwest. The Bookworm also prominently displays and heavily advertises Northwest's books. Northwest, in turn, gives The Bookworm a series of trade discounts amounting to 35/20/10. Calculate the net price of the order and the amount of the trade discount.

CHECK YOUR ANSWERS WITH THE SOLUTIONS ON PAGE 223.

CALCULATING THE NET PRICE OF A SERIES OF TRADE DISCOUNTS BY USING THE NET PRICE FACTOR, COMPLEMENT METHOD

7-7

As a shortcut, the net price can be calculated directly from the list price, bypassing the trade discount, by using the net price factor as before. Remember, the net price factor is the complement of the trade discount rate. With a series of discounts, we must find the complement of each trade discount to calculate the net price factor of the series.

The net price factor indicates to buyers what percent of the list price they actually *do* pay. For example, if the net price factor of a series of discounts is calculated to be .665, this means that the buyer is paying 66.5% of the list price.

STEPS FOR CALCULATING NET PRICE BY USING THE NET PRICE FACTOR

STEP 1. Find the complement of the trade discount rates in the series by subtracting each from 100% and converting them to decimal form.

STEP 2. Calculate the net price factor of the series by multiplying all the decimals together.

STEP 3. Calculate the net price by multiplying the list price by the net price factor.

Net price = List price × Net price factor

EXAMPLE7 CALCULATING NET PRICE FACTOR AND NET PRICE

The Crystal Gallery purchased merchandise from a manufacturer in Italy. The merchandise had a list price of $37,000 less trade discounts of 40/25/10. Calculate the net price factor and the net price of the order.

▶SOLUTIONSTRATEGY

Step 1. Subtract each trade discount from 100% and convert to decimals.

100%	100%	100%
− 40%	− 25%	− 10%
60% = .6	75% = .75	90% = .9

Step 2. Multiply all the complements together to get the net price factor.

Net price factor = .6 × .75 × .9

Net price factor = .405

Step 3. Net price = List price × Net price factor

Net price = 37,000 × .405

Net price = $14,985

▶TRYITEXERCISE 7

Something's Fishy, a pet shop, always gets a 30/20/12 series of trade discounts from the Clearview Fish Tank Company. In June, the shop ordered merchandise with a list price of $3,500. In September, the shop placed an additional order listing for $5,800.

a. What is the net price factor for the series of trade discounts?

b. What is the net price of the merchandise purchased in June?

c. What is the net price of the merchandise purchased in September?

CHECK YOUR ANSWERS WITH THE SOLUTIONS ON PAGE 223.

7-8   CALCULATING THE AMOUNT OF A TRADE DISCOUNT BY USING A SINGLE EQUIVALENT DISCOUNT

single equivalent discount A single trade discount that equates to all the discounts in a series or chain.

Sometimes retailers and wholesalers want to know the one single discount rate that equates to a series of trade discounts. This is known as the **single equivalent discount**. We have already learned that the trade discounts *cannot* simply be added together.

Here is the logic: The list price of the merchandise is 100%. If the net price factor is the part of the list price that is paid, then 100% minus the net price factor is the part of the list price that is the trade discount. The single equivalent discount, therefore, is the complement of the net price factor (100% – Net price factor percent).

IN THE Business World

Among other indicators, economists use **wholesale prices** as an important barometer of inflation as well as other economic trends. Rising wholesale prices inevitably lead to higher consumer prices and consequently inflation.

The Producer Price Index (PPI) is a weighted index of prices measured at the wholesale, or producer, level. A monthly release from the Bureau of Labor Statistics (BLS), the PPI shows trends in the wholesale markets for manufacturing industries and commodities markets. All of the physical goods-producing industries that make up the U.S. economy are included, but imports are not. The PPI was once called the Wholesale Price Index.

Source: www.investopedia.com

STEPS TO CALCULATE THE SINGLE EQUIVALENT DISCOUNT AND THE AMOUNT OF A TRADE DISCOUNT

STEP 1. Calculate the net price factor as before by subtracting each trade discount from 100% and multiplying them all together in decimal form.

STEP 2. Calculate the single equivalent discount by subtracting the net price factor in decimal form from 1.

Single equivalent discount = 1 − Net price factor

STEP 3. Find the amount of the trade discount by multiplying the list price by the single equivalent discount.

Trade discount = List price × Single equivalent discount

EXAMPLE8   CALCULATING THE SINGLE EQUIVALENT DISCOUNT AND THE AMOUNT OF A TRADE DISCOUNT

Calculate the single equivalent discount and amount of the trade discount on merchandise listing for $10,000 less trade discounts of 30/10/5.

▶SOLUTIONSTRATEGY

Step 1. Calculate the net price factor.

$$
\begin{array}{ccccc}
100\% & & 100\% & & 100\% \\
-\ 30\% & & -\ 10\% & & -\ 5\% \\
\hline
.70 & \times & .90 & \times & .95 \\
\end{array}
= .5985 = \text{Net price factor}
$$

Step 2. Calculate the single equivalent discount.

$$\text{Single equivalent discount} = 1 - \text{Net price factor}$$
$$\text{Single equivalent discount} = 1 - .5985 = \underline{.4015}$$

Note: 40.15% is the single equivalent discount of the series 30%, 10%, and 5%.

Step 3. Calculate the amount of the trade discount.

$$\text{Trade discount} = \text{List price} \times \text{Single equivalent discount}$$
$$\text{Trade discount} = 10,000 \times .4015 = \underline{\$4,015}$$

▶TRYITEXERCISE 8

The Rainbow Appliance Center purchased an order of dishwashers and ovens listing for $36,800. The manufacturer allows Rainbow a series of trade discounts of 25/15/10. What are the single equivalent discount and the amount of the trade discount?

CHECK YOUR ANSWERS WITH THE SOLUTIONS ON PAGE 223.

REVIEW EXERCISES

7

SECTION III

Calculate the following net price factors and net prices. For convenience, round net price factors to five decimal places when necessary.

	List Price	Trade Discount Rates	Net Price Factor	Net Price
1.	$360.00	12/10	.792	$285.12
2.	425.80	18/15/5	_____	_____
3.	81.75	20/10/10	_____	_____
4.	979.20	15/10/5	_____	_____
5.	7.25	$25/15/10\frac{1}{2}$	_____	_____
6.	.39	20/9/8	_____	_____

Calculate the following net price factors and single equivalent discounts. Round to five places when necessary.

	Trade Discount Rates	Net Price Factor	Single Equivalent Discount
7.	15/10	.765	.235
8.	20/15/12	_____	_____
9.	25/15/7	_____	_____
10.	30/5/5	_____	_____
11.	35/15/7.5	_____	_____

Complete the following table. Round net price factors to five decimal places when necessary.

	List Price	Trade Discount Rates	Net Price Factor	Single Equivalent Discount	Trade Discount	Net Price
12.	$7,800.00	15/5/5	.76713	.23287	$1,816.39	$5,983.61
13.	1,200.00	20/15/7	_____	_____	_____	_____
14.	560.70	25/15/5	_____	_____	_____	_____
15.	883.50	18/12/9	_____	_____	_____	_____
16.	4.89	12/10/10	_____	_____	_____	_____
17.	2,874.95	30/20/5.5	_____	_____	_____	_____

18. What is the net price factor of a 25/15 series of trade discounts?

19. What is the net price factor of a 35/20/15 series of discounts?

20. Kidzstuff.com ordered toys, games, and videos from a vendor. The order had a list price of $10,300 less trade discounts of 25/15/12.

   a. What is the net price factor?

   b. What is the net price of the order?

21. Legacy Designs places an order for furniture listing for $90,500 less trade discounts of 25/20.

   a. What is the net price factor?

   b. What is the net price of the order?

Satellite radio, also called digital radio, receives radio signals broadcast from a network of satellites more than 22,000 miles above the earth. In contrast, traditional radio reception is usually limited to 50–100 miles.

   Sirius XM Radio, Inc., offers a programming lineup of 135 channels of commercial-free music, sports, news, talk, entertainment, traffic, and weather. Subscribers can listen on more than 800 different types of devices for boats, cars, home, office, or a number of types of mobile devices. Sirius has agreements for the installation of satellite radio in vehicles with every major automaker.

22. Audio Giant received an order of Sirius XM satellite radios listing for $9,500 with trade discounts of 25/13/8.

   a. What is the net price factor?

   b. What is the single equivalent discount?

   c. What is the amount of the trade discount?

   d. What is the net price of the order?

23. The Speedy Auto Service Center can buy auto parts from Southeast Auto Supply at a series discount of 20/15/5 and from Northwest Auto Supply for 25/10/8.

   a. Which auto parts supplier offers a better discount to Speedy?

   b. If Speedy orders $15,000 in parts at list price per month, how much will it save in a year by choosing the lower-priced supplier?

24. Irazu Market buys supplies from Octet Distributors with a series discount of 35/20/10.

   a. What is the single equivalent discount?

   b. What is the amount of the trade discount on an order with a list price of $6,500?

25. Midtown Market received the following items at a discount of 25/20/10: 18 cases of canned peaches listing at $26.80 per case and 45 cases of canned pears listing at $22.50 per case.

    a. What is the total list price of this order?

    b. What is the amount of the trade discount?

    c. What is the net price of the order?

26. Shopper's Mart purchased the following items. Calculate the extended total after the trade discounts for each line, the invoice subtotal, and the invoice total.

Quantity	Unit	Merchandise	Unit List	Trade Discounts	Extended Total
150	ea.	Blenders	$59.95	20/15/15	_____
400	ea.	Toasters	$39.88	20/10/10	_____
18	doz.	Coffee Mills	$244.30	30/9/7	_____
12	doz.	Juicers	$460.00	25/10/5	_____
				Invoice subtotal	_____
		Extra $5\frac{1}{2}\%$ volume discount on total order			_____
				Invoice total	_____

The Pharmacy and Drug Store Industry in the United States retails a range of prescription and over-the-counter products. These include medicines; apothecaries; health and beauty items such as vitamin supplements, cosmetics, and toiletries; and photo processing services.

Top U.S. drug retailers include Rite Aid, CVS, Target, Kmart, Kroger, Safeway, Duane Reade, Supervalu, Walgreens, and Walmart.

27. Referring back to Exercise 26, you have just been hired as the buyer for the kitchen division of Shopper's Mart, a general merchandise retailer. After looking over the discounts offered to the previous buyer by the vendor, you decide to ask for better discounts.

    After negotiating with the vendor's salesperson, you now can buy blenders at trade discounts of 20/20/15 and juicers at 25/15/10. In addition, the vendor has increased the volume discount to $6\frac{1}{2}\%$.

    a. How much would have been saved with your new discounts based on the quantities of the previous order (Exercise 26)?

    b. As a result of your negotiations, the vendor has offered an additional discount of 2% of the total amount due if the invoice is paid within 15 days instead of the usual 30 days. What would be the amount of this discount?

BUSINESS DECISION: THE ULTIMATE TRADE DISCOUNT

28. A General Motors incentive program designed to reduce inventory of certain low-selling models offers a $7,000 extra dealer incentive for each of these vehicles that the dealer moved into its rental or service fleets.

    As the accountant for a dealership with a number of these vehicles left in stock, your manager has asked you to calculate certain invoice figures. The normal trade discount from GM is 18%. If the average sticker price (list price) of these remaining vehicles at your dealership is $23,500, calculate the following.

    a. What is the amount of the trade discount, including the incentive?

    b. What is the trade discount rate? Round to the nearest tenth of a percent.

    c. What is the net price (invoice price) to your dealership?

    d. If the cars were then sold from the fleets at $1,000 over "invoice" (net price), what is the total percentage savings to the consumer based on the list price? Round to the nearest tenth of a percent.

    e. (Optional) Although these incentive prices reflect extraordinary discounts to the consumer, what other factors should a consumer consider before purchasing a "discontinued" brand of vehicle?

SECTION IV **7** CASH DISCOUNTS AND TERMS OF SALE

terms of sale The details of when an invoice must be paid and if a cash discount is being offered.

credit period The time period that the seller allows the buyer to pay an invoice.

net date, or **due date** The last day of the credit period.

cash discount An extra discount offered by the seller as an incentive for early payment of an invoice.

invoice date The date an invoice is written. The beginning of the discount and credit periods when ordinary dating is used.

cash discount period The time period in which a buyer can take advantage of the cash discount.

discount date The last day of the discount period.

As merchandise physically arrives at the buyer's back door, the invoice ordinarily arrives by mail through the front door. Today more and more arrive by e-mail. What happens next? The invoice has a section entitled **terms of sale**. The terms of sale are the details of when the invoice must be paid and whether any additional discounts will be offered.

Commonly, manufacturers allow wholesalers and retailers 30 days or even longer to pay the bill. In certain industries, the time period is as much as 60 or 90 days. This is known as the **credit period**. This gives the buyer time to unpack and check the order and, more important, begin selling the merchandise. This credit period clearly gives the wholesaler and retailer an advantage. They can generate revenue by selling merchandise that they have not paid for yet.

To encourage them to pay the bill earlier than the **net date**, or **due date**, sellers frequently offer buyers an optional extra discount over and above the trade discounts. This is known as a **cash discount**. Cash discounts are an extra few percent offered as an incentive for early payment of the invoice, usually within 10 to 15 days after the **invoice date**. This is known as the **cash discount period**. The last date for a buyer to take advantage of a cash discount is known as the **discount date**.

THE IMPORTANCE OF CASH DISCOUNTS

Both buyers and sellers benefit from cash discounts. Sellers get their money much sooner, which improves their cash flow, whereas buyers get an additional discount, which lowers their merchandise cost, thereby raising their margin or gross profit.

Cash discounts generally range from an extra 1% to 5% off the net price of the merchandise. A 1% to 5% discount may not seem significant, but it is. Let's say that an invoice is due in 30 days; however, a distributor would like payment sooner. It might offer the retailer a cash discount of 2% if the bill is paid within 10 days rather than 30 days. If the retailer chooses to take the cash discount, he or she must pay the bill by the 10th day after the date of the invoice. Note that this is *20 days* earlier than the due date. The retailer is therefore receiving a 2% discount for paying the bill 20 days early.

The logic: There are 18.25 twenty-day periods in a year (365 days divided by 20 days). By multiplying the 2% discount by the 18.25 periods, we see that on a yearly basis, 2% cash discounts can *theoretically* amount to 36.5%. Very significant!

> ## Dollars AND Sense
>
> Cash discounts are so important to wholesalers' and retailers' "profit picture" that frequently they borrow the money on a short-term basis to take advantage of the cash discount savings. This procedure is covered in Chapter 10, "Simple Interest."

CALCULATING CASH DISCOUNTS AND NET AMOUNT DUE

7-9

Cash discounts are offered in the terms of sale. A transaction with no cash discount would have terms of sale of net 30, for example. This means the **net amount** of the invoice is due in 30 days. If a cash discount is offered, the terms of sale would be written as 2/10, n/30. This means a 2% cash discount may be taken if the invoice is paid within 10 days; if not, the net amount is due in 30 days. (See Exhibit 7-4.)

net amount The amount of money due from the buyer to the seller.

Exhibit 7-5 shows a time line of the discount period and credit period on an invoice dated October 15. The 2/10, n/30 terms of sale stipulate a cash discount if the bill is paid within 10 days. If not, the balance is due in 30 days. As you can see, the cash discount period runs for 10 days from the invoice date, October 15 to October 25. The credit period, 30 days, extends from the invoice date through November 14.

Sometimes two cash discounts are offered, such as 3/15, 1/25, n/60. This means a 3% cash discount is offered if the invoice is paid within 15 days, a 1% cash discount if the invoice is paid within 25 days, with the net amount due in 60 days.

Cash discounts cannot be taken on shipping charges or returned goods, only on the net price of the merchandise. If shipping charges are included in the amount of an invoice, they must be subtracted before the cash discount is taken. After the cash discount has been deducted, the shipping charges are added back to get the invoice total.

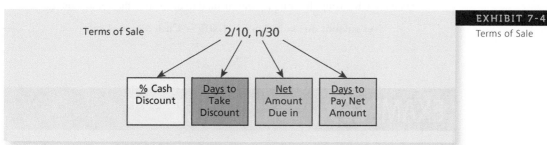

Terms of Sale   2/10, n/30

| % Cash Discount | Days to Take Discount | Net Amount Due in | Days to Pay Net Amount |

EXHIBIT 7-4
Terms of Sale

2/10, n/30 Terms of Sale

Invoice Date   Discount Date   Net Date

Cash Discount Period
10 Days

Oct. 15   Oct. 25   Nov. 14

Credit Period — 30 Days

EXHIBIT 7-5
Terms of Sale Time Line

© Randy Glasbergen.
www.glasbergen.com

GLASBERGEN —

Randy Glasbergen

"Our terms are net 30 days. If you don't pay
after 30 days, we come after you with a net!"

If arriving merchandise is damaged or is not what was ordered, those goods will be returned to the vendor. The amount of the returned goods must also be subtracted from the amount of the invoice. They are no longer a part of the transaction.

Learning Tip

Remember, shipping charges or returned items are not subject to cash discounts. These must be deducted from the invoice before the cash discount is applied. After the discount is taken, shipping charges, if any, are added back to get the invoice total.

STEPS TO CALCULATE CASH DISCOUNT AND NET AMOUNT DUE

STEP 1. Calculate the amount of the cash discount by multiplying the cash discount rate by the net price of the merchandise.

$$\text{Cash discount} = \text{Net price} \times \text{Cash discount rate}$$

STEP 2. Calculate the net amount due by subtracting the amount of the cash discount from the net price.

$$\text{Net amount due} = \text{Net price} - \text{Cash discount}$$

Note: As with trade discounts, buyers are frequently more interested in the net amount due than the amount of the discount. When that is the case, we can simplify the calculation by using the complement method to determine the net amount due.

$$\text{Net amount due} = \text{Net price} (100\% - \text{Cash discount rate})$$

EXAMPLE9   CALCULATING CASH DISCOUNT AND NET AMOUNT DUE

Rugs.com buys merchandise with an invoice amount of $16,000 from Karistan Carpet Mills. The terms of sale are 2/10, n/30. What is the amount of the cash discount? What is the net amount due on this order if the bill is paid by the 10th day?

► SOLUTIONSTRATEGY

Cash discount = Net price × Cash discount rate

$$\text{Cash discount} = 16,000 \times .02 = \underline{\$320}$$

Net amount due = Net price − Cash discount

$$\text{Net amount due} = 16,000 - 320 = \underline{\$15,680}$$

►TRYITEXERCISE 9

Valiant Plumbing ordered sinks from a supplier. The sinks had a net price of $8,300 and terms of sale of 3/15, n/45. What is the amount of the cash discount? What is the net amount due if the bill is paid by the 15th day?

CHECK YOUR ANSWERS WITH THE SOLUTIONS ON PAGE 223.

CALCULATING NET AMOUNT DUE, WITH CREDIT GIVEN FOR PARTIAL PAYMENT

7-10

Sometimes buyers do not have all the money needed to take advantage of the cash discount. Manufacturers and suppliers usually allow them to pay part of the invoice by the discount date and the balance by the end of the credit period. This **partial payment** earns partial cash discount credit. In this situation, we must calculate how much **partial payment credit** is given.

Here is how it works: Assume a cash discount of 4/15, n/45 is offered to a retailer. A 4% cash discount means that the retailer will pay 96% of the bill (100% − 4%) and receive 100% credit. Another way to look at it is that every $0.96 paid toward the invoice earns $1.00 credit. We must determine how many $0.96s are in the partial payment. This will tell us how many $1.00s of credit we receive.

partial payment When a portion of the invoice is paid within the discount period.

partial payment credit The amount of the invoice paid off by the partial payment.

STEPS TO CALCULATE PARTIAL PAYMENT CREDIT AND NET AMOUNT DUE

STEP 1. Calculate the amount of credit given for a partial payment by dividing the partial payment by the complement of the cash discount rate.

$$\text{Partial payment credit} = \frac{\text{Partial payment}}{100\% - \text{Cash discount rate}}$$

STEP 2. Calculate the net amount due by subtracting the partial payment credit from the net price.

$$\text{Net amount due} = \text{Net price} - \text{Partial payment credit}$$

IN THE Business World

The extension of partial payment credit by vendors is important to small retailers who don't always have the cash flow to take advantage of the full cash discount.

EXAMPLE10   CALCULATING NET AMOUNT DUE AFTER A PARTIAL PAYMENT

Happy Feet, a chain of children's shoe stores, receives an invoice from a tennis shoe manufacturer on September 3 with terms of 3/20, n/60. The net price of the order is $36,700. Happy Feet wants to send a partial payment of $10,000 by the discount date and the balance on the net date. How much credit does Happy Feet get for the partial payment? What is the remaining net amount due to the manufacturer?

►SOLUTIONSTRATEGY

$$\text{Partial payment credit} = \frac{\text{Partial payment}}{100\% - \text{Case discount rate}}$$

$$\text{Partial payment credit} = \frac{10,000}{100\% - 3\%} = \frac{10,000}{.97} = \underline{\$10,309.28}$$

$$\text{Net amount due} = \text{Net price} - \text{Partial payment credit}$$

$$\text{Net amount due} = \$36,700.00 - \$10,309.28 = \underline{\$26,390.72}$$

▶TRYITEXERCISE 10

All Pro Sports Center purchases $45,300 in baseball gloves from Spaulding on May 5. Spaulding allows 4/15, n/45. If All Pro sends a partial payment of $20,000 on the discount date, how much credit will be given for the partial payment? What is the net amount still due on the order?

CHECK YOUR ANSWERS WITH THE SOLUTIONS ON PAGE 223.

7-11 DETERMINING DISCOUNT DATE AND NET DATE BY USING VARIOUS TERMS OF SALE DATING METHODS

To determine the discount date and net date of an invoice, you must know how many days are in each month or use a calendar.

Following are two commonly used memory devices to help you remember how many days are in each month. Remember, in a leap year, February has 29 days. Leap years occur when the year is evenly divisible by 4 except if the year is also evenly divisible by 400. Therefore, 2016, 2020, and 2024 are examples of leap years, while 2000 was not a leap year.

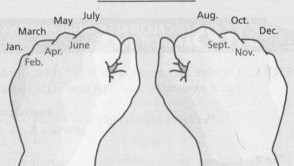

RHYME

Thirty days has September
April, June, and November
All the rest have thirty-one
Except February,
which has twenty-eight.

NAME THE KNUCKLES

Each month on a knuckle has 31 days and each month between knuckles has 30 days. February has 28.

Another way to find these dates is to use the days-in-a-year calendar shown in Exhibit 7-6. In Chapter 10, you will be able to use this calendar again to find future dates and calculate the number of days of a loan.

STEPS TO FINDING A FUTURE DATE USING A DAYS-IN-A-YEAR CALENDAR

STEP 1. Find the "day number" of the starting date.

Note: In leap years, add 1 to the day numbers beginning with March 1.

STEP 2. Add the number of days of the discount or credit period to that day number.

Note: If the new day number is over 365, subtract 365. This means the future date is in the next year.

STEP 3. Find the date by looking up the new day number from Step 2.

EXAMPLE11 FINDING THE NET DATE

If an invoice dated April 14 is due in 75 days, what is the net date?

►SOLUTIONSTRATEGY

Step 1. From the calendar, April 14 is day number 104.

Step 2. 104 + 75 = 179

Step 3. From the calendar, day number 179 is June 28.

►TRYITEXERCISE 11

If an invoice dated September 12 is due in 60 days, what is the net date?

CHECK YOUR ANSWER WITH THE SOLUTION ON PAGE 223.

EXHIBIT 7-6 Days-in-a-Year Calendar

Day of month	Jan.	Feb.	Mar.	Apr.	May	June	July	Aug.	Sept.	Oct.	Nov.	Dec.
1	1	32	60	91	121	152	182	213	244	274	305	335
2	2	33	61	92	122	153	183	214	245	275	306	336
3	3	34	62	93	123	154	184	215	246	276	307	337
4	4	35	63	94	124	155	185	216	247	277	308	338
5	5	36	64	95	125	156	186	217	248	278	309	339
6	6	37	65	96	126	157	187	218	249	279	310	340
7	7	38	66	97	127	158	188	219	250	280	311	341
8	8	39	67	98	128	159	189	220	251	281	312	342
9	9	40	68	99	129	160	190	221	252	282	313	343
10	10	41	69	100	130	161	191	222	253	283	314	344
11	11	42	70	101	131	162	192	223	254	284	315	345
12	12	43	71	102	132	163	193	224	255	285	316	346
13	13	44	72	103	133	164	194	225	256	286	317	347
14	14	45	73	104	134	165	195	226	257	287	318	348
15	15	46	74	105	135	166	196	227	258	288	319	349
16	16	47	75	106	136	167	197	228	259	289	320	350
17	17	48	76	107	137	168	198	229	260	290	321	351
18	18	49	77	108	138	169	199	230	261	291	322	352
19	19	50	78	109	139	170	200	231	262	292	323	353
20	20	51	79	110	140	171	201	232	263	293	324	354
21	21	52	80	111	141	172	202	233	264	294	325	355
22	22	53	81	112	142	173	203	234	265	295	326	356
23	23	54	82	113	143	174	204	235	266	296	327	357
24	24	55	83	114	144	175	205	236	267	297	328	358
25	25	56	84	115	145	176	206	237	268	298	329	359
26	26	57	85	116	146	177	207	238	269	299	330	360
27	27	58	86	117	147	178	208	239	270	300	331	361
28	28	59	87	118	148	179	209	240	271	301	332	362
29	29		88	119	149	180	210	241	272	302	333	363
30	30		89	120	150	181	211	242	273	303	334	364
31	31		90		151		212	243		304		365

During a leap year, add 1 to the day numbers beginning with March 1.

TERMS OF SALE—DATING METHODS

ORDINARY DATING

ordinary dating When the discount period and credit period start on the invoice date.

When the discount period and the credit period start on the date of the invoice, this is known as **ordinary dating**. It is the most common method of dating the terms of sale. The last day to take advantage of the cash discount, the discount date, is found by adding the number of days in the discount period to the date of the invoice. For example, to receive a cash discount, an invoice dated November 8 with terms of 2/10, n/30 should be paid no later than November 18 (November 8 + 10 days). The last day to pay the invoice, the net date, is found by adding the number of days in the credit period to the invoice date. With terms of 2/10, n/30, the net date would be December 8 (November 8 + 30 days). If the buyer does not pay the bill by the net date, the seller may impose a penalty charge for late payment.

EXAMPLE12   USING ORDINARY DATING

AccuCare Pharmacy receives an invoice dated August 19 from Bristol Drug Wholesalers for merchandise. The terms of sale are 3/10, n/45. If AccuCare elects to take the cash discount, what is the discount date? If AccuCare does not take the cash discount, what is the net date?

▶SOLUTIONSTRATEGY

Find the discount date by adding the number of days in the discount period to the date of the invoice.

$$\text{Discount date} = \text{August 19} + \text{10 days} = \underline{\text{August 29}}$$

If the discount is not taken, find the net date by adding the number of days in the credit period to the invoice date.

$$\text{August 19} + \text{45 days} = \begin{array}{l} \text{12 days left in August } (31-19) \\ + \text{ 30 days in September} \\ \underline{+ \quad \text{3 days in October}} \\ \text{45 days} \end{array}$$

The net date, the 45th day, is October 3.

▶TRYITEXERCISE 12

Great Impressions Printing buys ink and paper from a supplier. The invoice date of the purchase is June 11. If the terms of sale are 4/10, n/60, what are the discount date and the net date of the invoice?

CHECK YOUR ANSWERS WITH THE SOLUTIONS ON PAGE 223.

EOM OR PROXIMO DATING

EOM dating End-of-month dating. Depending on invoice date, terms of sale start at the end of the month of the invoice or the end of the following month.

proximo, or **prox** Another name for EOM dating. Means "in the following month."

EOM dating, or end-of-month dating, means that the terms of sale start *after* the end of the month of the invoice. Another name for this dating method is **proximo**, or **prox**. Proximo means "in the following month." For example, 2/10 EOM, or 2/10 proximo, means that a 2% cash discount will be allowed if the bill is paid 10 days after the *end of the month* of the invoice. This is the case for any invoice dated from the 1st to the 25th of a month. If an invoice is dated after the 25th of the month, the terms of sale begin *after* the end of the *following* month. Unless otherwise specified, the net amount is due *20 days* after the discount date.

EXAMPLE 13 — USING EOM DATING

As the shipping manager for World Imports, answer the following questions.

a. What are the discount date and the net date of an invoice dated March 3 with terms of 3/15 EOM?

b. What are the discount date and the net date of an invoice dated March 27 with terms of 3/15 EOM?

▶SOLUTIONSTRATEGY

a. Because the invoice date is between the 1st and the 25th of the month, March 3, the discount date on terms of 3/15 EOM would be 15 days *after* the end of the month of the invoice. The net date would be 20 days later.

$$\text{Discount date} = 15 \text{ days after the end of March} = \underline{\text{April 15}}$$

$$\text{Net date} = \text{April 15} + 20 \text{ days} = \underline{\text{May 5}}$$

b. Because the invoice date is after the 25th of the month, March 27, the discount date on terms of 3/15 EOM would be 15 days *after* the end of the month *following* the invoice month. The net date would be 20 days later.

$$\text{Discount date} = 15 \text{ days after the end of April} = \underline{\text{May 15}}$$

$$\text{Net date} = \text{May 15} + 20 \text{ days} = \underline{\text{June 4}}$$

▶TRYITEXERCISE 13

As the accounts receivable manager for River Bend Industries, answer the following questions.

a. What are the discount date and the net date of an invoice dated November 18 with terms of 3/15 EOM?

b. What are the discount date and the net date of an invoice dated November 27 with terms of 3/15 EOM?

CHECK YOUR ANSWERS WITH THE SOLUTIONS ON PAGE 223.

ROG DATING

Receipt of goods dating, or **ROG dating**, is a common method used when shipping times are long, such as with special or custom orders. When ROG dating is used, the terms of sale begin the day the goods are received at the buyer's location. With this method, the buyer does not have to pay for the merchandise before it arrives. An example would be 2/10 ROG. As usual, the net date is 20 days after the discount date.

ROG dating Receipt of goods dating. Terms of sale begin on the date the goods are received by the buyer.

EXAMPLE 14 — USING ROG DATING

What are the discount date and the net date for an invoice dated June 23 if the shipment arrives on August 16 and the terms are 3/15 ROG?

▶SOLUTIONSTRATEGY

In this case, the discount period starts on August 16, the date the shipment arrives. The net date will be 20 days after the discount date.

$$\text{Discount date} = \text{August 16} + 15 \text{ days} = \underline{\text{August 31}}$$

$$\text{Net date} = \text{August 31} + 20 \text{ days} = \underline{\text{September 20}}$$

▶TRYITEXERCISE 14

What are the discount date and the net date of an invoice dated October 11 if the shipment arrives on December 29 and the terms are 2/20 ROG?

CHECK YOUR ANSWERS WITH THE SOLUTIONS ON PAGE 223.

Extra, Ex, or **X dating** The buyer receives an extra discount period as an incentive to purchase slow-moving or out-of-season merchandise.

EXTRA DATING

The last dating method commonly used in business today is called **Extra, Ex,** or **X dating**. With this dating method, the seller offers an extra discount period to the buyer as an incentive for purchasing slow-moving or out-of-season merchandise, such as Christmas goods in July and bathing suits in January. An example would be 3/10, 60 extra. This means the buyer gets a 3% cash discount in 10 days plus 60 *extra* days, or a total of 70 days. Once again, unless otherwise specified, the net date is 20 days after the discount date.

EXAMPLE15   USING EXTRA DATING

What are the discount date and the net date of an invoice dated February 9 with terms of 3/15, 40 Extra?

SOLUTIONSTRATEGY

These terms, 3/15, 40 Extra, give the retailer 55 days (15 + 40) from February 9 to take the cash discount. The net date will be 20 days after the discount date.

$$\text{Discount date} = \text{February 9} + 55 \text{ days} = \underline{\text{April 5}}$$
$$\text{Net date} = \text{April 5} + 20 \text{ days} = \underline{\text{April 25}}$$

TRYITEXERCISE 15

What are the discount date and the net date of an invoice dated February 22 with terms of 4/20, 60 Extra?

CHECK YOUR ANSWERS WITH THE SOLUTIONS ON PAGE 223.

Learning Tip

Remember, when using extra dating, unless otherwise specified, the net date is 20 days after the discount date.

SECTION IV   7   REVIEW EXERCISES

Calculate the cash discount and the net amount due for each of the following transactions.

	Amount of Invoice	Terms of Sale	Cash Discount	Net Amount Due
1.	$15,800.00	3/15, n/30	$474.00	$15,326.00
2.	12,660.00	2/10, n/45	_____	_____
3.	2,421.00	4/10, n/30	_____	_____
4.	6,010.20	4/10, n/30	_____	_____
5.	9,121.44	$3\frac{1}{2}$/15, n/60	_____	_____

For the following transactions, calculate the credit given for the partial payment and the net amount due on the invoice.

	Amount of Invoice	Terms of Sale	Partial Payment	Credit for Partial Payment	Net Amount Due
6.	$8,303.00	2/10, n/30	$2,500	$2,551.02	$5,751.98
7.	1,344.60	3/10, n/45	460	_____	_____
8.	5,998.20	4/15, n/60	3,200	_____	_____
9.	7,232.08	$4\frac{1}{2}$/20, n/45	5,500	_____	_____

Using the ordinary dating method, calculate the discount date and the net date for the following transactions.

Date of Invoice	Terms of Sale	Discount Date(s)	Net Date
10. November 4	2/10, n/45	Nov. 14	Dec. 19
11. August 18	2/24, n/55	_____	_____
12. August 11	3/20, n/45	_____	_____
13. January 29	2/10, 1/20, n/60	_____	_____
14. July 8	4/25, n/90	_____	_____

Using the EOM, ROG, and Extra dating methods, calculate the discount date and the net date for the following transactions. Unless otherwise specified, the net date is 20 days after the discount date.

Date of Invoice	Terms of Sale	Discount Date	Net Date
15. December 5	2/10, EOM	Jan. 10	Jan. 30
16. June 27	3/15, EOM		
17. September 1	3/20, ROG		
	Rec'd Oct. 3		
18. February 11	2/10, 60 Extra		
19. May 18	4/25, EOM		
20. October 26	2/10, ROG		
	Rec'd Nov. 27		

21. The Apollo Company received an invoice from a vendor on April 12 in the amount of $1,420. The terms of sale were 2/15, n/45. The invoice included shipping charges of $108. The vendor sent $250 in merchandise that was not ordered. These goods will be returned by Apollo. (Remember, no discounts on shipping charges or returned goods.)

    a. What are the discount date and the net date?

    b. What is the amount of the cash discount?

    c. What is the net amount due?

22. An invoice is dated August 21 with terms of 4/18 EOM.

    a. What is the discount date?   b. What is the net date?

23. An invoice dated January 15 has terms of 3/20 ROG. The goods are delayed in shipment and arrive on March 2.

    a. What is the discount date?   b. What is the net date?

24. What payment should be made on an invoice in the amount of $3,400 dated August 7 if the terms of sale are 3/15, 2/30, n/45 and the bill is paid on

    a. August 19?

    b. September 3?

25. Red Tag Furniture received a SeaLand container of sofas from Thailand on April 14. The invoice, dated March 2, was for $46,230 in merchandise and $2,165 in shipping charges. The terms of sale were 3/15 ROG. Red Tag Furniture made a partial payment of $15,000 on April 27.

    a. What is the net amount due?

    b. What is the net date?

26. City Cellular purchased $28,900 in cell phones on April 25. The terms of sale were 4/20, 3/30, n/60. Freight terms were F.O.B. destination. Returned goods amounted to $650.

    a. What is the net amount due if City Cellular sends the manufacturer a partial payment of $5,000 on May 20?

    b. What is the net date?

    c. If the manufacturer charges a $4\frac{1}{2}$% late fee, how much would City Cellular owe if it did not pay the balance by the net date?

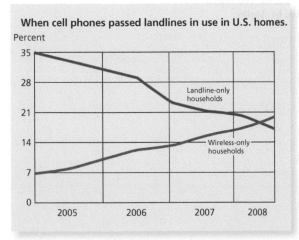

When cell phones passed landlines in use in U.S. homes.

In 2008, for the first time, the number of U.S. households opting for only cell phones outnumbered those that had just traditional landlines, and the trend has continued since that time.

Source: National Center for Health Statistics

BUSINESS DECISION: THE EMPLOYMENT TEST

27. As part of the employment interview for an accounting job at Sound Design, you have been asked to answer the questions below, based on an invoice from one of Sound Design's vendors, Target Electronic Wholesalers.

TARGET
ELECTRONIC WHOLESALERS
1979 N.E. 123 Street
Jacksonville, Florida 32204

Sold to: Sound Design
480 McDowell Rd.
Phoenix, AZ 85008

Invoice Date: June 28, 20XX

Terms of Sale: 3/15, n/30 ROG

Stock #	Description	Unit Price	Amount
4811V	Stereo Receivers	50 × $297.50 =	_____
511CX	Blu-ray Players	25 × $132.28 =	_____
6146M	Home Theater Systems	40 × $658.12 =	_____
1031A	LCD TVs	20 × $591.00 =	_____
		Merchandise Total	_____
		Insurance + Shipping	$1,150.00
		Invoice Total	_____

a. Extend each line and calculate the merchandise total and the total amount of the invoice, using the space provided on the invoice.

b. What are the discount date and the net date if the shipment arrived on July 16?

c. While in transit, five Blu-ray players and four LCD TVs were damaged and will be returned. What is the amount of the returned merchandise? What is the revised merchandise total?

d. What are the amount of the cash discount and the net amount due if the discount is taken?

e. If Sound Design sends in a partial payment of $20,000 within the discount period, what is the net balance still due?

CHAPTER FORMULAS

The Invoice

Extended total = Number of items × Cost per item

Trade Discounts—Single

Trade discount = List price × Trade discount rate

Net price = List price − Trade discount

Net price = List price (100% − Trade discount rate)

$$\text{Trade discount rate} = \frac{\text{Trade discount}}{\text{List price}}$$

Trade Discounts—Series

Net price = List price × Net price factor

Single equivalent discount = 1 − Net price factor

Trade discount = List price × Single equivalent discount

Cash Discounts and Terms of Sale

Net amount due = Net price (100% − Cash discount rate)

$$\text{Partial payment credit} = \frac{\text{Partial payment}}{100\% - \text{Cash discount rate}}$$

Net amount due = Net price − Partial payment credit

CHAPTER SUMMARY

Section I: The Invoice

Topic	Important Concepts	Illustrative Examples
Reading and Understanding the Parts of an Invoice **Performance Objective 7-1, Page 190**	Refer to Exhibits 7-1 to 7-3.	

Extending and Totaling an Invoice
 	
Performance Objective 7-2, Page 193
	Extended amount =
	    Number of items × Cost per item
	Invoice subtotal =
	    Total of extended amount column
	Invoice total =
	    Invoice subtotal + Other charges
		The Great Subversion, a sandwich shop, ordered 25 lb of ham at $3.69 per pound and 22 lb of cheese at $4.25 per pound. There is a $7.50 delivery charge. Extend each item and find the invoice subtotal and invoice total.
		
		25 × 3.69 = $92.25 Ham
		22 × 4.25 = 93.50 Cheese
		                    $185.75 Subtotal
		                    + 7.50 Delivery charge
		                    $193.25 Invoice total

Section II: Trade Discounts—Single

Topic	Important Concepts	Illustrative Examples
Calculating the Amount of a Single Trade Discount **Performance Objective 7-3, Page 197**	Trade discounts are reductions from the manufacturer's list price given to businesses in the trade for the performance of various marketing functions. Trade discount = List price × Trade discount rate	Sunglass King ordered merchandise with a list price of $12,700 from a manufacturer. Because it is in the trade, Sunglass King gets a 35% trade discount. What is the amount of the trade discount? Trade discount = 12,700 × .35 = $4,445

Section II (continued)

Topic	Important Concepts	Illustrative Examples

Calculating Net Price by Using the Net Price Factor, Complement Method
 	
Performance Objective 7-4, Page 197
	Net price factor =
	   100% − Trade discount rate
	Net price =
	   List price (100% − Trade discount rate)
		From the previous problem, use the net price factor to find the net price of the order for Sunglass King.
		
		Net price = 12,700 (100% − 35%)
		Net price = 12,700 × .65 = $8,255

Calculating Trade Discount Rate When List Price and Net Price Are Known **Performance Objective 7-5, Page 198**	Trade discount rate = $\dfrac{\text{Trade discount}}{\text{List price}}$	Cycle World Bike Shop orders merchandise listing for $5,300 from Schwinn. The net price of the order is $3,200. What is the trade discount rate? Trade discount = 5,300 − 3,200 = $2,100 Trade discount rate = $\dfrac{2,100}{5,300}$ = 39.6%

Section III: Trade Discounts—Series

Topic	Important Concepts	Illustrative Examples
Calculating Net Price and the Amount of a Trade Discount by Using a Series of Trade Discounts **Performance Objective 7-6, Page 202**	Net price is found by taking each trade discount in the series from the succeeding net price until all discounts have been deducted. Trade discount = List price − Net price	An invoice with merchandise listing for $4,700 was entitled to trade discounts of 20% and 15%. What is the net price and the amount of the trade discount? 4,700 × .20 = 940 4,700 − 940 = 3,760 3,760 × .15 = 564 3,760 − 564 = $3,196 Net price Trade discount = 4,700 − 3,196 = $1,504

Calculating Net Price of a Series of Trade Discounts by Using the Net Price Factor, Complement Method
 	
Performance Objective 7-7, Page 203
	Net price factor is found by subtracting each trade discount rate from 100% (complement) and multiplying these complements together.
	
	Net price = List price × Net price factor
		Use the net price factor method to verify your answer to the previous problem.
		
		    100% 100%
		  − 20% − 15%
		    .80 × .85 = .68 Net price factor
		
		Net price = 4,700 × .68 = $3,196

Calculating the Amount of a Trade Discount by Using a Single Equivalent Discount
 	
Performance Objective 7-8, Page 204
	Single equivalent discount =
	   1 − Net price factor
	Trade discount =
	   List price × Single equivalent discount
		What is the single equivalent discount and the amount of the trade discount in the previous problem?
		
		Use this to verify your trade discount answer.
		
		Single equivalent discount = 1 − .68 = .32
		Trade discount = 4,700 × .32 = $1,504

Section IV: Cash Discounts and Terms of Sale

Topic	Important Concepts	Illustrative Examples

Calculating Cash Discounts and Net Amount Due
 	
Performance Objective 7-9, Page 209
	Terms of sale specify when an invoice must be paid and if a cash discount is offered. Cash discount is an extra discount offered by the seller as an incentive for early payment of an invoice.
	
	Cash discount =
	   Net price × Cash discount rate
	Net amount due =
	   Net price − Cash discount
		Action Auto Parts orders merchandise for $1,800, including $100 in freight charges. Action gets a 3% cash discount. What is the amount of the cash discount and the net amount due?
		
		1,800 − 100 = $1,700 Net price
		Cash discount = 1,700 × .03 = $51
		
		1,700 − 51 = 1.649
		           + 100 Shipping charge
		          $1,749 Net amount due

Section IV (continued)

Topic	Important Concepts	Illustrative Examples

Calculating Net Amount Due, with Credit Given for Partial Payment
 	
Performance Objective 7-10, Page 211
	$$\text{Partial payment credit} = \frac{\text{Partial payment}}{100\% - \text{Cash discount rate}}$$
	
	Net amount due =
	    Net price − Partial payment credit
		Elite Fashions makes a partial payment of $3,000 on an invoice of $7,900. The terms of sale are 3/15, n/30. What is the amount of the partial payment credit, and how much does Elite Fashions still owe on the invoice?
		
		$$\text{Part pmt credit} = \frac{3,000}{100\% - 3\%} = \underline{\$3,092.78}$$
		
		Net amount due = 7,900.00
		    − 3,092.78
		    $\underline{\$4,807.22}$

Determining Discount Date and Net Date by Using Various Terms of Sale Dating Methods **Performance Objective 7-11, Page 212**	Discount date: last date to take advantage of a cash discount. Net date: last date to pay an invoice without incurring a penalty charge.	
Ordinary Dating Method **Performance Objective 7-11, Page 214**	Ordinary dating: discount period and the credit period start on the date of the invoice.	Galaxy Jewelers receives an invoice for merchandise on March 12 with terms of 3/15, n/30. What are the discount date and the net date? Disc date = March 12 + 15 days = <u>March 27</u> Net date = March 12 + 30 days = <u>April 11</u>

EOM or Proximo Dating Method
 	
Performance Objective 7-11, Page 214
	EOM means end of month. It is a dating method in which the terms of sale start *after* the end of the month of the invoice.
	    If the invoice is dated after the 25th of the month, the terms of sale start *after* the end of the *following* month.
	    Unless otherwise specified, the net date is *20 days* after the discount date.
	    Proximo, or prox, is another name for EOM dating. It means "in the following month."
		Majestic Cleaning Service buys supplies with terms of sale of 2/10, EOM. What are the discount date and the net date if the invoice date is
		
		a. May 5?
		
		b. May 27?
		
		a. May 5 invoice terms start *after* the end of May:
		
		    Discount date = <u>June 10</u>
		    Net date = June 10 + 20 days = <u>June 30</u>
		
		b. May 27 invoice terms start *after* the end of the *following* month, June:
		
		    Discount date = <u>July 10</u>
		    Net date = July 10 + 20 days = <u>July 30</u>

ROG Dating Method **Performance Objective 7-11, Page 215**	ROG means receipt of goods. It is a dating method in which the terms of sale begin on the date the goods are received rather than the invoice date. This is used to accommodate long shipping times. Unless otherwise specified, the net date is *20 days* after the discount date.	An invoice dated August 24 has terms of 3/10 ROG. If the merchandise arrives on October 1, what are the discount date and the net date? Disc date = October 1 + 10 days = <u>October 11</u> Net date = October 11 + 20 days = <u>October 31</u>
Extra Dating Method **Performance Objective 7-11, Page 216**	Extra, Ex, or X is a dating method in which the buyer receives an extra period of time before the terms of sale begin. Vendors use extra dating as an incentive to entice buyers to purchase out-of-season or slow-moving merchandise. Unless otherwise specified, the net date is *20 days* after the discount date.	Sugar Pine Candy Company buys merchandise from a vendor with terms of 3/15, 60 Extra. The invoice is dated December 11. What are the discount date and the net date? Disc. date = December 11 + 75 days = <u>February 24</u> Net date = February 24 + 20 days = <u>March 16</u>

TRY IT: EXERCISE SOLUTIONS FOR CHAPTER 7

1. a. Shutterbug Camera Shops   **h.** J. Herman

    b. 44929   **i.** Federal Express

    c. November 27, 20XX   **j.** Knoxville, TN

    d. $3,120.00   **k.** $125.00

    e. FotoFair Distributors   **l.** $5,632.80

    f. Net - 30 days   **m.** $345.00

    g. 1864 N.W. 123rd St., Chicago, IL 60613   **n.** $5,757.80

2.

Stock #	Quantity	Unit	Merchandise Description	Unit Price	Total
R443	125	ea.	Food Processors	$89.00	$11,125.00
B776	24	ea.	Microwave Ovens	$225.40	$5,409.60
Z133	6	doz.	12" Mixers	$54.12	$324.72
Z163	1	bx.	Mixer Covers	$166.30	$166.30
				Invoice Subtotal	$17,025.62
				Shipping Charges	+ $194.20
				Invoice Total	$17,219.82

3. Trade discount = List price × Trade discount rate

Trade discount = 7,600 × .30 = $2,280

4. Net price = List price (100% − Trade discount rate)

Net price = 2,100 (100% − 35%)

Net price = 2,100 × .65 = $1,365

5. Trade discount = List price − Net price

Trade discount = 109,500 − 63,300 = $46,200

Trade discount rate = $\dfrac{\text{Trade discount}}{\text{List price}} = \dfrac{46,200}{109,500} = .4219 = 42.2\%$

6.

$$\begin{array}{cccccc}
25,000 & 25,000 & 16,250 & 16,250 & 13,000 & 13,000 \\
\times\ \ .35 & -\ 8,750 & \times\ \ .20 & -\ 3,250 & \times\ \ .10 & -\ 1,300 \\
\hline
8,750 & 16,250 & 3,250 & 13,000 & 1,300 & \$11,700 = \text{Net price}
\end{array}$$

Trade discount = 25,000 − 11,700 = $13,300

7. a.

$$\begin{array}{ccc}
100\% & 100\% & 100\% \\
-\ 30\% & -\ 20\% & -\ 12\% \\
\hline
.7\ \times & .8\ \times & .88\ = .4928 = \text{Net price factor}
\end{array}$$

    b. Net price = List price × Net price factor

       Net price = 3,500 × .4928 = $1,724.80

    c. Net price = List price × Net price factor

       Net price = 5,800 × .4928 = $2,858.24

8.

$$\begin{array}{ccc}
100\% & 100\% & 100\% \\
-\ 25\% & -\ 15\% & -\ 10\% \\
\hline
.75\ \times & .85\ \times & .9\ = .57375 = \text{Net price factor}
\end{array}$$

Single equivalent discount = 1 − Net price factor

Single equivalent discount = 1 − .57375 = .42625

Trade discount = List price × Single equivalent discount

Trade discount = 36,800 × .42625 = $15,686

9. Cash discount = Net price × Cash discount rate

Cash discount = 8,300 × .03 = $249

Net amount due = Net price − Cash discount

Net amount due = 8,300 − 249 = $8,051

10. Partial payment credit = $\dfrac{\text{Partial payment}}{100\% - \text{Cash discount rate}}$

Partial payment credit = $\dfrac{20,000}{100\% - 4\%} = \dfrac{20,000}{.96} = \$20,833.33$

Net amount due = Net price − Partial payment credit

Net amount due = 45,300.00 − 20,833.33 = $24,466.67

11. From the calendar, September 12 is day number 255.

255 + 60 = 315

From the calendar, day number 315 is November 11.

12. Discount date = June 11 + 10 days = June 21

Net date = June 11 + 60 days

$$\begin{array}{rl}
30 & \text{Days in June} \\
-\ 11 & \text{Discount date} \\
\hline
19 & \text{June} \\
31 & \text{July} \\
+\ 10 & \text{Aug.} \longrightarrow \text{August 10} \\
\hline
60 & \text{Days}
\end{array}$$

13. a. Discount date = 15 days after end of November = December 15

       Net date = December 15 + 20 days = January 4

    b. Discount date = 15 days after end of December = January 15

       Net date = January 15 + 20 days = February 4

14. Discount date = December 29 + 20 days = January 18

Net date = January 18 + 20 days = February 7

15. Discount date = February 22 + 80 days = May 13

Net date = May 13 + 20 days = June 2

CONCEPT REVIEW

1. The document detailing a sales transaction is known as a(n) ____. (7-1)

2. F.O.B. shipping point and F.O.B. destination are shipping terms that specify where the merchandise ____ is transferred. (7-1)

3. To extend an invoice, for each line, we multiply the number of items by the ____ per item. (7-2)

4. To calculate the amount of a single trade discount, we multiply the ____ price by the trade discount rate. (7-3)

5. The ____ price is the amount a business actually pays for merchandise after the discount has been deducted. (7-4)

6. To calculate the net price factor, we subtract the trade discount rate from ____ . (7-4)

7. Write the formula for the trade discount rate. (7-5)

8. In a chain or ____ of trade discounts, we calculate the final net price by taking each discount one at a time from the previous net price. (7-6)

9. As a shortcut, we can use the net price ____ method to calculate the net price. (7-7)

10. To calculate the net price factor, we subtract each trade discount rate from 100% and then ____ all the complements together. (7-7)

11. A single trade discount that equates to all the discounts in a series or chain is called a single ____ discount. (7-8)

12. The "____ of sale" specify when an invoice must be paid and if a(n) ____ discount is being offered. (7-9)

13. To calculate the credit given for a partial payment, we divide the amount of the partial payment by 100% ____ the cash discount rate. (7-10)

14. The most common method for dating an invoice is when the discount period and the credit period start on the date of the invoice. This method is known as ____ dating. (7-11)

ASSESSMENT TEST

Answer the following questions based on the Leisure Time Industries invoice on the following page.

1. Who is the vendor?

2. What is the date of the invoice?

3. What is the stock number of rocker chairs?

4. What does dz. mean?

5. What is the unit price of plastic lounge covers?

6. What is the destination?

7. What is the extended total for chaise lounges with no armrest?

8. Who pays the freight if the terms are F.O.B. shipping point?

9. What is the invoice subtotal?

10. What is the invoice total?

LEISURE TIME INDUSTRIES
LTI

Patio Furniture Manufacturers
1930 Main Street
Fort Worth, Texas 76102

DATE: November 2, 20XX

SOLD TO: Patio Magic Stores
          3386 Fifth Avenue
          Raleigh, NC 27613

INVOICE # B-112743

TERMS OF SALE: Net 30 days

SHIPPING INFO: FedEx Freight

STOCK #	QUANTITY	UNIT	MERCHANDISE DESCRIPTION	UNIT PRICE	TOTAL
1455	40	ea.	Chaise Lounges with armrest	$169.00	_____
1475	20	ea.	Chaise Lounges—no armrest	$127.90	_____
4387	24	ea.	Rocker Chairs	$87.70	_____
8100	3	dz.	Plastic Lounge Covers	$46.55	_____

INVOICE SUBTOTAL: _____
Packing and Handling: $125.00
Shipping Charges: $477.50

INVOICE TOTAL: _____

11. The Fortunate Filly dress shop receives an invoice for the purchase of merchandise with a list price of $9,500 and receives a trade discount of 22%. What is the amount of the trade discount?

12. Stone Implement Supply buys chain saws that list for $395.95 less a 28% trade discount.

   a. What is the amount of the trade discount?

   b. What is the net price of each lawn mower?

13. Shorty's BBQ Restaurant places an order listing for $1,250 with a meat and poultry supplier. Shorty's receives a trade discount of $422 on the order. What is the trade discount rate on this transaction?

14. Fantasia Florist Shop purchases an order of imported roses with a list price of $2,375 less trade discounts of 15/20/20.

EXCEL 1

   a. What is the amount of the trade discount?

   b. What is the net amount of the order?

15. All-American Sports can purchase sneakers for $450 per dozen less trade discounts of 14/12 from Ideal Shoes. Fancy Footwear is offering the same sneakers for $435 less trade discounts of 18/6. Which supplier offers a lower net price?

16. a. What is the net price factor for trade discounts of 25/15/10?

b. Use that net price factor to find the net price of a TV listing for $600.

17. a. What is the net price factor of the trade discount series 20/15/11?

b. What is the single equivalent discount?

18. The Empire Carpet Company orders merchandise for $17,700, including $550 in shipping charges, from Mohawk Carpet Mills on May 4. Carpets valued at $1,390 will be returned because they are damaged. The terms of sale are 2/10, n/30 ROG. The shipment arrives on May 26, and Empire wants to take advantage of the cash discount.

a. By what date must Empire pay the invoice?

b. As the bookkeeper for Empire, how much will you send to Mohawk?

The U.S. Carpet Industry According to the Carpet and Rug Institute, carpet covers nearly 60% of all floors in the United States. Ninety percent of all domestic carpet is manufactured in Georgia, representing a significant economic impact to the state. Nationwide, the industry employs over 70,000 workers.

19. Lazy Days Laundry receives an invoice for detergent. The invoice is dated April 9 with terms of 3/15, n/30.

a. What is the discount date?

c. If the invoice terms are changed to 3/15 EOM, what is the new discount date?

b. What is the net date?

d. What is the new net date?

20. Ned's Sheds purchases building materials from Timbertown Lumber for $3,700 with terms of 4/15, n/30. The invoice is dated October 17. Ned's decides to send in a $2,000 partial payment.

a. By what date must the partial payment be sent to take advantage of the cash discount?

b. What is the net date?

c. If partial payment was sent by the discount date, what is the balance still due on the order?

21. A new sound system is being installed at Club Falcon. The invoice, dated June 9, shows the total cost of the equipment as $16,480. Shipping charges amount to $516, and insurance is $81.20. Terms of sale are 2/10 prox. If the invoice is paid on July 9, what is the net amount due?

BUSINESS DECISION: THE BUSY EXECUTIVE

22. You are a salesperson for Victory Lane Wholesale Auto Parts. You have just taken a phone order from one of your best customers, Champion Motors. Because you were busy when the call came in, you recorded the details of the order on a notepad.

Phone Order Notes

- The invoice date is April 4, 20XX.
- The customer order no. is 443B.
- Champion Motors's warehouse is located at 7011 N.W. 4th Avenue, Columbus, Ohio 43205.
- Terms of sale—3/15, n/45.
- The order will be filled by D. Watson.
- The goods will be shipped by truck.
- Champion Motors's home office is located next to the warehouse at 7013 N.W. 4th Avenue.
- Champion ordered 44 car batteries, stock #394, listing for $69.95 each and 24 truck batteries, stock #395, listing for $89.95 each. These items get trade discounts of 20/15.
- Champion also ordered 36 cases of 10W/30 motor oil, stock #838-W, listing for $11.97 per case, and 48 cases of 10W/40 super-oil, stock #1621-S, listing for $14.97 per case. These items get trade discounts of 20/20/12.
- The shipping charges for the order amount to $67.50.
- Insurance charges amount to $27.68.

a. Transfer your notes to the invoice on the following page, extend each line, and calculate the total.

b. What is the discount date of the invoice?

c. If Champion sends a partial payment of $1,200 by the discount date, what is the balance due on the invoice?

d. What is the net date of the invoice?

e. Your company has a policy of charging a 5% late fee if invoice payments are more than five days late. What is the amount of the late fee that Champion will be charged if it fails to pay the balance due on time?

Founded in 1928, **Genuine Parts Company** is a service organization engaged in the distribution of automotive replacement parts, industrial replacement parts, office products, and electrical/electronic materials. The company serves customers from more than 1,900 locations with approximately 31,700 employees.

NAPA, representing the Automotive Parts Group at Genuine Parts, is the central hub of company activity. The group consists of 58 NAPA distribution centers serving approximately 5,800 NAPA Auto Parts Stores, of which 1,000 are company-owned.

Source: Based on www.napaonline.com

INVOICE

Victory Lane
Wholesale Auto Parts
422 Riverfront Road
Cincinnati, Ohio 45244

Invoice #

Invoice Date:

Sold To:

Ship To:

Customer Order No.	Salesperson	Ship via	Terms of Sale	Filled by

Quantity Ordered	Stock Number	Description	Unit List Price	Trade Discounts	Extended Amount

Invoice Subtotal   _____
Shipping Charges   _____
Insurance   _____
Invoice Total   _____

COLLABORATIVE LEARNING ACTIVITY

Comparing Invoices and Discounts

1. As a team, collect invoices from a number of businesses in different industries in your area.

   a. How are they similar?

   b. How are they different?

2. Have each member of the team speak with a wholesaler or a retailer in your area.

   a. What are the typical trade discounts in that industry?

   b. What are the typical terms of sale in that industry?

CHAPTER 8 Markup and Markdown

PERFORMANCE OBJECTIVES

© Tiphoto/Shutterstock.com

SECTION I

8

MARKUP BASED ON COST

cost of goods sold The cost of the merchandise sold during an operating period. One of two major expense categories of a business.

operating expenses, or **overhead** All business expenses, other than cost of merchandise, required to operate a business, such as payroll, rent, utilities, and insurance.

markup, **markon**, or **margin** The amount added to the cost of an item to cover the operating expenses and profit. It is the difference between the cost and the selling price.

Determining an appropriate selling price for a company's goods or services is an extremely important function in business. The price must be attractive to potential customers, yet sufficient to cover expenses and provide the company with a reasonable profit.

In business, expenses are separated into two major categories. The first is the **cost of goods sold**. To a manufacturer, this expense would be the cost of production; to a wholesaler or retailer, the expense is the price paid to a manufacturer or distributor for the merchandise. The second category includes all the other expenses required to operate the business, such as salaries, rent, utilities, taxes, insurance, advertising, and maintenance. These expenses are known as **operating expenses**, overhead expenses, or simply **overhead**.

The amount added to the cost of an item to cover the operating expenses and profit is known as the **markup**, **markon**, or **margin**. It is the difference between the cost and the selling price of an item. Markup is applied at all levels of the marketing channels of distribution. This chapter deals with the business math applications involved in the pricing of goods and services.

8-1 UNDERSTANDING AND USING THE RETAILING EQUATION TO FIND COST, AMOUNT OF MARKUP, AND SELLING PRICE OF AN ITEM

retailing equation The selling price of an item is equal to the cost plus the markup.

The fundamental principle on which business operates is to sell goods and services for a price high enough to cover all expenses and provide the owners with a reasonable profit. The formula that describes this principle is known as the **retailing equation**. The equation states that the selling price of an item is equal to the cost plus the markup.

Selling price = Cost + Markup

Using the abbreviations C for cost, M for markup, and SP for selling price, the formula is written as

$$SP = C + M$$

To illustrate, if a camera costs a retailer $60 and a $50 markup is added to cover operating expenses and profit, the selling price of the camera would be $110.

$$\$60 \text{ (cost)} + \$50 \text{ (markup)} = \$110 \text{ (selling price)}$$

In Chapter 5, we learned that equations are solved by isolating the unknowns on one side and the knowns on the other. Using this theory, when the amount of markup is the unknown, the equation can be rewritten as

Markup = Selling price − Cost $M = SP - C$

When the cost is the unknown, the equation becomes

Cost = Selling price − Markup $C = SP - M$

The following examples illustrate how these formulas are used to determine the dollar amount of cost, markup, and selling price.

EXAMPLE1 — FINDING THE SELLING PRICE

Mementos Gift Shop pays $8.00 for a picture frame. If a markup of $6.50 is added, what is the selling price of the frame?

►SOLUTIONSTRATEGY

Because selling price is the unknown variable, we use the formula $SP = C + M$ as follows:

$$SP = C + M$$
$$SP = 8.00 + 6.50 = 14.50$$
$$\text{Selling price} = \underline{\$14.50}$$

►TRYITEXERCISE 1

For the following, use the basic retailing equation to solve for the unknown.

Hairbrushes cost the manufacturer $6.80 per unit to produce. If a markup of $9.40 is added to the cost, what is the selling price per brush?

CHECK YOUR ANSWER WITH THE SOLUTION ON PAGE 256.

EXAMPLE2 — FINDING THE AMOUNT OF MARKUP

Reliable Office Supply buys printing calculators from Taiwan for $22.50 each. If they are sold for $39.95, what is the amount of the markup?

►SOLUTIONSTRATEGY

Because the markup is the unknown variable, we use the formula $M = SP - C$ as follows:

$$M = SP - C$$
$$M = 39.95 - 22.50 = 17.45$$
$$\text{Markup} = \underline{\$17.45}$$

►TRYITEXERCISE 2

For the following, use the basic retailing equation to solve for the unknown.

The 19th Hole sells a dozen golf balls for $28.50. If the distributor was paid $16.75, what is the amount of the markup?

CHECK YOUR ANSWER WITH THE SOLUTION ON PAGE 256.

EXAMPLE3 — FINDING THE COST

Safeway Supermarkets sell Corn Crunchies for $3.29 per box. If the markup on this item is $2.12, how much did the store pay for the cereal?

▶ SOLUTIONSTRATEGY

Because the cost is the unknown variable in this problem, we use the formula $C = SP - M$.

$$C = SP - M$$
$$C = 3.29 - 2.12 = 1.17$$
$$\text{Cost} = \underline{\$1.17}$$

▶ TRYITEXERCISE 3

For the following, use the basic retailing equation to solve for the unknown.

After a wholesaler adds a markup of $75 to a television set, it is sold to a retail store for $290. What is the wholesaler's cost?

CHECK YOUR ANSWER WITH THE SOLUTION ON PAGE 256.

8-2 CALCULATING PERCENT MARKUP BASED ON COST

markup based on cost When cost is 100% and the markup is expressed as a percent of that cost.

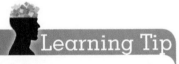

Learning Tip

A shortcut for calculating the factors of the retailing equation is to use the **markup table**. The cells represent cost, markup, and selling price in both dollars and percents.

Markup Table

	$	%
C		
+ MU		
SP		

In addition to being expressed in dollar amounts, markup is frequently expressed as a percent. There are two ways of representing markup as a percent: based on cost and based on selling price. Manufacturers and most wholesalers use cost as the base in calculating the percent markup because cost figures are readily available to them. When markup is based on cost, the cost is 100%, and the markup is expressed as a percent of that cost. Retailers, however, use selling price figures as the base of most calculations, including percent markup. In retailing, the selling price represents 100%, and the markup is expressed as a percent of that selling price.

In Chapter 6, we used the percentage formula Portion = Rate × Base. To review these variables, portion is a *part* of a whole amount; base is the *whole amount*; and rate, as a percent, describes what part the portion is of the base. When we calculate markup as a percent, we are actually solving a rate problem using the formula Rate = Portion ÷ Base.

When the markup is based on cost, the percent markup is the rate; the dollar amount of markup is the portion; and the cost, representing 100%, is the base. The answer will describe what percent the markup is of the cost; therefore, it is called percent **markup based on cost**. We use the formula:

Percent markup based on cost (rate) $= \dfrac{\text{Markup (portion)}}{\text{Cost (base)}}$ or $\%M_{\text{COST}} = \dfrac{M}{C}$

Learning Tip

Step 1. Fill in the given information using 100% for the base and *X* for this unknown. **(orange)**

Step 2. Calculate the figure for the remaining cell **(red)** in the column without the *X*.

$89.60 − $56.00 = $33.60

	$	%
C	56.00	100
+ MU	33.60	X
SP	89.60	

Then form a box. **(yellow)**

(continued on next page)

EXAMPLE4 CALCULATING PERCENT MARKUP BASED ON COST

Blanco Industries produces stainless steel sinks at a cost of $56.00 each. If the sinks are sold to distributors for $89.60 each, what are the amount of the markup and the percent markup based on cost?

▶ SOLUTIONSTRATEGY

$$M = SP - C$$
$$M = 89.60 - 56.00 = 33.60$$
$$\text{Markup} = \underline{\$33.60}$$

$$\%M_{\text{COST}} = \dfrac{M}{C}$$

$$\%M_{COST} = \frac{33.60}{56.00} = .6$$

Percent markup based on cost = <u>60%</u>

►TRYITEXERCISE 4

The Light Source buys lamps for $45 and sells them for $63. What are the amount of the markup and the percent markup based on cost?

CHECK YOUR ANSWERS WITH THE SOLUTIONS ON PAGE 256.

(continued from previous page)

The figures in the box form a proportion.

$$\frac{56}{33.60} = \frac{100}{X}$$

Step 3. Solve the proportion for X by cross-multiplying the corner figures in the box.

$$56X = 33.60\,(100)$$

$$X = \frac{3,360}{56} = 60\%$$

CALCULATING SELLING PRICE WHEN COST AND PERCENT MARKUP BASED ON COST ARE KNOWN

8-3

From the basic retailing equation, we know that the selling price is equal to the cost plus the markup. When the markup is based on cost, the cost equals 100%, and the selling price equals 100% plus the percent markup. If, for example, the percent markup is 30%, then

Selling price = Cost + Markup

Selling price = 100% + 30%

Selling price = 130% *of* the cost

Because *of* means multiply, we multiply the cost by (100% plus the percent markup).

Selling price = Cost (100% + Percent markup based on cost)

$$SP = C\,(100\% + \%M_{COST})$$

EXAMPLE5 CALCULATING THE SELLING PRICE

A wallet costs $50 to produce. If the manufacturer wants a 70% markup based on cost, what should be the selling price of the wallet?

►SOLUTIONSTRATEGY

$$SP = C\,(100\% + \%M_{COST})$$
$$SP = 50\,(100\% + 70\%)$$
$$SP = 50\,(170\%) = 50\,(1.7) = 85$$
Selling price = <u>$85</u>

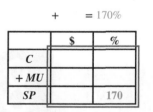

+		= 170%
	$	%
C		
+ *MU*		
SP		170

Note: When the brown box has six cells, use the four corner figures to form the proportion.

$$100X = 50\,(170)$$
$$X = \underline{\$85}$$

►TRYITEXERCISE 5

Superior Appliances buys toasters for $38. If a 65% markup based on cost is desired, what should be the selling price of the toaster?

CHECK YOUR ANSWER WITH THE SOLUTION ON PAGE 256.

8-4 CALCULATING COST WHEN SELLING PRICE AND PERCENT MARKUP BASED ON COST ARE KNOWN

To calculate cost when selling price and percent markup on cost are known, let's use our knowledge of solving equations from Chapter 5. Because we are dealing with the same three variables from the last section, simply solve the equation $SP = C(100\% + \%M_{COST})$ for the cost. Cost, the unknown, is isolated on one side of the equation by dividing both sides by (100% + Percent markup).

$$\text{Cost} = \frac{\text{Selling price}}{100\% + \text{Percent markup on cost}} \qquad C = \frac{SP}{100\% + \%M_{COST}}$$

EXAMPLE6 CALCULATING COST

American Eagle sells a blouse for $66. If a 50% markup based on cost is used, what is the cost of the blouse?

SOLUTIONSTRATEGY

	$	%
+ = 150%		
C		
+ MU		
SP		150

$$150X = 66(100)$$
$$X = \$44$$

$$\text{Cost} = \frac{\text{Selling price}}{100\% + \text{Percent markup on cost}}$$

$$\text{Cost} = \frac{66}{100\% + 50\%} = \frac{66}{150\%} = \frac{66}{1.5} = 44$$

$$\text{Cost} = \$44$$

TRYITEXERCISE 6

General Electric sells automatic coffeemakers to distributors for $39. If a 30% markup based on cost is used, how much did it cost to manufacture the coffee maker?

CHECK YOUR ANSWER WITH THE SOLUTIONS ON PAGE 256.

SECTION I 8 REVIEW EXERCISES

For the following items, calculate the missing information. Round dollars to the nearest cent and percents to the nearest tenth of a percent.

	Item	Cost	Amount of Markup	Selling Price	Percent Markup Based on Cost
1.	Television set	$161.50	$138.45	$299.95	85.7%
2.	Bookcase	$32.40	$21.50	_____	_____
3.	Automobile	_____	$5,400.00	$12,344.80	_____
4.	Dress	$75.00	_____	_____	80%
5.	Vacuum cleaner	_____	_____	$249.95	60%

Item	Cost	Amount of Markup	Selling Price	Percent Markup Based on Cost
6. Hat	$46.25	$50.00	$96.25	108.1%
7. Computer	$1,350.00	_____	$3,499.00	_____
8. Treadmill	_____	$880.00	$2,335.00	_____
9. 1 lb potatoes	$.58	_____	_____	130%
10. Wallet	_____	_____	$44.95	75%

Solve the following word problems. Round dollars to the nearest cent and percents to the nearest tenth of a percent.

11. Alarm clocks cost the manufacturer $56.10 per unit to produce. If a markup of $29.80 is added to the cost, what is the selling price per clock?

12. LooLoo Clothing Emporium sells scarves for $19.95. If the cost per scarf is $12.50, what is the amount of the markup?

13. After a wholesaler adds a markup of $420 to a TV, it sold for $949. What is the cost of the TV?

14. Amazon.com purchases flat-screen computer monitors from H.P. for $275.59 and sells them for $449.99.

 a. What is the amount of the markup?

 b. What is the percent markup based on cost?

15. The Holiday Card Shop purchased stationery for $2.44 per box. A $1.75 markup is added to the stationery.

 a. What is the selling price?

 b. What is the percent markup based on cost?

16. Staples adds a $4.60 markup to calculators and sells them for $9.95.

 a. What is the cost of the calculators?

 b. What is the percent markup based on cost?

17. a. What is the amount of markup on a skateboard from Flying Wheels Skate Shop if the cost is $58.25 and the selling price is $118.88?

 b. What is the percent markup based on cost?

AP Images/Mark Lennihan

Amazon.com, Inc., operates as an online retailer in North America and internationally. Its product categories include books, movies, music, and games; digital downloads; electronics and computers; home and garden; toys, kids, and baby; grocery; apparel, shoes, and jewelry; health and beauty; sports and outdoors; and tools, auto, and industrial products.

 The stated mission of Amazon.com is to "be Earth's most customer-centric company for four primary customer sets: consumers, sellers, enterprises, and content creators." In its first year, 1997, Amazon.com's net sales were $148 million. Ten years later net sales were $14 billion.

18. You are the manager of The Camera Connection. Use the advertisement for your store to answer the following questions.

    a. If the PowerShooter 1800 is marked up by $58.50, what is the cost and what is the percent markup based on cost?

    b. If the CyberShooter 2400 has a cost of $88.00, what are the amount of the markup and the percent markup based on cost?

    c. Which camera is more "profitable" to the store? Why?

    d. What other factors should be considered in determining profitability?

19. Crystal Auto Supply purchases water pumps from the distributor for $35.40 each. If Crystal adds a 120% markup based on cost, at what retail price should the pumps be sold?

20. Broadway Carpets sells designer rugs at retail for $875.88. If a 50% markup based on cost is added, what is the cost of the designer rugs?

21. What is the cost of a computer system that sells at retail for $850 with a 60% markup based on cost?

22. A real-wood filing cabinet from Office Solutions is marked up by $97.30 to $178.88.

    a. What is the cost?

    b. What is the percent markup based on cost?

23. The Green Thumb Garden Shop purchases automatic lawn sprinklers for $12.50 from the manufacturer. If a 75% markup based on cost is added, at what retail price should the sprinklers be marked?

24. a. What is the cost of a desk lamp at Urban Accents if the selling price is $49.95 and the markup is 70% based on the cost?

    b. What is the amount of the markup?

BUSINESS DECISION: KEYSTONE MARKUP

25. In department and specialty store retailing, a common markup strategy is to double the cost of an item to arrive at the selling price. This strategy is known as **keystoning** the markup and is widely used in apparel, cosmetics, fashion accessories, shoes, and other categories of merchandise.

    The reasoning for the high amount of markup is that these stores have particularly high operating expenses. In addition, they have a continuing need to update fixtures and remodel stores to attract customers.

    You are the buyer in the women's shoe department of the Roma Grande Department Store. You normally keystone your markups on certain shoes and handbags. This amount of markup allows you enough gross margin so that you can lower prices when "sales" occur and still have a profitable department.

    a. If you are looking for a line of handbags that will retail for $120, what is the most you can pay for the bags?

    b. At a women's wear trade show, you find a line of handbags that you like with a suggested retail price of $130. The vendor has offered you trade discounts of 30/20/5. Will this series of trade discounts allow you to keystone the handbags?

    c. (Challenge) The vendor tells you that the first two discounts, 30% and 20%, are fixed, but the 5% is negotiable. What trade discount, rounded to a whole percent, should you request in order to keystone the markup?

© Andre Blais/Shutterstock.com

Top U.S. Shopping Centers
Gross Leasable Area (GLA) in sq ft

King of Prussia Mall King of Prussia, Pennsylvania	2,856,000
Mall of America Bloomington, Minnesota	2,777,918
South Coast Plaza Costa Mesa, California	2,700,000
Mill Creek Mall Erie, Pennsylvania	2,600,000
Del Amo Fashion Center Torrance, California	2,500,000
Grand Canyon Parkway Las Vegas, Nevada	2,500,000
Aventura Mall Aventura, Florida	2,400,000
Sawgrass Mills Sunrise, Florida	2,383,906
The Galleria Houston, Texas	2,298,417

Source: www.shoppingcenters.com

MARKUP BASED ON SELLING PRICE

8

SECTION II

In Section I, we calculated markup as a percentage of the cost of an item. The cost was the base and represented 100%. As noted, this method is primarily used by manufacturers and wholesalers. In this section, the markup is calculated as a percentage of the selling price; therefore, the selling price will be the base and represent 100%. This practice is used by most retailers because most retail records and statistics are kept in sales dollars.

CALCULATING PERCENT MARKUP BASED ON SELLING PRICE

8-5

The calculation of percent **markup based on selling price** is the same as that for percent markup based on cost except that the base (the denominator) changes from cost to selling price. Remember, finding percent markup is a rate problem using the now familiar percentage formula Rate = Portion ÷ Base.

markup based on selling price When selling price is 100% and the markup is expressed as a percent of that selling price.

For this application of the formula, the percent markup based on selling price is the rate, the amount of the markup is the portion, and the selling price is the base. The formula is

$$\text{Percent markup based on selling price (rate)} = \frac{\text{Markup (portion)}}{\text{Selling price (base)}} \quad \text{or} \quad \%M_{SP} = \frac{M}{SP}$$

EXAMPLE 7 — CALCULATING THE PERCENT MARKUP BASED ON SELLING PRICE

Quality Hardware & Garden Supply purchases electric drills for $60 each. If it sells the drills for $125, what is the amount of the markup and what is the percent markup based on selling price?

SOLUTION STRATEGY

$$M = SP - C$$
$$M = 125 - 60 = 65$$
$$\text{Markup} = \underline{\$65}$$

$$\%M_{SP} = \frac{M}{SP}$$

$$\%M_{SP} = \frac{65}{125} = .52$$

Percent markup based on selling price = 52%

	–	= $65
	$	**%**
C		
+ MU	65	
SP		

$$125X = 65(100)$$
$$X = \underline{52\%}$$

TRY IT EXERCISE 7

Deals on Wheels buys bicycles from the distributor for $94.50 each. If the bikes sell for $157.50, what is the amount of the markup and what is the percent markup based on selling price?

CHECK YOUR ANSWERS WITH THE SOLUTIONS ON PAGE 256.

8-6 CALCULATING SELLING PRICE WHEN COST AND PERCENT MARKUP BASED ON SELLING PRICE ARE KNOWN

When the percent markup is based on selling price, remember that the selling price is the base and represents 100%. This means the percent cost plus the percent markup must equal 100%. If, for example, the markup is 25% of the selling price, the cost must be 75% of the selling price.

$$\text{Cost} + \text{Markup} = \text{Selling price}$$
$$75\% + 25\% = 100\%$$

Because the percent markup is known, the percent cost will always be the complement, or

% Cost = 100% − Percent markup based on selling price

Because the selling price is the base, we can solve for the selling price by using the percentage formula Base = Portion ÷ Rate, where the cost is the portion and the percent cost or (100% − Percent markup on selling price) is the rate.

$$\text{Selling price} = \frac{\text{Cost}}{100\% - \text{Percent markup on selling price}} \quad \text{or} \quad SP = \frac{C}{100\% - \%M_{SP}}$$

EXAMPLE8 CALCULATING SELLING PRICE

High Point Furniture purchases wall units from the manufacturer for $550. If the store policy is to mark up all merchandise 60% based on the selling price, what is the retail selling price of the wall units?

▶SOLUTIONSTRATEGY

$$SP = \frac{C}{100\% - \%M_{SP}}$$

$$SP = \frac{550}{100\% - 60\%} = \frac{550}{40\%} = 1{,}375$$

Selling price = $1,375

	−	= 40%
	$	%
C		40
+ *MU*		
SP		

$$40X = 550\ (100)$$
$$X = \$1{,}375$$

▶TRYITEXERCISE 8

Grand Prix Menswear buys suits for $169 from the manufacturer. If a 35% markup based on selling price is the objective, what should be the selling price of the suit?

CHECK YOUR ANSWER WITH THE SOLUTION ON PAGE 256.

CALCULATING COST WHEN SELLING PRICE AND PERCENT MARKUP BASED ON SELLING PRICE ARE KNOWN

8-7

Often retailers know how much their customers are willing to pay for an item. The following procedure is used to determine the most a retailer can pay for an item and still get the intended markup.

To calculate the cost of an item when the selling price and percent markup based on selling price are known, we use a variation of the formula used in the last section. To solve for cost, we must isolate cost on one side of the equation by multiplying both sides of the equation by (100% − Percent markup). This yields the equation for cost:

Cost = Selling price (100% − Percent markup on selling price)

$$C = SP\ (100\% - \%M_{SP})$$

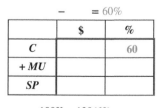

Learning Tip

The percent markup on cost is always *greater* than the corresponding percent markup on selling price because markup on cost uses cost as the base, which is *less* than the selling price. In the percentage formula, the lower the base, the greater the rate.

EXAMPLE9 CALCULATING COST

A buyer for a chain of boutiques is looking for a line of dresses to retail for $120. If a 40% markup based on selling price is the objective, what is the most the buyer can pay for these dresses and still get the intended markup?

▶SOLUTIONSTRATEGY

$$C = SP\ (100\% - \%M_{SP})$$
$$C = 120\ (100\% - 40\%) = 120\ (.6) = 72$$

Cost = $72

	−	= 60%
	$	%
C		60
+ *MU*		
SP		

$$100X = 120(60)$$
$$X = \$72$$

► TRYITEXERCISE 9

What is the most a gift shop buyer can pay for a set of wine glasses if he wants a 55% markup based on selling price and expects to sell the glasses for $79 at retail?

CHECK YOUR ANSWER WITH THE SOLUTION ON PAGE 256.

8-8 CONVERTING PERCENT MARKUP BASED ON COST TO PERCENT MARKUP BASED ON SELLING PRICE, AND VICE VERSA

CONVERTING PERCENT MARKUP BASED ON COST TO PERCENT MARKUP BASED ON SELLING PRICE

When percent markup is based on cost, it can be converted to percent markup based on selling price by using the following formula:

$$\text{Percent markup based on selling price} = \frac{\text{Percent markup based on cost}}{100\% + \text{Percent markup based on cost}}$$

EXAMPLE10 CONVERTING BETWEEN MARKUP TYPES

If a purse is marked up 60% based on cost, what is the corresponding percent markup based on selling price?

►SOLUTIONSTRATEGY

$$\text{Percent markup based on selling price} = \frac{\text{Percent markup based on cost}}{100\% + \text{Percent markup based on cost}}$$

$$\text{Percent markup based on selling price} = \frac{60\%}{100\% + 60\%} = \frac{.6}{1.6} = .375$$

$$\text{Percent markup based on selling price} = \underline{37.5\%}$$

► TRYITEXERCISE 10

A suitcase is marked up 50% based on cost. What is the corresponding percent markup based on selling price?

CHECK YOUR ANSWER WITH THE SOLUTION ON PAGE 256.

Learning Tip

This table provides a shortcut for converting between markup types. As before:

- Fill in the given information and also use 100% for the bases and X for the unknown. (orange)
- Calculate the figure for the remaining cell in the column without the X. (red)

$$100 + 60 = 160$$

- Form a proportion and solve for X.

	% C	% SP
C	100	
+ MU	60	X
SP	160	100

$$\frac{60}{160} = \frac{X}{100}$$
$$160X = 60(100)$$
$$X = \underline{37.5\%}$$

CONVERTING PERCENT MARKUP BASED ON SELLING PRICE TO PERCENT MARKUP BASED ON COST

When percent markup is based on selling price, it can be converted to percent markup based on cost by using the following formula:

$$\text{Percent markup based on cost} = \frac{\text{Percent markup based on selling price}}{100\% - \text{Percent markup based on selling price}}$$

EXAMPLE11 CONVERTING BETWEEN MARKUP TYPES

At Walmart, a Panasonic sound system is marked up 25% based on selling price. What is the corresponding percent markup based on cost? Round to the nearest tenth of a percent.

SOLUTIONSTRATEGY

$$\text{Percent markup based on cost} = \frac{\text{Percent markup based on selling price}}{100\% - \text{Percent markup based on selling price}}$$

$$\text{Percent markup based on cost} = \frac{25\%}{100\% - 25\%} = \frac{.25}{.75} = .3333$$

$$\text{Percent markup based on cost} = \underline{33.3\%}$$

	−	= 75%
	% C	**% SP**
C		75
+ MU		
SP		

$$75X = 25\,(100)$$
$$X = \underline{33.3\%}$$

TRYITEXERCISE 11

At Video Outlet, a PlayStation 4 game is marked up 75% based on selling price. What is the corresponding percent markup based on cost? Round to the nearest tenth of a percent.

CHECK YOUR ANSWER WITH THE SOLUTION ON PAGE 256.

---

8 REVIEW EXERCISES SECTION II

For the following items, calculate the missing information. Round dollars to the nearest cent and percents to the nearest tenth of a percent.

	Item	Cost	Amount of Markup	Selling Price	Percent Markup Based on Cost	Percent Markup Based on Selling Price	
1.	Sink	$65.00	$50.00	$115.00		43.5%	
2.	Textbook	$34.44	_____	$51.50		_____	
3.	Telephone	$75.00	_____	_____		45%	
4.	Bicycle	_____	_____	$133.50		60%	
5.	Magazine				60%	_____	
6.	Flashlight				_____	35%	
7.	Dollhouse	$71.25	$94.74	$165.99	133%	57.1%	
8.	Bar of soap	$1.18	$.79	_____	_____	_____	
9.	Truck	$15,449.00	_____	_____		38%	
10.	Sofa	_____	_____	$1,299.00		55%	
11.	Fan				150%	_____	
12.	Drill				_____	47%	

Solve the following word problems. Round dollars to the nearest cent and percents to the nearest tenth of a percent.

13. You are the manager of Midtown Hardware. If the EnergyMax batteries in your advertisement have a cost of $3.25,

   a. What is the amount of the markup on these batteries?

   b. What is your percent markup based on selling price?

   c. If the vendor reduces the cost to $2.90 as a promotional trade discount this week, what is your new amount of markup and what is the percent markup based on selling price?

14. A distributor purchases zero-turn mowers at a cost of $8,200 and sells them for $11,500.

   a. What is the amount of the markup?

   b. What is the percent markup based on selling price?

15. Waterbed City purchases beds from the manufacturer for $212.35. If the store policy is to mark up all merchandise 42% based on selling price, what is the retail selling price of the beds?

16. Video Depot uses a 40% markup based on selling price for its video game systems. On games and accessories, they use a 30% markup based on selling price. (See advertisement.)

   a. What is the cost and the amount of the markup of the video game system?

   b. What is the cost and the amount of the markup of the Sports Package game?

   c. As a promotion this month, the manufacturer is offering its dealers a rebate of $5.50 for each additional remote sold. What is the cost and percent markup (rounded to the nearest tenth of a percent) based on selling price?

17. Galaxy Tools manufactures an 18-volt drill at a cost of $38.32. It imports rechargeable battery packs for $20.84 each. Galaxy offers its distributors a "package deal" that includes a drill and two battery packs. The markup is 36% based on selling price. What is the selling price of the package?

18. You are the buyer for The Shoe Outlet. You are looking for a line of men's shoes to retail for $79.95. If your objective is a 55% markup based on selling price, what is the most that you can pay for the shoes to still get the desired markup?

19. If the markup on a sofa is 45% based on selling price, what is the corresponding percent markup based on cost?

20. If the markup on a scanner is 180% based on cost, what is the corresponding percent markup based on selling price?

21. A purse has a cost of $21.50 and a selling price of $51.99.

a. What is the amount of markup on the purse?

b. What is the percent markup based on cost?

c. What is the corresponding percent markup based on selling price?

22. As the manager of Speedy Supermarket, answer the following questions.

a. If 2-liter Bubbly-Cola products cost Speedy $16.50 per case of 24 bottles, what are the amount of the markup and the percent markup on selling price per case?

b. If 12-pack Bubbly-Cola products have a markup of $8.25 per case of six 12-packs at Speedy, what are the cost and the percent markup on selling price per case?

c. Why has Speedy Supermarket chosen to use markup based on selling price?

BUSINESS DECISION: INCREASING THE MARGIN

23. If Costco pays $37.50 for the vacuum cleaner shown here,

a. What is the percent markup based on selling price?

b. If Costco pays $1.50 to the insurance company for each product replacement policy sold, what is the percent markup based on selling price of the vacuum cleaner and policy combination?

c. If 6,000 vacuum cleaners are sold in a season and 40% are sold with the insurance policy, how many additional "markup dollars," the **gross margin**, was made by offering the policy?

d. (Optional) As a housewares buyer for Costco, what is your opinion of such insurance policies, considering their effect on the "profit picture" of the department? How can you sell more policies?

markdown A price reduction from the original selling price of merchandise.

The original selling price of merchandise usually represents only a temporary situation based on customer and competitor reaction to that price. A price reduction from the original selling price of merchandise is known as a **markdown**. Markdowns are frequently used in retailing because of errors in initial pricing or merchandise selection. For example, the original price may have been set too high or the buyer ordered the wrong styles, sizes, or quantities of merchandise.

Most markdowns should not be regarded as losses but as sales promotion opportunities used to increase sales and profits. When a sale has been concluded, raising prices back to the original selling price is known as a **markdown cancellation**. This section deals with the mathematics of markdowns, a series of markups and markdowns, and the pricing of perishable merchandise.

markdown cancellation Raising prices back to the original selling price after a sale is over.

8-9 DETERMINING THE AMOUNT OF MARKDOWN AND THE MARKDOWN PERCENT

sale price The promotional price of merchandise after a markdown.

A markdown is a reduction from the original selling price of an item to a new **sale price**. To determine the amount of a markdown, we use the following formula:

$$\text{Markdown} = \text{Original selling price} - \text{Sale price}$$

For example, if a sweater was originally marked at $89.95 and then was sale-priced at $59.95, the amount of the markdown would be $30.00 ($89.95 − $59.95 = $30.00).

To find the markdown percent, we use the percentage formula once again, Rate = Portion ÷ Base, where the markdown percent is the rate, the amount of the markdown is the portion, and the original selling price is the base:

$$\text{Markdown percent} = \frac{\text{Markdown}}{\text{Original selling price}}$$

Dollars AND Sense

Become a Prudent Shopper!
The price difference between two items is cash you get to put in your pocket. Even $10 saved this week will buy three dozen eggs next week. And saving $100 will give you $466.09 in 20 years at 8% interest.

Here are some of *Consumer Reports ShopSmart's* picks for the best sites to find deals:

- CouponWinner.com
- PricesandCoupons.com
- Savings.com
- Shop.com
- RetailMeNot.com
- Groupon.com
- 6pm.com
- TheOutnet.com

Sources: *The Miami Herald*, March 7, 2010, page 1E; *USA Today*, Sept. 18, 2009, page 3B.

Prudent shoppers often spend time comparing products in order to make informed buying decisions.

EXAMPLE 12 — DETERMINING THE MARKDOWN AND MARKDOWN PERCENT

A blender that originally sold for $60 was marked down and sold for $48. What is the amount of the markdown and the markdown percent?

▶ SOLUTIONSTRATEGY

$$\text{Markdown} = \text{Original selling price} - \text{Sale price}$$

$$\text{Markdown} = 60 - 48 = 12$$

$$\text{Markdown} = \underline{\$12}$$

$$\text{Markdown percent} = \frac{\text{Markdown}}{\text{Original selling price}} = \frac{12}{60} = .2$$

$$\text{Markdown percent} = \underline{20\%}$$

▶ TRYITEXERCISE 12

A tennis racquet that originally sold for $75 was marked down and sold for $56. What are the amount of the markdown and the markdown percent? Round your answer to the nearest tenth of a percent.

CHECK YOUR ANSWERS WITH THE SOLUTIONS ON PAGE 257.

> ### Learning Tip
>
> Note that *markdown percent* calculations are an application of *rate of decrease*, covered in Chapter 6.
>
> In the percentage formula, the markdown (portion) represents the amount of the decrease and the original selling price (base) represents the original amount.

DETERMINING THE SALE PRICE AFTER A MARKDOWN AND THE ORIGINAL PRICE BEFORE A MARKDOWN

8-10

DETERMINING SALE PRICE AFTER A MARKDOWN

In markdown calculations, the original selling price is the base, or 100%. After a markdown is subtracted from that price, the new price represents (100% − Markdown percent) *of* the original price. For example, if a chair is marked down 30%, the sale price would be 70% (100% − 30%) of the original price.

To find the new sale price after a markdown, we use the familiar percentage formula, Portion = Rate × Base, where the sale price is the portion, the original price is the base, and (100% − Markdown percent) is the rate.

> **Sale price = Original selling price (100% − Markdown percent)**

EXAMPLE 13 — DETERMINING THE SALE PRICE

Fernando's Hideaway, a men's clothing store, originally sold a line of ties for $55 each. If the manager decides to mark them down 40% for a clearance sale, what is the sale price of a tie?

▶ SOLUTIONSTRATEGY

Remember, if the markdown is 40%, the sale price must be 60% (100% − 40%) *of* the original price.

$$\text{Sale price} = \text{Original selling price}(100\% - \text{Markdown percent})$$

$$\text{Sale price} = \$55(100\% - 40\%) = 55(.6) = 33$$

$$\text{Sale price} = \underline{\$33}$$

► TRYITEXERCISE 13

Craftsman's Village originally sold paneling for $27.50 per sheet. When the stock was almost depleted, the price was marked down 60% to make room for incoming merchandise. What was the sale price per sheet of paneling?

CHECK YOUR ANSWER WITH THE SOLUTION ON PAGE 257.

DETERMINING THE ORIGINAL PRICE BEFORE A MARKDOWN

To find the original selling price before a markdown, we use the sale price formula solved for the original selling price. The original selling price is isolated to one side by dividing both sides of the equation by (100% − Markdown percent). *Note*: This is actually the percentage formula Base = Portion ÷ Rate with the original selling price as the base.

$$\text{Original selling price} = \frac{\text{Sale price}}{100\% - \text{Markdown percent}}$$

Wal-Mart Stores, Inc., serves customers and members more than 200 million times per week at more than 8,000 retail units under 53 different banners in 15 countries. Back in 1990, Walmart's net sales were $25 billion. Twenty years later net sales had grown to $405 billion.

Source: http://walmartstores.com

Marc F. Henning/Alamy

EXAMPLE14   DETERMINING THE ORIGINAL SELLING PRICE

What was the original selling price of a backpack at Walmart that is currently on sale for $99 after a 25% markdown?

SOLUTIONSTRATEGY

Reasoning: $99 = 75% (100% − 25%) *of* the original price. Solve for the original price.

$$\text{Original selling price} = \frac{\text{Sale price}}{100\% - \text{Markdown percent}} = \frac{99}{100\% - 25\%} = \frac{99}{.75} = 132$$

Original selling price = $132

► TRYITEXERCISE 14

What was the original selling price of a necklace currently on sale for $79 after a 35% markdown? Round your answer to the nearest cent.

CHECK YOUR ANSWER WITH THE SOLUTION ON PAGE 257.

8-11   COMPUTING THE FINAL SELLING PRICE AFTER A SERIES OF MARKUPS AND MARKDOWNS

staple goods Products considered basic and routinely purchased that do not undergo seasonal fluctuations in sales, such as food, tools, and furniture.

seasonal goods Products that undergo seasonal fluctuations in sales, such as fashion apparel and holiday merchandise.

Products that do not undergo seasonal fluctuations in sales, such as food, tools, tires, and furniture, are known as **staple goods**. These products are usually marked up once and perhaps marked down occasionally, on sale. **Seasonal goods**, such as men's and women's fashion items, snow shovels, bathing suits, and holiday merchandise, may undergo many markups and markdowns during their selling season. Merchants must continually adjust prices as the season progresses. Getting caught with an excessive amount of out-of-season inventory can ruin an otherwise bright profit picture. Christmas decorations in January and snow tires in June are virtually useless profit-wise!

EXAMPLE15 COMPUTING A SERIES OF MARKUPS AND MARKDOWNS

In March, Swim and Sport purchased designer bathing suits for $50 each. The original markup was 60% based on selling price. In May, the shop took a 25% markdown by having a sale. After three weeks, the sale was over and all merchandise was marked up 15%. By July, many of the bathing suits were still in stock, so the shop took a 30% markdown to stimulate sales. At the end of August, the balance of the bathing suits were put on clearance sale with a final markdown of another 25%. Compute the intermediate prices and the final selling price of the bathing suits. Round to the nearest cent.

▶ SOLUTIONSTRATEGY

When solving a series of markups and markdowns, remember that each should be based on the previous selling price. Use the formulas presented in this chapter and take each step one at a time.

Step 1. Find the original selling price, with markup based on selling price.

$$\text{Selling price} = \frac{\text{Cost}}{100\% - \text{Percent markup}} = \frac{50}{100\% - 60\%} = \frac{50}{.4} = 125$$

Original selling price = $125

Step 2. Calculate the 25% markdown in May.
Sale price = Original selling price(100% − Markdown percent)
Sale price = 125(100% − 25%) = 125(.75) = 93.75
Sale price = $93.75

Step 3. Calculate the after-sale 15% markup.
Remember, the base is the previous selling price, $93.75.
Selling price = Sale price(100% + Percent markup)
Selling price = 93.75(100% + 15%) = 93.75(1.15) = 107.81
Selling price = $107.81

Step 4. Calculate the July 30% markdown.
Sale price = Previous selling price(100% − Markdown percent)
Sale price = 107.81(100% − 30%) = 107.81(.7) = 75.47
Sale price = $75.47

Step 5. Calculate the final 25% markdown.
Sale price = Previous selling price(100% − Markdown percent)
Sale price = 75.47(100% − 25%) = 75.47(.75) = 56.60
Final sale price = $56.60

▶ TRYITEXERCISE 15

In September, Tire Depot in Chicago purchased snow tires from a distributor for $48.50 each. The original markup was 55% based on selling price. In November, the tires were marked down 30% and put on sale. In December, they were marked up 20%. In February, the tires were again on sale at 30% off, and in March, they cleared out with a final 25% markdown. What was the final selling price of the tires? Round to the nearest cent.

CHECK YOUR ANSWER WITH THE SOLUTION ON PAGE 257.

8-12   CALCULATING THE SELLING PRICE OF PERISHABLE GOODS

perishable goods Products that have a certain shelf life and then no value at all, such as fruits, vegetables, flowers, and dairy products.

Out-of-season merchandise still has some value, whereas **perishable goods** (such as fruits, vegetables, flowers, and dairy products) have a certain shelf life and then no value at all. For sellers of this type of merchandise to achieve their intended markups, the selling price must be based on the quantity of products sold at the original price. The quantity sold is calculated as total items less spoilage. For example, if a tomato vendor anticipates a 20% spoilage rate, the selling price of the tomatoes should be calculated based on 80% of the original stock. To calculate the selling price of perishables, use the following formula:

$$\text{Selling price of perishables} = \frac{\text{Total expected selling price}}{\text{Total quantity} - \text{Anticipated spoilage}}$$

EXAMPLE 16   CALCULATING THE SELLING PRICE OF PERISHABLE GOODS

The Farmer's Market buys 1,500 pounds of fresh bananas at a cost of $0.60 a pound. If a 15% spoilage rate is anticipated, at what price per pound should the bananas be sold to achieve a 50% markup based on selling price? Round to the nearest cent.

SOLUTIONSTRATEGY

Step 1. Find the total expected selling price: The total expected selling price is found by applying the selling price formula, $SP = C \div (100\% - \%M_{SP})$. The cost will be the total pounds times the price per pound, $1,500 \times \$.60 = \$900$.

$$SP = \frac{\text{Cost}}{100\% - \%M_{SP}} = \frac{900}{100\% - 50\%} = \frac{900}{.5} = 1,800$$

Total expected selling price = $\underline{\$1,800}$

Step 2. Find the anticipated spoilage: To find the amount of anticipated spoilage, use the formula

Anticipated spoilage = Total quantity × Spoilage rate
Anticipated spoilage = $1,500 \times 15\% = 1,500(.15) = 225$
Anticipated spoilage = $\underline{225 \text{ Pounds}}$

Step 3. Calculate the selling price of the perishables:

$$\text{Selling price of perishables} = \frac{\text{Total expected selling price}}{\text{Total quantity} - \text{Anticipated spoilage}}$$

$$\text{Selling price} = \frac{1,800}{1,500 - 225} = \frac{1,800}{1,275} = 1.411$$

Selling price of bananas = $\underline{\$1.41 \text{ Per pound}}$

TRYITEXERCISE 16

Enchanted Gardens, a chain of flower shops, purchases 800 dozen roses for Valentine's Day at a cost of $6.50 per dozen. If a 10% spoilage rate is anticipated, at what price per dozen should the roses be sold to achieve a 60% markup based on selling price? Round to the nearest cent.

CHECK YOUR ANSWER WITH THE SOLUTION ON PAGE 257.

REVIEW EXERCISES

8

For the following items, calculate the missing information. Round dollars to the nearest cent and percents to the nearest tenth of a percent.

	Item	Original Selling Price	Amount of Markdown	Sale Price	Markdown Percent
1.	Fish tank	$189.95	$28.50	$161.45	15%
2.	Sneakers	$53.88	_____	$37.50	_____
3.	Cantaloupe	_____	$.39	$1.29	_____
4.	CD player	$264.95	_____	_____	30%
5.	1 yd carpet	_____	_____	$24.66	40%
6.	Suitcase	$68.00	$16.01	$51.99	23.5%
7.	Chess set	$115.77	$35.50	_____	_____
8.	Necklace	_____	$155.00	$235.00	_____
9.	Copier	$1,599.88	_____	_____	35%
10.	Pen	_____	_____	$15.90	25%

Solve the following word problems, rounding dollars to the nearest cent and percents to the nearest tenth of a percent.

11. A home theater system that originally sold for $4,700 was marked down and sold for $3,900.

    a. What is the amount of the markdown?

    b. What is the markdown percent?

12. A soccer ball that originally sold for $24.66 at Target was marked down by $10.

    a. What is the sale price?

    b. What is the markdown percent?

13. a. A notebook that originally sold for $1.69 at Dollar General was marked down to $0.99. What is the amount of the markdown on these notebooks?

    b. What is the markdown percent?

    c. If the sale price is then marked up by 40%, what is the new selling price?

What would eventually become Target began in 1902 as Dayton's Dry Goods Company. The company entered the mass-market retail world in 1962, opening the very first Target. In 1995, the first SuperTarget, which includes an in-store grocery, opened. In 1999, architect Michael Graves, the first of more than 75 designers to do so, created an exclusive product line for Target. Typical Target annual revenues now exceed $60 billion.

14. You are shopping for a headset and webcam at the Micro-Electronics Warehouse so that you can video-chat with your friends.

    a. Verify the "regular price" (original price) of each headset in the ad and calculate which headset offers the greater markdown percent, the BuddyChat 200 or BuddyChat 300.

    b. What is the markdown percent on the BuddyCam HD webcam?

    c. You have decided to purchase the headset with the greatest markdown percent and the BuddyCam HD webcam in order to take advantage of an "Extra $15 Rebate" offer when you purchase both. What is the markdown percent on your total purchase including the rebate?

15. If a file cabinet selling for $98 is put on clearance sale at 60% off, what is the selling price?

16. Carousel Toys has Romper Buckaroos, wooden rocking horses for toddlers, on a 30% markdown sale for $72.09. What was the original price before they were marked down? Round to the nearest cent.

17. Lawn and Garden Galleria is having a 20% off sale on riding lawn mowers. The XL Deluxe model is on sale for $4,815. What was the original price of the mower?

18. From the Office Market coupon shown here,

    a. Calculate the markdown percent.

    b. If the offer was changed to "Buy 3, Get 2 Free," what would be the new markdown percent?

    c. Which offer is more profitable for the store? Explain.

19. In February, Golf World, a retail shop, purchased golf clubs for $453.50 per set. The original markup was 35% based on selling price. In April, the shop took a 20% markdown by having a special sale. After two weeks, the sale was over and the clubs were marked up 10%. In June, the shop offered a storewide sale of 15% off all merchandise, and in September, a final 10% markdown was taken on the clubs. What was the final selling price of the golf clubs?

20. Prestige Produce purchases 460 pounds of sweet potatoes at $0.76 per pound. If a 10% spoilage rate is anticipated, at what price per pound should the sweet potatoes be sold to achieve a 35% markup based on selling price?

21. A microwave oven cost The Appliance Warehouse $141.30 and was initially marked up by 55% based on selling price. In the next few months, the item was marked down 20%, marked up 15%, marked down 10%, and marked down a final 10%. What was the final selling price of the microwave oven?

22. The Flour Power Bakery makes 200 cherry cheesecakes at a cost of $2.45 each. If a spoilage rate of 5% is anticipated, at what price should the cakes be sold to achieve a 40% markup based on cost?

23. You have decided to purchase a set of four Good-Ride tires for your vehicle at the Tire Emporium.

    a. If the original price of these tires is $160.00 each, what are the amount of the markdown with rebate per tire and the markdown percent if you get the rebate and pay cash?

    b. What are the amount of the markdown per tire and the markdown percent if you decide to put the purchase on your Good-Ride credit card and get the double rebate?

TIRE EMPORIUM

Good-Ride Raven GT – Tire Sale

Sale Price: $115 + $20 Rebate

Double rebate when you use your Good-Ride Credit Card

c. When you purchased the set of four tires, you were offered an "Extra 5%" discount on the entire purchase if you also included wheel balancing at $5.75 per tire and a front-end alignment for $65.00. The sales tax in your state is 7.5%. What was the total amount of your purchase if you used your Good-Ride credit card? Use the unrounded markdown percent you found in part b in your calculations.

d. What are the advantages and disadvantages of using the credit card?

BUSINESS DECISION: THE PERMANENT MARKDOWN

EXCEL 3

24. You are the manager of World Wide Athlete, a chain of six sporting goods shops in your area. The shops sell 12 racing bikes per week at a retail price of $679.99. Recently, you put the bikes on sale at $599.99. At the sale price, 15 bikes were sold during the one-week sale.

a. What was your markdown percent on the bikes?

b. What is the percent increase in number of bikes sold during the sale?

c. How much more revenue would be earned in six months by permanently selling the bikes at the lower price rather than having a one-week sale each month? (6 sale weeks in 26 weeks)

d. (Optional) As manager of World Wide, would you recommend this permanent price reduction? Explain.

CHAPTER FORMULAS

Markup

Selling price = Cost + Markup

Cost = Selling price − Markup

Markup = Selling price − Cost

$$\text{Percent markup}_{\text{COST}} = \frac{\text{Markup}}{\text{Cost}}$$

$$\text{Percent markup}_{SP} = \frac{\text{Markup}}{\text{Selling price}}$$

Selling price = Cost(100% + %Markup$_{\text{COST}}$)

$$\text{Cost} = \frac{\text{Selling price}}{100\% + \%\text{Markup}_{\text{COST}}}$$

$$\text{Selling price} = \frac{\text{Cost}}{100\% - \%\text{Markup}_{SP}}$$

Cost = Selling price(100% − %Markup$_{SP}$)

$$\%\text{Markup}_{SP} = \frac{\%\text{Markup}_{\text{COST}}}{100\% + \%\text{Markup}_{\text{COST}}}$$

$$\%\text{Markup}_{\text{COST}} = \frac{\%\text{Markup}_{SP}}{100\% - \%\text{Markup}_{SP}}$$

Markdown

Markdown = Original selling price − Sale price

$$\text{Markdown}\% = \frac{\text{Markdown}}{\text{Original price}}$$

Sale price = Original price(100% − Markdown%)

$$\text{Original price} = \frac{\text{Sale price}}{100\% - \text{Markdown}\%}$$

Perishables

$$\text{Selling price}_{\text{Perishables}} = \frac{\text{Expected selling price}}{\text{Total quantity} - \text{Spoilage}}$$

CHAPTER SUMMARY

Section I: Markup Based on Cost

Topic	Important Concepts	Illustrative Examples
Using the Basic Retailing Equation **Performance Objective 8-1, Page 230**	The basic retailing equation is used to solve for selling price (*SP*), cost (*C*), and amount of markup (*M*). Selling price = Cost + Markup $SP = C + M$ Cost = Selling price − Markup $C = SP - M$ Markup = Selling price − Cost $M = SP - C$	1. What is the selling price of a blender that costs $86.00 and has a $55.99 markup? $SP = 86.00 + 55.99$ Selling price = $141.99 2. What is the cost of a radio that sells for $125.50 and has a $37.29 markup? $C = 125.50 - 37.29$ Cost = $88.21 3. What is the markup on a set of dishes costing $53.54 and selling for $89.95? $M = 89.95 - 53.54$ Markup = $36.41

Section I (continued)

Topic	Important Concepts	Illustrative Examples
Calculating Percent Markup Based on Cost **Performance Objective 8-2, Page 232**	$\%\text{Markup}_{\text{COST}} = \dfrac{\text{Markup}}{\text{Cost}}$ $\%M_{\text{COST}} = \dfrac{M}{C}$	A calculator costs \$25. If the markup is \$10, what is the percent markup based on cost? $\%M_{\text{COST}} = \dfrac{10}{25} = .4$ $\%M_{\text{COST}} = \underline{40\%}$
Calculating Selling Price **Performance Objective 8-3, Page 233**	$\text{Selling price} = \text{Cost}(100\% + \%\text{Markup}_{\text{COST}})$ $SP = C(100\% + \%M_{\text{COST}})$	A desk costs \$260 to manufacture. What should be the selling price if a 60% markup based on cost is desired? $SP = 260(100\% + 60\%)$ $SP = 260(1.6) = 416$ Selling price $= \underline{\$416}$
Calculating Cost **Performance Objective 8-4, Page 234**	$\text{Cost} = \dfrac{\text{Selling price}}{100\% + \%\text{Markup}_{\text{COST}}}$ $C = \dfrac{SP}{100\% + \%M_{\text{COST}}}$	What is the cost of a leather sofa with a selling price of \$250 and a 45% markup based on cost? $C = \dfrac{250}{100\% + 45\%} = \dfrac{250}{1.45}$ Cost $= \underline{\$172.41}$

Section II: Markup Based on Selling Price

Topic	Important Concepts	Illustrative Examples
Calculating Percent Markup Based on Selling Price **Performance Objective 8-5, Page 237**	$\%\text{Markup}_{SP} = \dfrac{\text{Markup}}{\text{Selling price}}$ $\%M_{SP} = \dfrac{M}{SP}$	What is the percent markup on the selling price of a Hewlett Packard printer with a selling price of \$400 and a markup of \$188? $\%M_{SP} = \dfrac{188}{400} = .47$ $\%M_{SP} = \underline{47\%}$
Calculating Selling Price **Performance Objective 8-6, Page 238**	$\text{Selling price} = \dfrac{\text{Cost}}{100\% - \%\text{Markup}_{SP}}$ $SP = \dfrac{C}{100\% - \%M_{SP}}$	What is the selling price of a marker pen with a cost of \$1.19 and a 43% markup based on selling price? $SP = \dfrac{1.19}{100\% - 43\%} = \dfrac{1.19}{.57}$ $SP = \underline{\$2.09}$
Calculating Cost **Performance Objective 8-7, Page 239**	$\text{Cost} = \text{Selling price}(100\% - \%\text{Markup}_{SP})$ $C = SP(100\% - \%M_{SP})$	What is the most a hardware store can pay for a drill if it will have a selling price of \$65.50 and a 45% markup based on selling price? $C = 65.50(100\% - 45\%)$ $C = 65.50(.55)$ Cost $= \underline{\$36.03}$
Converting Percent Markup Based on Cost to Percent Markup Based on Selling Price **Performance Objective 8-8, Page 240**	$\%\text{Markup}_{SP} = \dfrac{\%\text{Markup}_{\text{COST}}}{100\% + \%\text{Markup}_{\text{COST}}}$ $\%M_{SP} = \dfrac{\%M_{\text{COST}}}{100\% + \%M_{\text{COST}}}$	If a hair dryer is marked up 70% based on cost, what is the corresponding percent markup based on selling price? $\%M_{SP} = \dfrac{70\%}{100\% + 70\%} = \dfrac{.7}{1.7}$ $\%M_{SP} = .4118 = \underline{41.2\%}$

Section II (continued)

Topic	Important Concepts	Illustrative Examples
Converting Percent Markup Based on Selling Price to Percent Markup Based on Cost **Performance Objective 8-8, Page 240**	$$\%\text{Markup}_{COST} = \frac{\%\text{Markup}_{SP}}{100\% - \%\text{Markup}_{SP}}$$ $$\%M_{COST} = \frac{\%M_{SP}}{100\% - \%M_{SP}}$$	If a toaster is marked up 35% based on selling price, what is the corresponding percent markup based on cost? $$\%M_{COST} = \frac{35\%}{100\% - 35\%} = \frac{.35}{.65}$$ $$\%M_{COST} = .5384 = \underline{53.8\%}$$

Section III: Markdowns, Multiple Operations, and Perishable Goods

Topic	Important Concepts	Illustrative Examples
Calculating the Amount of Markdown and Markdown Percent **Performance Objective 8-9, Page 244**	Markdown = Original price − Sale price $MD = Orig - Sale$ $$\text{Markdown}\% = \frac{\text{Markdown}}{\text{Original price}}$$ $$MD\% = \frac{MD}{Orig}$$	Calculate the amount of markdown and the markdown percent of a television set that originally sold for \$425.00 and was then put on sale for \$299.95. Markdown = 425.00 − 299.95 Markdown = \underline{\$125.05} $$MD\% = \frac{125.05}{425.00} = .2942$$ Markdown% = \underline{29.4\%}
Determining the Sale Price after a Markdown **Performance Objective 8-10, Page 245**	Sale price = Original price(100% − Markdown%) Sale = Orig(100% − MD%)	What is the sale price of a computer that originally sold for \$2,500 and was then marked down by 35%? Sale = 2,500(100% − 35%) Sale = 2,500(.65) = 1,625 Sale price = \underline{\$1,625}
Determining the Original Selling Price before a Markdown **Performance Objective 8-10, Page 246**	$$\text{Original price} = \frac{\text{Sale price}}{100\% - \text{Markdown}\%}$$ $$Orig = \frac{Sale}{100\% - MD\%}$$	What is the original selling price of an exercise bicycle, which is currently on sale at Sears for \$235.88, after a 30% markdown? $$\text{Original price} = \frac{235.88}{100\% - 30\%} = \frac{235.88}{.7}$$ Original price = \underline{\$336.97}
Computing the Final Selling Price after a Series of Markups and Markdowns **Performance Objective 8-11, Page 246**	To solve for the final selling price after a series of markups and markdowns, calculate each step based on the previous selling price.	Compute the intermediate prices and the final selling price of an umbrella costing \$27.50 with the following seasonal activity: a. Initial markup, 40% on cost b. 20% markdown c. 15% markdown d. 10% markup e. Final clearance, 25% markdown a. Initial 40% markup: $$SP = C(100\% + \%M_{COST})$$ $$SP = 27.50(100\% + 40\%)$$ $$SP = 27.50(1.4) = 38.50$$ Original price = \underline{\$38.50} b. 20% markdown: $$Sale = Orig(100\% - MD\%)$$ $$Sale = 38.50(100\% - 20\%)$$ $$Sale = 38.50(.8)$$ Sale price = \underline{\$30.80}

Section III (continued)

Topic	Important Concepts	Illustrative Examples
		c. 15% markdown: $$\text{Sale} = \text{Orig}(100\% - MD\%)$$ $$\text{Sale} = 30.80(100\% - 15\%)$$ $$\text{Sale} = 30.80(.85)$$ $$\text{Sale price} = \underline{\$26.18}$$ d. 10% markup: $$SP = \text{sale price}(100\% + M\%)$$ $$SP = 26.18(100\% + 10\%)$$ $$SP = 26.18(1.10)$$ $$\text{Selling price} = \underline{\$28.80}$$ e. Final 25% markdown: $$\text{Sale} = \text{Orig}(100\% - MD\%)$$ $$\text{Sale} = 28.80(100\% - 25\%)$$ $$\text{Sale} = 28.80(.75)$$ $$\text{Final selling price} = \underline{\$21.60}$$
Calculating the Selling Price of Perishable Goods **Performance Objective 8-12, Page 248**	$\text{Selling price}_{\text{Perishables}}$ $$= \frac{\text{Total expected selling price}}{\text{Total quantity} - \text{Anticipated spoilage}}$$ $$SP_{\text{Perish.}} = \frac{\text{Exp. } SP}{\text{Quan.} - \text{Spoil.}}$$	A grocery store purchases 250 pounds of apples from a wholesaler for $.67 per pound. If a 10% spoilage rate is anticipated, what selling price per pound will yield a 45% markup based on cost? $$\text{Total cost} = 250 \text{ lb @ } \$.67 = \$167.50$$ $$\text{Exp } SP = C(100\% + M_{\text{COST}})$$ $$\text{Exp } SP = 167.50(100\% + 45\%)$$ $$\text{Exp } SP = 167.50(1.45) = \$242.88$$ $$SP_{\text{perish}} = \frac{242.88}{250 - 25} = \frac{242.88}{225}$$ $$SP_{\text{perish}} = \underline{\$1.08 \text{ Per pound}}$$

TRY IT: EXERCISE SOLUTIONS FOR CHAPTER 8

1. $SP = C + M = 6.80 + 9.40 = \underline{\$16.20}$

2. $M = SP - C = 28.50 - 16.75 = \underline{\$11.75}$

3. $C = SP - M = 290 - 75 = \underline{\$215}$

4. $M = SP - C = 63 - 45 = \underline{\$18}$

$\%M_{\text{COST}} = \dfrac{M}{C} = \dfrac{18}{45} = .4 = 40\%$

5. $SP = C(100\% + \%M_{\text{COST}}) = 38(100\% + 65\%) = 38(1.65) = \underline{\$62.70}$

6. $C = \dfrac{SP}{100\% + \%M_{\text{COST}}} = \dfrac{39}{100\% + 30\%} = \dfrac{39}{1.3} = \underline{\$30}$

7. $M = SP - C = 157.50 - 94.50 = \underline{\$63}$

$\%M_{SP} = \dfrac{M}{SP} = \dfrac{63.00}{157.50} = .40 = \underline{40\%}$

8. $SP = \dfrac{C}{100\% - \%M_{SP}} = \dfrac{169}{100\% - 35\%} = \dfrac{169}{.65} = \underline{\$260}$

9. $C = SP(100\% - \%M_{SP}) = 79(100\% - 55\%) = 79(.45) = \underline{\$35.55}$

10. $\%M_{SP} = \dfrac{\%M_{\text{COST}}}{100\% + \%M_{\text{COST}}} = \dfrac{50\%}{100\% + 50\%} = \dfrac{.5}{1.5} = .333 = \underline{33.3\%}$

11. $\%M_{\text{COST}} = \dfrac{\%M_{SP}}{100\% - \%M_{SP}} = \dfrac{75\%}{100\% - 75\%} = \dfrac{.75}{.25} = 3 = \underline{300\%}$

12. Markdown = Original price − Sale price = 75 − 56 = $\underline{\underline{\$19}}$

$$MD\% = \frac{MD}{\text{Original price}} = \frac{19}{75} = .2533 = \underline{\underline{25.3\%}}$$

13. Sale price = Original price(100% − MD%) = 27.50(100% − 60%) = 27.50(.4) = $\underline{\underline{\$11}}$

14. Original price = $\dfrac{\text{Sale price}}{100\% - MD\%} = \dfrac{79}{100\% - 35\%} = \dfrac{79}{.65} = \underline{\underline{\$121.54}}$

15. $SD = \dfrac{C}{100\% - \%M_{SP}} = \dfrac{48.50}{100\% - 55\%} = \dfrac{48.50}{.45} = \$107.78$

Markdown #1: Original price(100% − MD%) = 107.78(.7) = $75.45
20% markup: 75.45(100% + 20%) = 75.45(1.2) = $90.54
Markdown #2: Original price(100% − MD%) = 90.54(.7) = $63.38
Final markdown: Original price(100% − MD%) = 63.38(.75) = $\underline{\underline{\$47.54}}$

16. Total cost = 800 dozen @ $6.50 = $5,200

$$\text{Expected selling price} = \frac{C}{100\% - \%M_{SP}} = \frac{5,200}{100\% - 60\%} = \frac{5,200}{.4} = \$13,000$$

$$\text{Selling price}_{\text{Perishables}} = \frac{\text{Expected selling price}}{\text{Total quantity} - \text{Spoilage}} = \frac{13,000}{800 - 80} = \frac{13,000}{720} = \underline{\underline{\$18.06 \text{ per doz}}}$$

CONCEPT REVIEW

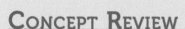

1. The retailing equation states that the selling price is equal to the _____ plus the _____. (8-1)

2. In business, expenses are separated into two major categories. The cost of _____ sold and _____ expenses. (8-1)

3. There are two ways of expressing markup as a percent: based on _____ and based on _____ _____. (8-2)

4. Write the formula for calculating the selling price when markup is based on cost. (8-3)

5. To calculate cost, we divide the _____ price by 100% plus the percent markup based on cost. (8-4)

6. The percent markup based on selling price is equal to the _____ divided by the selling price. (8-5)

7. When markup is based on selling price, the _____ price is the base and represents _____ percent. (8-6)

8. We use the formula for calculating _____ to find the most a retailer can pay for an item and still get the intended markup. (8-7)

9. To convert percent markup based on cost to percent markup based on selling price, we divide percent markup based on cost by 100% _____ the percent markup based on cost. (8-8)

10. To convert percent markup based on selling price to percent markup based on cost, we divide percent markup based on selling price by 100% _____ the percent markup based on selling price. (8-8)

11. A price reduction from the original selling price of merchandise is called a(n) _____. (8-9)

12. Write the formula for calculating the sale price after a markdown. (8-10)

13. In calculating a series of markups and markdowns, each calculation is based on the previous _____ price. (8-11)

14. Products that have a certain shelf life and then no value at all, such as fruit, vegetables, flowers, and dairy products, are known as _____ _____. (8-12)

ASSESSMENT TEST

Solve the following word problems. Round dollars to the nearest cent and percents to the nearest tenth of a percent.

1. A hair dryer is sold at wholesale for $12.50. If it is sold at retail with a markup of $7.25, what is the sales price?

2. Castle Mountain Furniture sells desks for $346.00. If the desks cost $212.66, what is the amount of the markup?

3. After Sunset Food Wholesalers adds a markup of $15.40 to a case of tomato sauce, it sells for $33.98. What is the wholesaler's cost per case?

4. Wyatt's Western Wear purchases shirts for $47.50 each. A $34.00 markup is added to the shirts.

    a. What is the selling price?

    b. What is the percent markup based on cost?

    c. What is the percent markup based on selling price?

5. As the manager of Dollar Depot, calculate the amount of the markup and the percent markup based on selling price per case if these Softies products cost your store $5.60 per case of 12 boxes.

6. Saks Fifth Avenue purchases a bracelet for $57.20. If the store policy is to mark up all merchandise in that department 42% based on selling price, what is the retail selling price of the perfume?

7. The Carpet Gallery is looking for a new line of nylon carpeting to retail at $39.88 per square yard. If management wants a 60% markup based on selling price, what is the most that can be paid for the carpeting to still get the desired markup?

8. a. At The Luminary, the markup on a halogen light fixture is 50% based on selling price. What is the corresponding percent markup based on cost?

    b. If the markup on a fluorescent light fixture transformer is 120% based on cost, what is the corresponding percent markup based on selling price?

9. A TV selling for $888 was marked down by $200 for a store-wide sale.

   a. What is the sale price of the TV?

   b. What is the markdown percent?

10. You are shopping for an executive desk chair at The Furniture Gallery.

    a. Calculate the original price and markdown percent of each chair to determine which has the greater markdown percent.

    b. With the purchase of either chair, The Furniture Gallery is offering a 15% discount on plastic chair mats. You have chosen a mat with an original price of $29.00. You also purchase a two-year leather protection plan on the chair for $19.95. If you choose the chair with the greater markdown percent and the sales tax in your area is 6.3%, what is the total amount of your purchase?

The Furniture Gallery

Save $40 instantly $79.99

OfficePro Model 20 High Back Leather Chair

Save $60 instantly $89.99

OfficePro Model 30 High Back Leather Chair

11. Macy's originally sold designer jackets for $277. If they are put on sale at a markdown of 22%, what is the sale price?

EXCEL 2

12. What was the original selling price of a treadmill currently on sale for $2,484 after a 20% markdown?

13. Backyard Bonanza advertised a line of inflatable pools for the summer season. The store uses a 55% markup based on selling price.

    a. If they were originally priced at $124.99, what was the cost?

    b. As the summer progressed, they were marked down 25%, marked up 15%, marked down 20%, and cleared out in October at a final 25%-off sale. What was the final selling price of the pools?

14. Epicure Market prepares fresh gourmet entrees each day. On Wednesday, 80 baked chicken dinners were made at a cost of $3.50 each. A 10% spoilage rate is anticipated.

    EXCEL 3

    a. At what price should the dinners be sold to achieve a 60% markup based on selling price?

Macy's is one of the nation's premier retailers, with typical annual sales exceeding $20 billion. The company operates more than 800 Macy's department stores and furniture galleries in 45 states, the District of Columbia, Guam, and Puerto Rico, as well as 40 Bloomingdale's stores in 12 states.

Macy's diverse workforce includes approximately 167,000 employees. The company also operates macys.com and bloomingdales.com.

Source: www.macysinc.com

    b. If Epicure offers a $1-off coupon in a newspaper advertisement, what markdown percent does the coupon represent?

CHAPTER 8

15. a. What is the original selling price of the guitar on sale at Music Mania if the $1,999.99 sale price represents 20% off?

b. How much did the store pay for the guitar if the initial markup was 150% based on cost?

c. What is the percent markup based on selling price?

d. If next month the guitar is scheduled to be on sale for $1,599.99, what is the markdown percent from the original price?

BUSINESS DECISION: MAINTAINED MARKUP

16. The markup that a retail store actually realizes on the sale of its goods is called **maintained markup**. It is what is achieved after "retail reductions" (markdowns) have been subtracted from the initial markup. Maintained markup is one of the "keys to profitability" in retailing. It is the difference between the actual selling price and the cost and therefore has a direct effect on net profits.

$$\text{Maintained markup} = \frac{\text{Actual selling price} - \text{Cost}}{\text{Actual selling price}}$$

You are the buyer for Four Aces Menswear, a chain of men's clothing stores. For the spring season, you purchased a line of men's casual shirts with a manufacturer's suggested retail price of $29.50. Your cost was $16.00 per shirt.

a. What is the initial percent markup based on selling price?

b. The shirts did not sell as expected at the regular price, so you marked them down to $21.99 and sold them out. What is the maintained markup on the shirts?

c. When you complained to the manufacturer's sales representative about having to take excessive markdowns in order to sell the merchandise, she offered a $2 rebate per shirt. What is your new maintained markup?

COLLABORATIVE LEARNING ACTIVITY

Retailing and the Demographic Generations

Understanding the shopping and media habits of different age groups can help marketers optimize product assortment, pricing, promotion, and advertising decisions by creating targeted strategies and special offers. As an example, consider the following.

According to *USA Today*, in the book *Gen buY: How Tweens, Teens, and Twenty-Somethings Are Revolutionizing Retail*, authors Kit Yarrow and Jane O'Donnell say Generation Y—today's teens, tweens, and twenty-somethings were the least likely to cut back spending during a recession.

What's more, the authors point out that the 84 million Generation Y'ers, born from 1978 through 2000, are so influential, they've changed shopping for all consumers. They call Gen Y "the taste-makers, influencers, and most enthusiastic buyers of today" who will become "the mature, high-income purchasers of the future."

Because of Gen Y, we now have, among other things:

- More creative, technically advanced websites
- A wide availability of online customer reviews
- A faster stream of product introductions
- Bigger, more comfortable dressing rooms

Source: *USA Today*, "Generation Y forces retailers to keep up with technology, new stuff," by Richard Eisenberg, Sept. 14, 2009, page 6B.

As a team, divide up the four major demographic generations: the Silent Generation: the Baby Boomers, Generation X, and Generation Y (aka the Millennials) to research the following questions and report your findings to the class. Use visual presentations whenever possible and be sure to site your sources.

1. How did each generation get its distinctive name? List any "subgroups" that have been defined, such as Baby Boomers – Young and Baby Boomers – Old.
2. Define each generation in terms of years born, size, income and purchasing power, lifestyle preferences, and particularly consumer buying behavior.
3. How and to what extent does each generation use the Internet?
4. How do manufacturers, retailers, and shopping malls use these demographic distinctions to "target" their marketing efforts to the various generations? Give specific examples.

Payroll

Minimum Wage Rates Over the Decades

Here's how the minimum wage has increased over the years and what an hour's work at minimum wage bought.

1950:
> Minimum wage: $0.75 per hour
> Gas: $0.27 or 22 minutes
> Movie ticket: $0.48 or 38 minutes
> Rent: $42 or 56 hours

1960:
> Minimum wage: $1 per hour
> Gas: $0.31 or 19 minutes
> Movie ticket: $0.69 or 41 minutes
> Rent: $71 or 71 hours

1970:
> Minimum wage: $1.60 per hour
> Gas: $0.36 or 14 minutes
> Movie ticket: $1.55 or 58 minutes
> Rent: $108 or 67.5 hours

1980:
> Minimum wage: $3.10 per hour
> Gas: $1.25 or 24 minutes
> Movie ticket: $2.60 or 50 minutes
> Rent: $243 or 78 hours

1990:
> Minimum wage: $3.80 per hour
> Gas: $1.13 or 18 minutes
> Movie ticket: $4.23 or 1 hour, 7 minutes
> Rent: $447 or 118 hours

2000:
> Minimum wage: $5.15 per hour
> Gas: $1.49 or 17 minutes
> Movie ticket: $5.39 or 1 hour, 3 minutes
> Rent: $602 or 117 hours

2010:
> Minimum wage: $7.25 per hour
> Gas: $2.78 or 23 minutes
> Movie ticket: $7.95 or 1 hour, 6 minutes
> Rent: $789 or 109 hours

Source: MSN.COM

PERFORMANCE OBJECTIVES

EMPLOYEE'S GROSS EARNINGS AND INCENTIVE PAY PLANS

9

SECTION I

Because payroll is frequently a company's largest operating expense, efficient payroll preparation and record keeping are extremely important functions in any business operation. Although today most businesses computerize their payroll functions, it is important for businesspeople to understand the processes and procedures involved.

Employers are responsible for paying employees for services rendered to the company over a period of time. In addition, the company is responsible for withholding certain taxes and other deductions from an employee's paycheck and depositing those taxes with the Internal Revenue Service (IRS) through authorized financial institutions. Other deductions, such as insurance premiums and charitable contributions, are also disbursed by the employer to the appropriate place.

In business, the term **gross pay**, or **gross earnings** means the *total* amount of earnings due an employee for work performed before payroll deductions are withheld. The **net pay**, **net earnings**, or **take-home pay** is the actual amount of the employee's paycheck after all payroll deductions have been withheld. This concept is easily visualized by the formula

gross pay, or **gross earnings** Total amount of earnings due an employee for work performed before payroll deductions are withheld.

net pay, **net earnings**, or **take-home pay** The actual amount of the employee's paycheck after all payroll deductions have been withheld.

Net pay = Gross pay − Total deductions

This chapter deals with the business math involved in payroll management: the computation of employee gross earnings; the calculation of withholding taxes and other deductions; and the associated governmental deposits, regulations, and record keeping requirements.

PRORATING ANNUAL SALARY ON THE BASIS OF WEEKLY, BIWEEKLY, SEMIMONTHLY, AND MONTHLY PAY PERIODS

9-1

Employee compensation takes on many forms in the business world. Employees who hold managerial, administrative, or professional positions are paid a salary. A **salary** is a fixed gross amount of pay equally distributed over periodic payments without regard to the number of hours worked. Salaries are usually expressed as an annual, or yearly, amount. For example, a corporate accountant might receive an annual salary of $50,000.

Although salaries may be stated as annual amounts, they are usually distributed to employees on a more timely basis. A once-a-year paycheck would be a real trick to manage! Employees are most commonly paid in one of the following ways:

salary A fixed gross amount of pay equally distributed over periodic payments without regard to the number of hours worked.

Weekly	52 paychecks per year	Annual salary ÷ 52
Biweekly	26 paychecks per year	Annual salary ÷ 26
Semimonthly	24 paychecks per year	Annual salary ÷ 24
Monthly	12 paychecks per year	Annual salary ÷ 12

EXAMPLE1 PRORATING ANNUAL SALARY

What is the weekly, biweekly, semimonthly, and monthly amount of gross pay for a corporate accountant with an annual salary of $50,000?

▶SOLUTIONSTRATEGY

The amount of gross pay per period is determined by dividing the annual salary by the number of pay periods per year.

$$\text{Weekly pay} = \frac{50,000}{52} = \underline{\$961.54}$$

$$\text{Biweekly pay} = \frac{50,000}{26} = \underline{\$1,923.08}$$

$$\text{Semimonthly pay} = \frac{50,000}{24} = \underline{\$2,083.33}$$

$$\text{Monthly pay} = \frac{50,000}{12} = \underline{\$4,166.67}$$

▶TRYITEXERCISE 1

An executive of a large manufacturing company earns a gross annual salary of $43,500. What is the weekly, biweekly, semimonthly, and monthly pay for this employee?

CHECK YOUR ANSWERS WITH THE SOLUTIONS ON PAGE 295.

9-2 CALCULATING GROSS PAY BY HOURLY WAGES, INCLUDING REGULAR AND OVERTIME RATES

wages Earnings for routine or manual work, usually based on the number of hours worked.

hourly wage, or **hourly rate** The amount an employee is paid for each hour worked.

overtime According to federal law, the amount an employee is paid for each hour worked over 40 hours per week.

Wages are earnings for routine or manual work, usually based on the number of hours worked. An **hourly wage**, or **hourly rate** is the amount an employee is paid for each hour worked. The hourly wage is the most frequently used pay method and is designed to compensate employees for the amount of time spent on the job. The Fair Labor Standards Act of 1938, a federal law, specifies that a standard work week is 40 hours and **overtime**, amounting to at least $1\frac{1}{2}$ times the hourly rate, must be paid for all hours worked over 40 hours per week. Paying an employee $1\frac{1}{2}$ times the hourly rate is known as time-and-a-half.

Many companies have taken overtime a step farther than required by compensating employees at time-and-a-half for all hours over 8 hours per day instead of 40 hours per week. Another common payroll benefit is when companies pay double time, twice the hourly rate, for holidays, midnight shifts, and weekend hours.

Minimum Wage Laws in the United States
U. S. Department of Labor—Wage and Hour Division (WHD)—January 1, 2014

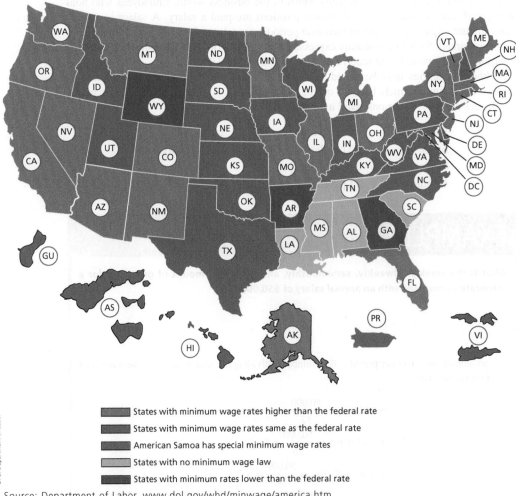

U. S. Department of Labor

States with minimum wage rates higher than the federal rate

States with minimum wage rates same as the federal rate

American Samoa has special minimum wage rates

States with no minimum wage law

States with minimum rates lower than the federal rate

Source: Department of Labor, www.dol.gov/whd/minwage/america.htm

According to the Department of Labor, as of January 2013, 16 states and Washington, D.C., had minimum wage rates higher than the federal minimum wage. Four states and Puerto Rico had minimum wage rates lower than the federal standard.

STEPS TO CALCULATE AN EMPLOYEE'S GROSS PAY BY HOURLY WAGES

STEP 1. Calculate an employee's regular gross pay for working 40 hours or less.

Regular pay = Hourly rate × Regular hours worked

STEP 2. Calculate an employee's overtime pay by chain multiplying the hourly rate by the overtime factor by the number of overtime hours.

Overtime pay = Hourly rate × Overtime factor × Overtime hours worked

STEP 3. Calculate total gross pay.

Total gross pay = Regular pay + Overtime pay

IN THE Business World

Payroll is a very important business responsibility. Employees must be paid on a regular basis, and accurate records must be kept for government reporting.

- Payroll is usually one of the largest "expense" categories of a company.
- The department responsible for the payroll function may be called Payroll, Personnel, or Human Resources.
- In recent years, companies have evolved that specialize in doing payroll. When a business hires an outside firm to perform a function such as payroll, this is known as *outsourcing*.

EXAMPLE2 CALCULATING HOURLY PAY

Karen Sullivan earns $8 per hour as a checker on an assembly line. If her overtime rate is time-and-a-half, what is her total gross pay for working 46 hours last week?

SOLUTIONSTRATEGY

To find Karen's total gross pay, compute her regular pay plus overtime pay.

Regular pay = Hourly rate × Regular hours worked
Regular pay = 8 × 40 = $320
Overtime pay = Hourly rate × Overtime factor × Overtime hours worked
Overtime pay = 8 × 1.5 × 6 = $72
Total gross pay = Regular pay + Overtime pay
Total gross pay = 320 + 72 = $392

TRYITEXERCISE 2

Rick Morton works as a delivery truck driver for $10.50 per hour with time-and-a-half for overtime and double time on Sundays. What was his total gross pay last week if he worked 45 hours on Monday through Saturday in addition to a four-hour shift on Sunday?

CHECK YOUR ANSWER WITH THE SOLUTION ON PAGE 295.

CALCULATING GROSS PAY BY STRAIGHT AND DIFFERENTIAL PIECEWORK SCHEDULES

9-3

A **piecework** pay rate schedule is based not on time but on production output. The incentive is that the more units the worker produces, the more money he or she makes. A **straight piecework plan** is when the worker receives a certain amount of pay per unit of output regardless of output quantity. A **differential piecework plan** gives workers a greater incentive to increase output because the rate per unit increases as output goes up. For example, a straight piecework plan might pay $3.15 per unit, whereas a differential plan might pay $3.05 for the first 50 units produced, $3.45 for units 51–100, and $3.90 for any units over 100.

piecework Pay rate schedule based on an employee's production output, not hours worked.

straight piecework plan Pay per unit of output regardless of output quantity.

differential piecework plan Greater incentive method of compensation than straight piecework, where pay per unit increases as output goes up.

STEPS TO CALCULATE GROSS PAY BY PIECEWORK

Straight Piecework:

STEP 1. Multiply the number of pieces or output units by the rate per unit.

Total gross pay = Output quantity × Rate per unit

Differential Piecework:

STEP 1. Multiply the number of output units at each level by the rate per unit at that level.

STEP 2. Find the total gross pay by adding the total from each level.

EXAMPLE3　CALCULATING PIECEWORK PAY

Barb Nelson works on a hat assembly line. Barb gets paid at a straight piecework rate of $0.35 per hat. What was Barb's total gross pay last week if she produced 1,655 hats?

▶ SOLUTIONSTRATEGY

Total gross pay = Output quantity × Rate per unit
Total gross pay = 1,655 × .35 = $579.25

▶ TRYITEXERCISE 3

George Lopez works at a tire manufacturing plant. He is on a straight piecework rate of $0.41 per tire. What was George's total gross pay last week if he produced 950 tires?

CHECK YOUR ANSWER WITH THE SOLUTION ON PAGE 295.

EXAMPLE4　CALCULATING DIFFERENTIAL PIECEWORK PAY

Paula Duke assembled 190 watches last week. Calculate her total gross pay based on the following differential piecework schedule.

Pay Level	Watches Assembled	Rate per Watch
1	1–100	$2.45
2	101–150	$2.75
3	Over 150	$3.10

▶ SOLUTIONSTRATEGY

To find Paula's total gross earnings, we calculate her earnings at each level of the pay schedule and add the totals. In this case, she will be paid for all of level 1,100 watches; for all of level 2, 50 watches; and for 40 watches at level 3 (190 − 150 = 40).

Level pay = Output × Rate per piece
Level 1 = 100 × 2.45 = $245
Level 2 = 50 × 2.75 = $137.50
Level 3 = 40 × 3.10 = $124
Total gross pay = Level 1 + Level 2 + Level 3
Total gross pay = 245 + 137.50 + 124 = $506.50

▶TRYITEXERCISE 4

You are the payroll manager for Trendy Toys, Inc., a manufacturer of small plastic toys. Your production workers are on a differential piecework schedule as follows.

Pay Level	Toys Produced	Rate per Toy
1	1–300	$0.68
2	301–500	$0.79
3	501–750	$0.86
4	Over 750	$0.94

Calculate last week's total gross pay for the following employees.

Name	Toys Produced	Total Gross Pay
C. Gomez	515	_____
L. Clifford	199	_____
M. Maken	448	_____
B. Nathan	804	_____

CHECK YOUR ANSWERS WITH THE SOLUTIONS ON PAGE 295.

CALCULATING GROSS PAY BY STRAIGHT AND INCREMENTAL COMMISSION, SALARY PLUS COMMISSION, AND DRAWING ACCOUNTS

9-4

STRAIGHT AND INCREMENTAL COMMISSION

Commission is a method of compensation primarily used to pay employees who sell a company's goods or services. **Straight commission** is based on a single specified percentage of the sales volume attained. For example, Delta Distributors pays its sales staff a commission of 8% on all sales. **Incremental commission** is much like the differential piecework rate whereby higher levels of sales earn increasing rates of commission. An example would be 5% commission on all sales up to $70,000, 6% on sales greater than $70,000 and up to $120,000, and 7% commission on any sales greater than $120,000.

commission Percentage method of compensation primarily used to pay employees who sell a company's goods and services.

straight commission Commission based on a specified percentage of the sales volume attained by an employee.

incremental commission Greater incentive method of compensation than straight commission whereby higher levels of sales earn increasing rates of commission.

STEPS TO CALCULATE GROSS PAY BY COMMISSION

Straight Commission:

STEP 1. Multiply the total sales by the commission rate.

$$\text{Total gross pay} = \text{Total sales} \times \text{Commission rate}$$

Incremental Commission:

STEP 1. Multiply the total sales at each level by the commission rate for that level.

STEP 2. Find the total gross pay by adding the total from each level.

EXAMPLE5 — CALCULATING COMMISSIONS

Diamond Industries pays its sales force a commission rate of 6% of all sales. What was the total gross pay for an employee who sold $113,500 last month?

SOLUTIONSTRATEGY

Total gross pay = Total sales × Commission rate
Total gross pay = 113,500 × .06 = $6,810

▶ TRYITEXERCISE 5

Alexa Walsh sells for Supreme Designs, a manufacturer of women's clothing. Alexa is paid a straight commission of 2.4%. If her sales volume last month was $233,760, what was her total gross pay?

CHECK YOUR ANSWER WITH THE SOLUTION ON PAGE 295.

EXAMPLE6 — CALCULATING INCREMENTAL COMMISSION

Vista Electronics pays its sales representatives on the following incremental commission schedule.

Level	Sales Volume	Commission Rate
1	$1–$50,000	4%
2	$50,001–$150,000	5%
3	Over $150,000	6.5%

What was the total gross pay for a sales rep who sold $162,400 last month?

SOLUTIONSTRATEGY

Using an incremental commission schedule, we find the pay for each level and then add the totals from each level. In this problem, the sales rep will be paid for all of level 1, $50,000; for all of level 2, $100,00; and for $12,400 of level 3 ($162,400 − $150,000 = $12,400).

Level pay = Sales per level × Commission rate
Level 1 pay = 50,000 × .04 = $2,000
Level 2 pay = 100,000 × .05 = $5,000
Level 3 pay = 12,400 × .065 = $806
Total gross pay = Level 1 + Level 2 + Level 3
Total gross pay = 2,000 + 5,000 + 806 = $7,806

▶ TRYITEXERCISE 6

Mike Lamb sells copiers for Royal Business Products. He is on an incremental commission schedule of 1.7% of sales up to $100,000 and 2.5% on sales greater than $100,000. What was Mike's total gross pay last month if his sales volume was $184,600?

CHECK YOUR ANSWER WITH THE SOLUTION ON PAGE 295.

IN THE Business World

Companies often give sales managers *override* commissions. This is a small commission on the total sales of the manager's sales force.

Example: Jim and Diane sell for Apex Electronics. They each receive 15% commission on their sales. John, their sales manager, receives a 3% override on their total sales. If Jim sells $20,000 and Diane sells $30,000 in June, how much commission does each person receive?

- Jim: $20,000 × 15% = $3,000
- Diane: $30,000 × 15% = $4,500
- John: $50,000 × 3% = $1,500

SALARY PLUS COMMISSION

A variation of straight and incremental commission pay schedules is the **salary plus commission** whereby the employee is paid a guaranteed salary plus a commission on sales over a specified amount. To calculate the total gross pay, find the amount of commission and add it to the salary.

salary plus commission A guaranteed salary plus a commission on sales over a specified amount.

EXAMPLE7 CALCULATING SALARY PLUS COMMISSION

Karie Jabe works on a pay schedule of $1,500 per month salary plus a 3% commission on all sales greater than $40,000. If she sold $60,000 last month, what was her total gross pay?

▶SOLUTIONSTRATEGY

To solve for Karie's total gross pay, add her monthly salary to her commission for the month.

$$\text{Commission} = \text{Commission rate} \times \text{Sales subject to commission}$$
$$\text{Commission} = 3\% \ (60,000 - 40,000)$$
$$\text{Commission} = .03 \times 20,000 = \$600$$
$$\text{Total gross pay} = \text{Salary} + \text{Commission}$$
$$\text{Total gross pay} = 1,500 + 600 = \underline{\$2,100}$$

▶TRYITEXERCISE 7

Ed Diamond is a sales representative for Jersey Shore Supply, Inc. He is paid a salary of $1,400 per month plus a commission of 4% on all sales greater than $20,000. If he sold $45,000 last month, what was his total gross earnings?

CHECK YOUR ANSWER WITH THE SOLUTION ON PAGE 295.

Dollars AND Sense

Education Pays
The unemployment rate in 2013 among people with a bachelor's degree or higher was 3.7%.
Among people whose education stopped short of a high school diploma, the rate was 11%.

Source: www.bls.gov

DRAW AGAINST COMMISSION

In certain industries and at certain times of the year, sales fluctuate significantly. To provide salespeople on commission with at least some income during slack periods of sales, a drawing account is used. A **drawing account**, or **draw against commission**, is a commission paid in advance of sales and later deducted from the commissions earned. If a period goes by when the salesperson does not earn enough commission to cover the draw, the unpaid balance carries over to the next period.

drawing account, or **draw against commission** Commission paid in advance of sales and later deducted from the commission earned.

EXAMPLE8 CALCULATING DRAW AGAINST COMMISSION

Bill Carpenter is a salesperson for Power Electronics. The company pays 8% commission on all sales and gives Bill a $1,500 per month draw against commission. If he receives his draw at the beginning of the month and then sells $58,000 during the month, how much commission is owed to Bill?

▶SOLUTIONSTRATEGY

To find the amount of commission owed to Bill, find the total amount of commission he earned and subtract $1,500, the amount of his draw against commission.

$$\text{Commission} = \text{Total sales} \times \text{Commission rate}$$
$$\text{Commission} = 58,000 \times 8\% = \underline{\$4,640}$$
$$\text{Commission owed} = \text{Commission} - \text{Amount of draw}$$
$$\text{Commission owed} = 4,640 - 1,500 = \underline{\$3,140}$$

▶ TRYITEXERCISE 8

Howard Lockwood sells for Catalina Designs, Inc. He is on a 3.5% straight commission with a $2,000 drawing account. If he is paid the draw at the beginning of the month and then sells $120,000 during the month, how much commission is owed to Howard?

CHECK YOUR ANSWER WITH THE SOLUTION ON PAGE 295.

SECTION I   9   REVIEW EXERCISES

Calculate the gross earnings per pay period for the following pay schedules.

	Annual Salary	Monthly	Semimonthly	Biweekly	Weekly
1.	$15,000	$1,250.00	$625.00	$576.92	$288.46
2.	$44,200				
3.	$100,000				
4.	$21,600	$1,800.00	$900.00	$830.77	$415.38
5.			$1,450.00		
6.				$875.00	
7.					$335.00

8. Mary Jo Prenaris is an office manager with gross earnings of $1,600 semimonthly. If her company switches pay schedules from semimonthly to biweekly, what are Mary Jo's new gross earnings?

9. Deb O'Connell is an accounting professional earning a salary of $58,000 at her firm. What is her equivalent weekly gross pay?

10. Jennifer Brunner works 40 hours per week as a chef's assistant. At the rate of $7.60 per hour, what are her gross weekly earnings?

11. Alan Kimball earns $22.34 per hour as a specialty chef at Le Bistro Restaurant. If he worked 53 hours last week and was paid time-and-a-half for weekly hours over 40, what was his gross pay?

12. Paul Curcio earns $8.25 per hour for regular time up to 40 hours, time-and-a-half for overtime, and double time for the midnight shift. Last week Paul worked 58 hours, including 6 hours on the midnight shift. What are his gross earnings?

As the payroll manager for Stargate Industries, your task is to complete the following weekly payroll record. The company pays overtime for all hours worked over 40 at the rate of time-and-a-half. Round to the nearest cent when necessary.

Employee	M	T	W	T	F	S	S	Hourly Rate	Total Hours	Overtime Hours	Regular Pay	Overtime Pay	Total Pay
13. Peters	7	8	5	8	8	0	0	$8.70	36	0	$313.20	0	$313.20
14. Sands	6	5	9	8	10	7	0	$9.50	___	___	___	___	___
15. Warner	8	6	11	7	12	0	4	$7.25	___	___	___	___	___
16. Lee	9	7	7	7	9	0	8	$14.75	___	___	___	___	___

17. Larry Jefferson gets paid a straight piecework rate of $3.15 for each alternator he assembles for Allied Mechanical Corp. If he assembled 226 units last week, what was his gross pay?

You are the payroll manager for Euro Couture, a manufacturer of women's apparel. Your workers are paid per garment sewn on a differential piecework schedule as follows.

Pay Level	Garments Produced	Rate per Garment
1	1–50	$3.60
2	51–100	$4.25
3	101–150	$4.50
4	Over 150	$5.10

Calculate last week's total gross pay for each of the following employees.

Employee	Garments Produced	Total Gross Pay
18. Goodrich, P.	109	$433.00
19. Walker, A.	83	___
20. Fox, B.	174	___

21. Katrina Byrd assembles motor mounts for C-207 executive planes. Her company has established a differential piecework scale as an incentive to increase production due to backlogged orders. The pay scale is $11.50 for the first 40 mounts, $12.35 for the next 30 mounts, $13.00 for the next 20 mounts, and $13.40 for all remaining mounts assembled during the week. Katrina assembled 96 mounts last week. What was her total gross pay?

22. Bob Farrell works for a company that manufactures small appliances. Bob is paid $2.00 for each toaster, $4.60 for each microwave oven, and $1.55 for each food blender he assembles. If he produced 56 toasters, 31 microwave ovens, and 79 blenders, what were his total weekly gross earnings?

23. What is the total gross pay for a salesperson on a straight commission of 4.7% if his or her sales volume is $123,200?

24. Pamela Mello is paid on an incremental commission schedule. She is paid 2.6% on the first $60,000 and 3.4% on any sales over $60,000. If her weekly sales volume was $89,400, what was her total commission?

25. Dory Schrader is a buyer for Oceans of Notions. She is paid a weekly salary of $885 plus a 4% commission on sales over $45,000. If her sales were $62,000 last week, what was her total gross pay?

26. Thomas Rendell's company pays him a straight 6% commission with a $1,350 drawing account each month. If his sales last month totaled $152,480, how much commission is owed to Thomas?

27. Katie Jergens works for Dynamic Designs selling clothing. She is on a salary of $140 per week plus a commission of 7% of her sales. Last week she sold 19 dresses at $79.95 each, 26 skirts at $24.75 each, and 17 jackets at $51.50 each. What were her total gross earnings for the week?

28. Jerry King is a server in a restaurant that pays a salary of $22 per day. He also averages tips of 18% of his total gross food orders. Last week he worked 6 days and had total food orders of $2,766.50. What was his total gross pay for the week?

BUSINESS DECISION: MINIMUM WAGE TIED TO INFLATION

29. In an effort to keep low-wage workers' salaries commensurate with the cost of living, a number of states have amended their constitutions to allow the minimum wage to be adjusted with inflation.

      You are the accountant for Delicious, Inc., a company that owns a chain of 18 fast-food restaurants in a state which adjusts the minimum wage for inflation. Each restaurant employs 35 workers, each averaging 20 hours per week at the current federal minimum wage, $7.25 per hour.

   a. How many hours at minimum wage are paid out each week by Delicious?

   b. At the current rate of $7.25 per hour, what is the amount of the weekly "minimum wage" portion of the restaurant's payroll?

   c. If the inflation rate this year is .7%, calculate the "adjusted" minimum wage rate to be paid next year.

    d. How much in "additional wages" will Delicious have to pay out next year at the adjusted rate?

    e. (Optional) Go to www.dol.gov/whd/minwage/america.htm and click on your state to find the current minimum wage. Calculate the weekly "minimum wage" portion of the restaurant's payroll assuming the restaurant is located in your state.

    f. (Optional) Suggest some ways that the restaurant chain or other small businesses can offset the increase in payroll and subsequent decrease in profit as a result of the minimum wage hike.

EMPLOYEE'S PAYROLL DEDUCTIONS

9

SECTION II

"Hey! What happened to my paycheck?" This is the typical reaction of employees on seeing their paychecks for the first time after a raise or a promotion. As we will see, gross pay is by no means the amount of money the employee takes home.

    Employers, by federal law, are required to deduct or withhold certain funds, known as **deductions** or **withholdings**, from an employee's paycheck. Employee payroll deductions fall into two categories: mandatory and voluntary. The three major **mandatory deductions** most workers in the United States are subject to are social security, Medicare, and federal income tax. Other mandatory deductions found only in some states are state income tax and state disability insurance.

    In addition to the mandatory deductions, employees may also choose to have **voluntary deductions** taken out of their paychecks. Some examples include payments for life or health insurance premiums, union or professional organization dues, credit union savings deposits or loan payments, stock or bond purchases, and charitable contributions.

    After all the deductions have been subtracted from the employee's gross earnings, the remaining amount is known as net, or take-home, pay.

deductions or **withholdings** Funds withheld from an employee's paycheck.

mandatory deductions Deductions withheld from an employee's paycheck by law: social security, Medicare, and federal income tax.

voluntary deductions Deductions withheld from an employee's paycheck by request of the employee, such as insurance premiums, dues, loan payments, and charitable contributions.

> **Net pay = Gross pay − Total deductions**

COMPUTING FICA TAXES, BOTH SOCIAL SECURITY AND MEDICARE, WITHHELD FROM AN EMPLOYEE'S PAYCHECK

9-5

In 1937 during the Great Depression, Congress enacted legislation known as the **Federal Insurance Contribution Act (FICA)** with the purpose of providing monthly benefits to retired and disabled workers and to the families of deceased workers. This social security tax, which is assessed to virtually every worker in the United States, is based on a certain percent of the worker's income up to a specified limit or **wage base** per year. When the tax began in 1937, the tax rate was 1% up to a wage base of $3,000. At that time, the maximum a worker could be taxed per year for social security was $30 (3,000 × .01).

    Today the FICA tax is divided into two categories. **Social security tax** (OASDI, which stands for Old Age, Survivors, and Disability Insurance) is a retirement plan, and **Medicare tax** is for health care and hospital insurance. The social security wage base changes every year. For the most current information, consult the Internal Revenue Service, *Circular E, Employer's Tax Guide*. As this is written, the following rates and wage base were in effect for the FICA tax and should be used for all exercises in this chapter:

Federal Insurance Contribution Act (FICA) Federal legislation enacted in 1937 during the Great Depression to provide retirement funds and hospital insurance for retired and disabled workers. Today FICA is divided into two categories, social security and Medicare.

wage base The amount of earnings up to which an employee must pay social security tax.

social security tax (OASDI) Old Age, Survivors, and Disability Insurance—a federal tax based on a percentage of a worker's income up to a specified limit or wage base for the purpose of providing monthly benefits to retired and disabled workers and to the families of deceased workers.

Medicare tax A federal tax used to provide health care benefits and hospital insurance to retired and disabled workers.

	Tax Rate	Wage Base
Social Security (OASDI)	6.2%	$117,000
Medicare	1.45%	no limit

When an employee reaches the wage base for the year, he or she is no longer subject to the tax. Based on the table on the previous page, the maximum social security tax per year is limited to $7,254 (117,000 × .062). There is no limit on the amount of Medicare tax. The 1.45% is in effect regardless of how much an employee earns.

EXAMPLE 9 — CALCULATING SOCIAL SECURITY AND MEDICARE WITHHOLDINGS

What are the withholdings for social security and Medicare for an employee with gross earnings of $650 per week? Round to the nearest cent.

▶ SOLUTION STRATEGY

To find the withholdings, we apply the tax rates for social security (6.2%) and Medicare (1.45%) to the gross earnings for the week:

$$\text{Social security tax} = \text{Gross earnings} \times 6.2\%$$
$$\text{Social security tax} = 650 \times .062 = \underline{\$40.30}$$
$$\text{Medicare tax} = \text{Gross earnings} \times 1.45\%$$
$$\text{Medicare tax} = 650 \times .0145 = 9.425 = \underline{\$9.43}$$

▶ TRY IT EXERCISE 9

What are the withholdings for social security and Medicare for an employee with gross earnings of $5,000 per month?

CHECK YOUR ANSWERS WITH THE SOLUTIONS ON PAGE 296.

REACHING THE WAGE BASE LIMIT

In the pay period when an employee's year-to-date (YTD) earnings reach and surpass the wage base for social security, the tax is applied only to the portion of the earnings below the limit.

EXAMPLE 10 — CALCULATING SOCIAL SECURITY WITH WAGE BASE LIMIT

Vickie Hirsh has earned $114,200 so far this year. Her next paycheck, $5,000, will put her earnings over the wage base limit for social security. What is the amount of Vickie's social security withholdings for that paycheck?

SOLUTION STRATEGY

To calculate Vickie's social security deduction, first determine how much more she must earn to reach the wage base of $117,000.

(continued)

Congress passed the Social Security Act in 1935 and passed Medicare into law in 1965.

Source: ssa.gov

Courtesy of Bob Brechner

Earnings subject to tax = Wage base − Year-to-date earnings

Earnings subject to tax = 117,000 − 114,200 = $2,800

Social security tax = Earnings subject to tax × 6.2%

Social security tax = 2,800 × .062 = $173.60

▶TRYITEXERCISE 10

Rick Nicotera has year-to-date earnings of $112,500. If his next paycheck is $6,000, what is the amount of his social security deduction?

CHECK YOUR ANSWER WITH THE SOLUTION ON PAGE 296.

CALCULATING AN EMPLOYEE'S FEDERAL INCOME TAX (FIT) WITHHOLDING BY THE PERCENTAGE METHOD

9-6

In addition to social security and Medicare tax withholdings, an employer is also responsible, by federal law, for withholding an appropriate amount of **federal income tax (FIT)** from each employee's paycheck. This graduated tax allows the government a steady flow of tax revenues throughout the year. Self-employed persons must send quarterly tax payments based on estimated earnings to the Internal Revenue Service. By IRS rules, 90% of the income tax due for a given calendar year must be paid within that year to avoid penalties.

The amount of income tax withheld from an employee's paycheck is determined by his or her amount of gross earnings, marital status, and the number of **withholding allowances**, or **exemptions**, claimed. Employees are allowed one exemption for themselves, one for their spouse if the spouse does not work, and one for each dependent child or elderly parent living with the taxpayer but not working.

Each employee is required to complete a form called W-4, Employee's Withholding Allowance Certificate. The information provided on this form is used by the employer in calculating the amount of income tax withheld from the paycheck. Employees should keep track of their tax liability during the year and adjust the number of exemptions as their personal situations change (i.e., marriage, divorce, or birth of a child).

The **percentage method** for determining the amount of federal income tax withheld from an employee's paycheck is used by companies whose payroll processing is on a computerized system. The amount of tax withheld is based on the amount of gross earnings, the marital status of the employee, and the number of withholding allowances claimed.

The percentage method of calculating federal income tax requires the use of two tables. The first is the Percentage Method Amount for One Withholding Allowance Table, as shown in Exhibit 9-1. This table shows the dollar amount of one withholding allowance for the various payroll periods. The second, as shown in Exhibit 9-2, is the Tables for Percentage Method of Withholding. These tables were in effect as this is written and should be used for the exercises in this chapter.

federal income tax (FIT) A graduated tax based on gross earnings, marital status, and number of exemptions that is paid by all workers earning over a certain amount in the United States.

withholding allowance, or **exemption** An amount that reduces an employee's taxable income. Employees are allowed one exemption for themselves, one for their spouse if the spouse does not work, and one for each dependent child or elderly parent living with the taxpayer but not working.

percentage method An alternative method to the wage bracket tables used to calculate the amount of an employee's federal income tax withholding.

Payroll Period	One Withholding Allowance
Weekly.	$ 76.00
Biweekly.	151.90
Semimonthly	164.60
Monthly	329.20
Quarterly	987.50
Semiannually	1,975.00
Annually	3,950.00
Daily or miscellaneous (each day of the payroll period)	15.20

EXHIBIT 9-1

Percentage Method Amount for One Withholding Allowance

EXHIBIT 9-2 Tables for Percentage Method of Withholding

Percentage Method Tables for Income Tax Withholding

(For Wages Paid in 20XX)

TABLE 1—WEEKLY Payroll Period

(a) SINGLE person (including head of household)—

If the amount of wages (after subtracting withholding allowances) is:

The amount of income tax to withhold is:

Not over $43 ....$0

Over—	But not over—		of excess over—
$43	—$218	......$0.00 plus 10%	—$43
$218	—$753	......$17.50 plus 15%	—$218
$753	—$1,762	......$97.75 plus 25%	—$753
$1,762	—$3,627	......$350.00 plus 28%	—$1,762
$3,627	—$7,834	......$872.20 plus 33%	—$3,627
$7,834	—$7,865	$2,260.51 plus 35%	—$7,834
$7,865	...............................$2,271.36 plus 39.6%		—$7,865

(b) MARRIED person—

If the amount of wages (after subtracting withholding allowances) is:

The amount of income tax to withhold is:

Not over $163 ....$0

Over—	But not over—		of excess over—
$163	—$512	......$0.00 plus 10%	—$163
$512	—$1,582	......$34.90 plus 15%	—$512
$1,582	—$3,025	......$195.40 plus 25%	—$1,582
$3,025	—$4,525	......$556.15 plus 28%	—$3,025
$4,525	—$7,953	......$976.15 plus 33%	—$4,525
$7,953	—$8,963	$2,107.39 plus 35%	—$7,953
$8,963	...............................$2,460.89 plus 39.6%		—$8,963

TABLE 2—BIWEEKLY Payroll Period

(a) SINGLE person (including head of household)—

If the amount of wages (after subtracting withholding allowances) is:

The amount of income tax to withhold is:

Not over $87 ....$0

Over—	But not over—		of excess over—
$87	—$436	......$0.00 plus 10%	—$87
$436	—$1,506	......$34.90 plus 15%	—$436
$1,506	—$3,523	......$195.40 plus 25%	—$1,506
$3,523	—$7,254	......$699.65 plus 28%	—$3,523
$7,254	—$15,667	......$1,744.33 plus 33%	—$7,254
$15,667	—$15,731	......$4,520.62 plus 35%	—$15,667
$15,731	...............................$4,543.02 plus 39.6%		—$15,731

(b) MARRIED person—

If the amount of wages (after subtracting withholding allowances) is:

The amount of income tax to withhold is:

Not over $325 ....$0

Over—	But not over—		of excess over—
$325	—$1,023	........$0.00 plus 10%	—$325
$1,023	—$3,163	........$69.80 plus 15%	—$1,023
$3,163	—$6,050	........$390.80 plus 25%	—$3,163
$6,050	—$9,050	........$1,112.55 plus 28%	—$6,050
$9,050	—$15,906	........$1,952.55 plus 33%	—$9,050
$15,906	—$17,925	........$4,215.03 plus 35%	—$15,906
$17,925	...............................$4,921.68 plus 39.6%		—$17,925

TABLE 3—SEMIMONTHLY Payroll Period

(a) SINGLE person (including head of household)—

If the amount of wages (after subtracting withholding allowances) is:

The amount of income tax to withhold is:

Not over $94 ....$0

Over—	But not over—		of excess over—
$94	—$472	......$0.00 plus 10%	—$94
$472	—$1,631	......$37.80 plus 15%	—$472
$1,631	—$3,817	......$211.65 plus 25%	—$1,631
$3,817	—$7,858	......$758.15 plus 28%	—$3,817
$7,858	—$16,973	......$1,889.63 plus 33%	—$7,858
$16,973	—$17,042	......$4,897.58 plus 35%	—$16,973
$17,042	...............................$4,921.73 plus 39.6%		—$17,042

(b) MARRIED person—

If the amount of wages (after subtracting withholding allowances) is:

The amount of income tax to withhold is:

Not over $352 ....$0

Over—	But not over—		of excess over—
$352	—$1,108	........$0.00 plus 10%	—$352
$1,108	—$3,427	........$75.60 plus 15%	—$1,108
$3,427	—$6,554	........$423.45 plus 25%	—$3,427
$6,554	—$9,804	........$1,205.20 plus 28%	—$6,554
$9,804	—$17,231	........$2,115.20 plus 33%	—$9,804
$17,231	—$19,419	........$4,566.11 plus 35%	—$17,231
$19,419	...............................$5,331.91 plus 39.6%		—$19,419

TABLE 4—MONTHLY Payroll Period

(a) SINGLE person (including head of household)—

If the amount of wages (after subtracting withholding allowances) is:

The amount of income tax to withhold is:

Not over $188 ....$0

Over—	But not over—		of excess over—
$188	—$944	......$0.00 plus 10%	—$188
$944	—$3,263	......$75.60 plus 15%	—$944
$3,263	—$7,633	......$423.45 plus 25%	—$3,263
$7,633	—$15,717	......$1,515.95 plus 28%	—$7,633
$15,717	—$33,946	......$3,779.47 plus 33%	—$15,717
$33,946	—$34,083	......$9,795.04 plus 35%	—$33,946
$34,083	...............................$9,842.99 plus 39.6%		—$34,083

(b) MARRIED person—

If the amount of wages (after subtracting withholding allowances) is:

The amount of income tax to withhold is:

Not over $692 ....$0

Over—	But not over—		of excess over—
$704	—$2,217	......$0.00 plus 10%	—$704
$2,217	—$6,854	......$151.30 plus 15%	—$2,217
$6,854	—$13,108	......$846.85 plus 25%	—$6,854
$13,108	—$19,608	......$2,410.35 plus 28%	—$13,108
$19,608	—$34,463	......$4,230.35 plus 33%	—$19,608
$34,463	—$38,838	......$9,132.50 plus 35%	—$34,463
$38,838	...............................$10,663.75 plus 39.6%		—$38,838

STEPS TO CALCULATE THE INCOME TAX WITHHELD BY THE PERCENTAGE METHOD

STEP 1. Using the proper payroll period, multiply one withholding allowance, Exhibit 9-1, by the number of allowances claimed by the employee.

STEP 2. Subtract that amount from the employee's gross earnings to find the wages subject to federal income tax.

STEP 3. From Exhibit 9-2, locate the proper segment (Table 1, 2, 3, or 4) corresponding to the employee's payroll period. Within that segment, use the *left* side (a) for single employees and the *right* side (b) for married employees.

STEP 4. Locate the "Over—" and "But not over—" brackets containing the employee's taxable wages from Step 2. The tax is listed to the right as a percent or a dollar amount and a percent.

EXAMPLE11 CALCULATING INCOME TAX WITHHOLDING

Lori Fast is a manager for Wayward Wind Travel. She is single and is paid $750 weekly. She claims two withholding allowances. Using the percentage method, calculate the amount of income tax that should be withheld from her paycheck each week.

SOLUTIONSTRATEGY

From Exhibit 9-1, the amount of one withholding allowance for an employee paid weekly is $76.00. Multiply this amount by the number of allowances claimed, two.

$$76.00 \times 2 = \$152.00$$

Subtract that amount from the gross earnings to get taxable income.

$$750.00 - 152.00 = \$598.00$$

From Exhibit 9-2, find the tax withheld from Lori's paycheck in Table 1(a), Weekly payroll period, Single person. Lori's taxable wages of $598.00 fall in the category "Over $218, but not over $753." The tax, therefore, is $17.50 plus 15% of the excess over $218.

$$\text{Tax} = 17.50 + .15(598.00 - 218.00)$$
$$\text{Tax} = 17.50 + .15(380.00)$$
$$\text{Tax} = 17.50 + 57.00 = \underline{\$74.50}$$

TRYITEXERCISE 11

Jan McMillan is married, claims five exemptions, and earns $5,670 per month. As the payroll manager of Jan's company, use the percentage method to calculate the amount of income tax that must be withheld from her paycheck.

CHECK YOUR ANSWER WITH THE SOLUTION ON PAGE 296.

9-7 DETERMINING AN EMPLOYEE'S TOTAL WITHHOLDING FOR FEDERAL INCOME TAX, SOCIAL SECURITY, AND MEDICARE USING THE COMBINED WAGE BRACKET TABLES

combined wage bracket tables IRS tables used to determine the combined amount of income tax, social security, and Medicare that must be withheld from an employee's gross earnings each pay period.

In 2001, the IRS introduced **combined wage bracket tables** that can be used to determine the combined amount of income tax, social security, and Medicare that must be withheld from an employee's gross earnings each pay period. These tables are found in *Publication 15-A, Employer's Supplemental Tax Guide*. This publication contains a complete set of tables for both single and married people, covering weekly, biweekly, semimonthly, monthly, and even daily pay periods.

Exhibit 9-3 shows a portion of the wage bracket tables for Married Persons—Weekly Payroll Period, and Exhibit 9-4 shows a portion of the wage bracket table for Single Persons—Monthly Payroll Period. These tables were in effect as this is written and should be used to solve wage bracket problems in this chapter.

STEPS TO FIND THE TOTAL INCOME TAX, SOCIAL SECURITY, AND MEDICARE WITHHELD USING THE COMBINED WAGE BRACKET TABLE

STEP 1. Based on the employee's marital status and period of payment, find the corresponding table (Exhibit 9-3 or 9-4).

STEP 2. Note that the two left-hand columns, labeled "At least" and "But less than," are the wage brackets. Scan down these columns until you find the bracket containing the gross pay of the employee.

STEP 3. Scan across the row of that wage bracket to the intersection of the column containing the number of withholding allowances claimed by the employee.

STEP 4. The number in that column on the wage bracket row is the amount of combined tax withheld.

EXAMPLE 12 USING THE COMBINED WAGE BRACKET TABLES

Use the combined wage bracket tables to determine the amount of income tax, social security, and Medicare withheld from the monthly paycheck of Erin Lane, a single employee claiming three withholding allowances and earning $2,975 per month.

SOLUTION STRATEGY

To find Erin Lane's monthly income tax withholding, choose the table for Single Persons—Monthly Payroll Period, Exhibit 9-4. Scanning down the "At least" and "But less than" columns, we find the wage bracket containing Erin's earnings: "At least 2,960—But less than 3,000."

Next, scan across that row from left to right to the "3" withholding allowances column. The number at that intersection, $460.97, is the total combined tax to be withheld from Erin's paycheck.

TRY IT EXERCISE 12

Using the combined wage bracket tables, what is the total amount of income tax, social security, and Medicare that should be withheld from Brent Andrus's weekly paycheck of $835 if he is married and claims two withholding allowances?

CHECK YOUR ANSWER WITH THE SOLUTION ON PAGE 296.

EXHIBIT 9-3 Payroll Deductions—Married, Paid Weekly

MARRIED Persons—WEEKLY Payroll Period
(For Wages Paid through December 20XX)

And the wages are—		And the number of withholding allowances claimed is—										
At least	But less than	0	1	2	3	4	5	6	7	8	9	10
		The amount of income, social security, and Medicare taxes to be withheld is—										
$800	$810	$140.58	$129.58	$117.58	$106.58	$95.58	$87.58	$80.58	$72.58	$64.58	$61.58	$61.58
810	820	142.35	131.35	120.35	108.35	97.35	89.35	82.35	74.35	66.35	62.35	62.35
820	830	145.11	134.11	122.11	111.11	99.11	91.11	84.11	76.11	68.11	63.11	63.11
830	840	146.88	135.88	124.88	112.88	101.88	92.88	85.88	77.88	69.88	63.88	63.88
840	850	149.64	138.64	126.64	115.64	103.64	94.64	87.64	79.64	71.64	64.64	64.64
850	860	151.41	140.41	129.41	117.41	106.41	96.41	89.41	81.41	73.41	66.41	65.41
860	870	154.17	143.17	131.17	120.17	108.17	98.17	91.17	83.17	75.17	68.17	66.17
870	880	155.94	144.94	133.94	121.94	110.94	99.94	92.94	84.94	76.94	69.94	66.94
880	890	158.70	147.70	135.70	124.70	112.70	101.70	94.70	86.70	78.70	71.70	67.70
890	900	160.47	149.47	138.47	126.47	115.47	103.47	96.47	88.47	80.47	73.47	68.47
900	910	163.23	152.23	140.23	129.23	117.23	106.23	98.23	90.23	82.23	75.23	69.23
910	920	165.00	154.00	143.00	131.00	120.00	108.00	100.00	92.00	84.00	77.00	70.00
920	930	167.76	156.76	144.76	133.76	121.76	110.76	101.76	93.76	85.76	78.76	70.76
930	940	169.53	158.53	147.53	135.53	124.53	112.53	103.53	95.53	87.53	80.53	72.53
940	950	172.29	161.29	149.29	138.29	126.29	115.29	105.29	97.29	89.29	82.29	74.29
950	960	174.06	163.06	152.06	140.06	129.06	117.06	107.06	99.06	91.06	84.06	76.06
960	970	176.82	165.82	153.82	142.82	130.82	119.82	108.82	100.82	92.82	85.82	77.82
970	980	178.59	167.59	156.59	144.59	133.59	121.59	110.59	102.59	94.59	87.59	79.59
980	990	181.35	170.35	158.35	147.35	135.35	124.35	113.35	104.35	96.35	89.35	81.35
990	1,000	183.12	172.12	161.12	149.12	138.12	126.12	115.12	106.12	98.12	91.12	83.12
1,000	1,010	185.88	174.88	162.88	151.88	139.88	128.88	117.88	107.88	99.88	92.88	84.88
1,010	1,020	187.65	176.65	165.65	153.65	142.65	130.65	119.65	109.65	101.65	94.65	86.65
1,020	1,030	190.41	179.41	167.41	156.41	144.41	133.41	122.41	111.41	103.41	96.41	88.41
1,030	1,040	192.18	181.18	170.18	158.18	147.18	135.18	124.18	113.18	105.18	98.18	90.18
1,040	1,050	194.94	183.94	171.94	160.94	148.94	137.94	126.94	114.94	106.94	99.94	91.94
1,050	1,060	196.71	185.71	174.71	162.71	151.71	139.71	128.71	117.71	108.71	101.71	93.71
1,060	1,070	199.47	188.47	176.47	165.47	153.47	142.47	131.47	119.47	110.47	103.47	95.47
1,070	1,080	201.24	190.24	179.24	167.24	156.24	144.24	133.24	122.24	112.24	105.24	97.24
1,080	1,090	204.00	193.00	181.00	170.00	158.00	147.00	136.00	124.00	114.00	107.00	99.00
1,090	1,100	205.77	194.77	183.77	171.77	160.77	148.77	137.77	126.77	115.77	108.77	100.77
1,100	1,110	208.53	197.53	185.53	174.53	162.53	151.53	140.53	128.53	117.53	110.53	102.53
1,110	1,120	210.30	199.30	188.30	176.30	165.30	153.30	142.30	131.30	119.30	112.30	104.30
1,120	1,130	213.06	202.06	190.06	179.06	167.06	156.06	145.06	133.06	122.06	114.06	106.06
1,130	1,140	214.83	203.83	192.83	180.83	169.83	157.83	146.83	135.83	123.83	115.83	107.83
1,140	1,150	217.59	206.59	194.59	183.59	171.59	160.59	149.59	137.59	126.59	117.59	109.59
1,150	1,160	219.36	208.36	197.36	185.36	174.36	162.36	151.36	140.36	128.36	119.36	111.36
1,160	1,170	222.12	211.12	199.12	188.12	176.12	165.12	154.12	142.12	131.12	121.12	113.12
1,170	1,180	223.89	212.89	201.89	189.89	178.89	166.89	155.89	144.89	132.89	122.89	114.89
1,180	1,190	226.65	215.65	203.65	192.65	180.65	169.65	158.65	146.65	135.65	124.65	116.65
1,190	1,200	228.42	217.42	206.42	194.42	183.42	171.42	160.42	149.42	137.42	126.42	118.42
1,200	1,210	231.18	220.18	208.18	197.18	185.18	174.18	163.18	151.18	140.18	128.18	120.18
1,210	1,220	232.95	221.95	210.95	198.95	187.95	175.95	164.95	153.95	141.95	130.95	121.95
1,220	1,230	235.71	224.71	212.71	201.71	189.71	178.71	167.71	155.71	144.71	132.71	123.71
1,230	1,240	237.48	226.48	215.48	203.48	192.48	180.48	169.48	158.48	146.48	135.48	125.48
1,240	1,250	240.24	229.24	217.24	206.24	194.24	183.24	172.24	160.24	149.24	137.24	127.24
1,250	1,260	242.01	231.01	220.01	208.01	197.01	185.01	174.01	163.01	151.01	140.01	129.01
1,260	1,270	244.77	233.77	221.77	210.77	198.77	187.77	176.77	164.77	153.77	141.77	130.77
1,270	1,280	246.54	235.54	224.54	212.54	201.54	189.54	178.54	167.54	155.54	144.54	132.54
1,280	1,290	249.30	238.30	226.30	215.30	203.30	192.30	181.30	169.30	158.30	146.30	135.30
1,290	1,300	251.07	240.07	229.07	217.07	206.07	194.07	183.07	172.07	160.07	149.07	137.07
1,300	1,310	253.83	242.83	230.83	219.83	207.83	196.83	185.83	173.83	162.83	150.83	139.83
1,310	1,320	255.60	244.60	233.60	221.60	210.60	198.60	187.60	176.60	164.60	153.60	141.60
1,320	1,330	258.36	247.36	235.36	224.36	212.36	201.36	190.36	178.36	167.36	155.36	144.36
1,330	1,340	260.13	249.13	238.13	226.13	215.13	203.13	192.13	181.13	169.13	158.13	146.13
1,340	1,350	262.89	251.89	239.89	228.89	216.89	205.89	194.89	182.89	171.89	159.89	148.89
1,350	1,360	264.66	253.66	242.66	230.66	219.66	207.66	196.66	185.66	173.66	162.66	150.66
1,360	1,370	267.42	256.42	244.42	233.42	221.42	210.42	199.42	187.42	176.42	164.42	153.42
1,370	1,380	269.19	258.19	247.19	235.19	224.19	212.19	201.19	190.19	178.19	167.19	155.19
1,380	1,390	271.95	260.95	248.95	237.95	225.95	214.95	203.95	191.95	180.95	168.95	157.95
1,390	1,400	273.72	262.72	251.72	239.72	228.72	216.72	205.72	194.72	182.72	171.72	159.72
1,400	1,410	276.48	265.48	253.48	242.48	230.48	219.48	208.48	196.48	185.48	173.48	162.48
1,410	1,420	278.25	267.25	256.25	244.25	233.25	221.25	210.25	199.25	187.25	176.25	164.25
1,420	1,430	281.01	270.01	258.01	247.01	235.01	224.01	213.01	201.01	190.01	178.01	167.01
1,430	1,440	282.78	271.78	260.78	248.78	237.78	225.78	214.78	203.78	191.78	180.78	168.78
1,440	1,450	285.54	274.54	262.54	251.54	239.54	228.54	217.54	205.54	194.54	182.54	171.54
1,450	1,460	287.31	276.31	265.31	253.31	242.31	230.31	219.31	208.31	196.31	185.31	173.31
1,460	1,470	290.07	279.07	267.07	256.07	244.07	233.07	222.07	210.07	199.07	187.07	176.07

EXHIBIT 9-4   Payroll Deductions—Single, Paid Monthly

SINGLE Persons—MONTHLY Payroll Period
(For Wages Paid through December 20XX)

And the wages are—		And the number of withholding allowances claimed is—										
At least	But less than	0	1	2	3	4	5	6	7	8	9	10
		The amount of income, social security, and Medicare taxes to be withheld is—										
$2,400	$2,440	$482.13	$433.13	$383.13	$334.13	$285.13	$244.13	$211.13	$185.13	$185.13	$185.13	$185.13
2,440	2,480	491.19	442.19	392.19	343.19	294.19	251.19	218.19	188.19	188.19	188.19	188.19
2,480	2,520	500.25	451.25	401.25	352.25	303.25	258.25	225.25	192.25	191.25	191.25	191.25
2,520	2,560	509.31	460.31	410.31	361.31	312.31	265.31	232.31	199.31	194.31	194.31	194.31
2,560	2,600	518.37	469.37	419.37	370.37	321.37	272.37	239.37	206.37	197.37	197.37	197.37
2,600	2,640	527.43	478.43	428.43	379.43	330.43	280.43	246.43	213.43	200.43	200.43	200.43
2,640	2,680	536.49	487.49	437.49	388.49	339.49	289.49	253.49	220.49	203.49	203.49	203.49
2,680	2,720	545.55	496.55	446.55	397.55	348.55	298.55	260.55	227.55	206.55	206.55	206.55
2,720	2,760	554.61	505.61	455.61	406.61	357.61	307.61	267.61	234.61	209.61	209.61	209.61
2,760	2,800	563.67	514.67	464.67	415.67	366.67	316.67	274.67	241.67	212.67	212.67	212.67
2,800	2,840	572.73	523.73	473.73	424.73	375.73	325.73	281.73	248.73	215.73	215.73	215.73
2,840	2,880	581.79	532.79	482.79	433.79	384.79	334.79	288.79	255.79	222.79	218.79	218.79
2,880	2,920	590.85	541.85	491.85	442.85	393.85	343.85	295.85	262.85	229.85	221.85	221.85
2,920	2,960	599.91	550.91	500.91	451.91	402.91	352.91	303.91	269.91	236.91	224.91	224.91
2,960	3,000	608.97	559.97	509.97	460.97	411.97	361.97	312.97	276.97	243.97	227.97	227.97
3,000	3,040	618.03	569.03	519.03	470.03	421.03	371.03	322.03	284.03	251.03	231.03	231.03
3,040	3,080	627.09	578.09	528.09	479.09	430.09	380.09	331.09	291.09	258.09	234.09	234.09
3,080	3,120	636.15	587.15	537.15	488.15	439.15	389.15	340.15	298.15	265.15	237.15	237.15
3,120	3,160	645.21	596.21	546.21	497.21	448.21	398.21	349.21	305.21	272.21	240.21	240.21
3,160	3,200	654.27	605.27	555.27	506.27	457.27	407.27	358.27	312.27	279.27	246.27	243.27
3,200	3,240	663.33	614.33	564.33	515.33	466.33	416.33	367.33	319.33	286.33	253.33	246.33
3,240	3,280	672.39	623.39	573.39	524.39	475.39	425.39	376.39	326.39	293.39	260.39	249.39
3,280	3,320	685.45	632.45	582.45	533.45	484.45	434.45	385.45	335.45	300.45	267.45	252.45
3,320	3,360	698.51	641.51	591.51	542.51	493.51	443.51	394.51	344.51	307.51	274.51	255.51
3,360	3,400	711.57	650.57	600.57	551.57	502.57	452.57	403.57	353.57	314.57	281.57	258.57
3,400	3,440	724.63	659.63	609.63	560.63	511.63	461.63	412.63	362.63	321.63	288.63	261.63
3,440	3,480	737.69	668.69	618.69	569.69	520.69	470.69	421.69	371.69	328.69	295.69	264.69
3,480	3,520	750.75	677.75	627.75	578.75	529.75	479.75	430.75	380.75	335.75	302.75	269.75
3,520	3,560	763.81	686.81	636.81	587.81	538.81	488.81	439.81	389.81	342.81	309.81	276.81
3,560	3,600	776.87	695.87	645.87	596.87	547.87	497.87	448.87	398.87	349.87	316.87	283.87
3,600	3,640	789.93	707.93	654.93	605.93	556.93	506.93	457.93	407.93	358.93	323.93	290.93
3,640	3,680	802.99	720.99	663.99	614.99	565.99	515.99	466.99	416.99	367.99	330.99	297.99
3,680	3,720	816.05	734.05	673.05	624.05	575.05	525.05	476.05	426.05	377.05	338.05	305.05
3,720	3,760	829.11	747.11	682.11	633.11	584.11	534.11	485.11	435.11	386.11	345.11	312.11
3,760	3,800	842.17	760.17	691.17	642.17	593.17	543.17	494.17	444.17	395.17	352.17	319.17
3,800	3,840	855.23	773.23	700.23	651.23	602.23	552.23	503.23	453.23	404.23	359.23	326.23
3,840	3,880	868.29	786.29	709.29	660.29	611.29	561.29	512.29	462.29	413.29	366.29	333.29
3,880	3,920	881.35	799.35	718.35	669.35	620.35	570.35	521.35	471.35	422.35	373.35	340.35
3,920	3,960	894.41	812.41	729.41	678.41	629.41	579.41	530.41	480.41	431.41	382.41	347.41
3,960	4,000	907.47	825.47	742.47	687.47	638.47	588.47	539.47	489.47	440.47	391.47	354.47
4,000	4,040	920.53	838.53	755.53	696.53	647.53	597.53	548.53	498.53	449.53	400.53	361.53
4,040	4,080	933.59	851.59	768.59	705.59	656.59	606.59	557.59	507.59	458.59	409.59	368.59
4,080	4,120	946.65	864.65	781.65	714.65	665.65	615.65	566.65	516.65	467.65	418.65	375.65
4,120	4,160	959.71	877.71	794.71	723.71	674.71	624.71	575.71	525.71	476.71	427.71	382.71
4,160	4,200	972.77	890.77	807.77	732.77	683.77	633.77	584.77	534.77	485.77	436.77	389.77
4,200	4,240	985.83	903.83	820.83	741.83	692.83	642.83	593.83	543.83	494.83	445.83	396.83
4,240	4,280	998.89	916.89	833.89	751.89	701.89	651.89	602.89	552.89	503.89	454.89	404.89
4,280	4,320	1,011.95	929.95	846.95	764.95	710.95	660.95	611.95	561.95	512.95	463.95	413.95
4,320	4,360	1,025.01	943.01	860.01	778.01	720.01	670.01	621.01	571.01	522.01	473.01	423.01
4,360	4,400	1,038.07	956.07	873.07	791.07	729.07	679.07	630.07	580.07	531.07	482.07	432.07
4,400	4,440	1,051.13	969.13	886.13	804.13	738.13	688.13	639.13	589.13	540.13	491.13	441.13
4,440	4,480	1,064.19	982.19	899.19	817.19	747.19	697.19	648.19	598.19	549.19	500.19	450.19
4,480	4,520	1,077.25	995.25	912.25	830.25	756.25	706.25	657.25	607.25	558.25	509.25	459.25
4,520	4,560	1,090.31	1,008.31	925.31	843.31	765.31	715.31	666.31	616.31	567.31	518.31	468.31
4,560	4,600	1,103.37	1,021.37	938.37	856.37	774.37	724.37	675.37	625.37	576.37	527.37	477.37
4,600	4,640	1,116.43	1,034.43	951.43	869.43	787.43	733.43	684.43	634.43	585.43	536.43	486.43
4,640	4,680	1,129.49	1,047.49	964.49	882.49	800.49	742.49	693.49	643.49	594.49	545.49	495.49
4,680	4,720	1,142.55	1,060.55	977.55	895.55	813.55	751.55	702.55	652.55	603.55	554.55	504.55
4,720	4,760	1,155.61	1,073.61	990.61	908.61	826.61	760.61	711.61	661.61	612.61	563.61	513.61
4,760	4,800	1,168.67	1,086.67	1,003.67	921.67	839.67	769.67	720.67	670.67	621.67	572.67	522.67
4,800	4,840	1,181.73	1,099.73	1,016.93	934.73	852.73	778.73	729.73	679.73	630.73	581.73	531.73
4,840	4,880	1,194.79	1,112.79	1,029.79	947.79	865.79	787.79	738.79	688.79	639.79	590.79	540.79
4,880	4,920	1,207.85	1,125.85	1,042.85	960.85	878.85	796.85	747.85	697.85	648.85	599.85	549.85
4,920	4,960	1,220.91	1,138.91	1,055.91	973.91	891.91	808.91	756.91	706.91	657.91	608.91	558.91
4,960	5,000	1,233.97	1,151.97	1,068.97	986.97	904.97	821.97	765.97	715.97	666.97	617.97	567.97
5,000	5,040	1,247.03	1,165.03	1,082.03	1,000.03	918.03	835.03	775.03	725.03	676.03	627.03	577.03

REVIEW EXERCISES

Solve the following problems using 6.2%, up to $117,000, for social security tax and 1.45%, no wage limit, for Medicare tax.

1. What are the withholdings for social security and Medicare for an employee with gross earnings of $825 per week?

   $825 \times .062 = \underline{\$51.15}$ Social security
   $825 \times .0145 = \underline{\$11.96}$ Medicare

2. What are the social security and Medicare withholdings for an executive whose annual gross earnings are $118,430?

3. Brian Hickman is an executive with Westco Distributors. His gross earnings are $9,800 per month.

   a. What are the withholdings for social security and Medicare for Brian in his January paycheck?

   b. In what month will Brian's salary reach the social security wage base limit?

   c. What are the social security and Medicare tax withholdings for Brian in the month named in part b?

4. Kristy Dunaway has biweekly gross earnings of $1,750. What are her total social security and Medicare tax withholdings for a whole year?

As the payroll manager for Freeport Enterprises, it is your task to calculate the monthly social security and Medicare withholdings for the following employees.

Employee	Year-to-Date Earnings	Current Month	Social Security	Medicare
5. Perez, J.	$23,446	$3,422	$212.16	$49.62
6. Graham, C.	$14,800	$1,540	_____	_____
7. Jagger, R.	$105,200	$4,700	_____	_____
8. Andretti, K.	$145,000	$12,450	_____	_____

Use the percentage method of income tax calculation to complete the following payroll roster.

Employee	Marital Status	Withholding Allowances	Pay Period	Gross Earnings	Income Tax Withholding
9. Randolph, B.	M	2	Weekly	$594	$27.90
10. White, W.	S	0	Semimonthly	$1,227	_____
11. Milian, B.	S	1	Monthly	$4,150	_____
12. Farley, D.	M	4	Biweekly	$1,849	_____

Use the combined wage bracket tables, Exhibits 9-3 and 9-4, to solve Exercises 13–19.

13. How much combined tax should be withheld from the paycheck of a married employee earning $1,075 per week and claiming four withholding allowances?

14. How much combined tax should be withheld from the paycheck of a single employee earning $3,185 per month and claiming zero withholding allowances?

15. Jeremy Dunn is single, claims two withholding allowances, and earns $4,025 per month. Calculate the amount of Jeremy's paycheck after his employer withholds social security, Medicare, and federal income tax.

Employee	Marital Status	Withholding Allowances	Pay Period	Gross Earnings	Combined Withholding
16. Alton, A.	S	3	Monthly	$4,633	$869.43
17. Emerson, P.	M	5	Weekly	$937	_____
18. Reese, S.	M	4	Weekly	$1,172	_____
19. Benson, K.	S	1	Monthly	$3,128	_____

BUSINESS DECISION: TAKE-HOME PAY

20. You are the payroll manager for the Canyon Ridge Resort. Mark Kelsch, the marketing director, earns a salary of $43,200 per year, payable monthly. He is married and claims four withholding allowances. His social security number is 444-44-4444.

In addition to federal income tax, social security, and Medicare, Mark pays 2.3% state income tax, $\frac{1}{2}$% for state disability insurance (both based on gross earnings), $23.74 for term life insurance, $122.14 to the credit union, and $40 to the United Way.

Fill out the following payroll voucher for Mark for the month of April.

Canyon Ridge Resort
Payroll Voucher

Employee: _____   Tax Filing Status: _____

SSN: _____   Withholding Allowances: ___

Full-time Pay Period From _____ To _____

Primary Withholdings: Additional Withholdings:

Federal income tax   _____   _____

Social security   _____   _____

Medicare   _____   _____

State income tax   _____

State disability   _____

Gross earnings: _____

– Total withholdings: _____

NET PAY   _____

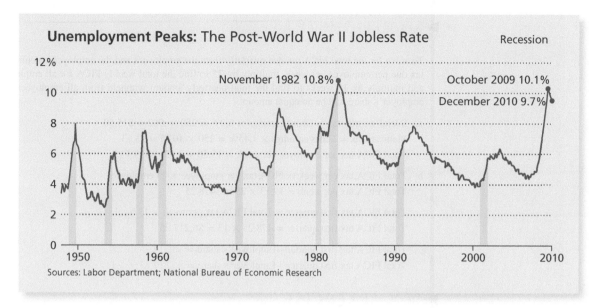

Unemployment Peaks: The Post-World War II Jobless Rate   Recession

November 1982 10.8%

October 2009 10.1%

December 2010 9.7%

Sources: Labor Department; National Bureau of Economic Research

EMPLOYER'S PAYROLL EXPENSES AND SELF-EMPLOYED PERSON'S TAX RESPONSIBILITY

9   SECTION III

To this point, we have discussed payroll deductions from the employee's point of view. Now let's take a look at the payroll expenses of the employer. According to the Fair Labor Standards Act, employers are required to maintain complete and up-to-date earnings records for each employee.

Employers are responsible for the payment of four payroll taxes: social security, Medicare, state unemployment tax (SUTA), and federal unemployment tax (FUTA). In addition, most employers are responsible for a variety of **fringe benefits** that are offered to their employees. These are benefits over and above an employee's normal earnings and can be a significant expense to the employer. Some typical examples are retirement plans, stock option plans, holiday leave, sick days, health and dental insurance, and tuition reimbursement. This section deals with the calculation of these employer taxes as well as the tax responsibility of self-employed persons.

fringe benefits Employer-provided benefits and service packages over and above an employee's paycheck, such as pension funds, paid vacations, sick leave, and health insurance.

COMPUTING FICA TAX FOR EMPLOYERS AND SELF-EMPLOYMENT TAX FOR SELF-EMPLOYED PERSONS

9-8

FICA TAX FOR EMPLOYERS

Employers are required to *match* all FICA tax payments, both social security and Medicare, made by each employee. For example, if a company withheld a total of $23,000 in FICA taxes from its employee paychecks this month, the company would be responsible for a matching share of $23,000.

EXAMPLE13   COMPUTING FICA TAX FOR EMPLOYEES AND THE EMPLOYER

Spectrum Engineering has 25 employees, each with gross earnings of $250 per week.

a. What are the total FICA (social security and Medicare) taxes that should be withheld from each employee's weekly paycheck?

b. At the end of the first quarter (13 weeks), what were the accumulated totals of the employee's share and the matching taxes for FICA that Spectrum had sent to the IRS?

SOLUTIONSTRATEGY

To solve for the total FICA tax due quarterly from the employees and the employer, calculate the tax due per employee per week, multiply by 25 to find the total weekly FICA for all employees, and multiply by 13 weeks to find the total quarterly amount withheld from all employees. The employer's share will be an equal amount.

a. Social security tax = Gross earnings × 6.2% = 250 × .062 = $15.50
    Medicare tax = Gross earnings × 1.45% = 250 × .0145 = $3.63
    Total FICA tax per employee per week = 15.50 + 3.63 = $19.13

b. Total FICA tax per week = FICA tax per employee × 25 employees
    Total FICA tax per week = 19.13 × 25 = $478.25

    Total FICA tax first quarter = Total FICA tax per week × 13 weeks
    Total FICA tax first quarter = 478.25 × 13 = $6,217.25

    Total FICA tax first quarter—Employee's share = $6,217.25
    Total FICA tax first quarter—Employer's share = $6,217.25

▶TRYITEXERCISE 13

Big Pine Tree Service has 18 employees, 12 with gross earnings of $350 per week and 6 with gross earnings of $425 per week. What are the employee's share and the employer's share of the social security and Medicare tax for the first quarter of the year?

CHECK YOUR ANSWERS WITH THE SOLUTIONS ON PAGE 296.

SELF-EMPLOYMENT TAX

The self-employment tax, officially known as the Self-Employment Contributions Act (SECA) tax, is the self-employed person's version of the FICA tax. It is due on the net earnings from self-employment.

Self-employed persons are responsible for social security and Medicare taxes at twice the rate deducted for employees. Technically, they are the employee and the employer and therefore must pay both shares. For a self-employed person, the social security and Medicare tax rates are twice the normal rates, as follows:

	Tax Rate	Wage Base
Social Security	12.4% (6.2% × 2)	$117,000
Medicare	2.9% (1.45% × 2)	No limit

EXAMPLE14   CALCULATING SELF-EMPLOYMENT TAX

What are the social security and Medicare taxes of a self-employed landscaper with net earnings of $43,800 per year?

▶SOLUTIONSTRATEGY

To find the amount of self-employment tax due, we apply the self-employed tax rates, 12.4% for social security and 2.9% for Medicare, to the net earnings.

Social security tax = Net earnings × Tax rate
Social security tax = 43,800 × .124 = $5,431.20
Medicare tax = Net earnings × Tax rate
Medicare tax = 43,800 × .029 = $1,270.20

▶ TRYITEXERCISE 14

Les Roberts, a self-employed commercial artist, had total net earnings of $60,000 last year. What was the amount of the social security and Medicare taxes Les was required to send the IRS last year?

CHECK YOUR ANSWERS WITH THE SOLUTIONS ON PAGE 296.

COMPUTING THE AMOUNT OF STATE UNEMPLOYMENT TAX (SUTA) AND FEDERAL UNEMPLOYMENT TAX (FUTA)

9-9

The **Federal Unemployment Tax Act (FUTA)**, together with state unemployment systems, provides for payments of unemployment compensation to workers who have lost their jobs. Most employers are responsible for both a federal and a state unemployment tax.

Generally, an employer can take a credit against the FUTA tax for amounts paid into state unemployment funds. These state taxes are commonly known as the **State Unemployment Tax Act (SUTA)**. This credit cannot be more than 5.4% of the first $7,000 of employees' taxable wages.

SUTA tax rates vary from state to state according to the employment record of the company. These merit-rating systems found in many states provide significant SUTA tax savings to companies with good employment records.

The FUTA may change from year to year. In this chapter we'll use a FUTA tax rate of .6%. (This assumes an unreduced FUTA tax of 6% for the first $7,000 of wages paid to each employee during the year reduced by a 5.4% SUTA credit. That is, 6% − 5.4% = .6% FUTA tax rate.)

Federal Unemployment Tax Act (FUTA) A federal tax that is paid by employers for each employee to provide unemployment compensation to workers who have lost their jobs.

State Unemployment Tax Act (SUTA) A state tax that is paid by employers for each employee to provide unemployment compensation to workers who have lost their jobs.

EXAMPLE15 CALCULATING SUTA AND FUTA TAXES

Uniphase Industries, Inc., had a total payroll of $50,000 last month. Uniphase pays a SUTA tax rate of 5.4% and a FUTA rate of 6.0% less the SUTA credit. If none of the employees had reached the $7,000 wage base, what is the amount of SUTA and FUTA tax the company must pay?

▶ SOLUTIONSTRATEGY

To calculate the SUTA and FUTA taxes, apply the appropriate tax rates to the gross earnings subject to the tax, in this case, all the gross earnings.

SUTA tax = Gross earnings × 5.4%
SUTA tax = 50,000 × .054 = $2,700

The FUTA tax rate will be .6%. Remember, it is actually 6.0% less the 5.4% credit.

FUTA tax = Gross earnings × .6%
FUTA tax = 50,000 × .006 = $300

▶ TRYITEXERCISE 15

Sunshine Catering had a total payroll of $10,000 last month. Sunshine pays a SUTA tax rate of 5.4% and a FUTA rate of 6.0% less the SUTA credit. If none of the employees had reached the $7,000 wage base, what is the amount of SUTA and FUTA tax the company must pay?

CHECK YOUR ANSWERS WITH THE SOLUTIONS ON PAGE 296.

9-10 CALCULATING EMPLOYER'S FRINGE BENEFIT EXPENSES

In addition to compensating employees with a paycheck, most companies today offer employee fringe benefit and services packages. These packages include a wide variety of benefits such as pension plans, paid vacations and sick leave, day-care centers, tuition assistance, and health insurance. Corporate executives may receive benefits such as company cars, first-class airline travel, and country club memberships. At the executive level of business, these benefits are known as **perquisites**, or **perks**.

Over the past decade, employee benefits have become increasingly important to workers. They have grown in size to the point where today total benefits may cost a company as much as 40% to 50% of payroll. Frequently, employees are given a *menu* of fringe benefits from which to choose up to a specified dollar amount. These plans are known as **cafeteria style**, or **flexible benefit programs**.

perquisites, or **perks** Executive-level fringe benefits such as first-class airline travel, company cars, and country club membership.

cafeteria style, or **flexible benefit programs** A plan whereby employees are given a menu of fringe benefits from which to choose up to a specified dollar amount.

IN THE Business World

Although paid vacations and health insurance are still the most popular among company-sponsored benefits, there is a trend today toward more "work-life initiatives." These are benefits that help employees balance their professional and personal lives, such as child-care assistance and flexible work hours.

STEPS TO CALCULATE EMPLOYER'S FRINGE BENEFITS EXPENSE

STEP 1. If the fringe benefit is a percent of gross payroll, multiply that percent by the amount of the gross payroll. If the fringe benefit is a dollar amount per employee, multiply that amount by the number of employees.

STEP 2. Find the total fringe benefits by adding all the individual fringe benefit amounts.

STEP 3. Calculate the fringe benefit percent by using the percentage formula Rate = Portion ÷ Base with total fringe benefits as the portion and gross payroll as the base (remember to convert your answer to a percent).

$$\text{Fringe benefit percent} = \frac{\text{Total fringe benefits}}{\text{Gross payroll}}$$

EXAMPLE16 CALCULATING FRINGE BENEFITS

In addition to its gross payroll of $150,000 per month, Premier Distributors, Inc., with 75 employees, pays 7% of payroll to a retirement fund, 9% for health insurance, and $25 per employee for a stock purchase plan.

a. What are the company's monthly fringe benefit expenses?

b. What percent of payroll does this represent?

▶SOLUTIONSTRATEGY

a. To solve for monthly fringe benefits, compute the amount of each benefit and add them to find the total.

Retirement fund expense = Gross payroll × 7%
Retirement fund expense = 150,000 × .07 = $10,500

Health insurance expense = Gross payroll × 9%
Health insurance expense = 150,000 × .09 = $13,500

Stock plan expense = Number of employees × $25
Stock plan expense = 75 × 25 = $1,875

Total fringe benefits = Retirement + Health + Stock
Total fringe benefits = 10,500 + 13,500 + 1,875 = $25,875

b. Fringe benefit percent = $\dfrac{\text{Total fringe benefits}}{\text{Gross payroll}} = \dfrac{25,875}{150,000} = .1725 = 17.25\%$

Paid vacation time is one of the many fringe benefits offered by employers today.

Courtesy of Bob Brechner

▶TRYITEXERCISE 16

Dynamo Productions employs 250 workers with a gross payroll of $123,400 per week. Fringe benefits are 5% of gross payroll for sick days and holiday leave, 8% for health insurance, and $12.40 per employee for dental insurance.

a. What is the total weekly cost of fringe benefits for Dynamo?

b. What percent of payroll does this represent?

c. What is the cost of these fringe benefits to the company for a year?

CHECK YOUR ANSWERS WITH THE SOLUTIONS ON PAGE 296.

CALCULATING QUARTERLY ESTIMATED TAX FOR SELF-EMPLOYED PERSONS

9-11

By IRS rules, you must pay self-employment tax if you had net earnings of $400 or more as a self-employed person. This is income that is not subject to withholding tax. Quarterly estimated tax is the method used to pay tax on these earnings. You may pay all of your estimated tax by April or in four equal amounts: in April, June, September, and January of the following year.

To calculate the quarterly estimated tax of a self-employed person, we divide the total of social security, Medicare, and income tax by 4. (There are 4 quarters in a year.) Internal Revenue Service form 1040 ES, Quarterly Estimated Tax Payment Voucher, shown in Exhibit 9-5, is used to file this tax with the IRS each quarter.

$$\text{Quarterly estimated tax} = \frac{\text{Social security} + \text{Medicare} + \text{Income tax}}{4}$$

EXHIBIT 9-5 Quarterly Estimated Tax Payment Voucher

Form **1040-ES**
Department of the Treasury
Internal Revenue Service

20XX Payment Voucher **4**

OMB No. 1545-0087

File only if you are making a payment of estimated tax by check or money order. Mail this voucher with your check or money order payable to the "**United States Treasury.**" Write your social security number and "20XX Form 1040-ES" on your check or money order. Do not send cash. Enclose, but do not staple or attach, your payment with this voucher.

Calendar year—Due Jan. 15,

Amount of estimated tax you are paying by check or money order.

$

Type or print

Your first name and initial	Your last name	Your social security number
If joint payment, complete for spouse		
Spouse's first name and initial	Spouse's last name	Spouse's social security number
Address (number, street, and apt. no.)		
City, state, and ZIP code (If a foreign address, enter city, province or state, postal code, and country.)		

For Privacy Act and Paperwork Reduction Act Notice, see instructions on page 5.
Page 6

Dollars AND Sense

You may use your American Express card, Discover card, MasterCard, or a debit card to make estimated tax payments. Call toll free or access by Internet one of the service providers listed below and follow the instructions. Each provider will charge a convenience fee based on the amount you are paying.

- Official Payments Corporation
  1-800-2PAY-TAX (1-800-272-9829)
  www.officialpayments.com/fed

- Link2GovCorporation 1-888-PAY1040
  (1-888-729-1040) www.PAY1040.com

EXAMPLE 17 CALCULATING QUARTERLY ESTIMATED TAX FOR SELF-EMPLOYED PERSONS

Ben Qualls is a self-employed marketing consultant. His estimated annual earnings this year are $118,000. His social security tax rate is 12.4% up to the wage base, Medicare is 2.9%, and his estimated federal income tax rate is 18%. How much estimated tax must he send to the IRS each quarter?

SOLUTIONSTRATEGY

Note that Ben's salary is above the social security wage base limit.

$$\text{Social security} = 117,000 \times .124 = \$14,508$$
$$\text{Medicare} = 118,000 \times .029 = \$3,422$$
$$\text{Income tax} = 118,000 \times .18 = \$21,240$$

$$\text{Quarterly estimated tax} = \frac{\text{Social security} + \text{Medicare} + \text{Income tax}}{4}$$

$$\text{Quarterly estimated tax} = \frac{14,508.00 + 3,422.00 + 21,240.00}{4} = \frac{39,170}{4} = \underline{\$9,792.50}$$

TRYITEXERCISE 17

Howard Lockwood is a self-employed freelance editor and project director for a large publishing company. His annual salary this year is estimated to be $120,000 with a federal income tax rate of 20%. What is the amount of estimated tax Howard must send to the IRS each quarter?

CHECK YOUR ANSWER WITH THE SOLUTION ON PAGE 296.

SECTION III 9 REVIEW EXERCISES

1. Westside Auto Supply has 8 delivery truck drivers, each with gross earnings of $570 per week.

   a. What are the total social security and Medicare taxes that should be withheld from these employees' paychecks each week?

   570 × 8 = $4,560 Gross earnings per week
   4,560 × .062 = $282.72 Total social security
   4,560 × .0145 = $66.12 Total Medicare

   b. What is the employer's share of these taxes for these employees for the first quarter of the year?

   282.72 × 13 = $3,675.36 Social security for the first quarter
   66.12 × 13 = $859.56 Medicare for the first quarter

2. Fandango Furniture Manufacturing, Inc., has 40 employees on the assembly line, each with gross earnings of $325 per week.

   a. What are the total social security and Medicare taxes that should be withheld from the employees' paychecks each week?

   b. What is the employer's share of these taxes for these employees for the first quarter of the year?

3. Arrow Asphalt & Paving Company has 24 employees, 15 with gross earnings of $345 per week and nine with gross earnings of $385 per week. What is the total social security and Medicare tax the company must send to the Internal Revenue Service for the first quarter of the year?

4. What are the social security and Medicare taxes due on gross earnings of $53,200 per year for Tricia Marvel, a self-employed commercial artist?

$53,200 \times .124 = \underline{\$6,596.80}$ Social security
$53,200 \times .029 = \underline{\$1,542.80}$ Medicare

5. What are the social security and Medicare taxes due on gross earnings of $42,600 per year for a self-employed person?

6. Lee Sutherlin is a self-employed electrical consultant. He estimates his annual net earnings at $38,700. How much social security and Medicare must he pay this year?

7. Barry Michaels earns $36,500 per year as the housewares manager at the Home Design Center.

a. If the SUTA tax rate is 5.4% of the first $7,000 earned each year, how much SUTA tax must the company pay each year for Barry?

$7,000 \times .054 = \underline{\$378}$ SUTA annually

b. If the FUTA tax rate is 6.0% of the first $7,000 earned in a year minus the SUTA tax paid, how much FUTA tax must the company pay each year for Barry?

$7,000 \times .006 = \underline{\$42}$ FUTA tax the company must pay annually

8. Dave O'Bannon earns $41,450 annually as a line supervisor for Redwood Manufacturers.

a. If the SUTA tax rate is 5.4% of the first $7,000 earned in a year, how much SUTA tax must Redwood pay each year for Dave?

b. If the FUTA tax rate is 6.0% of the first $7,000 earned in a year minus the SUTA tax paid, how much FUTA tax must the company pay each year for Dave?

9. Tanya Willis worked part time last year as a cashier in a Safeway Supermarket. Her total gross earnings were $6,440.

a. How much SUTA tax must the supermarket pay to the state for Tanya?

b. How much FUTA tax must be paid for her?

10. Amazon Appliance Company has three installers. Larry earns $355 per week, Curly earns $460 per week, and Moe earns $585 per week. The company's SUTA rate is 5.4%, and the FUTA rate is 6.0% minus the SUTA. As usual, these taxes are paid on the first $7,000 of each employee's earnings.

a. How much SUTA and FUTA tax does Amazon owe for the first quarter of the year?

b. How much SUTA and FUTA tax does Amazon owe for the second quarter of the year?

11. Jiffy Janitorial Service employs 48 workers and has a gross payroll of $25,200 per week. Fringe benefits are 6.4% for sick days and holiday leave, 5.8% for health and hospital insurance, and $14.50 per employee per week for uniform allowance.

a. What is the total weekly cost of fringe benefits for Jiffy?

$$25,200 \times .064 = \$1,612.80$$
$$25,200 \times .058 = 1,461.60$$
$$48 \times 14.50 = \underline{696.00}$$
$$\underline{\$3,770.40}$$

b. What percent of payroll does this represent?

$$R = \frac{P}{B} = \frac{3,770.40}{25,200.00} = .1496 = \underline{\underline{15\%}}$$

c. What is Jiffy's annual cost of fringe benefits?

$$3,770.40 \times 52 = \underline{\underline{\$196,060.80}}\text{ Annual cost of fringe benefits}$$

12. North Beach Limousine Service employs 166 workers and has a gross payroll of $154,330 per week. Fringe benefits are $4\frac{1}{2}\%$ of gross payroll for sick days and maternity leave, 7.4% for health insurance, 3.1% for the retirement fund, and $26.70 per employee per week for a stock purchase plan.

a. What is the total weekly cost of fringe benefits for the company?

b. What percent of payroll does this represent? Round to the nearest tenth of a percent.

c. What is the company's annual cost of fringe benefits?

13. Marc Batchelor, a self-employed sales consultant, has estimated annual earnings of $300,000 this year. His social security tax rate is 12.4% up to the wage base, Medicare is 2.9%, and his federal income tax rate is 24%.

   a. How much estimated tax must Marc send to the IRS each quarter?

   b. What form should he use?

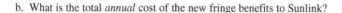

BUSINESS DECISION: NEW FRINGE BENEFITS

14. You are the human resource manager for Sunlink International, a cellular phone company with 800 employees. Top management has asked you to implement three additional fringe benefits that were negotiated with employee representatives and agreed upon by a majority of the employees. These include group term life insurance, a group legal services plan, and a wellness center.

   The life insurance is estimated to cost $260 per employee per quarter. The legal plan will cost $156 semiannually per employee. The company will contribute 40% to the life insurance premium and 75% to the cost of the legal services plan. The employees will pay the balance through payroll deductions from their biweekly paychecks. In addition, they will be charged $\frac{1}{4}$% of their gross earnings per paycheck for maintaining the wellness center. The company will pay the initial cost of $500,000 to build the center. This expense will be spread over 5 years.

   a. What total amount should be deducted *per paycheck* for these new fringe benefits for an employee earning $41,600 per year?

   b. What is the total *annual* cost of the new fringe benefits to Sunlink?

Human resource managers
handle or oversee all aspects of human resources work. Typical areas of responsibility include unemployment compensation, fringe benefits, training, and employee relations. They held about 904,900 jobs in 2008, with median annual earnings of $96,130. The middle 50% earned between $73,480 and $126,050.

CHAPTER 9

CHAPTER FORMULAS

Hourly Wages

Regular pay = Hourly rate × Regular hours worked

Overtime pay = Hourly rate × Overtime factor × Overtime hours worked

Total gross pay = Regular pay + Overtime pay

Piecework

Total gross pay = Output quantity × Rate per unit

Commission

Total gross pay = Total sales × Commission rate

Payroll Deductions

Total deductions = Social security + Medicare + Income tax + Voluntary deductions

Net pay = Gross pay − Total deductions

Fringe Benefits

$$\text{Fringe benefit percent} = \frac{\text{Total fringe benefits}}{\text{Gross payroll}}$$

Quarterly Estimated Tax

$$\text{Quarterly estimated tax} = \frac{\text{Social security} + \text{Medicare} + \text{Income tax}}{4}$$

CHAPTER SUMMARY

Section I: Employee's Gross Earnings and Incentive Pay Plans

Topic	Important Concepts	Illustrative Examples

Prorating Annual Salary to Various Pay Periods
 	
Performance Objective 9-1, Page 263
	Salaried employees are most commonly paid based on one of the following pay schedules:
	
	Weekly: 52 paychecks per year
	
	    Annual salary ÷ 52
	
	Biweekly: 26 paychecks per year
	
	    Annual salary ÷ 26
	
	Semimonthly: 24 paychecks per year
	
	    Annual salary ÷ 24
	
	Monthly: 12 paychecks per year
	
	    Annual salary ÷ 12
		What are the gross earnings of an employee with an annual salary of $40,000 based on weekly, biweekly, semimonthly, and monthly pay schedules?
		
		$\text{Weekly} = \dfrac{40,000}{52} = \$769.233$
		
		$\text{Biweekly} = \dfrac{40,000}{26} = \$1,538.46$
		
		$\text{Semimonthly} = \dfrac{40,000}{24} = \$1,666.67$
		
		$\text{Monthly} = \dfrac{40,000}{12} = \$3,333.33$

Calculating Gross Pay by Regular Hourly Wages and Overtime
 	
Performance Objective 9-2, Page 264
	An hourly wage is the amount an employee is paid for each hour worked.
	
	    Regular time specifies that a standard work week is 40 hours.
	
	    Overtime amounting to at least time-and-a-half must be paid for all hours over 40 hours. Some employers pay double time for weekend, holiday, and midnight shifts.
	
	Regular pay = Hourly rate × Hours worked
	
	Overtime pay = Hourly rate × Overtime factor × Hours worked
	
	Total gross pay = Regular pay + Overtime pay
		Sami Brady earns $9.50 per hour as a supervisor in a plant. If her overtime rate is time-and-a-half and holidays are double time, what is Sami's total gross pay for working 49 hours last week, including 4 holiday hours?
		
		Regular pay = 9.50 × 40 = $380.00
		
		Overtime pay =
		
		    9.50 × 1.5 × 5 = $71.25
		
		Double-time pay = 9.50 × 2 × 4 = $76.00
		
		Total gross pay =
		
		    380.00 + 71.25 + 76.00 = $527.25

Section I (continued)

Topic	Important Concepts	Illustrative Examples
Calculating Gross Pay by Straight and Differential Piecework Schedules **Performance Objective 9-3, Page 265**	A piecework pay rate schedule is based on production output, not time. Straight piecework pays the worker a certain amount of pay per unit regardless of quantity. In differential piecework, the rate per unit increases as output quantity goes up. Total gross pay = Output quantity × Rate per unit	Chemical Labs pays its workers $2.50 per unit of production. What is the gross pay of a worker producing 233 units? Gross pay = 233 × 2.50 = $582.50 Fortune Manufacturing pays its production workers $.54 per unit up to 5,000 units and $.67 per unit above 5,000 units. What is the gross pay of an employee who produces 6,500 units? 5,000 × .54 = 2,700 1,500 × .67 = 1,005 Total gross pay $3,705
Calculating Gross Pay by Straight and Incremental Commission **Performance Objective 9-4, Page 267**	Commission is a method of compensation primarily used to pay employees who sell goods and services. Straight commission is based on a single specified percentage of the sales volume attained. Incremental commission, like differential piecework, is when various levels of sales earn increasing rates of commission. Total gross pay = Total sales × Commission rate	Horizon Products pays 4% straight commission on all sales. What is the gross pay of an employee who sells $135,000? Gross pay = 135,000 × .04 = $5,400 Discovery Imports pays incremental commissions of 3.5% on sales up to $100,000 and 4.5% on all sales greater than $100,000. What is the gross pay of an employee selling $164,000? 100,000 × .035 = 3,500 64,000 × .045 = 2,880 Gross pay $6,380
Calculating Gross Pay by Salary Plus Commission **Performance Objective 9-4, Page 269**	Salary plus commission is a pay schedule whereby the employee receives a guaranteed salary in addition to a commission on sales over a specified amount.	An employee is paid a salary of $350 per week plus a 2% commission on sales greater than $8,000. If he sold $13,400 last week, how much did he earn? 350 + 2%(13,400 − 8,000) 350 + .02 × 5,400 350 + 108 = $458
Calculating Gross Pay with Drawing Accounts **Performance Objective 9-4, Page 269**	A drawing account, or draw against commission, is a commission paid in advance of sales and later deducted from the commission earned.	Steve Korb sells for a company that pays $6\frac{1}{2}\%$ commission with a $600 per month drawing account. If Steve takes the draw and then sells $16,400 in goods, how much commission is he owed? (16,400 × .065) − 600 1,066 − 600 = $466

Section II: Employee's Payroll Deductions

Topic	Important Concepts	Illustrative Examples
Computing FICA Taxes, Both Social Security and Medicare **Performance Objective 9-5, Page 273**	FICA taxes are divided into two categories: social security and Medicare. When employees reach the wage base for the year, they are no longer subject to the tax. <table><tr><td></td><td>**Tax Rate**</td><td>**Wage Base**</td></tr><tr><td>**Social Security**</td><td>6.2%</td><td>$117,000</td></tr><tr><td>**Medicare**</td><td>1.45%</td><td>no limit</td></tr></table>	What are the FICA tax withholdings for social security and Medicare for an employee with gross earnings of $760 per week? Social security = $760 × 6.2% = $47.12 Medicare = $760 × 1.45% = $11.02
Calculating Federal Income Tax Using Percentage Method *(continued)*	1. Multiply one withholding allowance, in Exhibit 9-1, by the number of allowances the employee claims.	Michelle Wolf is single, earns $1,800 per week as a loan officer for Bank of America, and claims three withholding allowances.

Section II (continued)

Topic	Important Concepts	Illustrative Examples
Performance Objective 9-6, Page 275	2. Subtract that amount from the employee's gross earnings to find the income subject to income tax. 3. Determine the amount of tax withheld from the appropriate section of Exhibit 9-2.	Calculate the amount of federal income tax withheld from Michelle's weekly paycheck. From Exhibit 9-1: $76.00 \times 3 = \$228.00$ Taxable income = $1{,}800 - 228.00 = \$1{,}572.00$ From Exhibit 9-2: Withholding tax = $97.75 + 25\%(1{,}572.00 - 753.00)$ $97.75 + .25(819.00)$ $97.75 + 204.75 = \underline{\$302.50}$
Determining an Employee's Total Withholding for Federal Income Tax, Social Security, and Medicare Using the Combined Wage Bracket Tables **Performance Objective 9-7, Page 278**	1. Based on marital status and payroll period, choose either Exhibit 9-3 or 9-4. 2. Scan down the left-hand columns until you find the bracket containing the gross pay of the employee. 3. Scan across the row of that wage bracket to the intersection of that employee's "withholding allowances claimed" column. 4. The number in that column on the wage bracket row is the amount of combined withholding tax.	What amount of combined tax should be withheld from the monthly paycheck of a single employee claiming two withholding allowances and earning $3,495 per month? Use Exhibit 9-4. Scan down the wage brackets to $3,480–$3,520. Scan across to "2" withholding allowances to find the tax, $627.75.

Section III: Employer's Payroll Expenses and Self-Employed Person's Tax Responsibility

Topic	Important Concepts	Illustrative Examples
Computing FICA Tax for Employers **Performance Objective 9-8, Page 283**	Employers are required to match all FICA tax payments made by each employee.	Last month Midland Services withheld a total of $3,400 in FICA taxes from employee paychecks. What is the company's FICA liability? The company is responsible for a matching amount withheld from the employees, $3,400.
Computing Self-Employment Tax **Performance Objective 9-8, Page 284**	Self-employed persons are responsible for social security and Medicare taxes at twice the rate deducted for employees. Technically, they are the employee and the employer; therefore, they must pay both shares, as follows: *Social Security* 12.4% (6.2% × 2), wage base $117,000 *Medicare* 2.9% (1.45% × 2), no limit	What are the social security and Medicare taxes due on gross earnings of $4,260 per month for a self-employed person? *Social security* Gross earnings × 12.4% = $4{,}260 \times .124 = \underline{\$528.24}$ *Medicare* Gross earnings × 2.9% = $4{,}260 \times .029 = \underline{123.54}$
Computing the Amount of State Unemployment Tax (SUTA) and Federal Unemployment Tax (FUTA) **Performance Objective 9-9, Page 285**	SUTA and FUTA taxes provide for unemployment compensation to workers who have lost their jobs. These taxes are paid by the employer. The SUTA tax rate is 5.4% of the first $7,000 of earnings per year by each employee. The FUTA tax rate used in this chapter is 6.0% of the first $7,000 minus the SUTA tax paid (6.0% − 5.4% = 0.6%).	Trans Lux, Inc., had a total payroll of $40,000 last month. If none of the employees has reached the $7,000 wage base, what is the amount of SUTA and FUTA tax due? $\text{SUTA} = 40{,}000 \times 5.4\% = \underline{\$2{,}160}$ $\text{FUTA} = 40{,}000 \times .6\% = \underline{\$240}$

Section III (continued)

Topic	Important Concepts	Illustrative Examples
Calculating Employer's Fringe Benefit Expenses **Performance Objective 9-10, Page 286**	In addition to compensating employees with a paycheck, most companies offer benefit packages that may include pensions, paid sick days, tuition assistance, and health insurance. Fringe benefits represent a significant expense to employers. $$\text{Fringe benefit percent} = \frac{\text{Total fringe benefits}}{\text{Gross payroll}}$$	Linear Industries employs 48 workers and has a monthly gross payroll of \$120,000. In addition, the company pays 6.8% to a pension fund, 8.7% for health insurance, and \$30 per employee for a stock purchase plan. What are Linear's monthly fringe benefit expenses? What percent of payroll does this represent? $120,000 \times 6.8\% = 8,160$ $120,000 \times 8.7\% = 10,440$ $48 \times \$30 = +1,440$ Total fringe benefits $\underline{\$20,040}$ $$\text{Fringe benefit \%} = \frac{20,040}{120,000} = \underline{16.7\%}$$
Calculating Quarterly Estimated Tax for Self-Employed Persons **Performance Objective 9-11, Page 287**	Each quarter self-employed persons must send to the IRS Form 1040-ES along with a tax payment for social security, Medicare, and income tax. Quarterly estimated tax $$= \frac{\text{Social security} + \text{Medicare} + \text{Income tax}}{4}$$	Amanda Turner is a self-employed decorator. She estimates her annual net earnings at \$44,000 for the year. Her income tax rate is 10%. What is the amount of her quarterly estimated tax? $44,000 \times .124 = \$5,456$ Social security $44,000 \times .029 = \$1,276$ Medicare $44,000 \times .10 = \$4,400$ Income tax $$\text{Quarterly estimated tax} = \frac{5,456 + 1,276 + 4,400}{4}$$ $$= \frac{11,132}{4} = \underline{\$2,783}$$

TRY IT: EXERCISE SOLUTIONS FOR CHAPTER 9

1. Weekly pay $= \dfrac{\text{Annual salary}}{50} = \dfrac{43,500}{52} = \underline{\$836.54}$

Biweekly pay $= \dfrac{\text{Annual salary}}{26} = \dfrac{43,500}{26} = \underline{\$1,673.08}$

Semimonthly pay $= \dfrac{\text{Annual salary}}{24} = \dfrac{43,500}{24} = \underline{\$1,812.50}$

Monthly pay $= \dfrac{\text{Annual salary}}{12} = \dfrac{43,500}{12} = \underline{\$3,625.00}$

2. Regular pay = Hourly rate × Regular hours worked
Regular pay = 10.50 × 40 = $\underline{\$420}$

Overtime pay
  = Hourly rate × Overtime factor × Hours worked
Overtime pay = 10.50 × 1.5 × 5 = $\underline{\$78.75}$

Double-time pay
  = Hourly rate × Overtime factor × Hours worked
Double-time pay = 10.50 × 2 × 4 = $\underline{\$84}$

Total gross pay = Regular pay + Overtime pay
Total gross pay = 420.00 + 78.75 + 84.00 = $\underline{\$582.75}$

3. Total gross pay = Output quantity × Rate per unit
Total gross pay = 950 × .41 = $\underline{\$389.50}$

4. Level pay = Output rate per piece
Gomez: 300 × .68 = 204.00
        200 × .79 = 158.00
         15 × .86 = + 12.90
                $\underline{\$374.90}$ Total gross pay

Clifford: 199 × .68 = $\underline{\$135.32}$ Total gross pay

Maken: 300 × .68 = 204.00
         148 × .79 = + 116.92
                 $320.92 Total gross pay

Nathan: 300 × .68 = 204.00
         200 × .79 = 158.00
         250 × .86 = 215.00
          54 × .94 = + 50.76
                 $627.76 Total gross pay

5. Total gross pay = Total sales × Commission rate
Total gross pay = 233,760 × .024 = $\underline{\$5,610.24}$

6. Level pay = Sales per level × Commission rate
Level pay = 100,000 × .017 = $1,700
         84,600 × .025 = + 2,115
                 $\underline{\$3,815}$

7. Commission = Commission rate × Sales subject to commission
Commission = 4%(45,000 − 20,000)
Commission = .04 × 25,000 = $1,000

Total gross pay = Salary + Commission
Total gross pay = 1,400 + 1,000 = $\underline{\$2,400}$

8. Commission = Total sales × Commission rate
Commission = 120,000 × 3.5% = $4,200

Commission owed = Commission − Amount of draw
Commission owed = 4,200 − 2,000 = $\underline{\$2,200}$

9. Social security tax = Gross earnings × 6.2%
    Social security tax = 5,000 × .062 = $310

    Medicare tax = Gross earnings × 1.45%
    Medicare tax = 5,000 × .0145 = $72.50

10. Earnings subject to tax = Wage base − Year-to-date earnings
    Earnings subject to tax = 117,000 − 112,500 = $4,500

    Social security tax = Earnings subject to tax × 6.2%
    Social security tax = 4,500 × .062 = $279.00

11. From Exhibit 9-1
    Withholding allowance = 1 allowance × Exemptions
    Withholding allowance = $329.20 × 5 = $1,646

    Taxable income = Gross pay − Withholding allowance
    Taxable income = 5,670 − 1,646 = $4,024

    From Exhibit 9-2, Table 4(b):
    Category $2,217 to $6,854

    Withholding Tax = 151.30 + 15% of amount greater than $2,217
    Withholding Tax = 151.30 + .15(4,024 − 2,217)
    Withholding Tax = 151.30 + .15(1,807)
    Withholding Tax = 151.30 + 271.05 = $422.35

12. From Exhibit 9-3
    $835 Weekly, married, 2 allowances = $124.88

13. *12 employees @ $350*

    Social security = 350 × .062 = $21.70
    Medicare = 350 × .0145 = $5.08

    Total FICA per employee = 21.70 + 5.08 = $26.78
    Total FICA per week = 26.78 × 12 employees = $321.36
    Total FICA per quarter = 321.36 × 13 weeks = $4,177.68

    6 employees @ $425

    Social security = 425 × .062 = $26.35
    Medicare = 425 × .0145 = $6.16

    Total FICA per employee = 26.35 + 6.16 = $32.51
    Total FICA per week = 32.51 × 6 employees = $195.06
    Total FICA per quarter = 195.06 × 13 weeks = $2,535.78

Total FICA per quarter:
    Employees' share = 4,177.68 + 2,535.78 = $6,713.46
    Employer's share = 4,177.68 + 2,535.78 = $6,713.46

14. Social security = 60,000 × .124 = $7,440
    Medicare = 60,000 × .029 = $1,740

15. SUTA tax = Gross earnings × 5.4%
    SUTA tax = 10,000 × .054 = $540

    FUTA tax = Gross earnings × .6%
    FUTA tax = 10,000 × .006 = $60

16. a. Fringe benefits
        Sick days = Gross payroll × 5%
        Sick days = 123,400 × .05 = $6,170

        Health insurance = Gross payroll × 8%
        Health insurance = 123,400 × .08 = $9,872

        Dental insurance = Number of employees × 12.40
        Dental insurance = 250 × 12.40 = $3,100

        Total fringe benefits = 6,170 + 9,872 + 3,100 = $19,142

    b. Fringe benefit percent = $\dfrac{\text{Total fringe benefit}}{\text{Gross payroll}}$

        Fringe benefit percent = $\dfrac{19,142}{123,400}$ = .155 = 15.5%

    c. Yearly fringe benefits = Weekly total × 52
        Yearly fringe benefits = 19,142 × 52 = $995,384

17. Social security = 117,000 × .124 = $14,508
    Medicare = 120,000 × .029 = $3,480.00
    Income tax = 120,000 × .2 = $24,000.00

    Quarterly estimated tax = $\dfrac{\text{Social security} + \text{Medicare} + \text{Income tax}}{4}$

    Quarterly estimated tax = $\dfrac{14,508.00 + 3,480.00 + 24,000.00}{4}$

    $= \dfrac{41,988}{4} = \$10,497$

CONCEPT REVIEW

1. Gross pay is the amount of earnings before payroll _____ are withheld; net pay is the actual amount of the _____. (9.1)

2. Annual salaries are commonly prorated to be paid weekly, biweekly, _____, and _____. (9-1)

3. Total gross pay includes regular pay and _____ pay, which according to federal law is for hours worked over _____ hours per week. (9-2)

4. When employees are paid on their production output, not hours worked, this is called _____. (9-3)

5. To calculate total gross pay for an employee paid on commission, we multiply the total _____ by the commission rate. (9-4)

6. A draw against commission is commission paid in _____ of sales and later _____ from the commission earned. (9-4)

7. The current employee tax rate for social security is _____ percent of gross earnings; the current tax rate for Medicare is _____ percent of gross earnings. (9-5)

8. The wage base limit for social security used in this chapter is _____. (9-5)

9. In addition to social security and Medicare tax withholdings, an employer is also responsible, by federal law, for withholding an appropriate amount of federal _____ tax from each employee's paycheck. (9-6)

10. The combined wage bracket table is based on the _____ status of the employee and the _____ period used. The columns list the combined taxes to be withheld based on the number of withholding _____ claimed. (9-7)

11. Self-employed persons are responsible for social security and Medicare taxes at _____ the rate deducted for employees. This amounts to _____ percent for social security and _____ percent for Medicare. (9-8)

12. For companies with full and timely payments to the state unemployment system, the SUTA tax rate is _____ percent of gross earnings and the FUTA tax rate is _____ percent of gross earnings. (9-9)

13. A plan whereby employees are given a menu of fringe benefits from which to choose is known as the _____ style or _____ benefit program. (9-10)

14. Write the formula for quarterly estimated tax for self-employed persons. (9-11)

ASSESSMENT TEST

1. Bill Pearson earns $2,800 semimonthly as a congressional aide for a senator in the state legislature.

    a. How much are his annual gross earnings?

    b. If the senator switches pay schedules from semimonthly to biweekly, what will Bill's new gross earnings be per payroll period?

2. Barbara Sultan works 40 hours per week as a registered nurse. At the rate of $31.50 per hour, what are her gross weekly earnings?

3. Eric Shotwell's company pays him $18.92 per hour for regular time up to 40 hours and time-and-a-half for overtime. His time card for Monday through Friday last week had 8.3, 8.8, 7.9, 9.4, and 10.6 hours. What was Eric's total gross pay?

4. Mitch Anderson is a security guard. He earns $7.45 per hour for regular time up to 40 hours, time-and-a-half for overtime, and double time for the midnight shift. If Mitch worked 56 hours last week, including 4 hours on the midnight shift, how much were his gross earnings?

© StockLite/Shutterstock.com

5. Fergie Nelson assembles toasters for the Gold Coast Corporation. She is paid on a differential piecework rate of $2.70 per toaster for the first 160 toasters and $3.25 for each toaster over 160. If she assembled 229 units last week, how much were her gross earnings?

EXCEL 2

Registered nurses (RNs) treat patients, educate patients and the public about various medical conditions, and provide advice and emotional support to patients' family members. RNs record patients' medical histories and symptoms, help perform diagnostic tests and analyze results, operate medical machinery, administer treatment and medications, and help with patient follow-up and rehabilitation.

    Overall job opportunities for registered nurses are excellent. Employment of registered nurses is expected to grow by 22% from 2008 to 2018, much faster than the average for all other occupations.

6. You work in the payroll department of Universal Manufacturing. The following piece rate schedule is used for computing earnings for assembly line workers. As an overtime bonus, on Saturdays, each unit produced counts as $1\frac{1}{2}$ units.

1–100	$2.30
101–150	2.60
151–200	2.80
over 200	3.20

CHAPTER
9

Calculate the gross earnings for the following Universal Manufacturing employees.

	Employee	Mon.	Tues.	Wed.	Thurs.	Fri.	Sat.	Total Units	Gross Earnings
a.	Shane	0	32	16	36	27	12	_____	_____
b.	Gonzales	18	26	24	10	13	0	_____	_____
c.	Bethards	26	42	49	51	34	20	_____	_____

7. Kate Fitzgerald's company pays differential piecework for electronic product manufacturing. Production pay rates for a particular circuit board assembly and soldering are $18.20 per board for the first 14 boards, $19.55 each for boards 15–30, $20.05 each for boards 31–45, and $20.48 each for boards 46 and up. If Kate assembled and soldered 52 boards last week, what was her total gross pay?

8. Foremost Fish Market pays a straight commission of 18% on gross sales, divided equally among the three employees working the counter. If Foremost sold $22,350 in seafood last week, how much was each counter employee's total gross pay?

9. Bryan Vincent booked $431,000 in new sales last month. Commission rates are 1% for the first $150,000, 1.8% for the next $200,000, and 2.3% for amounts over $350,000. What was Bryan's total gross pay?

10. Spencer Morris works in the telemarketing division for a company that pays a salary of $735 per month plus a commission of $3\frac{1}{2}\%$ of all sales greater than $15,500. If he sold $45,900 last month, what was his total gross pay?

11. Bonnie Woodruff is on a 2.1% straight commission with a $700 drawing account. If she is paid the draw at the beginning of the month and then sells $142,100 during the month, how much commission is owed to Bonnie?

12. Arturo Muina is the captain on a charter fishing boat. He is paid a salary of $140 per day. He also averages tips amounting to 12% of the $475 daily charter rate. Last month during a fishing tournament, Arturo worked 22 days. What were his total gross earnings for the month?

Regardless of what they sell, **telemarketers** are responsible for initiating telephone sales calls to potential clients, using a prepared selling script. They are usually paid on a commission based on the amount of their sales volume or number of new "leads" they generate.

CHAPTER
9

Solve the following problems using 6.2% up to $117,000 for social security withholding and 1.45% for Medicare.

13. What are the withholdings for social security and Medicare for an employee with gross earnings of $725 per week?

14. Dan Dietrich is an executive with Coronado Distributors. His gross earnings are $17,300 per month.

    a. What are the withholdings for social security and Medicare for Dan's January paycheck?

    b. In what month will his salary reach the social security wage base limit?

    c. What are the social security and Medicare tax withholdings for Dan in the month named in part b?

Use the *percentage method* to solve the following.

15. Larry Alison is single, claims one withholding allowance, and earns $2,450 per month.

    a. What is the amount of Larry's paycheck after his employer withholds social security, Medicare, and income tax?

    b. If Larry gets married and changes to two withholding allowances, what will be the new amount of his paycheck?

    c. If he then gets a 15% raise, what is the new amount of his paycheck?

IN THE
Business world

Consider the tax implications of a pay raise. In part c, Larry got a 15% raise, but his total deductions increased by 21.9%! His net pay raise, after taxes, was 14.1%

Use the *combined wage bracket tables*, Exhibits 9-3 and 9-4, for Exercises 16 and 17.

16. How much combined tax should be withheld from the paycheck of a married employee earning $910 per week and claiming three withholding allowances?

17. How much combined tax should be withheld from the paycheck of a single employee earning $4,458 per month and claiming zero withholding allowances?

18. Fran Mallory is married, claims five withholding allowances, and earns $3,500 per month. In addition to social security, Medicare, and FIT, Fran pays 2.1% state income tax, $\frac{1}{2}$% for state disability insurance (both based on gross income), $43.11 for life insurance, and $72.30 to the credit union. As payroll manager for Fran's company, calculate her net take-home pay per month.

19. Vanguard Fabricators has 83 employees on the assembly line, each with gross earnings of $329 per week.

    a. What are the total social security and Medicare taxes that should be withheld from the employee paychecks each week?

    b. At the end of the first quarter (13 weeks), what are the accumulated totals of the employee's share and the *matching* taxes for FICA that Vanguard had sent to the IRS?

20. Paul Warren is a self-employed mechanic. Last year he had total gross earnings of $44,260. What are Paul's quarterly social security and Medicare payments due to the IRS?

21. Tim Ries earns $48,320 annually as a supervisor for the Lakeside Bank.

    a. If the SUTA tax rate is 5.4% of the first $7,000 earned in a year, how much SUTA tax must the bank pay each year for Tim?

    b. If the FUTA tax rate is 6.0% of the first $7,000 earned in a year minus the SUTA tax paid, how much FUTA tax must the bank pay each year for Tim?

22. Universal Exporting has three warehouse employees: John Abner earns $422 per week, Anne Clark earns $510 per week, and Todd Corbin earns $695 per week. The company's SUTA tax rate is 5.4%, and the FUTA rate is 6.0% minus the SUTA. As usual, these taxes are paid on the first $7,000 of each employee's earnings.

    a. How much SUTA and FUTA tax did the company pay for these employees in the first quarter of the year?

    b. How much SUTA and FUTA tax did Universal pay in the second quarter of the year?

23. Sky High Crane Company employs 150 workers and has a gross payroll of $282,100 per week. Fringe benefits are $6\frac{1}{2}\%$ of gross payroll for sick days and holiday leave, 9.1% for health and hospital insurance, 4.6% for the retirement fund, and $10.70 per employee per week for a stock purchase plan.

    a. What is the total weekly cost of fringe benefits for the company?

    b. What percent of payroll does this represent?

    c. What is the company's annual cost of fringe benefits?

24. Ransford Alda is a self-employed security consultant with estimated annual earnings of $90,000. His social security tax rate is 12.4%, Medicare is 2.9%, and his federal income tax rate is 14%.

    a. How much estimated tax must Ransford send to the IRS each quarter?

    b. What form should he use?

BUSINESS DECISION: THE BRIDE, THE GROOM, AND THE TAX MAN

25. Two of your friends, Chuck and Joan, have been dating for a year. Chuck earns $3,000 per month as the manager of an Aeropostale store. Joan is a sophomore in college and is not currently working. They plan to marry but cannot decide whether to get married now or wait a year or two.

    After studying the payroll chapter in your business math class, you inform Chuck that married couples generally pay less income taxes and that if they got married now instead of waiting, he would have less income tax withheld from his paychecks. Chuck's current tax filing status is single, one exemption. If he and Joan got married, he could file as married, two exemptions. Use the percentage method and Exhibits 9-1 and 9-2 to calculate the following:

    a. How much income tax is withheld from Chuck's paycheck each month now?

    b. How much income tax would be withheld from Chuck's check if he and Joan got married?

c. Assuming Joan has three more years of full-time college before going to work and Chuck expects a 10% raise in one year and a 15% raise the year after, what is the total three-year tax advantage of their getting married now?

COLLABORATIVE LEARNING ACTIVITY

Researching the Job Market

1. As a team, collect "Help Wanted" ads from the classified section of your local newspaper. (Note: Weekend editions are usually the most comprehensive.) Find examples of various jobs that are paid by salary, hourly rate, piece rate, and commission. Answer the following for similar jobs.

   a. How much do they pay?

   b. What pay periods are used?

   c. What fringe benefits are being offered?

2. As a team, research the Internet or library for the following payroll information. Present your findings to the class. List your sources for the answers.

   a. Starting salaries of employees in various industries and in government occupations.

   b. Personal and household income by area of the country or by state. How does your area or state compare?

   c. Starting salaries by amount of education for various professions.

Business Math JOURNAL

BUSINESS, MATH, AND MORE ...

The Alphabet of Internet Commerce

E-Commerce

Electronic commerce, commonly known as e-commerce or e-business, consists of the buying and selling of products and services over the Internet. Electronic commerce that is conducted between businesses is referred to as business-to-business, or B2B. Electronic commerce that is conducted between businesses and consumers, on the other hand, is referred to as business-to-consumer, or B2C.

Online retailers are sometimes known as e-tailers, and online retail is referred to as e-tail. Today most big retailers have an electronic commerce presence on the Internet.

According to Forrester Research,

Estimates of the number of people in the United States making purchases online:

- 167 million—more than half the population—in 2011
- 192 million in 2016
- Estimates of average yearly online spending:
- $1,207 in 2011
- $1,738 in 2016

U.S. Online Retail Sales Estimates ($ billions)

	2009	2010	2011	2012	2013	2014
	$155.2	$172.9	$191.7	$210.0	$229.8	$248.7
% of total U.S. retail sales	6%	7%	7%	7%	8%	8%

Source: Forrester Research

You'll see, Chet; sales will pick up as soon as this whole Internet fad blows over.

© original artist Reproduction rights obtainable from www.CartoonStock.com

M-Commerce

Mobile commerce, also known as m-commerce, is the ability to conduct commerce using a mobile device, such as a mobile phone, a personal digital assistant (PDA), or a smartphone.

Mobile commerce began in 1997 when the first two mobile-phone-enabled Coca Cola vending machines were installed in the Helsinki area in Finland. The machines accepted payment via SMS text messages. The first banking service based on mobile phones was launched in 1997 by Merita Bank of Finland, also using SMS.

Sources: www.wikipedia.org; www.internetretailer.com, Paul Demery, "Big Retailers See Big Impact of Mobile on Web and Store Sales," Oct. 10, 2010.

Estimated Annual Mobile Visits to the Top 500 Mobile Commerce Sites

Year	Visits (billions)
2010	1.3
2011	5.0
2012	10.1
2013	17.6
2014	26.4
2015	33.0

Source: Internet Retailer, www.internetretailer.com, Bill Siwicki, April 21, 2012

Issues & Activities

1. Use the chart at the left to respond to the following:
   a. Calculate the percent increase in sales from year to year to determine which year is estimated to have the greatest increase.
   b. In 2014, online retail sales of $248.7 billion have been estimated to represent 8% of total retail sales. Using these figures, calculate the estimated total retail sales in 2014.
2. Use the table above to find the estimated percent age increase from 2010 to 2015.
3. In teams, research the Internet to find current trends in "Internet Commerce" statistics. List your sources and visually report your findings to the class.

Brainteaser—"Work, Don't Work"

You have agreed to work under the conditions that you are to be paid $55 for every day you work and you must pay back $66 for every day you don't work. If after 30 days you have earned $924, how many days did you work?

See the end of Appendix A for the solution.

Simple Interest and Promissory Notes

PERFORMANCE OBJECTIVES

UNDERSTANDING AND COMPUTING SIMPLE INTEREST

10   SECTION I

The practice of borrowing and lending money dates back in history for thousands of years. Today institutions such as banks, savings and loans, and credit unions are specifically in business to borrow and lend money. They constitute a significant portion of the service sector of the American economy.

Interest is the rental fee charged by a lender to a business or an individual for the use of money. The amount of interest charged is determined by three factors: the amount of money being borrowed or invested, known as the **principal**; the percent of interest charged on the money per year, known as the **rate**; and the length of time of the loan, known as **time**. The manner in which the interest is computed is an additional factor that influences the amount of interest. The two most commonly used methods in business today for computing interest are simple and compound.

Simple interest means that the interest is calculated *only once* for the entire time period of the loan. At the end of the time period, the borrower repays the principal plus the interest. Simple interest loans are usually made for short periods of time, such as a few days, weeks, or months. **Compound interest** means that the interest is calculated *more than once* during the time period of the loan. When compound interest is applied to a loan, each succeeding time period accumulates interest on the previous interest in addition to interest on the principal. Compound interest loans are generally for time periods of a year or longer.

This chapter discusses the concepts of simple interest; simple discount, which is a variation of a simple interest loan; and promissory notes. Chapter 11 covers the concepts and calculations related to compound interest and present value.

interest The price or rental fee charged by a lender to a borrower for the use of money.

principal A sum of money, either invested or borrowed, on which interest is calculated.

rate The percent that is charged or earned for the use of money per year.

time Length of time, expressed in days, months, or years, of an investment or loan.

simple interest Interest calculated solely on the principal amount borrowed or invested. It is calculated only once for the entire time period of the loan.

compound interest Interest calculated at regular intervals on the principal and previously earned interest. Covered in Chapter 11.

COMPUTING SIMPLE INTEREST FOR LOANS WITH TERMS OF YEARS OR MONTHS

10-1

Simple interest is calculated by using a formula known as the simple interest formula. It is stated as follows:

$$\text{Interest} = \text{Principal} \times \text{Rate} \times \text{Time}$$
$$I = PRT$$

When using the simple interest formula, the time factor, T, must be expressed in years or a fraction of a year.

SIMPLE INTEREST FORMULA—YEARS OR MONTHS

Years

When the time period of a loan is a year or longer, use the number of years as the time factor, converting fractional parts to decimals. For example, the time factor for a 2-year loan is 2, 3 years is 3, $1\frac{1}{2}$ years is 1.5, $4\frac{3}{4}$ years is 4.75, and so on.

Months

When the time period of a loan is for a specified number of months, express the time factor as a fraction of a year. The number of months is the numerator, and 12 months (1 year) is the denominator. A loan for 1 month would have a time factor of $\frac{1}{12}$; a loan for 2 months would have a factor of $\frac{2}{12}$, or $\frac{1}{6}$; a 5-month loan would use $\frac{5}{12}$ as the factor; a loan for 18 months would use $\frac{18}{12}$, or $1\frac{1}{2}$, written as 1.5.

Banking institutions all over the world are in business specifically to borrow and lend money at a profitable rate of interest.

DBImages/Alamy

EXAMPLE1 CALCULATING SIMPLE INTEREST

a. What is the amount of interest for a loan of $8,000 at 9% interest for 1 year?

►SOLUTIONSTRATEGY

To solve this problem, we apply the simple interest formula:

$$\text{Interest} = \text{Principal} \times \text{Rate} \times \text{Time}$$
$$\text{Interest} = 8{,}000 \times 9\% \times 1$$
$$\text{Interest} = 8{,}000 \times .09 \times 1$$
$$\text{Interest} = \underline{\$720}$$

b. What is the amount of interest for a loan of $16,500 at $12\frac{1}{2}\%$ interest for 7 months?

►SOLUTIONSTRATEGY

In this example, the rate is converted to .125 and the time factor is expressed as a fraction of a year, $\frac{7}{12}$.

$$\text{Interest} = \text{Principal} \times \text{Rate} \times \text{Time}$$
$$\text{Interest} = 16{,}500 \times .125 \times \frac{7}{12}$$
$$\text{Interest} = \underline{\$1{,}203.13}$$

Calculator Sequence: 16500 ⊠ .125 ⊠ 7 ⊡ 12 ▣ $1,203.13

►TRYITEXERCISE 1

Find the amount of interest on each of the following loans.

	Principal	Rate	Time
a.	$4,000	7%	$2\frac{1}{4}$ years
b.	$45,000	$9\frac{3}{4}\%$	3 months
c.	$130,000	10.4%	42 months

CHECK YOUR ANSWERS WITH THE SOLUTIONS ON PAGE 334.

10-2 CALCULATING SIMPLE INTEREST FOR LOANS WITH TERMS OF DAYS BY USING THE EXACT INTEREST AND ORDINARY INTEREST METHODS

There are two methods for calculating the time factor, T, when applying the simple interest formula using days. Because time must be expressed in years, loans whose terms are given in days must be made into a fractional part of a year. This is done by dividing the days of a loan by the number of days in a year.

SIMPLE INTEREST FORMULA—DAYS

Exact Interest

exact interest Interest calculation method using 365 days (366 in leap year) as the time factor denominator.

The first method for calculating the time factor is known as **exact interest**. Exact interest uses *365 days* as the time factor denominator. This method is used by government agencies, the Federal Reserve Bank, and most credit unions.

$$\text{Time} = \frac{\textbf{Number of days of a loan}}{365}$$

Ordinary Interest

The second method for calculating the time factor is known as **ordinary interest**. Ordinary interest uses *360 days* as the denominator of the time factor. This method dates back to the time before electronic calculators and computers. In the past, when calculating the time factor manually, a denominator of 360 was easier to use than 365.

Regardless of today's electronic sophistication, banks and most other lending institutions still use ordinary interest because it yields a somewhat higher amount of interest than does the exact interest method. Over the years, ordinary interest has become known as the **banker's rule**.

ordinary interest or **banker's rule**
Interest calculation method using 360 days as the time factor denominator.

$$\text{Time} = \frac{\text{Number of days of a loan}}{360}$$

EXAMPLE2 CALCULATING EXACT INTEREST

Using the exact interest method, what is the amount of interest on a loan of $4,000 at 7% interest for 88 days?

►SOLUTIONSTRATEGY

Because we are looking for exact interest, we will use 365 days as the denominator of the time factor in the simple interest formula:

$$\text{Interest} = \text{Principal} \times \text{Rate} \times \text{Time}$$

$$\text{Interest} = 4,000 \times .07 \times \frac{88}{365}$$

$$\text{Interest} = 67.506849$$

$$\text{Interest} = \underline{\$67.51}$$

Calculator Sequence: 4000 ☒ .07 ☒ 88 ÷ 365 ＝ $67.51

►TRYITEXERCISE 2

Joe Hale goes to a credit union and borrows $23,000 at 8% for 119 days. If the credit union calculates interest by the exact interest method, what is the amount of interest on the loan?

CHECK YOUR ANSWER WITH THE SOLUTION ON PAGE 334.

EXAMPLE3 CALCULATING ORDINARY INTEREST

Using the ordinary interest method, what is the amount of interest on a loan of $19,500 at 6% interest for 160 days?

►SOLUTIONSTRATEGY

Because we are looking for ordinary interest, we will use 360 days as the denominator of the time factor in the simple interest formula:

$$\text{Interest} = \text{Principal} \times \text{Rate} \times \text{Time}$$

$$\text{Interest} = 19,500 \times .06 \times \frac{160}{360}$$

$$\text{Interest} = \underline{\$520}$$

Calculator Sequence: 19500 ☒ .06 ☒ 160 ÷ 360 ＝ $520

►TRYITEXERCISE 3

Karen Mitroff goes to the bank and borrows $15,000 at $9\frac{1}{2}$% for 250 days. If the bank uses the ordinary interest method, how much interest will Karen have to pay?

CHECK YOUR ANSWER WITH THE SOLUTION ON PAGE 334.

10-3 CALCULATING THE MATURITY VALUE OF A LOAN

maturity value The total payback of principal and interest of an investment or a loan.

Learning Tip

When using the maturity value formula, $MV = P(1 + RT)$, the order of operation is
- Multiply Rate by Time
- Add the 1
- Multiply by the Principal

When the time period of a loan is over, the loan is said to mature. At that time, the borrower repays the original principal plus the interest. The total payback of principal and interest is known as the **maturity value** of a loan. Once the interest has been calculated, the maturity value can be found by using the following formula:

$$\text{Maturity value} = \text{Principal} + \text{Interest}$$
$$MV = P + I$$

For example, if a loan for $50,000 had interest of $8,600, the maturity value would be found by adding the principal and the interest: $50,000 + 8,600 = \$58,600$.

Maturity value can also be calculated directly without first calculating the interest by using the following formula:

$$\text{Maturity value} = \text{Principal} (1 + \text{Rate} \times \text{Time})$$
$$MV = P (1 + RT)$$

EXAMPLE4   CALCULATING MATURITY VALUE

What is the maturity value of a loan for $25,000 at 11% for $2\frac{1}{2}$ years?

SOLUTIONSTRATEGY

Because this example asks for the maturity value, not the amount of interest, we will use the formula for finding maturity value directly, $MV = P (1 + RT)$. Remember to multiply the rate and time first, then add the 1. Note that the time, $2\frac{1}{2}$ years, should be converted to the decimal equivalent 2.5 for ease in calculation.

$$\begin{aligned}
\text{Maturity value} &= \text{Principal} (1 + \text{Rate} \times \text{Time}) \\
\text{Maturity value} &= 25{,}000 (1 + .11 \times 2.5) \\
\text{Maturity value} &= 25{,}000 (1 + .275) \\
\text{Maturity value} &= 25{,}000 (1.275) \\
\text{Maturity value} &= \underline{\$31{,}875}
\end{aligned}$$

TRYITEXERCISE 4

a. What is the amount of interest and the maturity value of a loan for $15,400 at $6\frac{1}{2}$% simple interest for 24 months? (Use the formula $MV = P + I$.)

b. Apollo Air Taxi Service borrowed $450,000 at 8% simple interest for 9 months to purchase a new airplane. Use the formula $MV = P (1 + RT)$ to find the maturity value of the loan.

CHECK YOUR ANSWERS WITH THE SOLUTIONS ON PAGE 334.

CALCULATING THE NUMBER OF DAYS OF A LOAN

10-4

The first day of a loan is known as the **loan date**, and the last day is known as the **due date** or **maturity date**. When these dates are known, the number of days of the loan can be calculated by using the "Days in Each Month" chart and the steps that follow.

loan date The first day of a loan.

due date or **maturity date** The last day of a loan.

Days in Each Month

28 Days	30 Days	31 Days
February	April	January
(29 leap year)	June	March
	September	May
	November	July
		August
		October
		December

STEPS FOR DETERMINING THE NUMBER OF DAYS OF A LOAN

STEP 1. Determine the number of days remaining in the first month by subtracting the loan date from the number of days in that month.

STEP 2. List the number of days for each succeeding whole month.

STEP 3. List the number of loan days in the last month.

STEP 4. Add the days from Steps 1, 2, and 3.

EXAMPLE5   CALCULATING DAYS OF A LOAN

Kevin Krease borrowed money from the Charter Bank on August 18 and repaid the loan on November 27. What was the number of days of the loan?

SOLUTIONSTRATEGY

The number of days from August 18 to November 27 would be calculated as follows:

Step 1.	Days remaining in first month	Aug. 31		
		Aug. −18		
		13 ——→ August	13 days
Step 2.	Days in succeeding whole months ——→ September		30 days
	——→ October		31 days
Step 3.	Days of loan in last month ————→ November		+ 27 days
Step 4.	Add the days		Total 101 days

Learning Tip

An alternative method for calculating the number of days of a loan is to use the Days-in-a-Year Calendar, Exhibit 7-6, page 213.

- Subtract the "day number" of the loan date from the "day number" of the maturity date.
- If the maturity date is in the next year, add 365 to that day number, then subtract. *Note:* In leap years, add 1 to the day numbers beginning with March 1.

TRYITEXERCISE 5

a. A loan was made on April 4 and had a due date of July 18. What was the number of days of the loan?

b. Ryan McPherson borrowed $3,500 on June 15 at 11% interest. If the loan was due on October 9, what was the amount of interest on Ryan's loan using the exact interest method?

CHECK YOUR ANSWERS WITH THE SOLUTIONS ON PAGE 334.

10-5 DETERMINING THE MATURITY DATE OF A LOAN

When the loan date and number of days of the loan are known, the maturity date can be found as follows:

STEPS FOR DETERMINING THE MATURITY DATE OF A LOAN

STEP 1. Find the number of days remaining in the first month by subtracting the loan date from the number of days in that month.

STEP 2. Subtract the days remaining in the first month (Step 1) from the number of days of the loan.

STEP 3. Continue subtracting days in each succeeding whole month until you reach a month with a difference less than the total days in that month. At that point, the maturity date will be the day that corresponds to the difference.

EXAMPLE6 DETERMINING MATURITY DATE OF A LOAN

What is the maturity date of a loan taken out on April 14 for 85 days?

SOLUTIONSTRATEGY

Step 1. Days remaining in first month

           30 Days in April
        −14 Loan date April 14
      Days remaining in April   16

Step 2. Subtract remaining days in first month from days of the loan

      85 Days of the loan
   −16 Days remaining in April
     Difference   69

Step 3. Subtract succeeding whole months

      69 Difference
  −31 Days in May
    Difference   38

      38 Difference
  −30 Days in June
    Difference   8

At this point, the difference, 8, is less than the number of days in the next month, July; therefore, the maturity date is July 8.

TRYITEXERCISE 6

a. What is the maturity date of a loan taken out on September 9 for 125 days?

b. On October 21, Jill Voorhis went to the Regal National Bank and took out a loan for $9,000 at 10% ordinary interest for 80 days. What is the maturity value and maturity date of this loan?

CHECK YOUR ANSWERS WITH THE SOLUTIONS ON PAGE 334.

SECTION I 10 REVIEW EXERCISES

Find the amount of interest on each of the following loans.

	Principal	Rate (%)	Time	Interest
1.	$5,000	8	2 years	$800.00
2.	$60,000	$6\frac{3}{4}$	9 months	_____
3.	$100,000	5.5	18 months	_____

Principal	Rate (%)	Time	Interest
4. $80,000	6	$3\frac{1}{2}$ years	_____
5. $6,440	$5\frac{1}{2}$	7 months	_____
6. $13,200	9.2	$4\frac{3}{4}$ years	_____

Use the exact interest method (365 days) and the ordinary interest method (360 days) to compare the amount of interest for the following loans.

Principal	Rate (%)	Time (days)	Exact Interest	Ordinary Interest
7. $45,000	13	100	$1,602.74	$1,625.00
8. $184,500	7.75	58	_____	_____
9. $32,400	8.6	241	_____	_____
10. $7,230	9	18	_____	_____
11. $900	$10\frac{1}{4}$	60	_____	_____
12. $100,000	10	1	_____	_____
13. $2,500	6	74	_____	_____
14. $350	14.1	230	_____	_____
15. $50,490	$9\frac{1}{4}$	69	_____	_____
16. $486,000	$13\frac{1}{2}$	127	_____	_____

Find the amount of interest and the maturity value of the following loans. Use the formula $MV = P + I$ to find the maturity values.

Principal	Rate (%)	Time	Interest	Maturity Value
17. $54,000	11.9	2 years	$12,852.00	$66,852.00
18. $125,000	$12\frac{1}{2}$	5 months	_____	_____
19. $33,750	8.4	10 months	_____	_____
20. $91,000	$9\frac{1}{4}$	$2\frac{1}{2}$ years	_____	_____
21. $56,200	10.2	4 years	_____	_____
22. $135,000	7.7	18 months	_____	_____

Find the maturity value of the following loans. Use $MV = P(1 + RT)$ to find the maturity values.

Principal	Rate (%)	Time	Maturity Value
23. $1,500	9	2 years	$1,770.00
24. $18,620	$10\frac{1}{2}$	30 months	_____
25. $1,000,000	11	3 years	_____
26. $750,000	13.35	11 months	_____
27. $128,400	8.3	2.5 years	_____
28. $5,200	7.4	16 months	_____

From the following information, determine the number of days of each loan.

	Loan Date	Due Date	Number of Days
29.	September 5	December 12	98
30.	June 27	October 15	_____
31.	January 23	November 8	_____
32.	March 9	July 30	_____
33.	August 2	September 18	_____
34.	November 18	March 2	_____

From the following information, determine the maturity date of each loan.

JUMP START WWW

	Loan Date	Time of Loan (days)	Maturity Date
35.	October 19	45	December 3
36.	February 5	110	_____
37.	May 26	29	_____
38.	July 21	200	_____
39.	December 6	79	_____
40.	January 13	87	_____
41.	April 27	158	_____

Solve the following word problems. Round to the nearest cent when necessary.

42. On April 12, Michelle Lizaro borrowed $5,000 from her credit union at 9% for 80 days. The credit union uses the ordinary interest method.

    a.   What is the amount of interest on the loan?

    b.   What is the maturity value of the loan?

    c.   What is the maturity date of the loan?

Credit unions differ from banks and other financial institutions in that the members who are account holders are the owners of the credit union. Credit unions serve groups that share something in common, such as where they work or where they live. The largest credit union in the United States is Navy Federal Credit Union in Vienna, Virginia, with $36.4 billion in assets and 3.2 million members.

43. What is the maturity value of a $60,000 loan for 100 days at 6.1% interest using the exact interest method?

EXCEL 2

44. Central Auto Parts borrowed $350,000 at 9% interest on July 19 for 120 days.

    a.   If the bank uses the ordinary interest method, what is the amount of interest on the loan?

    b.   What is the maturity date?

45. Emil Benson missed an income tax payment of $9,000. The Internal Revenue Service charges a 13% simple interest penalty calculated by the exact interest method. If the tax was due on April 15 but was paid on August 19, what was the amount of the penalty charge?

46. At the City National Credit Union, a 7%, $8,000 loan for 180 days had interest charges of $276.16. What type of interest did City National use, ordinary or exact?

47. Kyle Rohrs borrowed $1,080 on June 16 at 9.2% exact interest from the Wells Fargo Bank. On August 10, Kyle repaid the loan. How much interest did he pay?

BUSINESS DECISION: COMPETING BANKS

EXCEL 3

48. You are the accounting manager for Kool Ragz, Inc., a manufacturer of men's and women's clothing. The company needs to borrow $1,800,000 for 90 days in order to purchase a large quantity of material at "closeout" prices. The interest rate for such loans at your bank, Rimrock Bank, is 11% using ordinary interest.

   a. What is the amount of interest on this loan?

   b. After making a few "shopping" calls, you find that Southside National Bank will lend at 11% using exact interest. What is the amount of interest on this offer?

   c. So that you can keep your business, Rimrock Bank has offered a loan at 10.5% using ordinary interest. What is the amount of interest on this offer?

   d. (Challenge) If Southside National wants to beat Rimrock's last offer (part c) by charging $1,250 less interest, what rate, rounded to the nearest hundredths of a percent, must it quote using exact interest?

There are approximately 7,000 commercial banks in the United States. Roughly 25% of these banks have assets in excess of $300 million.

USING THE SIMPLE INTEREST FORMULA

10

SECTION II

In Section I, we used the simple interest formula, $I = PRT$, to solve for the interest. Frequently in business, however, the principal, rate, or time might be the unknown factor. Remember from Chapter 5 that an equation can be solved for any of the variables by isolating that variable to one side of the equation. In this section, we convert the simple interest formula to equations that solve for each of the other variable factors.

If you find this procedure difficult to remember, use the magic triangle, as we did in Chapter 6, to calculate the portion, rate, and base. Remember, to use the Magic Triangle, cover the variable you are solving for and the new formula will "magically" appear!

Magic Triangle
Simple Interest Formula

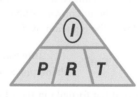

$$I = PRT$$

SOLVING FOR THE PRINCIPAL

10-6

When using the simple interest formula to solve for principal, P, we isolate the P on one side of the equation by dividing both sides of the equation by RT. This yields the new equation as follows:

$$\text{Principal} = \frac{\text{Interest}}{\text{Rate} \times \text{Time}} \qquad P = \frac{I}{RT}$$

We can also find the formula in the Magic Triangle by covering the unknown variable, P, as follows:

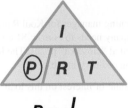

**Magic Triangle
Solving for Principal**

$$P = \frac{I}{RT}$$

EXAMPLE7 FINDING THE PRINCIPAL OF A LOAN

Allied Bank loaned Checkpoint Industries money at 8% interest for 90 days. If the amount of interest was \$4,000, use the ordinary interest method to find the amount of principal borrowed.

▶SOLUTIONSTRATEGY

To solve for the principal, we use the formula $P = \frac{I}{RT}$.

$P = \frac{I}{RT}$ Substitute the known variables into the equation.

$P = \dfrac{4,000}{.08 \times \frac{90}{360}}$ Calculate the denominator first.
Calculator sequence: .08 ✕ 90 ÷ 360 = M+

$P = \dfrac{4,000}{.02}$ Next, divide the numerator by the denominator.
Calculator sequence: 4000 ÷ MR = 200,000

Principal = $200,000   The company borrowed $200,000 from the bank.

▶TRYITEXERCISE 7

Telex Electronics borrowed money at 9% interest for 125 days. If the interest charge was \$560, use the ordinary interest method to calculate the amount of principal of the loan.

CHECK YOUR ANSWER WITH THE SOLUTION ON PAGE 334.

10-7 SOLVING FOR THE RATE

When we solve the simple formula for rate, the answer will be a decimal that must be converted to a percent. In business, interest rates are always expressed as a percent.

When the rate is the unknown variable, we isolate the R on one side of the equation by dividing both sides of the equation by PT. This yields the new equation as follows:

$$\text{Rate} = \frac{\text{Interest}}{\text{Principal} \times \text{Time}} \qquad R = \frac{I}{PT}$$

We can also find the formula in the Magic Triangle by covering the unknown variable, R, as follows:

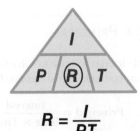

**Magic Triangle
Solving for Rate**

$$R = \frac{I}{PT}$$

EXAMPLE8   FINDING THE RATE OF A LOAN

Using the ordinary interest method, what is the rate of interest on a loan of $5,000 for 125 days if the amount of interest is $166? Round your answer to the nearest hundredth of a percent.

SOLUTIONSTRATEGY

To solve for the rate, we use the formula $R = \dfrac{I}{PT}$.

$R = \dfrac{I}{PT}$ Substitute the known variables into the equation.

$R = \dfrac{166}{5{,}000 \times \dfrac{125}{360}}$ Calculate the denominator first.
Calculator sequence: 5000 ⊠ 125 ÷ 360 = M+
Next, divide the numerator by the denominator.

$R = \dfrac{166}{1{,}736.111111}$ *Note:* Don't round the denominator.
Calculator sequence: 166 ÷ MR = .095616

$R = .095616$ Round the answer to the nearest hundredth of a percent.

Rate = <u>9.56%</u>   The bank charged <u>9.56%</u> interest.

TRYITEXERCISE 8

Using the ordinary interest method, what is the rate of interest on a loan of $25,000 for 245 days if the amount of interest is $1,960? Round your answer to the nearest hundredth of a percent.

CHECK YOUR ANSWER WITH THE SOLUTION ON PAGE 334.

SOLVING FOR THE TIME

10-8

When solving the simple interest formula for time, a whole number in the answer represents years and a decimal represents a portion of a year. The decimal should be converted to days by multiplying it by 360 for ordinary interest or by 365 for exact interest. Lending institutions consider any part of a day to be a full day. Therefore, any fraction of a day is rounded up to the next higher day even if it is less than .5.

For example, an answer of 3 means 3 years. An answer of 3.22 means 3 years and .22 of the next year. Assuming ordinary interest, multiply the decimal portion of the answer, .22, by 360. This gives 79.2, which represents the number of days. The total time of the loan would be 3 years and 80 days. Remember to always round up any fraction of a day.

When using the simple interest formula to solve for time, T, we isolate the T on one side of the equation by dividing both sides of the equation by PR. This yields the new equation as follows:

$$\text{Time} = \frac{\text{Interest}}{\text{Principal} \times \text{Rate}} \qquad T = \frac{I}{PR}$$

We can also find the formula in the Magic Triangle by covering the unknown variable, T, as follows:

**Magic Triangle
Solving for Time**

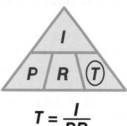

$$T = \frac{I}{PR}$$

> **Learning Tip**
>
> Remember, when time, T, is calculated, any fraction of a day is rounded up to the next higher day even if it is less than .5.
>
> For example, 25.1 days would round up to 26 days.

EXAMPLE9   FINDING THE TIME PERIOD OF A LOAN

What would be the time period of a loan for $7,600 at 11% ordinary interest if the amount of interest is $290?

SOLUTIONSTRATEGY

To solve for the time, we use the formula $T = \dfrac{I}{PR}$.

$T = \dfrac{I}{PR}$	Substitute the known variables into the equation.
$T = \dfrac{290}{7,600 \times .11}$	Calculate the denominator first. Calculator sequence: 7600 $\times$ .11 $=$ M+
$T = \dfrac{290}{836}$	Next, divide the numerator by the denominator. Calculator sequence: 290 $\div$ MR $=$ .3468899
$T = .3468899$ years	Because the answer is a decimal, the time is less than 1 year. Using ordinary interest, we multiply the entire decimal by 360 to find the number of days of the loan.
$T = .3468899 \times 360$	Calculator Sequence: .3468899 $\times$ 360 $=$ 124.8 or <u>125 days</u>

Time = 124.8 days, or <u>125 days</u>

TRYITEXERCISE 9

What is the time period of a loan for $15,000 at 9.5% ordinary interest if the amount of interest is $650?

CHECK YOUR ANSWER WITH THE SOLUTION ON PAGE 334.

10-9   CALCULATING LOANS INVOLVING PARTIAL PAYMENTS BEFORE MATURITY

Frequently, businesses and individuals who have borrowed money for a specified length of time find that they want to save some interest by making one or more partial payments on the loan before the maturity date. The most commonly used method for this calculation is known as the **U.S. rule**. The rule states that when a partial payment is made on a loan, the payment is first used to pay off the accumulated interest to date and the balance is used to reduce the principal. In this application, the ordinary interest method (360 days) will be used for all calculations.

U.S. rule Method for distributing early partial payments of a loan whereby the payment is first used to pay off the accumulated interest to date, with the balance used to reduce the principal.

STEPS FOR CALCULATING MATURITY VALUE OF A LOAN AFTER ONE OR MORE PARTIAL PAYMENTS

STEP 1. Using the simple interest formula with *ordinary* interest, compute the amount of interest due from the date of the loan to the date of the partial payment.

STEP 2. Subtract the interest from Step 1 from the partial payment. This pays the interest to date.

STEP 3. Subtract the balance of the partial payment after Step 2 from the original principal of the loan. This gives the adjusted principal.

STEP 4. If another partial payment is made, repeat Steps 1, 2, and 3 using the adjusted principal and the number of days since the last partial payment.

STEP 5. The maturity value is computed by adding the interest since the last partial payment to the adjusted principal.

Learning Tip

Remember to use *ordinary interest*, 360 days, for all calculations involving partial payments.

To help you visualize the details of a loan with partial payments, construct a timeline such as the one illustrated in Exhibit 10-1.

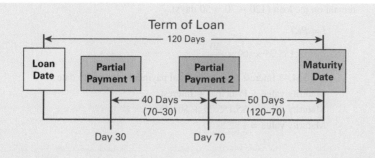

EXHIBIT 10-1
Partial Payment Timeline

EXAMPLE10 — CALCULATING LOANS INVOLVING PARTIAL PAYMENTS

Ray Windsor borrowed $10,000 at 9% interest for 120 days. On day 30, Ray made a partial payment of $2,000. On day 70, he made a second partial payment of $3,000. What is the maturity value of the loan after the partial payments?

▶SOLUTIONSTRATEGY

Step 1. Compute the interest from the date of the loan to the partial payment. In this problem, the first partial payment was made on day 30.

$$I = PRT$$

$$I = 10,000 \times .09 \times \frac{30}{360} = 75$$

$$I = \$75$$

Step 2. Subtract the interest from the partial payment.

$2,000 Partial payment
− 75 Accumulated interest
$1,925 Amount of partial payment left to reduce the principal

Step 3. Reduce the principal.

$10,000 Original principal
− 1,925 Amount of partial payment used to reduce principal
$8,075 Adjusted principal

Step 4. A second partial payment of $3,000 was made on day 70. We now repeat Steps 1, 2, and 3 to credit the second partial payment properly. Remember, use the adjusted principal and 40 days (70 − 30 = 40) for this calculation.

Step 1.

$$I = PRT$$

$$I = \$8,075 \times .09 \times \frac{40}{360}$$

$$I = \$80.75 \quad \text{Accumulated interest since last partial payment}$$

Step 2.

$3,000.00 Partial payment
− 80.75 Accumulated interest
$2,919.25 Amount of partial payment left to reduce principal

Step 3.

$8,075.00 Principal
− 2,919.25 Amount of partial payment used to reduce principal
$5,155.75 Adjusted principal

Step 5. Once all partial payments have been credited, we find the maturity value of the loan by calculating the interest due from the last partial payment to the maturity date and adding it to the last adjusted principal.

Note: The last partial payment was made on day 70 of the loan; therefore, 50 days remain on the loan (120 − 70 = 50 days).

$$I = PRT$$

$$I = \$5{,}155.75 \times .09 \times \frac{50}{360}$$

$I = \$64.45$ Interest from last partial payment to maturity date

Maturity value = Principal + Interest

Maturity value = $5,155.75 + $64.45

Maturity value = $5,220.20

▶TRYITEXERCISE 10

Rita Peterson borrowed $15,000 at 12% ordinary interest for 100 days. On day 20 of the loan, she made a partial payment of $4,000. On day 60, she made another partial payment of $5,000. What is the maturity value of the loan after the partial payments?

CHECK YOUR ANSWER WITH THE SOLUTION ON PAGE 334.

SECTION II 10 REVIEW EXERCISES

Compute the principal for the following loans. Use ordinary interest when time is stated in days.

	Principal	Rate (%)	Time	Interest
1.	$1,250	12	2 years	$300
2.	_____	9	$1\frac{1}{2}$ years	$675
3.	_____	8	9 months	$3,000
4.	_____	8.6	90 days	$4,950
5.	_____	5	210 days	$917
6.	_____	6	6 months	$2,250
7.	_____	10.5	3 years	$8,190

Compute the rate for the following loans. Round answers to the nearest tenth of a percent; use ordinary interest when time is stated in days.

	Principal	Rate (%)	Time	Interest
8.	$5,000	8	3 years	$1,200
9.	$1,800	____	5 months	$105
10.	$48,000	____	60 days	$728
11.	$54,000	___	72 days	$732
12.	$125,000	____	2 years	$18,750
13.	$36,700	____	190 days	$2,000
14.	$295,500	___	14 months	$39,800

Use the ordinary interest method to compute the time for the following loans. Round answers to the next higher day when necessary.

	Principal	Rate (%)	Time	Interest
15.	$18,000	12	158 days	$948
16.	$7,900	10.4	_____	$228
17.	$4,500	$9\frac{3}{4}$	_____	$375
18.	$25,000	8.9	_____	$4,450
19.	$7,400	9.6	_____	$200
20.	$41,000	6.4	_____	$3,936
21.	$3,600	14.3	_____	$125

Calculate the missing information for the following loans. Round percents to the nearest tenth and days to the next higher day when necessary.

	Principal	Rate (%)	Time (days)	Interest Method	Interest	Maturity Value
22.	$16,000	13	___	Ordinary	$760	_____
23.	_____	9.5	100	Exact	$340	_____
24.	$3,800	___	165	Exact	$220	_____
25.	$25,500	$11\frac{1}{4}$	300	Ordinary	_____	_____
26.	_____	10.4	___	Exact	$4,000	$59,000

Solve the following word problems. Round answers to the nearest cent when necessary.

27. Kendall Motors, a Buick dealership, borrowed $225,000 on April 16 to purchase a shipment of new cars. The interest rate was 9.3% using the ordinary interest method. The amount of interest was $9,600.

   a. For how many days was the loan?

   b. What was the maturity date of the loan?

28. Mike Drago took out a loan for $3,500 at the Gold Coast Bank for 270 days. If the bank uses the ordinary interest method, what rate of interest was charged if the amount of interest was $269? Round your answer to the nearest tenth of a percent.

29. Tiffany Francis borrowed money from her credit union to buy a car at 13.5% simple interest. If the loan was repaid in 2 years and the amount of interest was $2,700, how much did Tiffany borrow?

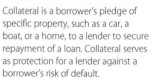

Dollars AND Sense

Collateral is a borrower's pledge of specific property, such as a car, a boat, or a home, to a lender to secure repayment of a loan. Collateral serves as protection for a lender against a borrower's risk of default.

   If a borrower defaults on a loan, that borrower forfeits (gives up) the property pledged as collateral—and the lender then becomes the owner of the collateral. In a typical mortgage loan transaction, for instance, the real estate that is acquired with the help of the loan serves as collateral.

30. What is the maturity date of a loan for $5,000 at 15% exact interest taken out on June 3? The amount of interest on the loan was $150.

31. You are the owner of a Supercuts Hair Salon. What rate of interest were you charged on an ordinary interest loan for $135,000 in equipment if the interest was $4,400 and the time period was from January 16 to April 27? Round your answer to the nearest tenth of a percent.

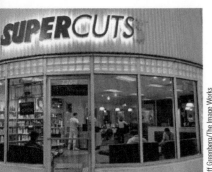

Jeff Greenberg/The Image Works

Supercuts, with over 2,300 locations, has been ranked the number one hair care franchise in the United States and the fifth best franchise opportunity overall in *Entrepreneur* magazine's annual "Franchise 500" issue.

Initial investment to franchise a Supercuts salon is $111,000–$239,700. Financial requirements are $100,000 liquid assets and $300,000 net worth. The franchise fee is $22,500 for the first salon and $12,500 for each additional salon.

Supercuts is owned by **Regis Corporation,** global leader in salon and hair care services.

Since its inception in 1922, Regis has grown to over 60 distinct brands of salons, education centers, and specialized hair service centers, serving 160 million customers annually through 12,800 worldwide locations. With approximately 55,000 full-time employees, typical annual revenues for Regis Corporation total over $2 billion dollars.

32. Michelle Payne deposited $8,000 in a savings account paying 6.25% simple interest. How long will it take for her investment to amount to $10,000?

33. The Actor's Playhouse theater borrowed $100,000 at 8% ordinary interest for 90 days to purchase new stage lighting equipment. On day 40 of the loan, the theater made a partial payment of $35,000. What is the new maturity value of the loan?

$$I = PRT = 100,000 \times .08 \times \frac{40}{360} = \$888.89$$

$35,000.00 Paid	$100,000.00
− 888.89 Interest	− 34,111.11
$34,111.11	$65,888.89
	Adjusted principal

$$MV = P(1 + RT) = 65,888.89 \left(1 + .08 \times \frac{50}{360}\right) = \underline{\$66,620.99}$$

34. Steve Perry borrowed $10,000 at 12% ordinary interest for 60 days. On day 20 of the loan, Steve made a partial payment of $4,000. What is the new maturity value of the loan?

35. Pamela Boyd borrowed $20,000 at 6.5% ordinary interest for 150 days. On day 30 of the loan, she made a partial payment of $8,000. What is the new maturity value of the loan?

36. The Mutt Hut Pet Shop borrowed $60,000 on March 15 for 90 days. The rate was 13% using the ordinary interest method. On day 25 of the loan, The Mutt Hut made a partial payment of $16,000, and on day 55 of the loan, The Mutt Hut made a second partial payment of $12,000.

   a. What is the new maturity value of the loan?

b. What is the maturity date of the loan?

37. a. How many years will it take $5,000 invested at 8% simple interest to double to $10,000?

b. How long will it take if the interest rate is increased to 10%?

Gerrit de Heus/Alamy

Taco Bell serves more than 2 billion consumers each year in more than 5,800 restaurants in the United States. The initial investment to franchise a Taco Bell is $1.3 million –$2.3 million. Franchise fees are $45,000 initial fee, then 5.5% monthly royalty fees and 4.5% monthly advertising fees.

Yum! Brands, Inc., based in Louisville, Kentucky, is the world's largest restaurant company in terms of system restaurants, with more than 37,000 restaurants in over 110 countries and territories and more than 1 million associates. Yum! is ranked in the top 250 companies on the Fortune 500 list. Four of the restaurant brands—KFC, Pizza Hut, Taco Bell, and Long John Silver's—are the global leaders of the chicken, pizza, Mexican-style food, and quick-service seafood categories, respectively.

BUSINESS DECISION: THE OPPORTUNITY COST

38. You are the owner of four Taco Bell restaurant locations. You have a business loan with Citizens Bank taken out 60 days ago that is due in 90 days. The amount of the loan is $40,000, and the rate is 9.5% using ordinary interest.

You currently have some excess cash. You have the choice of sending Citizens $25,000 now as a partial payment on your loan or purchasing an additional $25,000 of serving supplies such as food containers, cups, and plastic dinnerware for your inventory at a special discount price that is "10% off" your normal cost of these items.

a. How much interest will you save on this loan if you make the partial payment and don't purchase the additional serving supplies?

b. How much will you save by purchasing the discounted serving supplies and not making the partial payment?

c. (Optional) What other factors should you consider before making this decision?

SECTION III

10 UNDERSTANDING PROMISSORY NOTES AND DISCOUNTING

promissory note A debt instrument in which one party agrees to repay money to another within a specified period of time. Promissory notes may be noninterest-bearing at no interest or interest-bearing at a specified rate of interest.

Technically, the document that states the details of a loan and is signed by the borrower is known as a **promissory note**. *Promissory* means it is a promise to pay the principal back to the lender on a certain date. *Note* means that the document is a negotiable instrument and can be transferred or sold to others not involved in the original loan. Much like a check, with proper endorsement by the payee, the note can be transferred to another person, company, or lending institution.

Promissory notes are either noninterest-bearing or interest-bearing. When a note is noninterest-bearing, the maturity value equals the principal because there is no interest being charged. With interest-bearing notes, the maturity value equals the principal plus the interest.

Exhibit 10-2 is an example of a typical promissory note with its parts labeled. Notice the similarity between a note and a check. A list explaining the labels follows.

Maker: The person or company borrowing the money and issuing the note.

Payee: The person or institution lending the money and receiving the payment.

Term: The time period of the note, usually stated in days. (Use ordinary interest.)

Date: The date that the note is issued.

Face Value or Principal: The amount of money borrowed.

Interest Rate: The annual rate of interest being charged.

Maturity Date or Due Date: The date when maturity value is due to the payee.

EXHIBIT 10-2   Interest-Bearing Promissory Note

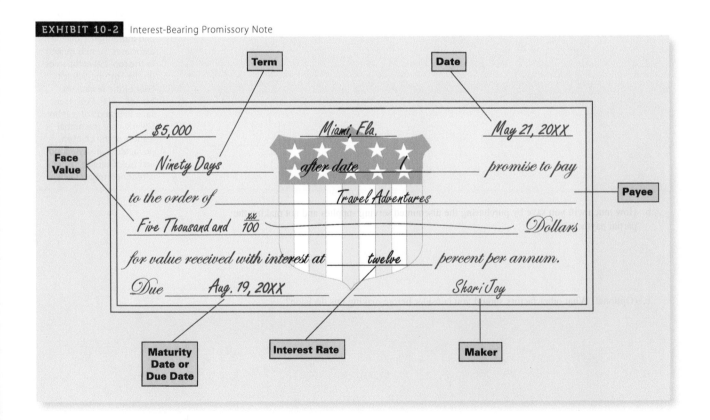

CALCULATING BANK DISCOUNT AND PROCEEDS FOR A SIMPLE DISCOUNT NOTE

10-10

To this point, we have been dealing with *simple interest notes* in which the interest was added to the principal to determine the maturity value. Another way of lending money is to deduct the interest from the principal at the beginning of the loan and give the borrower the difference. These are known as **simple discount notes**. When this method is used, the amount of interest charged is known as the **bank discount** and the amount that the borrower receives is known as the **proceeds**. When the term of the note is over, the borrower will repay the entire principal, or face value, of the note as the maturity value.

For example, Julie goes to a bank and signs a simple interest note for $5,000. If the interest charge amounts to $500, she will receive $5,000 at the beginning of the note and repay $5,500 on maturity of the note. If the bank used a simple discount note for Julie's loan, the bank discount (interest) would be deducted from the face value (principal). Julie's proceeds on the loan would be $4,500, and on maturity she would pay $5,000.

simple discount notes Promissory notes in which the interest is deducted from the principal at the beginning of the loan.

bank discount The amount of interest charged (deducted from the principal) on a discounted promissory note.

proceeds The amount of money that the borrower receives at the time a discounted note is made.

BANK DISCOUNT

Because bank discount is the same as interest, we use the formula $I = PRT$ as before, substituting bank discount for interest, face value for principal, and discount rate for interest rate. *Note:* Use ordinary interest, 360 days, for simple discount notes whose terms are stated in days.

> **Bank discount = Face value × Discount rate × Time**

PROCEEDS

The proceeds of a note are calculated using the following formula:

> **Proceeds = Face value − Bank discount**

EXAMPLE11 — CALCULATING BANK DISCOUNT AND PROCEEDS

What are the bank discount and proceeds of a $7,000 note at a 7% discount rate for 270 days?

SOLUTIONSTRATEGY

$$\text{Bank discount} = \text{Face value} \times \text{Discount rate} \times \text{Time}$$

$$\text{Bank discount} = \$7,000 \times .07 \times \frac{270}{360}$$

$$\text{Bank discount} = \underline{\$367.50}$$

$$\text{Proceeds} = \text{Face value} - \text{Bank discount}$$

$$\text{Proceeds} = \$7,000 - \$367.50$$

$$\text{Proceeds} = \underline{\$6,632.50}$$

TRYITEXERCISE 11

Erin Lang signed a $20,000 simple discount promissory note at the Sovereign Bank for a student loan. The discount rate is 13%, and the term of the note is 330 days. What is the amount of the bank discount, and what are Erin's proceeds on the loan?

CHECK YOUR ANSWERS WITH THE SOLUTIONS ON PAGE 334.

Dollars AND Sense

Student Aid

The U.S. Department of Education student aid programs are the largest source of student aid in America. The Free Application for Federal Student Aid (FAFSA) is the form used by virtually all two- and four-year colleges, universities, and career schools for federal, state, and college aid.

A number of student loans allow for a grace period before the loan must be repaid. However, interest may accrue during this time. For more information, visit www.fafsa.ed.gov and http://ibrinfo.org.

10-11 CALCULATING TRUE, OR EFFECTIVE, RATE OF INTEREST FOR A SIMPLE DISCOUNT NOTE

In a simple interest note, the borrower receives the full face value, whereas with a simple discount note, the borrower receives only the proceeds. Because the proceeds are less than the face value, the stated discount rate is not the true or actual interest rate of the note.

true, or **effective**, **interest rate**
The actual interest rate charged on a discounted note. Takes into account the fact that the borrower does not receive the full amount of the principal.

To protect the consumer, the U.S. Congress has passed legislation requiring all lending institutions to quote the **true**, or **effective**, **interest rate** for all loans. Effective interest rate is calculated by substituting the bank discount for interest and the proceeds for principal in the rate formula,

$$\text{Effective interest rate} = \frac{\text{Bank discount}}{\text{Proceeds} \times \text{Time}}$$

EXAMPLE12 CALCULATING EFFECTIVE INTEREST RATE

What is the effective interest rate of a simple discount note for $10,000 at a bank discount rate of 14% for a period of 90 days? Round to the nearest tenth of a percent.

►SOLUTIONSTRATEGY

To find the effective interest rate, we must first calculate the amount of the bank discount and the proceeds of the note, then substitute these numbers in the effective interest rate formula.

Step 1. Bank Discount

$$\text{Bank discount} = \text{Face value} \times \text{Discount rate} \times \text{Time}$$
$$\text{Bank discount} = \$10,000 \times .14 \times \frac{90}{360}$$
$$\text{Bank discount} = \$350$$

Step 2. Proceeds

$$\text{Proceeds} = \text{Face value} - \text{Bank discount}$$
$$\text{Proceeds} = 10,000 - 350$$
$$\text{Proceeds} = \$9,650$$

Step 3. Effective Interest Rate

$$\text{Effective interest rate} = \frac{\text{Bank discount}}{\text{Proceeds} \times \text{Time}}$$
$$\text{Effective interest rate} = \frac{350}{9,650 \times \frac{90}{360}}$$
$$\text{Effective interest rate} = \frac{350}{2,412.50}$$
$$\text{Effective interest rate} = .14507, \text{ or } \underline{14.5\%}$$

►TRYITEXERCISE 12

What is the effective interest rate of a simple discount note for $40,000 at a bank discount rate of 11% for a period of 270 days? Round your answer to the nearest hundredth of a percent.

CHECK YOUR ANSWER WITH THE SOLUTION ON PAGE 334.

10-12 DISCOUNTING NOTES BEFORE MATURITY

Frequently in business, companies extend credit to their customers by accepting short-term promissory notes as payment for goods or services. These notes are simple interest and are usually for less than one year. Prior to the maturity date of these notes, the payee (lender) may take the note to a bank and sell it. This is a convenient way for a company or individual to *cash in* a note at any time before maturity. This process is known as **discounting a note**.

When a note is discounted at a bank, the original payee receives the proceeds of the discounted note and the bank (the new payee) receives the maturity value of the note when it matures. The time period used to calculate the proceeds is from the date the note is discounted to the maturity date. This is known as the **discount period**.

Exhibit 10-3 illustrates the timeline for a 90-day simple interest note discounted on the 60th day.

discounting a note A process whereby a company or an individual can cash in or sell a promissory note at a discount at any time before maturity.

discount period The time period between the date a note is discounted and the maturity date. Used to calculate the proceeds of a discounted note.

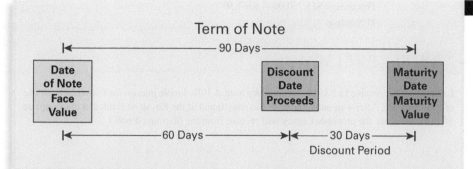

STEPS FOR DISCOUNTING A NOTE BEFORE MATURITY

STEP 1. Calculate the maturity value of the note. If the original note was noninterest-bearing, the maturity value will be the same as the face value. If the original note was interest-bearing, the maturity value should be calculated as usual:

Maturity value = Principal$(1 + \text{Rate} \times \text{Time})$

STEP 2. Determine the number of days or months of the discount period. The discount period is used as the numerator of the time in Step 3.

STEP 3. Calculate the amount of the bank discount by using the following formula. *Note*: Use ordinary interest, 360 days, for discounting a note before maturity, when the terms are stated in days.

Bank discount = Maturity value $\times$ Discount rate $\times$ Time

STEP 4. Calculate the proceeds of the note by using the following formula:

Proceeds = Maturity value − Bank discount

EXAMPLE13   CALCULATING PROCEEDS OF A DISCOUNTED NOTE

Continental Industries received a **$15,000** promissory note for **150 days** at **12%** simple interest from one of its customers. After 90 days, Continental needed cash, so it discounted the note at the InterAmerican Bank at a discount rate of 14%. What are the proceeds Continental will receive from the discounted note?

▶SOLUTIONSTRATEGY

Step 1. Calculate the maturity value of the original note:

$$\text{Maturity value} = \text{Principal}\,(1 + \text{Rate} \times \text{Time})$$

$$\text{Maturity value} = 15{,}000\left(1 + .12 \times \frac{150}{360}\right)$$

$$\text{Maturity value} = 15{,}000\,(1 + .05) = 15{,}000(1.05)$$

$$\text{Maturity value} = \$15{,}750$$

Step 2. Find the number of days of the discount period: In this example, the note was discounted after 90 days of a 150-day note; therefore, the discount period is 60 days $(150 - 90 = 60)$.

Step 3. Calculate the amount of the bank discount:

$$\text{Bank discount} = \text{Maturity value} \times \text{Discount rate} \times \text{Time}$$

$$\text{Bank discount} = \$15,750 \times .14 \times \frac{60}{360}$$

$$\text{Bank discount} = \$367.50$$

Step 4. Calculate the proceeds of the discounted note:

$$\text{Proceeds} = \text{Maturity value} - \text{Bank discount}$$

$$\text{Proceeds} = \$15,750.00 - \$367.50$$

$$\text{Proceeds} = \underline{\$15,382.50}$$

▶TRYITEXERCISE 13

Legacy Lumber received a $35,000 promissory note at 10% simple interest for 6 months from one of its customers. After 4 months, the note was discounted at the Keystone Bank at a discount rate of 14%. What are the proceeds Legacy will receive from the discounted note?

CHECK YOUR ANSWER WITH THE SOLUTION ON PAGE 335.

10-13   PURCHASING U.S. TREASURY BILLS

U.S. Treasury bills, or **T-bills** Short-term government securities that represent loans to the U.S. government.

U.S. Treasury bills, or **T-bills**, are short-term government securities with maturities of 4 weeks, 13 weeks, and 26 weeks. Sold by banks, brokers, and dealers in increments of $1,000, these securities represent loans to the U.S. government and are considered to be among the safest of investments. Just like discounted bank notes, T-bills are sold at a discount from their face value.

For example, you might pay $970 for a T-bill with a face value of $1,000. When the bill matures, you would be paid its face value, $1,000. Your interest is the difference between the face value and the purchase price—in this example, $30. The interest is determined by the discount rate, which is set when the bills are initially auctioned by the U.S. Treasury.

When comparing T-bills to discounted bank notes, the interest of a T-bill is the equivalent of the bank discount of a note; the face value of a T-bill is the equivalent of the proceeds of a note. Use the following formulas for T-bill calculations:

$$\textbf{Interest} = \textbf{Face value} \times \textbf{Discount rate} \times \textbf{Time}$$

$$\textbf{Purchase price} = \textbf{Face value} - \textbf{Interest}$$

$$\textbf{Effective interest rate} = \frac{\textbf{Interest}}{\textbf{Purchase price} \times \textbf{Time}}$$

EXAMPLE14   PURCHASING U.S. TREASURY BILLS

Peggy Estes purchased $5,000 in U.S. Treasury bills with a discount rate of 4% for a period of 13 weeks.

a. How much interest did Peggy earn on the T-bill investment?

b. How much was the purchase price of Peggy's T-bills?

c. What was the effective interest rate of Peggy's T-bill investment? Round to the nearest hundredth of a percent.

▶SOLUTIONSTRATEGY

a. Interest = Face value × Discount rate × Time

$$\text{Interest} = \$5,000 \times .04 \times \frac{13}{52} = \underline{\$50}$$

Dollars AND Sense

For more information about Treasury bills, go to www.ustreas.gov.

b. Purchase price = Face value − Interest
   Purchase price = 5,000 − 50 = $4,950

c. Effective interest rate = $\dfrac{\text{Interest}}{\text{Purchase price} \times \text{Time}}$

   Effective interest rate = $\dfrac{50}{4,950 \times \dfrac{13}{52}}$ = .040404 = 4.04%

▶ TRYITEXERCISE 14

Bob Schaller purchased $10,000 in U.S. Treasury bills with a discount rate of 4.6% for a period of 26 weeks.

a. How much interest did Bob earn on the T-bill investment?

b. How much was the purchase price of Bob's T-bills?

c. What was the effective interest rate of Bob's T-bill investment? Round to the nearest hundredth of a percent.

CHECK YOUR ANSWERS WITH THE SOLUTIONS ON PAGE 335.

REVIEW EXERCISES

10   SECTION III

Calculate the bank discount and proceeds for the following simple discount notes. Use the ordinary interest method, 360 days, when applicable.

	Face Value	Discount Rate (%)	Term	Bank Discount	Proceeds
1.	$4,500	13	6 months	$292.50	$4,207.50
2.	$235	11.3	50 days	_____	_____
3.	$2,000	$7\frac{1}{2}$	1 year	_____	_____
4.	$35,000	9.65	11 months	_____	_____
5.	$7,800	$8\frac{1}{4}$	130 days	_____	_____

Using ordinary interest, 360 days, calculate the missing information for the following simple discount notes.

	Face Value	Discount Rate (%)	Date of Note	Term (days)	Maturity Date	Bank Discount	Proceeds
6.	$16,800	10	June 3	80	Aug. 22	$373.33	$16,426.67
7.	$5,000	14.7	April 16	_____	July 9	_____	_____
8.	$800	12.1	Sept. 3	109		_____	_____
9.	$1,300	$9\frac{1}{2}$	Aug. 19	_____	Nov. 27	_____	_____
10.	$75,000	5	May 7	53		_____	_____

Using ordinary interest, 360 days, calculate the bank discount, proceeds, and effective rate for the following simple discount notes. Round effective rate to the nearest hundredth of a percent.

	Face Value	Discount Rate (%)	Term (days)	Bank Discount	Proceeds	Effective Rate (%)
11.	$2,700	14	126	$132.30	$2,567.70	14.72
12.	$6,505	10.39	73	_____	_____	_____

	Face Value	Discount Rate (%)	Term (days)	Bank Discount	Proceeds	Effective Rate (%)
13.	$3,800	7.25	140	_____	_____	_____
14.	$95,000	9.7	45	_____	_____	_____
15.	$57,500	$12\frac{3}{4}$	230	_____	_____	_____

The following interest-bearing promissory notes were discounted at a bank by the payee before maturity. Use the ordinary interest method, 360 days, to calculate the missing information.

	Face Value	Interest Rate (%)	Date of Note	Term of Note (days)	Maturity Date	Maturity Value	Date of Discount	Discount Period (days)	Discount Rate (%)	Proceeds
16.	$2,500	12	Mar. 4	70	May 13	$2,558.33	Apr. 15	28	13	$2,532.46
17.	$4,000	10.4	Dec. 12	50	_____	_____	Jan. 19	_____	15	_____
18.	$850	$13\frac{1}{2}$	June 7	125	_____	_____	Sept. 3	_____	16.5	_____
19.	$8,000	9	May 10	90	_____	_____	July 5	_____	10.2	_____
20.	$1,240	7.6	Sept. 12	140	_____	_____	Dec. 5	_____	11.8	_____

Calculate the interest, purchase price, and effective interest rate of the following Treasury bill (T-bill) purchases. Round effective interest rate to the nearest hundredth of a percent.

	Face Value	Discount Rate (%)	Term (weeks)	Interest	Purchase Price	Effective Rate (%)
21.	$15,000	5.20	13	$195	$14,805	5.27
22.	$50,000	4.40	26	_____	_____	____
23.	$80,000	4.82	13	_____	_____	____
24.	$35,000	3.80	4	_____	_____	____
25.	$100,000	4.15	26	_____	_____	____

Use the ordinary interest method, 360 days, to solve the following word problems. Round to the nearest cent when necessary.

26. Roni Lockard signed a $22,500 simple discount promissory note at the Pacific National Bank. The discount rate was 11%, and the note was made on February 17 (not in a leap-year) for 107 days.

a. What proceeds will Roni receive on the note?

b. What is the maturity date of the note?

27. Boz Foster signed a $10,000 simple discount promissory note at a bank discount rate of 6%. If the term of the note was 125 days, what was the effective interest rate of the note? Round your answer to the nearest hundredth of a percent.

28. Pinnacle Manufacturing received a $40,000 promissory note at 12% simple interest for 95 days from one of its customers. On day 70, Pinnacle discounted the note at the Berryville Bank at a discount rate of 15%. The note was made on September 12.

   a. What was the maturity date of the note?

   b. What was the maturity value of the note?

   c. What was the discount date of the note?

   d. What proceeds did Pinnacle receive after discounting the note?

29. Christy Thomas purchased $150,000 in U.S. Treasury bills with a discount rate of 4.2% for a period of 4 weeks.

   a. How much interest did Christy earn on the T-bill investment?

   b. How much was the purchase price of Christy's T-bills?

   c. What was the effective interest rate of Christy's T-bill investment? Round to the nearest hundredth of a percent.

BUSINESS DECISION: FINANCING THE DEALERS

30. Richie Powers is the owner of American Eagle Boats, a manufacturer of custom pleasure boats. Because of the economic recession and slow boat sales recently, American Eagle has begun accepting promissory notes from its dealers to help finance large orders. This morning American Eagle accepted a 90-day, 9.5% promissory note for $600,000 from Champion Marine, one of its sales dealers.

   You are a manager for Atlantic Bank, and Richie is one of your clients. Atlantic's discount rate is currently 16%. Richie's goal is to discount the note as soon as possible, but not until the proceeds are at least equal to the face value of the note, $600,000.

   a. As his banker, Richie has asked you to "run the numbers" at ten-day intervals starting with day 20 and advise him as to when he can discount the note and still receive his $600,000.

According to the National Marine Manufacturers Association, the top five boating states are Florida, Texas, California, North Carolina, and New York. Typical sales and service expenditures for recreational boating exceed $30 billion annually.

b. (Challenge) Calculate the exact day the note should be discounted to meet Richie's goal.

CHAPTER FORMULAS

Simple Interest

Interest = Principal × Rate × Time

$$\text{Time (exact interest)} = \frac{\text{Number of days of a loan}}{365}$$

$$\text{Time (ordinary interest)} = \frac{\text{Number of days of a loan}}{360}$$

Maturity value = Principal + Interest

Maturity value = Principal(1 + Rate × Time)

The Simple Interest Formula

$$\text{Principal} = \frac{\text{Interest}}{\text{Rate} \times \text{Time}}$$

$$\text{Rate} = \frac{\text{Interest}}{\text{Principal} \times \text{Time}}$$

$$\text{Time} = \frac{\text{Interest}}{\text{Principal} \times \text{Rate}}$$

Simple Discount Notes

Bank discount = Face value × Discount rate × Time

Proceeds = Face value − Bank discount

$$\text{Effective interest rate} = \frac{\text{Bank discount}}{\text{Proceeds} \times \text{Time}}$$

Discounting a Note before Maturity

Bank discount = Maturity value × Discount rate × Time

Proceeds = Maturity value − Bank discount

Purchasing U.S. Treasury Bills

Interest = Face value × Discount rate × Time

Purchase price = Face value − Interest

$$\text{Effective interest rate} = \frac{\text{Interest}}{\text{Purchase price} \times \text{Time}}$$

CHAPTER SUMMARY

Section I: Understanding and Computing Simple Interest

Topic	Important Concepts	Illustrative Examples
Computing Simple Interest for Loans with Terms of Years or Months **Performance Objective 10-1, Page 305**	Simple interest is calculated by using the formula $I = PRT$. $$\text{Interest} = \text{Principal} \times \text{Rate} \times \text{Time}$$ *Note*: Time is always expressed in years or fractions of a year.	What is the amount of interest for a loan of $20,000 at 12% simple interest for 9 months? $$I = 20{,}000 \times .12 \times \frac{9}{12}$$ Interest = $1,800
Calculating Simple Interest for Loans with Terms of Days by Using the Exact Interest Method **Performance Objective 10-2, Page 306**	Exact interest uses *365 days* as the time factor denominator. $$\frac{\text{Number of days of a loan}}{365}$$	Using the exact interest method, what is the amount of interest on a loan of $5,000 at 8% for 95 days? $$I = PRT$$ $$I = 5{,}000 \times .08 \times \frac{95}{365}$$ Interest = $104.11
Calculating Simple Interest for Loans with Terms of Days by Using the Ordinary Interest Method **Performance Objective 10-2, Page 307**	Ordinary interest uses *360 days* as the time factor denominator. $$\frac{\text{Number of days of a loan}}{360}$$	Using the ordinary interest method, what is the amount of interest on a loan of $8,000 at 9% for 120 days? $$I = PRT$$ $$I = 8{,}000 \times .09 \times \frac{120}{360}$$ Interest = $240
Calculating the Maturity Value of a Loan **Performance Objective 10-3, Page 308**	When the time period of a loan is over, the loan is said to mature. The total payback of principal and interest is known as the maturity value of a loan. $$\text{Maturity value} = \text{Principal} + \text{Interest}$$ $$\text{Maturity value} = \text{Principal}(1 + \text{Rate} \times \text{Time})$$	What is the maturity value of a loan for $50,000 at 12% interest for 3 years? $$MV = 50{,}000(1 + .12 \times 3)$$ $$MV = 50{,}000(1.36)$$ Maturity value = $68,000

Calculating the Number of Days of a Loan
 	
Performance Objective 10-4, Page 309
	1. Determine the number of days remaining in the first month by subtracting the loan date from the number of days in that month.
	2. List the number of days for each succeeding whole month.
	3. List the number of loan days in the last month.
	4. Add the days from Steps 1, 2, and 3.
		Steve Adams borrowed money from the Republic Bank on May 5 and repaid the loan on August 19. For how many days was this loan?
		
		May 31
		− May 5
		    26 Days in May
		    61 June–July
		  +19 August
		  106 Days

Determining the Maturity Date of a Loan
 	
Performance Objective 10-5, Page 310
	1. Determine the number of days remaining in the first month.
	2. Subtract days from Step 1 from number of days in the loan.
	3. Subtract days in each succeeding whole month until you reach a month in which the difference is less than the days in that month. The maturity date will be the day of that month that corresponds to the difference.
		What is the maturity date of a loan taken out on June 9 for 100 days?
		
		June 30 100 Days of the loan
		June −9 − 21 Days in June
		  21 Days in June 79
		             − 31 Days in July
		             48
		             − 31 Days in August
		             17
		At this point, the difference, 17, is less than the days in September; therefore, the maturity date is September 17.

Section II: Using the Simple Interest Formula

Topic	Important Concepts	Illustrative Examples
Solving for the Principal **Performance Objective 10-6, Page 313**	$\dfrac{\text{Interest}}{\text{Rate} \times \text{Time}}$ (P) R T triangle with I on top	Kye Morrow borrowed money at 10% interest for 2 years. If the interest charge was $800, how much principal did Kye borrow? $\text{Principal} = \dfrac{800}{.10 \times 2} = \dfrac{800}{.2}$ $\text{Principal} = \underline{\$4{,}000}$
Solving for the Rate **Performance Objective 10-7, Page 314**	$\dfrac{\text{Interest}}{\text{Principal} \times \text{Time}}$ P (R) T triangle with I on top	Arnold Parker borrowed $3,000 for 75 days. If the interest was $90 using ordinary interest, what was the rate on Arnold's loan? $\text{Rate} = \dfrac{90}{3{,}000 \times \dfrac{75}{360}} = \dfrac{90}{625}$ $\text{Rate} = .144 = \underline{14.4\%}$
Solving for the Time **Performance Objective 10-8, Page 315**	When solving for time, whole numbers are years and decimals are multiplied by 360 or 365 to get days. Any fraction of a day should be rounded up to the next higher day because lending institutions consider any portion of a day to be another day. $\dfrac{\text{Interest}}{\text{Principal} \times \text{Rate}}$ P R (T) triangle with I on top	What is the time period of a loan for $20,000 at 9% ordinary interest if the amount of interest is $1,000? $\text{Time} = \dfrac{1{,}000}{20{,}000 \times .09} = \dfrac{1{,}000}{1{,}800} = .555555$ $\text{Time} = .555555 \times 360 = 199.99 = \underline{200 \text{ Days}}$
Calculating Loans Involving Partial Payments before Maturity **Performance Objective 10-9, Page 316**	1. Using the simple interest formula with *ordinary* interest, compute the amount of interest due from the date of the loan to the date of the partial payment. 2. Subtract the interest from Step 1 from the partial payment. This pays the interest to date. 3. Subtract the balance of the partial payment after Step 2 from the original principal of the loan. This gives the adjusted principal. 4. If another partial payment is made, repeat Steps 1, 2, and 3 using the adjusted principal and the number of days since the last partial payment. 5. The maturity value is computed by adding the interest since the last partial payment to the adjusted principal.	Sue Williams borrowed $7,000 at 10% ordinary interest for 120 days. On day 90, Sue made a partial payment of $3,000. What was the new maturity value of the loan? $I = PRT$ $I = 7{,}000 \times .10 \times \dfrac{90}{360} = \$175$ $\begin{array}{ll}\$3{,}000 & \text{Partial payment} \\ -\ 175 & \text{Accumulated interest} \\ \hline \$2{,}825 & \text{Reduces principal} \\ \$7{,}000 & \text{Original principal} \\ -2{,}825 & \\ \hline \$4{,}175 & \text{Adjusted principal}\end{array}$ Days remaining = $120 - 90 = 30$ $I = PRT$ $I = 4{,}175 \times .10 \times \dfrac{30}{360} = \$34.79$ Maturity value = $P + I$ $MV = 4{,}175 + 34.79$ Maturity value = $\underline{\$4{,}209.79}$

Section III: Understanding Promissory Notes and Discounting

Topic	Important Concepts	Illustrative Examples
Calculating Bank Discount and Proceeds for a Simple Discount Note **Performance Objective 10-10, Page 323**	With discounting, the interest, known as the bank discount, is deducted from the face value of the loan. The borrower gets the difference, known as the proceeds. Bank discount = $\qquad$ Face value × Discount rate × Time Proceeds = Face value − Bank discount	What are the bank discount and proceeds of a $10,000 note discounted at 12% for 6 months? Bank discount = $10,000 \times .12 \times \dfrac{6}{12}$ Bank discount = $600 $\qquad$ Proceeds = $10,000 − 600 = \underline{\$9,400}$
Calculating True, or Effective, Rate of Interest for a Simple Discount Note **Performance Objective 10-11, Page 324**	Because the proceeds are less than the face value of a loan, the true, or effective, interest rate is higher than the stated bank discount rate. $\dfrac{\text{Bank discount}}{\text{Proceeds} \times \text{Time}}$	What is the effective rate of a simple discount note for $20,000 at a bank discount of 15% for a period of 9 months? Bank discount = $FV \times R \times T$ Bank discount = $20,000 \times .15 \times \dfrac{9}{12}$ Bank discount = $2,250 Proceeds = Face value − Bank discount Proceeds = 20,000 − 2,250 Proceeds = $17,750 Effective interest rate = $\dfrac{2,250}{17,750 \times \dfrac{9}{12}}$ Effective interest rate = $\underline{16.9\%}$
Discounting Notes before Maturity **Performance Objective 10-12, Page 324**	Frequently, companies extend credit to their customers by accepting short-term promissory notes as payment for goods or services. These notes can be cashed in early by discounting them at a bank and receiving the proceeds. 1. Calculate the maturity value. $\qquad MV = P(1 + RT)$ 2. Determine the discount period. 3. Calculate the bank discount. $\qquad$ Bank discount = $MV \times R \times T$ 4. Calculate the proceeds. $\qquad$ Proceeds = MV − Bank discount	Reliable Food Wholesalers received a $100,000 promissory note for 6 months at 11% interest from SuperSaver Supermarkets. If Reliable discounts the note after 4 months at a discount rate of 15%, what proceeds will it receive? $MV = 100,000 \left(1 + .11 \times \dfrac{6}{12}\right)$ $MV = \$105,500$ Discount period = 2 months (6 − 4) Bank discount = $105,500 \times .15 \times \dfrac{2}{12}$ Bank discount = $2,637.50 Proceeds = 105,500.00 − 2,637.50 Proceeds = $\underline{\$102,862.50}$
Purchasing U.S. Treasury Bills **Performance Objective 10-13, Page 326**	U.S. Treasury bills, or T-bills, are short-term government securities with maturities of 4 weeks, 13 weeks, and 26 weeks. Sold by banks, brokers, and dealers in increments of $1,000, these securities represent loans to the U.S. government. Just like discounted bank notes, T-bills are sold at a discount from their face value. Interest = Face value × Discount rate × Time Purchase price = Face value − Interest Effective interest rate = $\dfrac{\text{Interest}}{\text{Purchase price} \times \text{Time}}$	Cindy Lane purchased $3,000 in U.S. Treasury bills with a discount rate of 5% for a period of 26 weeks. a. How much interest did Cindy earn on the T-bill investment? $\qquad$ Interest = $3,000 \times .05 \times \dfrac{26}{52} = \underline{\$75}$ b. How much was the purchase price of Cindy's T-bills? $\qquad$ Purchase price = $3,000 − 75 = \underline{\$2,925}$ c. What was the effective interest rate of Cindy's T-bill investment? Round to the nearest hundredth of a percent. $\qquad$ Effective interest rate = $\dfrac{75}{2,925 \times \dfrac{26}{52}}$ $\qquad = .05128 = \underline{5.13\%}$

TRY IT: EXERCISE SOLUTIONS FOR CHAPTER 10

1a. $I = PRT = 4,000 \times .07 \times 2.25 = \underline{\$630}$

1b. $I = PRT = 45,000 \times .0975 \times \dfrac{3}{12} = \underline{\$1,096.88}$

1c. $I = PRT = 130,000 \times .104 \times \dfrac{42}{12} = \underline{\$47,320}$

2. $I = PRT = 23,000 \times .08 \times \dfrac{119}{365} = \underline{\$599.89}$

3. $I = PRT = 15,000 \times .095 \times \dfrac{250}{360} = \underline{\$989.58}$

4a. $I = PRT = 15,400 \times .065 \times \dfrac{24}{12} = \underline{\$2,002}$

$MV = P + I = 15,400 + 2,002 = \underline{\$17,402}$

4b. $MV = P(1 + RT) = 450,000 \left(1 + .08 \times \dfrac{9}{12}\right) = \underline{\$477,000}$

5a.
$$\begin{array}{l} 30 \\ \underline{-\ 4} \\ 26 \text{ Days} \end{array} \nearrow \begin{array}{l} 26 \text{ April} \\ 61 \text{ May–June} \\ \underline{+18} \text{ July} \\ \underline{105} \text{ Days} \end{array}$$

5b.
$$\begin{array}{l} 30 \\ \underline{-15} \\ 15 \text{ Days} \end{array} \nearrow \begin{array}{l} 15 \text{ June} \\ 92 \text{ July–Sept.} \\ \underline{+9} \text{ Oct.} \\ \underline{116} \text{ Days} \end{array}$$

$I = PRT = 3,500 \times .11 \times \dfrac{116}{365} = \underline{\$122.36}$

6a.
$$\begin{array}{ll} \text{Days in Sept.} & 30 \\ \text{Loan date} & \underline{-9} \\ \text{Days of Sept.} & 21 \end{array} \nearrow \begin{array}{l} 125 \text{ Days of loan} \\ \underline{-21} \text{ Days of Sept.} \\ 104 \\ \underline{-31} \text{ October} \\ 73 \\ \underline{-30} \text{ November} \\ 43 \\ \underline{-31} \text{ December} \\ 12 \longrightarrow \underline{\text{January 12}} \end{array}$$

6b. $MV = P(1 + RT) = 9,000 \left(1 + .10 \times \dfrac{80}{360}\right) = \underline{\$9,200}$

$$\begin{array}{l} 31 \\ \underline{-21} \\ 10 \text{ Days} \end{array} \nearrow \begin{array}{l} 10 \text{ Oct.} \\ 61 \text{ Nov.–Dec.} \\ \underline{+9} \text{ Jan.} \longrightarrow \underline{\text{January 9}} \\ \underline{80} \text{ Days} \end{array}$$

7. $P = \dfrac{I}{RT} = \dfrac{560}{.09 \times \dfrac{125}{360}} = \underline{\$17,920}$

8. $R = \dfrac{I}{PT} = \dfrac{1,960}{25,000 \times \dfrac{245}{360}} = .1152 = \underline{11.52\%}$

9. $I = \dfrac{I}{PR} = \dfrac{650}{15,000 \times .095} = \begin{array}{r} .4561404 \\ \times \ \ 360 \\ \hline 164.2 = \underline{165 \text{ Days}} \end{array}$

10. $I = PRT = 15,000 \times .12 \times \dfrac{20}{360} = \$100$ 1st partial payment = 20 Days

$$\begin{array}{ll} 4,000 \text{ Payment} & 15,000 \\ \underline{-100} \text{ Interest} & \underline{-3,900} \\ 3,900 & 11,100 \text{ Adjustment principal} \end{array}$$

$I = PRT = 11,100 \times .12 \times \dfrac{40}{360} = \$148$ 2nd partial payment = 40 Days $(60 - 20)$

$$\begin{array}{ll} 5,000 \text{ Payment} & 11,100 \\ \underline{-\ 148} \text{ Interest} & \underline{-4,852} \\ 4,852 & 6,248 \text{ Adjustment principal} \end{array}$$ Days remaining = 40 $(100 - 60)$

$I = PRT = 6,248 \times .12 \times \dfrac{40}{360} = \$83.31$

Final due = $P + I = 6,248.00 + 83.31 = \underline{\$6,331.31}$

11. Bank discount = $FV \times R \times T = 20,000 \times .13 \times \dfrac{330}{360} = \underline{\$2,383.33}$

Proceeds = Face value − Bank discount = $20,000.00 - 2,383.33 = \underline{\$17,616.67}$

12. Bank discount = $FV \times R \times T = 40,000 \times .11 \times \dfrac{270}{360} = \underline{\$3,300}$

Proceeds = Face value − Bank discount = $40,000 - 3,300 = \$36,700$

Effective interest rate = $\dfrac{\text{Bank discount}}{\text{Proceeds} \times \text{Time}} = \dfrac{3,300}{36,700 \times \dfrac{270}{360}} = \underline{11.99\%}$

13. $MV = P(1 + RT) = 35,000 \left(1 + .10 \times \dfrac{6}{12}\right) = \underline{\underline{\$36,750}}$

$$\begin{array}{r} 6 \text{ months} \\ - 4 \text{ months} \\ \hline \text{Discount period} = \quad 2 \text{ months} \end{array}$$

Bank discount $= MV \times R \times T = 36,750 \times .14 \times \dfrac{2}{12} = \$857.50$

Proceeds $=$ Maturity value $-$ Bank discount $= \$36,750.00 - 857.50 = \underline{\underline{\$35,892.50}}$

14. a. Interest $=$ Face value $\times$ Discount rate $\times$ Time $= 10,000 \times .046 \times \dfrac{26}{52} = \underline{\underline{\$230}}$

 b. Purchase price $=$ Face value $-$ Interest $= 10,000 - 230 = \underline{\underline{\$9,770}}$

 c. Effective interest rate $= \dfrac{\text{Interest}}{\text{Purchase price} \times \text{Time}} = \dfrac{230}{9,770 \times \dfrac{26}{52}} = .04708 = \underline{\underline{4.71\%}}$

Concept Review

1. The price or rental fee charged by a lender to a borrower for the use of money is known as _____. (10-1)

2. List the three factors that determine the amount of interest charged on a loan. (10-1)

3. Interest calculated solely on the principal amount borrowed is known as _____ interest, whereas interest calculated at regular intervals on the principal and previously earned interest is known as _____ interest. (10-1)

4. The interest calculation method that uses 365 days (366 in leap year) as the time factor denominator is known as _____ interest. (10-2)

5. The interest calculation method that uses 360 days as the time factor denominator is known as _____ interest. (10-2)

6. Maturity value is the total payback of principal and interest of a loan. List the two formulas for calculating maturity value. (10-3)

7. The first day of a loan is known as the _____ date; the last day of a loan is known as the _____ date. (10-4, 10-5)

8. Write the formula for calculating simple interest. (10-6)

9. When solving the simple interest formula for principal, rate, or time, the _____ is always the numerator. (10-6, 10-7, 10-8)

10. The U.S. rule states that when a partial payment is made on a loan, the payment is first used to pay off the accumulated _____ to date and the balance is used to reduce the _____. (10-9)

11. The amount of money that the borrower receives at the time a discounted note is made is known as the _____. (10-10)

12. The actual interest rate charged on a discounted note is known as the _____, or _____, interest rate. (10-11)

13. When a note is discounted before maturity, the proceeds are calculated by subtracting the amount of the bank discount from the _____ value of the loan. (10-12)

14. Discounted short-term loans made to the U.S. government are known as U.S. Treasury _____. (10-13)

ASSESSMENT TEST

Using the exact interest method (365 days), find the amount of interest on the following loans.

	Principal	Rate (%)	Time (days)	Exact Interest
1.	$15,000	13	120	_____
2.	$1,700	$12\frac{1}{2}$	33	_____

Using the ordinary interest method (360 days), find the amount of interest on the following loans.

	Principal	Rate (%)	Time (days)	Ordinary Interest
3.	$20,600	12	98	_____
4.	$286,000	$13\frac{1}{2}$	224	_____

What is the maturity value of the following loans? Use $MV = P(1 + RT)$ to find the maturity values.

	Principal	Rate (%)	Time	Maturity Value
5.	$15,800	7	4 years	_____
6.	$100,000	$6\frac{3}{4}$	7 months	_____

From the following information, determine the number of days of each loan.

	Loan Date	Due Date	Number of Days
7.	April 16	August 1	_____
8.	October 20	December 18	_____

From the following information, determine the maturity date of each loan.

	Loan Date	Time Loan (days)	Maturity Date
9.	November 30	55	_____
10.	May 15	111	_____

Compute the principal for the following loans. Round answers to the nearest cent.

	Principal	Rate (%)	Time	Interest
11.	_____	7	2 years	$2,800
12.	_____	$10\frac{1}{2}$	10 months	$5,900

Compute the rate for the following loans. Round answers to the nearest tenth of a percent.

	Principal	Rate (%)	Time	Interest
13.	$2,200	_____	4 years	$800
14.	$50,000	_____	9 months	$4,500

Use the ordinary interest method to compute the time for the following loans. Round answers to the next higher day when necessary.

	Principal	Rate (%)	Time (days)	Interest
15.	$13,500	6	_____	$350
16.	$7,900	10.4	_____	$625

Calculate the missing information for the following loans. Round percents to the nearest tenth and days to the next higher day when necessary.

	Principal	Rate (%)	Time (days)	Interest Method	Interest	Maturity Value
17.	$13,000	14	_____	Ordinary	$960	_____
18.	_____	12.2	133	Exact	$1,790	_____
19.	$2,500	_____	280	Ordinary	$295	_____

Using ordinary interest, calculate the missing information for the following simple discount notes.

	Face Value	Discount Rate (%)	Date of Note	Term (days)	Maturity Date	Bank Discount	Proceeds
20.	$50,000	13	Apr. 5	_____	Aug. 14	_____	_____
21.	$875,000	$9\frac{1}{2}$	Oct. 25	87		_____	_____

Using ordinary interest (360 days), calculate the bank discount, proceeds, and effective rate for the following simple discount notes. Round effective rate to the nearest hundredth of a percent.

	Face Value	Discount Rate (%)	Term (days)	Bank Discount	Proceeds	Effective Rate (%)
22.	$22,500	$10\frac{1}{2}$	60	_____	_____	_____
23.	$290,000	11.9	110	_____	_____	_____

The following interest-bearing promissory notes were discounted at a bank by the payee before maturity. Use the ordinary interest method (360 days) to solve for the missing information.

	Face Value	Interest Rate (%)	Date of Note	Term of Note (days)	Maturity Date	Maturity Value	Date Note Discounted	Discount Period (days)	Discount Rate (%)	Proceeds
24.	$8,000	11	Jan. 12	83	_____	_____	Mar. 1	_____	15	_____
25.	$5,500	$13\frac{1}{2}$	June 17	69	_____	_____	July 22	_____	13.7	_____

Calculate the interest, purchase price, and effective interest rate of the following Treasury bill (T-bill) purchases. Round effective interest rate to the nearest hundredth of a percent.

	Face Value	Discount Rate (%)	Term (weeks)	Interest	Purchase Price	Effective Rate (%)
26.	$75,000	5.15	4	_____	_____	_____
27.	$28,000	4.90	26	_____	_____	_____

Solve the following word problems. Round to the nearest cent when necessary.

28. On May 23, Samantha Best borrowed $4,000 from the Tri City Credit Union at 13% for 160 days. The credit union uses the exact interest method.

   a. What was the amount of interest on the loan?

   b. What was the maturity value of the loan?

   c. What is the maturity date of the loan?

29. Ronald Brown missed an income tax payment of $2,600. The Internal Revenue Service charges a 15% simple interest penalty calculated by the exact interest method. If the tax was due on April 15 but was paid on July 17, what was the amount of the penalty charge?

30. Katie Chalmers borrowed money from her credit union at 13.2% simple interest to buy furniture. If the loan was repaid in $2\frac{1}{2}$ years and the amount of interest was $1,320, how much did Katie borrow?

CHAPTER
10

31. Ryan Roberts took out a loan for $5,880 at the Linville Ridge Bank for 110 days. The bank uses the ordinary method for calculating interest. What rate of interest was charged if the amount of interest was $152? Round to the nearest tenth of a percent.

32. Alicia Eastman deposited $2,000 in a savings account at the Biltmone Bank paying 6% ordinary interest. How long will it take for her investment to amount to $2,600?

33. Laurie Carron borrowed $16,000 at 14% ordinary interest for 88 days. On day 30 of the loan, she made a partial payment of $7,000. What was the new maturity value of the loan?

34. Euromart Tile Company borrowed $40,000 on April 6 for 66 days. The rate was 14% using the ordinary interest method. On day 25 of the loan, Euromart made a partial payment of $15,000, and on day 45 of the loan, Euromart made a second partial payment of $10,000.

a. What was the new maturity value of the loan?

b. What was the maturity date of the loan?

35. Brandi Lee signed a $30,000 simple discount promissory note at the Signature Bank. The discount rate was 13% ordinary interest, and the note was made on August 9 for 95 days.

a. What proceeds did Brandi receive on the note?

b. What was the maturity date of the note?

c. What was the effective interest rate of the note? Round the answer to the nearest hundredth of a percent.

36. Varsity Press, a publisher of college textbooks, received a $70,000 promissory note at 12% ordinary interest for 60 days from one of its customers, Reader's Choice Bookstores. After 20 days, Varsity Press discounted the note at the Grove Isle Bank at a discount rate of 14.5%. The note was made on March 21.

a. What was the maturity date of the note?

b. What was the maturity value of the note?

c. What was the discount date of the note?

d. What proceeds did Varsity Press receive after discounting the note?

37. Fernando Rodriguez purchased $64,000 in U.S. Treasury bills with a discount rate of 4.7% for a period of 13 weeks.

a. How much interest did Fernando earn on the T-bill investment?

b. How much was the purchase price of Fernando's T-bills?

c. What was the effective interest rate of Fernando's T-bill investment? Round to the nearest hundredth of a percent.

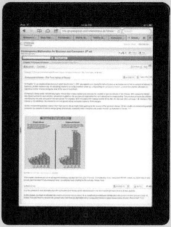

On-campus and online **bookstores** are the main sources of textbooks for college students. Electronic textbooks represent an ever increasing portion of total textbook sales. Some digital textbooks can be made to expire anywhere from 6 to 18 months after the date of purchase.

BUSINESS DECISION: BORROWING TO TAKE ADVANTAGE OF A CASH DISCOUNT

38. You are the accountant for Suite Dreams, a retail furniture store. Recently, an order of sofas and chairs was received from a manufacturer with terms of 3/15, n/45. The order amounted to $230,000, and Suite Dreams can borrow money at 13% ordinary interest.

a. How much can be saved by borrowing the funds for 30 days to take advantage of the cash discount? (Remember, Suite Dreams must borrow only the net amount due after the cash discount is taken.)

b. What would you recommend?

EXCEL 3

Dollars AND Sense

This Business Decision illustrates an important business concept—borrowing money to take advantage of a cash discount.

Note how much can be saved by taking the cash discount even if the money is borrowed.

For a review of cash discounts, see Section IV in Chapter 7.

COLLABORATIVE LEARNING ACTIVITY

The Automobile Loan

As a team, choose a particular type of automobile category that you want to research (such as sport utility vehicle, sports car, hybrid, or luxury sedan). Then have each member of the team choose a different manufacturer's model within that category.

For example, if the team picked sport utility vehicle, individual choices might include Chevy Equinox, Mazda CX-7, Ford Escape, or Honda CRV.

a. From your local newspaper and the Internet, collect advertisements and offers for the purchase of the model you have chosen.

b. Visit or call a dealership for the vehicle you picked. Speak with a salesperson about the types of "deals" currently being offered on that model.

- What loan rates and terms are available from the dealer?
- Who is the actual lender?

c. Contact various lending institutions (banks, finance companies, credit unions) and inquire about vehicle loans.

- What loan rates and terms are being offered?
- Which lending institution is offering the best deal? Why?
- How do these rates and terms compare with those from the dealership?

4 HOUR ATM

DATE 01-11-2014	TIME 04:51

CERTIFICATE OF DEPOSIT	INTEREST RATES	APY
3 MONTH CD	0.50	0.50
6 MONTH CD	0.55	0.55
12 MONTH CD	0.75	.75
24 MONTH CD	1.05	.05
36 MONTH CD	1.24	.25
48 MONTH CD	1.49	.50
60 MONTH CD	1.59	.60

SAVINGS ACCOUNT	INTEREST RATES	APY
SUPER SAVERS 10K +	.25	.25

MONEY MARKET CHECKING	INTEREST RATES	APY
MONEY MARKET 10K +	.15	.15
MONEY MARKET 25K +	.25	.25
MONEY MARKET 50K +	.35	.35

CHECKING ACCOUNT	INTEREST RATES	APY
N.O.W. ACCOUNT	.15	.15

Member FDIC

THIS IS MY BANK

Robert K. Chin/Alamy

PERFORMANCE OBJECTIVES

SECTION I: Compound Interest—The Time Value of Money

11-1: Manually calculating compound amount (future value) and compound interest (p. 343)

11-2: Computing compound amount (future value) and compound interest by using compound interest tables (p. 344)

11-3: Creating compound interest table factors for periods beyond the table (p. 347)

11-4: Calculating annual percentage yield (APY) or effective interest rate (p. 348)

11-5: Calculating compound amount (future value) by using the compound interest formula (p. 349)

SECTION II: Present Value

11-6: Calculating the present value of a future amount by using present value tables (p. 354)

11-7: Creating present value table factors for periods beyond the table (p. 356)

11-8: Calculating present value of a future amount by using the present value formula (p. 357)

SECTION I | **11** | COMPOUND INTEREST—THE TIME VALUE OF MONEY

compound interest Interest that is applied a number of times during the term of a loan or an investment. Interest paid on principal and previously earned interest.

In Chapter 10, we studied simple interest in which the formula $I = PRT$ was applied once during the term of a loan or an investment to find the amount of interest. In business, another common way of calculating interest is by using a method known as *compounding*, or **compound interest**, in which the interest calculation is applied a number of times during the term of the loan or investment.

Compound interest yields considerably higher interest than simple interest does because the investor is earning interest on the interest. With compound interest, the interest earned for each period is reinvested or added to the previous principal before the next calculation or compounding. The previous principal plus interest then becomes the new principal for the next period. For example, $100 invested at 8% interest is worth $108 after the first year ($100 principal + $8 interest). If the interest is not withdrawn, the interest for the next period will be calculated based on $108 principal.

As this compounding process repeats itself each period, the principal keeps growing by the amount of the previous interest. As the number of compounding periods increases, the amount of interest earned grows dramatically, especially when compared with simple interest, as illustrated in Exhibit 11-1.

EXHIBIT 11-1 The Time Value of Money

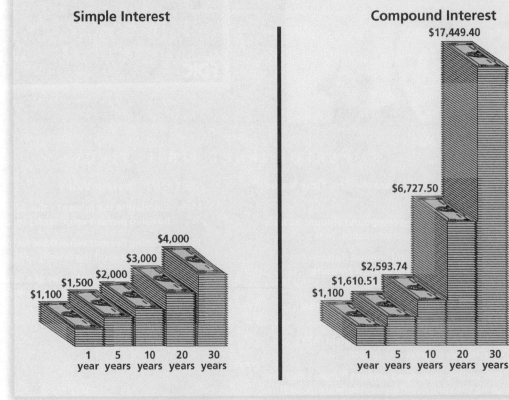

THE VALUE OF COMPOUND INTEREST

The growth of an investment may vary greatly depending on whether simple or compound interest is involved. For example, the chart below shows the growth of $1,000 invested in an account paying 10% annual simple interest versus the same amount invested in an account paying 10% annual compound interest. As this chart shows, compound interest yields more than four times the value generated by simple interest over 30 years.

Simple Interest

$1,100
$1,500
$2,000
$3,000
$4,000

1 year   5 years   10 years   20 years   30 years

Compound Interest

$17,449.40
$6,727.50
$2,593.74
$1,610.51
$1,100

1 year   5 years   10 years   20 years   30 years

time value of money The idea that money "now," or in the present, is more desirable than the same amount of money in the future because it can be invested and earn interest as time goes by.

This chapter introduces you to an all-important business concept, the **time value of money**. Consider this: If you were owed $1,000, would you rather have it now or 1 year from now? If you answered "now," you already have a feeling for the concept. Money "now," or in the *present*, is more desirable than the same amount of money in the *future* because it can be invested and earn interest as time goes by.

In this chapter, you learn to calculate the **compound amount (future value)** of an investment at compound interest when the **present amount (present value)** is known. You also learn to calculate the present value that must be deposited now at compound interest to yield a known future amount. (See Exhibit 11-2.)

compound amount, or **future value (FV)** The total amount of principal and accumulated interest at the end of a loan or an investment.

present amount, or **present value (PV)** An amount of money that must be deposited today at compound interest to provide a specified lump sum of money in the future.

EXHIBIT 11-2 Present Value and Future Value at Compound Interest

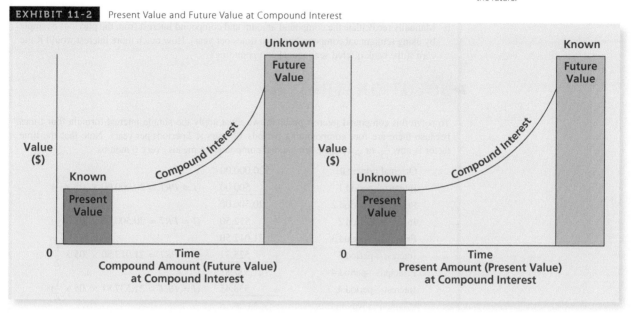

MANUALLY CALCULATING COMPOUND AMOUNT (FUTURE VALUE) AND COMPOUND INTEREST

11-1

Compounding divides the time of a loan or an investment into compounding periods or simply periods. To manually calculate the compound amount or future value of an investment, we must compound or calculate the interest as many times as there are compounding periods at the interest rate per period.

For example, an investment made for 5 years at 6% compounded annually (once per year) would have five compounding periods (5 years × 1 period per year), each at 6%. If the same investment was compounded semiannually (two times per year), there would be 10 compounding periods (5 years × 2 periods per year), each at 3% (6% annual rate ÷ 2 periods per year).

The amount of compound interest is calculated by subtracting the principal from the compound amount.

> **Compound interest = Compound amount − Principal**

The Time Value of Money

EXAMPLE1 MANUALLY CALCULATING COMPOUND INTEREST

a. Katie Trotta invested $20,000 in a passbook savings account at 5% interest compounded annually for 2 years. Manually calculate the compound amount of the investment and the total amount of compound interest Katie earned.

SOLUTIONSTRATEGY

To solve this compound interest problem manually, we must apply the simple interest formula twice because there are two compounding periods (2 years × 1 period per year). Note how the interest from the first period is reinvested or added to the original principal to earn interest in the second period.

Original principal	$20,000.00	
Interest—period 1	+ 1,000.00	$(I = PRT = 20,000.00 \times .05 \times 1)$
Principal—period 2	21,000.00	
Interest—period 2	+ 1,050.00	$(I = PRT = 21,000.00 \times .05 \times 1)$
Compound Amount	$22,050.00	
Compound amount	$22,050.00	
Principal	− 20,000.00	
Compound Interest Earned	$2,050.00	

b. Manually recalculate the compound amount and compound interest from the previous example by using semiannual compounding (two times per year). How much more interest would Katie earn if the bank offered semiannual compounding?

▶SOLUTIONSTRATEGY

To solve this compound interest problem, we must apply the simple interest formula four times because there are four compounding periods (2 years × 2 periods per year). Note that the time factor is now $\frac{6}{12}$, or $\frac{1}{2}$, because semiannual compounding means every 6 months.

Original principal	$20,000.00	
Interest—period 1	+ 500.00	$(I = PRT = 20,000.00 \times .05 \times \frac{1}{2})$
Principal—period 2	20,500.00	
Interest—period 2	+ 512.50	$(I = PRT = 20,500.00 \times .05 \times \frac{1}{2})$
Principal—period 3	21,012.50	
Interest—period 3	+ 525.31	$(I = PRT = 21,012.50 \times .05 \times \frac{1}{2})$
Principal—period 4	21,537.81	
Interest—period 4	+ 538.45	$(I = PRT = 21,537.81 \times .05 \times \frac{1}{2})$
Compound Amount	$22,076.26	
Compound amount	$22,076.26	
Principal	− 20,000.00	
Compound Interest	$2,076.26	

For the same investment values, semiannual compounding yields $26.26 more than annual compounding:

Interest with semiannual compounding	2,076.26
Interest with annual compounding	− 2,050.00
	$26.26

▶TRYITEXERCISE 1

Gail Parker invested $10,000 at 6% interest compounded semiannually for 3 years. Manually calculate the compound amount and the compound interest of Gail's investment.

CHECK YOUR ANSWERS WITH THE SOLUTIONS ON PAGE 363.

11-2 COMPUTING COMPOUND AMOUNT (FUTURE VALUE) AND COMPOUND INTEREST BY USING COMPOUND INTEREST TABLES

You do not have to work many compound interest problems manually, particularly those with numerous compounding periods, before you start wishing for an easier way! In actuality, there are two other methods for solving compound interest problems. The first uses a compound interest formula, and the second uses compound interest tables.

The compound interest formula, $A = P(1 + i)^n$, contains an exponent and therefore requires the use of a calculator with an exponential function key. The use of the compound interest formula is covered in Performance Objective 11-5.

A compound interest table, such as Table 11-1 on page 345, is a useful set of factors that represent the future values of $1 at various interest rates for a number of compounding periods. Because these factors are based on $1, the future values of other principal amounts are found by multiplying the appropriate table factor by the number of dollars of principal.

TABLE 11-1 Compound Interest Table (Future Value of $1 at Compound Interest)

Periods	$\frac{1}{2}$%	1%	$1\frac{1}{2}$%	2%	3%	4%	5%	6%	7%	8%	Periods
1	1.00500	1.01000	1.01500	1.02000	1.03000	1.04000	1.05000	1.06000	1.07000	1.08000	1
2	1.01003	1.02010	1.03023	1.04040	1.06090	1.08160	1.10250	1.12360	1.14490	1.16640	2
3	1.01508	1.03030	1.04568	1.06121	1.09273	1.12486	1.15763	1.19102	1.22504	1.25971	3
4	1.02015	1.04060	1.06136	1.08243	1.12551	1.16986	1.21551	1.26248	1.31080	1.36049	4
5	1.02525	1.05101	1.07728	1.10408	1.15927	1.21665	1.27628	1.33823	1.40255	1.46933	5
6	1.03038	1.06152	1.09344	1.12616	1.19405	1.26532	1.34010	1.41852	1.50073	1.58687	6
7	1.03553	1.07214	1.10984	1.14869	1.22987	1.31593	1.40710	1.50363	1.60578	1.71382	7
8	1.04071	1.08286	1.12649	1.17166	1.26677	1.36857	1.47746	1.59385	1.71819	1.85093	8
9	1.04591	1.09369	1.14339	1.19509	1.30477	1.42331	1.55133	1.68948	1.83846	1.99900	9
10	1.05114	1.10462	1.16054	1.21899	1.34392	1.48024	1.62889	1.79085	1.96715	2.15892	10
11	1.05640	1.11567	1.17795	1.24337	1.38423	1.53945	1.71034	1.89830	2.10485	2.33164	11
12	1.06168	1.12683	1.19562	1.26824	1.42576	1.60103	1.79586	2.01220	2.25219	2.51817	12
13	1.06699	1.13809	1.21355	1.29361	1.46853	1.66507	1.88565	2.13293	2.40985	2.71962	13
14	1.07232	1.14947	1.23176	1.31948	1.51259	1.73168	1.97993	2.26090	2.57853	2.93719	14
15	1.07768	1.16097	1.25023	1.34587	1.55797	1.80094	2.07893	2.39656	2.75903	3.17217	15
16	1.08307	1.17258	1.26899	1.37279	1.60471	1.87298	2.18287	2.54035	2.95216	3.42594	16
17	1.08849	1.18430	1.28802	1.40024	1.65285	1.94790	2.29202	2.69277	3.15882	3.70002	17
18	1.09393	1.19615	1.30734	1.42825	1.70243	2.02582	2.40662	2.85434	3.37993	3.99602	18
19	1.09940	1.20811	1.32695	1.45681	1.75351	2.10685	2.52695	3.02560	3.61653	4.31570	19
20	1.10490	1.22019	1.34686	1.48595	1.80611	2.19112	2.65330	3.20714	3.86968	4.66096	20
21	1.11042	1.23239	1.36706	1.51567	1.86029	2.27877	2.78596	3.39956	4.14056	5.03383	21
22	1.11597	1.24472	1.38756	1.54598	1.91610	2.36992	2.92526	3.60354	4.43040	5.43654	22
23	1.12155	1.25716	1.40838	1.57690	1.97359	2.46472	3.07152	3.81975	4.74053	5.87146	23
24	1.12716	1.26973	1.42950	1.60844	2.03279	2.56330	3.22510	4.04893	5.07237	6.34118	24
25	1.13280	1.28243	1.45095	1.64061	2.09378	2.66584	3.38635	4.29187	5.42743	6.84848	25

Periods	9%	10%	11%	12%	13%	14%	15%	16%	17%	18%	Periods
1	1.09000	1.10000	1.11000	1.12000	1.13000	1.14000	1.15000	1.16000	1.17000	1.18000	1
2	1.18810	1.21000	1.23210	1.25440	1.27690	1.29960	1.32250	1.34560	1.36890	1.39240	2
3	1.29503	1.33100	1.36763	1.40493	1.44290	1.48154	1.52088	1.56090	1.60161	1.64303	3
4	1.41158	1.46410	1.51807	1.57352	1.63047	1.68896	1.74901	1.81064	1.87389	1.93878	4
5	1.53862	1.61051	1.68506	1.76234	1.84244	1.92541	2.01136	2.10034	2.19245	2.28776	5
6	1.67710	1.77156	1.87041	1.97382	2.08195	2.19497	2.31306	2.43640	2.56516	2.69955	6
7	1.82804	1.94872	2.07616	2.21068	2.35261	2.50227	2.66002	2.82622	3.00124	3.18547	7
8	1.99256	2.14359	2.30454	2.47596	2.65844	2.85259	3.05902	3.27841	3.51145	3.75886	8
9	2.17189	2.35795	2.55804	2.77308	3.00404	3.25195	3.51788	3.80296	4.10840	4.43545	9
10	2.36736	2.59374	2.83942	3.10585	3.39457	3.70722	4.04556	4.41144	4.80683	5.23384	10
11	2.58043	2.85312	3.15176	3.47855	3.83586	4.22623	4.65239	5.11726	5.62399	6.17593	11
12	2.81266	3.13843	3.49845	3.89598	4.33452	4.81790	5.35025	5.93603	6.58007	7.28759	12
13	3.06580	3.45227	3.88328	4.36349	4.89801	5.49241	6.15279	6.88579	7.69868	8.59936	13
14	3.34173	3.79750	4.31044	4.88711	5.53475	6.26135	7.07571	7.98752	9.00745	10.14724	14
15	3.64248	4.17725	4.78459	5.47357	6.25427	7.13794	8.13706	9.26552	10.53872	11.97375	15
16	3.97031	4.59497	5.31089	6.13039	7.06733	8.13725	9.35762	10.74800	12.33030	14.12902	16
17	4.32763	5.05447	5.89509	6.86604	7.98608	9.27646	10.76126	12.46768	14.42646	16.67225	17
18	4.71712	5.55992	6.54355	7.68997	9.02427	10.57517	12.37545	14.46251	16.87895	19.67325	18
19	5.14166	6.11591	7.26334	8.61276	10.19742	12.05569	14.23177	16.77652	19.74838	23.21444	19
20	5.60441	6.72750	8.06231	9.64629	11.52309	13.74349	16.36654	19.46076	23.10560	27.39303	20
21	6.10881	7.40025	8.94917	10.80385	13.02109	15.66758	18.82152	22.57448	27.03355	32.32378	21
22	6.65860	8.14027	9.93357	12.10031	14.71383	17.86104	21.64475	26.18640	31.62925	38.14206	22
23	7.25787	8.95430	11.02627	13.55235	16.62663	20.36158	24.89146	30.37622	37.00623	45.00763	23
24	7.91108	9.84973	12.23916	15.17863	18.78809	23.21221	28.62518	35.23642	43.29729	53.10901	24
25	8.62308	10.83471	13.58546	17.00006	21.23054	26.46192	32.91895	40.87424	50.65783	62.66863	25

The values in Table 11-1 were generated by the formula $FV = (1 + i)^n$ rounded to five decimal places, where i is the interest rate per period and n is the total number of periods.

EXHIBIT 11-3

Compounding Periods per Year

Interest Compounded		Compounding Periods per Year
Annually	Every year	1
Semiannually	Every 6 months	2
Quarterly	Every 3 months	4
Monthly	Every month	12
Daily	Every day	365
Continuously		Infinite

$$\text{Compound amount (future value)} = \text{Table factor} \times \text{Principal}$$

To use the compound interest tables, we must know the number of compounding periods and the interest rate per period. Exhibit 11-3 above shows the various compounding options and the corresponding number of periods per year. *Note*: The greater the number of compounding periods per year, the higher the interest earned on the investment. Today interest can actually be calculated on a continuous basis—that is, up to the minute. In competitive markets, many banks offer continuous compounding as an incentive to attract new deposits.

To find the number of compounding periods of an investment, multiply the number of years by the number of periods per year.

$$\text{Compounding periods} = \text{Years} \times \text{Periods per year}$$

To find the interest rate per period, divide the annual, or nominal, rate by the number of periods per year.

$$\text{Interest rate per period} = \frac{\text{Nominal rate}}{\text{Period per year}}$$

STEPS FOR USING COMPOUND INTEREST TABLES

STEP 1. Scan across the top row to find the interest rate per period.

STEP 2. Look down that column to the row corresponding to the number of periods.

STEP 3. The table factor at the intersection of the rate-per-period column and the number-of-periods row is the future value of $1 at compound interest. Multiply the table factor by the principal to determine the compound amount.

$$\text{Compound amount} = \text{Table factor} \times \text{Principal}$$

EXAMPLE2   USING COMPOUND INTEREST TABLES

John Anderson invested $1,200 in an account at 8% interest compounded quarterly for 5 years. Use Table 11-1 to find the compound amount of John's investment. What is the amount of the compound interest?

SOLUTIONSTRATEGY

To solve this compound interest problem, we must first find the interest rate per period and the number of compounding periods.

$$\text{Interest rate per period} = \frac{\text{Nominal rate}}{\text{Periods per year}}$$

$$\text{Interest rate per period} = \frac{8\%}{4} = 2\%$$

$$\text{Compounding periods} = \text{Years} \times \text{Periods per year}$$

$$\text{Compounding periods} = 5 \times 4 = 20$$

Now find the table factor by scanning across the top row of the compound interest table to 2% and down the 2% column to 20 periods. The table factor at that intersection is 1.48595. The compound amount is found by multiplying the table factor by the principal:

$$\text{Compound amount} = \text{Table factor} \times \text{Principal}$$
$$\text{Compound amount} = 1.48595 \times 1{,}200 = \$1{,}783.14$$

The amount of interest is found by subtracting the principal from the compound amount.

$$\text{Compound interest} = \text{Compound amount} - \text{Principal}$$
$$\text{Compound interest} = 1{,}783.14 - 1{,}200.00 = \$583.14$$

▶TRYITEXERCISE 2

Jenny Chao invested $20,000 at 6% interest compounded semiannually for 8 years. Use Table 11-1 to find the compound amount of her investment. What is the amount of compound interest Jenny earned?

CHECK YOUR ANSWERS WITH THE SOLUTIONS ON PAGE 363.

CREATING COMPOUND INTEREST TABLE FACTORS FOR PERIODS BEYOND THE TABLE

11-3

When the number of periods of an investment is greater than the number of periods provided by the compound interest table, you can compute a new table factor by multiplying the factors for any two periods that add up to the number of periods required. For answer consistency in this chapter, use the two table factors that represent *half*, or values as close as possible to half, of the periods required. For example,

```
20 periods ──┐
             ├──▶ 40 periods
20 periods ──┘
```

```
20 periods ──┐
             ├──▶ 41 periods
21 periods ──┘
```

STEPS FOR CREATING NEW COMPOUND INTEREST TABLE FACTORS

STEP 1. For the stated interest rate per period, find the two table factors that represent *half*, or values as close as possible to half, of the periods required.

STEP 2. Multiply the two table factors from Step 1 to form the new factor.

STEP 3. Round the new factor to five decimal places.

EXAMPLE3 CALCULATING COMPOUND AMOUNT FOR PERIODS BEYOND THE TABLE

Calculate a new table factor and find the compound amount of $10,000 invested at 6% compounded monthly for 3 years.

▶SOLUTIONSTRATEGY

This investment requires a table factor for 36 periods (12 periods per year for 3 years). Because Table 11-1 provides factors only up to 25 periods, we must create one using the steps above.

Step 1. At 6% interest compounded monthly, the rate per period is $\frac{1}{2}\%$. Because we are looking for 36 periods, we will use the factors for 18 and 18 periods at $\frac{1}{2}\%$.

Table factor for 18 periods, $\frac{1}{2}\% = 1.09393$

Table factor for 18 periods, $\frac{1}{2}\% = 1.09393$

Step 2. Multiply the factors for 18 and 18 periods.

$$1.09393 \times 1.09393 = 1.196682$$

Step 3. Round to five decimal places.

The new table factor for 36 periods is 1.19668.

The compound amount of the $10,000 investment is

Compound amount = Table factor × Principal

Compound amount = 1.19668 × 10,000 = $11,966.80

▶ TRYITEXERCISE 3

Stan Gray invests $3,500 at 8% interest compounded quarterly for 7 years. Calculate a new table factor and find the compound amount of Stan's investment.

CHECK YOUR ANSWERS WITH THE SOLUTIONS ON PAGE 363.

IN THE Business World

The Rule of 72

There is an easy method for calculating approximately how long it takes an amount of money to double in value at compound interest. Simply divide the number 72 by the interest rate. The result is the number of years it takes to double in value.

$$\text{Years to double} = \frac{72}{\text{Compound interest rate}}$$

- For example, if you invested money at 6% compound interest, it would take 12 years ($\frac{72}{6} = 12$) to double your money.

- If you were able to find an investment that paid 9% interest, you could double your money in 8 years ($\frac{72}{9} = 8$).

INTERFOTO/Personalities/Alamy

Source: www.hetemeel.com

11-4 CALCULATING ANNUAL PERCENTAGE YIELD (APY) OR EFFECTIVE INTEREST RATE

annual, or **nominal**, **rate** The advertised or stated interest rate of an investment or loan. The rate used to calculate the compound interest.

In describing investments and loans, the advertised or stated interest rate is known as the **annual**, or **nominal**, **rate**. It is also the rate used to calculate the compound interest. Consider, however, what happens to an investment of $100 at 12% nominal interest.

As we learned in Performance Objective 11-2, the greater the number of compounding periods per year, the higher the amount of interest earned. (See Exhibit 11-4.) Although the nominal interest rate is 12%, with monthly compounding, the $100 earns more than 12%. This is why many investment offers today advertise daily or continuous compounding. How much are these investments really earning?

EXHIBIT 11-4

Compound Interest Earned on $100 at 12%

Compounding	Interest Earned
Annually	$12.00
Semiannually	$12.36
Quarterly	$12.55
Monthly	$12.68

The **annual percentage yield (APY)**, or **effective rate**, reflects the real rate of return on an investment. APY is calculated by finding the total compound interest earned in 1 year and dividing by the principal. *Note*: This is actually the simple interest formula (from Chapter 10) solved for rate $R = I \div PT$, where T is equal to 1.

$$\text{Annual percentage (APY)} = \frac{\text{Total compound interest earned in 1 year}}{\text{Principal}}$$

From Exhibit 11-4, we can see that the annual percentage yield is the same as the nominal rate when interest is compounded annually; however, it jumps to 12.36% ($12.36) when the compounding is changed to semiannually and to 12.68 % ($12.68) when compounded monthly.

> **annual percentage yield (APY), or effective rate** The real or true rate of return on an investment. It is the total compound interest earned in 1 year divided by the principal. The more compounding periods per year, the higher the APY.

EXAMPLE 4 — CALCULATING APY

What is the compound amount, compound interest, and annual percentage yield of $4,000 invested for 1 year at 8% compounded semiannually?

▶ SOLUTION STRATEGY

First, we must find the total compound interest earned in 1 year. We can find the compound amount using the factor for 4%, two periods, from Table 11-1.

Compound amount = Table factor × Principal
Compound amount = 1.08160 × 4,000 = $4,326.40

Compound interest = Compound amount − Principal
Compound interest = 4,326.40 − 4,000 = $326.40

$$\text{Annual percentage yield} = \frac{\text{Total compound interest earned in 1 year}}{\text{Principal}}$$

$$\text{Annual percentage yield} = \frac{326.40}{4,000.00} = 8.16\%$$

▶ TRY IT EXERCISE 4

Jill Quinn invested $7,000 in a certificate of deposit for 1 year at 6% interest compounded quarterly. What is the compound amount, compound interest, and annual percentage yield of Jill's investment? Round the APY to the nearest hundredth of a percent.

CHECK YOUR ANSWERS WITH THE SOLUTIONS ON PAGE 363.

Dollars AND Sense

Regulation DD of the Truth in Savings Law, enacted by Congress in 1993, requires banks and other depository institutions to fully disclose the terms of deposit accounts to consumers. The major provisions of the regulation require institutions to:

* Provide consumer account holders with written information about important terms of an account, including the **annual percentage yield**.
* Provide fee and other information on any periodic statement sent to consumers.
* Use prescribed methods to determine the balance on which interest is calculated.
* Comply with special requirements when advertising deposit accounts.

CALCULATING COMPOUND AMOUNT (FUTURE VALUE) BY USING THE COMPOUND INTEREST FORMULA

11-5

If your calculator has an exponential function key, y^x, you can calculate the compound amount of an investment by using the compound interest formula.

The compound interest formula states:

$$A = P(1 + i)^n$$

where:

A = **Compound amount**

P = **Principal**

i = **Interest rate per period (expressed as a decimal)**

n = **Total compounding periods (years × periods per year)**

STEPS FOR SOLVING THE COMPOUND INTEREST FORMULA

STEP 1. Add the 1 and the interest rate per period, i.

STEP 2. Raise the sum from Step 1 to the nth (number of compounding periods) power by using the y^x key on your calculator.

STEP 3. Multiply the principal, P, by the answer from Step 2.

Calculator Sequence: 1 $\boxed{+}$ i $\boxed{=}$ $\boxed{y^x}$ n $\boxed{\times}$ P $\boxed{=}$ A

EXAMPLE5   USING THE COMPOUND INTEREST FORMULA

Use the compound interest formula to calculate the compound amount of $5,000 invested at 10% interest compounded semiannually for 3 years.

SOLUTIONSTRATEGY

This problem is solved by substituting the investment information into the compound interest formula. It is important to solve the formula using the sequence of steps outlined above. Note that the rate per period, i, is 5% (10% ÷ 2 periods per year). The total number of periods, the exponent n, is 6 (3 years × 2 periods per year).

$$A = P(1 + i)^n$$
$$A = 5{,}000\,(1 + .05)^6$$
$$A = 5{,}000\,(1.05)^6$$
$$A = 5{,}000\,(1.3400956) = 6{,}700.4782 = \underline{\$6{,}700.48}$$

Calculator Sequence: 1 $\boxed{+}$ .05 $\boxed{=}$ $\boxed{y^x}$ 6 $\boxed{\times}$ 5000 $\boxed{=}$ $6,700.4782 = $6,700.48

▶TRYITEXERCISE 5

Use the compound interest formula to calculate the compound amount of $3,000 invested at 8% interest compounded quarterly for 5 years.

CHECK YOUR ANSWER WITH THE SOLUTION ON PAGE 363.

SECTION I 11 REVIEW EXERCISES

For the following investments, find the total number of compounding periods and the interest rate per period.

	Term of Investment	Nominal (Annual) Rate (%)	Interest Compounded	Compounding Periods	Rate per Period (%)
1.	3 years	13	annually	3	13
2.	5 years	4	quarterly	_____	_____
3.	12 years	8	semiannually	_____	_____
4.	6 years	6	monthly	_____	_____
5.	4 years	6	quarterly	_____	_____
6.	9 years	5.5	semiannually	_____	_____
7.	9 months	4	quarterly	_____	_____

Manually calculate the compound amount and compound interest for the following investments.

	Principal	Time Period (years)	Nominal Rate (%)	Interest Compounded	Compound Amount	Compound Interest
8.	$4,000	2	10	annually	$4,840.00	$840.00
9.	$10,000	1	4	quarterly	_____	_____
10.	$8,000	3	8	semiannually	_____	_____
11.	$2,000	4	6	annually	_____	_____

Using Table 11-1, calculate the compound amount and compound interest for the following investments.

	Principal	Time Period (years)	Nominal Rate (%)	Interest Compounded	Compound Amount	Compound Interest
12.	$7,000	4	13	annually	$11,413.29	$4,413.29
13.	$11,000	6	4	semiannually	_____	_____
14.	$5,300	3	8	quarterly	_____	_____
15.	$67,000	2	18	monthly	_____	_____
16.	$25,000	15	5	annually	_____	_____
17.	$400	2	6	monthly	_____	_____
18.	$8,800	$12\frac{1}{2}$	10	semiannually	_____	_____

The following investments require table factors for periods beyond the table. Create the new table factor, rounded to five places, and calculate the compound amount for each.

	Principal	Time Period (years)	Nominal Rate (%)	Interest Compounded	New Table Factor	Compound Amount
19.	$13,000	3	12	monthly	1.43077	$18,600.01
20.	$19,000	29	9	annually	_____	_____
21.	$34,700	11	4	quarterly	_____	_____
22.	$10,000	40	3	annually	_____	_____
23.	$1,000	16	6	semiannually	_____	_____

For the following investments, compute the amount of compound interest earned in 1 year and the annual percentage yield (APY).

	Principal	Nominal Rate (%)	Interest Compounded	Compound Interest Earned in 1 Year	Annual Percentage Yield (APY)
24.	$5,000	10	semiannually	$512.50	10.25%
25.	$2,000	4	annually	_____	_____
26.	$36,000	12	monthly	_____	_____
27.	$1,000	8	quarterly	_____	_____
28.	$8,000	6	semiannually	_____	_____

Solve the following word problems by using Table 11-1.

29. Sherry Smith invested $3,000 at the Horizon Bank at 6% interest compounded quarterly.

    a. What is the annual percentage yield of this investment?

b. What will Sherry's investment be worth after 6 years?

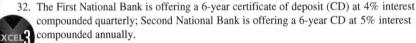

30. As a savings plan for college, when their son Bob was born, the Wilburs deposited $10,000 in an account paying 8% compounded annually. How much will the account be worth when Bob is 18 years old?

31. You are the owner of a UPS Store franchise. You have just deposited $12,000 in an investment account earning 12% compounded monthly. This account is intended to pay for store improvements in $2\frac{1}{2}$ years. At that rate, how much will be available in the account for the project?

EXCEL 2

32. The First National Bank is offering a 6-year certificate of deposit (CD) at 4% interest compounded quarterly; Second National Bank is offering a 6-year CD at 5% interest compounded annually.

EXCEL 3

   a. If you were interested in investing $8,000 in one of these CDs, calculate the compound amount of each offer.

   b. What is the annual percentage yield of each CD?

   c. (Optional) If Third National Bank has a 6-year CD at 4.5% interest compounded monthly, use the compound interest formula to calculate the compound amount of this offer.

33. A certain animal husbandry program has a flock of sheep that increases in size by 15% every year. If there are currently 48 sheep, how many sheep are expected to be in the flock in 5 years? Round to the nearest whole sheep.

34. The rate of bacteria growth in a laboratory experiment was measured at 16% per hour. If this experiment is repeated and begins with 5 grams of bacteria, how much bacteria should be expected after 12 hours? Round to the nearest tenth of a gram.

SG cityscapes/Alamy

UPS Store franchises have consistently been recognized as leading opportunities in this sector. With 4,300 locations, the minimum requirements are $60,000–$100,000 in cash or liquid assets.

Some of the products and services UPS Stores provide include packing and shipping services, mailbox and postal services, copying, faxing, notary services, finishing and printing services, and packaging and moving supplies.

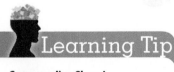

Learning Tip

Compounding Sheep!
The concept of compounding may also be used to compound "other variables" besides money. Use the compound interest table or formula for Exercises 33 and 34.

Solve the following exercises and word problems by using the compound interest formula.

	Principal	Time Period (years)	Nominal Rate (%)	Interest Compounded	Compound Amount	Compound Interest
35.	$5,000	4	4.2	semiannually	$5,904.40	$904.40
36.	$700	8	1.5	monthly	_____	_____
37.	$2,800	$2\frac{1}{2}$	3.1	quarterly	_____	_____
38.	$12,450	10	2.6	annually	_____	_____

39. Gabriel Hopen, a 32-year-old commercial artist, has just signed a contract with an advertising agency. Gabriel's starting salary is $47,800. The agency has agreed to increase his salary by 8.5% annually. How much will Gabriel's salary be after 5 years? Round to the nearest whole dollar.

40. The FernRod Motorcycle Company invested $250,000 at 4.5% compounded monthly to be used for the expansion of their manufacturing facilities. How much money will be available for the project in $3\frac{1}{2}$ years?

BUSINESS DECISION: DAILY COMPOUNDING

41. As an incentive to attract savings deposits, most financial institutions today offer **daily** and even **continuous compounding**. This means that savings, or passbook, accounts, as well as CDs, earn interest compounded each day or even more frequently, such as every hour or even every minute. (Continuous compounding, in which compounding occurs every instant, involves a different formula that is derived from the formula we've been using.) Let's take a look at daily compounding.

   To calculate the compound amount, A, of an investment with daily compounding, use the compound interest formula modified as follows:

   - Rate per period (daily) $= \dfrac{i}{365}$ (nominal interest rate, i, divided by 365)
   - Number of periods (days), n, = number of days of the investment.

$$A = P\left(1 + \frac{i}{365}\right)^n$$

Calculator Sequence: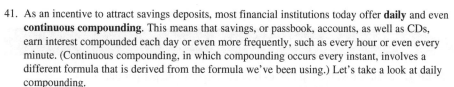
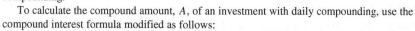

   a. On April 19, Thomas Ash deposited $2,700 in a passbook savings account at 3.5% interest compounded daily. What is the compound amount of his account on August 5?

   b. Using daily compounding, recalculate the compound amount for each of the three certificates of deposit in Exercise 32.

11

SECTION II   PRESENT VALUE

In Section I, we learned how to find a future value when the present value was known. Let's take a look at the reverse situation, also commonly found in business. When a future value (an amount needed in the future) is known, the present value is the amount that must be invested today to accumulate with compound interest to that future value. For example, if a corporation wants $100,000 in 5 years (future value—known) to replace its fleet of trucks, what amount must be invested today (present value—unknown) at 8% compounded quarterly to achieve this goal? (See Exhibit 11-5.)

EXHIBIT 11-5

Present Value to Future Value

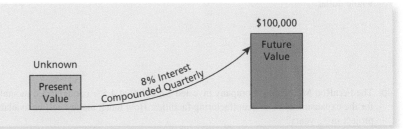

11-6   CALCULATING THE PRESENT VALUE OF A FUTURE AMOUNT BY USING PRESENT VALUE TABLES

Just as there are compound interest tables to aid in the calculation of compound amounts, present value tables help calculate the present value of a known future amount. Table 11-2 is such a table. Note that this table is similar to the compound interest table in that the table factors are based on the interest rate per period and the number of compounding periods.

STEPS FOR USING PRESENT VALUE TABLES

STEP 1. Scan across the top row to find the interest rate per period.

STEP 2. Look down that column to the row corresponding to the number of periods.

STEP 3. The table factor found at the intersection of the rate-per-period column and the number-of-periods row is the present value of $1 at compound interest. Multiply the table factor by the compound amount to determine the present value.

Present value = Table factor × Compound amount (future value)

EXAMPLE6   CALCULATING PRESENT VALUE

Charlie Watson will need $5,000 in 8 years. Use Table 11-2 to find how much he must invest now at 6% interest compounded semiannually to have $5,000, 8 years from now.

►SOLUTIONSTRATEGY

To solve this present value problem, we will use 3% per period (6% nominal rate ÷ 2 periods per year) and 16 periods (8 years × 2 periods per year).

Step 1. Scan the top row of the present value table to 3%.

Step 2. Look down that column to the row corresponding to 16 periods.

TABLE 11-2 Present Value Table (Present Value of $1 at Compound Interest)

Periods	$\frac{1}{2}$%	1%	$1\frac{1}{2}$%	2%	3%	4%	5%	6%	7%	8%	Periods
1	0.99502	0.99010	0.98522	0.98039	0.97087	0.96154	0.95238	0.94340	0.93458	0.92593	1
2	0.99007	0.98030	0.97066	0.96117	0.94260	0.92456	0.90703	0.89000	0.87344	0.85734	2
3	0.98515	0.97059	0.95632	0.94232	0.91514	0.88900	0.86384	0.83962	0.81630	0.79383	3
4	0.98025	0.96098	0.94218	0.92385	0.88849	0.85480	0.82270	0.79209	0.76290	0.73503	4
5	0.97537	0.95147	0.92826	0.90573	0.86261	0.82193	0.78353	0.74726	0.71299	0.68058	5
6	0.97052	0.94205	0.91454	0.88797	0.83748	0.79031	0.74622	0.70496	0.66634	0.63017	6
7	0.96569	0.93272	0.90103	0.87056	0.81309	0.75992	0.71068	0.66506	0.62275	0.58349	7
8	0.96089	0.92348	0.88771	0.85349	0.78941	0.73069	0.67684	0.62741	0.58201	0.54027	8
9	0.95610	0.91434	0.87459	0.83676	0.76642	0.70259	0.64461	0.59190	0.54393	0.50025	9
10	0.95135	0.90529	0.86167	0.82035	0.74409	0.67556	0.61391	0.55839	0.50835	0.46319	10
11	0.94661	0.89632	0.84893	0.80426	0.72242	0.64958	0.58468	0.52679	0.47509	0.42888	11
12	0.94191	0.88745	0.83639	0.78849	0.70138	0.62460	0.55684	0.49697	0.44401	0.39711	12
13	0.93722	0.87866	0.82403	0.77303	0.68095	0.60057	0.53032	0.46884	0.41496	0.36770	13
14	0.93256	0.86996	0.81185	0.75788	0.66112	0.57748	0.50507	0.44230	0.38782	0.34046	14
15	0.92792	0.86135	0.79985	0.74301	0.64186	0.55526	0.48102	0.41727	0.36245	0.31524	15
16	0.92330	0.85282	0.78803	0.72845	0.62317	0.53391	0.45811	0.39365	0.33873	0.29189	16
17	0.91871	0.84438	0.77639	0.71416	0.60502	0.51337	0.43630	0.37136	0.31657	0.27027	17
18	0.91414	0.83602	0.76491	0.70016	0.58739	0.49363	0.41552	0.35034	0.29586	0.25025	18
19	0.90959	0.82774	0.75361	0.68643	0.57029	0.47464	0.39573	0.33051	0.27651	0.23171	19
20	0.90506	0.81954	0.74247	0.67297	0.55368	0.45639	0.37689	0.31180	0.25842	0.21455	20
21	0.90056	0.81143	0.73150	0.65978	0.53755	0.43883	0.35894	0.29416	0.24151	0.19866	21
22	0.89608	0.80340	0.72069	0.64684	0.52189	0.42196	0.34185	0.27751	0.22571	0.18394	22
23	0.89162	0.79544	0.71004	0.63416	0.50669	0.40573	0.32557	0.26180	0.21095	0.17032	23
24	0.88719	0.78757	0.69954	0.62172	0.49193	0.39012	0.31007	0.24698	0.19715	0.15770	24
25	0.88277	0.77977	0.68921	0.60953	0.47761	0.37512	0.29530	0.23300	0.18425	0.14602	25

Periods	9%	10%	11%	12%	13%	14%	15%	16%	17%	18%	Periods
1	0.91743	0.90909	0.90090	0.89286	0.88496	0.87719	0.86957	0.86207	0.85470	0.84746	1
2	0.84168	0.82645	0.81162	0.79719	0.78315	0.76947	0.75614	0.74316	0.73051	0.71818	2
3	0.77218	0.75131	0.73119	0.71178	0.69305	0.67497	0.65752	0.64066	0.62437	0.60863	3
4	0.70843	0.68301	0.65873	0.63552	0.61332	0.59208	0.57175	0.55229	0.53365	0.51579	4
5	0.64993	0.62092	0.59345	0.56743	0.54276	0.51937	0.49718	0.47611	0.45611	0.43711	5
6	0.59627	0.56447	0.53464	0.50663	0.48032	0.45559	0.43233	0.41044	0.38984	0.37043	6
7	0.54703	0.51316	0.48166	0.45235	0.42506	0.39964	0.37594	0.35383	0.33320	0.31393	7
8	0.50187	0.46651	0.43393	0.40388	0.37616	0.35056	0.32690	0.30503	0.28478	0.26604	8
9	0.46043	0.42410	0.39092	0.36061	0.33288	0.30751	0.28426	0.26295	0.24340	0.22546	9
10	0.42241	0.38554	0.35218	0.32197	0.29459	0.26974	0.24718	0.22668	0.20804	0.19106	10
11	0.38753	0.35049	0.31728	0.28748	0.26070	0.23662	0.21494	0.19542	0.17781	0.16192	11
12	0.35553	0.31863	0.28584	0.25668	0.23071	0.20756	0.18691	0.16846	0.15197	0.13722	12
13	0.32618	0.28966	0.25751	0.22917	0.20416	0.18207	0.16253	0.14523	0.12989	0.11629	13
14	0.29925	0.26333	0.23199	0.20462	0.18068	0.15971	0.14133	0.12520	0.11102	0.09855	14
15	0.27454	0.23939	0.20900	0.18270	0.15989	0.14010	0.12289	0.10793	0.09489	0.08352	15
16	0.25187	0.21763	0.18829	0.16312	0.14150	0.12289	0.10686	0.09304	0.08110	0.07078	16
17	0.23107	0.19784	0.16963	0.14564	0.12522	0.10780	0.09293	0.08021	0.06932	0.05998	17
18	0.21199	0.17986	0.15282	0.13004	0.11081	0.09456	0.08081	0.06914	0.05925	0.05083	18
19	0.19449	0.16351	0.13768	0.11611	0.09806	0.08295	0.07027	0.05961	0.05064	0.04308	19
20	0.17843	0.14864	0.12403	0.10367	0.08678	0.07276	0.06110	0.05139	0.04328	0.03651	20
21	0.16370	0.13513	0.11174	0.09256	0.07680	0.06383	0.05313	0.04430	0.03699	0.03094	21
22	0.15018	0.12285	0.10067	0.08264	0.06796	0.05599	0.04620	0.03819	0.03162	0.02622	22
23	0.13778	0.11168	0.09069	0.07379	0.06014	0.04911	0.04017	0.03292	0.02702	0.02222	23
24	0.12640	0.10153	0.08170	0.06588	0.05323	0.04308	0.03493	0.02838	0.02310	0.01883	24
25	0.11597	0.09230	0.07361	0.05882	0.04710	0.03779	0.03038	0.02447	0.01974	0.01596	25

The values in Table 11-2 were generated by the formula $PV = \dfrac{1}{(1 + i)^n}$ rounded to five decimal places, where i is the interest rate per period and n is the total number of periods.

Step 3. Find the table factor at the intersection of Steps 1 and 2 and multiply it by the compound amount to find the present value. Table factor = .62317.

$$\text{Present value} = \text{Table factor} \times \text{Compound amount}$$
$$\text{Present value} = .62317 \times 5,000 = \underline{\$3,115.85}$$

▶ TRYITEXERCISE 6

Count Gustav wants to renovate his castle in Boulogne in 3 years. He estimates the cost to be $3,000,000. Use Table 11-2 to find how much Count Gustav must invest now at 8% interest compounded quarterly to have $3,000,000, 3 years from now.

CHECK YOUR ANSWER WITH THE SOLUTION ON PAGE 363.

11-7 CREATING PRESENT VALUE TABLE FACTORS FOR PERIODS BEYOND THE TABLE

Just as with the compound interest tables, there may be times when the number of periods of an investment or a loan is greater than the number of periods provided by the present value tables. When this occurs, you can create a new table factor by multiplying the table factors for any two periods that add up to the number of periods required.

For answer consistency in this chapter, use the two table factors that represent *half*, or values as close as possible to half, of the periods required. For example,

STEPS FOR CREATING NEW TABLE FACTORS

STEP 1. For the stated interest rate per period, find the two table factors that represent *half*, or values as close as possible to half, of the periods required.

STEP 2. Multiply the two table factors from Step 1 to form the new factor.

STEP 3. Round the new factor to five decimal places.

EXAMPLE7   CREATING PRESENT VALUE TABLE FACTORS

Calculate a new table factor and find the present value of $2,000 if the interest rate is 6% compounded quarterly for 8 years.

▶ SOLUTIONSTRATEGY

This investment requires a table factor for 32 periods, four periods per year for 8 years. Because Table 11-2 provides factors only up to 25 periods, we must create one by using the steps above.

Step 1. At 6% interest compounded quarterly, the rate per period is $1\frac{1}{2}\%$. Because we are looking for 32 periods, we will use the factors for 16 and 16 periods at $1\frac{1}{2}\%$.

Table factor for 16 periods, $1\frac{1}{2}\% = .78803$

Table factor for 16 periods, $1\frac{1}{2}\% = .78803$

Step 2. Multiply the factors for 16 and 16 periods:

$$.78803 \times .78803 = .620991$$

Step 3. Rounding to five decimal places, the new table factor for 32 periods is .62099. The present value of the $2,000 investment is

Present value = Table factor × Compound amount
Present value = .62099 × 2,000 = $1,241.98

▶TRYITEXERCISE 7

Calculate a new table factor and find the present value of $8,500 if the interest rate is 6% compounded quarterly for 10 years.

CHECK YOUR ANSWERS WITH THE SOLUTIONS ON PAGE 363.

CALCULATING PRESENT VALUE OF A FUTURE AMOUNT BY USING THE PRESENT VALUE FORMULA

11-8

If your calculator has an exponential function key, y^x, you can calculate the present value of an investment by using the present value formula.

The present value formula states:

$$PV = \frac{A}{(1 + i)^n}$$

where:

PV = **Present value**

A = **Compound amount**

i = **Interest rate per period (expressed as a decimal)**

n = **Total compounding periods (years × periods per year)**

STEPS FOR SOLVING THE PRESENT VALUE FORMULA

STEP 1. Add the 1 and the interest rate per period, i.

STEP 2. Raise the sum from Step 1 to the nth power by using the y^x key on your calculator.

STEP 3. Divide the compound amount, A, by the answer from Step 2.

Calculator sequence 1 ⊞ i ⊟ y^x n ⊟ M+ A ÷ MR ⊟ PV

EXAMPLE8   USING THE PRESENT VALUE FORMULA

Use the present value formula to calculate the present value of $3,000 if the interest rate is 8% compounded quarterly for 6 years.

▶SOLUTIONSTRATEGY

This problem is solved by substituting the investment information into the present value formula. It is important to solve the formula using the sequence of steps outlined. Note the rate per period, i, is 2% (8% ÷ 4 periods per year). The total number of periods, the exponent n, is 24 (6 years × 4 periods per year).

$$\text{Present value} = \frac{A}{(1 + i)^n}$$

$$\text{Present value} = \frac{3,000}{(1 + .02)^{24}}$$

$$\text{Present value} = \frac{3,000}{(1.02)^{24}}$$

$$\text{Present value} = \frac{3,000}{1.608437249} = \$1,865.16$$

Calculator Sequence: 1 ⊞ .02 ⊟ y^x 24 ⊟ M+ 3000 ÷ MR ⊟ $1,865.16

► TRYITEXERCISE 8

Sam and Rosa Alonso want to accumulate $30,000, 17 years from now as a college fund for their baby son, Michael. Use the present value formula to calculate how much they must invest now at an interest rate of 8% compounded semiannually to have $30,000 in 17 years.

CHECK YOUR ANSWER WITH THE SOLUTION ON PAGE 363.

SECTION II   11   REVIEW EXERCISES

For the following investments, calculate the present value (principal) and the compound interest. Use Table 11-2. Round your answers to the nearest cent.

	Compound Amount	Term of Investment	Nominal Rate (%)	Interest Compounded	Present Value	Compound Interest
1.	$6,000	3 years	9	annually	$4,633.08	$1,366.92
2.	$24,000	6 years	4	semiannually	_____	_____
3.	$650	5 years	8	quarterly	_____	_____
4.	$2,000	12 years	6	semiannually	_____	_____
►5.	$50,000	25 years	11	annually	_____	_____
6.	$14,500	18 months	4	semiannually	_____	_____
►7.	$9,800	4 years	12	quarterly	_____	_____
8.	$100,000	10 years	4	annually	_____	_____
9.	$250	1 year	6	monthly	_____	_____
10.	$4,000	27 months	8	quarterly	_____	_____

The following investments require table factors for periods beyond the table. Create the new table factor rounded to five places and calculate the present value for each.

	Compound Amount	Term of Investment (years)	Nominal Rate (%)	Interest Compounded	New Table Factor	Present Value
11.	$12,000	10	16	quarterly	.20829	$2,499.48
12.	$33,000	38	7	annually	_____	_____
13.	$1,400	12	6	quarterly	_____	_____
14.	$1,000	45	3	annually	_____	_____
►15.	$110,000	17	8	semiannually	_____	_____

Solve the following word problems by using Table 11-2.

16. How much must be invested today at 6% compounded quarterly to have $8,000 in 3 years?

17. Samantha Wimberly is planning a vacation in Europe in 4 years, after graduation. She estimates that she will need $3,500 for the trip.

   a. If her bank is offering 4-year certificates of deposit with 8% interest compounded quarterly, how much must Samantha invest now to have the money for the trip?

   b. How much compound interest will be earned on the investment?

© Ford Motor Company

18. Pinnacle Homes, a real estate development company, is planning to build five homes, each costing $125,000, in $2\frac{1}{2}$ years. The Galaxy Bank pays 6% interest compounded semiannually. How much should the company invest now to have sufficient funds to build the homes in the future?

Corporate bonds are debt obligations, or IOUs, issued by private and public corporations. They are typically issued in multiples of $1,000. Bonds are commonly used to finance company modernization and expansion programs.

   When you buy a bond, you are lending money to the corporation that issued it. The corporation promises to return your money (or principal) on a specified maturity date. Until that time, it also pays you a stated rate of interest.

19. Tri-Star Airlines intends to pay off a $20,000,000 corporate bond issue that comes due in 4 years. How much must the company set aside now at 6% interest compounded monthly to accumulate the required amount of money?

20. Stuart Daniels estimates that he will need $25,000 to set up a small business in 7 years.

   a. How much must Stuart invest now at 8% interest compounded quarterly to achieve his goal?

   b. How much compound interest will he earn on the investment?

21. Summertime songbird population within the Mid-America flyway is predicted to increase over the next 8 years at the rate of 2% per year. If the songbird population is predicted to reach 55 million in 8 years, how many songbirds are there today? Round to the nearest million.

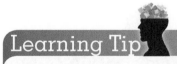

Learning Tip

Present Value of a Songbird!
Just as with compounding, the concept of present value of a future amount may also be applied to "other variables" besides money. Use the present value table or formula for Exercises 21 and 22.

22. The requirement for computer server capacity at Acme Industries is expected to increase at a rate of 15% per year for the next 5 years. If the server capacity is expected to be 1,400 gigabytes in 5 years, how many gigabytes of capacity are there today? Round to the nearest whole gigabyte.

Solve the following exercises and word problems by using the present value formula

	Compound Amount	Term of Investment	Nominal Rate (%)	Interest Compounded	Present Value	Compound Interest
23.	$4,500	7 years	3.8	annually	$3,466.02	$1,033.98
24.	$15,000	8 years	4.5	monthly	_____	_____
25.	$18,900	10 years	1.9	semiannually	_____	_____
26.	$675	15 months	2.7	quarterly	_____	_____

27. Alana and Eva Rodriguez are planning a cross-country road trip in 3 years. They estimate $6,000 will be needed to cover expenses. The National Bank of Pinecrest is offering a 3-year CD paying 3.62% interest compounded quarterly.

     a. How much should they set aside now to achieve their goal? Round to the nearest whole dollar.

     b. How much interest will Alana and Eva earn on the CD?

28. Mike Gioulis would like to have $25,000 in 4 years to pay off a balloon payment on his business mortgage. His money market account is paying 1.825% compounded daily. Disregarding leap years, how much money must Mike put in his account now to achieve his goal? Round to the nearest whole dollar.

BUSINESS DECISION: THE INFLATION FACTOR

29. You are the finance manager for Olympia Industries. The company plans to purchase $1,000,000 in new assembly line machinery in 5 years.

     a. How much must be set aside now at 6% interest compounded semiannually to accumulate the $1,000,000 in 5 years?

     b. If the inflation rate on this type of equipment is 4% per year, what will be the cost of the equipment in 5 years, adjusted for inflation?

     c. Use the inflation-adjusted cost of the equipment to calculate how much must be set aside now.

     d. Use the present value formula to calculate how much would be required now if you found a bank that offered 6% interest compounded daily.

Dollars AND Sense

Inflation should be taken into account when making financial plans that cover time periods longer than a year.

CHAPTER FORMULAS

Compound Interest

Compound interest = Compound amount − Principal

Compounding periods = Years × Periods per year

Interest rate per period = $\dfrac{\text{Nominal rate}}{\text{Periods per year}}$

Compound amount = Table factor × Principal

Annual percentage yield (APY) = $\dfrac{\text{Total compound interest earned in 1 year}}{\text{Principal}}$

Compound amount = Principal$(1 + \text{Interest rate per period})^{\text{periods}}$

Present Value

Present value = Table factor × Compound amount

Present value = $\dfrac{\text{Compound amount}}{(1 + \text{Interest rate per period})^{\text{periods}}}$

CHAPTER SUMMARY

Section I: Compound Interest—The Time Value of Money

Topic	Important Concepts	Illustrative Examples
Manually Calculating Compound Amount (Future Value) **Performance Objective 11-1, Page 343**	In compound interest, the interest is applied a number of times during the term of an investment. Compound interest yields considerably higher interest than simple interest does because the investor is earning interest on the interest. Interest can be compounded annually, semiannually, quarterly, monthly, daily, and continuously. 1. Determine the number of compounding periods (years × periods per year). 2. Apply the simple interest formula, $I = PRT$, as many times as there are compounding periods, adding interest to principal before each succeeding calculation.	Manually calculate the compound amount of a $1,000 investment at 8% interest compounded annually for 2 years. Original principal 1,000.00 Interest — period 1 + 80.00 Principal — period 2 1,080.00 Interest — period 2 + 86.40 Compound amount $1,166.40
Calculating Amount of Compound Interest **Performance Objective 11-1, Page 343**	Amount of compound interest is calculated by subtracting the original principal from the compound amount. Compound interest = Compound amount − Principal	What is the amount of compound interest earned in the problem above? $1,166.40 − 1,000.00 = $166.40
Computing Compound Amount (Future Value) by Using Compound Interest Tables **Performance Objective 11-2, Page 344**	1. Scan across the top row of Table 11-1 to find the interest rate per period. 2. Look down that column to the row corresponding to the number of compounding periods. 3. The table factor found at the intersection of the rate-per-period column and the number-of-periods row is the future value of $1.00 at compound interest. Compound amount = Table factor × Principal	Use Table 11-1 to find the compound amount of an investment of $2,000 at 12% interest compounded quarterly for 6 years. Rate = 3% per period (12% ÷ 4) Periods = 24 (6 years × 4) Table factor = 2.03279 Compound amount = 2.03279 × 2,000 = $4,065.58
Creating Compound Interest Table Factors for Periods beyond the Table **Performance Objective 11-3, Page 347**	1. For the stated interest rate per period, find the two table factors that represent *half*, or values as close as possible to half, of the periods required. 2. Multiply the two table factors from Step 1 to form the new factor. 3. Round the new factor to five decimal places.	Create a new table factor for 5% interest for 30 periods. Multiply the 5% factors for 15 and 15 periods from Table 11-1. 5%, 15 periods = 2.07893 5%, 15 periods = × 2.07893 30 periods 4.3219499 New factor rounded = 4.32195

Section I (continued)

Topic	Important Concepts	Illustrative Examples
Calculating Annual Percentage Yield (APY) or Effective Interest Rate **Performance Objective 11-4, Page 348**	To calculate annual percentage yield, divide total compound interest earned in 1 year by the principal. $$\text{Annual percentage yield (APY)} = \frac{1 \text{ year compound interest}}{\text{Principal}}$$	What is the annual percentage yield of $5,000 invested for 1 year at 12% compounded monthly? From Table 11-1, we use the table factor for 12 periods, 1%, to find the compound amount: $1.12683 \times 5,000 = 5,634.15$ Interest = Cmp. amt. − Principal Interest = $5,634.15 - 5,000.00 = 634.15$ $$\text{APY} = \frac{634.15}{5,000} = 12.68\%$$

Calculating Compound Amount (Future Value) by Using the Compound Interest Formula
 	
Performance Objective 11-5, Page 349
	In addition to the compound interest tables, another method for calculating compound amount is by using the compound interest formula.
	
	$A = P(1 + i)^n$
	where:
	  A = Compound amount
	  P = Principal
	  i = Interest rate per period (decimal form)
	  n = Number of compounding periods
		What is the compound amount of $3,000 invested at 8% interest compounded quarterly for 10 years?
		$A = P(1 + i)^n$
		$A = 3,000(1 + .02)^{40}$
		$A = 3,000(1.02)^{40}$
		$A = 3,000(2.2080396)$
		$A = \$6,624.12$

Section II: Present Value

Topic	Important Concepts	Illustrative Examples

Calculating the Present Value of a Future Amount by Using Present Value Tables
 	
Performance Objective 11-6, Page 354
	When the future value, an amount needed in the future, is known, the present value is the amount that must be invested today to accumulate, with compound interest, to that future value.
	
	1. Scan across the top row of Table 11-2 to find the rate per period.
	2. Look down that column to the row corresponding to the number of periods.
	3. The table factor found at the intersection of the rate-per-period column and the number-of-periods row is the present value of $1 at compound interest.
	
	    Present value
	       = Table factor × Compound amount
		How much must be invested now at 10% interest compounded semiannually to have $8,000, 9 years from now?
		Rate = 5% (10% ÷ 2)
		Periods = 18 (9 years × 2)
		Table factor = .41552
		Present value = .41552 × 8,000
		Present value = $3,324.16

Creating Present Value Table Factors for Periods beyond the Table
 	
Performance Objective 11-7, Page 356
	1. For the stated interest rate per period, find the two table factors that represent *half*, or values as close as possible to half, of the periods required.
	2. Multiply the two table factors from Step 1 for the new factor.
	3. Round the new factor to five decimal places.
		Create a new table factor for 6% interest for 41 periods.
		   Multiply the 6% factors for 21 and 20 periods from Table 11-2.
		6%, 21 periods = .29416
		6%, <u>20</u> periods = <u>× .31180</u>
		   41 periods .0917191
		New factor rounded = .09172

Calculating Present Value of a Future Amount by Using the Present Value Formula
 	
Performance Objective 11-8, Page 357
	If your calculator has an exponential function key, y^x, you can calculate the present value of an investment by using the present value formula.
	
	$$PV = \frac{A}{(1 + i)^n}$$
	where:
	  PV = Present value
	  A = Compound amount
	  i = Interest rate per period (decimal form)
	  n = Total compounding periods
		How much must be invested now to have $12,000 in 10 years if the interest rate is 12% compounded quarterly?
		$$\text{Present value} = \frac{12,000}{(1 + .03)^{40}}$$
		$$PV = \frac{12,000}{(1.03)^{40}} = \frac{12,000}{3.2620378}$$
		Present value = $3,678.68

TRY IT: EXERCISE SOLUTIONS FOR CHAPTER 11

1. 10,000.00 Original principal

$\underline{+\ \ 300.00}$ $(I = PRT = 10,000 \times .06 \times \frac{1}{2} = 300)$

10,300.00 Principal period 2

$\underline{+\ \ 309.00}$ $(I = PRT = 10,300.00 \times .06 \times \frac{1}{2} = 309)$

10,609.00 Principal period 3

$\underline{+\ \ 318.27}$ $(I = PRT = 10,609.00 \times .06 \times \frac{1}{2} = 318.27)$

10,927.27 Principal period 4

$\underline{+\ \ 327.82}$ $(I = PRT = 10,927.27 \times .06 \times \frac{1}{2} = 327.82)$

11,255.09 Principal period 5

$\underline{+\ \ 337.65}$ $(I = PRT = 11,255.09 \times .06 \times \frac{1}{2} = 337.65)$

11,592.74 Principal period 6

$\underline{+\ \ 347.78}$ $(I = PRT = 11,592.74 \times .06 \times \frac{1}{2} = 347.78)$

$\underline{\$11,940.52}$ Compound amount

Compound Interest = 11,940.52 − 10,000.00 = $\underline{\$1,940.52}$

2. 3%, 16 periods

Compound amount = Table factor × Principal

Compound amount = 1.60471 × 20,000 = $\underline{\$32,094.20}$

Compound interest = Compound amount − Principal

Compound interest = 32,094.20 − 20,000.00 = $\underline{\$12,094.20}$

3. Table factor required = 2%, 28 periods

2%, 14 periods: 1.31948

2%, 14 periods: $\underline{\times\ 1.31948}$

28 periods $1.74102747 = \underline{1.74103}$ New table factor

2%, 28 periods

Compound amount = 1.74103 × 3,500 = $\underline{\$6,093.61}$

4. $1\frac{1}{2}$%, 4 periods

Compound amount = 1.06136 × 7,000 = $\underline{\$7,429.52}$

Compound interest = 7,429.52 − 7,000.00 = $\underline{\$429.52}$

$\text{Annual percentage yield} = \frac{\text{1 year compound interest}}{\text{Principal}} = \frac{429.52}{7,000.00} = \underline{6.14\%}$

5. $A = P(1 + i)^n$ $P = \$3,000$

$i = \frac{8\%}{4} = .02$

$n = 5 \times 4 = 20$

$A = 3,000\,(1 + .02)^{20}$

$A = 3,000\,(1.02)^{20}$

$A = 3,000\,(1.4859474)$

$A = \underline{\$4,457.84}$

6. 2%, 12 periods

Present value = Table factor × Compound amount

Present value = .78849 × 3,000,000 = $\underline{\$2,365,470}$

7. Table factor required = $1\frac{1}{2}$%, 40 periods

$1\frac{1}{2}$%, 20 periods: .74247

$1\frac{1}{2}$%, 20 periods: $\underline{\times\ .74247}$

40 periods = $.5512617 = \underline{.55126}$ New table factor

$1\frac{1}{2}$%, 40 periods

Present value = .55126 × 8,500 = $\underline{\$4,685.71}$

8. $PV = \dfrac{A}{(1 + i)^n}$ $A = 30,000$

$i = \frac{8\%}{2} = .04$

$n = 17 \times 2 = 34$

$PV = \dfrac{30,000}{(1 + .04)^{34}}$

$PV = \dfrac{30,000}{(1.04)^{34}}$

$PV = \dfrac{30,000}{3.7943163} = \underline{\$7,906.56}$

CONCEPT REVIEW

1. Interest calculated solely on the principal is known as _____ interest, whereas interest calculated on the principal and previously earned interest is known as _____ interest. (11-1)

2. The concept that money "now," or in the present, is more desirable than the same amount of money in the future because it can be invested and earn interest as time goes by is known as the _____ of money. (11-1)

3. The total amount of principal and accumulated interest at the end of a loan or an investment is known as the _____ amount or _____ value. (11-1)

4. An amount of money that must be deposited today at compound interest to provide a specified lump sum of money in the future is known as the _____ amount or _____ value. (11-1, 11-6)

5. The amount of compound interest is calculated by subtracting the _____ from the compound amount. (11-1)

6. Compound interest is actually the _____ interest formula applied a number of times. (11-1)

7. A compound interest table is a useful set of factors that represent the future value of _____ at various interest rates for a number of compounding periods. (11-2)

8. A shortcut method for calculating approximately how long it takes money to double in value at compound interest is called the Rule of _____. (11-3)

9. Write the formula for calculating the number of compounding periods of a loan or an investment. (11-2)

10. Write the formula for calculating the interest rate per period of a loan or an investment. (11-2)

11. Newly created table factors for compound interest and present value should be rounded to _____ decimal places. (11-3, 11-7)

12. The annual percentage yield (APY) is equal to the total compound interest earned in _____ year divided by the _____. (11-4)

13. When using the compound interest table or the present value table, the factor is found at the intersection of the rate-per-_____ column and the number-of-_____ row. (11-2, 11-6)

14. To use the compound interest formula and the present value formula, you need a calculator with a(n) _____ function (y^x) key. (11-5, 11-8)

ASSESSMENT TEST

Note: Round to the nearest cent when necessary.

Using Table 11-1, calculate the compound amount and compound interest for the following investments.

	Principal	Time Period (years)	Nominal Rate (%)	Interest Compounded	Compound Amount	Compound Interest
1.	$14,000	6	4	semiannually		
2.	$7,700	5	6	quarterly		
3.	$3,000	1	6	monthly		
4.	$42,000	19	11	annually		

The following investments require table factors for periods beyond the table. Create the new table factor and calculate the compound amount for each.

	Principal	Time Period (years)	Nominal Rate (%)	Interest Compounded	New Table Factor	Compound Amount
5.	$20,000	11	8	quarterly		
6.	$10,000	4	6	monthly		

For the following investments, compute the amount of compound interest earned in 1 year and the annual percentage yield. Round APY to the nearest hundredth of a percent.

	Principal	Nominal Rate (%)	Interest Compounded	Compound Interest Earned in 1 Year	Annual Percentage Yield (APY)
7.	$8,500	12	monthly		
8.	$1,000,000	8	quarterly		

Calculate the present value (principal) and the compound interest for the following investments. Use Table 11-2. Round answers to the nearest cent.

	Compound Amount	Term of Investment	Nominal Rate (%)	Interest Compounded	Present Value	Compound Interest
9.	$150,000	22 years	15	annually		
10.	$20,000	30 months	4	semiannually		
11.	$900	$1\frac{3}{4}$ years	18	monthly		
12.	$5,500	15 months	8	quarterly		

The following investments require table factors for periods beyond the table. Create the new table factor and the present value for each.

	Compound Amount	Time Period (years)	Nominal Rate (%)	Interest Compounded	New Table Factor	Present Value
13.	$1,300	4	12	monthly		
14.	$100,000	50	5	annually		

Solve the following word problems by using Table 11-1 or 11-2. When necessary, create new table factors. Round dollars to the nearest cent and percents to the nearest hundredth of a percent.

15. What is the compound amount and compound interest of $36,000 invested at 12% compounded semiannually for 7 years?

EXCEL 1

16. What is the present value of $73,000 in 11 years if the interest rate is 8% compounded semiannually?

EXCEL 2

17. What is the compound amount and compound interest of $15,000 invested at 6% compounded quarterly for 27 months?

18. What is the annual percentage yield of a $10,000 investment for 1 year at 6% interest compounded monthly?

19. City Wide Delivery Service uses vans costing $24,800 each. How much will the company have to invest today to accumulate enough money to buy six new vans at the end of 4 years? City Wide's bank is currently paying 12% interest compounded quarterly.

LL26 /iStockphoto.com

20. You are the owner of a Jani-King cleaning service franchise. Your accountant has determined that the business will need $27,500 in new equipment in 3 years. If your bank is paying 6% interest compounded monthly, how much must you invest today to meet this financial goal? Round to the nearest whole dollar.

Jani-King is the world's largest commercial cleaning franchise company with over 12,000 owners worldwide. Jani-King contracts commercial cleaning services for many different facilities including healthcare, office, hotel/resort, manufacturing, restaurant, and sporting venues.

Jani-King has been rated the #1 Commercial Cleaning Franchise Company for 23 years in a row by *Entrepreneur Magazine*. In most regions, one may start a Jani-King franchise for as little as $3,000. Cleaning services is a $100 billion industry and is projected to grow to more than $155 billion. The U.S. Bureau of Labor Statistics reports that professional cleaning specialists will be the fastest-growing occupation in this decade.

21. Valerie Walton invested $8,800 at the Northern Trust Credit Union at 12% interest compounded quarterly.

   a. What is the annual percentage yield of this investment?

   b. What will Valerie's investment be worth after 6 years?

22. Bob and Joy Salkind want to save $50,000 in $5\frac{1}{2}$ years for home improvement projects. If the Bank of Aventura is paying 8% interest compounded quarterly, how much must they deposit now to have the money for the project?

CHAPTER
11

23. While rummaging through the attic, you discover a savings account left to you by a relative. When you were 5 years old, he invested $20,000 in your name at 6% interest compounded semiannually. If you are now 20 years old, how much is the account worth?

24. Applegate Industries is planning to expand its production facility in a few years. New plant construction costs are estimated to be $4.50 per square foot. The company invests $850,000 today at 8% interest compounded quarterly.

   a. How many square feet of new facility could be built after $3\frac{1}{2}$ years? Round to the nearest whole square foot.

   b. If the company waits 5 years and construction costs increase to $5.25 per square foot, how many square feet could be built? Round to the nearest whole square foot. What do you recommend?

25. Over the past 10 years, you've made the following investments:
   1. Deposited $10,000 at 8% compounded semiannually in a 3-year certificate of deposit.
   2. After 3 years, you took the maturity value (principal and interest) of that CD and added another $5,000 to buy a 4-year, 6% certificate compounded quarterly.
   3. When that certificate matured, you added another $8,000 and bought a 3-year, 7% certificate compounded annually.

      a. What was the total worth of your investment when the last certificate matured?

      b. What is the total amount of compound interest earned over the 10-year period?

26. Fred North owns Redlands Farms, a successful strawberry farm. The strawberry plants increase at a compound rate of 12% per year. Each year Fred brings new land under cultivation for the new strawberry plants. If the farm has 50 acres of strawberry plants today, how many acres of strawberry plants will the farm have in 8 years? Round to the nearest whole acre.

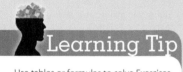

Learning Tip

Use tables or formulas to solve Exercises 26 and 27.

27. At Reliable Trucking, Inc., annual sales are predicted to increase over the next 3 years at a rate of 6% per year. Sales equate to "fleet miles." If Reliable's fleet miles are predicted to reach 4.4 million in 3 years, what is the number of fleet miles today? Round to the nearest tenth of a million.

Solve the following exercises and word problems using formulas.

	Principal	Time Period (years)	Nominal Rate (%)	Interest Compounded	Compound Amount	Compound Interest
28.	$3,425	11	6.6	monthly	_____	_____
29.	$21,800	6	2.9	semiannually	_____	_____
30.	$400	$2\frac{1}{2}$	4.2	quarterly	_____	_____
31.	$9,630	5	3.1	annually	_____	_____

	Principal	Term of Investment	Nominal Rate (%)	Interest Compounded	Present Value	Compound Interest
32.	$6,300	14 years	6.3	annually	_____	_____
33.	$80,200	9 months	4.8	quarterly	_____	_____
34.	$27,500	10 years	3.6	semiannually	_____	_____
35.	$2,440	5 years	1.5	monthly	_____	_____

36. What is the compound amount and compound interest of a $73,000 investment earning 2.9% interest compounded semiannually for 4 years? Round to the nearest whole dollar.

37. Jorge Rodriguez would like to pay off his condo when he retires. How much must he invest now at 2.3% interest compounded quarterly to have $125,000 in 11 years? Round to the nearest whole dollar.

38. Quinn and Julius inherited $50,000 each from their great-grandmother's estate. Quinn invested her money in a 5-year CD paying 1.6% interest compounded semiannually. Julius deposited his money in a money market account paying 1.05% compounded monthly.

   a. How much money will each have in 5 years? Round to the nearest whole dollar.

   b. How much compound interest will they each have earned at the end of 5 years?

39. Greg and Verena Sava need $20,000 in 3 years to expand their goat cheese business. The Bank of Sutton is offering a 3-year CD paying 3.9% compounded monthly. How much should they invest now to achieve their goal? Round to the nearest whole dollar.

CHAPTER 11

BUSINESS DECISION: PAY ME NOW, PAY ME LATER

Dollars AND Sense

Pay Me Now, Pay Me Later is a good example of how the "time value of money" concept can be applied in business.

Remember: *When interest can be earned, money today is more desirable than the same amount of money in the future.*

40. You are the owner of an apartment building that is being offered for sale for $1,500,000. You receive an offer from a prospective buyer who wants to pay you $500,000 now, $500,000 in 6 months, and $500,000 in 1 year.

    a. What is the actual present value of this offer considering you can earn 12% interest compounded monthly on your money?

    b. If another buyer offers to pay you $1,425,000 cash now, which is a better deal?

    c. Because you understand the "time value of money" concept, you have negotiated a deal with the original buyer from part a whereby you will accept the three-payment offer but will charge 12% interest compounded monthly on the two delayed payments. Calculate the total purchase price under this new arrangement.

    d. Now calculate the present value of the new deal to verify that you will receive the original asking price of $1,500,000 for your apartment building.

COLLABORATIVE LEARNING ACTIVITY

Putting Your Money to Work

As a team, research financial institutions in your area (brick-and-mortar banks), as well as Internet-only institutions (virtual banks and e-banks), to find and list various certificates of deposit currently being offered. Assume that you want to invest $10,000 for 12 months.

    a. What interest rates do these CDs pay? How often is interest compounded?
    b. What is the early withdrawal penalty?
    c. Are these CDs insured? If so, by whom? What is the limit per account?
    d. Overall, which institution offers the CD that would earn the most interest after 12 months?

CHAPTER 12 Annuities

PERFORMANCE OBJECTIVES

12

FUTURE VALUE OF AN ANNUITY: ORDINARY AND ANNUITY DUE

annuity Payment or receipt of equal amounts of money per period for a specified amount of time.

The concepts relating to compound interest in Chapter 11 were mainly concerned with lump sum investments or payments. Frequently in business, situations involve a series of equal periodic payments or receipts rather than lump sums. These are known as annuities. An **annuity** is the payment or receipt of *equal* cash amounts per period for a specified amount of time. Some common applications are insurance and retirement plan premiums and payouts; loan payments; and savings plans for future events such as starting a business, going to college, or purchasing expensive items (e.g., real estate or business equipment).

In this chapter, you learn to calculate the future value of an annuity, the amount accumulated at compound interest from a series of equal periodic payments. You also learn to calculate the present value of an annuity, the amount that must be deposited now at compound interest to yield a series of equal periodic payments. Exhibit 12-1 graphically shows the difference between the future value of an annuity and the present value of an annuity.

simple annuities Annuities in which the number of compounding periods per year coincides with the number of annuity payments per year.

complex annuities Annuities in which the annuity payments and compounding periods do not coincide.

All the exercises in this chapter are of the type known as **simple annuities**. This means that the number of compounding periods per year coincides with the number of annuity payments per year. For example, if the annuity payments are monthly, the interest is compounded monthly; if the annuity payments are made every six months, the interest is compounded semiannually. **Complex annuities** are those in which the annuity payments and compounding periods do not coincide.

As with compound interest, annuities can be calculated manually, by tables, and by formulas. Manual computation is useful for illustrative purposes; however, it is too tedious because it requires a calculation for each period. The table method is the easiest and most widely used and is the basis for this chapter's exercises. As in Chapter 11, there are formulas to calculate annuities; however, they require calculators with the exponential function key, y^x, and the change-of-sign key, $+/-$. These optional Performance Objectives are for students with business, financial, or scientific calculators.

12-1 CALCULATING THE FUTURE VALUE OF AN ORDINARY ANNUITY BY USING TABLES

annuities certain Annuities that have a specified number of time periods.

contingent annuities Annuities based on an uncertain time period, such as the life of a person.

Annuities are categorized into annuities certain and contingent annuities. **Annuities certain** are annuities that have a specified number of periods, such as $200 per month for 5 years or $500 semiannually for 10 years. **Contingent annuities** are based on an uncertain time period, such as a retirement plan that is payable only for the lifetime of the retiree. This chapter is concerned only with annuities certain.

EXHIBIT 12-1 Timeline Illustrating Present and Future Value of an Annuity

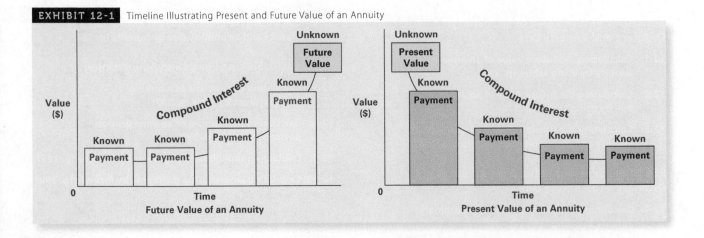

When the annuity payment is made at the end of each period, it is known as an **ordinary annuity**. When the payment is made at the beginning of each period, it is called an **annuity due**. A salary paid at the end of each month is an example of an ordinary annuity. A mortgage payment or rent paid at the beginning of each month is an example of an annuity due.

The **future value of an annuity** is also known as the **amount of an annuity**. It is the total of the annuity payments plus the accumulated compound interest on those payments.

For illustrative purposes, consider the following annuity calculated manually.

What is the future value of an ordinary annuity of $10,000 per year for 4 years at 6% interest compounded annually?

Because this is an ordinary annuity, the payment is made at the *end* of each period (in this case, years). Each interest calculation uses $I = PRT$, with $R = .06$ and $T = 1$ year.

Time	Balance	
Beginning of period 1	0	
	+ 10,000.00	First annuity payment (end of period 1)
End of period 1	10,000.00	
Beginning of period 2	10,000.00	
	600.00	Interest earned, period 2 (10,000.00 × .06 × 1)
	+ 10,000.00	Second annuity payment (end of period 2)
End of period 2	20,600.00	
Beginning of period 3	20,600.00	
	1,236.00	Interest earned, period 3 (20,600.00 × .06 × 1)
	+ 10,000.00	Third annuity payment (end of period 3)
End of period 3	31,836.00	
Beginning of period 4	31,836.00	
	1,910.16	Interest earned, period 4 (31,836.00 × .06 × 1)
	+ 10,000.00	Fourth annuity payment (end of period 4)
End of period 4	$43,746.16	Future value of the ordinary annuity

As you can see, calculating annuities this way is tedious. An annuity of 10 years with payments made monthly would require 120 calculations. As with compound interest, we will use tables to calculate the future value (amount) of an annuity.

STEPS FOR CALCULATING FUTURE VALUE (AMOUNT) OF AN ORDINARY ANNUITY

STEP 1. Calculate the interest rate per period for the annuity (nominal rate ÷ periods per year).

STEP 2. Determine the number of periods of the annuity (years × periods per year).

STEP 3. From Table 12-1 on pages 372–373, locate the ordinary annuity table factor at the intersection of the rate-per-period column and the number-of-periods row.

STEP 4. Calculate the future value of the ordinary annuity.

$$\text{Future value (ordinary annuity)} = \text{Ordinary annuity table factor} \times \text{Annuity payment}$$

ordinary annuity Annuity that is paid or received at the end of each time period.

annuity due Annuity that is paid or received at the beginning of each time period.

future value of an annuity, or **amount of an annuity** The total amount of the annuity payments and the accumulated interest on those payments.

Learning Tip

The procedure for using the annuity tables, Tables 12-1 and 12-2, is the same as we used with the compound interest and present value tables in Chapter 11.

Table factors are found at the intersection of the rate-per-period column and the number-of-periods row.

TABLE 12-1 Future Value (Amount) of an Ordinary Annuity of $1

Periods	$\frac{1}{2}\%$	1%	$1\frac{1}{2}\%$	2%	3%	4%	5%	6%	7%	8%	Periods
1	1.00000	1.00000	1.00000	1.00000	1.00000	1.00000	1.00000	1.00000	1.00000	1.00000	1
2	2.00500	2.01000	2.01500	2.02000	2.03000	2.04000	2.05000	2.06000	2.07000	2.08000	2
3	3.01502	3.03010	3.04522	3.06040	3.09090	3.12160	3.15250	3.18360	3.21490	3.24640	3
4	4.03010	4.06040	4.09090	4.12161	4.18363	4.24646	4.31013	4.37462	4.43994	4.50611	4
5	5.05025	5.10101	5.15227	5.20404	5.30914	5.41632	5.52563	5.63709	5.75074	5.86660	5
6	6.07550	6.15202	6.22955	6.30812	6.46841	6.63298	6.80191	6.97532	7.15329	7.33593	6
7	7.10588	7.21354	7.32299	7.43428	7.66246	7.89829	8.14201	8.39384	8.65402	8.92280	7
8	8.14141	8.28567	8.43284	8.58297	8.89234	9.21423	9.54911	9.89747	10.25980	10.63663	8
9	9.18212	9.36853	9.55933	9.75463	10.15911	10.58280	11.02656	11.49132	11.97799	12.48756	9
10	10.22803	10.46221	10.70272	10.94972	11.46388	12.00611	12.57789	13.18079	13.81645	14.48656	10
11	11.27917	11.56683	11.86326	12.16872	12.80780	13.48635	14.20679	14.97164	15.78360	16.64549	11
12	12.33556	12.68250	13.04121	13.41209	14.19203	15.02581	15.91713	16.86994	17.88845	18.97713	12
13	13.39724	13.80933	14.23683	14.68033	15.61779	16.62684	17.71298	18.88214	20.14064	21.49530	13
14	14.46423	14.94742	15.45038	15.97394	17.08632	18.29191	19.59863	21.01507	22.55049	24.21492	14
15	15.53655	16.09690	16.68214	17.29342	18.59891	20.02359	21.57856	23.27597	25.12902	27.15211	15
16	16.61423	17.25786	17.93237	18.63929	20.15688	21.82453	23.65749	25.67253	27.88805	30.32428	16
17	17.69730	18.43044	19.20136	20.01207	21.76159	23.69751	25.84037	28.21288	30.84022	33.75023	17
18	18.78579	19.61475	20.48938	21.41231	23.41444	25.64541	28.13238	30.90565	33.99903	37.45024	18
19	19.87972	20.81090	21.79672	22.84056	25.11687	27.67123	30.53900	33.75999	37.37896	41.44626	19
20	20.97912	22.01900	23.12367	24.29737	26.87037	29.77808	33.06595	36.78559	40.99549	45.76196	20
21	22.08401	23.23919	24.47052	25.78332	28.67649	31.96920	35.71925	39.99273	44.86518	50.42292	21
22	23.19443	24.47159	25.83758	27.29898	30.53678	34.24797	38.50521	43.39229	49.00574	55.45676	22
23	24.31040	25.71630	27.22514	28.84496	32.45288	36.61789	41.43048	46.99583	53.43614	60.89330	23
24	25.43196	26.97346	28.63352	30.42186	34.42647	39.08260	44.50200	50.81558	58.17667	66.76476	24
25	26.55912	28.24320	30.06302	32.03030	36.45926	41.64591	47.72710	54.86451	63.24904	73.10594	25
26	27.69191	29.52563	31.51397	33.67091	38.55304	44.31174	51.11345	59.15638	68.67647	79.95442	26
27	28.83037	30.82089	32.98668	35.34432	40.70963	47.08421	54.66913	63.70577	74.48382	87.35077	27
28	29.97452	32.12910	34.48148	37.05121	42.93092	49.96758	58.40258	68.52811	80.69769	95.33883	28
29	31.12439	33.45039	35.99870	38.79223	45.21885	52.96629	62.32271	73.63980	87.34653	103.96594	29
30	32.28002	34.78489	37.53868	40.56808	47.57542	56.08494	66.43885	79.05819	94.46079	113.28321	30
31	33.44142	36.13274	39.10176	42.37944	50.00268	59.32834	70.76079	84.80168	102.07304	123.34587	31
32	34.60862	37.49407	40.68829	44.22703	52.50276	62.70147	75.29883	90.88978	110.21815	134.21354	32
33	35.78167	38.86901	42.29861	46.11157	55.07784	66.20953	80.06377	97.34316	118.93343	145.95062	33
34	36.96058	40.25770	43.93309	48.03380	57.73018	69.85791	85.06696	104.18375	128.25876	158.62667	34
35	38.14538	41.66028	45.59209	49.99448	60.46208	73.65222	90.32031	111.43478	138.23688	172.31680	35
36	39.33610	43.07688	47.27597	51.99437	63.27594	77.59831	95.83632	119.12087	148.91346	187.10215	36

The values in Table 12-1 were generated by the formula $\dfrac{(1+i)^n - 1}{i}$ and rounded to five decimal places, where i is the interest rate per period and n is the total number of periods.

TABLE 12-1 Future Value (Amount) of an Ordinary Annuity of $1 *(Continued)*

Periods	9%	10%	11%	12%	13%	14%	15%	16%	17%	18%	Periods
1	1.00000	1.00000	1.00000	1.00000	1.00000	1.00000	1.00000	1.00000	1.00000	1.00000	1
2	2.09000	2.10000	2.11000	2.12000	2.13000	2.14000	2.15000	2.16000	2.17000	2.18000	2
3	3.27810	3.31000	3.34210	3.37440	3.40690	3.43960	3.47250	3.50560	3.53890	3.57240	3
4	4.57313	4.64100	4.70973	4.77933	4.84980	4.92114	4.99338	5.06650	5.14051	5.21543	4
5	5.98471	6.10510	6.22780	6.35285	6.48027	6.61010	6.74238	6.87714	7.01440	7.15421	5
6	7.52333	7.71561	7.91286	8.11519	8.32271	8.53552	8.75374	8.97748	9.20685	9.44197	6
7	9.20043	9.48717	9.78327	10.08901	10.40466	10.73049	11.06680	11.41387	11.77201	12.14152	7
8	11.02847	11.43589	11.85943	12.29969	12.75726	13.23276	13.72682	14.24009	14.77325	15.32700	8
9	13.02104	13.57948	14.16397	14.77566	15.41571	16.08535	16.78584	17.51851	18.28471	19.08585	9
10	15.19293	15.93742	16.72201	17.54874	18.41975	19.33730	20.30372	21.32147	22.39311	23.52131	10
11	17.56029	18.53117	19.56143	20.65458	21.81432	23.04452	24.34928	25.73290	27.19994	28.75514	11
12	20.14072	21.38428	22.71319	24.13313	25.65018	27.27075	29.00167	30.85017	32.82393	34.93107	12
13	22.95338	24.52271	26.21164	28.02911	29.98470	32.08865	34.35192	36.78620	39.40399	42.21866	13
14	26.01919	27.97498	30.09492	32.39260	34.88271	37.58107	40.50471	43.67199	47.10267	50.81802	14
15	29.36092	31.77248	34.40536	37.27971	40.41746	43.84241	47.58041	51.65951	56.11013	60.96527	15
16	33.00340	35.94973	39.18995	42.75328	46.67173	50.98035	55.71747	60.92503	66.64885	72.93901	16
17	36.97370	40.54470	44.50084	48.88367	53.73906	59.11760	65.07509	71.67303	78.97915	87.06804	17
18	41.30134	45.59917	50.39594	55.74971	61.72514	68.39407	75.83636	84.14072	93.40561	103.74028	18
19	46.01846	51.15909	56.93949	63.43968	70.74941	78.96923	88.21181	98.60323	110.28456	123.41353	19
20	51.16012	57.27500	64.20283	72.05244	80.94683	91.02493	102.44358	115.37975	130.03294	146.62797	20
21	56.76453	64.00250	72.26514	81.69874	92.46992	104.76842	118.81012	134.84051	153.13854	174.02100	21
22	62.87334	71.40275	81.21431	92.50258	105.49101	120.43600	137.63164	157.41499	180.17209	206.34479	22
23	69.53194	79.54302	91.14788	104.60289	120.20484	138.29704	159.27638	183.60138	211.80134	244.48685	23
24	76.78981	88.49733	102.17415	118.15524	136.83147	158.65862	184.16784	213.97761	248.80757	289.49448	24
25	84.70090	98.34706	114.41331	133.33387	155.61956	181.87083	212.79302	249.21402	292.10486	342.60349	25
26	93.32398	109.18177	127.99877	150.33393	176.85010	208.33274	245.71197	290.08827	342.76268	405.27211	26
27	102.72313	121.09994	143.07864	169.37401	200.84061	238.49933	283.56877	337.50239	402.03234	479.22109	27
28	112.96822	134.20994	159.81729	190.69889	227.94989	272.88923	327.10408	392.50277	471.37783	566.48089	28
29	124.13536	148.63093	178.39719	214.58275	258.58338	312.09373	377.16969	456.30322	552.51207	669.44745	29
30	136.30754	164.49402	199.02088	241.33268	293.19922	356.78685	434.74515	530.31173	647.43912	790.94799	30
31	149.57522	181.94342	221.91317	271.29261	332.31511	407.73701	500.95692	616.16161	758.50377	934.31863	31
32	164.03699	201.13777	247.32362	304.84772	376.51608	465.82019	577.10046	715.74746	888.44941	1103.49598	32
33	179.80032	222.25154	275.52922	342.42945	426.46317	532.03501	664.66552	831.26706	1040.48581	1303.12526	33
34	196.98234	245.47670	306.83744	384.52098	482.90338	607.51991	765.36535	965.26979	1218.36839	1538.68781	34
35	215.71075	271.02437	341.58955	431.66350	546.68082	693.57270	881.17016	1120.71295	1426.49102	1816.65161	35
36	236.12472	299.12681	380.16441	484.46312	618.74933	791.67288	1014.34568	1301.02703	1669.99450	2144.64890	36

The values in Table 12-1 were generated by the formula $\dfrac{(1+i)^n - 1}{i}$ and rounded to five decimal places, where i is the interest rate per period and n is the total number of periods.

EXAMPLE 1   CALCULATING THE FUTURE VALUE OF AN ORDINARY ANNUITY

Stuart Daniels deposited $3,000 at the *end* of each year for 8 years in his savings account. If his bank paid 5% interest compounded annually, use Table 12-1 to find the future value of Stuart's account.

SOLUTIONSTRATEGY

Step 1. The rate period is 5% (5% ÷ 1 period per year).

Step 2. The number of periods is eight (8 years × 1 period per year).

Step 3. From Table 12-1, the table factor for 5%, eight periods is 9.54911.

Step 4. Future value = Ordinary annuity table factor × Annuity payment

Future value = 9.54911 × 3,000 = $28,647.33

TRYITEXERCISE 1

Freeport Bank is paying 8% interest compounded quarterly. Use Table 12-1 to find the future value of $1,000 deposited at the *end* of every 3 months for 6 years.

CHECK YOUR ANSWER WITH THE SOLUTION ON PAGE 398.

12-2   CALCULATING THE FUTURE VALUE OF AN ANNUITY DUE BY USING TABLES

Once again, for illustrative purposes, let's manually calculate the future value of the annuity. This time, however, it is an annuity due.

What is the amount of an annuity due of $10,000 per year for 4 years at 6% interest compounded annually?

Because this is an annuity due, the payment is made at the *beginning* of each period. Each interest calculation uses $I = PRT$, with $R = .06$ and $T = 1$ year.

Time	Balance	
Beginning of period 1	10,000.00	First annuity payment (beginning of period 1)
	+ 600.00	Interest earned, period 1 (10,000.00 × .06 × 1)
End of period 1	10,600.00	
Beginning of period 2	10,600.00	
	10,000.00	Second annuity payment (beginning of period 2)
	+ 1,236.00	Interest earned, period 2 (20,600.00 × .06 × 1)
End of period 2	21,836.00	
Beginning of period 3	21,836.00	
	10,000.00	Third annuity payment (beginning of period 3)
	+ 1,910.16	Interest earned, period 3 (31,836.00 × .06 × 1)
End of period 3	33,746.16	
Beginning of period 4	33,746.16	
	10,000.00	Fourth annuity payment (beginning of period 4)
	+ 2,624.77	Interest earned, period 4 (43,746.16 × .06 × 1)
End of period 4	$46,370.93	Future value of the annuity due

When the future value of an annuity due is calculated, the table factor is found by using the same table as ordinary annuities (Table 12-1), with some modifications in the steps. With annuities due, you must *add* one period to the number of periods and *subtract* 1.00000 from the table factor.

STEPS FOR CALCULATING FUTURE VALUE (AMOUNT) OF AN ANNUITY DUE

STEP 1. Calculate the number of periods of the annuity (years × periods per year) and *add* one period to the total.

STEP 2. Calculate the interest rate per period (nominal rate ÷ periods per year).

STEP 3. From Table 12-1, locate the table factor at the intersection of the rate-per-period column and the number-of-periods row.

STEP 4. *Subtract* 1.00000 from the ordinary annuity table factor to get the annuity due table factor.

STEP 5. Calculate the future value of the annuity due.

Future value (annuity due) = Annuity due table factor × Annuity payment

Saving for College

If parents save and invest $10 per workday at 12% interest from the birth date of their child, when the child is 18 and ready for college, the parents would have $150,000 accumulated—through the power of compounding.

EXAMPLE2 CALCULATING THE FUTURE VALUE OF AN ANNUITY DUE

Chris Manning deposited $60 at the *beginning* of each month for 2 years at his credit union. If the interest rate was 12% compounded monthly, use Table 12-1 to calculate the future value of Chris's account.

SOLUTIONSTRATEGY

Step 1. Number of periods of the annuity due is 24 (2 × 12) + 1 for a total of 25.

Step 2. Interest rate per period is 1% (12% ÷ 12).

Step 3. The ordinary annuity table factor at the intersection of the rate column and the periods row is 28.24320.

Step 4. Subtract 1.00000 from the table factor:

$$\begin{array}{ll} 28.24320 & \text{ordinary annuity table factor} \\ -1.00000 & \\ \hline 27.24320 & \text{annuity due table factor} \end{array}$$

Step 5. Future value = Annuity due table factor × Annuity payment

Future value = 27.24320 × 60 = $1,634.59

TRYITEXERCISE 2

Vista Savings & Loan is paying 6% interest compounded quarterly. Use Table 12-1 to calculate the future value of $1,000 deposited at the *beginning* of every 3 months for 5 years.

CHECK YOUR ANSWER WITH THE SOLUTION ON PAGE 398.

CALCULATING THE FUTURE VALUE OF AN ORDINARY ANNUITY AND AN ANNUITY DUE BY FORMULA

12-3

Students with financial, business, or scientific calculators may use the following formulas to solve for the future value of an ordinary annuity and the future value of an annuity due.

Future value of an ordinary annuity	Future value of an annuity due
$FV = Pmt \times \dfrac{(1 + i)^n - 1}{i}$	$FV = Pmt \times \dfrac{(1 + i)^n - 1}{i} \times (1 + i)$

Learning Tip

Note that the annuity due formula is the same as the ordinary annuity formula except that it is multiplied by $(1 + i)$. This is to account for the additional period of the annuity due.

where:

FV = **future value**
Pmt = **annuity payment**
i = **interest rate per period (nominal rate ÷ periods per year)**
n = **number of periods (years × periods per year)**

Ordinary Annuity
Calculator Sequence: 1 $\boxed{+}$ i $\boxed{=}$ $\boxed{y^x}$ n $\boxed{-}$ 1 $\boxed{=}$ $\boxed{÷}$ i $\boxed{×}$ Pmt $\boxed{=}$ $FV_{\text{ordinary annuity}}$

Annuity Due
Calculator Sequence: 1 $\boxed{+}$ i $\boxed{=}$ $\boxed{×}$ $FV_{\text{ordinary annuity}}$ $\boxed{=}$ $FV_{\text{annuity due}}$

EXAMPLE3 USING FORMULAS TO CALCULATE ANNUITIES

a. What is the future value of an ordinary annuity of $100 per month for 3 years at 6% interest compounded monthly?

b. What is the future value of this investment if it is an annuity due?

SOLUTIONSTRATEGY

a. For this future value of an ordinary annuity problem, we use $i = .5\% (6\% ÷ 12)$ and $n = 36$ periods (3 years × 12 periods per year).

$$FV = Pmt \times \frac{(1 + i)^n - 1}{i}$$

$$FV = 100 \times \frac{(1 + .005)^{36} - 1}{.005}$$

$$FV = 100 \times \frac{(1.005)^{36} - 1}{.005}$$

$$FV = 100 \times \frac{1.196680525 - 1}{.005}$$

$$FV = 100 \times \frac{.196680525}{.005}$$

$$FV = 100 \times 39.336105 = \underline{\$3,933.61}$$

Calculator Sequence: 1 $\boxed{+}$ .005 $\boxed{=}$ $\boxed{y^x}$ 36 $\boxed{-}$ 1 $\boxed{=}$ $\boxed{÷}$ .005 $\boxed{×}$ 100 $\boxed{=}$ $\underline{\$3,933.61}$

b. To solve the problem as an annuity due rather than an ordinary annuity, multiply $(1 + i)$, for one extra compounding period, by the future value of the ordinary annuity.

$$FV_{\text{annuity due}} = (1 + i) \times FV_{\text{ordinary annuity}}$$

$$FV_{\text{annuity due}} = (1 + .005) \times 3,933.61$$

$$FV_{\text{annuity due}} = (1.005) \times 3,933.61 = \underline{\$3,953.28}$$

Calculator Sequence: 1 $\boxed{+}$ .005 $\boxed{=}$ $\boxed{×}$ 3,933.61 $\boxed{=}$ $\underline{\$3,953.28}$

TRYITEXERCISE 3

Katrina Byrd invested $250 at the *end* of every 3-month period for 5 years at 8% interest compounded quarterly.

a. How much is Katrina's investment worth after 5 years?

b. If Katrina had invested the money at the *beginning* of each 3-month period rather than at the end, how much would be in the account?

CHECK YOUR ANSWERS WITH THE SOLUTIONS ON PAGE 398.

REVIEW EXERCISES

12 SECTION I

Note: Round to the nearest cent when necessary.

Use Table 12-1 to calculate the future value of the following ordinary annuities.

	Annuity Payment	Payment Frequency	Time Period (years)	Nominal Rate (%)	Interest Compounded	Future Value of the Annuity
1.	$1,000	every 3 months	4	8	quarterly	$18,639.29
2.	$2,500	every 6 months	5	4	semiannually	_____
3.	$10,000	every year	10	9	annually	_____
4.	$200	every month	2	6	monthly	_____
5.	$1,500	every 3 months	7	6	quarterly	_____

Use Table 12-1 to calculate the future value of the following annuities due.

	Annuity Payment	Payment Frequency	Time Period (years)	Nominal Rate (%)	Interest Compounded	Future Value of the Annuity
6.	$400	every 6 months	12	10	semiannually	$18,690.84
7.	$1,000	every 3 months	3	8	quarterly	_____
8.	$50	every month	$2\frac{1}{2}$	6	monthly	_____
9.	$2,000	every year	25	5	annually	_____
10.	$4,400	every 6 months	8	6	semiannually	_____

Solve the following exercises by using Table 12-1.

11. Paragon Savings & Loan is paying 6% interest compounded monthly. How much will $100 deposited at the *end* of each month be worth after 2 years?

12. Suntech Distributors, Inc. deposits $5,000 at the *beginning* of each 3-month period for 6 years in an account paying 8% interest compounded quarterly.

    a. How much will be in the account at the end of the 6-year period?

    b. What is the total amount of interest earned in this account?

13. Jess Thomas deposits $100 each payday into an account at 6% interest compounded monthly. She gets paid on the last day of each month. How much will her account be worth at the end of 30 months?

14. Jorge Otero has set up an annuity due with the United Credit Union. At the beginning of each month, $170 is electronically debited from his checking account and placed into a savings account earning 6% interest compounded monthly. What is the value of Jorge's account after 18 months?

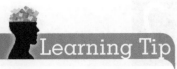

15. When Ben Taylor was born, his parents began depositing $500 at the *beginning* of every year into an annuity to save for his college education. If the account paid 7% interest compounded annually for the first 10 years and then dropped to 5% for the next 8 years, how much is the account worth now that Ben is 18 years old and ready for college?

Solve the following exercises by using formulas.

Ordinary Annuities

	Annuity Payment	Payment Frequency	Time Period (years)	Nominal Rate (%)	Interest Compounded	Future Value of the Annuity
16.	$2,000	every 6 months	3	3.0	semiannually	$12,459.10
17.	$300	every month	8	6.0	monthly	_____
18.	$1,800	every 3 months	$3\frac{1}{2}$	4.0	quarterly	_____

Annuities Due

	Annuity Payment	Payment Frequency	Time Period (years)	Nominal Rate (%)	Interest Compounded	Future Value of the Annuity
19.	$675	every month	5	1.5	monthly	$42,082.72
20.	$4,800	every 3 months	3	6.0	quarterly	_____
21.	$7,000	every year	10	3.2	annually	_____

22. To establish a "rainy day" cash reserve account, Bonanza Industries deposits $10,000 of its profit at the end of each quarter into a money market account that pays 1.75% interest compounded quarterly.

    a. How much will the account be worth in 3 years?

    b. How much will the account be worth in $4\frac{1}{2}$ years?

23. As a part of his retirement planning strategy, Mark Woodson deposits $125 each payday into an investment account at 3% interest compounded monthly. Mark gets paid on the first day of each month.

    a. How much will his account be worth in 5 years?

    b. How much will his account be worth in 15 years?

24. Hi-Tech Hardware has been in business for a few years and is doing well. The owner has decided to save for a future expansion to a second location. He invests $1,000 at the *end* of every month at 12% interest compounded monthly.

a. How much will be available for the second store after $2\frac{1}{2}$ years?

b. How much would be in the account if the owner saved for 5 years?

c. How much would be in the account after 5 years if it had been an annuity due?

BUSINESS DECISION: PLANNING YOUR NEST EGG

25. As part of your retirement plan, you have decided to deposit $3,000 at the *beginning* of each year into an account paying 5% interest compounded annually.

a. How much would the account be worth after 10 years?

b. How much would the account be worth after 20 years?

c. When you retire in 30 years, what will be the total worth of the account?

d. If you found a bank that paid 6% interest compounded annually rather than 5%, how much would you have in the account after 30 years?

e. Use the future value of an annuity due formula to calculate how much you would have in the account after 30 years if the bank in part d switched from annual compounding to monthly compounding and you deposited $250 at the *beginning* of each month instead of $3,000 at the *beginning* of each year.

Dollars AND Sense

In 1950, 16 workers contributed to the Social Security benefit of a single retiree. Today, approximately 3.3 workers pay for a retiree's Social Security benefit and by 2025 that number is projected to fall to just 2.

Feb. 28, 2010, page 35, Gregory Bresiger.

PRESENT VALUE OF AN ANNUITY: ORDINARY AND ANNUITY DUE

12 SECTION II

In Section I of this chapter, we learned to calculate the future value of an annuity. This business situation requires that a series of equal payments be made into an account, such as a savings account. The annuity starts with nothing and accumulates at compound interest to a future amount. Now consider the opposite situation. What if we wanted an account from which we could withdraw a series of equal payments over a period of time? This business situation requires that a lump sum amount be deposited at compound interest now to yield the specified annuity payments. The lump sum that is required up front is known as the **present value of an annuity**.

Let's look at a business situation using this type of annuity. A company owes $10,000 interest to bondholders at the end of each month for the next 3 years. The company decides to set up an account with a lump sum deposit now, which at compound interest will yield the $10,000 monthly payments for 3 years. After 3 years, the debt will have been paid and the account will be zero.

Just as in Section I, these annuities can be ordinary, whereby withdrawals from the account are made at the *end* of each period, or annuity due, in which the withdrawals are made at the *beginning*. As with the future value of an annuity, we will use tables to calculate the present value of an annuity. Once again, in addition to tables, these annuities can be solved by using formulas requiring a calculator with a y^x key.

12-4   CALCULATING THE PRESENT VALUE OF AN ORDINARY ANNUITY BY USING TABLES

Table 12-2 on pages 382 and 383 is used to calculate the lump sum required to be deposited now to yield the specified annuity payment.

STEPS FOR CALCULATING PRESENT VALUE OF AN ORDINARY ANNUITY

STEP 1. Calculate the interest rate per period for the annuity (nominal rate ÷ periods per year).

STEP 2. Determine the number of periods of the annuity (years × periods per year).

STEP 3. From Table 12-2, locate the present value table factor at the intersection of the rate-per-period column and the number-of-periods row.

STEP 4. Calculate the present value of the ordinary annuity.

$$\text{Present value (ordinary annuity)} = \text{Ordinary annuity table factor} \times \text{Annuity payment}$$

EXAMPLE 4   CALCULATING THE PRESENT VALUE OF AN ORDINARY ANNUITY

How much must be deposited now at 9% compounded annually to yield an annuity payment of $5,000 at the end of each year for 10 years?

SOLUTIONSTRATEGY

Step 1.   The rate per period is 9% (9% ÷ 1 period per year).

Step 2.   The number of periods is 10 (10 years × 1 period per year).

Step 3.   From Table 12-2, the table factor for 9%, 10 periods is 6.41766.

Step 4.   Present value = Ordinary annuity table factor × Annuity payment
Present value = 6.41766 × 5,000 = $32,088.30

TRYITEXERCISE 4

The Broadway Movieplex needs $20,000 at the end of each 6-month movie season for renovations and new projection equipment. How much must be deposited now at 8% compounded semiannually to yield this annuity payment for the next 6 years?

CHECK YOUR ANSWER WITH THE SOLUTION ON PAGE 398.

CALCULATING THE PRESENT VALUE OF AN ANNUITY DUE BY USING TABLES

12-5

The present value of an annuity due is calculated by using the same table as ordinary annuities, with some modifications in the steps.

STEPS FOR CALCULATING PRESENT VALUE OF AN ANNUITY DUE

STEP 1. Calculate the number of periods of the annuity (years × periods per year) and *subtract* one period from the total.

STEP 2. Calculate the interest rate per period (nominal rate ÷ periods per year).

STEP 3. From Table 12-2, locate the table factor at the intersection of the rate-per-period column and the number-of-periods row.

STEP 4. *Add* 1.00000 to the ordinary annuity table factor to get the annuity due table factor.

STEP 5. Calculate the present value of the annuity due.

$$\text{Present value (annuity due)} = \text{Annuity due table factor} \times \text{Annuity payment}$$

Learning Tip

The procedure for finding the present value table factor for an annuity due is the *opposite* of that for future value factors. This time you must *subtract* a period and *add* a 1.00000.

EXAMPLE5 CALCULATING THE PRESENT VALUE OF AN ANNUITY DUE

How much must be deposited now at 10% compounded semiannually to yield an annuity payment of $2,000 at the beginning of each 6-month period for 7 years?

SOLUTIONSTRATEGY

Step 1. The number of periods for the annuity due is 14 (7 years × 2 periods per year) less 1 period = 13.

Step 2. The rate per period is 5% (10% ÷ 2 periods per year).

Step 3. From Table 12-2, the ordinary annuity table factor for 5%, 13 periods is 9.39357.

Step 4. Add 1 to the table factor from Step 3 to get 10.39357, the annuity due table factor.

Step 5. Present value (annuity due) = Annuity due table factor × Annuity payment
Present value = 10.39357 × 2,000 = $20,787.14

TRYITEXERCISE 5

You are the accountant at Supreme Lumber, Inc. Based on sales and expense forecasts, you have estimated that $10,000 must be sent to the Internal Revenue Service for income tax payments at the *beginning* of each 3-month period for the next 3 years. How much must be deposited now at 6% compounded quarterly to yield the annuity payment needed?

CHECK YOUR ANSWER WITH THE SOLUTION ON PAGE 398.

TABLE 12-2   Present Value (Amount) of an Ordinary Annuity of $1

Periods	$\frac{1}{2}\%$	1%	$1\frac{1}{2}\%$	2%	3%	4%	5%	6%	7%	8%	Periods
1	0.99502	0.99010	0.98522	0.98039	0.97087	0.96154	0.95238	0.94340	0.93458	0.92593	1
2	1.98510	1.97040	1.95588	1.94156	1.91347	1.88609	1.85941	1.83339	1.80802	1.78326	2
3	2.97025	2.94099	2.91220	2.88388	2.82861	2.77509	2.72325	2.67301	2.62432	2.57710	3
4	3.95050	3.90197	3.85438	3.80773	3.71710	3.62990	3.54595	3.46511	3.38721	3.31213	4
5	4.92587	4.85343	4.78264	4.71346	4.57971	4.45182	4.32948	4.21236	4.10020	3.99271	5
6	5.89638	5.79548	5.69719	5.60143	5.41719	5.24214	5.07569	4.91732	4.76654	4.62288	6
7	6.86207	6.72819	6.59821	6.47199	6.23028	6.00205	5.78637	5.58238	5.38929	5.20637	7
8	7.82296	7.65168	7.48593	7.32548	7.01969	6.73274	6.46321	6.20979	5.97130	5.74664	8
9	8.77906	8.56602	8.36052	8.16224	7.78611	7.43533	7.10782	6.80169	6.51523	6.24689	9
10	9.73041	9.47130	9.22218	8.98259	8.53020	8.11090	7.72173	7.36009	7.02358	6.71008	10
11	10.67703	10.36763	10.07112	9.78685	9.25262	8.76048	8.30641	7.88687	7.49867	7.13896	11
12	11.61893	11.25508	10.90751	10.57534	9.95400	9.38507	8.86325	8.38384	7.94269	7.53608	12
13	12.55615	12.13374	11.73153	11.34837	10.63496	9.98565	9.39357	8.85268	8.35765	7.90378	13
14	13.48871	13.00370	12.54338	12.10625	11.29607	10.56312	9.89864	9.29498	8.74547	8.24424	14
15	14.41662	13.86505	13.34323	12.84926	11.93794	11.11839	10.37966	9.71225	9.10791	8.55948	15
16	15.33993	14.71787	14.13126	13.57771	12.56110	11.65230	10.83777	10.10590	9.44665	8.85137	16
17	16.25863	15.56225	14.90765	14.29187	13.16612	12.16567	11.27407	10.47726	9.76322	9.12164	17
18	17.17277	16.39827	15.67256	14.99203	13.75351	12.65930	11.68959	10.82760	10.05909	9.37189	18
19	18.08236	17.22601	16.42617	15.67846	14.32380	13.13394	12.08532	11.15812	10.33560	9.60360	19
20	18.98742	18.04555	17.16864	16.35143	14.87747	13.59033	12.46221	11.46992	10.59401	9.81815	20
21	19.88798	18.85698	17.90014	17.01121	15.41502	14.02916	12.82115	11.76408	10.83553	10.01680	21
22	20.78406	19.66038	18.62082	17.65805	15.93692	14.45112	13.16300	12.04158	11.06124	10.20074	22
23	21.67568	20.45582	19.33086	18.29220	16.44361	14.85684	13.48857	12.30338	11.27219	10.37106	23
24	22.56287	21.24339	20.03041	18.91393	16.93554	15.24696	13.79864	12.55036	11.46933	10.52876	24
25	23.44564	22.02316	20.71961	19.52346	17.41315	15.62208	14.09394	12.78336	11.65358	10.67478	25
26	24.32402	22.79520	21.39863	20.12104	17.87684	15.98277	14.37519	13.00317	11.82578	10.80998	26
27	25.19803	23.55961	22.06762	20.70690	18.32703	16.32959	14.64303	13.21053	11.98671	10.93516	27
28	26.06769	24.31644	22.72672	21.28127	18.76411	16.66306	14.89813	13.40616	12.13711	11.05108	28
29	26.93302	25.06579	23.37608	21.84438	19.18845	16.98371	15.14107	13.59072	12.27767	11.15841	29
30	27.79405	25.80771	24.01584	22.39646	19.60044	17.29203	15.37245	13.76483	12.40904	11.25778	30
31	28.65080	26.54229	24.64615	22.93770	20.00043	17.58849	15.59281	13.92909	12.53181	11.34980	31
32	29.50328	27.26959	25.26714	23.46833	20.38877	17.87355	15.80268	14.08404	12.64656	11.43500	32
33	30.35153	27.98969	25.87895	23.98856	20.76579	18.14765	16.00255	14.23023	12.75379	11.51389	33
34	31.19555	28.70267	26.48173	24.49859	21.13184	18.41120	16.19290	14.36814	12.85401	11.58693	34
35	32.03537	29.40858	27.07559	24.99862	21.48722	18.66461	16.37419	14.49825	12.94767	11.65457	35
36	32.87102	30.10751	27.66068	25.48884	21.83225	18.90828	16.54685	14.62099	13.03521	11.71719	36

The values in Table 12-2 were generated by the formula $\dfrac{(1+i)^n - 1}{i(1+i)^n}$ and rounded to five decimal places, where i is the interest rate per period and n is the total number of periods.

TABLE 12-2 Present Value (Amount) of an Ordinary Annuity of $1 *(Continued)*

Periods	9%	10%	11%	12%	13%	14%	15%	16%	17%	18%	Periods
1	0.91743	0.90909	0.90090	0.89286	0.88496	0.87719	0.86957	0.86207	0.85470	0.84746	1
2	1.75911	1.73554	1.71252	1.69005	1.66810	1.64666	1.62571	1.60523	1.58521	1.56564	2
3	2.53129	2.48685	2.44371	2.40183	2.36115	2.32163	2.28323	2.24589	2.20958	2.17427	3
4	3.23972	3.16987	3.10245	3.03735	2.97447	2.91371	2.85498	2.79818	2.74324	2.69006	4
5	3.88965	3.79079	3.69590	3.60478	3.51723	3.43308	3.35216	3.27429	3.19935	3.12717	5
6	4.48592	4.35526	4.23054	4.11141	3.99755	3.88867	3.78448	3.68474	3.58918	3.49760	6
7	5.03295	4.86842	4.71220	4.56376	4.42261	4.28830	4.16042	4.03857	3.92238	3.81153	7
8	5.53482	5.33493	5.14612	4.96764	4.79877	4.63886	4.48732	4.34359	4.20716	4.07757	8
9	5.99525	5.75902	5.53705	5.32825	5.13166	4.94637	4.77158	4.60654	4.45057	4.30302	9
10	6.41766	6.14457	5.88923	5.65022	5.42624	5.21612	5.01877	4.83323	4.65860	4.49409	10
11	6.80519	6.49506	6.20652	5.93770	5.68694	5.45273	5.23371	5.02864	4.83641	4.65601	11
12	7.16073	6.81369	6.49236	6.19437	5.91765	5.66029	5.42062	5.19711	4.98839	4.79322	12
13	7.48690	7.10336	6.74987	6.42355	6.12181	5.84236	5.58315	5.34233	5.11828	4.90951	13
14	7.78615	7.36669	6.98187	6.62817	6.30249	6.00207	5.72448	5.46753	5.22930	5.00806	14
15	8.06069	7.60608	7.19087	6.81086	6.46238	6.14217	5.84737	5.57546	5.32419	5.09158	15
16	8.31256	7.82371	7.37916	6.97399	6.60388	6.26506	5.95423	5.66850	5.40529	5.16235	16
17	8.54363	8.02155	7.54879	7.11963	6.72909	6.37286	6.04716	5.74870	5.47461	5.22233	17
18	8.75563	8.20141	7.70162	7.24967	6.83991	6.46742	6.12797	5.81785	5.53385	5.27316	18
19	8.95011	8.36492	7.83929	7.36578	6.93797	6.55037	6.19823	5.87746	5.58449	5.31624	19
20	9.12855	8.51356	7.96333	7.46944	7.02475	6.62313	6.25933	5.92884	5.62777	5.35275	20
21	9.29224	8.64869	8.07507	7.56200	7.10155	6.68696	6.31246	5.97314	5.66476	5.38368	21
22	9.44243	8.77154	8.17574	7.64465	7.16951	6.74294	6.35866	6.01133	5.69637	5.40990	22
23	9.58021	8.88322	8.26643	7.71843	7.22966	6.79206	6.39884	6.04425	5.72340	5.43212	23
24	9.70661	8.98474	8.34814	7.78432	7.28288	6.83514	6.43377	6.07263	5.74649	5.45095	24
25	9.82258	9.07704	8.42174	7.84314	7.32998	6.87293	6.46415	6.09709	5.76623	5.46691	25
26	9.92897	9.16095	8.48806	7.89566	7.37167	6.90608	6.49056	6.11818	5.78311	5.48043	26
27	10.02658	9.23722	8.54780	7.94255	7.40856	6.93515	6.51353	6.13636	5.79753	5.49189	27
28	10.11613	9.30657	8.60162	7.98442	7.44120	6.96066	6.53351	6.15204	5.80985	5.50160	28
29	10.19828	9.36961	8.65011	8.02181	7.47009	6.98304	6.55088	6.16555	5.82039	5.50983	29
30	10.27365	9.42691	8.69379	8.05518	7.49565	7.00266	6.56598	6.17720	5.82939	5.51681	30
31	10.34280	9.47901	8.73315	8.08499	7.51828	7.01988	6.57911	6.18724	5.83709	5.52272	31
32	10.40624	9.52638	8.76860	8.11159	7.53830	7.03498	6.59053	6.19590	5.84366	5.52773	32
33	10.46444	9.56943	8.80054	8.13535	7.55602	7.04823	6.60046	6.20336	5.84928	5.53197	33
34	10.51784	9.60857	8.82932	8.15656	7.57170	7.05985	6.60910	6.20979	5.85409	5.53557	34
35	10.56682	9.64416	8.85524	8.17550	7.58557	7.07005	6.61661	6.21534	5.85820	5.53862	35
36	10.61176	9.67651	8.87859	8.19241	7.59785	7.07899	6.62314	6.22012	5.86171	5.54120	36

The values in Table 12-2 were generated by the formula $\dfrac{(1+i)^n - 1}{i(1+i)^n}$ and rounded to five decimal places, where i is the interest rate per period and n is the total number of periods.

12-6 CALCULATING THE PRESENT VALUE OF AN ORDINARY ANNUITY AND AN ANNUITY DUE BY FORMULA

Students with financial, business, or scientific calculators may use the following formulas to solve for the present value of an ordinary annuity and the present value of an annuity due. Note that the annuity due formula is the same as the ordinary annuity formula except that it is multiplied by $(1 + i)$. This is to account for the fact that with an annuity due, each payment earns interest for one additional period because payments are made at the beginning of each period, not the end.

Present value of an ordinary annuity

$$PV = Pmt \times \frac{1 - (1 + i)^{-n}}{i}$$

Present value of an annuity due

$$PV = Pmt \times \frac{1 - (1 + i)^{-n}}{i} \times (1 + i)$$

where:

PV = **present value (lump sum)**
Pmt = **annuity payment**
i = **interest rate per period (nominal rate ÷ periods per year)**
n = **number of periods (years × periods per year)**

Ordinary Annuity
Calculator Sequence: 1 $+$ i $=$ y^x n $+/-$ $=$ M+ 1 $-$ MR $=$ $÷$ i $\times$ Pmt $=$ PV

Annuity Due
Calculator Sequence: 1 $+$ i $=$ $\times$ $PV_{\text{ordinary annuity}}$ $=$ $PV_{\text{annuity due}}$

EXAMPLE6   CALCULATING PRESENT VALUE OF AN ANNUITY BY FORMULA

a. What is the present value of an ordinary annuity of $100 per month for 4 years at 6% interest compounded monthly?

b. What is the present value of this investment if it is an annuity due?

►SOLUTIONSTRATEGY

a. For this present value of an ordinary annuity problem, we use $i = .5\%$ (6% ÷ 12) and $n = 48$ periods (4 years × 12 periods per year).

$$PV = Pmt \times \frac{1 - (1 + i)^{-n}}{i}$$

$$PV = 100 \times \frac{1 - (1 + .005)^{-48}}{.005}$$

$$PV = 100 \times \frac{1 - (1.005)^{-48}}{.005}$$

$$PV = 100 \times \frac{1 - .7870984111}{.005}$$

$$PV = 100 \times \frac{.2129015889}{.005}$$

$$PV = 100 \times 42.58031778 = \$4,258.03$$

Calculator Sequence:

1 $+$ .005 $=$ y^x 48 $+/-$ $=$ M+ 1 $-$ MR $=$ $÷$ .005 $\times$ 100 $=$ $4,258.03

b. To solve as an annuity due rather than an ordinary annuity, multiply the present value of the ordinary annuity by $(1 + i)$ for one extra compounding period.

$$PV_{\text{annuity due}} = (1 + i) \times PV_{\text{ordinary annuity}}$$
$$PV_{\text{annuity due}} = (1 + .005) \times 4,258.03$$
$$PV_{\text{annuity due}} = (1.005) \times 4,258.03 = \$4,279.32$$

Calculator Sequence: 1 $+$ .005 $=$ $\times$ 4,258.03 $=$ $4,279.32

▶ TRYITEXERCISE 6

Use the present value of an annuity formula to solve the following.

a. Angus McDonald wants $500 at the *end* of each 3-month period for the next 6 years. If Angus's bank is paying 8% interest compounded quarterly, how much must he deposit now to receive the desired ordinary annuity?

b. If Angus wants the payments at the *beginning* of each 3-month period rather than at the end, how much should he deposit?

CHECK YOUR ANSWERS WITH THE SOLUTIONS ON PAGE 398.

REVIEW EXERCISES

12 SECTION II

Note: Round to the nearest cent when necessary.

Use Table 12-2 to calculate the present value of the following ordinary annuities.

	Annuity Payment	Payment Frequency	Time Period (years)	Nominal Rate (%)	Interest Compounded	Present Value of the Annuity
1.	$300	every 6 months	7	10	semiannually	$2,969.59
2.	$2,000	every year	20	7	annually	_____
3.	$4,000	every 3 months	6	8	quarterly	_____
4.	$1,000	every month	$1\frac{3}{4}$	6	monthly	_____
5.	$8,500	every 3 months	3	4	quarterly	_____

Use Table 12-2 to calculate the present value of the following annuities due.

	Annuity Payment	Payment Frequency	Time Period (years)	Nominal Rate (%)	Interest Compounded	Present Value of the Annuity
6.	$1,400	every year	10	11	annually	$9,151.87
7.	$2,500	every 3 months	5	4	quarterly	_____
8.	$500	every month	$2\frac{1}{4}$	6	monthly	_____
9.	$6,000	every 6 months	15	2	semiannually	_____
10.	$4,000	every year	18	7	annually	_____

Solve the following exercises by using Table 12-2.

11. Diamond Savings & Loan is paying 6% interest compounded monthly. How much must be deposited now to withdraw an annuity of $400 at the end of each month for 2 years?

12. Jami Minard wants to receive an annuity of $2,000 at the beginning of each year for the next 10 years. How much should be deposited now at 6% compounded annually to accomplish this goal?

13. As the chief accountant for Proline Industries, you have estimated that the company must pay $100,000 income tax to the IRS at the end of each quarter this year. How much should be deposited now at 8% interest compounded quarterly to meet this tax obligation?

14. Ron Sample is the grand prize winner in a college tuition essay contest awarded through a local organization's scholarship fund. The winner receives $2,000 at the beginning of each year for the next 4 years. How much should be invested at 7% interest compounded annually to award the prize?

15. Silver Tip Golf Course management has contracted to pay a golf green maintenance specialist a $680 monthly fee at the end of each month to provide advice on improving the quality of the greens on its 18-hole course. How much should be deposited now into an account that earns 6% compounded monthly to be able to make monthly payments to the consultant for the next year?

16. Analysts at Sky West Airlines did a 3-year projection of expenses. They calculated that the company will need $15,800 at the *beginning* of each 6-month period to buy fuel, oil, lube, and parts for aircraft operations and maintenance. Sky West can get 6% interest compounded semi-annually from its bank. How much should Sky West deposit now to support the next 3 years of operations and maintenance expenses?

Solve the following exercises by using formulas.

Present value of an ordinary annuity

	Annuity Payment	Payment Frequency	Time Period (yrs)	Nominal Rate (%)	Interest Compounded	Present Value of the Annuity
17.	$500	every 3 months	$3\frac{1}{4}$	6.0	quarterly	$5,865.77
18.	$280	every month	5	3.0	monthly	_____
19.	$950	every year	8	2.9	annually	_____

Present value of an annuity due

	Annuity Payment	Payment Frequency	Time Period (yrs)	Nominal Rate (%)	Interest Compounded	Present Value of the Annuity
20.	$1,100	every year	5	5.8	annually	$4,929.14
21.	$425	every month	$4\frac{3}{4}$	4.5	monthly	_____
22.	$700	every 6 months	7	3.6	semiannually	_____

23. As part of an inheritance, Joan Townsend will receive an annuity of $1,500 at the *end* of each month for the next 6 years. What is the present value of this inheritance at a rate of 2.4% interest compounded monthly?

24. Norm Legend has been awarded a scholarship from Canmore College. For the next 4 years, he will receive $3,500 for tuition and books at the *beginning* of each quarter. How much must the school set aside now in an account earning 3% interest compounded quarterly to pay Norm's scholarship?

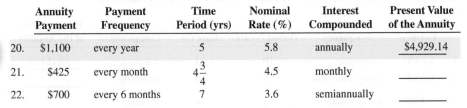

BUSINESS DECISION: THE INSURANCE SETTLEMENT

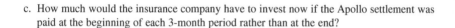

25. Apollo Enterprises has been awarded an insurance settlement of $5,000 at the end of each 6-month period for the next 10 years.

    a. As the accountant, calculate how much the insurance company must set aside now at 6% interest compounded semiannually to pay this obligation to Apollo.

    b. How much would the insurance company have to invest now if the Apollo settlement was changed to $2,500 at the end of each 3-month period for 10 years and the insurance company earned 8% interest compounded quarterly?

    c. How much would the insurance company have to invest now if the Apollo settlement was paid at the beginning of each 3-month period rather than at the end?

SINKING FUNDS AND AMORTIZATION

12

SECTION III

Sinking funds and amortization are two common applications of annuities. In the previous sections of this chapter, the amount of the annuity payment was known and you were asked to calculate the future or present value (lump sum) of the annuity. In this section, the future or present value of the annuity is known and the amount of the payments is calculated.

A sinking fund situation occurs when the future value of an annuity is known and the payment required each period to amount to that future value is the unknown. **Sinking funds** are accounts used to set aside equal amounts of money at the end of each period at compound interest for the purpose of saving for a future obligation. Businesses use sinking funds to accumulate money for such things as new equipment, facility expansion, and other expensive items needed in the future. Another common use is to retire financial obligations such as bond issues that come due at a future date. Individuals can use sinking funds to save for a college education, a car, the down payment on a house, or a vacation.

Amortization is the opposite of a sinking fund. **Amortization** is a financial arrangement whereby a lump-sum obligation is incurred at compound interest now (present value) and is paid off or liquidated by a series of equal periodic payments for a specified amount of time. With amortization, the amount of the loan or obligation is given and the equal payments that will amortize, or pay off, the obligation must be calculated. Some business uses of amortization include paying off loans and liquidating insurance or retirement funds.

In this section, you learn to calculate the sinking fund payment required to save for a future amount and the amortization payment required to liquidate a present amount. We assume that all annuities are ordinary, with payments made at the *end* of each period. As in previous sections, these exercises can be calculated by tables or by formulas.

sinking funds Accounts used to set aside equal amounts of money at the end of each period at compound interest for the purpose of saving for a future obligation.

amortization A financial arrangement whereby a lump-sum obligation is incurred at compound interest now, such as a loan, and is paid off or liquidated by a series of equal periodic payments for a specified amount of time.

IN THE
Business World

Mortgages, which are real estate loans, are a common example of amortization. More detailed coverage, including the preparation of amortization schedules, is found in Chapter 14.

CALCULATING THE AMOUNT OF A SINKING FUND PAYMENT BY TABLE

12-7

In a sinking fund, the future value is known; therefore, we use the future value of an annuity table (Table 12-1) to calculate the amount of the payment.

STEPS FOR CALCULATING THE AMOUNT OF A SINKING FUND PAYMENT

STEP 1. Using the appropriate rate per period and number of periods of the sinking fund, find the future value table factor from Table 12-1.

STEP 2. Calculate the amount of the sinking fund payment.

$$\text{Sinking fund payment} = \frac{\text{Future value of the sinking fund}}{\text{Future value table factor}}$$

EXAMPLE7 · CALCULATING THE AMOUNT OF A SINKING FUND PAYMENT

What sinking fund payment is required at the end of each 6-month period at 6% interest compounded semiannually to amount to $12,000 in 4 years?

►SOLUTIONSTRATEGY

Step 1. This sinking fund is for 8 periods (4 years × 2 periods per year) at 3% per period (6% ÷ 2 periods per year). From Table 12-1, 8 periods, 3% per period gives a future value table factor of 8.89234.

Step 2. Sinking fund payment $= \dfrac{\text{Future value of the sinking fund}}{\text{Future value table factor}}$

Sinking fund payment $= \dfrac{12,000}{8.89234} = \$1,349.48$

►TRYITEXERCISE 7

Magi Khoo wants to accumulate $8,000 in 5 years for a trip to Europe. If Magi has an investment paying 12% interest compounded quarterly, how much must she deposit at the end of each 3-month period in a sinking fund to reach her desired goal?

CHECK YOUR ANSWER WITH THE SOLUTION ON PAGE 399.

Sinking funds enable businesses to plan for future purchases of expensive equipment.

© Gilles Lougassi/Shutterstock.com

CALCULATING THE AMOUNT OF AN AMORTIZATION PAYMENT BY TABLE

12-8

Amortization is the process of "paying off" a financial obligation with a series of equal and regular payments over a period of time. With amortization, the original amount of the loan or obligation is known (present value); therefore, we use the present value table (Table 12-2) to calculate the amount of the payment.

STEPS FOR CALCULATING THE AMOUNT OF AN AMORTIZATION PAYMENT

STEP 1. Using the appropriate rate per period and number of periods of the amortization, find the present value table factor from Table 12-2.

STEP 2. Calculate the amount of the amortization payment.

$$\text{Amortization payment} = \frac{\text{Original amount of obligation}}{\text{Present value table factor}}$$

EXAMPLE8 CALCULATING THE AMOUNT OF AN AMORTIZATION PAYMENT

What amortization payments are required each month at 12% interest to pay off a $10,000 loan in 2 years?

▶SOLUTIONSTRATEGY

Step 1. This amortization is for 24 periods (2 years × 12 periods per year) at 1% per period (12% ÷ 12 periods per year). From Table 12-2, 24 periods, 1% per period gives a present value table factor of 21.24339.

Step 2. $\text{Amortization payment} = \dfrac{\text{Original amount of obligation}}{\text{Present value table factor}}$

$\text{Amortization payment} = \dfrac{10,000}{21.24339} = \$470.73$

▶TRYITEXERCISE 8

Captain Bob Albrecht purchased a new fishing boat for $130,000. He made a $20,000 down payment and financed the balance at his bank for 7 years. What amortization payments are required every 3 months at 16% interest to pay off the boat loan?

CHECK YOUR ANSWER WITH THE SOLUTION ON PAGE 399.

CALCULATING SINKING FUND PAYMENTS BY FORMULA

12-9

In addition to using Table 12-1, sinking fund payments may be calculated by using the following formula:

$$\text{Sinking fund payment} = FV \times \frac{i}{(1+i)^n - 1}$$

where:

> FV = amount needed in the future
>
> i = interest rate per period (nominal rate ÷ periods per year)
>
> n = number of periods (years × periods per year)

Calculator Sequence:

1 $+$ i $=$ y^x n $-$ 1 $=$ M+ i $÷$ MR $×$ FV $=$ Sinking fund payment

---

EXAMPLE9 — CALCULATING SINKING FUND PAYMENTS BY FORMULA

Ocean Air Corporation needs $100,000 in 5 years to pay off a bond issue. What sinking fund payment is required at the end of each month at 12% interest compounded monthly to meet this financial obligation?

▶ SOLUTIONSTRATEGY

To solve this sinking fund problem, we use 1% interest rate per period (12% ÷ 12) and 60 periods (5 years × 12 periods per year).

$$\text{Sinking fund payment} = \text{Future value} \times \frac{i}{(1+i)^n - 1}$$

$$\text{Sinking fund payment} = 100{,}000 \times \frac{.01}{(1+.01)^{60} - 1}$$

$$\text{Sinking fund payment} = 100{,}000 \times \frac{.01}{.8166967}$$

$$\text{Sinking fund payment} = 100{,}000 \times .0122444 = \underline{\$1{,}224.44}$$

Calculator Sequence:

1 $+$ .01 $=$ y^x 60 $-$ 1 $=$ M+ .01 $÷$ MR $×$ 100,000 $=$ $\underline{\$1{,}224.44}$

▶ TRYITEXERCISE 9

Big Sky Ski Rental Center will need $40,000 in 6 years to replace aging equipment. What sinking fund payment is required at the end of each month at 6% interest compounded monthly to amount to the $40,000 in 6 years?

CHECK YOUR ANSWER WITH THE SOLUTION ON PAGE 399.

12-10 CALCULATING AMORTIZATION PAYMENTS BY FORMULA

In addition to using Table 12-2, amortization payments may be calculated by using the following formula:

$$\textbf{Amortization payment} = PV \times \frac{i}{1 - (1+i)^{-n}}$$

where:

> PV = amount of the loan or obligation
>
> i = interest rate per period (nominal rate ÷ periods per year)
>
> n = number of periods (years × periods per year)

Calculator Sequence:

1 $+$ i $=$ y^x n $+/-$ $=$ M+ 1 $-$ MR $=$ MC M+ i $÷$ MR $×$ PV $=$ Amortization payment

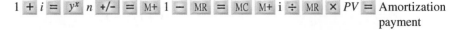

EXAMPLE10 · CALCULATING AMORTIZATION PAYMENTS BY FORMULA

What amortization payment is required each month at 18% interest to pay off $5,000 in 3 years?

►SOLUTIONSTRATEGY

To solve this amortization problem, we use 1.5% interest rate per period (18% ÷ 12) and 36 periods (3 years × 12 periods per year).

$$\text{Amortization payment} = \text{Present value} \times \frac{i}{1 - (1 + i)^{-n}}$$

$$\text{Amortization payment} = 5{,}000 \times \frac{.015}{1 - (1 + .015)^{-36}}$$

$$\text{Amortization payment} = 5{,}000 \times \frac{.015}{.4149103}$$

$$\text{Amortization payment} = 5{,}000 \times .0361524 = \underline{\$180.76}$$

Calculator Sequence:

1 $+$ .015 $=$ y^x 36 $+/-$ $=$ M+ 1 $-$ MR $=$ MC M+ .015 $\div$ MR $\times$ 5,000 $=$

$\underline{\$180.76}$

►TRYITEXERCISE 10

Apex Manufacturing recently purchased a new computer system for $150,000. What amortization payment is required each month at 12% interest to pay off this obligation in 8 years?

CHECK YOUR ANSWER WITH THE SOLUTION ON PAGE 399.

REVIEW EXERCISES

12 SECTION III

Note: Round to the nearest cent when necessary.

For the following sinking funds, use Table 12-1 to calculate the amount of the periodic payments needed to amount to the financial objective (future value of the annuity).

	Sinking Fund Payment	Payment Frequency	Time Period (years)	Nominal Rate (%)	Interest Compounded	Future Value (Objective)
1.	$2,113.50	every 6 months	8	10	semiannually	$50,000
2.	_____	every year	14	9	annually	$250,000
3.	_____	every 3 months	5	4	quarterly	$1,500
4.	_____	every month	$1\frac{1}{2}$	6	monthly	$4,000
5.	_____	every 3 months	4	4	quarterly	$18,750

You have just been hired as a loan officer at the Eagle National Bank. Your first assignment is to calculate the amount of the periodic payment required to amortize (pay off) the following loans being considered by the bank (use Table 12-2).

	Loan Payment	Payment Period	Term of Loan (years)	Nominal Rate (%)	Present Value (Amount of Loan)
6.	$4,189.52	every year	12	9	$30,000
7.	_____	every 3 months	5	8	$5,500

	Loan Payment	Payment Period	Term of Loan (years)	Nominal Rate (%)	Present Value (Amount of Loan)
8.	_____	every month	$1\frac{3}{4}$	6	$10,000
9.	_____	every 6 months	8	6	$13,660
10.	_____	every month	1.5	12	$850

Solve the following exercises by using tables.

11. Everest Industries established a sinking fund to pay off a $10,000,000 loan that comes due in 8 years for a corporate yacht.

   a. What equal payments must be deposited into the fund every 3 months at 6% interest compounded quarterly for Everest to meet this financial obligation?

   b. What is the total amount of interest earned in this sinking fund account?

Corporate yachts provide companies with ways to recognize employees; secure the undivided attention of valued clients; perform product launches; hold meetings, conferences, and presentations; and serve as handsome tax write-offs.

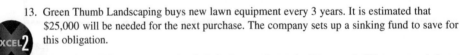

12. Jennifer Kaufman bought a used Toyota Prius for $15,500. She made a $2,500 down payment and is financing the balance at Imperial Bank over a 3-year period at 12% interest. As her banker, calculate what equal monthly payments will be required by Jennifer to amortize the car loan.

13. Green Thumb Landscaping buys new lawn equipment every 3 years. It is estimated that $25,000 will be needed for the next purchase. The company sets up a sinking fund to save for this obligation.

   a. What equal payments must be deposited every 6 months if interest is 8% compounded semiannually?

   b. What is the total amount of interest earned by the sinking fund?

14. Paul and Donna Kelsch are planning a Mediterranean cruise in 4 years and will need $7,500 for the trip. They decide to set up a "sinking fund" savings account for the vacation. They intend to make regular payments at the end of each 3-month period into the account that pays 6% interest compounded quarterly. What periodic sinking fund payment will allow them to achieve their vacation goal?

15. Valerie Ross is ready to retire and has saved $200,000 for that purpose. She wants to amortize (liquidate) that amount in a retirement fund so that she will receive equal annual payments over the next 25 years. At the end of the 25 years, no funds will be left in the account. If the fund earns 4% interest, how much will Valerie receive each year?

Solve the following exercises by using the sinking fund or amortization formula.

Sinking fund payment

	Sinking Fund Payment	Payment Frequency	Time Period (years)	Nominal Rate (%)	Interest Compounded	Future Value (Objective)
16.	$345.97	every 3 months	5	6.0	quarterly	$8,000
17.	_____	every month	8	1.5	monthly	$5,500
18.	_____	every 6 months	$3\frac{1}{2}$	4.0	semiannually	$1,900

Amortization payment

	Loan Payment	Payment Frequency	Time Period (years)	Nominal Rate (%)	Present Value (Amount of Loan)
19.	$3,756.68	every year	10	10.6	$22,500
20.	_____	every 3 months	4	8.8	$9,000
21.	_____	every month	6	9.0	$4,380

22. Turnberry Manufacturing has determined that it will need $500,000 in 8 years for a new roof on its southeastern regional warehouse. A sinking fund is established for the roof at 3.4% compounded semiannually. What equal payments are required every 6 months to accumulate the needed funds for the roof?

23. Randy Scott purchased a motorcycle for $8,500 with a loan amortized over 5 years at 7.2% interest. What equal monthly payments are required to amortize this loan?

24. Betty Price purchased a new home for $225,000 with a 20% down payment and the remainder amortized over a 15-year period at 9% interest.

   a. What amount did Betty finance?

   b. What equal monthly payments are required to amortize this loan over 15 years?

   c. What equal monthly payments are required if Betty decides to take a 20-year loan rather than a 15-year loan?

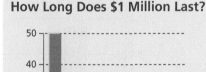

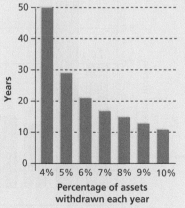

How Long Does $1 Million Last?

This chart shows the number of years a $1 million portfolio with an annual return of 8.7% can last based on percentage of assets withdrawn each year.

25. The Shangri-La Hotel has a financial obligation of $1,000,000 due in 5 years for kitchen equipment. A sinking fund is established to meet this obligation at 7.5% interest compounded monthly.

   a. What equal monthly sinking fund payments are required to accumulate the needed amount?

   b. What is the total amount of interest earned in the account?

BUSINESS DECISION: DON'T FORGET INFLATION!

26. You are the vice president of finance for Neptune Enterprises, Inc., a manufacturer of scuba diving gear. The company is planning a major plant expansion in 5 years. You have decided to start a sinking fund to accumulate the funds necessary for the project. Your company's investments yield 8% compounded quarterly. It is estimated that $2,000,000 in today's dollars will be required; however, the inflation rate on construction costs and plant equipment is expected to average 5% per year for the next 5 years.

   a. Use the compound interest concept from Chapter 11 to determine how much will be required for the project, taking inflation into account.

   b. What sinking fund payments will be required at the end of every 3-month period to accumulate the necessary funds?

Dollars AND Sense

This Business Decision, "Don't Forget Inflation," illustrates how inflation can affect long-range financial planning in business. Notice how much more the project will cost in 5 years because of rising prices.

At www.bls.gov, the Bureau of Labor Statistics provides an inflation calculator that you can use to enter a year and a dollar amount of buying power and then calculate how much buying power would be required for the same amount of goods or services in a subsequent year after inflation.

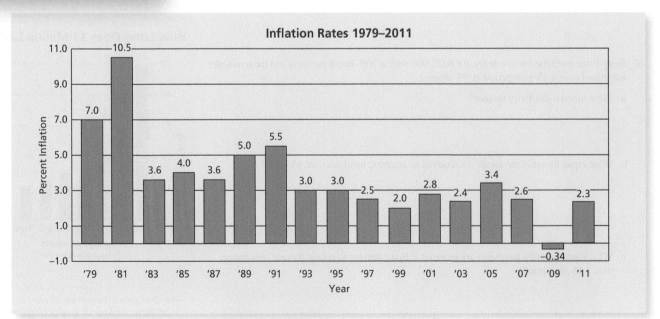

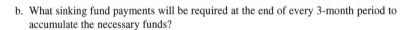

CHAPTER FORMULAS

Future Value of an Annuity

Future value (ordinary annuity) = Ordinary annuity table factor × Annuity payment

$$FV \text{ (ordinary annuity)} = \text{Payment} \times \frac{(1 + i)^n - 1}{i}$$

Future value (annuity due) = Annuity due table factor × Annuity payment

$$FV \text{ (annuity due)} = \text{Payment} \times \frac{(1 + i)^n - 1}{i} \times (1 + i)$$

Present Value of an Annuity

Present value (ordinary annuity) = Ordinary annuity table factor × Annuity payment

$$PV \text{ (ordinary annuity)} = \text{Payment} \times \frac{1 - (1 + i)^{-n}}{i}$$

Present value (annuity due) = Annuity due table factor × Annuity payment

$$PV \text{ (annuity due)} = \text{Payment} \times \frac{1 - (1 + i)^{-n}}{i} \times (1 + i)$$

Sinking Fund

$$\text{Sinking fund payment} = \frac{\text{Future value of the sinking fund}}{\text{Future value table factor}}$$

$$\text{Sinking fund payment} = \text{Future value} \times \frac{i}{(1 + i)^n - 1}$$

Amortization

$$\text{Amortization payment} = \frac{\text{Original amount of obligation}}{\text{Present value table factor}}$$

$$\text{Amortization payment} = \text{Present value} \times \frac{i}{1 - (1 + i)^{-n}}$$

CHAPTER SUMMARY

Section I: Future Value of an Annuity: Ordinary and Annuity Due

Topic	Important Concepts	Illustrative Examples
Calculating the Future Value of an Ordinary Annuity by Using Tables **Performance Objective 12-1, Page 370**	An annuity is the payment or receipt of *equal* cash amounts per period for a specified amount of time. 1. Calculate the interest rate per period for the annuity (nominal rate ÷ periods per year). 2. Determine the number of periods of the annuity (years × periods per year). 3. From Table 12-1, locate the ordinary annuity table factor at the intersection of the rate column and the periods row. 4. Calculate the future value of an ordinary annuity by Future value (ordinary annuity) = Table factor × Annuity payment	Calculate the future value of an ordinary annuity of $500 every 6 months for 5 years at 12% interest compounded semiannually. Rate per period = 6% (12% ÷ 2 periods per year) Periods = 10 (5 years × 2 periods per year) Table factor 6%, 10 periods = 13.18079 Future value = 13.18079 × 500 Future value = $6,590.40

Section I (continued)

Topic	Important Concepts	Illustrative Examples
Calculating the Future Value of an Annuity Due by Using Tables **Performance Objective 12-2, Page 374**	1. Calculate the number of periods of the annuity (years × periods per year) and add one period to the total. 2. Calculate the interest rate per period (nominal rate ÷ periods per year). 3. Locate the table factor at the intersection of the rate column and the periods row. 4. Subtract 1 from the ordinary annuity table factor to get the annuity due table factor. 5. Calculate the future value of an annuity due by Future value (annuity due) = Table factor × Annuity payment	Calculate the future value of an annuity due to $100 per month for 2 years at 12% interest compounded monthly. Periods = (2 × 12) + 1 for a total of 25 Rate per period = 1%, (12% ÷ 12) Table factor 1%, 25 periods = 28.24320 28.24320 − 1 = 27.24320 Future value = 27.24320 × 100 Future value = $2,724.32
Calculating the Future Value of an Ordinary Annuity and an Annuity Due by Formula **Performance Objective 12-3, Page 375**	*Future Value: Ordinary Annuity* $$FV = Pmt \times \frac{(1+i)^n - 1}{i}$$ *Future Value: Annuity Due* $$FV = Pmt \times \frac{(1+i)^n - 1}{i} \times (1+i)$$ where: FV = future value Pmt = annuity payment i = interest rate per period (nominal rate ÷ periods per year) n = number of periods (years × periods per year)	a. What is the future value of an *ordinary annuity* of $200 per month for 4 years at 12% interest compounded monthly? $$FV = 200 \times \frac{(1+.01)^{48} - 1}{.01}$$ $$FV = 200 \times 61.222608$$ $$FV = \$12,244.52$$ b. What is the future value of this investment if it is an *annuity due*? $$FV = 12,244.52 \times (1 + .01)$$ $$FV = 12,244.52 \times 1.01$$ $$FV = \$12,366.97$$

Section II: Present Value of an Annuity: Ordinary and Annuity Due

Topic	Important Concepts	Illustrative Examples
Calculating the Present Value of an Ordinary Annuity by Using Tables **Performance Objective 12-4, Page 380**	1. Calculate the interest rate per period for the annuity (nominal rate ÷ periods per year). 2. Determine the number of periods of the annuity (years × periods per year). 3. From Table 12-2, locate the present value table factor at the intersection of the rate column and the periods row. 4. Calculate the present value of an ordinary annuity by Present value (ordinary annuity) = Table factor × Annuity payment	How much must be deposited now at 5% compounded annually to yield an annuity payment of $1,000 at the end of each year for 11 years? Rate per period = 5% (5% ÷ 1 period per year) Number of periods = 11 (11 years × 1 period per year) Table factor 5%, 11 periods is 8.30641 Present value = 8.30641 × 1,000 Present value = $8,306.41
Calculating the Present Value of an Annuity Due by Using Tables **Performance Objective 12-5, Page 381**	1. Calculate the number of periods (years × periods per year) and subtract 1 from the total. 2. Calculate rate per period (nominal rate ÷ periods per year). 3. Locate the table factor at the intersection of the rate column and the periods row. 4. Add 1 to the ordinary annuity table factor to get the annuity due table factor. 5. Calculate the present value of an annuity due by Present value (annuity due) = Table factor × Annuity payment	How much must be deposited now at 8% compounded semiannually to yield an annuity payment of $1,000 at the beginning of each 6-month period for 5 years? Number of periods = 10 (5 × 2) less 1 period = 9 Rate per period = 4% (8% ÷ 2) Table factor 4%, 9 periods = 7.43533 7.43533 + 1 = 8.43533 Present value = 8.43533 × 1,000 Present value = $8,435.33

Section II (continued)

Topic	Important Concepts	Illustrative Examples
Calculating the Present Value of an Ordinary Annuity and an Annuity Due by Formula **Performance Objective 12-6, Page 384**	*Present Value: Ordinary Annuity* $PV = Pmt \times \dfrac{1 - (1 + i)^{-n}}{i}$ *Present Value: Annuity Due* $PV = Pmt \times \dfrac{1 - (1 + i)^{-n}}{i} \times (1 + i)$ where: $\quad PV$ = present value $\quad Pmt$ = annuity payment $\quad i$ = interest rate per period $\quad$ (nominal rate ÷ periods per year) $\quad n$ = number of periods $\quad$ (years × periods per year)	a. What is the present value of an ordinary annuity of \$100 per month for 5 years at 12% interest compounded monthly? $\quad PV = 100 \times \dfrac{1 - (1 + .01)^{-60}}{.01}$ $\quad PV = 100 \times 44.955038$ $\quad PV = \underline{\$4,495.50}$ b. What is the present value of this investment if it is an annuity due? $\quad PV_{\text{annuity due}} = PV_{\text{ordinary annuity}} \times (1 + i)$ $\quad PV = 4,495.50 \times (1 + .01)$ $\quad PV = 4,495.50 \times 1.01$ $\quad PV = \underline{\$4,540.46}$

Section III: Sinking Funds and Amortization

Topic	Important Concepts	Illustrative Examples
Calculating the Amount of a Sinking Fund Payment by Table **Performance Objective 12-7, Page 387**	Sinking funds are accounts used to set aside equal amounts of money at the end of each period at compound interest for the purpose of saving for a known future financial obligation. 1. Using the appropriate rate per period and number of periods, find the future value table factor from Table 12-1. 2. Calculate the amount of the sinking fund payment by $\quad$ Sinking fund payment = $\quad\quad \dfrac{\text{Future value of sinking fund}}{\text{Future value table factor}}$	What sinking fund payment is required at the end of each 6-month period at 10% interest compounded semiannually to amount to \$10,000 in 7 years? Number of periods = 14 (7 years × 2 periods per year) Rate per period = 5% (10% ÷ 2 periods per year) Table factor 14 periods, 5% = 19.59863 $\text{Payment} = \dfrac{10,000}{19.59863}$ Payment = $\underline{\$510.24}$
Calculating the Amount of an Amortization Payment by Table **Performance Objective 12-8, Page 389**	Amortization is a financial arrangement whereby a lump-sum obligation is incurred now (present value) and is paid off or liquidated by a series of equal periodic payments for a specified amount of time. 1. Using the appropriate rate per period and number of periods of the amortization, find the present value table factor from Table 12-2. 2. Calculate the amount of the amortization payment by $\quad$ Amortization payment = $\quad\quad \dfrac{\text{Original amount obligation}}{\text{Present value table factor}}$	What amortization payments are required at the end of each month at 18% interest to pay off a \$15,000 loan in 3 years? Number of periods = 36 (3 years × 12 periods per year) Rate per period = 1.5% (18% ÷ 12 periods per year) Table factor 36 periods, 1.5% = 27.66068 $\text{Amortization payment} = \dfrac{15,000}{27.66068}$ Amortization payment = $\underline{\$542.29}$

Section III (continued)

Topic	Important Concepts	Illustrative Examples
Calculating Sinking Fund Payments by Formula **Performance Objective 12-9, Page 389**	Sinking fund payments can be calculated by using the following formula $$Pmt = FV \times \frac{i}{(1+i)^n - 1}$$ where: Pmt = sinking fund payment FV = future value, amount needed in the future i = interest rate per period (nominal rate ÷ periods per year) n = number of periods (years × periods per year)	What sinking fund payment is required at the end of each month at 12% interest compounded monthly to amount to $10,000 in 4 years? Rate per period = 1% (12% ÷ 12) Periods = 48 (4 × 12) $$Pmt = 10,000 \times \frac{.01}{(1+.01)^{48} - 1}$$ $$Pmt = 10,000 \times \frac{.01}{.6122261}$$ $$Pmt = 10,000 \times .0163338$$ Sinking fund payment = $163.34
Calculating Amortization Payments by Formula **Performance Objective 12-10, Page 390**	Amortization payments are calculated by using the following formula: $$Pmt = PV \times \frac{i}{1-(1+i)^{-n}}$$ where: Pmt = amortization payment PV = present value, amount of the loan or obligation i = interest rate per period (nominal rate ÷ periods per year) n = number of periods (years × periods per year)	What amortization payment is required each month at 18% interest to pay off $3,000 in 2 years? Rate = 1.5% (18% ÷ 12) Periods = 24 (2 × 12) $$Pmt = 3,000 \times \frac{.015}{1-(1+.015)^{-24}}$$ $$Pmt = 3,000 \times \frac{.015}{.3004561}$$ $$Pmt = 3,000 \times .0499241$$ Amortization payment = $149.77

TRY IT: EXERCISE SOLUTIONS FOR CHAPTER 12

1. 2%, 24 periods

Future value = Table factor × Annuity payment

Future value = 30.42186 × 1,000 = $30,421.86

2. Periods = 20 (5 × 4) + 1 = 21

Rate = $\frac{6\%}{4} = 1\frac{1}{2}\%$

Table factor = 24.47052

$\underline{\quad - 1.00000}$

23.47052

Future value = Table factor × Annuity payment

Future value = 23.47052 × 1,000 = $23,470.52

3. a. 2%, 20 periods

$$FV = Pmt \times \frac{(1+i)^n - 1}{i}$$

$$FV = 250 \times \frac{(1+.02)^{20} - 1}{.02} = 250 \times \frac{(1.02)^{20} - 1}{.02}$$

$$FV = 250 \times 24.297369 = \$6,074.34$$

b. $FV_{\text{annuity due}} = (1+i) \times FV_{\text{ordinary annuity}}$

$FV_{\text{annuity due}} = (1+.02) \times 6,074.34 = \underline{\$6,195.83}$

4. 4%, 12 periods

Present value = Table factor × Annuity payment

Present value = 9.38507 × 20,000 = $187,701.40

5. Periods = 12 (3 × 4) − 1 = 11

Rate = $\frac{6\%}{4} = 1\frac{1}{2}\%$

Table factor = 10.07112

$\underline{\quad + 1.00000}$

11.07112

Present value = Table factor × Annuity payment

Present value = 11.07112 × 10,000 = $110,711.20

6. a. 2%, 24 periods

$$PV = Pmt \times \frac{1-(1+i)^{-n}}{i}$$

$$PV = 500 \times \frac{1-(1+.02)^{-24}}{.02} = 500 \times \frac{1-.6217215}{.02}$$

$$PV = 500 \times 18.913925 = \$9,456.96$$

b. $PV_{\text{annuity due}} = (1+i) \times PV_{\text{ordinary annuity}}$

$PV_{\text{annuity due}} = (1+.02) \times 9,456.96 = \underline{\$9,646.10}$

7. 3%, 20 periods

$$\text{Sinking fund payment} = \frac{\text{Future value of sinking fund}}{\text{Future value table factor}}$$

$$\text{Sinking fund payment} = \frac{8,000}{26.87037} = \underline{\underline{\$297.73}}$$

8. Amount financed = 130,000 − 20,000 = $110,000

4%, 28 periods

$$\text{Amortization payment} = \frac{\text{Original amount of obligation}}{\text{Present value table factor}}$$

$$\text{Amortization payment} = \frac{110,000}{16.66306} = \underline{\underline{\$6,601.43}}$$

9. .5%, 72 periods

$$\text{Sinking fund payment} = FV \times \frac{i}{(1+i)^n - 1}$$

$$\text{Sinking fund payment} = 40,000 \times \frac{.005}{(1+.005)^{72} - 1}$$

$$\text{Sinking fund payment} = 40,000 \times .0115729 = \underline{\underline{\$462.92}}$$

10. 1%, 96 periods

$$\text{Amortization payment} = PV \times \frac{i}{1 - (1+i)^{-n}}$$

$$\text{Amortization payment} = 150,000 \times \frac{.01}{1 - (1+.01)^{-96}}$$

$$\text{Amortization payment} = 150,000 \times .0162528 = \underline{\underline{\$2,437.93}}$$

Concept Review

1. Payment or receipt of equal amounts of money per period for a specified amount of time is known as a(n) _____. (12-1)

2. In a simple annuity, the number of compounding _____ per year coincides with the number of annuity _____ per year. (12-1)

3. An ordinary annuity is paid or received at the _____ of each time period. (12-1, 12-2)

4. An annuity due is paid or received at the _____ of each time period. (12-1, 12-2)

5. The total amount of the annuity payments and the accumulated interest on those payments is known as the _____ value of an annuity. (12-1)

6. The table factor for an annuity due is found by _____ one period to the number of periods of the annuity and then subtracting _____ from the resulting table factor. (12-2)

7. Write the formula for calculating the future value of an ordinary annuity when using a calculator with an exponential function, y^x, key. (12-3)

8. Write the formula for calculating the future value of an annuity due when using a calculator with an exponential function, (y^x), key. (12-3)

9. The lump sum amount of money that must be deposited today to provide a specified series of equal payments (annuity) in the future is known as the _____ value of an annuity. (12-4)

10. The table factor for the present value of an annuity due is found by _____ one period from the number of periods of the annuity and then adding _____ to the resulting table factor. (12-5)

11. A(n) _____ fund is an account used to set aside equal amounts of money at compound interest for the purpose of saving for a future obligation. (12-7)

12. _____ is a financial arrangement whereby a lump-sum obligation is incurred at compound interest now, such as a loan, and is then paid off by a series of equal periodic payments. (12-7, 12-8)

13. Write the formula for calculating a sinking fund payment by table. (12-7)

14. Write the formula for calculating an amortization payment by table. (12-8)

ASSESSMENT TEST

Note: Round to the nearest cent when necessary.

Use Table 12-1 to calculate the future value of the following ordinary annuities.

	Annuity Payment	Payment Frequency	Time Period (years)	Nominal Rate (%)	Interest Compounded	Future Value of the Annuity
1.	$4,000	every 3 months	6	8	quarterly	_____
2.	$10,000	every year	20	5	annually	_____

Use Table 12-1 to calculate the future value of the following annuities due.

	Annuity Payment	Payment Frequency	Time Period (years)	Nominal Rate (%)	Interest Compounded	Future Value of the Annuity
3.	$1,850	every 6 months	12	10	semiannually	_____
4.	$200	every month	$1\frac{3}{4}$	6	monthly	_____

Use Table 12-2 to calculate the present value of the following ordinary annuities.

	Annuity Payment	Payment Frequency	Time Period (years)	Nominal Rate (%)	Interest Compounded	Present Value of the Annuity
5.	$6,000	every year	9	5	annually	_____
6.	$125,000	every 3 months	3	6	quarterly	_____

Use Table 12-2 to calculate the present value of the following annuities due.

	Annuity Payment	Payment Frequency	Time Period (years)	Nominal Rate (%)	Interest Compounded	Present Value of the Annuity
7.	$700	every month	$1\frac{1}{2}$	6	monthly	_____
8.	$2,000	every 6 months	6	4	semiannually	_____

Use Table 12-1 to calculate the amount of the periodic payments needed to amount to the financial objective (future value of the annuity) for the following sinking funds.

	Sinking Fund Payment	Payment Frequency	Time Period (years)	Nominal Rate (%)	Interest Compounded	Future Value (Objective)
9.	_____	every year	13	7	annually	$20,000
10.	_____	every month	$2\frac{1}{4}$	6	monthly	$7,000

Use Table 12-2 to calculate the amount of the periodic payment required to amortize (pay off) the following loans.

	Loan Payment	Payment Period	Term of Loan (years)	Nominal Rate (%)	Interest Compounded	Present Value (Amount of Loan)
11.	_____	every 3 months	8	8	quarterly	$6,000
12.	_____	every month	$2\frac{1}{2}$	6	monthly	$20,000

Solve the following exercises by using tables.

13. How much will $800 deposited into a savings account at the *end* of each month be worth after 2 years at 6% interest compounded monthly?

14. How much will $3,500 deposited at the *beginning* of each 3-month period be worth after 7 years at 12% interest compounded quarterly?

15. What amount must be deposited now to withdraw $200 at the *beginning* of each month for 3 years if interest is 12% compounded monthly?

16. How much must be deposited now to withdraw $4,000 at the *end* of each year for 20 years if interest is 7% compounded annually?

17. Mary Evans plans to buy a used car when she starts college three years from now. She can make deposits at the end of each month into a 6% sinking fund account compounded monthly. If she wants to have $14,500 available to buy the car, what should be the amount of her monthly sinking fund payments?

18. A sinking fund is established by Alliance Industries at 8% interest compounded semiannually to meet a financial obligation of $1,800,000 in 4 years.

   a. What periodic sinking fund payment is required every 6 months to reach the company's goal?

   b. How much greater would the payment be if the interest rate was 6% compounded semiannually rather than 8%?

19. Lucky Strike, a bowling alley, purchased new equipment from Brunswick in the amount of $850,000. Brunswick is allowing Lucky Strike to amortize the cost of the equipment with monthly payments over 2 years at 12% interest. What equal monthly payments will be required to amortize this loan?

20. Aaron Grider buys a home for $120,500. After a 15% down payment, the balance is financed at 8% interest for 9 years.

   a. What equal quarterly payments will be required to amortize this mortgage loan?

   b. What is the total amount of interest Aaron will pay on the loan?

CHAPTER
12

Solve the following exercises by using formulas.

Ordinary annuity

	Annuity Payment	Payment Frequency	Time Period (years)	Nominal Rate (%)	Interest Compounded	Future Value of the Annuity
21.	$150	every month	4	3.0	monthly	_____
22.	$5,600	every year	9	1.8	annually	_____

Annuity due

	Annuity Payment	Payment Frequency	Time Period (years)	Nominal Rate (%)	Interest Compounded	Future Value of the Annuity
23.	$500	every 6 months	5	3.0	semiannually	_____
24.	$185	every month	$1\frac{1}{2}$	6.0	monthly	_____

Present value of an ordinary annuity

	Annuity Payment	Payment Frequency	Time Period (years)	Nominal Rate (%)	Interest Compounded	Present Value of the Annuity
25.	$1,500	every month	4	1.5	monthly	_____
26.	$375	every 6 months	2	3	semiannually	_____

Present value of an annuity due

	Annuity Payment	Payment Frequency	Time Period (years)	Nominal Rate (%)	Interest Compounded	Present Value of the Annuity
27.	$2,400	every 3 months	4	10	quarterly	_____
28.	$600	every year	20	4.3	annually	_____

Sinking fund payment

	Sinking Fund Payment	Payment Frequency	Time Period (years)	Nominal Rate (%)	Interest Compounded	Future Value (Objective)
29.	_____	every year	4	3.7	annually	$25,000
30.	_____	every 3 months	3	2	quarterly	$3,600

Amortization payment

	Loan Payment	Payment Frequency	Time Period (years)	Nominal Rate (%)	Present Value (Amount of Loan)
31.	_____	every 6 months	$2\frac{1}{2}$	12.0	$10,400
32.	_____	every month	4	13.5	$2,200

33. The town of Bay Harbor is planning to buy five new hybrid police cars in 4 years. The cars are expected to cost $38,500 each.

   a. What equal quarterly payments must the city deposit into a sinking fund at 3.5% interest compounded quarterly to achieve its goal?

   b. What is the total amount of interest earned in the account?

EXCEL 2

Hybrid vehicles run off a rechargeable battery and gasoline. With each hybrid burning 20%–30% less gasoline than comparably sized conventional models, they are in great demand by consumers.
   Lithium-ion battery packs are expected to become the dominant power source for hybrids with projected sales increasing from $21 billion in 2015 to $74 billion in 2020.

Source: Based on evrsoll.com

© GyuAki Gyula/Shutterstock.com

34. The Mesa Grande Bank is paying 9% interest compounded monthly.

    a. If you deposit $100 into a savings plan at the beginning of each month, how much will it be worth in 10 years?

    b. How much would the account be worth if the payments were made at the end of each month rather than at the beginning?

35. Sandpiper Savings & Loan is offering mortgages at 7.32% interest. What monthly payments would be required to amortize a loan of $200,000 for 25 years?

 EXCEL 3

BUSINESS DECISION: TIME IS MONEY!

36. You are one of the retirement counselors at the Valley View Bank. You have been asked to give a presentation to a class of high school seniors about the importance of saving for retirement. Your boss, the vice president of the trust division, has designed an example for you to use in your presentation. The students are shown five retirement scenarios and are asked to guess which yields the most money. *Note:* All annuities are *ordinary*. Although some people stop investing, the money remains in the account at 10% interest compounded annually.

    a. Look over each scenario and make an educated guess as to which investor will have the largest accumulation of money invested at 10% over the next 40 years. Then for your presentation, calculate the final value for each scenario.

        • Venus invests $1,200 per year and stops after 15 years.

        • Kevin waits 15 years, invests $1,200 per year for 15 years, and stops.

        • Rafael waits 15 years, then invests $1,200 per year for 25 years.

        • Magda waits 10 years, invests $1,500 per year for 15 years, and stops.

        • Heather waits 10 years, then invests $1,500 per year for 30 years.

    b. Based on the results, what message will this presentation convey to the students?

    c. Recalculate each scenario as an annuity due.

    d. How can the results be used in your presentation?

Dollars AND Sense

Saving for your child's college education

There are many ways to "grow" money—tax free—for your child's college education using annuities. Here are three popular options:

• **529 Savings Plans**—A 529 plan is a tax-advantaged savings plan designed to encourage saving for future college costs. These "qualified tuition plans" are sponsored by states, state agencies, or educational institutions. www.sec.gov/investor/pubs/intro529.htm

• **Coverdell Education Savings Accounts**—Coverdell accounts work like IRAs: you make annual contributions to an investment account, and the investment grows free of federal taxes. www.savingforcollege.com

• **Zero Coupon Bonds**—Municipal bonds (also known as "munis") represent investments in state and local government projects such as schools, highways, hospitals, and other important public projects. www.investinginbonds.com

Source: Adapted from: *The Miami Herald*, Oct. 25, 2009, page 1E, "5 Ways to Save for College."

CHAPTER
12

COLLABORATIVE LEARNING ACTIVITY

The "Personal" Sinking Fund

1. As a team, design a "personal" sinking fund for something to save for in the future.

   a. What are the amount and the purpose of the fund?

   b. What savings account interest rates are currently being offered at banks and credit unions in your area?

   c. Choose the best rate and calculate what monthly payments would be required to accumulate the desired amount in 1 year, 2 years, and 5 years.

2. As a team, research the annual reports or speak with accountants of corporations in your area that use sinking funds to accumulate money for future obligations. Answer the following questions about those sinking funds.

   a. What is the name of the corporation?

   b. What is the purpose and the amount of the sinking fund?

   c. For how many years is the fund?

   d. How much are the periodic payments?

   e. At what interest rate are these funds growing?

Growing Money

Refer to the "Dollars and Sense" tip on the previous page that discusses how to save for a child's college education. Divide into teams to further research and report to the class on the following.

a. What is the current status of the three tax-free savings plans?

   • 529 plans
   • Coverdell Education Savings Accounts
   • zero coupon bonds

b. What are the current interest rates and contribution limits of the various plans?

c. Speak with a certified financial planner to research other alternatives, such as custodial accounts and IRAs, that are available to those who want to save for their child's college education.

Business Math JOURNAL

BUSINESS, MATH, AND MORE ...

Managing Your Money

7 New Rules to Live By

Why is there so much month left at the end of the money? In recent years, our economy has undergone some dramatic changes. The "Great Recession" has significantly altered the financial planning parameters for individuals and families seeking financial freedom.

Here are some new planning guidelines from the editors of *Money* magazine and Bank of America to help you attain your long-term financial goals.

- **Savings**—Save at least 15% (and ideally 20%) of your income for long-term goals. The old rule was 10%, but that was when you could count on pension plans, shorter retirement periods, and better market returns.
- **Debt**—Keep your debt-to-income ratio under 30%. That's down from 36% so that you can direct more cash flow toward emergency and retirement savings. As a cushion, keep a six-month reserve of cash in a high-yield savings account and any additional emergency money in a short-term bond index fund.
- **Home**—Look at refinancing when rates are one percentage point lower than your current rate, not two as in years past when closing costs were higher. You should plan to live in the house for at least as long as it will take to pay off the closing costs and fees with the reduction in payment. (See the Mortgage Refinancing Worksheet on page 472 in Chapter 14.)
- **Spending**—Keep discretionary spending (clothes, dining out, movies) under 20% of your take-home pay. Before the recession, you could play with up to 30%, but average debt obligations have risen.
- **Investments**—Invest no more than 5% of your portfolio in your company stock or any single stock. The old yardstick was 10%, but you'll be safer with more diversification.
- **Allocation**—To determine how much of your portfolio should be in stocks, subtract your age from 110. The old formula subtracted your age from 100, but rising medical costs and increasing life spans necessitate being more aggressive. If you are comfortable with even more risk, subtract your age from 120.
- **Retirement**—To figure out how big a nest egg you'll need, multiply your ideal annual income by 30. (First, subtract any pension and Social Security income you will receive.) That's up from the previous rule of 25 because of increased longevity.

"We are spending entirely too much on bills."

Source: *Make Peace With Your Money*, "Money & Main St." guidebook series. Bank of America, *Money* Magazine, 7 New Rules to Live By, page 6.

Helpful Websites

The Internet can be a valuable source of money management information. Some helpful websites are www.bankrate.com, www.creditinfocenter.com, www.moneymanagement.org, www.betterbudgeting.com, and http://moneycentral.msn.com.

Issues & Activities

1. Use the chart below to:
   a. Distribute the various expenditure categories for a family with annual earnings of $55,000.
   b. Distribute your annual earnings for each expenditure category.
   c. Determine which of your expenditure categories are higher than average and which are lower than average.
   d. List some ways you can save on your annual expenditures.
2. For a family with annual earnings of $64,000, use the "7 New Rules to Live By" to answer the following questions.
   a. Ideally, how much should the family save?
   b. What should the family's debt limit be?
   c. If the family's portfolio amounts to $93,000, what should their limit be on any single stock?
   d. If the family's ideal annual income is $45,000 after pensions and Social Security, how big of a nest egg will they need?
3. In teams, use the websites listed above and other Internet sites to find current trends in "financial planning." List your sources and visually report your findings to the class.

Brainteaser—"Sky-High Debt!"

If a stack of 1,000 thousand dollar bills ($1 million) is 4 inches thick, how high would the stack be if it was equal to $13.72 trillion, the national debt as of December 2010?

See the end of Appendix A for the solution.

Average Annual Consumer Expenditures

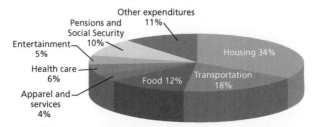

Other expenditures 11%
Pensions and Social Security 10%
Entertainment 5%
Health care 6%
Apparel and services 4%
Food 12%
Transportation 18%
Housing 34%

Source: U.S. Department of Commerce, *Statistical Abstract of the United States 2010.* Consumer Expenditures in 2007, Table 668, page 440.

CHAPTER 14 Mortgages

PERFORMANCE OBJECTIVES

SECTION I 14 MORTGAGES—FIXED-RATE AND ADJUSTABLE-RATE

real estate Land, including any permanent improvements such as homes, apartment buildings, factories, hotels, shopping centers, or any other "real" structures.

Mortgage A loan in which real property is used as security for a debt.

Federal Housing Administration (FHA) A government agency within the U.S. Department of Housing and Urban Development (HUD) that sets construction standards and insures residential mortgage loans made by approved lenders.

VA mortgages or **GI Loans** Long-term, low-down-payment home loans made by private lenders to eligible veterans, the payment of which is guaranteed by the Veterans Administration in the event of a default.

conventional loans Real estate loans made by private lenders that are not FHA-insured or VA-guaranteed.

private mortgage insurance (PMI) A special form of insurance primarily on mortgages for single-family homes, allowing the buyer to borrow more by putting down a smaller down payment.

adjustable-rate mortgage (ARM) A mortgage loan in which the interest rate changes periodically, usually in relation to a predetermined economic index.

Real estate is defined as "land, including the air above and the earth below, plus any permanent improvements to the land, such as homes, apartment buildings, factories, hotels, shopping centers, or any other 'real' property." Whether for commercial or residential property, practically all real estate transactions today involve some type of financing. The mortgage loan is the most popular method of financing real estate purchases.

A **mortgage** is any loan in which real property is used as security for a debt. During the term of the loan, the property becomes security, or collateral, for the lender, sufficient to ensure recovery of the amount loaned.

Mortgages today fall into one of three categories: FHA-insured, VA-guaranteed, and conventional. The National Housing Act of 1934 created the **Federal Housing Administration (FHA)** to encourage reluctant lenders to invest their money in the mortgage market, thereby stimulating the depressed construction industry. Today the FHA is a government agency within the Department of Housing and Urban Development (HUD). The FHA insures private mortgage loans made by approved lenders.

In 1944, the Servicemen's Readjustment Act (GI Bill of Rights) was passed to help returning World War II veterans purchase homes. Special mortgages were established known as **Veterans Affairs (VA) mortgages** or **GI Loans**. Under this and subsequent legislation, the government guarantees payment of a mortgage loan made by a private lender to a veteran/buyer should the veteran default on the loan.

VA loans may be used by eligible veterans, surviving spouses, and active service members to buy, construct, or refinance homes, farm residences, or condominiums. Down payments by veterans are not required but are left to the discretion of lenders, whereas FHA and conventional loans require a down payment from all buyers.

Conventional loans are made by private lenders and generally have a higher interest rate than either an FHA or VA loan. Most conventional lenders are restricted to loaning 80% of the appraised value of a property, thus requiring a 20% down payment. If the borrower agrees to pay the premium for **private mortgage insurance (PMI)**, the conventional lender can lend up to 95% of the appraised value of the property.

Historically, high interest rates in the early 1980s caused mortgage payments to skyrocket beyond the financial reach of the average home buyer. To revitalize the slumping mortgage industry, the **adjustable-rate mortgage (ARM)** was created. These are mortgage loans under which the interest rate is periodically adjusted to more closely coincide with changing

Mortgage loans are the most common form of loan made for real estate property purchases.

Courtesy of Bob Brechner

economic conditions. ARMs are very attractive, particularly to first-time buyers, because a low teaser rate may be offered for the first few years and then adjusted upward to a higher rate later in the loan. Today the adjustable-rate mortgage has become the most widely accepted option to the traditional 15- and 30-year fixed-rate mortgages.

Extra charges known as **mortgage discount points** are frequently added to the cost of a loan as a rate adjustment factor. This allows lenders to increase their yield without showing an increase in the mortgage interest rate. Each discount point is equal to 1% of the amount of the loan.

By their nature, mortgage loans involve large amounts of money and long periods of time. Consequently, the monthly payments and the amount of interest paid over the years can be considerable. Exhibit 14-1 illustrates the 30-year mortgage rates in the United States from 1974 to 2010 and the monthly payment on a $100,000 mortgage at various interest rate levels.

In reality, the higher interest mortgages would have been refinanced as rates declined, but consider the "housing affordability" factor. In 1982, payments on a $100,000 mortgage were $1,548 per month, compared with $457 in 2010!

In this section, you learn to calculate the monthly payments of a mortgage and prepare a partial amortization schedule of that loan. You also calculate the amount of property tax and insurance required as part of each monthly payment. In addition, you learn about the **closing**, the all-important final step in a real estate transaction, and the calculation of the closing costs. Finally, you learn about the important components of an adjustable-rate mortgage: the index, the lender's margin, the interest rate, and the cost caps.

mortgage discount points Extra charges frequently added to the cost of a mortgage, allowing lenders to increase their yield without showing an increase in the mortgage interest rate.

closing A meeting at which the buyer and seller of real estate conclude all matters pertaining to the transaction. At the closing, the funds are transferred to the seller and the ownership or title is transferred to the buyer.

CALCULATING THE MONTHLY PAYMENT AND TOTAL INTEREST PAID ON A FIXED-RATE MORTGAGE

14-1

In Chapter 12, we learned that amortization is the process of paying off a financial obligation in a series of equal, regular payments over a period of time. We calculated the amount of an amortization payment by using the present value of an annuity table or the optional amortization formula.

Because mortgages run for relatively long periods of time, we can also use a special present-value table in which the periods are listed in years. The table factors represent the monthly payment required per $1,000 of debt to amortize a mortgage. The monthly payment includes mortgage interest and an amount to reduce the principal. (See Table 14-1.)

Dollars
AND Sense

As a result of declining mortgage rates in recent years, a record 68.8% of families own their own homes today. That amounts to nearly 76 million households.

Purchasing and financing a home is one of the most important financial decisions a person will ever make. Substantial research should be done and much care taken in choosing the correct time to buy, the right property to buy, and the best financial offer to accept. (See Exhibit 14-2, "Mortgage Shopping Worksheet," pages 459–460.)

EXHIBIT 14-1 Historical Mortgage Rates and Monthly Payments

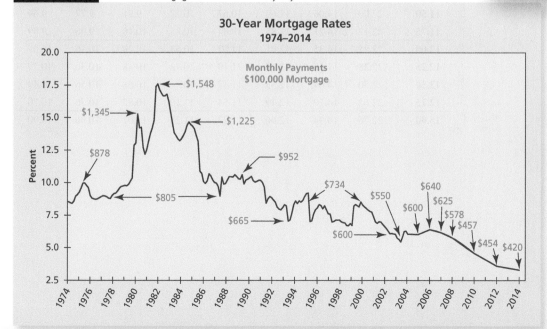

TABLE 14-1	Monthly Payments to Amortize Principal and Interest per $1,000 Financed

Monthly Payments
(Necessary to amortize a loan of $1,000)

Interest Rate (%)	5 Years	10 Years	15 Years	20 Years	25 Years	30 Years	35 Years	40 Years
3.50	$18.19	$9.89	$7.15	$5.80	$5.01	$4.49	$4.13	$3.87
3.75	18.30	10.01	7.27	5.93	5.14	4.63	4.28	4.03
4.00	18.42	10.12	7.40	6.06	5.28	4.77	4.43	4.18
4.25	18.53	10.24	7.52	6.19	5.42	4.92	4.58	4.34
4.50	18.64	10.36	7.65	6.33	5.56	5.07	4.73	4.50
4.75	18.76	10.48	7.78	6.46	5.70	5.22	4.89	4.66
5.00	18.88	10.61	7.91	6.60	5.85	5.37	5.05	4.83
5.25	18.99	10.73	8.04	6.74	6.00	5.53	5.21	4.99
5.50	19.11	10.86	8.18	6.88	6.15	5.68	5.38	5.16
5.75	19.22	10.98	8.31	7.03	6.30	5.84	5.54	5.33
6.00	19.34	11.11	8.44	7.17	6.45	6.00	5.71	5.51
6.25	19.45	11.23	8.58	7.31	6.60	6.16	5.88	5.68
6.50	19.57	11.36	8.72	7.46	6.76	6.33	6.05	5.86
6.75	19.69	11.49	8.85	7.61	6.91	6.49	6.22	6.04
7.00	19.81	11.62	8.99	7.76	7.07	6.66	6.39	6.22
7.25	19.92	11.75	9.13	7.91	7.23	6.83	6.57	6.40
7.50	20.04	11.88	9.28	8.06	7.39	7.00	6.75	6.59
7.75	20.16	12.01	9.42	8.21	7.56	7.17	6.93	6.77
8.00	20.28	12.14	9.56	8.37	7.72	7.34	7.11	6.96
8.25	20.40	12.27	9.71	8.53	7.89	7.52	7.29	7.15
8.50	20.52	12.40	9.85	8.68	8.06	7.69	7.47	7.34
8.75	20.64	12.54	10.00	8.84	8.23	7.87	7.66	7.53
9.00	20.76	12.67	10.15	9.00	8.40	8.05	7.84	7.72
9.25	20.88	12.81	10.30	9.16	8.57	8.23	8.03	7.91
9.50	21.01	12.94	10.45	9.33	8.74	8.41	8.22	8.11
9.75	21.13	13.08	10.60	9.49	8.92	8.60	8.41	8.30
10.00	21.25	13.22	10.75	9.66	9.09	8.78	8.60	8.50
10.25	21.38	13.36	10.90	9.82	9.27	8.97	8.79	8.69
10.50	21.50	13.50	11.06	9.99	9.45	9.15	8.99	8.89
10.75	21.62	13.64	11.21	10.16	9.63	9.34	9.18	9.09
11.00	21.75	13.78	11.37	10.33	9.81	9.53	9.37	9.29
11.25	21.87	13.92	11.53	10.50	9.99	9.72	9.57	9.49
11.50	22.00	14.06	11.69	10.67	10.17	9.91	9.77	9.69
11.75	22.12	14.21	11.85	10.84	10.35	10.10	9.96	9.89
12.00	22.25	14.35	12.01	11.02	10.54	10.29	10.16	10.09
12.25	22.38	14.50	12.17	11.19	10.72	10.48	10.36	10.29
12.50	22.50	14.64	12.33	11.37	10.91	10.68	10.56	10.49
12.75	22.63	14.79	12.49	11.54	11.10	10.87	10.76	10.70
13.00	22.76	14.94	12.66	11.72	11.28	11.07	10.96	10.90

Learning Tip

Remember that the table values represent monthly payments "per $1,000" financed. When calculating the amount of the monthly payment, you must first determine the number of $1,000s being financed, then multiply that figure by the table factor.

STEPS TO FIND THE MONTHLY MORTGAGE PAYMENT BY USING AN AMORTIZATION TABLE AND TO FIND TOTAL INTEREST

STEP 1. Find the number of $1,000s financed.

$$\text{Number of \$1,000s financed} = \frac{\text{Amount financed}}{1,000}$$

STEP 2. Using Table 14-1, locate the table factor, monthly payment per $1,000 financed, at the intersection of the number-of-years column and the interest-rate row.

STEP 3. Calculate the monthly payment.

$$\text{Monthly payment} = \text{Number of \$1,000s financed} \times \text{Table factor}$$

STEP 4. Find the total interest of the loan.

$$\text{Total interest} = (\text{Monthly payment} \times \text{Number of payments}) - \text{Amount financed}$$

EXAMPLE1 CALCULATING MONTHLY PAYMENT AND TOTAL INTEREST

What is the monthly payment and total interest on a $150,000 mortgage at 5% for 30 years?

SOLUTIONSTRATEGY

Step 1. Number of $1,000s financed $= \dfrac{\text{Amount financed}}{1,000} = \dfrac{150,000}{1,000} = 150$

Step 2. Table factor for 5%, 30 years is 5.37.

Step 3. Monthly payment = Number of $1,000s financed × Table factor
Monthly payment = 150 × 5.37
Monthly payment = $805.50

Step 4. Total interest = (Monthly payment × Number of payments) − Amount financed
Total interest = (805.50 × 360) − 150,000
Total interest = 289,980 − 150,000
Total interest = $139,980

TRYITEXERCISE 1

What is the monthly payment and total interest on an $85,500 mortgage at 4.5% for 25 years?

CHECK YOUR ANSWERS WITH THE SOLUTION ON PAGE 475.

PREPARING A PARTIAL AMORTIZATION SCHEDULE OF A MORTGAGE

14-2

Mortgages used to purchase residential property generally require regular, equal payments. A portion of the payment is used to pay interest on the loan; the balance of the payment is used to reduce the principal. This type of mortgage is called a **level-payment plan** because the amount of the payment remains the same for the duration of the loan. The amount of the payment that is interest gradually decreases, while the amount that reduces the debt gradually increases.

level-payment plan Mortgages with regular, equal payments over a specified period of time.

amortization schedule A chart that shows the month-by-month breakdown of each mortgage payment into interest and principal and the outstanding balance of the loan.

An **amortization schedule** is a chart that shows the status of the mortgage loan after each payment. The schedule illustrates month by month how much of the mortgage payment is interest and how much is left to reduce to principal. The schedule also shows the outstanding balance of the loan after each payment.

In reality, amortization schedules are long because they show the loan status for each month. A 30-year mortgage, for example, would require a schedule with 360 lines (12 months × 30 years = 360 payments).

Dollars AND Sense

In most cases, mortgage interest expense is tax-deductible. To increase your deductions for the current year, make your January mortgage payment by December 20. This will allow time for the payment to be credited to your account in December, giving you an extra month of interest deduction this year.

STEPS TO CREATE AN AMORTIZATION SCHEDULE FOR A LOAN

STEP 1. Use Table 14-1 to calculate the amount of the monthly payment.

STEP 2. Calculate the amount of interest for the current month using $I = PRT$, where P is the current outstanding balance of the loan, R is the annual interest rate, and T is $\frac{1}{12}$.

STEP 3. Find the portion of the payment used to reduce principal.

Portion of payment reducing principal = Monthly payment − Interest

STEP 4. Calculate the outstanding balance of the mortgage loan.

Outstanding balance = Previous balance − Portion of payment reducing principal

STEP 5. Repeat Steps 2, 3, and 4 for each succeeding month and enter the values on a schedule with columns labeled as follows.

| Payment Number | Monthly Payment | Monthly Interest | Portion Used to Reduce Principal | Loan Balance |

EXAMPLE2 PREPARING A PARTIAL AMORTIZATION SCHEDULE

Prepare an amortization schedule for the first three months of the $150,000 mortgage at 5% for 30 years from Example 1. Remember, you have already calculated the monthly payment to be $805.50.

SOLUTIONSTRATEGY

Step 1. $805.50 (from Example 1, page 455)

Step 2. **Month 1:**
Interest = Principal × Rate × Time
Interest = $150,000 \times .05 \times \frac{1}{12}$
Interest = $625.00

Step 3. Portion of payment reducing principal = Monthly payment − Interest
Portion of payment reducing principal = 805.50 − 625.00
Portion of payment reducing principal = $180.50

Step 4. Outstanding balance = Previous balance − Portion of payment reducing principal
Outstanding balance = 150,000.00 − 180.50
Outstanding balance after one payment = $149,819.50

Step 5. Repeat Steps 2, 3, and 4, for two more payments and enter the values on the schedule.
Month 2:
Interest = $149,819.50 \times .05 \times \frac{1}{12} = $624.25
(*Note:* Although very slightly, interest decreased.)

Portion reducing principal = 805.50 − 624.25 = $181.25

Outstanding balance after two payments = 149,819.50 − 181.25 = $149,638.25

Month 3:

Interest = $149,638.25 \times .05 \times \frac{1}{12}$ = $623.49

Portion reducing principal = 805.50 − 623.49 = $182.01

Outstanding balance after three payments = 149,638.25 − 182.01 = $149,456.24

Amortization Schedule
$150,000 Loan, 5%, 30 years

Payment Number	Monthly Payment	Monthly Interest	Portion Used to Reduce Principal	Loan Balance
0				$150,000.00
1	$805.50	$625.00	$180.50	$149,819.50
2	$805.50	$624.25	$181.25	$149,638.25
3	$805.50	$623.49	$182.01	$149,456.24

▶ TRYITEXERCISE 2

Prepare an amortization schedule of the first four payments of a $125,000 mortgage at 6% for 15 years. Use Table 14-1 to calculate the amount of the monthly payment.

CHECK YOUR ANSWERS WITH THE SOLUTIONS ON PAGES 475–476.

CALCULATING THE MONTHLY PITI OF A MORTGAGE LOAN

14-3

In reality, mortgage payments include four parts: principal, interest, taxes, and insurance—thus the abbreviation PITI. VA, FHA, and most conventional loans require borrowers to pay $\frac{1}{12}$ of the estimated annual property taxes and hazard insurance with each month's mortgage payment. Each month the taxes and insurance portions of the payment are placed in a type of savings account for safekeeping known as an **escrow account**. Each year when the property taxes and hazard insurance premiums are due, the lender disburses those payments from the borrower's escrow account. During the next 12 months, the account again builds up to pay the next year's taxes and insurance.

PITI An abbreviation for the total amount of a mortgage payment; includes principal, interest, property taxes, and hazard insurance.

escrow account Bank account used by mortgage lenders for the safekeeping of the funds accumulating to pay next year's property taxes and hazard insurance.

STEPS TO CALCULATE THE PITI OF A MORTGAGE

STEP 1. Calculate the principal and interest portion, PI, of the payment as before, using the amortization table, Table 14-1.

STEP 2. Calculate the monthly tax and insurance portion, TI.

$$\text{Monthly TI} = \frac{\text{Estimated property tax + Hazard insurance}}{12}$$

STEP 3. Calculate the total monthly PITI.

$$\text{Monthly PITI} = \text{Monthly PI} + \text{Monthly TI}$$

IN THE Business World

Typically, over the years of a mortgage, property taxes and insurance premiums rise. When this happens, the lender must increase the portion set aside in the escrow account by increasing the taxes and insurance parts of the monthly payment.

EXAMPLE 3   CALCULATING THE MONTHLY PITI OF A MORTGAGE

Lorie Kojian purchased a home with a mortgage of $87,500 at 7.5% for 30 years. The property taxes are $2,350 per year, and the hazard insurance premium is $567.48. What is the monthly PITI payment of Lorie's loan?

SOLUTIONSTRATEGY

Step 1. From the amortization table, Table 14-1, the factor for 7.5%, 30 years is 7.00. When we divide the amount of Lorie's loan by 1,000, we get 87.5 as the number of 1,000s financed. The principal and interest portion, PI, is therefore $87.5 \times 7.00 = \$612.50$.

Step 2.
$$\text{Monthly TI} = \frac{\text{Estimated property tax} + \text{Hazard insurance}}{12}$$

$$\text{Monthly TI} = \frac{2,350.00 + 567.48}{12} = \frac{2,917.48}{12} = \$243.12$$

Step 3. Monthly PITI = PI + TI
Monthly PITI = 612.50 + 243.12
Monthly PITI = $855.62

TRYITEXERCISE 3

Michael Veteramo purchased a home with a mortgage of $125,600 at 6.25% for 20 years. The property taxes are $3,250 per year, and the hazard insurance premium is $765. What is the monthly PITI payment of Michael's loan?

CHECK YOUR ANSWER WITH THE SOLUTION ON PAGE 476.

14-4   UNDERSTANDING CLOSING COSTS AND CALCULATING THE AMOUNT DUE AT CLOSING

title or **deed** The official document representing the right of ownership of real property.

closing costs Expenses incurred in conjunction with the sale of real estate, including loan origination fees, credit reports, appraisal fees, title search, title insurance, inspections, attorney's fees, recording fees, and broker's commission.

settlement or **closing statement** A document that provides a detailed accounting of payments, credits, and closing costs of a real estate transaction.

The term *closing* or *settlement* is used to describe the final step in a real estate transaction. This is a meeting at which time documents are signed; the buyer pays the agreed-upon purchase price; and the seller delivers the **title**, or right of ownership, to the buyer. The official document conveying ownership is known as the **deed**.

Closing costs are the expenses incurred in conjunction with the sale of real estate. In the typical real estate transaction, both the buyer and the seller are responsible for a number of costs that are paid for at the time of closing. The party obligated for paying a particular closing cost is often determined by local custom or by negotiation. Some closing costs are expressed as dollar amounts, whereas others are a percent of the amount financed or amount of the purchase price.

At closing, the buyer is responsible for the purchase price (mortgage + down payment) plus closing costs. The amount received by the seller after all expenses have been paid is known as the proceeds. The **settlement statement** or **closing statement** is a document, usually prepared by an attorney, that provides a detailed breakdown of the real estate transaction. This document itemizes closing costs and indicates how they are allocated between the buyer and the seller.

Exhibit 14-2, "Mortgage Shopping Worksheet," can be used to compare mortgage offers from various lenders. It provides a comprehensive checklist of important loan information, typical fees, closing and settlement costs, and other questions and considerations people should be aware of when shopping for a mortgage loan.

EXHIBIT 14-2 Mortgage Shopping Worksheet

Mortgage Shopping Worksheet

	Lender 1	Lender 2
Name of Lender		
Name of Contact		
Date of Contact		
Mortgage Amount		

Basic Information on the Loans

	Lender 1	Lender 2
Type of mortgage: fixed rate, adjustable rate, conventional, FHA, other? If adjustable, see page 460.		
Minimum down payment required		
Loan term (length of loan)		
Contract interest rate..		
Annual percentage rate (APR)		
Points (may be called loan discount points)		
Monthly private mortgage insurance (PMI) premiums...........		
How long must you keep PMI?.....................................		
Estimated monthly escrow for taxes and hazard insurance		
Estimated monthly payment (principal, interest, taxes, insurance, PMI)..........		

Fees

Different institutions may have different names for some fees and may charge different fees. We have listed some typical fees you may see on loan documents.

	Lender 1	Lender 2
Appraisal fee or loan processing fee................................		
Origination fee or underwriting fee		
Lender fee or funding fee		
Appraisal fee...		
Attorney's fees		
Document preparation and recording fees		
Broker's fees (may be quoted as points, origination fees, or interest rate add-on)...		
Credit report fee		
Other fees		
Name of Lender		

Other Costs at Closing/Settlement

	Lender 1	Lender 2
Title search/title insurance		
For lender...		
For you..		
Estimated prepaid amounts for interest, taxes, hazard insurance, payments to escrow.........................		
State and local taxes, stamp taxes, transfer taxes		
Flood determination		
Prepaid private mortgage insurance (PMI)........................		
Surveys and home inspections		
Total Fees and Other Closing/Settlement Cost Estimates		

Other Questions and Considerations about the Loan

	Lender 1	Lender 2
Are any of the fees or costs waivable?		
Prepayment penalties		
Is there a prepayment penalty?.....................................		
If so, how much is it?		
How long does the penalty period last? (for example, three years? five years?)		
Are extra principal payments allowed?............................		

(Continued)

EXHIBIT 14-2 Mortgage Shopping Worksheet (*Continued*)

Mortgage Shopping Worksheet

	Lender 1	Lender 2
Lock-ins		
Is the lock-in agreement in writing?.	_____	_____
Is there a fee to lock in?.	_____	_____
When does the lock-in occur—at application, approval, or another time?.	_____	_____
How long will the lock-in last?.	_____	_____
If the rate drops before closing, can you lock in at a lower rate?.	_____	_____
If the loan is an adjustable rate mortgage:		
What is the initial rate?.	_____	_____
What is the maximum the rate could be next year?.	_____	_____
What are the rate and payment caps for each year and over the life of the loan?.	_____	_____
What is the frequency of rate change and of any changes to the monthly payment?.	_____	_____
What index will the lender use?.	_____	_____
What margin will the lender add to the index?.	_____	_____
Credit life insurance		
Does the monthly amount quoted to you include a charge for credit life insurance?.	_____	_____
If so, does the lender require credit life insurance as a condition of the loan?.	_____	_____
How much does the credit life insurance cost?.	_____	_____
How much lower would your monthly payment be without the credit life insurance?.	_____	_____
If the lender does not require credit life insurance and you still want to buy it, what rates can you get from other insurance providers?.	_____	_____

Dollars AND Sense

The amount of interest paid and the length of a mortgage can be dramatically reduced by making **biweekly payments** (every two weeks) instead of monthly. By choosing this mortgage payment option, you are taking advantage of the all-important "time value of money" concept.

Here's an example. A 30-year, 7% mortgage for $100,000 has monthly payments of $666. The total interest you will pay on the loan is $139,509. If, instead, you make biweekly payments of $333, you would pay off the loan in 23 years and the total interest would be $103,959. The biweekly option saves you $35,550 in interest and seven years of payments!

To see how this option can be applied to your mortgage, go to www.bankrate.com and type *biweekly mortgage calculator* in the search box.

EXAMPLE4 CALCULATING MORTGAGE CLOSING COSTS

Barry and Donna Rae Schwartz are purchasing a $180,000 home. The down payment is 25%, and the balance will be financed with a 25-year fixed-rate mortgage at 6.5% and 2 discount points (each point is 1% of the amount financed). When Barry and Donna Rae signed the sales contract, they put down a deposit of $15,000, which will be credited to their down payment at the time of the closing. In addition, they must pay the following expenses: credit report, $80; appraisal fee, $150; title insurance premium, $\frac{1}{2}$% of amount financed; title search, $200; and attorney's fees, $450.

a. Calculate the amount due from Barry and Donna Rae at the closing.

b. If the sellers are responsible for the broker's commission, which is 6% of the purchase price, $900 in other closing costs, and the existing mortgage with a balance of $50,000, what proceeds will they receive on the sale of the property?

▶SOLUTIONSTRATEGY

a. Down payment = 180,000 × 25% = $45,000

Amount financed = 180,000 − 45,000 = $135,000

Closing Costs, Buyer

Discount points (135,000 × 2%)	$ 2,700
Down payment (45,000 − 15,000 deposit)	30,000
Credit report	80
Appraisal fee	150
Title insurance (135,000 × $\frac{1}{2}$%)	675
Title search	200
Attorney's fees	450
Due at closing	$34,255

b.

Proceeds, Seller

Sale price		$180,000
Less: Broker's commission:		
180,000 × 6%	$10,800	
Closing costs	900	
Mortgage payoff	50,000	
		−61,700
Proceeds to seller		$118,300

▶ TRYITEXERCISE 4

Jonathan Monahan is purchasing a townhouse for $120,000. The down payment is 20%, and the balance will be financed with a 15-year fixed-rate mortgage at 9% and 3 discount points (each point is 1% of the amount financed). When Jonathan signed the sales contract, he put down a deposit of $10,000, which will be credited to his down payment at the time of the closing. In addition, he must pay the following expenses: loan application fee, $100; property transfer fee, $190; title insurance premium, $\frac{3}{4}$% of amount financed; hazard insurance premium, $420; prepaid taxes, $310; and attorney's fees, $500.

a. Calculate the amount due from Jonathan at the closing.

b. If the seller is responsible for the broker's commission, which is $5\frac{1}{2}$% of the purchase price, $670 in other closing costs, and the existing mortgage balance of $65,000, what proceeds will the seller receive on the sale of the property?

CHECK YOUR ANSWERS WITH THE SOLUTIONS ON PAGE 476.

CALCULATING THE INTEREST RATE OF AN ADJUSTABLE-RATE MORTGAGE (ARM)

14-5

With a fixed-rate mortgage, the interest rate stays the same during the life of the loan. With an adjustable-rate mortgage (ARM), the interest rate changes periodically, usually in relation to an index, and payments may go up or down accordingly. In recent years, the ARM has become the most widely accepted alternative to the traditional 30-year fixed-rate mortgage.

The primary components of an ARM are the index, lender's margin, calculated interest rate, initial interest rate, and cost caps. With most ARMs, the interest rate and monthly payment change every year, every three years, or every five years. The period between one rate change and the next is known as the **adjustment period**. A loan with an adjustment period of one year, for example, is called a one-year ARM.

Most lenders tie ARM interest rate changes to changes in an **index rate**. These indexes usually go up and down with the general movement of interest rates in the nation's economy. When the index goes up, so does the mortgage rate, resulting in higher monthly payments. When the index goes down, the mortgage rate may or may not go down.

adjustment period The amount of time between one rate change and the next on an adjustable-rate mortgage; generally one, two, or three years.

index rate The economic index to which the interest rate on an adjustable-rate mortgage is tied.

lender's margin or **spread** The percentage points added to an index rate to get the interest rate of an adjustable-rate mortgage.

calculated or **initial ARM interest rate** The interest rate of an adjustable-rate mortgage to which all future adjustments and caps apply.

teaser rate A discounted interest rate for the first adjustment period of an adjustable-rate mortgage that is below the current market rate of interest.

interest-rate caps Limits on the amount the interest rate can increase on an ARM.

periodic rate caps Limits on the amount the interest rate of an ARM can increase per adjustment period.

overall rate caps Limits on the amount the interest rate of an ARM can increase over the life of the loan.

To calculate the interest rate on an ARM, lenders add a few points called the **lender's margin** or **spread** to the index rate. The amount of the margin can differ among lenders and can make a significant difference in the amount of interest paid over the life of a loan.

> **Calculated ARM interest rate = Index rate + Lender's margin**

The **calculated** or **initial ARM interest rate** is usually the rate to which all future adjustments and caps apply, although this rate may be discounted by the lender during the first payment period to attract and qualify more potential borrowers. This low initial interest rate, sometimes known as a **teaser rate**, is one of the main appeals of the ARM; however, without some protection from rapidly rising interest rates, borrowers might be put in a position of not being able to afford the rising mortgage payments. To prevent this situation, standards have been established requiring limits or caps on increases.

Interest-rate caps place a limit on the amount the interest rate can increase. These may come in the form of **periodic rate caps**, which limit the increase from one adjustment period to the next, and **overall rate caps**, which limit the increase over the life of the mortgage. The following formulas can be used to find the maximum interest rates of an ARM:

> **Maximum rate per adjustment period = Previous rate + Periodic rate cap**
>
> **Maximum overall ARM rate = Initial rate + Overall rate cap**

EXAMPLE5 CALCULATING ARM RATES

Florence Powers bought a home with an adjustable-rate mortgage. The lender's margin on the loan is 2.5%, and the overall rate cap is 6% over the life of the loan.

a. If the current index rate is 4.9%, what is the calculated interest rate of the ARM?

b. What is the maximum overall rate of the loan?

▶SOLUTIONSTRATEGY

a. Because the loan interest rate is tied to an index, we use the formula

Calculated ARM interest rate = Index rate + Lender's margin
Calculated ARM interest rate = 4.9% + 2.5%
Calculated ARM interest rate = 7.4%

b.

Maximum overall rate = Calculated rate + Overall rate cap
Maximum overall rate = 7.4% + 6%
Maximum overall rate = 13.4%

▶TRYITEXERCISE 5

Kate Fitzgerald bought a home with an adjustable-rate mortgage. The lender's margin on the loan is 3.4%, and the overall rate cap is 7% over the life of the loan. The current index rate is 3.2%.

a. What is the initial interest rate of the ARM?

b. What is the maximum overall rate of the loan?

CHECK YOUR ANSWERS WITH THE SOLUTIONS ON PAGE 476.

REVIEW EXERCISES

14 SECTION I

Using Table 14-1 as needed, calculate the required information for the following mortgages.

	Amount Financed	Interest Rate	Term of Loan (years)	Number of $1,000s Financed	Table Factor	Monthly Payment	Total Interest
1.	$80,000	9.00%	20	80	9.00	$720.00	$92,800.00
2.	$72,500	6.00%	30				
3.	$164,900	4.50%	25				
4.	$154,300	4.75%	15				
5.	$96,800	7.75%	30				
6.	$422,100	5.50%	20				
7.	$184,300	6.25%	15				

8. Marc Bove purchased a home with a $78,500 mortgage at 9% for 15 years. Calculate the monthly payment and prepare an amortization schedule for the first four months of Marc's loan.

Payment Number	Monthly Payment	Monthly Interest	Portion Used to Reduce Principal	Loan Balance
0				$78,500.00
1				
2				
3				
4				

As one of the loan officers for Grove Gate Bank, calculate the monthly principal and interest, PI, using Table 14-1 and the monthly PITI for the following mortgages.

	Amount Financed	Interest Rate	Term of Loan (years)	Monthly PI	Annual Property Tax	Annual Insurance	Monthly PITI
9.	$76,400	8.00%	20	$639.47	$1,317	$866	$821.39
10.	$128,800	4.75%	15		$2,440	$1,215	
11.	$224,500	5.25%	30		$3,506	$1,431	
12.	$250,000	4.50%	25		$6,553	$2,196	
13.	$164,500	6.75%	30		$3,125	$1,569	
14.	$140,500	4.25%	10		$2,842	$1,460	

15. Ben and Mal Scott plan to buy a home for $272,900. They will make a 10% down payment and qualify for a 25-year, 7% mortgage loan.

a. What is the amount of their monthly payment?

b. How much interest will they pay over the life of the loan?

16. Michael Sanchez purchased a condominium for $88,000. He made a 20% down payment and financed the balance with a 30-year, 9% fixed-rate mortgage.

   a. What is the amount of the monthly principal and interest portion, PI, of Michael's loan?

   b. Construct an amortization schedule for the first four months of Michael's mortgage.

Payment Number	Monthly Payment	Monthly Interest	Portion Used to Reduce Principal	Loan Balance
0				_____
1	_____	_____	_____	_____
2	_____	_____	_____	_____
3	_____	_____	_____	_____
4	_____	_____	_____	_____

   c. If the annual property taxes are $1,650 and the hazard insurance premium is $780 per year, what is the total monthly PITI of Michael's loan?

17. Luis Schambach is shopping for a 15-year mortgage for $150,000. Currently, the Fortune Bank is offering an 8.5% mortgage with 4 discount points and the Northern Trust Bank is offering an 8.75% mortgage with no points. Luis is unsure which mortgage is a better deal and has asked you to help him decide. (Remember, each discount point is equal to 1% of the amount financed.)

   a. What is the total interest paid on each loan?

   b. Taking into account the closing points, which bank is offering a better deal and by how much?

18. Phil Pittman is interested in a fixed-rate mortgage for $100,000. He is undecided whether to choose a 15- or 30-year mortgage. The current mortgage rate is 5.5% for the 15-year mortgage and 6.5% for the 30-year mortgage.

   a. What are the monthly principal and interest payments for each loan?

b. What is the total amount of interest paid on each loan?

c. Overall, how much more interest is paid by choosing the 30-year mortgage?

19. Larry and Cindy Lynden purchased a townhome in Alison Estates with an adjustable-rate mortgage. The lender's margin on the loan is 4.1%, and the overall rate cap is 5% over the life of the loan. The current index rate is the prime rate, 3.25%.

a. What is the calculated interest rate of the ARM?
    Calculated ARM interest rate = Index rate + Lender's margin
    Calculated ARM interest rate = 3.25 + 4.1 = <u>7.35%</u>

b. What is the maximum overall rate of the loan?
    Maximum overall ARM rate = Initial rate + Overall rate cap
    Maximum overall ARM rate = 7.35 + 5.0 = <u>12.35%</u>

20. Heather Gott bought a home with an adjustable-rate mortgage. The lender's margin on the loan is 3.5%, and the overall rate cap is 8% over the life of the loan.

a. If the current index rate is 3.75%, what is the calculated interest rate of the ARM?

b. What is the maximum overall ARM rate of Heather's loan?

21. Joe and Gloria Moutran are purchasing a house in Winter Springs financed with an adjustable-rate mortgage. The lender's margin on the loan is 2.75%, and the overall rate cap is 6.2% over the life of the loan. The current index rate is 5.8%.

a. What is the calculated interest rate of the ARM?

b. What is the maximum overall ARM rate of the loan?

22. You are a real estate broker for Aurora Realty. One of your clients, Erica Heston, has agreed to purchase one of the homes your office has listed for sale for a negotiated price of $235,000. The down payment is 20%, and the balance will be financed with a 15-year fixed-rate mortgage at 8.75% and $3\frac{1}{2}$ discount points. The annual property tax is $5,475, and the hazard insurance premium is $2,110. When Erica signed the original contract, she put down a deposit of $5,000, which will be credited to her down payment. In addition, at the time of closing, Erica must pay the following expenses:

Appraisal fee	$215
Credit report	$65
Roof inspection	$50
Mortgage insurance premium	$\frac{1}{2}$% of amount financed
Title search	$125
Attorney's fees	$680
Escrow fee	$210
Prepaid interest	$630

As Erica's real estate broker, she has asked you the following questions:

a. What is the total monthly PITI of the mortgage loan?

b. What is the total amount of interest that will be paid on the loan?

c. How much is due from Erica at the time of the closing?

d. If your real estate office is entitled to a commission from the seller of $6\frac{1}{2}\%$ of the price of the home, how much commission is made on the sale?

BUSINESS DECISION: BUYING DOWN THE MORTGAGE

23. The buyer of a piece of real estate is often given the option of buying down the loan. This option gives the buyer a choice of loan terms in which various combinations of interest rates and discount points are offered. The choice of how many points and what rate is optimal is often a matter of how long the buyer intends to keep the property.

    Darrell Frye is planning to buy an office building at a cost of $988,000. He must pay 10% down and has a choice of financing terms. He can select from a 7% 30-year loan and pay 4 discount points, a 7.25% 30-year loan and pay 3 discount points, or a 7.5% 30-year loan and pay 2 discount points. Darrell expects to hold the building for four years and then sell it. Except for the three rate and discount point combinations, all other costs of purchasing and selling are fixed and identical.

    a. What is the amount being financed?

    b. If Darrell chooses the 4-point 7% loan, what will be his total outlay in points and payments after 48 months?

    c. If Darrell chooses the 3-point 7.25% loan, what will be his total outlay in points and payments after 48 months?

    d. If Darrell chooses the 2-point 7.5% loan, what will be his total outlay in points and payments after 48 months?

    e. Of the three choices for a loan, which results in the lowest total outlay for Darrell?

SECOND MORTGAGES—HOME EQUITY LOANS AND LINES OF CREDIT

After the "housing crisis" brought on by the recession of 2008, the Mortgage Bankers Association reported that more than 1 in 10 homeowners with a mortgage were in foreclosure or were behind in their payments. (See Exhibit 14-3.)

Despite these statistics, homeowners today may use the *equity* in their homes to qualify for a sizable amount of credit at interest rates that are historically low. In addition, under existing law, the interest may be tax-deductible because the debt is secured by the home.

A **home equity loan** is a lump-sum second mortgage loan based on the available equity in a home. A **home equity line of credit** is a form of revolving credit also based on the available equity. Because the home is likely to be a consumer's largest asset, many homeowners use these loans and credit lines only for major expenditures such as debt consolidation, education, home improvements, business expansion, medical bills, and vacations.

With home equity lines of credit, the borrower will be approved for a specific amount of credit known as the **credit limit**. This is the maximum amount that can be borrowed at any one time on that line of credit.

home equity loan A lump-sum second mortgage loan based on the available equity in a home.

home equity line of credit A revolving credit second mortgage loan made on the available equity in a home.

credit limit A pre-approved limit on the amount of a home equity line of credit.

CALCULATING THE POTENTIAL AMOUNT OF CREDIT AVAILABLE TO A BORROWER

14-6

Most lenders set the credit limit on a home equity loan or line by taking a percentage of the appraised value of the house and subtracting the balance owed on the existing mortgage. In determining your actual credit limit, the lender also will consider your ability to repay by looking at your income, debts, and other financial obligations as well as your credit history.

STEPS TO CALCULATE THE POTENTIAL AMOUNT OF CREDIT AVAILABLE TO A BORROWER

STEP 1. Calculate the percentage of appraised value.

Percentage of appraised value = Appraised value × Lender's percentage

STEP 2. Find the potential amount of credit available.

Potential credit = Percentage of appraised value − First mortgage balance

EXAMPLE 6 CALCULATING POTENTIAL CREDIT OF A HOME EQUITY LOAN

Terri Alexander owns a house that was recently appraised for $115,700. The balance on her existing mortgage is $67,875. If her bank is willing to loan up to 75% of the appraised value, what is the potential amount of credit available to Terri on a home equity loan?

SOLUTIONSTRATEGY

Step 1. Percentage of appraised value = Appraised value × Lender's percentage
Percentage of appraised value = 115,700 × .75
Percentage of appraised value = $86,775

Step 2. Potential credit = Percentage of appraised value − First mortgage balance
Potential credit = 86,775 − 67,875
Potential credit = $18,900

▶TRYITEXERCISE 6

Justin Schaefer owns a home that was recently appraised for $92,900. The balance on his existing first mortgage is $32,440. If his credit union is willing to loan up to 80% of the appraised value, what is the potential amount of credit available to Justin on a home equity line of credit?

CHECK YOUR ANSWER WITH THE SOLUTION ON PAGE 476.

EXHIBIT 14-3
Home Equity Lending

Dollars AND Sense

In 2010, the signing of the financial reform bill into law meant real financial reform had finally become a reality. Almost two years after the near collapse of the financial system, Congress put new rules in place to prevent the abusive lending practices responsible for the crisis. Highlights of the new law include:

- A Consumer Financial Protection Bureau (CFPB) to stop unfair lending practices
- Governmental authority to step in and safely shut down failing financial firms
- Prohibitions on abusive mortgage lending practices such as kickbacks for steering people into high-rate loans when they qualify for lower rates
- Stronger foreclosure prevention, including an emergency loan fund to help families at risk of losing their home because of unemployment or illness

Source: www.responsiblelending.org

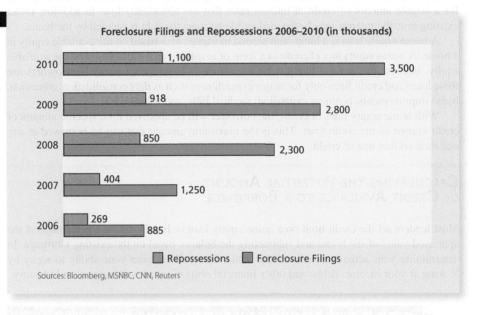

Foreclosure Filings and Repossessions 2006–2010 (in thousands)

Year	Repossessions	Foreclosure Filings
2010	1,100	3,500
2009	918	2,800
2008	850	2,300
2007	404	1,250
2006	269	885

Sources: Bloomberg, MSNBC, CNN, Reuters

14-7 CALCULATING THE HOUSING EXPENSE RATIO AND THE TOTAL OBLIGATIONS RATIO OF A BORROWER

qualifying ratios Ratios used by lenders to determine whether borrowers have the economic ability to repay loans.

housing expense ratio The ratio of a borrower's monthly housing expense (PITI) to monthly gross income.

total obligations ratio The ratio of a borrower's total monthly financial obligations to monthly gross income.

Mortgage lenders use ratios to determine whether borrowers have the economic ability to repay the loan. FHA, VA, and conventional lenders all use monthly gross income as the base for calculating these **qualifying ratios**. Two important ratios used for this purpose are the **housing expense ratio** and the **total obligations ratio**. These ratios are expressed as percents and are calculated by using the following formulas:

$$\text{Housing expense ratio} = \frac{\text{Monthly housing expense (PITI)}}{\text{Monthly gross income}}$$

$$\text{Total obligations ratio} = \frac{\text{Total monthly financial obligations}}{\text{Monthly gross income}}$$

The mortgage business uses widely accepted guidelines for these ratios that should not be exceeded. The ratio guidelines are shown in Exhibit 14-4.

EXHIBIT 14-4
Lending Ratio Guidelines

Mortgage Type	Housing Expense Ratio	Total Obligations Ratio
FHA	29%	41%
Conventional	28%	36%

Note that the ratio formulas are an application of the percentage formula; the ratio is the rate, the PITI or total obligations are the portion, and the monthly gross income is the base. With this in mind, we are able to solve for any of the variables.

EXAMPLE7   CALCULATING MORTGAGE LENDING RATIOS

Sue Harper earns a gross income of $2,490 per month. She has applied for a mortgage with a monthly PITI of $556. Sue has other financial obligations totaling $387.50 per month.

a. What is Sue's housing expense ratio?

b. What is Sue's total obligations ratio?

c. According to the Lending Ratio Guidelines in Exhibit 14-4, for what type of mortgage would she qualify, if any?

►SOLUTIONSTRATEGY

a. $\text{Housing expense ratio} = \dfrac{\text{Monthly housing expense (PITI)}}{\text{Monthly gross income}}$

$\text{Housing expense ratio} = \dfrac{556}{2,490}$

$\text{Housing expense ratio} = .2232 = \underline{22.3\%}$

b. $\text{Total obligations ratio} = \dfrac{\text{Total monthly financial obligations}}{\text{Monthly gross income}}$

$\text{Total obligations ratio} = \dfrac{556.00 + 387.50}{2,490} = \dfrac{943.50}{2,490}$

$\text{Total obligations ratio} = .3789 = \underline{37.9\%}$

c. According to the Lending Ratio Guidelines, Sue would qualify for an FHA mortgage but not a conventional mortgage; her total obligations ratio is 37.9%, which is above the limit for conventional mortgages.

►TRYITEXERCISE 7

Roman Bass earns a gross income of $3,100 per month. He has made application at the Golden Gables Bank for a mortgage with a monthly PITI of $669. Roman has other financial obligations totaling $375 per month.

a. What is Roman's housing expense ratio?

b. What is Roman's total obligations ratio?

c. According to the Lending Ratio Guidelines in Exhibit 14-4, for what type of mortgage would he qualify, if any?

CHECK YOUR ANSWERS WITH THE SOLUTIONS ON PAGE 477.

Note: Round all answers to the nearest cent when necessary.

For the following second mortgage applications, calculate the percentage of appraised value and the potential credit.

	Appraised Value	Lender's Percentage	Percentage of Appraised Value	Balance of First Mortgage	Potential Credit
1.	$118,700	75%	$89,025	$67,900	$21,125
2.	$124,500	70%	_____	$53,400	_____
3.	$141,200	80%	_____	$99,100	_____
4.	$324,600	75%	_____	$197,500	_____
5.	$105,000	65%	_____	$70,000	_____
6.	$243,800	60%	_____	$101,340	_____
7.	$1,329,000	70%	_____	$514,180	_____

Calculate the housing expense ratio and the total obligations ratio for the following mortgage applications.

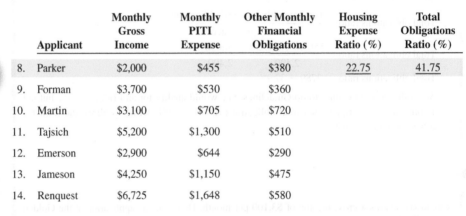

	Applicant	Monthly Gross Income	Monthly PITI Expense	Other Monthly Financial Obligations	Housing Expense Ratio (%)	Total Obligations Ratio (%)
8.	Parker	$2,000	$455	$380	22.75	41.75
9.	Forman	$3,700	$530	$360		
10.	Martin	$3,100	$705	$720		
11.	Tajsich	$5,200	$1,300	$510		
12.	Emerson	$2,900	$644	$290		
13.	Jameson	$4,250	$1,150	$475		
14.	Renquest	$6,725	$1,648	$580		

15. Use Exhibit 14-4, Lending Ratio Guidelines, on page 468 to answer the following questions:

   a. Which of the applicants in Exercises 8–14 would *not* qualify for a conventional mortgage?

   b. Which of the applicants in Exercises 8–14 would *not* qualify for any mortgage?

16. Ronald and Samantha Brady recently had their condominium in Port Isaac appraised for $324,600. The balance on their existing first mortgage is $145,920. If their bank is willing to loan up to 75% of the appraised value, what is the amount of credit available to the Bradys on a home equity line of credit?

   $$324,600 \times .75 = \$243,450$$
   $$-145,920$$
   Available credit $\underline{\$97,530}$

17. The Barclays own a home that was recently appraised for $219,000. The balance on their existing first mortgage is $143,250. If their bank is willing to loan up to 65% of the appraised value, what is the potential amount of credit available to the Barclays on a home equity loan?

18. Ransford and Alda Mariano own a home recently appraised for $418,500. The balance on their existing mortgage is $123,872. If their bank is willing to loan up to 80% of the appraised value, what is the amount of credit available to them?

19. Michelle Heaster is thinking about building an addition on her home. The house was recently appraised for $154,000, and the balance on her existing first mortgage is $88,600. If Michelle's bank is willing to loan up to 70% of the appraised value, does she have enough equity in the house to finance a $25,000 addition?

20. Jamie and Alice Newmark have a combined monthly gross income of $9,702 and monthly expenses totaling $2,811. They plan to buy a home with a mortgage whose monthly PITI will be $2,002.

    a. What is Jamie and Alice's combined housing expense ratio?

    b. What is their total obligations ratio?

    c. For what kind of mortgage can they qualify, if any?

    d. (Optional challenge) By how much would they need to reduce their monthly expenses in order to qualify for an FHA mortgage?

Mortgage brokers are real estate financing professionals acting as the intermediary between consumers and lenders during mortgage transactions. A mortgage broker works with consumers to help them through the complex mortgage origination process.

Brokers earn commissions in exchange for bringing borrowers and lenders together and receive payment when the mortgage loan is closed.

21. You are a mortgage broker at Interamerican Bank. One of your clients, Bill Cramer, has submitted an application for a mortgage with a monthly PITI of $1,259. His other financial obligations total $654.50 per month. Bill earns a gross income of $4,890 per month.

    a. What is his housing expense ratio?

    b. What is his total obligations ratio?

c. According to the Lending Ratio Guidelines on page 468, for what type of mortgage would Bill qualify, if any?

d. If Bill decided to get a part-time job so that he could qualify for a conventional mortgage, how much additional monthly income would he need?

BUSINESS DECISION: DOES IT PAY TO REFINANCE YOUR MORTGAGE?

22. According to money.CNN.com, with mortgage rates near 35-year lows, you may be able to cut your payments sharply by refinancing your loan. To qualify for the best rates, you need a credit score of 740 or higher and usually at least 20% equity.

Even if you have to settle for a higher rate, a new loan may save you money. The main consideration is whether you will live in your home long enough to offset the refinance closing costs.

Your current mortgage payment is $1,458.50 per month, with a balance of $214,800. You have a chance to refinance at the Biltmore Bank with a 30-year, 5.5% mortgage. The closing costs of the loan are application fee, $90; credit report, $165; title insurance, .4% of the amount financed; title search, $360; and attorney's fees, $580.

You plan to live in your home for at least four more years. Use the Mortgage Refinancing Worksheet below to see if it makes sense to refinance your mortgage.

MORTGAGE REFINANCING WORKSHEET

STEP 1. Current monthly mortgage payment.. ☐

STEP 2. New monthly mortgage payment if you refinance........................ ☐

New rate ____   Current mortgage balance ____
☐ Table 14-1 factor ____ × # of 1,000s to borrow ____

STEP 3. Monthly savings.. ☐

☐ Step 1. ____ − Step 2. ____

STEP 4. Total refinance closing costs (appraisal, title search, etc.).............. ☐

STEP 5. Total months needed to recoup your costs.................................. ☐

☐ Step 4 result ÷ Step 3 result ____

STEP 6. Total months you plan to live in your home............................... ☐

The Bottom Line—If you plan to live in your home longer than the result in Step 5, it makes sense to refinance.

CHAPTER FORMULAS

Fixed-Rate Mortgages

Monthly payment = Number of $1,000s financed × Table 14-1 factor

Total interest = (Monthly payment × Number of payments) − Amount financed

$$\text{Monthly taxes and Insurance (TI)} = \frac{\text{Estimated property tax + Hazard insurance}}{12}$$

Monthly PITI = Monthly PI + Monthly TI

Adjustable-Rate Mortgages

Calculated interest rate = Index rate + Lender's margin

Maximum rate per adjustment period = Previous rate + Periodic rate cap

Maximum overall rate = Initial rate + Overall rate cap

Home Equity Loans and Lines of Credit

Percentage of appraised value = Appraised value × Lender's percentage

Second mortgage potential credit = Percentage of appraised value − First mortgage balance

$$\text{Housing expense ratio} = \frac{\text{Monthly housing expense (PITI)}}{\text{Monthly gross income}}$$

$$\text{Total obligations ratio} = \frac{\text{Total monthly financial obligations}}{\text{Monthly gross income}}$$

CHAPTER SUMMARY

Section I: Mortgages—Fixed-Rate and Adjustable-Rate

Topic	Important Concepts	Illustrative Examples
Calculating the Monthly Payment and Total Interest Paid on a Fixed-Rate Mortgage **Performance Objective 14-1, Page 453**	1. Find the number of $1,000s financed by $$\text{Number of }\$1,000s = \frac{\text{Amount financed}}{1,000}$$ 2. From Table 14-1, locate the table factor, monthly payment per $1,000 financed, at the intersection of the number-of-years column and the interest-rate row. 3. Calculate the monthly payment by Monthly payment = Number of 1,000s financed × Table factor 4. Find the total interest of the loan by $$\text{Total interest} = \left(\begin{array}{c}\text{Monthly}\\\text{payments}\end{array} \times \begin{array}{c}\text{Number of}\\\text{payments}\end{array}\right) - \begin{array}{c}\text{Amount}\\\text{financed}\end{array}$$	What is the monthly payment and total interest on a $100,000 mortgage at 9.5% for 30 years? $$\text{Number of 1,000s} = \frac{100,000}{1,000} = 100$$ Table factor: $9\frac{1}{2}\%$, 30 years = 8.41 Monthly payment = 100 × 8.41 = $\underline{\$841}$ Total interest of the loan = (841 × 360) − 100,000 $$= 302,760 - 100,000$$ $$= \underline{\$202,760}$$
Preparing a Partial Amortization Schedule of a Mortgage **Performance Objective 14-2, Page 455**	1. Calculate the monthly payment of the loan as before. 2. Calculate the amount of interest for the current month using $I = PRT$, where P is the current outstanding balance of the loan, R is the annual interest rate, and T is $\frac{1}{12}$. 3. Find the portion of the payment used to reduce principal by $$\begin{array}{c}\text{Portion of}\\\text{payment reducing}\\\text{principal}\end{array} = \begin{array}{c}\text{Monthly}\\\text{payment}\end{array} - \text{Interest}$$ 4. Calculate outstanding balance of the loan by $$\begin{array}{c}\text{Outstanding}\\\text{balance}\end{array} = \begin{array}{c}\text{Previous}\\\text{balance}\end{array} - \begin{array}{c}\text{Portion of payment}\\\text{reducing principal}\end{array}$$ 5. Repeat Steps 2, 3, and 4 for each succeeding month and enter the values on a schedule labeled appropriately.	Prepare an amortization schedule for the first month of a $70,000 mortgage at 9% for 20 years. Using Table 14-1, we find the monthly payment of the mortgage to be $\underline{\$630}$. *Month 1:* Interest = Principal × Rate × Time Interest = 70,000 × .09 × $\frac{1}{12}$ Interest = $\underline{\$525}$ Portion of payment reducing principal 630 − 525 = $\underline{\$105}$ Outstanding balance after one payment 70,000 − 105 = $\underline{\$69,895}$ An amortization schedule can now be prepared from these data.

Section I (continued)

Topic	Important Concepts	Illustrative Examples

Calculating the Monthly PITI of a Mortgage Loan
 	
Performance Objective 14-3, Page 457
	In reality, mortgage payments include four elements: principal, interest, taxes, and insurance—thus the abbreviation PITI.
	
	Monthly PITI of a mortgage:
	
	1. Calculate the principal and interest portion (PI) of the payment as before using Table 14-1.
	2. Calculate the monthly tax and insurance portion (TI) by
	
	$$\text{Monthly TI} = \frac{\text{Estimated properly tax} + \text{Hazard insurance}}{12}$$
	
	3. Calculate the total monthly PITI by
	
	Monthly PITI = Monthly PI + Monthly TI
		Maureen Cassidy purchased a home for $97,500 with a mortgage at 8.5% for 15 years. The property taxes are $1,950 per year, and the hazard insurance premium is $466. What is the monthly PITI payment of Maureen's loan?
		   Using a table factor of 9.85 from Table 14-1, we find the monthly PI for this 8.5%, 15-year mortgage to be $960.38.
		
		$$\text{Monthly TI} = \frac{1{,}950 + 466}{12}$$
		$$= \frac{2{,}416}{12} = \$201.33$$
		
		Monthly PITI = PI + TI
		   = 960.38 + 201.33 = $\underline{\$1{,}161.71}$

Calculating the Amount Due at Closing
 	
Performance Objective 14-4, Page 458
	Closing costs are the expenses incurred in conjunction with the sale of real estate. Both buyer and seller are responsible for specific costs.
	   The party responsible for paying a particular closing cost is often determined by local custom or by negotiation.
	   Some closing costs are expressed as dollar amounts, whereas others are a percent of the amount financed or amount of the purchase price.
	   At closing, the buyer is responsible for the purchase price (mortgage and down payment) plus closing costs.
	   The amount received by the seller after all expenses have been paid is known as the proceeds.
		Typical Closing Costs
		Buyer: Attorney's fee, inspections, credit report, appraisal fee, hazard insurance premium, title exam and insurance premium, escrow fee, prepaid taxes, and interest
		Seller: Attorney's fee, broker's commission, survey expense, inspections, abstract of title, certificate of title, escrow fee, prepayment penalty—existing loan, documentary stamps

Calculating the Interest Rate of an Adjustable-Rate Mortgage (ARM) **Performance Objective 14-5, Page 461**	Use the following formulas to find the various components of an ARM: $$\text{Calculated interest rate} = \text{Index rate} + \text{Lender's margin}$$ $$\text{Max rate per period} = \text{Previous rate} + \text{Periodic cap}$$ $$\text{Maximum overall rate of ARM} = \text{Initial rate} + \text{Overall cap}$$	Howard Gold bought a home with an adjustable-rate mortgage. The margin on the loan is 3.5%, and the rate cap is 8% over the life of the loan. If the current index rate is 3.6%, what is the calculated interest rate and the maximum overall rate of the loan? Calculated interest rate = 3.6% + 3.5% = $\underline{7.1\%}$ Maximum overall rate = 7.1% + 8% = $\underline{15.1\%}$

Section II: Second Mortgages—Home Equity Loans and Lines of Credit

Topic	Important Concepts	Illustrative Examples
Calculating the Potential Amount of Credit Available to a Borrower **Performance Objective 14-6, Page 467**	Most lenders set the credit limit on a home equity loan or line by taking a percentage of the appraised value of the home and subtracting the balance owed on the existing first mortgage. In determining your actual credit limit, the lender also will consider your ability to repay by looking at your income, debts, and other financial obligations, as well as your credit history. *Potential amount of credit available to borrower:* 1. Calculate the percentage of appraised value by $$\text{Percentage of appraised value} = \text{Appraised value} \times \text{Lender's percentage}$$ 2. Find the potential amount of credit available by $$\text{Potential credit} = \text{Percentage of appraised value} - \text{First mortgage debt}$$	The McCartneys own a home that was recently appraised for $134,800. The balance on their existing first mortgage is $76,550. If their bank is willing to loan up to 70% of the appraised value, what is the amount of credit available to the McCartneys on a home equity loan? Percentage of appraisal value = 134,800 × .70 = $94,360 Available credit = 94,360 − 76,550 = $\underline{\$17{,}810}$

Section II (continued)

Topic	Important Concepts	Illustrative Examples
Calculating the Housing Expense Ratio and the Total Obligations Ratio of a Borrower **Performance Objective 14-7, Page 468**	Mortgage lenders use ratios to determine whether borrowers have the economic ability to repay the loan. Two important ratios used for this purpose are the housing expense ratio and the total obligations ratio. These ratios are expressed as percents and are calculated by using the following formulas: $\text{Housing expense ratio} = \dfrac{\text{Monthly housing expense (PITI)}}{\text{Monthly gross income}}$ $\text{Total obligations ratio} = \dfrac{\text{Total monthly financial obligations}}{\text{Monthly gross income}}$	Vickie Howard earns a gross income of $3,750 per month. She has made application for a mortgage with a monthly PITI of $956. Vickie has other financial obligations totaling $447 per month. a. What is her housing expense ratio? b. What is her total obligations ratio? c. According to the Lending Ratio Guidelines on page 468, for what type of mortgage would Vickie qualify, if any? $\text{Housing expense ratio} = \dfrac{956}{3,750} = 25.5\%$ $\text{Total obligation ratio} = \dfrac{1,403}{3,750} = 37.4\%$ According to the Lending Ratio Guidelines, Vickie would qualify for an FHA mortgage but not a conventional mortgage; her total obligations ratio is 37.4%, which is above the limit for conventional mortgages.

TRY IT: EXERCISE SOLUTIONS FOR CHAPTER 14

1. $\text{Number of 1,000s financed} = \dfrac{\text{Amount financed}}{1,000}$

    $\text{Number of 1,000s financed} = \dfrac{85,500}{1,000} = 85.5$

    Table factor 4.5%, 25 years = 5.56

    Monthly payment = Number of 1,000s financed × Table factor

    Monthly payment = 85.5 × 5.56 = $475.38

    Total interest = (Monthly payment × Number of payments) − Amount financed

    Total interest = (475.38 × 300) − 85,500

    Total interest = 142,614 − 85,500 = $57,114

2. $\text{Number of 1,000s financed} = \dfrac{125,000}{1,000} = 125$

    Table factor 6%, 15 years = 8.44

    Monthly payment = 125 × 8.44 = $1055.00

    Month 1

    $I = PRT = 125,000 \times .06 \times \dfrac{1}{12} = \$625.00$

    Portion of payment reducing principal = $1055.00 − 625.00 = $430.00

    Outstanding balance = 125,000.00 − 430.00 = $124,570.00

    Month 2

    $I = PRT = 124,570.00 \times .06 \times \dfrac{1}{12} = \$622.85$

    Portion of payment reducing principal = $1055.00 − 622.85 = $432.15

    Outstanding balance = 124,570.00 − 432.15 = $124,137.85

    Month 3

    $I = PRT = 124,137.85 \times .06 \times \dfrac{1}{12} = \$620.69$

    Portion of payment reducing principal = 1055.00 − 620.69 = $434.31

    Outstanding balance = 124,137.85 − 434.31 = $123,703.54

Month 4

$$I = PRT = 123{,}703.54 \times .06 \times \frac{1}{12} = \$618.52$$

Portion of payment reducing principal = 1055.00 − 618.52 = $436.48

Outstanding balance = 123,703.54 − 436.48 = $123,267.06

Amortization Schedule
$125,000, 6%, 15 years

Payment Number	Monthly Payment	Monthly Interest	Portion Used to Reduce Principal	Loan Balance
0				$125,000.00
1	$1055.00	$625.00	$430.00	$124,570.00
2	$1055.00	$622.85	$432.15	$124,137.85
3	$1055.00	$620.69	$434.31	$123,703.54
4	$1055.00	$618.52	$436.48	$123,267.06

3.

Number of 1,000s $= \dfrac{125{,}600}{1{,}000} = 125.6$

Table factor 6.25%, 20 years = 7.31

Monthly payment (PI) = 125.6 × 7.31 = $918.14

Monthly TI $= \dfrac{\text{Property tax} + \text{Hazard insurance}}{12}$

Monthly TI $= \dfrac{3{,}250 + 765}{12} = \dfrac{4{,}015}{12} = \$334.58$

Monthly PITI = PI + TI = 918.14 + 334.58 = $\underline{\$1{,}252.72}$

4.　a.　Down payment = 120,000 × 20% = $24,000

Amount financed = 120,000 − 24,000 = $96,000

Closing Costs, Buyer:

Discount points (96,000 × 3%)	$ 2,880
Down payment (24,000 − 10,000)	14,000
Application fee	100
Condominium transfer fee	190
Title insurance (96,000 × $\frac{3}{4}$%)	720
Hazard insurance	420
Prepaid taxes	310
Attorney's fees	500
Due at closing	$19,120

b.　*Proceeds, Seller:*

Purchase price	$120,000
Less: Broker's commission	
120,000 × 5$\frac{1}{2}$%	$ 6,600
Closing costs	670
Mortgage payoff	65,000
	− 72,270
Proceeds to seller	$47,730

5.　a.　Calculated ARM rate = Index rate + Lender's margin

Calculated ARM rate = 3.2 + 3.4 = $\underline{6.6\%}$

b.　Maximum overall rate = Calculated ARM rate + Overall rate cap

Maximum overall rate = 6.6 + 7.0 = $\underline{13.6\%}$

6.　Percentage of appraised value = Appraised value × Lender's percentage

Percentage of appraised value = 92,900 × 80% = $74,320

Potential credit = Percentage of appraised value − First mortgage balance

Potential credit = 74,320 − 32,440 = $\underline{\$41{,}880}$

7. a. Housing expense ratio $= \dfrac{\text{Monthly housing expense (PITI)}}{\text{Monthly gross income}}$

    Housing expense ratio $= \dfrac{669}{3{,}100} = 21.6\%$

    b. Total obligations ratio $= \dfrac{\text{Total monthly financial obligation}}{\text{Monthly gross income}}$

    Total obligations ratio $= \dfrac{669 + 375}{3{,}100} = \dfrac{1{,}044}{3{,}100} = 33.7\%$

    c. According to the guidelines, Roman qualifies for both <u>FHA and conventional mortgages</u>.

CONCEPT REVIEW

1. Land, including permanent improvements on that land, is known as _____. (14-1)

2. A(n) _____ is a loan in which real property is used as security for a debt. (14-1)

3. Mortgage _____ points are an extra charge frequently added to the cost of a mortgage. (14-1, 14-4)

4. A chart that shows the month-by-month breakdown of each mortgage payment into interest and principal is known as a(n) _____ schedule. (14-2)

5. A(n) _____ account is a bank account used by mortgage lenders to accumulate next year's property taxes and hazard insurance. (14-3)

6. Today most mortgage payments include four parts, abbreviated PITI. Name these parts. (14-3)

7. The final step in a real estate transaction is a meeting at which time the buyer pays the agreed-upon purchase price and the seller delivers the ownership documents. This meeting is known as the _____. (14-4)

8. The official document representing the right of ownership of real property is known as the _____ or the _____. (14-4)

9. List four mortgage loan closing costs. (14-4)

10. A mortgage in which the interest rate changes periodically, usually in relation to a predetermined economic index, is known as a(n) _____ rate mortgage. (14-5)

11. A home equity _____ is a lump-sum second mortgage based on the available equity in a home. (14-6)

12. A home equity _____ of credit is a revolving credit second mortgage loan on the equity in a home. (14-6)

13. Write the formula for the housing expense ratio. (14-7)

14. Write the formula for the total obligations ratio. (14-7)

ASSESSMENT TEST

You are one of the branch managers of the Insignia Bank. Today two loan applications were submitted to your office. Calculate the requested information for each loan.

	Amount Financed	Interest Rate	Term of Loan	Number of $1,000s Financed	Table Factor	Monthly Payment	Total Interest
1.	$155,900	4.50%	25 years	____	____	_____	_____
2.	$98,500	5.25%	20 years	____	____	_____	_____

Here are some popular real estate websites that buyers, sellers, and renters can use to research locations in which they are interested.

- Realtor.com
- Zillow.com
- Redfin.com
- HotPads.com
- PropertyShark.com

3. Suzanne Arthurs purchased a home with a $146,100 mortgage at 6.5% for 30 years. Calculate the monthly payment and prepare an amortization schedule for the first three months of Suzanne's loan.

Payment Number	Monthly Payment	Monthly Interest	Portion Used to Reduce Principal	Loan Balance
0				$146,100.00
1	_____	_____	_____	_____
2	_____	_____	_____	_____
3	_____	_____	_____	_____

Use Table 14-1 to calculate the monthly principal and interest and calculate the monthly PITI for the following mortgages.

	Amount Financed	Interest Rate	Term of Loan	Monthly PI	Annual Property Tax	Annual Insurance	Monthly PITI
4.	$54,200	4.75%	25 years	_____	$719	$459	_____
5.	$162,100	5.50%	15 years	_____	$2,275	$1,033	_____

For the following second mortgage applications, calculate the percentage of appraised value and the potential credit.

	Appraised Value	Lender's Percentage	Percentage of Appraised Value	Balance of First Mortgage	Potential Credit
6.	$114,500	65%	_____	$77,900	_____
7.	$51,500	80%	_____	$27,400	_____
8.	$81,200	70%	_____	$36,000	_____

For the following mortgage applications, calculate the housing expense ratio and the total expense ratio.

Applicant	Monthly Gross Income	Monthly PITI Expense	Other Monthly Financial Obligations	Housing Expense Ratio (%)	Total Obligations Ratio (%)
9. Morton	$5,300	$1,288	$840	_____	_____
10. Hauser	$3,750	$952	$329	_____	_____

11. As a loan officer using the Lending Ratio Guidelines on page 468, what type of mortgage can you offer Morton and Hauser from Exercises 9 and 10?

12. Dale Evans bought the Lazy D Ranch with an adjustable-rate mortgage. The lender's margin on the loan is 3.9%, and the overall rate cap is 6% over the life of the loan.

   a. If the current index rate is 4.45%, what is the calculated interest rate of the ARM?

   b. What is the maximum overall rate of Dale's loan?

13. Diversified Investments purchased a 24-unit apartment building for $650,000. After a 20% down payment, the balance was financed with a 20-year, 7.75% fixed-rate mortgage.

   a. What is the amount of the monthly principal and interest portion of the loan?

b. As Diversified's loan officer, construct an amortization schedule for the first two months of the mortgage.

Payment Number	Monthly Payment	Monthly Interest	Portion Used to Reduce Principal	Loan Balance
0				_____
1	_____	_____	_____	_____
2	_____	_____	_____	_____

c. If the annual property taxes are $9,177 and the hazard insurance premium is $2,253 per year, what is the total monthly PITI of the loan?

d. If each apartment rents for $825 per month, how much income will Diversified make per month after the PITI is paid on the building?

14. Larry Mager purchased a ski lodge in Telluride for $850,000. His bank is willing to finance 70% of the purchase price. As part of the mortgage closing costs, Larry had to pay $4\frac{1}{4}$ discount points. How much did this amount to?

Denny's Corporation, through its subsidiaries, engages in the ownership and operation of a chain of family-style restaurants primarily in the United States. Its restaurants offer traditional American-style food. The company owns and operates its restaurants under the Denny's brand name.

In a typical year, total revenue from company restaurant sales and franchise and license sales exceeds $530 million.

Source: www.dennys.com

15. A Denny's Restaurant franchisee is looking for a 20-year mortgage with 90% financing to build a new location costing $775,000. The Spring Creek Bank is offering an 8% mortgage with $1\frac{1}{2}$ discount points; Foremost Savings & Loan is offering a 7.5% mortgage with 4 discount points. The franchisee is unsure which mortgage is the better deal and has asked for your help.

a. What is the total interest paid on each loan?

b. Taking into account the discount points, which lender is offering a better deal and by how much?

16. How much more total interest will be paid on a 30-year fixed-rate mortgage for $100,000 at 9.25% compared with a 15-year mortgage at 8.5%?

17. Adam Marsh is purchasing a $134,000 condominium apartment. The down payment is 20%, and the balance will be financed with a 20-year fixed-rate mortgage at 8.75% and 3 discount points. The annual property tax is $1,940, and the hazard insurance premium is $1,460. When Adam signed the original sales contract, he put down a deposit of $10,000, which will be credited to his down payment. In addition, at the time of closing, he must pay the following expenses:

Appraisal fee	$165
Credit report	$75
Attorney's fees	$490
Roof inspection	$50
Termite inspection	$88
Title search	$119
Mortgage insurance premium	1.2% of amount financed
Documentary stamps	$\frac{1}{4}$% of amount financed

As Adam's real estate agent, he has asked you the following questions:

a. What is the total monthly PITI of the mortgage loan?

b. What is the total amount of interest that Adam will pay on the loan?

c. How much is due at the time of the closing?

d. If the sellers are responsible for the 6% broker's commission, $900 in closing costs, and the existing first mortgage with a balance of $45,000, what proceeds will be received on the sale of the property?

18. Martin Ellingham is negotiating to buy a vacation cottage in Port Wenn. The seller of the cottage is asking $186,000. Martin offered him a cash deal, owner-seller (no broker) only if the seller would reduce the price by 12%. The seller agreed. Martin must pay a 10% down payment upon signing the agreement of sale. At closing, he must pay the balance of the agreed-upon sale price, a $500 attorney's fee, a $68 utility transfer fee, a title search and transfer fee of $35 plus $\frac{3}{4}$% of the selling price, and the first six months of the annual insurance of $1,460 per year. How much does Martin owe at closing?

19. The Randolphs own a home that recently appraised for $161,400. The balance on their existing first mortgage is $115,200. If their bank is willing to loan up to 70% of the appraised value, what is the amount of credit available to the Randolphs on a home equity line of credit?

20. Jonathan and Kimberly Schwartz live in a home to which they want to make major improvements. They plan to replace the existing heating and cooling system, remodel the kitchen, and add a room above the garage. To pay for this renovation, they plan to get a home equity line of credit. Their home currently appraises for $298,000. They owe $68,340 on the first mortgage. How much credit will their bank provide if the limit is 75% of their home's value?

21. Phil Armstrong earns a gross income of $5,355 per month. He has submitted an application for a fixed-rate mortgage with a monthly PITI of $1,492. Phil has other financial obligations totaling $625 per month.

a. What is his housing expense ratio?

b. What is his total obligations ratio?

c. According to the Lending Ratio Guidelines on page 468, for what type of mortgage would Phil qualify, if any?

22. Magda Leon is applying for a home mortgage with a monthly PITI of $724. She currently has a gross income of $2,856 and other monthly expenses of $411.

a. What is Magda's housing expense ratio?

b. What is her total obligations ratio?

c. According to the lending ratio guidelines, for what type of mortgage would Magda qualify, if any?

BUSINESS DECISION: FOR WHAT SIZE MORTGAGE CAN YOU QUALIFY?

23. You are applying for a conventional mortgage from the Americana Bank. Your monthly gross income is $3,500, and the bank uses the 28% housing expense ratio guideline.

a. What is the highest PITI for which you can qualify? *Hint:* Solve the housing expense ratio formula for PITI. Remember, this is an application of the percentage formula, Portion = Rate × Base, where PITI is the portion, the expense ratio is the rate, and your monthly gross income is the base.

b. Based on your answer from part a, if you are applying for a 30-year, 9% mortgage and the taxes and insurance portion of PITI is $175 per month, use Table 14-1 to calculate the size of the mortgage for which you qualify. *Hint:* Subtract TI from PITI. Divide the PI by the appropriate table factor to determine the number of $1,000s for which you qualify.

c. Based on your answer from part b, if you are planning on a 20% down payment, what is the most expensive house you can afford? *Hint:* Use the percentage formula again. The purchase price of the house is the base, the amount financed is the portion, and the percent financed is the rate.

COLLABORATIVE LEARNING ACTIVITY

The Hypothetical Mortgage

Speak with the loan officers at mortgage lending institutions in your area and ask for their help with a business math class project.

Your assignment is to research the various types of financing deals currently being offered for a hypothetical condominium you plan to buy. The following assumptions apply to this project:

- The purchase price of the condo you plan to buy is $200,000.
- The condo was recently appraised for $220,000.
- You plan to make a 25% down payment ($50,000) and are seeking a $150,000 mortgage.
- You have a job that qualifies you for that size mortgage.

As a team, your assignment is to compare the current interest rates, costs, and features associated with a 15-year fixed-rate mortgage, a 30-year fixed-rate mortgage, and an adjustable-rate mortgage.

a. What are the current interest rates and discount points of the 15- and 30-year fixed-rate mortgages?

b. What are the monthly payments of the fixed-rate mortgages?

c. What is the initial (teaser) rate, discount points, adjustment period, rate caps, margin, and index for the adjustable-rate mortgage?

d. What are the fees or charges for the loan application, property appraisal, survey, credit report, inspections, title search, title insurance, and document preparation?

e. What other charges or fees can be expected at closing?

f. Which type of mortgage does your team think is the best deal at this time? Why?

g. Which bank would you choose for the mortgage? Why?

CHAPTER 15 Financial Statements and Ratios

PERFORMANCE OBJECTIVES

SECTION I 15 THE BALANCE SHEET

financial statements A series of accounting reports summarizing a company's financial data compiled from business activity over a period of time. The four most common are the balance sheet, the income statement, the owner's equity statement, and the cash flow statement.

Financial statements are the periodic report cards of how a business is doing from a monetary perspective. After all, money is the primary way in which the score is kept in the competitive arena of business. These important statements are a summary of a company's financial data compiled from business activity over a period of time.

The four major financial statements used in business today are the balance sheet, the income statement, the owner's equity statement, and the cash flow statement. Together they tell a story about how a company has performed in the past and is likely to perform in the near future. In this chapter, we focus our attention on the preparation and analysis of the balance sheet and the income statement. The Business Decisions at the ends of the review exercises and the Assessment Test feature actual financial statements from recent annual reports of well-known companies representing various industries. These financial statements provide an opportunity to examine real-world statements and apply your own analytical skills.

Typically, a company's accounting department prepares financial statements quarterly for the purpose of management review and government reporting of income tax information. At the end of each year, the accounting department prepares annual financial statements to present the company's yearly financial position and performance. Public corporations, those whose stock can be bought and sold by the general investing public, are required by law to make their statements available to the stockholders and the financial community in the form of quarterly and annual reports. Because it is public information, condensed versions of these reports often appear in financial publications such as the *Wall Street Journal, Business Week, Forbes,* and *Fortune.*

financial analysis The assessment of a company's past, present, and anticipated future financial condition based on the information found on the financial statements.

Financial analysis is the assessment of a company's past, present, and anticipated future financial condition based on the information found on the financial statements. Financial ratios are the primary tool of this analysis. These ratios are a way of standardizing financial data so that they may be compared with ratios from previous operating periods of the same firm or from other similar-size firms in the same industry.

Internally, owners and managers rely on this analysis to evaluate a company's financial strengths and weaknesses and to help make sound business decisions. From outside the firm, creditors and investors use financial statements and ratios to determine a company's creditworthiness or investment potential.

balance sheet A financial statement illustrating the financial position of a company in terms of assets, liabilities, and owner's equity as of a certain date.

financial position The economic resources owned by a company and the claims against those resources at a specific point in time.

The **balance sheet** is the financial statement that lists a company's financial position on a certain date, usually at the end of a month, a quarter, or a year. To fully understand the balance sheet, we must first examine some basic accounting theory.

Financial position refers to the economic resources owned by a company and the claims against those resources at a specific point in time. *Equities* is another term for *claims.* Keep in mind that a firm's economic resources must be equal to its equities. A business enterprise can therefore be pictured as an equation:

$$\text{Economic resources} = \text{Equities}$$

creditors Those to whom money is owed.

liabilities Debts or obligations of a business resulting from past transactions that require the company to pay money, provide goods, or perform services in the future.

owner's equity The resources claimed by the owner against the assets of a business: Owner's equity = Assets − Liabilities. Also called proprietorship, capital, or net worth.

There are two types of equities: the rights of the **creditors** (those who are owed money by the business) and the rights of the owners. The rights of the creditors are known as **liabilities** and represent debts of the business. The rights of the owners are known as **owner's equity.** Owner's equity represents the resources invested in the business by the owners. Theoretically, owner's equity is what would be left over after all liabilities were paid to the creditors. We can now enhance our equation:

$$\text{Economic resources} = \text{Liabilities} + \text{Owner's equity}$$

assets Economic resources (for example, cash; inventories; and land, buildings, and equipment) owned by a business.

In accounting terminology, the economic resources owned by a business are known as the **assets.** Our equation now becomes

$$\text{Assets} = \text{Liabilities} + \text{Owner's Equity}$$

accounting equation Algebraic expression of a company's financial position: Assets = Liabilities + Owner's equity.

This all-important equation is known as the **accounting equation.** The balance sheet is a visual presentation of this equation at a point in time. Some balance sheets display the assets on the left and the liabilities and owner's equity on the right. Another popular format lists the assets on top and the liabilities and owner's equity below. Remember, on a balance sheet, the assets must be equal to the liabilities plus owner's equity.

PREPARING A BALANCE SHEET

15-1

Let's begin by looking at an example of a typical balance sheet and then examining each section and its components more closely. A balance sheet for a corporation, Hypothetical Enterprises, Inc., follows. Carefully look over the statement. Then read the descriptions of the balance sheet components, which begin below, and "Steps to Prepare a Balance Sheet," page 487. Finally, follow the example and attempt the Try-It Exercise.

Hypothetical Enterprises, Inc.
Balance Sheet
December 31, 20XX

Assets

Current Assets

Cash	$ 13,000	
Accounts Receivable	32,500	
Merchandise Inventory	50,600	
Prepaid Expenses	1,200	
Supplies	4,000	
Total Current Assets		$101,300

Property, Plant, and Equipment

Land	40,000	
Buildings	125,000	
Machinery and Equipment	60,000	
Total Property, Plant, and Equipment		225,000

Investments and Other Assets

Investments	10,000	
Intangible Assets	5,000	
Total Investments and Other Assets		15,000
Total Assets		$341,300

Liabilities and Owner's Equity

Current Liabilities

Accounts Payable	$ 17,500	
Salaries Payable	5,400	
Taxes Payable	6,500	
Total Current Liabilities		$ 29,400

Long-Term Liabilities

Mortgage Payable	115,000	
Debenture Bond	20,000	
Total Long-Term Liabilities		135,000
Total Liabilities		164,400

Stockholders' Equity

Capital Stock	126,900	
Retained Earnings	50,000	
Total Stockholders' Equity		176,900
Total Liabilities and Stockholders' Equity		$341,300

Annual Meeting The annual meeting is a company gathering usually held at the end of each fiscal year at which the previous year and the outlook for the future are discussed and directors are elected by vote of the common stockholders.

Shortly before each annual meeting, the corporation sends out a document called a proxy statement to each stockholder. The proxy statement contains a list of the business concerns to be addressed at the meeting and a ballot for voting on company initiatives and electing the new board of directors.

BALANCE SHEET COMPONENTS

ASSETS The asset section of a balance sheet is divided into three components: Current Assets; Property, Plant, and Equipment; and Investments and Other Assets.

Current Assets Cash or assets that will be sold, used, or converted to cash within one year. The following are typical examples of current assets:

- Cash—Cash on hand in the form of bills, coins, checking accounts, and savings accounts.
- Marketable securities—Investments in short-term securities that can be quickly converted to cash, such as stocks and bonds.

- Accounts receivable—Money owed by customers to the firm for goods and services sold on credit.
- Notes receivable—Money owed to the business involving promissory notes.
- Merchandise inventory—The cost of goods a business has on hand for resale to its customers.
- Prepaid expenses—Money paid in advance by the firm for benefits and services not yet received, such as prepaid insurance premiums or prepaid rent.
- Supplies—Cost of assets used in the day-to-day operation of the business. These might include office supplies such as paper, pencils, pens, CDs, and DVDs or maintenance supplies such as paper towels, soap, lubricants, lightbulbs, and batteries.

Property, Plant, and Equipment   Also known as fixed or long-term assets. These assets will be used by the firm in the operation of the business for a period of time longer than one year. Some examples follow:

- Land—The original purchase price of land owned by the company. Land is an asset that does not depreciate (or lose its value) over a period of time.
- Buildings—The cost of the buildings owned by the firm less the accumulated depreciation (or total loss in value) on those buildings since they were new. This is known as the book value of the buildings.
- Machinery and equipment—The book value (or original cost less accumulated depreciation) of all machinery, fixtures, vehicles, and equipment used in the operation of a business.

Investments and Other Assets   This category lists the firm's investments and all other assets.

- Investments—Investments made by the firm and held for periods longer than one year.
- Other assets—A catch-all category for any assets not previously listed.
- Intangibles—Long-term assets that have no physical substance but have a value based on rights and privileges claimed by the owner. Some examples are copyrights, patents, royalties, and goodwill.

LIABILITIES AND OWNER'S EQUITY   The liabilities and owner's equity section of the balance sheet lists the current and long-term liabilities incurred by the company as well as the owner's *net worth* or claim against the assets of the business. From the accounting equation, it is the difference between the total assets and the total liabilities.

Current Liabilities   Debts and financial obligations of the company that are due to be paid within one year. Some examples follow:

- Accounts payable—Debts owed by the firm to creditors for goods and services purchased with less than one year of credit. These might include 30-, 60-, or 90-day terms of sale extended by suppliers and vendors.
- Notes payable—Debts owed by the firm involving promissory notes. An example is a short-term loan from a bank.
- Salaries payable—Compensation to employees that has been earned but not yet paid.
- Taxes payable—Taxes owed by the firm but not yet paid by the date of the statement.

Long-Term Liabilities   Debts and financial obligations of the company that are due to be paid in one year or more or are to be paid out of non-current assets. Some examples follow:

- Mortgage payable—The total obligation a firm owes for the long-term financing of land and buildings.
- Debenture bonds—The total amount a firm owes on bonds at maturity to bondholders for money borrowed on the general credit of the company.

Owner's Equity   When a business is organized as a sole proprietorship or partnership, the equity section of the balance sheet is known as owner's equity. The ownership is labeled with the name of the owners or business and the word *capital*. Some examples follow:

- Paul Kelsch, capital
- Lost Sock Laundry, capital.

Stockholders' Equity When the business is a corporation, the equity section of the balance sheet is known as stockholders' equity. The ownership is represented in two categories, capital stock and retained earnings.

- Capital stock—This represents money acquired by selling stock to investors who become stockholders. Capital stock is divided into preferred stock, which has preference over common stock regarding dividends, and common stock, representing the most basic rights to ownership of a corporation.
- Retained earnings—Profits from the operation of the business that have not been distributed to the stockholders in the form of dividends.

Learning Tip

Don't be overwhelmed by the amount of new terminology associated with financial statements. Start by understanding the function and basic structure of each statement. Then learn the purpose of each major category. This should help you determine in which category of the statement each component is listed.

STEPS TO PREPARE A BALANCE SHEET

STEP 1. Centered at the top of the page, write the company name, type of statement, and date.

STEP 2. In a section labeled ASSETS, list and total all of the Current Assets; Property, Plant, and Equipment; and Investments and Other Assets.

STEP 3. Add the three components of the Assets section to get Total Assets.

STEP 4. Double-underline Total Assets.

STEP 5. In a section labeled LIABILITIES AND OWNER'S EQUITY, list and total all Current Liabilities and Long-Term Liabilities.

STEP 6. Add the two components of the Liabilities section to get Total Liabilities.

STEP 7. List and total the Owner's or Stockholders' Equity.

STEP 8. Add the Total Liabilities and Owner's Equity.

STEP 9. Double-underline Total Liabilities and Owner's Equity.

Note: In accordance with the accounting equation, check to be sure that

$$\text{Assets} = \text{Liabilities} + \text{Owner's Equity}$$

EXAMPLE1 PREPARING A BALANCE SHEET

Use the following financial information to prepare a balance sheet for Royal Equipment Supply, Inc., as of June 30, 2016: cash, $3,400; accounts receivable, $5,600; merchandise inventory, $98,700; prepaid insurance, $455; supplies, $800; land and building, $147,000; fixtures, $8,600; delivery vehicles, $27,000; forklift, $7,000; goodwill, $10,000; accounts payable, $16,500; notes payable, $10,000; mortgage payable, $67,000; common stock, $185,055; and retained earnings, $30,000.

SOLUTIONSTRATEGY

The balance sheet for Royal Equipment Supply, Inc. follows. Note that the assets are equal to the liabilities plus stockholders' equity.

Royal Equipment Supply, Inc.
Balance Sheet
June 30, 2016

Assets

Current Assets

Cash	$3,400	
Accounts Receivable	5,600	
Merchandise Inventory	98,700	
Prepaid Insurance	455	
Supplies	800	
Total Current Assets		$108,955

Property, Plant, and Equipment

Land and Building	$147,000	
Fixtures	8,600	
Delivery Vehicles	27,000	
Forklift	7,000	
Total Property, Plant, and Equipment		189,600

Investments and Other Assets

Goodwill	10,000	
Total Investments and Other Assets		10,000
Total Assets		$308,555

Liabilities and Stockholders' Equity

Current Liabilities

Accounts Payable	$16,500	
Notes Payable	10,000	
Total Current Liabilities		$ 26,500

Long-Term Liabilities

Mortgage Payable	67,000	
Total Long-Term Liabilities		67,000
Total Liabilities		93,500

Stockholders' Equity

Common Stock	185,055	
Retained Earnings	30,000	
Total Stockholders' Equity		215,055
Total Liabilities and Stockholders' Equity		$308,555

IN THE Business World

The stockholders are the owners of a corporation; therefore, the *owner's equity* on the balance sheet of a corporation is known as *stockholders' equity*.

▶ TRYITEXERCISE 1

Use the following financial information to prepare a balance sheet as of December 31, 2016, for Keystone Auto Repair, a sole proprietorship owned by Blake Williams: cash, $5,200; accounts receivable, $2,800; merchandise inventory, $2,700; prepaid salary, $235; supplies, $3,900; land, $35,000; building, $74,000; fixtures, $1,200; tow truck, $33,600; tools and equipment, $45,000; accounts payable, $6,800; notes payable, $17,600; taxes payable, $3,540; mortgage payable, $51,000; Blake Williams, capital, $124,695.

CHECK YOUR STATEMENT WITH THE SOLUTION ON PAGE 520.

15-2   PREPARING A VERTICAL ANALYSIS OF A BALANCE SHEET

vertical analysis A percentage method of analyzing financial statements whereby each item on the statement is expressed as a percent of a base amount. On balance sheet analysis, the base is total assets; on income statement analysis, the base is net sales.

common-size balance sheets Special forms of balance sheets that list only the vertical analysis percentages, not the dollar figures. All items are expressed as a percent of total assets.

Once the balance sheet has been prepared, a number of analytical procedures can be applied to the data to further evaluate a company's financial condition. One common method of analysis of a single financial statement is known as **vertical analysis**. In vertical analysis, each item on the balance sheet is expressed as a percent of total assets (total assets = 100%).

Once the vertical analysis has been completed, the figures show the relationship of each item on the balance sheet to total assets. For analysis purposes, these percents can then be compared with previous statements of the same company, with competitors' figures, or with published industry averages for similar-size companies.

A special form of balance sheet known as a common-size balance sheet is frequently used in financial analysis. **Common-size balance sheets** list only the vertical analysis percentages, not the dollar figures.

STEPS **TO PREPARE A VERTICAL ANALYSIS**
OF A BALANCE SHEET

STEP 1. Use the percentage formula, Rate = Portion ÷ Base, to find the percentage of
each item on the balance sheet. Use each item as the portion and total assets
as the base.

STEP 2. Round each answer to the nearest tenth of a percent.

Note: A 0.1% differential may sometimes occur due to rounding.

STEP 3. List the percent of each balance sheet item in a column to the right of the
monetary amount.

EXAMPLE2   PREPARING A VERTICAL ANALYSIS OF A BALANCE SHEET

**Prepare a vertical analysis of the balance sheet for Hypothetical Enterprises, Inc., on
page 485.**

SOLUTIONSTRATEGY

Using the steps for vertical analysis, perform the following calculation for each balance sheet item
and enter the results on the statement:

$$\frac{\text{Cash}}{\text{Total assets}} = \frac{13,000}{341,300} = .038 = 3.8\%$$

Hypothetical Enterprises, Inc.
Balance Sheet
December 31, 20XX

Assets

Current Assets

Cash	$13,000	3.8%
Accounts Receivable	32,500	9.5
Merchandise Inventory	50,600	14.8
Prepaid Expenses	1,200	0.4
Supplies	4,000	1.2
Total Current Assets	101,300	29.7

Property, Plant, and Equipment

Land	40,000	11.7
Buildings	125,000	36.6
Machinery and Equipment	60,000	17.6
Total Property, Plant, and Equipment	225,000	65.9

Investments and Other Assets

Investments	10,000	2.9
Intangible Assets	5,000	1.5
Total Investments and Other Assets	15,000	4.4
Total Assets	$341,300	100.0%

Liabilities and Stockholders' Equity

Current Liabilities

Accounts Payable	$17,500	5.1%
Salaries Payable	5,400	1.6
Taxes Payable	6,500	1.9
Total Current Liabilities	29,400	8.6

Long-Term Liabilities

Mortgage Payable	115,000	33.7
Debenture Bond	20,000	5.9
Total Long-Term Liabilities	135,000	39.6
Total Liabilities	164,400	48.2

Learning Tip

In vertical analysis, remember that each
item on the balance sheet is the *portion*
and Total Assets is the *base*.

Because of rounding, the percents
may not always add up to 100%. There
may be a 0.1% differential.

Stockholders' Equity

Capital Stock	126,900	37.2
Retained Earnings	50,000	14.6
Total Stockholders' Equity	176,900	51.8
Total Liabilities and Stockholders' Equity	$341,300	100.0%

►TRYITEXERCISE 2

Prepare a vertical analysis of the balance sheet for Royal Equipment Supply, Inc., on pages 487–488.

CHECK YOUR ANSWERS WITH THE SOLUTIONS ON PAGE 521.

15-3 PREPARING A HORIZONTAL ANALYSIS OF A BALANCE SHEET

comparative balance sheet Balance sheet prepared with the data from the current year or operating period side by side with the figures from one or more previous periods.

horizontal analysis Method of analyzing financial statements whereby each item of the current period is compared in dollars and percent with the corresponding item from a previous period.

Frequently, balance sheets are prepared with the data from the current year or operating period side by side with the figures from one or more previous periods. This type of presentation is known as a **comparative balance sheet** because the data from different periods can be readily compared. This information provides managers, creditors, and investors with important data concerning the progress of the company over a period of time, financial trends that may be developing, and the likelihood of future success.

Comparative balance sheets use horizontal analysis to measure the increases and decreases that have taken place in the financial data between two operating periods. In **horizontal analysis**, each item of the current period is compared in dollars and percent with the corresponding item from a previous period.

STEPS TO PREPARE A HORIZONTAL ANALYSIS OF A BALANCE SHEET

STEP 1. Set up a comparative balance sheet format with the current period listed first and the previous period listed next.

STEP 2. Label the next two columns:

Increase (Decrease)	
Amount	Percent

STEP 3. For each item on the balance sheet, calculate the dollar difference between the current and previous periods and enter this figure in the Amount column. Enter all decreases in parentheses.

STEP 4. Calculate the percent change (increase or decrease) using the percentage formula:

$$\text{Percent change (rate)} = \frac{\text{Amount of change, Step 3 (portion)}}{\text{Previous period amount (base)}}$$

STEP 5. Enter the percent change (rounded to the nearest tenth of a percent) in the Percent column. Once again, enter all decreases in parentheses.

EXAMPLE3 PREPARING A HORIZONTAL ANALYSIS OF A BALANCE SHEET

Using the following comparative balance sheet for the Supreme Construction Company as of December 31, 2015 and 2016, prepare a horizontal analysis of this balance sheet for the owner, Randy McQueen.

Supreme Construction Company
Comparative Balance Sheet
December 31, 2015 and 2016

Assets	2016	2015
Current Assets		
Cash	$ 3,500	$ 2,900
Accounts Receivable	12,450	7,680
Supplies	2,140	3,200
Total Current Assets	18,090	13,780
Property, Plant, and Equipment		
Land	15,000	15,000
Buildings	54,000	61,000
Machinery and Equipment	134,200	123,400
Total Property, Plant, and Equipment	203,200	199,400
Total Assets	$ 221,290	$ 213,180
Liabilities and Owner's Equity		
Current Liabilities		
Accounts Payable	$ 5,300	$ 4,100
Notes Payable	8,500	9,400
Total Current Liabilities	13,800	13,500
Long-Term Liabilities		
Mortgage Payable	26,330	28,500
Note Payable on Equipment (5-year)	10,250	11,430
Total Long-Term Liabilities	36,580	39,930
Total Liabilities	50,380	53,430
Owner's Equity		
Randy McQueen, Capital	170,910	159,750
Total Liabilities and Owner's Equity	$ 221,290	$ 213,180

►SOLUTIONSTRATEGY

Using the steps for horizontal analysis, perform the following operation on all balance sheet items and then enter the results on the statement.

Cash

2014 amount − 2013 amount = 3,500 − 2,900

= $600 Increase

$$\text{Percent change} = \frac{\text{Amount of change}}{\text{Previous period amount}} = \frac{600}{2,900} = .20689 = 20.7\%$$

Supreme Construction Company
Comparative Balance Sheet
December 31, 2015 and 2016

Assets	2016	2015	Increase (Decrease) Amount	Percent
Current Assets				
Cash	$ 3,500	$ 2,900	$ 600	20.7%
Accounts Receivable	12,450	7,680	4,770	62.1
Supplies	2,140	3,200	(1,060)	(33.1)
Total Current Assets	18,090	13,780	4,310	31.3
Property, Plant, and Equipment				
Land	15,000	15,000	0	0
Buildings	54,000	61,000	(7,000)	(11.5)
Machinery and Equipment	134,200	123,400	10,800	8.8
Total Property, Plant, and Equipment	203,200	199,400	3,800	1.9
Total Assets	$221,290	$213,180	$8,110	3.8%

Liabilities and Owner's Equity

Current Liabilities				
Accounts Payable	$ 5,300	$ 4,100	$ 1,200	29.3%
Notes Payable	8,500	9,400	(900)	(9.6)
Total Current Liabilities	13,800	13,500	300	2.2
Long-Term Liabilities				
Mortgage Payable	26,330	28,500	(2,170)	(7.6)
Note Payable on Equipment (5-year)	10,250	11,430	(1,180)	(10.3)
Total Long-Term Liabilities	36,580	39,930	(3,350)	(8.4)
Total Liabilities	50,380	53,430	(3,050)	(5.7)
Owner's Equity				
Randy McQueen, Capital	170,910	159,750	11,160	7.0
Total Liabilities and Owner's Equity	$221,290	$213,180	$ 8,110	3.8%

▶ TRYITEXERCISE 3

Complete the following comparative balance sheet with horizontal analysis for Calypso Industries, Inc.

Calypso Industries, Inc.
Comparative Balance Sheet
December 31, 2015 and 2016

			Increase (Decrease)	
Assets	**2016**	**2015**	**Amount**	**Percent**
Current Assets				
Cash	$ 8,700	$ 5,430	____	____
Accounts Receivable	23,110	18,450	____	____
Notes Receivable	2,900	3,400	____	____
Supplies	4,540	3,980	____	____
Total Current Assets			____	____
Property, Plant, and Equipment				
Land	34,000	34,000	____	____
Buildings	76,300	79,800	____	____
Machinery and Equipment	54,700	48,900	____	____
Total Property, Plant, and Equipment			____	____
Investments and Other Assets	54,230	49,810	____	____
Total Assets			____	____
Liabilities and Stockholders' Equity				
Current Liabilities				
Accounts Payable	$ 15,330	$ 19,650	____	____
Salaries Payable	7,680	7,190	____	____
Total Current Liabilities			____	____
Long-Term Liabilities				
Mortgage Payable	53,010	54,200	____	____
Note Payable (3-year)	32,400	33,560	____	____
Total Long-Term Liabilities			____	____
Total Liabilities			____	____
Liabilities and Stockholders' Equity	**2016**	**2015**		
Stockholders' Equity				
Common Stock	$130,060	$120,170	____	____
Retained Earnings	20,000	9,000	____	____
Total Liabilities and Stockholders' Equity			____	____

CHECK YOUR ANSWERS WITH THE SOLUTIONS ON PAGE 521–522.

REVIEW EXERCISES

Calculate the following values according to the accounting equation.

	Assets	Liabilities	Owner's Equity
1.	$283,000	$121,400	$161,600
2.	$548,900	$335,900	$213,000
3.	$45,300	$29,000	$16,300
4.	$657,300	$241,100	_____
5.	_____	$1,366,500	$2,117,000
6.	$830,400	_____	$210,800
7.	_____	$406,000	$2,000,200
8.	$15,909,000	$6,339,100	_____

Calculate the missing balance sheet items for Exercise 9, The Home Depot; Exercise 10, Amazon.com; and Exercise 11, Gap. Complete each company's column; then move on to the next column.

	THE BALANCE SHEET (in millions)		
	Exercise 9	Exercise 10	Exercise 11
Company Date	The Home Depot, Inc. February 2, 2014	Amazon.com, Inc. December 31, 2013	Gap Inc. February 1, 2014
Current Assets	$15,279	$24,625	_____
Fixed and Other Assets—net	25,239	_____	3,419
Total Assets	_____	40,159	7,849
Current Liabilities	10,749	22,980	_____
Long-Term and Other Liabilities	17,247	_____	2,342
Total Liabilities	_____	30,413	4,787
Stockholders' Equity	_____	_____	_____

For the following balance sheet items, check the appropriate category.

		Current Asset	Fixed Asset	Current Liability	Long-Term Liability	Owner's Equity
12.	Land	____	____	____	____	____
13.	Supplies	____	____	____	____	____
14.	Marketable securities	____	____	____	____	____
15.	Retained earnings	____	____	____	____	____
16.	Buildings	____	____	____	____	____
17.	Mortgage payable	____	____	____	____	____
18.	Cash	____	____	____	____	____
19.	Notes payable	____	____	____	____	____
20.	Equipment	____	____	____	____	____
21.	Note receivable (3-month)	____	____	____	____	____
22.	Prepaid expenses	____	____	____	____	____
23.	Merchandise inventory	____	____	____	____	____
24.	Common stock	____	____	____	____	____
25.	Trucks	____	____	____	____	____
26.	Debenture bonds	____	____	____	____	____
27.	Accounts receivable	____	____	____	____	____
28.	Salaries payable	____	____	____	____	____

	Current Asset	Fixed Asset	Current Liability	Long-Term Liability	Owner's Equity
29. R. Smith, capital	___	___	___	___	___
30. Savings account	___	___	___	___	___
31. Preferred stock	___	___	___	___	___
32. Note payable (2-year)	___	___	___	___	___
33. Taxes payable	___	___	___	___	___

Prepare the following statements on separate sheets of paper.

34. a. Use the following financial information to calculate the owner's equity and prepare a balance sheet with vertical analysis as of December 31, 2015, for Victory Lane Sporting Goods, a sole proprietorship owned by Kyle Pressman: current assets, $157,600; property, plant, and equipment, $42,000; investments and other assets, $35,700; current liabilities, $21,200; and long-term liabilities, $53,400.

Victory Lane Sporting Goods
Balance Sheet
December 31, 2015

    b. The following financial information is for Victory Lane Sporting Goods as of December 31, 2016: current assets, $175,300; property, plant, and equipment, $43,600; investments and other assets, $39,200; current liabilities, $27,700; and long-term liabilities, $51,000.

       Calculate the owner's equity for 2016 and prepare a comparative balance sheet with horizontal analysis for 2015 and 2016.

Victory Lane Sporting Goods
Comparative Balance Sheet
December 31, 2015 and 2016

35. a. Use the following financial information to prepare a balance sheet with vertical analysis as of June 30, 2015, for Stargate Industries, Inc.: cash, $44,300; accounts receivable, $127,600; merchandise inventory, $88,100; prepaid maintenance, $4,100; office supplies, $4,000; land, $154,000; building, $237,000; fixtures, $21,400; vehicles, $64,000; computers, $13,000; goodwill, $20,000; investments, $32,000; accounts payable, $55,700; salaries payable, $23,200; notes payable (6-month), $38,000; mortgage payable, $91,300; debenture bonds, $165,000; common stock, $350,000; and retained earnings, $86,300.

Stargate Industries, Inc.
Balance Sheet
June 30, 2015

    b. The following financial information is for Stargate Industries as of June 30, 2016: cash, $40,200; accounts receivable, $131,400; merchandise inventory, $92,200; prepaid maintenance, $3,700; office supplies, $6,200; land, $154,000; building, $231,700; fixtures, $23,900; vehicles, $55,100; computers, $16,800; goodwill, $22,000; investments, $36,400; accounts payable, $51,800; salaries payable, $25,100; notes payable (6-month), $19,000; mortgage payable, $88,900; debenture bonds, $165,000; common stock, $350,000; and retained earnings, $113,800.

       Prepare a comparative balance sheet with horizontal analysis for 2015 and 2016.

Stargate Industries, Inc.
Comparative Balance Sheet
June 30, 2015 and 2016

BUSINESS DECISION: THE BALANCE SHEET

36. From the consolidated balance sheets for Macy's on the following page,

    a. Prepare a horizontal analysis of the Current Assets section comparing February 2, 2013 and February 1, 2014.

    b. Prepare a vertical analysis of the Current Liabilities section for February 1, 2014.

Curved Light USA/Alamy

Macy's, established in 1858, opened as a small, fancy dry goods store on the corner of 14th Street and 6th Avenue in New York City. With corporate offices in Cincinnati and New York, today Macy's is one of the nation's premier retailers. Together with its subsidiaries, Macy's, Inc. operates 850 stores in 45 states, the District of Columbia, Guam, and Puerto Rico under the names Macy's and Bloomingdale's, as well as the websites www.macys.com and www.bloomingdales.com.

The company's retail stores and websites sell a range of merchandise, including men's, women's, and children's apparel and accessories and cosmetics, home furnishings, and other consumer goods. The company, formerly known as Federated Department Stores, Inc., changed its name to Macy's, Inc. in June 2007.

MACY'S, INC.
CONSOLIDATED BALANCE SHEETS
(in millions)

	February 1, 2014	February 2, 2013
ASSETS		
Current Assets:		
Cash and Cash Equivalents	$ 2,273	$ 1,836
Receivables	438	371
Merchandise Inventories	5,557	5,308
Prepaid Expenses and Other Current Assets	420	361
Total Current Assets	8,688	7,876
Property and Equipment—Net	7,930	8,196
Goodwill	3,743	3,743
Other Intangible Assets—Net	527	561
Other Assets	746	615
Total Assets	$21,634	$20,991
LIABILITIES AND SHAREHOLDERS' EQUITY		
Current Liabilities:		
Short-Term Debt	$ 463	$ 124
Merchandise Accounts Payable	1,691	1,579
Accounts Payable and Accrued Liabilities	2,810	2,610
Income Taxes	362	355
Deferred Income Taxes	400	407
Total Current Liabilities	5,726	5,075
Long-Term Debt	6,728	6,806
Deferred Income Taxes	1,273	1,238
Other Liabilities	1,658	1,821
Shareholders' Equity	6,249	6,051
Total Liabilities and Shareholders' Equity	$21,634	$20,991

SECTION II

15

THE INCOME STATEMENT

THE BOTTOM LINE

income, **operating**, or **profit and loss statement** Financial statement summarizing the operations of a business over a period of time. Illustrates the amount of revenue earned, expenses incurred, and the resulting profit or loss: Revenue − Total Expenses = Profit (or loss).

revenue The primary source of money, both cash and credit, flowing into the business from its customers for goods sold or services rendered over a period of time.

expenses Costs incurred by a business in the process of earning revenue.

When all is said and done, the question is how well did the business do. The real score is found on the income statement. An **income statement**, also known as an **operating statement** or **profit and loss statement**, is a summary of the operations of a business over a period of time—usually a month, a quarter, or a year. For any business to exist, it must have earnings as well as expenses in the form of either cash or credit. The income statement shows the **revenue**, or earnings, of the business from the sale of goods and services; the **expenses**, the costs incurred to generate that revenue; and the bottom line **profit** or **loss**, the difference between revenue and expenses.

$$\text{Profit (or Loss)} = \text{Revenue} - \text{Total Expenses}$$

where: Revenue = Earnings (either cash or credit) from sales during the period

Total expenses = Cost of goods sold + Operating expenses + Taxes

15-4   PREPARING AN INCOME STATEMENT

profit or **loss** The difference between revenue earned and expenses incurred during an operating period—profit when revenue is greater than expenses; loss when expenses are greater than revenue. Profit is also known as earnings or income.

Once again, let's begin by looking at a typical income statement. As before, we will use Hypothetical Enterprises, Inc. to illustrate. Carefully look over the following income statement and then read the descriptions of each section and its components.

Keep in mind that an income statement covers a *period* of time, whereas a balance sheet covers a *moment* in time.

Hypothetical Enterprises, Inc.
Income Statement for the Year Ended December 31, 20XX

Revenue		
Gross Sales	$923,444	
Less: Sales Returns and Allowances	22,875	
Sales Discounts	3,625	
Net Sales		$896,944
Cost of Goods Sold		
Merchandise Inventory, Jan. 1	220,350	
Net Purchases	337,400	
Freight In	12,350	
Goods Available for Sale	570,100	
Less: Merchandise Inventory, Dec. 31	88,560	
Cost of Goods Sold		481,540
Gross Margin		415,404
Operating Expenses		
Salaries and Benefits	152,600	
Rent and Utilities	35,778	
Advertising and Promotion	32,871	
Insurance	8,258	
General and Administrative Expenses	41,340	
Depreciation	19,890	
Miscellaneous Expenses	14,790	
Total Operating Expenses		305,527
Income before Taxes		109,877
Income Tax		18,609
Net Income		$91,268

INCOME STATEMENT COMPONENTS

REVENUE   The revenue section of the income statement represents the primary source of money, both cash and credit, flowing into the business from its customers for goods sold or services rendered.

> Gross sales
> − Sales returns and allowances
> − Sales discounts
> ─────────────────────
> Net sales

- Gross sales—Total sales of goods and services achieved by the company during the operating period.
- Sales returns and allowances—Amount of merchandise returned for cash or credit by customers for various reasons.
- Sales discounts—Cash discounts given to customers by the business as an incentive for early payment of an invoice (for example, 3/15, n/45, where a 3% extra discount is given if the invoice is paid within 15 days rather than the net date of 45 days).
- Net sales—Amount received after taking into consideration returned goods, allowances, and sales discounts.

COST OF GOODS SOLD   The cost of goods sold section represents the cost to the business of the merchandise that was sold during the operating period.

> Merchandise inventory (beginning)
> + Net purchases
> + Freight in
> ─────────────────────
> Goods available for sale
> − Merchandise inventory (ending)
> ─────────────────────
> Cost of goods sold

- Merchandise inventory (beginning of operating period)—Total value of the goods in inventory at the beginning of the operating period. This *beginning inventory* is last period's ending inventory.
- Net purchases—Amount, at cost, of merchandise purchased during the period for resale to customers after purchase returns and allowances and purchase discounts earned are deducted.
- Freight in—Total amount of the freight or transportation charges incurred for the net purchases.
- Goods available for sale—The total amount of the goods available to be sold during the operating period. It is the sum of beginning inventory, net purchases, and freight in.
- Merchandise inventory (end of operating period)—Total value of the goods remaining in inventory at the end of the operating period. This *ending inventory* is next period's beginning inventory.
- Cost of goods sold—Total value of the goods that were sold during the period. It is the difference between goods available for sale and the ending merchandise inventory.

GROSS MARGIN   Gross margin, also known as gross profit, represents the difference between net sales and cost of goods sold.

> Net sales
> − Cost of goods sold
> ─────────────────────
> Gross margin

TOTAL OPERATING EXPENSES   Total operating expenses are the sum of all expenses incurred by the business during the operating period except the cost of goods sold and taxes. Operating expenses differ from company to company. Some typical examples are salaries and benefits, sales commissions, rent and utilities, advertising and promotion, insurance, general and administrative expenses, depreciation, and miscellaneous expenses.

INCOME BEFORE TAXES   This figure represents the money a company made before paying income tax. It is the difference between gross margin and total operating expenses.

> Gross margin
> − Total operating expenses
> ─────────────────────
> Income before taxes

IN THE Business World

The phrase *all to the good* is derived from an old accounting term. The word *good* was used in the nineteenth century to mean *profit*. Thus, after expenses were taken out, the rest "went to the good!"

INCOME TAX   This expense figure is the amount of income tax, both state and federal, that is paid by the business during the operating period.

NET INCOME, NET PROFIT, or NET LOSS   Literally the bottom line of the income statement. It is the difference between income before taxes and the income tax paid.

$$\begin{array}{r} \text{Income before taxes} \\ -\ \text{Income tax} \\ \hline \text{Net income (loss)} \end{array}$$

STEPS TO PREPARE AN INCOME STATEMENT

STEP 1.   Centered at the top of the page, write the company name, type of statement, and period of time covered by the statement (for example, "Year ended Dec. 31, 2016" or "April 2016").

STEP 2.   In a two-column format as illustrated on page 496, calculate:

   a.   *Net Sales:*

$$\begin{array}{r} \text{Gross sales} \\ -\ \text{Sales returns and allowances} \\ -\ \text{Sales discounts} \\ \hline \text{Net sales} \end{array}$$

   b.   *Cost of Goods Sold:*

$$\begin{array}{r} \text{Merchandise inventory (beginning)} \\ +\ \text{Net purchases} \\ +\ \text{Freight in} \\ \hline \text{Goods available for sale} \\ -\ \text{Merchandise inventory (ending)} \\ \hline \text{Cost of goods sold} \end{array}$$

   c.   *Gross Margin:*

$$\begin{array}{r} \text{Net sales} \\ -\ \text{Cost of goods sold} \\ \hline \text{Gross margin} \end{array}$$

   d.   *Total Operating Expenses:* Sum of all operating expenses

   e.   *Income before Taxes:*

$$\begin{array}{r} \text{Gross margin} \\ -\ \text{Total operating expenses} \\ \hline \text{Income before taxes} \end{array}$$

   f.   *Net Income:*

$$\begin{array}{r} \text{Income before taxes} \\ -\ \text{Income tax} \\ \hline \text{Net income (loss)} \end{array}$$

EXAMPLE 4   PREPARING AN INCOME STATEMENT

Use the following financial information to prepare an income statement for Royal Equipment Supply, Inc. for the year ended December 31, 2016: gross sales, $458,400; sales returns and allowances, $13,200; sales discounts, $1,244; merchandise inventory, Jan. 1, 2016, $198,700; merchandise inventory, Dec. 31, 2016, $76,400; net purchases, $86,760; freight in, $875; salaries, $124,200; rent, $21,000; utilities, $1,780; advertising, $5,400; insurance, $2,340; administrative expenses, $14,500; miscellaneous expenses, $6,000; and income tax, $17,335.

SOLUTIONSTRATEGY

The income statement for Royal Equipment Supply, Inc. follows.

Royal Equipment Supply, Inc.
Income Statement
For the Year Ended December 31, 2016

Revenue		
Gross Sales	$458,400	
Less: Sales Returns and Allowances	13,200	
Sales Discounts	1,244	
Net Sales		$443,956
Cost of Goods Sold		
Merchandise Inventory, Jan. 1	198,700	
Net Purchases	86,760	
Freight In	875	
Goods Available for Sale	286,335	
Less: Merchandise Inventory, Dec. 31	76,400	
Cost of Goods Sold		209,935
Gross Margin		234,021
Operating Expenses		
Salaries	124,200	
Rent	21,000	
Utilities	1,780	
Advertising	5,400	
Insurance	2,340	
Administrative Expenses	14,500	
Miscellaneous Expenses	6,000	
Total Operating Expenses		175,220
Income before Taxes		58,801
Income Tax		17,335
Net Income		$ 41,466

▶TRYITEXERCISE 4

Use the following financial information to prepare an income statement for Cutting Edge Manufacturing, Inc., for the year ended December 31, 2016: gross sales, $1,356,000; sales returns and allowances, $93,100; sales discounts, $4,268; merchandise inventory, Jan. 1, 2016, $324,800; merchandise inventory, Dec. 31, 2016, $179,100; net purchases, $255,320; freight in, $3,911; salaries, $375,900; rent, $166,000; utilities, $7,730; advertising, $73,300; insurance, $22,940; administrative expenses, $84,500; miscellaneous expenses, $24,900; and income tax, $34,760.

CHECK YOUR STATEMENT WITH THE SOLUTION ON PAGE 522.

IN THE Business World

The popular business term *bottom line* literally comes from the structure of an income statement:

Total revenue
−Total expenses
Income (loss) ◀——— Bottom line

PREPARING A VERTICAL ANALYSIS OF AN INCOME STATEMENT

15-5

Vertical analysis can be applied to the income statement just as it was to the balance sheet. Each figure on the income statement is expressed as a percent of net sales (net sales = 100%). The resulting figures describe how net sales were distributed among the expenses and what percent was left as net profit. For analysis purposes, this information can then be compared with the figures from previous operating periods for the company, with competitors' figures, or with published industry averages for similar-size companies.

As with balance sheets, income statements with vertical analysis can be displayed in the format known as **common-size**, in which all figures on the statement appear as percentages.

common-size income statement
A special form of income statement that lists only the vertical analysis percentages, not the dollar figures. All items are expressed as a percent of net sales.

STEPS TO PREPARE A VERTICAL ANALYSIS OF AN INCOME STATEMENT

STEP 1. Use the percentage formula, Rate = Portion ÷ Base, to find the rate of each item on the income statement. Use each item as the portion and net sales as the base.

STEP 2. Round each answer to the nearest tenth of a percent.

Note: A 0.1% differential may sometimes occur due to rounding.

STEP 3. List the percentage of each statement item in a column to the right of the monetary amount.

EXAMPLE5 PREPARING A VERTICAL ANALYSIS OF AN INCOME STATEMENT

Prepare a vertical analysis of the income statement for Hypothetical Enterprises, Inc., on page 496.

SOLUTIONSTRATEGY

Using the steps for vertical analysis, perform the following calculation for each income statement item and enter the results on the income statement as follows:

$$\frac{\text{Gross sales}}{\text{Net sales}} = \frac{923,444}{896,944} = 1.0295 = 103.0\%$$

Hypothetical Enterprises, Inc.
Income Statement for the Year Ended December 31, 20XX

Revenue		
Gross Sales	$923,444	103.0%
Less: Sales Returns and Allowances	22,875	2.6
Sales Discounts	3,625	.4
Net Sales	896,944	100.0%
Cost of Goods Sold		
Merchandise Inventory, Jan. 1	220,350	24.6
Net Purchases	337,400	37.6
Freight In	12,350	1.4
Goods Available for Sale	570,100	63.6
Less: Merchandise Inventory, Dec. 31	88,560	9.9
Cost of Goods Sold	481,540	53.7
Gross Margin	415,404	46.3
Operating Expenses		
Salaries and Benefits	152,600	17.0
Rent and Utilities	35,778	4.0
Advertising and Promotion	32,871	3.7
Insurance	8,258	.9
General and Administrative Expenses	41,340	4.6
Depreciation	19,890	2.2
Miscellaneous Expenses	14,790	1.6
Total Operating Expenses	305,527	34.1
Income before Taxes	109,877	12.3
Income Tax	18,609	2.1
Net Income	$ 91,268	10.2%

TRYITEXERCISE 5

Prepare a vertical analysis of the income statement for Royal Equipment Supply, Inc., on page 499.

CHECK YOUR STATEMENT WITH THE SOLUTION ON PAGE 522.

PREPARING A HORIZONTAL ANALYSIS OF AN INCOME STATEMENT

15-6

As with the balance sheet, the income statement can be prepared in a format that compares the financial data of the business from one operating period to another. This horizontal analysis provides percent increase or decrease information for each item on the income statement. Such information provides a useful progress report of the company. As before, the previous or original period figure is the base.

STEPS TO PREPARE A HORIZONTAL ANALYSIS OF AN INCOME STATEMENT

STEP 1. Set up a comparative income statement format with the current period listed first and the previous period listed next.

STEP 2. Label the next two columns: $\dfrac{\text{Increase (Decrease)}}{\text{Amount} \quad \text{Percent}}$

STEP 3. For each item on the income statement, calculate the dollar difference between the current and the previous period and enter this figure in the Amount column. Enter all decreases in parentheses.

STEP 4. Calculate the percent change (increase or decrease) by the percentage formula:

$$\text{Percent change (rate)} = \frac{\text{Amount of change, Step 3 (portion)}}{\text{Previous period amount (base)}}$$

STEP 5. Enter the percent change, rounded to the nearest tenth of a percent, in the Percent column. Once again, enter all decreases in parentheses.

EXAMPLE6 PREPARING A HORIZONTAL ANALYSIS OF AN INCOME STATEMENT

A comparative income statement for Foremost Furniture, Inc. for 2015 and 2016 follows. Prepare a horizontal analysis of the statement for the company.

Foremost Furniture, Inc.
Comparative Income Statement

	2016	2015
Revenue		
Gross Sales	$623,247	$599,650
Less: Sales Returns and Allowances	8,550	9,470
Sales Discounts	3,400	1,233
Net Sales	611,297	588,947
Cost of Goods Sold		
Merchandise Inventory, Jan. 1	158,540	134,270
Purchases	117,290	111,208
Freight In	2,460	1,980
Goods Available for Sale	278,290	247,458
Less: Merchandise Inventory, Dec. 31	149,900	158,540
Cost of Goods Sold	128,390	88,918
Gross Margin	482,907	500,029
Operating Expenses		
Salaries and Benefits	165,300	161,200
Rent and Utilities	77,550	76,850
Depreciation	74,350	75,040
Insurance	4,560	3,900
Office Expenses	34,000	41,200
Warehouse Expenses	41,370	67,400
Total Operating Expenses	397,130	425,590
Income before Taxes	85,777	74,439
Income Tax	27,400	19,700
Net Income	$ 58,377	$ 54,739

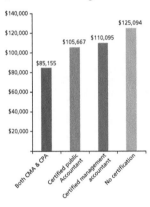

SOLUTIONSTRATEGY

Using the steps for horizontal analysis, perform the following operation on all income statement items and then enter the results on the statement.

Gross Sales   2016 amount − 2015 amount = Amount of change

$$623,247 - 599,650 = \$23,597 \text{ increase}$$

$$\text{Percent change} = \frac{\text{Amount of change}}{\text{Previous period amount}} = \frac{23,597}{599,650} = 3.9\%$$

Foremost Furniture, Inc.
Comparative Income Statement

	2016	2015	Increase (Decrease) Amount	Percent
Revenue				
Gross Sales	$623,247	$599,650	$23,597	3.9%
Less: Sales Returns and Allowances	8,550	9,470	(920)	(9.7)
Sales Discounts	3,400	1,233	2,167	175.8
Net Sales	611,297	588,947	22,350	3.8
Cost of Goods Sold				
Merchandise Inventory, Jan. 1	158,540	134,270	24,270	18.1
Purchases	117,290	111,208	6,082	5.5
Freight In	2,460	1,980	480	24.2
Goods Available for Sale	278,290	247,458	30,832	12.5
Less: Merchandise Inventory, Dec. 31	149,900	158,540	(8,640)	(5.4)
Cost of Goods Sold	128,390	88,918	39,472	44.4
Gross Margin	482,907	500,029	(17,122)	(3.4)
Operating Expenses				
Salaries and Benefits	165,300	161,200	4,100	2.5
Rent and Utilities	77,550	76,850	700	.9
Depreciation	74,350	75,040	(690)	(.9)
Insurance	4,560	3,900	660	16.9
Office Expenses	34,000	41,200	(7,200)	(17.5)
Warehouse Expenses	41,370	67,400	(26,030)	(38.6)
Total Operating Expenses	397,130	425,590	(28,460)	(6.7)
Income before Taxes	85,777	74,439	11,338	15.2
Income Tax	27,400	19,700	7,700	39.1
Net Income	$ 58,377	$ 54,739	$ 3,638	6.6%

▶TRYITEXERCISE 6

Complete the following comparative income statement with horizontal analysis for Timely Watch Company, Inc.

Timely Watch Company, Inc.
Comparative Income Statement

	2016	2015	Increase (Decrease) Amount	Percent
Revenue				
Gross Sales	$1,223,000	$996,500	____	____
Less: Sales Returns and Allowances	121,340	99,600	____	____
Sales Discounts	63,120	51,237	____	____
Net Sales	____	____	____	____
Cost of Goods Sold				
Merchandise Inventory, Jan. 1	311,200	331,000	____	____
Purchases	603,290	271,128	____	____
Freight In	18,640	13,400	____	____
Goods Available for Sale			____	____
Less: Merchandise Inventory, Dec. 31	585,400	311,200	____	____
Cost of Goods Sold	____	____	____	____
Gross Margin	____	____	____	____

	2016	2015	Increase (Decrease)	
			Amount	Percent
Operating Expenses				
Salaries and Benefits	215,200	121,800	_____	_____
Rent and Utilities	124,650	124,650	_____	_____
Depreciation	43,500	41,230	_____	_____
Insurance	24,970	23,800	_____	_____
Administrative Store Expenses	58,200	33,900	_____	_____
Warehouse Expenses	42,380	45,450	_____	_____
Total Operating Expenses				
Income before Taxes				
Income Tax	66,280	41,670	_____	_____
Net Income				

CHECK YOUR ANSWERS WITH THE SOLUTIONS ON PAGE 522–523.

15 REVIEW EXERCISES   SECTION II

Calculate the missing information based on the format of the income statement.

	Net Sales	Cost of Goods Sold	Gross Margin	Operating Expenses	Net Profit
1.	$565,700	$244,600	$321,100	$276,400	$44,700
2.	$4,232,000	$2,362,000	$1,870,000	$1,210,500	$659,500
3.	$705,300	$398,450	$306,850	$196,525	$110,325
4.	$334,500	$132,300	_____	$108,000	_____
5.	$1,640,000	_____	$760,000	$354,780	_____
6.	_____	$257,000	$418,530	_____	$84,370
7.	$341,300	$186,740	_____	_____	$68,050
8.	$7.64 million	_____	$2.75 million	$1.68 million	_____

Calculate the missing income statement items for Exercise 9, CVS Caremark; Exercise 10, AutoZone; and Exercise 11, PetSmart. Complete each company's column; then move on to the next column.

THE INCOME STATEMENT			
	Exercise 9	**Exercise 10**	**Exercise 11**
Company Year Ended	**CVS Caremark** December 31, 2012 (in millions)	**AutoZone** December 31, 2014 (in thousands)	**PetSmart** February 3, 2013 (in thousands)
Revenue	$123,133	$9,475,313	_____
Cost of Goods Sold	100,627	_____	4,696,098
Gross Margin	_____	4,934,907	2,062,139
Operating Expenses	15,278	3,104,684	_____
Income before Taxes	_____	_____	651,217
Income Tax*	3,351	_____	_____
Net Income (loss)	_____	1,069,744	389,529

*Also includes interest expense and other income and losses.

12. For the third quarter, Micro Tech had gross sales of $315,450, sales returns and allowances of $23,100, and sales discounts of $18,700. What were the net sales?

13. For August, Island Traders, Inc. had the following financial information: merchandise inventory, August 1, $244,500; merchandise inventory, August 31, $193,440; gross purchases, $79,350; purchase returns and allowances, $8,700; and freight in, $970.

   a. What is the amount of the goods available for sale?

   b. What is the cost of goods sold for August?

   c. If net sales were $335,000, what was the gross margin for August?

   d. If total operating expenses were $167,200, what was the net profit?

Prepare the following statements on separate sheets of paper.

14. a. As the assistant accounting manager for Jefferson Airplane Parts, Inc., construct an income statement with vertical analysis for the first quarter of 2016 from the following information: gross sales, $240,000; sales discounts, $43,500; beginning inventory, Jan. 1, $86,400; ending inventory, March 31, $103,200; net purchases, $76,900; total operating expenses, $108,000; and income tax, $14,550.

Jefferson Airplane Parts, Inc.
Income Statement
January 1 to March 31, 2016

   b. You have just received a report with the second-quarter figures. Prepare a comparative income statement with horizontal analysis for the first and second quarter of 2016: gross sales, $297,000; sales discounts, $41,300; beginning inventory, April 1, $103,200; ending inventory, June 30, $96,580; net purchases, $84,320; total operating expenses, $126,700; and income tax, $16,400.

Jefferson Airplane Parts, Inc.
Comparative Income Statement
First and Second Quarter, 2016

15. a. Use the following financial information to construct a 2015 income statement with vertical analysis for the Sweets & Treats Candy Company, Inc.: gross sales, $2,249,000; sales returns and allowances, $143,500; sales discounts, $54,290; merchandise inventory, Jan. 1, $875,330; merchandise inventory, Dec. 31, $716,090; net purchases, $546,920; freight in, $11,320; salaries, $319,800; rent, $213,100; depreciation, $51,200; utilities, $35,660; advertising, $249,600; insurance, $39,410; administrative expenses, $91,700; miscellaneous expenses, $107,500; and income tax, $38,450.

Sweets & Treats Candy Company, Inc.
Income Statement, 2015

b. The following data represents Sweets & Treats' operating results for 2016. Prepare a comparative income statement with horizontal analysis for 2014 and 2015: gross sales, $2,125,000; sales returns and allowances, $126,400; sales discounts, $73,380; merchandise inventory, Jan. 1, 2016, $716,090; merchandise inventory, Dec. 31, 2016, $584,550; net purchases, $482,620; freight in, $9,220; salaries, $340,900; rent, $215,000; depreciation, $56,300; utilities, $29,690; advertising, $217,300; insurance, $39,410; administrative expenses, $95,850; miscellaneous expenses, $102,500; and income tax, $44,530.

Sweets & Treats Candy Company, Inc.
Comparative Income Statement, 2015 and 2016

BUSINESS DECISION: THE INCOME STATEMENT

16. From the following consolidated statements of income for Comcast Corporation.

a. Prepare a horizontal analysis of the net income comparing 2012 and 2013.
b. Prepare a vertical analysis of the costs and expenses for 2013.

COMCAST CORPORATION
CONSOLIDATED STATEMENT OF INCOME

Year ended December 31 (in millions, except per share data)	2013	2012	2011
Revenue	$64,657	$62,570	$55,842
Costs and Expenses:			
Programming and production	19,670	19,929	16,596
Other operating and administrative	18,584	17,833	16,646
Advertising, marketing and promotion	4,969	4,831	4,243
Depreciation	6,254	6,150	6,040
Amortization	1,617	1,648	1,596
	51,094	50,391	45,121
Operating Income	13,563	12,179	10,721
Other Income (Expense):			
Interest expense	(2,574)	(2,521)	(2,505)
Investment income (loss), net	576	219	159
Equity in net income (losses) of investees, net	(86)	959	(35)
Other income (expense), net	(364)	773	(133)
	(2,448)	(570)	(2,514)
Income before income taxes	11,115	11,609	8,207
Income tax expense	(3,980)	(3,744)	(3,050)
Net income	7,135	7,865	5,157
Net (income) loss attributable to noncontrolling interests and redeemable subsidiary preferred stock	(319)	(1,662)	(997)
Net Income Attributable to Comcast Corporation	$6,816	$6,203	$4,160
Basic earnings per common share attributable to Comcast Corporation shareholders	$2.60	$2.32	$1.51
Diluted earnings per common share attributable to Comcast Corporation shareholders	$2.56	$2.28	$1.50
Dividends declared per common share	$0.78	$0.65	$0.45

Comcast Corporation (Nasdaq: CMCSA, CMCSK) (www.comcast.com) is one of the world's leading media, entertainment, and communications companies. Comcast is principally involved in the operation of cable systems through Comcast Cable and in the development, production, and distribution of entertainment, news, sports, and other content for global audiences through NBCUniversal. Comcast Cable is one of the nation's largest video, high-speed Internet, and phone providers to residential and business customers. Comcast is the majority owner and manager of NBCUniversal, which owns and operates entertainment and news cable networks, the NBC and Telemundo broadcast networks, local television station groups, television production operations, a major motion picture company, and theme parks.

Source: Comcast Corporation

financial ratios A series of comparisons of financial statement components in ratio form used by analysts to evaluate the operating performance of a company.

In addition to vertical and horizontal analysis of financial statements, managers, creditors, and investors also study comparisons among various components on the statements. These comparisons are expressed as ratios and are known as **financial ratios**.

Basically, financial ratios represent an effort by analysts to standardize financial information, which in turn makes comparisons more meaningful. The fundamental purpose of ratio analysis is to indicate areas requiring further investigation. Think of them as signals indicating areas of potential strength or weakness of the firm. Frequently, financial ratios have to be examined more closely to discover their true meaning. A high ratio, for example, might indicate that the numerator figure is too high or the denominator figure is too low.

Financial ratios fall into four major categories:

- **Liquidity ratios** tell how well a company can pay off its short-term debts and meet unexpected needs for cash.

- **Efficiency ratios** indicate how effectively a company uses its resources to generate sales.

- **Leverage ratios** show how and to what degree a company has financed its assets.

- **Profitability ratios** tell how much of each dollar of sales, assets, and stockholders' investment resulted in bottom-line net profit.

15-7 CALCULATING FINANCIAL RATIOS

ratio A comparison of one amount to another.

As we learned in Chapter 5, a **ratio** is a comparison of one amount to another. A financial ratio is simply a ratio whose numerator and denominator are financial information taken from the balance sheet, the income statement, or other important business data.

Ratios may be stated a number of ways. For example, a ratio of credit sales, $40,000, to total sales, $100,000, in a retail store may be stated as follows:

a. Credit sales ratio is $\dfrac{40,000}{100,000}$,

or 4 to 10,

or 2 to 5 (written 2:5).

b. Credit sales are $\dfrac{4}{10}$, or 40% of total sales.

c. For every $1.00 of sales, $0.40 is on credit.

Conversely, the ratio of total sales, $100,000, to credit sales, $40,000, in a retail store may be stated as follows:

a. Total sales ratio is $\dfrac{100,000}{40,000}$,

or 10 to 4,

or 2.5 to 1 (written 2.5:1).

b. Total sales are $\dfrac{10}{4}$, or 250% of credit sales.

c. For every $2.50 of sales, $1.00 is on credit.

To illustrate how ratios are used in financial analysis, let's apply this concept to Hypothetical Enterprises, Inc., a company introduced in Sections I and II of this chapter.

Managers analyze financial statement data to determine strengths and weaknesses of a business.

EXAMPLE7   CALCULATING FINANCIAL RATIOS

Calculate the financial ratios for Hypothetical Enterprises, Inc., using the data from the financial statements presented on pages 485 and 496.

▶SOLUTIONSTRATEGY

Liquidity Ratios

Businesses must have enough cash on hand to pay their bills as they come due. The **liquidity ratios** examine the relationship between a firm's current assets and its maturing obligations. The amount of a firm's working capital and these ratios are good indicators of a firm's ability to pay its bills over the next few months. Short-term creditors pay particular attention to these figures.

The term **working capital** refers to the difference between current assets and current liabilities at a point in time. Theoretically, it is the amount of money that would be left over if all current liabilities were paid off by current assets.

liquidity ratios Financial ratios that tell how well a company can pay off its short-term debts and meet unexpected needs for cash.

working capital The difference between current assets and current liabilities at a point in time. Theoretically, the amount of money left over if all current liabilities are paid off by current assets.

$$\text{Working capital} = \text{Current assets} - \text{Current liabilities}$$

Current ratio or **working capital ratio** is the comparison of a firm's current assets to current liabilities. This ratio indicates the amount of current assets available to pay off $1 of current debt. A current ratio of 2:1 or greater is considered by banks and other lending institutions to be an acceptable ratio.

current ratio or **working capital ratio** The comparison of a firm's current assets to current liabilities.

$$\text{Current ratio} = \frac{\text{Current assets}}{\text{Current liabilities}}$$

Hypothetical Enterprises, Inc.:

$$\text{Working capital} = 101{,}300 - 29{,}400 = \$71{,}900$$

$$\text{Current ratio} = \frac{101{,}300}{29{,}400} = 3.45 = 3.45{:}1$$

Analysis: This ratio shows that Hypothetical has $3.45 in current assets for each $1.00 it owes in current liabilities. A current ratio of 3.45:1 indicates that the company has more than sufficient means of covering short-term debts and is therefore in a strong liquidity position.

Acid test or **quick ratio** indicates a firm's ability to quickly liquidate assets to pay off current debt. This ratio recognizes that a firm's inventories are one of the least liquid current assets. Merchandise inventories and prepaid expenses are not part of quick assets because they are not readily convertible to cash. An acid test ratio of 1:1 or greater is considered acceptable.

acid test or **quick ratio** A ratio that indicates a firm's ability to quickly liquidate assets to pay off current debt.

$$\text{Quick assets} = \text{Cash} + \text{Marketable securities} + \text{Receivables}$$

$$\text{Acid test ratio} = \frac{\text{Quick assets}}{\text{Current liabilities}}$$

Hypothetical Enterprises, Inc. (*Note:* Hypothetical has no marketable securities):

$$\text{Quick assets} = 13{,}000 + 32{,}500 = \$45{,}500$$

$$\text{Acid test ratio} = \frac{45{,}500}{29{,}400} = 1.55 = 1.55{:}1$$

Analysis: An acid test ratio of 1.55:1 also indicates a strong liquidity position. It means that Hypothetical has the ability to meet all short-term debt obligations immediately if necessary.

Efficiency Ratios

Efficiency ratios provide the basis for determining how effectively the firm is using its resources to generate sales. A firm with $500,000 in assets producing $1,000,000 in sales is using its resources more efficiently than a firm producing the same sales with $2,000,000 invested in assets.

Average collection period indicates how quickly a firm's credit accounts are being collected and is a good measure of how efficiently a firm is managing its accounts receivable. *Note:* When credit sales figures are not available, net sales may be used instead.

efficiency ratios Financial ratios that indicate how effectively a company uses its resources to generate sales.

average collection period Indicator of how quickly a firm's credit accounts are being collected. Expressed in days.

$$\text{Average collection period} = \frac{\text{Accounts receivable} \times 365}{\text{Credit sales}}$$

Hypothetical Enterprises, Inc.:

$$\text{Average collection period} = \frac{32{,}500 \times 365}{896{,}944} = \frac{11{,}862{,}500}{896{,}944} = 13.23 = 13\ \text{Days}$$

Analysis: This ratio tells us that on average, Hypothetical's credit customers take 13 days to pay their bills. Because most industries average between 30 and 60 days, the firm's 13-day collection period is favorable and shows considerable efficiency in handling credit accounts.

inventory turnover The number of times during an operating period that the average inventory was sold.

Inventory turnover is the number of times during an operating period that the average inventory was sold.

$$\text{Average inventory} = \frac{\text{Beginning inventory} + \text{Ending inventory}}{2}$$

$$\text{Inventory turnover} = \frac{\text{Cost of goods sold}}{\text{Average inventory}}$$

Hypothetical Enterprises, Inc.:

$$\text{Average inventory} = \frac{220{,}350 + 88{,}560}{2} = \$154{,}455$$

$$\text{Inventory turnover} = \frac{481{,}540}{154{,}455} = 3.12 = 3.1\ \text{Times}$$

Analysis: Inventory turnover is one ratio that should be compared with the data from previous operating periods and with published industry averages for similar-size firms in the same industry to draw meaningful conclusions. When inventory turnover is below average, it may be a signal that the company is carrying too much inventory. Carrying excess inventory can lead to extra expenses such as warehouse costs and insurance. It also ties up money that could be used more efficiently elsewhere.

asset turnover ratio Ratio that tells the number of dollars in sales a firm generates from each dollar it has invested in assets.

Asset turnover ratio tells the number of dollars in sales the firm generates from each dollar it has invested in assets. This ratio is an important measure of a company's efficiency in managing its assets.

$$\text{Asset turnover ratio} = \frac{\text{Net sales}}{\text{Total assets}}$$

Hypothetical Enterprises, Inc.:

$$\text{Asset turnover ratio} = \frac{896{,}944}{341{,}300} = 2.63 = 2.63{:}1$$

Analysis: Asset turnover is another ratio best compared with those of previous operating periods and industry averages to reach any meaningful conclusions. Hypothetical's 2.63:1 ratio means that the company is generating $2.63 in sales for every $1.00 in assets.

Leverage Ratios

When firms borrow money to finance assets, they are using financial leverage. Investors and creditors alike are particularly interested in the **leverage ratios** because the greater the leverage a firm has used, the greater the risk of default on interest and principal payments. Such situations could lead the firm into eventual bankruptcy.

leverage ratios Financial ratios that show how and to what degree a company has financed its assets.

debt-to-assets ratio Ratio that measures to what degree the assets of the firm have been financed with borrowed funds, or leveraged. It is commonly expressed as a percent.

Debt-to-assets ratio measures to what degree the assets of the firm have been financed with borrowed funds, or leveraged. This ratio identifies the claim on assets by the creditors. It is commonly expressed as a percent.

$$\text{Debt-to-assets ratio} = \frac{\text{Total liabilities}}{\text{Total assets}}$$

Hypothetical Enterprises, Inc.:

$$\text{Debt-to-assets ratio} = \frac{164{,}400}{341{,}300} = .4817 = 48.2\%$$

Analysis: This ratio indicates that Hypothetical's creditors have claim to 48.2% of the company assets, or for each $1.00 of assets, the company owes $0.48 to its creditors.

debt-to-equity ratio A ratio that compares the total debt of a firm to the owner's equity. It is commonly expressed as a percent.

Debt-to-equity ratio is used as a safety-factor measure for potential creditors. The ratio compares the total debt of the firm with the owner's equity. It tells the amount of debt incurred by the company for each $1 of equity. It is commonly expressed as a percent.

$$\text{Debt-to-equity ratio} = \frac{\text{Total liabilities}}{\text{Owner's equity}}$$

Hypothetical Enterprises, Inc.:

$$\text{Debt-to-equity ratio} = \frac{164,400}{176,900} = .929 = \underline{.929:1 \text{ or } 92.9\%}$$

Analysis: This ratio indicates that for each $1.00 of owner's equity, Hypothetical has financed $0.93 in assets. As the debt-to-equity ratio increases, so does the risk factor to potential creditors and investors. This ratio should be compared with previous periods and industry norms.

Profitability Ratios

The **profitability ratios** are important to anyone whose economic interests are tied to the long-range success of the firm. Investors expect a return on their investment in the form of dividends and stock price appreciation. Without adequate profits, firms quickly fall out of favor with current and future investors.

profitability ratios Financial ratios that tell how much of each dollar of sales, assets, and owner's investment resulted in net profit.

Gross profit margin is an assessment of how well the cost of goods sold category of expenses was controlled. In particular, this measure spotlights a firm's management of its purchasing and pricing functions. Gross profit margin is expressed as a percent of net sales.

gross profit margin An assessment of how well the cost of goods sold category of expenses was controlled. Expressed as a percent of net sales.

$$\text{Gross profit margin} = \frac{\text{Gross profit}}{\text{Net sales}}$$

Hypothetical Enterprises, Inc.:

$$\text{Gross profit margin} = \frac{415,404}{896,944} = .463 = \underline{46.3\%}$$

Analysis: Hypothetical's gross profit constitutes 46.3% of the company's sales, which means that for each $1.00 of sales, $0.46 remains as gross margin. For a meaningful analysis, this ratio should be compared with previous operating periods and industry averages.

Net profit margin is an assessment of management's overall ability to control the cost of goods sold and the operating expenses of the firm. This ratio is the bottom-line score of a firm's profitability and is one of the most important and most frequently used ratios. Net profit margin can be calculated either before or after income tax. As with gross profit margin, it is expressed as a percent.

net profit margin An assessment of management's overall ability to control the cost of goods sold and the operating expenses of a firm. Expressed as a percent of net sales.

$$\text{Net profit margin} = \frac{\text{Net income}}{\text{Net sales}}$$

Hypothetical Enterprises, Inc.:

$$\text{Net profit margin} = \frac{91,268}{896,944} = .1018 = \underline{10.2\%}$$

Analysis: This means that for each $1.00 of net sales, Hypothetical was able to generate $0.10 in net profit. Most firms today have net profit margins between 1% and 8% depending on the industry. Regardless of industry, Hypothetical's 10.2% net profit margin would be considered very profitable.

Return on investment is the amount of profit generated by the firm in relation to the amount invested by the owners. Abbreviated ROI, this ratio is commonly expressed as a percent.

return on investment The amount of profit generated by a firm in relation to the amount invested by the owners. Expressed as a percent of owner's equity.

$$\text{Return on investment} = \frac{\text{Net income}}{\text{Owner's equity}}$$

Hypothetical Enterprises, Inc.:

$$\text{Return on investment} = \frac{91,268}{176,900} = .5159 = \underline{51.6\%}$$

Analysis: This ratio indicates that Hypothetical generated $0.52 in net profit for each $1.00 invested by the owners. Most investors would consider 51.6% an excellent return on their money.

►TRYITEXERCISE 7

Use the balance sheet and income statement on pages 487–488 and 499 to calculate the financial ratios for Royal Equipment Supply, Inc.

CHECK YOUR ANSWERS WITH THE SOLUTIONS ON PAGE 523.

15-8 PREPARING A TREND ANALYSIS OF FINANCIAL DATA

trend analysis The use of index numbers to calculate percentage changes of a company's financial data for several successive operating periods.

index numbers Numbers used in trend analysis indicating changes in magnitude of financial data over a period of time. Calculated by setting a base period equal to 100% and calculating other periods in relation to the base period.

In Sections I and II of this chapter, we used horizontal analysis to calculate and report the *amount* and *percent* change in various balance sheet and income statement items from one operating period to another. When these percentage changes are tracked for a number of successive periods, it is known as **trend analysis**. Trend analysis introduces the element of time into financial analysis. Whereas data from one statement gives a firm's financial position at a given point in time, trend analysis provides a dynamic picture of the firm by showing its financial direction over a period of time.

Index numbers are used in trend analysis to show the percentage change in various financial statement items. With index numbers, a base year is chosen and is equal to 100%. All other years' figures are measured as a percentage of the base year. Once again, we encounter the now familiar percentage formula Rate = Portion ÷ Base. The index number should be expressed as a percent rounded to the nearest tenth.

$$\text{Index number (rate)} = \frac{\text{Yearly amount (portion)}}{\text{Base year amount (base)}}$$

For example, if a company had sales of \$50,000 in the base year and \$60,000 in the index year, the index number would be 1.2, or 120% (60,000 ÷ 50,000). The index number means that the sales for the index year were 1.2 times, or 120%, of the base year.

STEPS FOR PREPARING A TREND ANALYSIS

STEP 1. Choose a base year and let it equal 100%.

STEP 2. Calculate the index number for each succeeding year.

$$\text{Index number} = \frac{\text{Yearly amount}}{\text{Base year amount}}$$

STEP 3. Round each index number to the nearest tenth of a percent.

EXAMPLE8 PREPARING A TREND ANALYSIS

From the following data, prepare a 5-year trend analysis of net sales, net income, and total assets for Hypothetical Enterprises, Inc.

Hypothetical Enterprises, Inc.
5-Year Selected Financial Data

	2015	2014	2013	2012	2011
Net Sales	\$896,944	\$881,325	\$790,430	\$855,690	\$825,100
Net Income	91,268	95,550	56,400	75,350	70,100
Total Assets	341,300	320,100	315,600	314,200	303,550

▶ SOLUTIONSTRATEGY

To prepare the trend analysis, we will calculate the index number for each year by using the percentage formula and then enter the figures in a trend analysis table. The earliest year, 2011, will be the base year (100%). The first calculation, 2012 net sales index number, is as follows:

$$2012 \text{ net sales index number} = \frac{855,690}{825,100} = 1.037 = 103.7\%$$

Trend Analysis (in percentages)

	2015	2014	2013	2012	2011
Net Sales	108.7	106.8	95.8	103.7	100.0
Net Income	130.2	136.3	80.5	107.5	100.0
Total Assets	112.4	105.5	104.0	103.5	100.0

In addition to the table form of presentation, trend analysis frequently uses charts to visually present the financial data. Multiple-line charts are a particularly good way of presenting comparative data. For even more meaningful analysis, company data can be graphed on the same coordinates as industry averages.

The chart below illustrates Hypothetical's trend analysis figures in a multiple-line-chart format.

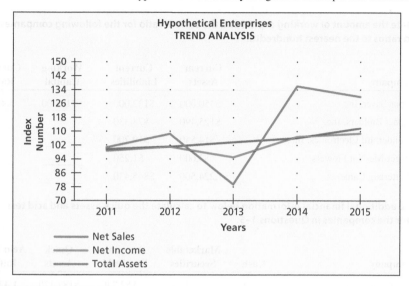

▶**TRYITEXERCISE 8**

Prepare a trend analysis from the following financial data for Precision Engineering, Inc., and prepare a multiple-line chart of the net sales, total assets, and stockholders' equity.

Precision Engineering, Inc.
5-Year Selected Financial Data

	2015	2014	2013	2012	2011
Net Sales	$245,760	$265,850	$239,953	$211,231	$215,000
Total Assets	444,300	489,320	440,230	425,820	419,418
Stockholders' Equity	276,440	287,500	256,239	223,245	247,680

Precision Engineering, Inc.
Trend Analysis (in percentages)

	2015	2014	2013	2012	2011
Net Sales	_____	_____	_____	_____	_____
Total Assets	_____	_____	_____	_____	_____
Stockholders' Equity	_____	_____	_____	_____	_____

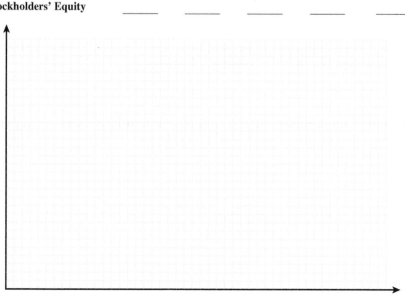

Calculate the amount of working capital and the current ratio for the following companies. Round ratios to the nearest hundredth.

Company	Current Assets	Current Liabilities	Working Capital	Current Ratio
1. Super-Saver, Inc.	$450,000	$132,000	$318,000	3.41:1
2. Impact Builders, Inc.	$125,490	$74,330	_____	_____
3. Thunderbird Electronics, Inc.	$14,540	$19,700	_____	_____
4. Forget-Me-Not Flowers	$3,600	$1,250	_____	_____
5. Shutterbug Cameras	$1,224,500	$845,430	_____	_____

Use the additional financial information below to calculate the quick assets and acid test ratio for the companies in Questions 1–5.

Company	Cash	Marketable Securities	Accounts Receivable	Quick Assets	Acid Test Ratio
6. Super-Saver, Inc.	$39,350	$95,000	$52,770	$187,120	1.42:1
7. Impact Builders, Inc.	$12,320	$30,000	$53,600	_____	_____
8. Thunderbird Electronics, Inc.	$2,690	0	$4,330	_____	_____
9. Forget-Me-Not Flowers	$1,180	0	$985	_____	_____
10. Shutterbug Cameras	$24,400	$140,000	$750,300	_____	_____

11. Calculate the average collection period for Super-Saver, Inc. from Exercise 6 assuming that the credit sales for the year amounted to $770,442.

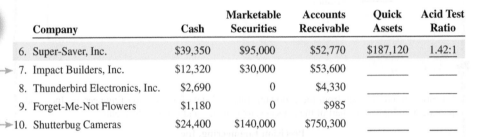

$$\text{Average collection period} = \frac{\text{Accounts receivable} \times 365}{\text{Credit sales}}$$

$$\text{Average collection period} = \frac{52,770 \times 365}{770,442} = \frac{19,261,050}{770,442} = \underline{\underline{25 \text{ Days}}}$$

12. Calculate the average collection period for Impact Builders, Inc. from Exercise 7 assuming that the credit sales for the year amounted to $445,000.

13. a. Calculate the average collection period for Shutterbug Cameras from Exercise 10 assuming that the credit sales for the year amounted to $8,550,000.

    b. Assuming that the industry average for similar firms is 48 days, evaluate the company's ratio.

Calculate the average inventory and inventory turnover ratio for the following companies.

Company	Beginning Inventory	Ending Inventory	Average Inventory	Cost of Goods Sold	Inventory Turnover
14. High-Line Jewelers	$1,547,800	$1,366,000	$1,456,900	$6,500,000	4.5
15. Summit Gas	$90,125	$58,770	_____	$487,640	_____
16. Skyline Gifts	$856,430	$944,380	_____	$3,437,500	_____
17. Certified Fabrics	$121,400	$89,900	_____	$659,000	_____
18. Prestige Hardware	$313,240	$300,050	_____	$4,356,470	_____

19. The Organic Market had net sales of $650,000 last year. If the total assets of the company are $2,450,000, what is the asset turnover ratio?

$$\text{Asset turnover ratio} = \frac{\text{Net sales}}{\text{Total assets}} = \frac{650,000}{2,450,000} = .27 = \underline{\underline{.27:1}}$$

20. Heads or Tails Coin Shop had net sales of $1,354,600 last year. If the total assets of the company are $2,329,500, what is the asset turnover ratio?

Calculate the amount of owner's equity and the two leverage ratios for the following companies.

Company	Total Assets	Total Liabilities	Owner's Equity	Debt-to-Assets Ratio	Debt-to-Equity Ratio
21. Royal Rugs	$1,400.000	$535,000	$865,000	.38:1	.62:1
22. Gateway Imports	$232,430	$115,320	_____	_____	_____
23. Reader's Choice Books	$512,900	$357,510	_____	_____	_____
24. Café Europa	$2,875,000	$2,189,100	_____	_____	_____

Calculate the gross and net profits and the two profit margins for the following companies.

Company	Net Sales	Cost of Goods Sold	Gross Profit	Operating Expenses	Net Profit	Gross Profit Margin (%)	Net Profit Margin (%)
25. Plant World	$640,000	$414,000	$226,000	$112,600	$113,400	35.3	17.7
26. Timberline Marble	$743,500	$489,560	_____	$175,410	_____	_____	_____
27. Sundance Plumbing	$324,100	$174,690	_____	$99,200	_____	_____	_____
28. Dynamic Optical	$316,735	$203,655	_____	$85,921	_____	_____	_____

Using the owner's equity information below, calculate the return on investment for the companies in Exercises 25–28.

	Owner's Equity	Return on Investment (%)
29. Plant World	$525,000	21.6
30. Timberline Marble	$434,210	_____
31. Sundance Plumbing	$615,400	_____
32. Dynamic Optical	$397,000	_____

33. Prepare a trend analysis from the following financial data for Hook, Line, and Sinker Fishing Supply.

Hook, Line, and Sinker Fishing Supply
5-Year Selected Financial Data

	2015	2014	2013	2012	2011
Net Sales	$238,339	$282,283	$239,448	$215,430	$221,800
Net Income	68,770	71,125	55,010	57,680	55,343
Total Assets	513,220	502,126	491,100	457,050	467,720
Stockholders' Equity	254,769	289,560	256,070	227,390	240,600

Hook, Line, and Sinker Fishing Supply
Trend Analysis (in percentages)

	2015	2014	2013	2012	2011
Net Sales	_____	_____	_____	_____	_____
Net Income	_____	_____	_____	_____	_____
Total Assets	_____	_____	_____	_____	_____
Stockholders' Equity	_____	_____	_____	_____	_____

BUSINESS DECISION: FINANCIAL RATIOS

The years 2005 to 2009 were a period of rapid growth for Starbucks and the company's revenues grew by more than 50% during that period. Use the financial data for Starbucks on the following page for Exercises 34a–34e.

34. a. Calculate the asset turnover ratio for 2008 and 2009.

b. Calculate the net profit margin for 2007, 2008, and 2009.

Starbucks is the world's #1 specialty coffee retailer. Its story began in 1971 when it was a roaster and retailer of whole bean and ground coffee, tea, and spices with a single store in Seattle's Pike Place Market. Starbucks Corporation was founded in 1985, and it remains based in Seattle, Washington.

Starbucks engages in the purchase, roasting, and sale of whole bean coffees worldwide. It offers brewed coffees, Italian-style espresso beverages, cold blended beverages, various complementary food items, and a selection of premium teas, as well as beverage-related accessories and equipment through its retail stores. In addition, it produces ready-to-drink beverages and ice cream for sale in retail stores.

In 2000, net revenues were $2.2 million ($2,169,218). Just 10 years later, in 2010, net revenues were $10.7 billion. Of this, beverage sales accounted for 75% of net revenues, food accounted for 19%, whole bean and soluble coffees accounted for 4%, and coffee-making equipment and other merchandise comprised 2%.

c. Calculate the return on investment for 2007, 2008, and 2009.

d. Prepare a trend analysis of the net revenue and total assets for 2005 through 2009.

e. Extra credit: Prepare a trend analysis multiple-line chart for the information in part d.

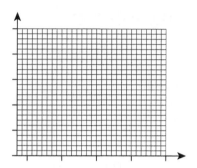

Starbucks—Selected Financial Data
(In millions, except earnings per share)

As of and for the fiscal year ended	Sept. 27, 2009 (52 wks)	Sept. 28, 2008 (52 wks)	Sept. 30, 2007 (52 wks)	Oct. 1, 2006 (52 wks)	Oct. 2, 2005 (52 wks)
Results of Operations					
Net revenues:					
Company-operated retail	$8,180.1	$ 8,771.9	$7,998.3	$6,583.1	$5,391.9
Specialty:					
Licensing	1,222.3	1,171.6	1,026.3	860.6	673.0
Food service and other	372.2	439.5	386.9	343.2	304.4
Total specialty	1,594.5	1,611.1	1,413.2	1,203.8	977.4
Total net revenues	$9,774.6	$10,383.0	$9,411.5	$7,786.9	$6,369.3
Operating income	$562.0	$ 503.9	$1,053.9	$ 894.0	$ 780.5
Earnings before cumulative effect of change in accounting principle	390.8	315.5	672.6	581.5	494.4
Cumulative effect of accounting change for asset retirement obligations, net of taxes	—	—	—	17.2	—
Net earnings	$ 390.8	$ 315.5	$ 672.6	$ 564.3	$ 494.4
Earnings per common share before cumulative effect of change in accounting principle—diluted ("EPS")	$ 0.52	$ 0.43	$ 0.87	$ 0.73	$ 0.61
Cumulative effect of accounting change for asset retirement obligations, net of taxes—per common share	—	—	—	0.02	—
EPS—diluted	$ 0.52	$ 0.43	$ 0.87	$ 0.71	$ 0.61
Net cash provided by operating activities	$1,389.0	$ 1,258.7	$1,331.2	$1,131.6	$ 922.9
Capital expenditures (additions to property, plant, and equipment)	$ 445.6	$ 984.5	$1,080.3	$ 771.2	$ 643.3
Balance Sheet					
Total assets	$5,576.8	$ 5,672.6	$5,343.9	$4,428.9	$3,513.7
Short-term borrowings	—	713.0	710.3	700.0	277.0
Long-term debt (including current portion)	549.5	550.3	550.9	2.7	3.6
Shareholders' equity	$3,045.7	$ 2,490.9	$2,284.1	$2,228.5	$2,090.3

**CHAPTER
15**

CHAPTER FORMULAS

Liquidity Ratios

Working capital = Current assets − Current liabilities

$$\text{Current ratio} = \frac{\text{Current assets}}{\text{Current liabilities}}$$

Quick assets = Cash + Marketable securities + Receivables

$$\text{Acid test ratio} = \frac{\text{Quick assets}}{\text{Current liabilities}}$$

Efficiency Ratios

$$\text{Average collection period} = \frac{\text{Accounts receivable} \times 365}{\text{Credit sales}}$$

$$\text{Average inventory} = \frac{\text{Beginning inventory} + \text{Ending inventory}}{2}$$

$$\text{Inventory turnover} = \frac{\text{Cost of goods sold}}{\text{Average inventory}} \qquad \text{Asset turnover ratio} = \frac{\text{Net sales}}{\text{Total assets}}$$

Leverage Ratios

$$\text{Debt-to-assets ratio} = \frac{\text{Total liabilities}}{\text{Total assets}} \qquad \text{Debt-to-equity ratio} = \frac{\text{Total liabilities}}{\text{Owner's equity}}$$

Profitability Ratios

$$\text{Gross profit margin} = \frac{\text{Gross profit}}{\text{Net sales}} \qquad \text{Net profit margin} = \frac{\text{Net income}}{\text{Net sales}}$$

$$\text{Return on investment} = \frac{\text{Net income}}{\text{Owner's equity}}$$

CHAPTER SUMMARY

Section I: The Balance Sheet

Topic	Important Concepts	Illustrative Examples
Preparing a Balance Sheet **Performance Objective 15-1, Page 485**	The balance sheet is a financial statement that shows a company's financial position on a certain date. It is based on the fundamental accounting equation: Assets = Liabilities + Owner's equity *Balance sheet preparation:* 1. *List and total:* 　　　Current assets 　+ Property, plant, and equipment 　+ Investments and other assets 　　　Total assets 2. *List and total:* 　　　Current liabilities 　+ Long-term liabilities 　　　Total liabilities 3. *List and total:* 　　　Owner's equity 4. Add the Total liabilities and the Owner's equity. This total should equal the Total assets.	*International Industries, Inc.* Balance Sheet December 31, 2015 Assets Cash ... $ 24,000 Receivables ... 92,000 Inventory ... 68,500 Supplies ... 12,100 　Total current assets ... $196,600 Land and building ... $546,700 Fixtures & equipment ... 88,400 Vehicles ... 124,200 　Total property & equipment ... $759,300 　　Total assets ... $955,900 Liabilities & Owner's Equity Accounts payable ... $ 82,400 Note payable (3-month) ... 31,300 　Total current liabilities ... $113,700 Mortgage payable ... $213,400 Note payable (2-year) ... 65,800 　Total long-term liabilities ... $279,200 Total liabilities ... $392,900 Owner's equity ... 563,000 　Total liabilities & 　　owner's equity ... $955,900

Section I (continued)

Topic	Important Concepts	Illustrative Examples
Preparing a Vertical Analysis of a Balance Sheet **Performance Objective 15-2, Page 488**	In vertical analysis, each item on the balance sheet is expressed as a percent of total assets. *Vertical analysis preparation:* 1. Use the percentage formula, $$\text{Rate} = \text{Portion} \div \text{Base}$$ Use each balance sheet item as the portion and total assets as the base. 2. Round each answer to the nearest tenth of a percent. *Note*: A 0.1% differential may occur due to rounding.	International Industries, Inc. Balance Sheet—Asset Section December 31, 2015 <table><tr><td>Cash</td><td>$ 24,000</td><td>2.5%</td></tr><tr><td>Receivables</td><td>92,000</td><td>9.6</td></tr><tr><td>Inventory</td><td>68,500</td><td>7.2</td></tr><tr><td>Supplies</td><td>12,100</td><td>1.3</td></tr><tr><td>Current assets</td><td>$196,600</td><td>20.6</td></tr><tr><td>Land & building</td><td>$546,700</td><td>57.2</td></tr><tr><td>Fixtures & equipment</td><td>88,400</td><td>9.2</td></tr><tr><td>Vehicles</td><td>124,200</td><td>13.0</td></tr><tr><td>Property & equipment</td><td>$759,300</td><td>79.4</td></tr><tr><td>Total assets</td><td>$955,900</td><td>100.0%</td></tr></table>
Preparing a Horizontal Analysis of a Balance Sheet **Performance Objective 15-3, Page 490**	Comparative balance sheets display data from the current period side by side with the figures from one or more previous periods. In horizontal analysis, each item of the current period is compared in dollars and percent with the corresponding item from the previous period. *Horizontal analysis preparation:* 1. Set up a comparative balance sheet format with the current period listed first. 2. Label the next two columns: **Increase (Decrease)** **Amount Percent** 3. For each item, calculate the dollar difference between the current and previous period and enter this figure in the Amount column. Enter all decreases in parentheses. 4. Calculate the percent change using $$\frac{\text{Percent}}{\text{change}} = \frac{\text{Amount of change (portion)}}{\text{Previous period amount (base)}}$$ 5. Enter the percent change in the Percent column. Round to the nearest tenth of a percent. Enter all decreases in parentheses.	If the 2014 cash figure for International Industries, Inc. was $21,300, the comparative balance sheet horizontal analysis would be listed as follows: Cash |		Increase (Decrease)	
2015	2014	Amount	Percent
$24,000	$21,300	$2,700	12.7	 $$\frac{2,700}{21,300} = 12.7\%$$ For a comprehensive example of a comparative balance sheet with horizontal analysis, see pages 491–492, Supreme Construction Company.

Section II: The Income Statement

Topic	Important Concepts	Illustrative Examples

Preparing an Income Statement
 	
Performance Objective 15-4, Page 496
	An income statement is a summary of the operations of a business over a period of time. It is based on the equation
	
	$$\text{Profit} = \text{Revenue} - \text{Total expenses}$$
	
	Income Statement preparation:
	
	1. Label the top of the statement with the company name and period of time covered.
	2. In a two-column format, calculate
	
	  a. *Net sales*
	
	    Gross sales
	    − Sales returns & allowances
	    − Sales discounts
	    Net sales
		International Industries, Inc.
		Income Statement
		Year Ended December 31, 2015
		(in thousands)
		
		<table><tr><td>Gross sales</td><td>$435.3</td><td></td></tr><tr><td>Sales returns</td><td>11.1</td><td></td></tr><tr><td>Sales discounts</td><td>8.0</td><td></td></tr><tr><td>Net sales</td><td></td><td>$416.2</td></tr><tr><td>Inventory, Jan. 1</td><td>124.2</td><td></td></tr><tr><td>Net purchases</td><td>165.8</td><td></td></tr><tr><td>Freight in</td><td>2.7</td><td></td></tr><tr><td>Goods available</td><td>292.7</td><td></td></tr><tr><td>Inventory, Dec. 31</td><td>118.1</td><td></td></tr><tr><td>Cost of goods sold</td><td></td><td>174.6</td></tr><tr><td>Gross margin</td><td></td><td>241.6</td></tr><tr><td>Salaries</td><td>87.6</td><td></td></tr><tr><td>Rent & utilities</td><td>22.5</td><td></td></tr><tr><td>Other expenses</td><td>101.7</td><td></td></tr><tr><td>Total operating expenses</td><td></td><td>211.8</td></tr><tr><td>Net income</td><td></td><td>$ 29.8</td></tr></table>

Section II (continued)

Topic	Important Concepts	Illustrative Examples

	b. *Cost of goods sold*
	
	Beginning inventory
	+ Net purchases
	+ Freight in
	   Goods available for sale
	− Ending inventory
	   Cost of goods sold
	
	c. *Gross margin*
	
	Net sales
	− Cost of goods sold
	   Gross margin
	
	d. *Net income*
	
	Gross margin
	− Total operating expenses
	   Net income	

Topic	Important Concepts	Illustrative Examples

Preparing a Vertical Analysis of an Income Statement
 	
Performance Objective 15-5, Page 499
	In vertical analysis of an income statement, each figure is expressed as a percent of net sales.
	
	Vertical analysis preparation:
	
	1. Use the percentage formula,
	
	    Rate = Portion ÷ Base
	
	   Use each income statement item as the portion and net sales as the base.
	2. Round each answer to the nearest tenth of a percent.
	
	   Note: A 0.1% differential may occur due to rounding.
		International Industries, Inc.
		Income Statement—2015
		(in thousands)

Gross sales	$435.3	104.6%
Sales returns	11.1	2.7
Sales discounts	8.0	1.9
Net sales	416.2	100.0
Inventory, Jan. 1	124.2	29.8
Net purchases	165.8	39.8
Freight in	2.7	.6
Goods available for sale	292.7	70.3
Inventory, Dec. 31	118.1	28.4
Cost of goods sold	174.6	42.0
Gross margin	241.6	58.0
Salaries	87.6	21.0
Rent & utilities	22.5	5.4
Other expenses	101.7	24.4
Total operating expenses	211.8	50.9
Net income	$ 29.8	7.2%

Topic	Important Concepts	Illustrative Examples

Preparing a Horizontal Analysis of an Income Statement
 	
Performance Objective 15-6, Page 501
	In horizontal analysis of a comparative income statement, each item of the current period is compared in dollars and percent with the corresponding item from the previous period.
	
	Horizontal analysis preparation:
	
	1. Set up a comparative income statement format with the current period listed first.
	2. Label the next two columns:
	
	    Increase (Decrease)
	    Amount Percent
	
	3. For each item, calculate the dollar difference between the current and previous period and enter this figure in the Amount column. Enter all decreases in parentheses.
	4. Calculate the percent change by using
	
	$$\text{Percent change (rate)} = \frac{\text{Amount of change (portion)}}{\text{Previous period amount (base)}}$$
	
	5. Enter the percent change in the Percent column. Round to the nearest tenth of a percent. Enter all decreases in parentheses.
		If the 2014 net income figure for International Industries, Inc. was $23,100, the comparative income statement horizontal analysis would be listed as follows:
		
		Net Income

		Increase (Decrease)	
2015	**2014**	**Amount**	**Percent**
$29,800	$23,100	$6,700	29.0

$$\frac{6,700}{23,100} = 29.0\%$$

For a comprehensive example of a comparative income statement with horizontal analysis, see pages 501–502, Foremost Furniture, Inc.

Section III: Financial Ratios and Trend Analysis

Topic	Important Concepts	Illustrative Examples
Calculating Financial Ratios **Performance Objective 15-7, Page 506**	Financial ratios are standardized comparisons of various items from the balance sheet and the income statement. When compared with ratios of previous operating periods and industry averages, they can be used as signals to analysts of potential strengths or weaknesses of the firm.	A company had net sales of $100,000 and net income of $10,000. Express these data as a ratio. $$\frac{100,000}{10,000} = 10$$ 1. The ratio of sales to income is 10 to 1, written 10:1. 2. Net income is $\frac{1}{10}$, or 10%, of net sales. 3. For every $1.00 of net sales, the company generates $0.10 in net income.
Liquidity Ratios **Performance Objective 15-7, Page 507**	Liquidity ratios examine the relationship between a firm's current assets and its maturing obligation. They are a good indicator of a firm's ability to pay its bills over the next few months. $$\text{Current ratio} = \frac{\text{Current assets}}{\text{Current liabilities}}$$ $$\text{Acid test ratio} \times \frac{\text{Cash} + \text{Marketable securities} + \text{Accounts receivable}}{\text{Current liabilities}}$$	International Industries, Inc. Financial Ratios 2015 $$\text{Current ratio} = \frac{196,600}{113,700} = 1.73 = 1.73{:}1$$ $$\text{Acid test ratio} = \frac{24,000 + 92,000}{113,700} = 1.02 = 1.02{:}1$$
Efficiency Ratios **Performance Objective 15-7, Page 507**	Efficiency ratios provide the basis for determining how effectively a firm uses its resources to generate sales. $$\text{Average collection period} = \frac{\text{Accounts receivable} \times 365}{\text{Credit sales}}$$ $$\text{Inventory turnover} = \frac{\text{Cost of goods sold}}{(\text{Beg inventory} + \text{End inventory})/2}$$ $$\text{Asset turnover ratio} = \frac{\text{Net sales}}{\text{Total assets}}$$	Credit sales for International Industries, Inc. are 50% of net sales. Average collection period = $$\frac{92,000 \times 365}{208,100} = 161 \text{ Days}$$ Inventory turnover = $$\frac{174,000}{(124,200 + 118,100)/2} = 1.44 \text{ Times}$$ $$\text{Asset turnover ratio} = \frac{416,200}{955,900} = .44 = .44{:}1$$
Leverage Ratios **Performance Objective 15-7, Page 508**	Leverage ratios provide information about the amount of money a company has borrowed to finance its assets. $$\text{Debt-to-assets ratio} = \frac{\text{Total liabilities}}{\text{Total assets}}$$ $$\text{Debt-to-equity ratio} = \frac{\text{Total liabilities}}{\text{Owner's equity}}$$	$$\text{Debt-to-assets ratio} = \frac{392,900}{955,900} = .411 = 41.1\%$$ $$\text{Debt-to-equity ratio} = \frac{392,900}{563,000} = .698 = 69.8\%$$
Profitability Ratios **Performance Objective 15-7, Page 509**	Profitability ratios show a firm's ability to generate profits and provide its investors with a return on their investment. $$\text{Gross profit margin} = \frac{\text{Gross profit}}{\text{Net sales}}$$ $$\text{Net profit margin} = \frac{\text{Net income}}{\text{Net sales}}$$ $$\text{Return on investment} = \frac{\text{Net income}}{\text{Owner's equity}}$$	$$\text{Gross profit margin} = \frac{241,600}{416,200} = .580 = 58.0\%$$ $$\text{Net profit margin} = \frac{29,800}{416,200} = .072 = 7.2\%$$ $$\text{Return on investment} = \frac{29,800}{563,000} = .053 = 5.3\%$$
Preparing a Trend Analysis of Financial Data **Performance Objective 15-8, Page 510**	Trend analysis is the process of tracking changes in financial statement items for three or more operating periods. Trend analysis figures can be displayed on a chart using index numbers or more visually as a line graph or bar chart.	Prepare a trend analysis for International Industries, Inc. net sales data. *International Industries, Inc.* Net Sales (in thousands) | 2015 | 2014 | 2013 | 2012 | 2011 | | 416.2 | 401.6 | 365.4 | 388.3 | 375.1 |

Section III (continued)

Topic	Important Concepts	Illustrative Examples
	Trend analysis preparation: 1. Choose a base year (usually the earliest year) and let it equal 100%. 2. Calculate the index number for each succeeding year by using $$\text{Index number (rate)} = \frac{\text{Yearly amount (portion)}}{\text{Base year amount (base)}}$$ 3. Round each index number to the nearest tenth of a percent. 4. *Optional:* Graph the index numbers or the raw data on a line chart.	For this trend analysis, we will use 2011 as the base year, 100%. Each subsequent year's index number is calculated by using the yearly amount as the portion and the 2011 amount as the base. For example, 2012 index number = $$\frac{388.3}{375.1} = 103.5\%$$ <table><tr><td>2015</td><td>2014</td><td>2013</td><td>2012</td><td>2011</td></tr><tr><td>111.0</td><td>107.1</td><td>97.4</td><td>103.5</td><td>100.0</td></tr></table>

International Industries, Inc. Trend Analysis — line chart of Index Number (95.0 to 120.0) vs Years (2011–2015): 2011 = 100.0, 2012 = 103.5, 2013 = 97.5, 2014 = 107.5, 2015 = 111.0.

TRY IT: EXERCISE SOLUTIONS FOR CHAPTER 15

1.

Keystone Auto Repair
Balance Sheet
December 31, 2016

Assets

Current Assets

Cash	$5,200	
Accounts Receivable	2,800	
Merchandise Inventory	2,700	
Prepaid Salary	235	
Supplies	3,900	
Total Current Assets		$ 14,835

Property, Plant, and Equipment

Land	35,000	
Building	74,000	
Fixtures	1,200	
Tow Truck	33,600	
Tools and Equipment	45,000	
Total Property, Plant, and Equipment		188,800
Total Assets		$203,635

Liabilities and Owner's Equity

Current Liabilities

Accounts Payable	$ 6,800	
Notes Payable	17,600	
Taxes Payable	3,540	
Total Current Liabilities		$ 27,940

Long-Term Liabilities

Mortgage Payable	51,000	
Total Long-Term Liabilities		51,000
Total Liabilities		78,940

Owner's Equity

Blake Williams, Capital	124,695	
Total Owner's Equity		124,695
Total Liabilities and Owner's Equity		$203,635

2.

Royal Equipment Supply, Inc.
Balance Sheet
June 30, 2016

Assets

Current Assets

Cash	$ 3,400	1.1%
Accounts Receivable	5,600	1.8
Merchandise Inventory	98,700	32.0
Prepaid Insurance	455	.1
Supplies	800	.3
Total Current Assets	108,955	35.3

Property, Plant, and Equipment

Land and Building	147,000	47.6
Fixtures	8,600	2.8
Delivery Vehicles	27,000	8.8
Forklift	7,000	2.3
Total Property, Plant, and Equipment	189,600	61.4

Investments and Other Assets

Goodwill	10,000	3.2
Total Investments and Other Assets	10,000	3.2
Total Assets	$308,555	100.0%

Liabilities and Stockholders' Equity

Current Liabilities

Accounts Payable	$ 16,500	5.3%
Notes Payable	10,000	3.2
Total Current Liabilities	26,500	8.6

Long-Term Liabilities

Mortgage Payable	67,000	21.7
Total Long-Term Liabilities	67,000	21.7
Total Liabilities	93,500	30.3

Stockholders' Equity

Common Stock	185,055	60.0
Retained Earnings	30,000	9.7
Total Stockholders' Equity	215,055	69.7
Total Liabilities and Stockholders' Equity	$308,555	100.0%

3.

Calypso Industries, Inc.
Comparative Balance Sheet
December 31, 2015 and 2016

Assets	2016	2015	Increase (Decrease) Amount	Increase (Decrease) Percent
Current Assets				
Cash	$ 8,700	$ 5,430	$ 3,270	60.2%
Accounts Receivable	23,110	18,450	4,660	25.3
Notes Receivable	2,900	3,400	(500)	(14.7)
Supplies	4,540	3,980	560	14.1
Total Current Assets	39,250	31,260	7,990	25.6
Property, Plant, and Equipment				
Land	34,000	34,000	0	0
Buildings	76,300	79,800	(3,500)	(4.4)
Machinery and Equipment	54,700	48,900	5,800	11.9
Total Prop., Plant, and Equipment	165,000	162,700	2,300	1.4
Investments and Other Assets	54,230	49,810	4,420	8.9
Total Assets	$258,480	$243,770	$14,710	6.0%

Liabilities and Stockholders' Equity	2016	2015	Increase (Decrease) Amount	Percent
Current Liabilities				
Accounts Payable	$ 15,330	$ 19,650	($4,320)	(22.0%)
Salaries Payable	7,680	7,190	490	6.8
Total Current Liabilities	23,010	26,840	(3,830)	(14.3)
Long-Term Liabilities				
Mortgage Payable	53,010	54,200	(1,190)	(2.2)
Note Payable (3-year)	32,400	33,560	(1,160)	(3.5)
Total Long-Term Liabilities	85,410	87,760	(2,350)	(2.7)
Total Liabilities	108,420	114,600	(6,180)	(5.4)
Stockholders' Equity				
Common Stock	130,060	120,170	9,890	8.2
Retained Earnings	20,000	9,000	11,000	122.2
Total Liabilities and Stockholders' Equity	$258,480	$243,770	$14,710	6.0%

4.

Cutting Edge Manufacturing, Inc.
Income Statement
December 31, 2016

Revenue		
Gross Sales	$1,356,000	
Less: Sales Returns and Allowances	93,100	
Sales Discounts	4,268	
Net Sales		$1,258,632
Cost of Goods Sold		
Merchandise Inventory, Jan. 1	324,800	
Net Purchases	255,320	
Freight In	3,911	
Goods Available for Sale	584,031	
Less: Merchandise Inventory, Dec. 31	179,100	
Cost of Goods Sold		404,931
Gross Margin		853,701
Operating Expenses		
Salaries	375,900	
Rent	166,000	
Utilities	7,730	
Advertising	73,300	
Insurance	22,940	
Administrative Expenses	84,500	
Miscellaneous Expenses	24,900	
Total Operating Expenses		755,270
Income before Taxes		98,431
Income Tax		34,760
Net Income		$ 63,671

5.

Royal Equipment Supply, Inc.
Income Statement
December 31, 2016

Revenue		
Gross Sales	$458,400	103.3%
Less: Sales Returns and Allowances	13,200	3.0
Sales Discounts	1,244	.3
Net Sales	$443,956	100.0%
Cost of Goods Sold		
Merchandise Inventory, Jan. 1	198,700	44.8
Net Purchases	86,760	19.5
Freight In	875	.2
Goods Available for Sale	286,335	64.5
Less: Merchandise Inventory, Dec. 31	76,400	17.2
Cost of Goods Sold	209,935	47.3
Gross Margin	234,021	52.7
Operating Expenses		
Salaries	124,200	28.0
Rent	21,000	4.7
Utilities	1,780	.4
Advertising	5,400	1.2
Insurance	2,340	.5
Administrative Expenses	14,500	3.3
Miscellaneous Expenses	6,000	1.4
Total Operating Expenses	175,220	39.5
Income before Taxes	58,801	13.2
Income Tax	17,335	3.9
Net Income	$ 41,466	9.3%

6.

Timely Watch Company, Inc.
Comparative Income Statement
For the Years Ended December 31, 2015 and 2016

	2016	2015	Increase (Decrease) Amount	Percent
Revenue				
Gross Sales	$1,223,000	$996,500	$226,500	22.7%
Less: Sales Returns and Allowances	121,340	99,600	21,740	21.8
Sales Discounts	63,120	51,237	11,883	23.2
Net Sales	1,038,540	845,663	192,877	22.8
Cost of Goods Sold				
Merchandise Inventory, Jan. 1	311,200	331,000	(19,800)	(6.0)
Purchases	603,290	271,128	332,162	122.5
Freight In	18,640	13,400	5,240	39.1
Goods Available for Sale	933,130	615,528	317,602	51.6
Less: Merchandise Inventory, Dec. 31	585,400	311,200	274,200	88.1
Cost of Goods Sold	347,730	304,328	43,402	14.3
Gross Margin	690,810	541,335	149,475	27.6

Operating Expenses

Salaries and Benefits	215,200	121,800	93,400	76.7
Rent and Utilities	124,650	124,650	0	0
Depreciation	43,500	41,230	2,270	5.5
Insurance	24,970	23,800	1,170	4.9
Administrative Store Expenses	58,200	33,900	24,300	71.7
Warehouse Expenses	42,380	45,450	(3,070)	(6.8)
Total Operating Expenses	508,900	390,830	118,070	30.2
Income before Taxes	181,910	150,505	31,405	20.9
Income Tax	66,280	41,670	24,610	59.1
Net Income	$115,630	$108,835	$ 6,795	6.2%

7. *Royal Equipment Supply—Financial Ratios 2011*

Working capital = Current assets − Current liabilities = 108,955 − 26,500 = $82,455

$$\text{Current ratio} = \frac{\text{Current assets}}{\text{Current liabilities}} = \frac{108,955}{26,500} = 4.11:1$$

$$\text{Acid test ratio} = \frac{\text{Cash + Marketable securities + Receivables}}{\text{Current liabilities}} = \frac{3,400 + 5,600}{26,500} = .34:1$$

$$\text{Average collection period} = \frac{\text{Accounts receivable} \times 365}{\text{Net sales}} = \frac{5,600 \times 365}{443,956} = 4.6 \text{ days}$$

$$\text{Average inventory} = \frac{\text{Beginning inventory + Ending inventory}}{2} = \frac{198,700 + 76,400}{2} = \$137,550$$

$$\text{Inventory turnover} = \frac{\text{Cost of goods sold}}{\text{Average inventory}} = \frac{209,935}{137,550} = 1.5 \text{ times}$$

$$\text{Asset turnover ratio} = \frac{\text{Net sales}}{\text{Total assets}} = \frac{443,956}{308,555} = 1.44:1$$

$$\text{Debt-to-assets ratio} = \frac{\text{Total liabilities}}{\text{Total assets}} = \frac{93,500}{308,555} = .303 = 30.3\%$$

$$\text{Debt-to-equity ratio} = \frac{\text{Total liabilities}}{\text{Owner's equity}} = \frac{93,500}{215,055} = .435 = 43.5\%$$

$$\text{Gross profit margin} = \frac{\text{Gross profit}}{\text{Net sales}} = \frac{234,021}{443,956} = .527 = 52.7\%$$

$$\text{Net profit margin} = \frac{\text{Net income}}{\text{Net sales}} = \frac{41,446}{443,956} = .093 = 9.3\%$$

$$\text{Return on investment} = \frac{\text{Net income}}{\text{Owner's equity}} = \frac{41,466}{215,055} = .193 = 19.3\%$$

8.

Precision Engineering, Inc.
Trend Analysis (in percentages)

	2015	2014	2013	2012	2011
Net Sales	114.3	123.7	111.6	98.2	100.0
Total Assets	105.9	116.7	105.0	101.5	100.0
Stockholders' Equity	111.6	116.1	103.5	90.1	100.0

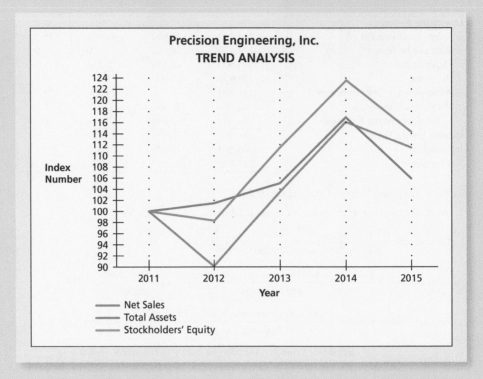

CONCEPT REVIEW

1. In accounting, economic resources owned by a company are known as _____, whereas debts or obligations of a company are known as _____. (15-1)

2. The financial statement that illustrates the financial position of a company in terms of assets, liabilities, and owner's equity as of a certain date is known as a(n) _____ sheet. (15-1)

3. The balance sheet is a visual presentation of the all-important "accounting equation." Write this equation. (15-1)

4. In vertical analysis of a balance sheet, each figure on the statement is expressed as a percent of _____ _____. (15-2)

5. A financial statement prepared with the data from the current operating period side by side with the figures from one or more previous periods is known as a(n) _____ statement. (15-3, 15-6)

6. Horizontal analysis is a method of analyzing financial statements whereby each item of the current period is compared in _____ and _____ with the corresponding item from a previous period. (15-3, 15-6)

7. A financial statement summarizing the operations of a business over a period of time is known as an income statement, an operating statement, or a(n) _____ and _____ statement. (15-4)

8. Write the formula that illustrates the structure of an income statement. (15-4)

9. In vertical analysis of an income statement, each figure on the statement is expressed as a percent of _____ _____. (15-5)

10. Name the four major categories of financial ratios. (15-7)

11. Write the formulas for the current ratio and inventory turnover. (15-7)

12. Write the formulas for the debt-to-assets ratio and return on investment. (15-7)

13. The use of index numbers to track percentage changes of a company's financial data over successive operating periods is known as _____ analysis. (15-8)

14. With index numbers, a base period is chosen and is equal to _____ percent. (15-8)

ASSESSMENT TEST

CHAPTER 15

Prepare the following statements on separate sheets of paper.

Calculate the missing balance sheet items for Exercise 1, Hershey Co. and Exercise 2, Lowe's, Inc. Complete each company's column; then move on to the next column.

THE BALANCE SHEET (in millions)		
	Exercise 1	Exercise 2
Company Date	Hershey Co. December 31, 2013	Lowe's, Inc. January 31, 2014
Current Assets	$2,487	$10,296
Fixed Assets	2,870	_____
Total Assets	_____	32,732
Current Liabilities	1,408	8,876
Long-Term Liabilities	2,345	_____
Total Liabilities	_____	20,879
Stockholders' Equity	_____	_____

Calculate the missing income statement items for Exercise 3, Target, and Exercise 4, Advance Auto Parts. Complete each company's column; then move on to the next column.

THE INCOME STATEMENT (in millions)		
	Exercise 3	Exercise 4
Company Year Ended	Target December 31, 2013	Advance Auto Parts December 31, 2013
Revenue	$72,596	_____
Cost of Goods Sold	51,160	3,242
Gross Margin	_____	3,252
Operating Expenses	4,229	_____
Income before Taxes	_____	626
Income Tax*	15,236	_____
Net Income (loss)	_____	392

*Also includes interest expense and other income and losses.

5. **a.** Use the following financial information to calculate the owner's equity and prepare a balance sheet with vertical analysis as of December 31, 2014, for Uniflex Fabricators, Inc., a sole proprietorship owned by Paul Provost: current assets, $132,500; property, plant, and equipment, $88,760; investments and other assets, $32,400; current liabilities, $51,150; and long-term liabilities, $87,490.

Uniflex Fabricators, Inc.
Balance Sheet
As of December 31, 2014

   b. The following financial information is for Uniflex Fabricators, Inc., as of December 31, 2015. Calculate the owner's equity for 2015 and prepare a comparative balance sheet with horizontal analysis for 2014 and 2015: current assets, $154,300; property, plant, and equipment, $124,650; investments and other assets, $20,000; current liabilities, $65,210; and long-term liabilities, $83,800.

EXCEL2

Uniflex Fabricators, Inc.
Comparative Balance Sheet
As of December 31, 2014 and 2015

6. **a.** Use the following financial information to prepare a balance sheet with vertical analysis as of October 31, 2014, for Sticks & Stones Builders Mart: cash, $45,260; accounts receivable, $267,580; merchandise inventory, $213,200; prepaid expenses, $13,400; supplies, $5,300; land, $87,600; building, $237,200; equipment, $85,630; vehicles, $54,700; computers, $31,100; investments, $53,100; accounts payable, $43,200; salaries payable, $16,500; notes payable (6-month), $102,400; mortgage payable, $124,300; notes payable (3-year), $200,000; common stock, $422,000; and retained earnings, $185,670.

Sticks & Stones Builders Mart
Balance Sheet
As of October 31, 2014

b. The following financial information is for Sticks & Stones Builders Mart as of October 31, 2015. Prepare a comparative balance sheet with horizontal analysis for 2014 and 2015: cash, $47,870; accounts receivable, $251,400; merchandise inventory, $223,290; prepaid expenses, $8,500; supplies, $6,430; land, $87,600; building, $234,500; equipment, $88,960; vehicles, $68,800; computers, $33,270; investments, $55,640; accounts payable, $48,700; salaries payable, $9,780; notes payable (6-month), $96,700; mortgage payable, $121,540; notes payable (3-year), $190,000; common stock, $450,000; and retained earnings, $189,540.

Sticks & Stones Builders Mart
Comparative Balance Sheet
As of October 31, 2014 and 2015

7. For the second quarter, Evergreen Plant Nursery had gross sales of $214,300, sales returns and allowances of $26,540, and sales discounts of $1,988. What were Evergreen's net sales?

8. For the month of January, Consolidated Engine Parts, Inc. had the following financial information: merchandise inventory, January 1, $322,000; merchandise inventory, January 31, $316,400; gross purchases, $243,460; purchase returns and allowances, $26,880; and freight in, $3,430.

    a. What are Consolidated's goods available for sale?

    b. What is the cost of goods sold for January?

    c. If net sales were $389,450, what was the gross margin for January?

    d. If total operating expenses were $179,800, what was the net profit or loss?

395

CHAPTER
15

Prepare the following statements on separate sheets of paper.

9. **a.** From the following third-quarter 2015 information for Woof & Meow Pet Supply, construct an income statement with vertical analysis: gross sales, $224,400; sales returns and allowances, $14,300; beginning inventory, July 1, $165,000; ending inventory, September 30, $143,320; net purchases, $76,500; total operating expenses, $68,600; and income tax, $8,790.

Woof & Meow Pet Supply
Income Statement
Third Quarter, 2015

b. The following financial information is for the fourth quarter of 2015 for Woof & Meow Pet Supply. Prepare a comparative income statement with horizontal analysis for the third and fourth quarters: gross sales, $218,200; sales returns and allowances, $9,500; beginning inventory, October 1, $143,320; ending inventory, December 31, $125,300; net purchases, $81,200; total operating expenses, $77,300; and income tax, $11,340.

Woof & Meow Pet Supply
Comparative Income Statement
Third and Fourth Quarters, 2015

10. **a.** Use the following financial information to construct a 2013 income statement with vertical analysis for Jazzline Jewelers: gross sales, $1,243,000; sales returns and allowances, $76,540; sales discounts, $21,300; merchandise inventory, Jan. 1, 2013, $654,410; merchandise inventory, Dec. 31, 2013, $413,200; net purchases, $318,000; freight in, $3,450; salaries, $92,350; rent, $83,100; depreciation, $87,700; utilities, $21,350; advertising, $130,440; insurance, $7,920; miscellaneous expenses, $105,900; and income tax, $18,580.

Jazzline Jewelers
Income Statement
For the Year Ended December 31, 2013

b. The following data represent Jazzline's operating results for 2014. Prepare a comparative income statement with horizontal analysis for 2013 and 2014: gross sales, $1,286,500; sales returns and allowances, $78,950; sales discounts, $18,700; merchandise inventory, Jan. 1, 2014, $687,300; merchandise inventory, Dec. 31, 2014, $401,210; net purchases, $325,400; freight in, $3,980; salaries, $99,340; rent, $85,600; depreciation, $81,200; utilities, $21,340; advertising, $124,390; insurance, $8,700; miscellaneous expenses, $101,230; and income tax, $12,650.

Jazzline Jewelers
Comparative Income Statement
For the Years Ended December 31, 2013 and 2014

As the accounting manager of Spring Creek Plastics, Inc., you have been asked to calculate the following financial ratios for the company's 2015 annual report. Use the balance sheet and the income statement on page 528 for Spring Creek.

11. Working capital:

12. Current ratio:

13. Acid test ratio:

14. Average collection period (credit sales are 60% of net sales):

15. Inventory turnover:

16. Asset turnover ratio:

17. Debt-to-assets ratio:

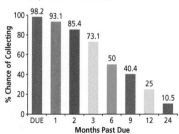

Dollars AND Sense

According to Burt & Associates, one of America's premiere collection agencies, the following chart illustrates the percent chance of collecting accounts receivable from financially distressed companies.

CHAPTER 15

18. Debt-to-equity ratio:

19. Gross profit margin:

20. Net profit margin:

21. Return on investment:

Spring Creek Plastics, Inc.
Balance Sheet
As of December 31, 2015

Assets

Cash	$ 250,000	
Accounts Receivable	325,400	
Merchandise Inventory	416,800	
Marketable Securities	88,700	
Supplies	12,100	
Total Current Assets		$1,093,000
Land and Building	1,147,000	
Fixtures and Equipment	868,200	
Total Property, Plant, and Equipment		2,015,200
Total Assets		$3,108,200

Liabilities and Owner's Equity

Accounts Payable	$ 286,500	
Notes Payable (6-month)	153,200	
Total Current Liabilities		$439,700
Mortgage Payable	325,700	
Notes Payable (4-year)	413,100	
Total Long-Term Liabilities		738,800
Total Liabilities		1,178,500
Owner's Equity		1,929,700
Total Liabilities and Owner's Equity		$3,108,200

Spring Creek Plastics, Inc.
Income Statement, 2015

Net Sales		$1,695,900
Merchandise Inventory, Jan. 1	$ 767,800	
Net Purchases	314,900	
Freight In	33,100	
Goods Available for Sale	1,115,800	
Merchandise Inventory, Dec. 31	239,300	
Cost of Goods Sold		876,500
Gross Margin		819,400
Total Operating Expenses		702,300
Income before Taxes		117,100
Taxes		35,200
Net Income		$ 81,900

22. Prepare a trend analysis from the financial data listed below for Coastal Marine International.

Coastal Marine International
4-Year Selected Financial Data

	2014	2013	2012	2011
Net Sales	$ 898,700	$ 829,100	$ 836,200	$ 801,600
Net Income	96,300	92,100	94,400	89,700
Total Assets	2,334,000	2,311,000	2,148,700	1,998,900
Stockholders' Equity	615,000	586,000	597,200	550,400

Coastal Marine International
Trend Analysis (in percentages)

	2014	2013	2012	2011
Net Sales	____	____	____	____
Net Income	____	____	____	____
Total Assets	____	____	____	____
Stockholders' Equity	____	____	____	____

23. As part of the trend analysis for Coastal Marine International, prepare a multiple-line chart for the annual report comparing net sales and net income for the years 2011 through 2014.

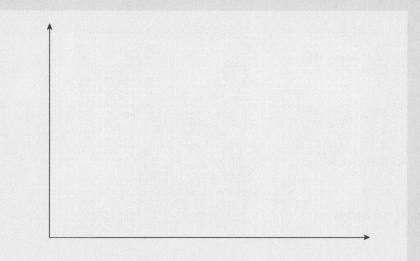

24. From the following consolidated statements of earnings for Netflix, Inc., prepare a vertical analysis in the form of a common-size income statement (percentages only) for 2013.

NETFLIX, INC.
CONSOLIDATED STATEMENTS OF OPERATIONS
(in thousands)

	Twelve Months Ended December 31, 2013
Revenues	$4,374,562
Cost of revenues	3,083,256
Marketing	503,889
Technology and development	378,769
General and administrative	180,301
Operating income	228,347
Other income (expense)	
Interest expense	(29,142)
Interest and other	(3,002)
Loss on extinguishment of debt	(25,129)
Income before income taxes	171,074
Provision for income taxes	58,671
Net income	$ 112,403

Mphillips007/iStockphoto.com

Netflix, Inc. is the world's largest video subscription service, streaming movies, TV episodes, and original content over the Internet and sending DVDs and Blu-ray high-definition discs by mail. The company was founded in 1997 and had its first profitable year in 2003. With the rise of streaming videos, by 2010 Netflix had morphed from being the U.S. Postal Service's most rapidly growing first-class customer to being the biggest source of evening Internet traffic in North America.

CHAPTER 15

Business Decision: Evaluating Financial Performance

25. In 2010 Apple introduced the iPad, and the sales of this device helped boost Apple revenues significantly. From the consolidated statements of income and balance sheets for Apple on the following page, prepare the following financial ratios for 2010 and 2011.

    a. Current ratio

    b. Acid test ratio

    c. Asset turnover ratio

    d. Debt-to-assets ratio

    e. Debt-to-equity ratio

    f. Net profit margin

    g. Return on investment

    h. Based on your calculations of the financial ratios for Apple, for each ratio, determine whether the 2011 figure was better or worse than the ratio for 2010.

    i. How would you rate Apple's financial ratios in 2010 and 2011?

Apple was founded in 1976 with the goal of developing and selling personal computers. It has since expanded to offer the wide range of consumer electronics products used by many people around the world. In 2014, Apple became the first company in the world to reach a valuation (based on stock price times number of shares) of more than $700 billion.

Oleksiy Maksymenko Photography/Alamy

Apple Inc.
CONSOLIDATED BALANCE SHEETS
(In millions, except number of shares which are reflected in thousands)

Assets:	September 24, 2011
Current assets:	
Cash and cash equivalents	$ 9,815
Short-term marketable securities	16,137
Accounts receivable, less allowances of $53 and $55, respectively	5,369
Inventories	776
Deferred tax assets	2,014
Vendor non-trade receivables	6,348
Other current assets	4,529
Total current assets	44,988
Long-term marketable securities	55,618
Property, plant and equipment, net	7,777
Goodwill	896
Acquired intangible assets, net	3,536
Other assets	3,556
Total assets	$ 116,371

Liabilities and Shareholders' Equity:	
Current liabilities:	
Accounts payable	$ 14,632
Accrued expenses	9,247
Deferred revenue	4,091
Total current liabilities	27,970
Deferred revenue—non-current	1,686
Other non-current liabilities	10,100
Total liabilities	39,756
Commitments and contingencies	
Shareholders' equity:	
Common stock, no par value; 1,800,000 shares authorized; 929,277 and 915,970 shares issued and outstanding, respectively	13,331
Retained earnings	62,841
Accumulated other comprehensive income/(loss)	443
Total shareholders' equity	76,615
Total liabilities and shareholders' equity	$ 116,371

CONSOLIDATED STATEMENTS
OF OPERATIONS
(In millions, except number of shares which are reflected in thousands and per share amounts)

Three Years Ended September 24, 2011	2011	2010
Net sales	$ 108,249	$ 65,225
Cost of sales	64,431	39,541
Gross margin	43,818	25,684
Operating expenses:		
Research and development	2,429	1,782
Selling, general and administrative	7,599	5,517
Total operating expenses	10,028	7,299
Operating income	33,790	18,385
Other income and expense	415	155
Income before provision for income taxes	34,205	18,540
Provision for income taxes	8,283	4,527
Net income	$ 25,922	$ 14,013
Earnings per common share:		
Basic	$ 28.05	$ 15.41
Diluted	$ 27.68	$ 15.15
Shares used in computing earnings per share:		
Basic	924,258	909,461
Diluted	936,645	924,712

COLLABORATIVE LEARNING ACTIVITY

1. How Are They Doing Now?

Work as teams to research the latest balance sheet and income statement figures for the following companies for which you calculated figures in the chapter.

- Page 493 – Home Depot, Amazon.com, and Gap
- Page 503 – CVS Caremark, AutoZone, and PetSmart
- Page 525 – Hershey, Lowe's, Target, and Advance Auto Parts.

a. Using your favorite search engine, enter the company name and the words *investor relations* to locate the latest company 10K report filed with the Securities and Exchange Commission (SEC). This document contains the most recent company information, including balance sheet and income statement figures.

b. For each company, compare the balance sheet and income statement figures over the last three years.

c. Report your findings to the class using horizontal analysis and a visual presentation.

d. (optional) For each company, compare the earnings per share and stock price figures over the last three years. Use a trend analysis and line charts for your presentation of this data to the class.

2. Analyzing a Company

As a team, choose an industry you want to research, such as airlines, beverage, computers, entertainment, food, motor vehicles, retail, or wholesale. Then choose three public companies that directly compete in that industry.

Using the Internet, research key business ratios and other available information about that industry. This may be found in the government's publication the *Survey of Current Business* or from private sources such as Moody's Index, Dun & Bradstreet, or Standard & Poors.

Obtain the most recent annual report and quarterly report for each company from its website. This information is usually available under a section entitled "Investor Information." Based on the information your team has accumulated:

a. Calculate the current and previous years' financial ratios for each company.

b. Compare each company's ratios to the industry averages.

c. Evaluate each company's financial condition regarding liquidity, efficiency, leverage, and profitability.

d. If your team were going to invest in only one of these companies, which would you choose? Why?

Business Math JOURNAL

BUSINESS, MATH, AND MORE ...

Identity Theft

What Is It?

According to SpendOnLife.com, identity theft is defined as "the process of using someone else's personal information for your own personal gain."

The Javelin Strategy & Research Center has been studying identity theft closely since 2004. Each year it releases its findings. The 2011 study revealed that:

- Identity theft affected 11.6 million victims, or 4.8% of the U.S. population, in 2011.
- The number of victims in 2011 was 13% more than in 2010.
- The average out-of-pocket cost to resolve the problem was $373 per victim and took an average of 21 hours.
- 13% of identity fraud crimes were committed by someone the victim knew.

Identity Theft Tips for Students

- Don't conduct financial transactions, manage bank accounts, or input personal information using library or shared computers.
- Log off a public computer after using it, whether it is in the school lab or in a shared dorm room or apartment.
- Don't post personal details such as your phone number and address on Facebook or other social networking sites.
- Password-protect your cell phone and laptop. Use a password that is at least six digits long and contains special characters, numbers, and letters. Never use personal information like your birth date or birth year as your password. Change passwords frequently and use a different password for each device.
- Look for a pop-up window that asks if you'd like to save your password when you log in to accounts on the computer. Never check this box, even if you are the only person who uses the computer. That way the password isn't stored.

- Download the latest updates for your antivirus software as soon as they become available. This will help keep your machine virus-free and protect it from the newest versions of malware and spyware.
- Don't trust a new roommate until you know him or her better. At least keep your personally identifiable information secure.
- Consider an identity theft protection service. Many cost only about a quarter per day. An identity protection plan is exponentially better than having no protection.

Source: www.identitytheftlabs.com

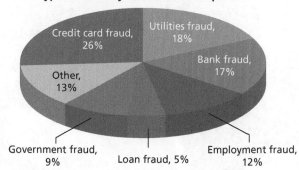

Types of Identity Theft Fraud Complaints

- Credit card fraud, 26%
- Utilities fraud, 18%
- Bank fraud, 17%
- Other, 13%
- Government fraud, 9%
- Loan fraud, 5%
- Employment fraud, 12%

Source: Federal Trade Commission, Consumer Sentinel Network Fraud Complaints, 2009. www.spendonlife.com.

Issues & Activities

1. Use the Javelin Strategy & Research Center statistics in the first column to find the number of identity theft victims in 2011 (rounded to the nearest ten million).
2. Use the chart above and the Javelin statistics to find how many identity theft victims were in the credit card, employment fraud, and government fraud categories in 2011.
3. In teams, research the Internet to find current trends in "identity theft" statistics. List your sources and visually report your findings to the class.

Brainteaser—"I See the Light"

If a digital clock is the only light in an otherwise totally dark room, at what time will the room be the darkest? The brightest?

See the end of Appendix A for the solution.

"Please look them over VERY carefully, Mr. Lamson, and let us know if you see the man who stole your identity."

© John McPherson/Distributed by Universal Uclick via CartoonStock.com 4-22

Inventory

PERFORMANCE OBJECTIVES

INVENTORY VALUATION

As noted on howstuffworks.com, the next time you visit a mega-retailer such as Walmart, you will see one of businesses' greatest logistical triumphs: billion dollar inventory management systems. Retailers such as Target, Lowe's, Home Depot, and Best Buy stock tens of thousands of items from all over the world. Walmart alone stocks items made in more than 70 countries and at any given time manages an average of $32 billion in inventory.

With those kinds of numbers, having an effective and efficient inventory management system is imperative. Walmart's system helps it maintain its signature "everyday low prices" by telling store managers which products are selling and which are simply taking up valuable shelf and warehouse space. Inventory management systems are the rule for such enterprises, but smaller businesses and vendors use them, too. These systems ensure that customers always have enough of what they want and balance that goal against a retailer's financial need to maintain as little inventory as possible.

In business, the term **inventory** is used to describe the goods that a company has in its possession at any given time. For companies engaged in manufacturing activities, inventories are divided into raw materials (used to make other products), partially completed products (work in process), and finished goods (ready for sale to the trade).

Manufacturers sell their finished goods to wholesalers and retailers. These goods, purchased and held expressly for resale, are commonly known as **merchandise inventory**. For wholesalers and retailers, the primary source of revenue is from the sale of this merchandise. In terms of dollars, merchandise inventory is one of the largest and most important assets of a merchandising company. As an expense, the cost of goods sold is the largest deduction from sales in the determination of a company's profit, often larger than the total of operating or overhead expenses.

Interestingly, merchandise inventory is an account that is found on both the balance sheet and the income statement. The method used to determine the value of this inventory has a significant impact on a company's bottom-line results. In addition to appearing on the financial statements, the value of the merchandise inventory must also be determined for income tax purposes and insurance and as a business indicator to management.

To place a value on a merchandise inventory, we must first know the quantity and the cost of the goods remaining at the end of an operating period. Merchandise held for sale must be physically counted at least once a year. Many businesses take inventory on a quarterly or even monthly basis. This is known as a **periodic inventory system** because the physical inventory is counted periodically.

Today most companies use computers to keep track of merchandise inventory on a continuous, or perpetual, basis. This is known as a **perpetual inventory system**. For each merchandise category, the purchases made by the company are added to inventory, whereas the sales to customers are subtracted. These balances are known as the **book inventory** of the items held for sale. As accurate as the perpetual system may be, it must be confirmed with an actual physical count at least once a year.

Taking inventory consists of physically counting, weighing, or measuring the items on hand; placing a price on each item; and multiplying the number of items by the price to determine the total cost. The counting part of taking inventory, although tedious, is not difficult. The pricing part, however, is an important and often controversial business decision. To this day, accountants have varying opinions on the subject of inventory valuation techniques.

In most industries, the prices that businesses pay for goods frequently change. A hardware store, for example, may buy a dozen lightbulbs for $10.00 one month and $12.50 the next. A gasoline station may pay $1.75 per gallon on Tuesday and $1.69 on Thursday. When inventory is taken, it is virtually impossible to determine what price was paid for those items that remain in inventory. This means that the *flow of goods* in and out of a business does not always match the *flow of costs* in and out of the business.

The one method of pricing inventory that actually matches the flow of costs to the flow of goods is known as the **specific identification method**. This method is feasible only when the variety of merchandise carried in stock and the volume of sales are relatively low, such as

inventory Goods that a company has in its possession at any given time. May be in the form of raw materials, partially finished goods, or goods available for sale.

merchandise inventory Goods purchased by wholesalers and retailers for resale.

periodic inventory system Inventory system in which merchandise is physically counted at least once a year to determine the value of the goods available for sale.

perpetual inventory system Inventory system in which goods available for sale are updated on a continuous basis by computer. Purchases by the company are added to inventory, whereas sales to customers are subtracted from inventory.

book inventory The balance of a perpetual inventory system at any given time. Must be confirmed with an actual physical count at least once a year.

specific identification method Inventory valuation method in which each item in inventory is matched or coded with its actual cost. Feasible only for low-volume merchandise flow such as automobiles, boats, and other expensive items.

When a cashier scans a product being purchased, a laser reads the **Universal Product Code (UPC),** a 12-digit bar code on each product's package or label. The digits identify the manufacturer, the product, the size, and product attributes such as flavor or color.

Originally invented by a Toyota subsidiary to track vehicles during production, **QR (Quick Response) Codes** are used for inventory control as well as advertising and many other uses. Both UPC and QR Codes are used for maintaining perpetual inventory systems.

with automobiles and other expensive items. Each car, for example, has a specific vehicle identification number, or serial number, that makes inventory valuation accurate. A list of the vehicles in stock at any given time with their corresponding costs can easily be totaled to arrive at an inventory figure.

In reality, most businesses have a wide variety of merchandise and find this method too expensive because implementation would require sophisticated computer bar-coding systems. For this reason, it is customary to use an *assumption* as to the flow of costs of merchandise in and out of a business. The three most common cost flow assumptions or inventory pricing methods are as follows:

1. **First-in, first-out (FIFO):** Cost flow is in the order in which the costs were incurred.
2. **Last-in, first-out (LIFO):** Cost flow is in the reverse order in which the costs were incurred.
3. **Average cost:** Cost flow is an average of the costs incurred.

Although cost is the primary basis for the valuation of inventory, when market prices or current replacement costs fall below the actual cost of the items in inventory, the company has incurred a loss. For example, let's say a computer retailer purchases a large quantity of DVD drives at a cost of $200 each. A few months later, due to advances in technology, a faster model is introduced costing only $175 each. Under these market conditions, companies are permitted to choose a method for pricing inventory known as the lower-of-cost-or-market (LCM) rule.

All the inventory valuation methods listed above are acceptable for both income tax reporting and a company's financial statements. As we see in this section, each of these methods has advantages and disadvantages. Economic conditions such as whether merchandise prices are rising (inflation) or falling (deflation) play an important role in the decision of which method to adopt.

For income tax reporting, once a method has been chosen, the Internal Revenue Service (IRS) requires that it be used consistently from one year to the next. Any changes in the method used for inventory valuation must be for a good reason and must be approved by the IRS.

16-1 PRICING INVENTORY BY USING THE FIRST-IN, FIRST-OUT (FIFO) METHOD

first-in, first-out (FIFO) method
Inventory valuation method that assumes the items purchased by a company *first* are the *first* items to be sold. Items remaining in ending inventory at the end of an accounting period are therefore considered as if they were the most recently purchased.

The **first-in, first-out (FIFO) method,** illustrated in Exhibit 16-1, assumes that the items purchased *first* are the *first* items sold. The items in inventory at the end of the year are matched with the costs of items of the same type that were most recently purchased. This method closely approximates the manner in which most businesses reduce their inventory, especially when the merchandise is perishable or subject to frequent style or model changes.

Essentially, this method involves taking physical inventory at the end of the year or accounting period and assigning cost in reverse order in which the purchases were received.

> **STEPS TO CALCULATE THE VALUE OF ENDING INVENTORY BY USING FIFO**
>
> **STEP 1.** List the number of units on hand at the end of the year and their corresponding costs starting with the ending balance and working *backward* through the incoming shipments.
>
> **STEP 2.** Multiply the number of units by the corresponding cost per unit for each purchase.
>
> **STEP 3.** Calculate the value of ending inventory by totaling the extensions from Step 2.

EXHIBIT 16-1

First-In, First-Out—FIFO

First-In, First-Out—FIFO

To illustrate the application of the FIFO method of inventory pricing as well as the other methods in this section, we will use the following annual inventory data for 8 × 10 picture frames at Target.

Target

January 1	Beginning Inventory	400 units @ $5	$ 2,000
April 9	Purchase	200 units @ $6	1,200
July 19	Purchase	500 units @ $7	3,500
October 15	Purchase	300 units @ $8	2,400
December 8	Purchase	200 units @ $9	1,800
Picture frames available for sale during the year		1,600	$10,900

Target is an upscale discounter that provides high-quality, on-trend merchandise at attractive prices in spacious and guest-friendly stores. In addition, Target operates an online business, Target.com.

The Target merchandise mix includes 23% household essentials, 22% hardlines, 20% apparel and accessories, 19% home furnishings and décor, and 16% food and pet supplies.

Helen Sessions/Alamy

EXAMPLE1 PRICING INVENTORY BY USING THE FIFO METHOD

When physical inventory of the picture frames was taken at Target on December 31, it was found that 700 remained in inventory. Using the FIFO method of inventory pricing, what is the dollar value of this ending inventory?

SOLUTIONSTRATEGY

With the assumption under FIFO that the inventory cost flow is made up of the *most recent* costs, the 700 picture frames in ending inventory would be valued as follows:

Step 1. Set up a table listing the 700 picture frames with costs in reverse order of acquisition.

200 units @ $9 from the December 8 purchase
300 units @ $8 from the October 15 purchase
200 units @ $7 from the July 19 purchase
700 Inventory, December 31

IN THE Business World

The value placed on inventory can have a significant effect on the *net income* of a company. Because net income is the basis of calculating federal income tax, accountants frequently must decide whether to value inventory to reflect higher net profit to entice investors or lower net profit to minimize income taxes.

Steps 2 & 3. Extend each purchase, multiplying the number of units by the cost per unit, and find the total of the extensions.

Units	Cost/Unit	Total
200	$9	$1,800
300	8	2,400
200	7	1,400
700		$5,600 Ending inventory using FIFO

TRYITEXERCISE 1

You are the merchandise manager at Best Buy. The following data represent your records of the annual inventory figures for a particular video game.

Best Buy

January 1	Beginning Inventory	200 units @ $8.00	$1,600
May 14	Purchase	100 units @ $8.50	850
August 27	Purchase	250 units @ $9.00	2,250
November 18	Purchase	300 units @ $8.75	2,625
Video games available for sale		850	$7,325

Using the FIFO method of inventory pricing, what is the dollar value of ending inventory if 380 video games were on hand on December 31?

CHECK YOUR ANSWER WITH THE SOLUTION ON PAGE 562.

16-2 PRICING INVENTORY BY USING THE LAST-IN, FIRST-OUT (LIFO) METHOD

last-in, first-out (LIFO) method
Inventory valuation method that assumes the items purchased by a company *last* are the *first* items to be sold. Items remaining in ending inventory at the end of an accounting period are therefore considered as if they were the oldest goods.

The **last-in, first-out (LIFO) method**, illustrated in Exhibit 16-2, assumes that the items purchased *last* are sold or removed from inventory *first*. The items in inventory at the end of the year are matched with the cost of items of the same type that were purchased earliest. Therefore, items included in the ending inventory are considered to be those from the beginning inventory plus those acquired first from purchases.

This method involves taking physical inventory at the end of the year or accounting period and assigning cost in the same order in which the purchases were received.

STEPS TO CALCULATE THE VALUE OF ENDING INVENTORY BY USING LIFO

STEP 1. List the number of units on hand at the end of the year and their corresponding costs starting with the beginning inventory and working *forward* through the incoming shipments.

STEP 2. Multiply the number of units by the corresponding cost per unit for each purchase.

STEP 3. Calculate the value of ending inventory by totaling the extensions from Step 2.

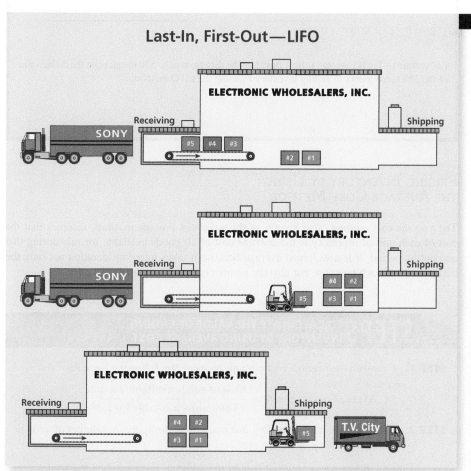

Last-In, First-Out—LIFO

EXHIBIT 16-2
Last-In, First-Out—LIFO

IN THE Business World

One of the main reasons for choosing a particular inventory valuation method is for the calculation of income for tax purposes.

- When costs are *rising*:
  FIFO → Higher gross profit
  LIFO → Lower gross profit

- When costs are *decreasing*:
  FIFO → Lower gross profit
  LIFO → Higher gross profit

EXAMPLE2 — PRICING INVENTORY BY USING THE LIFO METHOD

Let's return to the previous example about the 8 × 10 picture frames from Target, page 537. Once again, when physical inventory was taken on December 31, it was found that 700 remained in inventory. Using the LIFO method of inventory pricing, what is the dollar value of this ending inventory?

▶ SOLUTIONSTRATEGY

With the assumption under LIFO that the inventory cost flow is made up of the *earliest* costs, the 700 picture frames in ending inventory would be valued as follows:

Step 1. Set up a table listing the 700 picture frames with costs in the order in which they were acquired.

> 400 units @ $5 from the January 1 beginning inventory
> 200 units @ $6 from the April 9 purchase
> 100 units @ $7 from the July 19 purchase
> 700 Inventory, December 31

Steps 2 & 3. Extend each purchase, multiplying the number of units by the cost per unit, and find the total of the extensions.

Units	Cost/Unit	Total
400	$5	$2,000
200	6	1,200
100	7	700
700		$3,900 — Ending inventory using LIFO

► TRYITEXERCISE 2

Let's return to Try It Exercise 1, Best Buy. Use the data from page 538 to calculate the dollar value of the 380 video games in ending inventory by using the LIFO method.

CHECK YOUR ANSWER WITH THE SOLUTION ON PAGE 562.

16-3   PRICING INVENTORY BY USING THE AVERAGE COST METHOD

average cost, or **weighted average**, **method** Inventory valuation method that assumes the cost of each unit of inventory is the *average* cost of all goods available for sale during that accounting period.

The **average cost method**, also known as **the weighted average method**, assumes that the cost of each unit of inventory is the *average* cost of all goods available for sale during that accounting period. It is a weighted average because it takes into consideration not only the cost per unit in each purchase but also the number of units purchased at each cost.

STEPS TO CALCULATE THE VALUE OF ENDING INVENTORY BY USING AVERAGE COST

STEP 1. Calculate the average cost per unit by using the following formula.

$$\text{Average cost per unit} = \frac{\text{Cost of goods available for sale}}{\text{Total units available for sale}}$$

STEP 2. Calculate the value of ending inventory by multiplying the number of units in ending inventory by the average cost per unit.

$$\text{Ending inventory} = \text{Units in ending inventory} \times \text{Average cost per unit}$$

EXAMPLE3   PRICING INVENTORY BY USING AVERAGE COST

Let's return once again to the example of the 8 × 10 picture frames from Target, page 537. Using the average cost method of inventory pricing, what is the dollar value of the 700 frames on hand in ending inventory?

►SOLUTIONSTRATEGY

Under the weighted average cost method, the 700 frames in ending inventory would be valued as follows:

Step 1. Calculate the average cost per unit:

$$\text{Average cost per unit} = \frac{\text{Cost of goods available for sale}}{\text{Total units available for sale}}$$

$$\text{Average cost per unit} = \frac{10,900}{1,600} = \$6.81$$

Step 2. Ending inventory = Units in ending inventory × Average cost per unit

Ending inventory = 700 × 6.81 = $4,767

►TRYITEXERCISE 3

Once again, let's use the Best Buy example. This time use the data from page 538 to calculate the value of the 380 video games in ending inventory by using the average cost method.

CHECK YOUR ANSWER WITH THE SOLUTION ON PAGE 562.

PRICING INVENTORY BY USING THE LOWER-OF-COST-OR-MARKET (LCM) RULE

16-4

The three methods of pricing inventory discussed to this point—FIFO, LIFO, and weighted average—have been based on the cost of the merchandise. When the market price or current replacement price of an inventory item declines below the actual price paid for that item, companies are permitted to use a method known as the **lower-of-cost-or-market (LCM) rule**. This method takes into account such market conditions as severely falling prices, changing fashions or styles, and obsolescence of inventory items. The use of the LCM rule assumes that decreases in replacement costs will be accompanied by proportionate decreases in selling prices.

The lower of cost or market means comparing the market value (current replacement cost) of each item on hand with its cost, using the lower amount as its inventory value. Under ordinary circumstances, market value means the usual price paid based on the volume of merchandise normally ordered by the firm.

lower-of-cost-or-market (LCM) rule
Inventory valuation method whereby items in inventory are valued at their actual cost or their current replacement value, whichever is lower. This method is permitted under conditions of falling prices or merchandise obsolescence.

STEPS TO CALCULATE THE VALUE OF ENDING INVENTORY BY USING THE LOWER-OF-COST-OR-MARKET RULE

STEP 1. Calculate the cost for each item in the inventory by using one of the acceptable methods: FIFO, LIFO, or weighted average.

STEP 2. Determine the market price or current replacement cost for each item.

STEP 3. For each item, select the basis for valuation, cost or market, by choosing the lower figure.

STEP 4. Calculate the total amount for each inventory item by multiplying the number of items by the valuation price chosen in Step 3.

STEP 5. Calculate the total value of the inventory by adding all the figures in the Amount column.

EXAMPLE4 PRICING INVENTORY BY USING THE LCM RULE

The following data represent the inventory figures of the Sundance Boutique. Use the lower-of-cost-or-market rule to calculate the extended amount for each item and the total value of the inventory.

Item	Description	Quantity	Cost	Market	Valuation Basis	Amount
Blouses	Style #44	40	$ 27.50	$ 31.25	_____	_____
	Style #54	54	36.40	33.20	_____	_____
Slacks	Style #20	68	42.10	39.80	_____	_____
	Style #30	50	57.65	59.18	_____	_____
Jackets	Suede	30	141.50	130.05	_____	_____
	Wool	35	88.15	85.45	_____	_____
				Total Value of Inventory		_____

►SOLUTIONSTRATEGY

In this example, the cost and market price are given. We begin by choosing the lower of cost or market and then extending each item to the Amount column. For example, the Style #44 blouse will be valued at the cost, $27.50, because it is less than the market price, $31.25. The extension would be 40 × $27.50 = $1,100.00.

Item	Description	Quantity	Unit Price Cost	Unit Price Market	Valuation Basis	Amount
Blouses	Style #44	40	$ 27.50	$ 31.25	Cost	$ 1,100.00 ◄
	Style #54	54	36.40	33.20	Market	1,792.80
Slacks	Style #20	68	42.10	39.80	Market	2,706.40
	Style #30	50	57.65	59.18	Cost	2,882.50
Jackets	Suede	30	141.50	130.05	Market	3,901.50
	Wool	35	88.15	85.45	Market	2,990.75
					Total Value of Inventory	**$15,373.95**

►TRYITEXERCISE 4

Determine the value of the following inventory for the Personal Touch Gift Shop by using the lower-of-cost-or-market rule.

Description	Quantity	Unit Price Cost	Unit Price Market	Valuation Basis	Amount
Lamps	75	$ 9.50	$ 9.20	_____	_____
Jewelry Boxes	120	26.30	27.15	_____	_____
16" Vases	88	42.40	39.70	_____	_____
12" Vases	64	23.65	21.40	_____	_____
Fruit Bowls	42	36.90	42.00	_____	_____
				Total Value of Inventory	_____

CHECK YOUR ANSWERS WITH THE SOLUTIONS ON PAGE 563.

SECTION I **16** REVIEW EXERCISES

1. Calculate the total number of Sonic Blu-ray players available for sale and the cost of goods available for sale from the following inventory figures at Superior Electronics.

Superior Electronics
Sonic Blu-ray Player Inventory

Date	Units Purchased	Cost per Unit	Total Cost
Beginning Inventory, January 1	40	$125	$5,000
Purchase, February 20	32	118	3,776
Purchase, April 16	30	146	4,380
Purchase, June 8	25	135	3,375
Blu-ray Players Available for Sale	**127**	**Cost of Goods Available for Sale**	**$16,531**

2. When the buyer for Superior Electronics (Exercise 1) took physical inventory of the Blu-ray players on July 31, 64 units remained in inventory.

a. Calculate the dollar value of the 64 Blu-ray players by using FIFO.

Units	Cost/Unit	Total	
25	$135	$3,375	
30	146	4,380	
9	118	1,062	
64		$8,817	FIFO

b. Calculate the dollar value of the 64 Blu-ray players by using LIFO.

Units	Cost/Unit	Total	
40	$125	$5,000	
24	118	2,832	
64		$7,832	LIFO

c. Calculate the dollar value of the 64 Blu-ray players by using the average cost method. Round average cost to the nearest cent.

$$\text{Average cost} = \frac{16,531}{127} = 130.165 = \$130.17 \text{ each}$$

Inventory value = 64 × 130.17 = $8,330.88

Advance Auto Parts began as a two-store operation in 1932 in Virginia. It now operates over 3,700 locations in forty states plus Puerto Rico and the Virgin Islands.

EXCEL 1

3. Calculate the total number of units available for sale and the cost of goods available for sale from the following inventory of oil filters for Advance Auto Parts.

Advance Auto Parts
Oil Filter Inventory

Date	Units Purchased	Cost per Unit	Total Cost
Beginning Inventory, January 1	160	$1.45	_____
Purchase, March 14	210	1.65	_____
Purchase, May 25	190	1.52	_____
Purchase, August 19	300	1.77	_____
Purchase, October 24	250	1.60	_____
Total Units Available	══	**Cost of Goods Available for Sale**	══

EXCEL 2

4. When the merchandise manager of Advance Auto Parts took physical inventory of the oil filters on December 31, it was found that 550 remained in inventory.

a. Calculate the dollar value of the 550 oil filters by using FIFO.

b. Calculate the dollar value of the 550 oil filters by using LIFO.

c. Calculate the dollar value of the 550 filters by using the average cost method.

5. The following data represents the inventory for home burglar alarm systems at First Alert
    Security Corporation.

First Alert Security Corporation
Burglar Alarm Systems Inventory

Date	Units	Cost per Unit	Total Cost
Beginning Inventory, January 1	235	$140.00	_____
Purchase, March 10	152	143.50	_____
Purchase, May 16	135	146.80	_____
Purchase, October 9	78	150.00	_____
Alarm Systems Available for Sale		**Cost of Goods Available for Sale**	

a. How many alarm systems did First Alert Security have available for sale?

b. What is the total cost of the alarm systems available for sale?

c. If physical inventory on December 31 showed 167 alarm systems on hand, calculate
    their dollar value by using FIFO.

d. Calculate the value of the 167 alarm systems by using LIFO.

e. Calculate the dollar value of the 167 alarm systems by using the average cost method.

6. The following data represent the inventory figures for 55-gallon fish tanks at Something's
    Fishy.

Something's Fishy
55-Gallon Fish Tanks Inventory

			Amount
January 1	Beginning Inventory	42 units @ $38.00	_____
March 12	Purchase	80 units @ $36.50	_____
July 19	Purchase	125 units @ $39.70	_____
September 2	Purchase	75 units @ $41.75	_____
Fish Tanks Available for Sale	_____	**Cost of Tanks Available for Sale**	_____

a. How many fish tanks did Something's Fishy have available for sale?

b. Calculate the total cost of the tanks available for sale.

c. If physical inventory on December 31 showed 88 tanks on hand, calculate their dollar value
    by using FIFO.

d. Calculate the value of the 88 tanks by using LIFO.

e. Calculate the dollar value of the 88 tanks by using the average cost method.

7. Determine the value of the following inventory for A Nose for Clothes Boutique by using the lower-of-cost-or-market rule.

A Nose for Clothes Boutique

Description	Quantity	Unit Price Cost	Unit Price Market	Valuation Basis	Amount
Jackets	56	$124	$128	Cost	$ 6,944
Slacks	88	58	53	Market	4,664
Belts	162	19	17	Market	2,754
Blouses	125	41	45	Cost	5,125
				Total Value of Inventory	**$19,487**

8. Determine the value of the following inventory for Nichols Hardware by using the lower-of-cost-or-market rule.

True Value Hardware
Power Tool Inventory

Description	Quantity	Unit Price Cost	Unit Price Market	Valuation Basis	Amount
10-piece drill bit set	14	$25.60	$26.20	_____	_____
$\frac{1}{2}$" Drill	19	42.33	39.17	_____	_____
7" Circular Saw	12	32.29	34.50	_____	_____
$\frac{3}{8}$" Router	8	55.30	54.22	_____	_____
5" Rotary Sander	15	27.60	27.10	_____	_____
9" Belt Sander	11	32.50	34.51	_____	_____
				Total Value of Inventory	_____

9. Determine the value of the following inventory for the Rainbow Gardens Emporium by using the lower-of-cost-or-market rule.

Rainbow Gardens Emporium

Description	Quantity	Unit Price Cost	Unit Price Market	Valuation Basis	Amount
Dish Sets	220	$36	$33	_____	_____
Tablecloths	180	13	14	_____	_____
Barbeque Tools	428	35	33	_____	_____
Outdoor Lamps	278	56	50	_____	_____
Ceramic Statues	318	22	17	_____	_____
				Total Value of Inventory	_____

True Value, headquartered in Chicago, is one of the world's largest retailer-owned hardware cooperatives. True Value's cooperative serves 54 countries with more than 5,000 stores, 12 regional distribution centers, and 3,000 associates.

A cooperative, or co-operative, is a retailer-owned buying group consisting of members. It's not a franchise, but a group of individual store owners. Collectively, store operators own their wholesale distributor, which is True Value Company. To become a member, you must purchase 60 shares of Class A common stock per store. In addition to acquiring the stock, there are other financial considerations to be made in order to cover inventory, fixtures, equipment, and start-up costs.

BUSINESS DECISION: IN OR OUT?

10. You are the accounting manager of Kleen and Green Janitorial Supply, Inc., of Chicago. One of your junior accountants is working on the December 31 year-end inventory figures and has asked for your help in determining which of several transactions belong in the ending inventory. From the following inventory scenarios, decide which *should* be included in the year-end inventory and which *should not. Hint:* Refer to Exhibit 7-3, Shipping Terms, page 193.

   a. An order for a floor buffer and three different floor conditioning attachments shipped on December 31, FOB Chicago, and is expected to arrive on January 4.
   b. An order for six drums of floor wax and four drums of wax stripper was shipped to a Detroit customer on December 31, FOB Detroit, and should arrive on January 2.
   c. An order for 5 foot-operated mop buckets and 12 rag mops will be shipped on January 3.
   d. A floor cleaning machine was returned on December 28 for warranty repair and is scheduled to be return-shipped on January 6.
   e. Two cases of window wipes were shipped on December 30 FOB destination and are due to arrive on January 5.
   f. A carton of 12 one-gallon bottles of window washing solution and 8 boxes of streak-free window washing cloths were ordered on December 30 and are due to be shipped on January 3.

SECTION II   **16** INVENTORY ESTIMATION

IN THE Business World

In business today, it is common practice for retail stores to use the retail method of inventory valuation, whereas manufacturers and wholesalers use the gross profit method.

In Section I of this chapter, we learned to calculate the value of ending inventory with several methods using a physical count at the end of the accounting year. Most companies, however, require inventory figures more frequently than the once-a-year physical inventory. Monthly and quarterly financial statements, for example, may be prepared with inventory estimates rather than expensive physical counts or perpetual inventory systems. In addition, when physical inventories are destroyed by fire or other disasters, estimates must be made for insurance claims purposes.

The two generally accepted methods for *estimating* the value of an inventory are the retail method and the gross profit method. For these methods to closely approximate the actual value of inventory, the markup rate for all items bought and sold by the company must be consistent. If they are not, the estimates should be calculated separately for each product category. For example, if a toy store gets a 30% markup on tricycles and 50% on bicycles, these categories should be calculated separately.

16-5 ESTIMATING THE VALUE OF ENDING INVENTORY BY USING THE RETAIL METHOD

retail method Method of inventory estimation used by most retailers based on a comparison of goods available for sale at cost and at retail.

The **retail method** of inventory estimation is used by retail businesses of all types and sizes, from Walmart and Sears to the corner grocery store. To use this method, the company must have certain figures in its accounting records, including the following:

a. *Beginning inventory* at cost price and at retail (selling price)

b. *Purchases* during the period at cost price and at retail

c. *Net sales* for the period

From these figures, the goods available for sale are determined at both cost and retail. We then calculate a ratio known as the **cost to retail price ratio**, or simply **cost ratio**, by the formula:

cost to retail price ratio, or **cost ratio** Ratio of goods available for sale at cost to the goods available for sale at retail. Used in the retail method of inventory estimation to represent the cost of each dollar of retail sales.

$$\text{Cost ratio} = \frac{\text{Goods available for sale at cost}}{\text{Goods available for sale at retail}}$$

This ratio represents the cost of each dollar of retail sales. For example, if the cost ratio for a company is .6, or 60%, this means that $.60 is the cost of each $1.00 of retail sales.

STEPS TO ESTIMATE THE VALUE OF ENDING INVENTORY BY USING THE RETAIL METHOD

STEP 1. List beginning inventory and purchases at both cost and retail.

STEP 2. Add purchases to beginning inventory to determine goods available for sale at both cost and retail.

> Beginning inventory
> + Purchases
> ─────────────
> Goods available for sale

STEP 3. Calculate the cost ratio.

$$\text{Cost ratio} = \frac{\textbf{Goods available for sale at cost}}{\textbf{Goods available for sale at retail}}$$

STEP 4. Subtract net sales from goods available for sale at retail to get ending inventory at retail.

> Goods available for sale at retail
> − Net sales
> ─────────────
> Ending inventory at retail

STEP 5. Convert ending inventory at retail to ending inventory at cost by multiplying the ending inventory at retail by the cost ratio.

Ending inventory at cost = Ending inventory at retail × Cost ratio

EXAMPLE5 ESTIMATING INVENTORY USING THE RETAIL METHOD

Using the retail method, estimate the value of the ending inventory at cost on June 30 from the following information for Dependable Distributors, Inc.

Dependable Distributors, Inc.
Financial Highlights
June 1–June 30

	Cost	Retail
Beginning Inventory	$200,000	$400,000
Net Purchases (June)	150,000	300,000
Net Sales (June) $500,000		

►SOLUTIONSTRATEGY

Steps 1 & 2. List the beginning inventory and purchases and calculate the goods available for sale.

	Cost	Retail
Beginning Inventory	$200,000	$400,000
+ Net Purchases (June)	+ 150,000	+ 300,000
Goods Available for Sale	$350,000	$700,000

Step 3. $\text{Cost ratio} = \dfrac{\text{Goods available for sale at cost}}{\text{Goods available for sale at retail}}$

$\text{Cost ratio} = \dfrac{350,000}{700,000} = .5 = 50\%$

Remember, this 50% figure means that $.50 was the cost of each $1.00 of retail sales.

Step 4. Find ending inventory at retail.

Goods available for sale at retail	$700,000
– Net sales	– 500,000
Ending inventory at retail	$200,000

Step 5. Convert the inventory at retail to inventory at cost by using the cost ratio.

Ending inventory at cost = Ending inventory at retail × Cost ratio

Ending inventory at cost = 200,000 × .5 = $100,000

▶TRYITEXERCISE 5

Using the retail method, estimate the value of the ending inventory at cost on August 31 from the following information for Ripe 'N Ready Fruit Wholesalers, Inc.

Ripe 'N Ready Fruit Wholesalers, Inc.
Financial Highlights
August 1–August 31

	Cost	Retail
Beginning Inventory	$600,000	$800,000
Net Purchases (August)	285,000	380,000
Net Sales (August) $744,000		

CHECK YOUR ANSWER WITH THE SOLUTION ON PAGE 563.

16-6   ESTIMATING THE VALUE OF ENDING INVENTORY BY USING THE GROSS PROFIT METHOD

gross profit or **gross margin method**
Method of inventory estimation using a company's gross margin percent to estimate the ending inventory. This method assumes that a company maintains approximately the same gross margin from year to year.

The **gross profit** or **gross margin method** uses a company's gross margin percent to estimate the ending inventory. This method assumes that a company maintains approximately the same gross margin from year to year. Inventories estimated in this manner are frequently used for interim reports and insurance claims; however, this method is not acceptable for inventory valuation on a company's annual financial statements.

From Chapter 15, remember that net sales comprises the cost of goods sold and gross margin.

Net sales (100%) = Cost of goods sold (%) + Gross margin (%)

From this equation, we see that when the gross margin percent is known, the cost of goods sold percent would be its complement because together they equal net sales, which is 100%.

Cost of goods sold percent = 100% – Gross margin percent

Knowing the cost of goods sold percent is the key to this calculation. We use this percent to find the cost of goods sold, which when subtracted from goods available for sale, gives us the estimated ending inventory.

STEPS TO ESTIMATE THE VALUE OF ENDING INVENTORY BY USING THE GROSS PROFIT METHOD

STEP 1. Calculate the goods available for sale.

$$\begin{array}{r} \text{Beginning inventory} \\ +\,\underline{\text{Net Purchases}} \\ \text{Goods available for sale} \end{array}$$

STEP 2. Find the estimated cost of goods sold by multiplying net sales by the cost of goods sold percent (complement of gross margin percent).

Estimated cost of goods sold = Net sales (100% − Gross margin%)

STEP 3. Calculate the estimate of ending inventory by subtracting the estimated cost of goods sold from the goods available for sale.

$$\begin{array}{r} \text{Goods available for sale} \\ -\,\underline{\text{Estimated cost of goods sold}} \\ \text{Estimated ending inventory} \end{array}$$

EXAMPLE6 ESTIMATING INVENTORY BY USING THE GROSS PROFIT METHOD

Angler's Fishing Supply, Inc., maintains a gross margin of 45% on all its wholesale supplies. In April, Angler's had a beginning inventory of $80,000, net purchases of $320,000, and net sales of $500,000. Use the gross profit method to estimate Angler's cost of ending inventory.

►SOLUTIONSTRATEGY

Step 1.

Beginning inventory (April 1)	$ 80,000
+ Net purchases	320,000
Goods available for sale	$400,000

Step 2. Estimated cost of goods sold = Net sales (100% − Gross margin %)

Estimated cost of goods sold = $500,000 (100% − 45%) = $275,000

Step 3.

Goods available for sale	$400,000
− Estimated cost of goods sold	275,000
Estimated ending inventory (April 30)	$125,000

►TRYITEXERCISE 6

Fantasy Beauty Products, Inc., maintains a gross margin of 39% on all its wholesale beauty supplies. In November, the company had a beginning inventory of $137,000, net purchases of $220,000, and net sales of $410,000. Use the gross profit method to estimate the cost of ending inventory for November.

CHECK YOUR ANSWER WITH THE SOLUTION ON PAGE 563.

SECTION II **16** **REVIEW EXERCISES**

1. Using the retail method, estimate the value of the ending inventory at cost on June 30 from the following information for Perfume Bazaar. Round the cost ratio to the nearest whole percent.

Perfume Bazaar
Financial Highlights
June 1–June 30

	Cost	Retail
Beginning inventory, June 1	$43,000	$92,000
Net purchases (June)	26,000	55,300
Net sales (June) $132,400		

	Cost	Retail		
Beginning inventory, June 1	$43,000	$92,000	Goods available for sale at retail	$147,300
Net purchases (June)	26,000	55,300	Net sales	– 132,400
Goods available for sale	$69,000	$147,300	Ending inventory at retail	$14,900

$$\text{Cost ratio} = \frac{69,000}{147,300} = .468 = 47\%$$

Ending inventory at cost = 14,900 × 47%
= $7,003

2. Using the retail method, estimate the value of the ending inventory at cost on September 30 from the following information for Scandinavian Furniture Designs, Inc. Round the cost ratio to the nearest tenth of a percent.

Scandinavian Furniture Designs, Inc.
September 1–September 30

	Cost	Retail
Beginning Inventory, September 1	$150,000	$450,000
Purchases (September)	90,000	270,000
Net Sales (September) $395,000		

3. Using the retail method, estimate the value of the ending inventory at cost on November 30 from the following information for Imperial Imports. Round the cost ratio to the nearest whole percent.

Imperial Imports
Financial Highlights
November 1–November 30

	Cost	Retail
Beginning inventory, November 1	$137,211	$328,500
Net purchases (November)	138,849	313,500
Net sales (November) $205,400		

4. Rambo Plumbing Supply maintains a gross margin of 40% on all of its kitchen sinks and faucet sets. In November, Rambo had a beginning inventory of $178,400, net purchases of $91,200, and net sales of $215,800. Use the gross profit method to estimate the cost of ending inventory.

Beginning inventory, Nov. 1	$178,400	Estimated cost of goods sold	$= 215,800(100\% - 40\%)$
Net purchases (Nov.)	+ 91,200		$= 215,800 \times .6 = \$129,480$
Goods available for sale	$269,600		

Goods available for sale	$269,600
Cost of goods sold	− 129,480
Estimated ending inventory	$140,120

5. Omni Fitness Equipment, Inc., maintains a gross margin of 55% on all its weight training products. In April, Omni had a beginning inventory of $146,000, net purchases of $208,000, and net sales of $437,000. Use the gross profit method to estimate the cost of ending inventory.

6. Hirst Electrical Supplies maintains a gross margin of 58% on all of its merchandise. In June, the company had a beginning inventory of $468,500, net purchases of $88,600, and net sales of $127,700. Use the gross profit method to estimate the cost of ending inventory as of June 30.

7. The following data represent the inventory figures for Hot Shot Welding Supply, Inc. Using the retail method, estimate the value of the ending inventory at cost on January 31. Round the cost ratio to the nearest tenth of a percent.

Hot Shot Welding Supply, Inc.
January 1–January 31

	Cost	Retail
Beginning Inventory, January 1	$50,000	$120,000
Net purchases (January)	90,000	216,000
Net Sales (January) $188,000		

8. You are the warehouse manager for Discovery Kitchen Supplies. On a Sunday in May, you receive a phone call from the owner. He states that the entire building and contents were destroyed by fire. For the police report and the insurance claim, the owner has asked you to estimate the value of the lost inventory. Your records, which luckily were backed up on the hard drive of your home computer, indicate that at the time of the fire, the net sales to date were $615,400 and the purchases were $232,600. The beginning inventory on January 1 was $312,000. For the past three years, the company has operated at a gross margin of 60%. Use the gross profit method to calculate your answer.

BUSINESS DECISION: OVER OR UNDER?

9. You own Bristol Marine, a retailer of boats, motors, and marine accessories. The store manager has just informed you that the amount of the physical inventory was incorrectly reported as $540,000 instead of the correct amount of $450,000. Unfortunately, yesterday you sent the quarterly financial statements to the stockholders. Now you must send revised statements and a letter of explanation.

a. What effect did the error have on the items of the balance sheet for Bristol? Express your answer as *overstated* or *understated* for the items affected by the error.

b. What effect will the error have on the items of the income statement for Bristol?

c. Did this error make the Bristol quarterly results look better or worse than they actually were?

SECTION III **16** INVENTORY TURNOVER AND TARGETS

---

inventory, or **stock**, **turnover** The number of times during an operating period that the average dollars invested in merchandise inventory was theoretically sold out or turned over. May be calculated in retail dollars or in cost dollars.

In Chapter 15, we learned to use inventory turnover as one of the financial statement efficiency ratios. To review, **inventory turnover**, or **stock turnover**, is the number of times during an operating period that the average dollars invested in merchandise inventory was theoretically sold out or turned over.

Generally, the more expensive the item, the lower the turnover rate. For example, furniture and fine jewelry items might have a turnover rate of three or four times per year, whereas a grocery store might have a turnover of 15 or 20 times per year, or more. In this section, we revisit the concept of inventory turnover and learn to calculate it at retail and at cost.

Although a company must maintain inventory quantities large enough to meet the day-to-day demands of its operations, it is important to keep the amount invested in inventory to a minimum. In this section, we also learn to calculate target inventories for companies based on published industry standards.

Regardless of the method used to determine inventory turnover, the procedure always involves dividing some measure of sales volume by a measure of the typical or average inventory. This **average inventory** is commonly found by adding the beginning and ending inventories of the operating period and dividing by 2.

average inventory An estimate of a company's typical inventory at any given time that is calculated by dividing the total of all inventories taken during an operating period by the number of times inventory was taken.

$$\text{Average inventory} = \frac{\text{Beginning inventory} + \text{Ending inventory}}{2}$$

Whenever possible, additional interim inventories should be used to increase the accuracy of the average inventory figure. For example, if a mid-year inventory was taken, this figure would be added to the beginning and ending inventories and the total divided by 3. If monthly inventories were available, they would be added and the total divided by 12.

CALCULATING INVENTORY TURNOVER RATE AT RETAIL

16-7

When inventory turnover rate is calculated at retail, the measure of sales volume used is net sales. The average inventory is expressed in retail sales dollars by using the beginning and ending inventories at retail. The inventory turnover rate is expressed in number of *times* the inventory was sold out during the period.

STEPS TO CALCULATE INVENTORY TURNOVER RATE AT RETAIL

STEP 1. Calculate average inventory at retail.

$$\text{Average inventory}_{\text{at retail}} = \frac{\text{Beginning inventory at retail} + \text{Ending inventory at retail}}{2}$$

STEP 2. Calculate the inventory turnover at retail. Round to the nearest tenth when necessary.

$$\text{Inventory turnover}_{\text{at retail}} = \frac{\text{Net sales}}{\text{Average inventory at retail}}$$

IN THE Business World

Inventory turnover is an important business indicator, particularly when compared with turnover rates from previous operating periods and with published industry statistics for similar-sized companies.

EXAMPLE7 CALCULATING INVENTORY TURNOVER RATE AT RETAIL

Hobby Town had net sales of $650,900 for the year. If the beginning inventory at retail was $143,000 and the ending inventory at retail was $232,100, what are the average inventory at retail and the inventory turnover at retail rounded to the nearest tenth?

SOLUTIONSTRATEGY

Step 1.
$$\text{Average inventory}_{\text{at retail}} = \frac{\text{Beginning inventory at retail} + \text{Ending inventory at retail}}{2}$$

$$\text{Average inventory}_{\text{at retail}} = \frac{143,000 + 232,100}{2} = \frac{375,100}{2} = \$187,550$$

Step 2.
$$\text{Inventory turnover}_{\text{at retail}} = \frac{\text{Net sales}}{\text{Average inventory at retail}}$$

$$\text{Inventory turnover}_{\text{at retail}} = \frac{650,900}{187,550} = 3.47 = 3.5 \text{ times}$$

TRYITEXERCISE 7

Exotic Gardens had net sales of $260,700 for the year. If the beginning inventory at retail was $65,100 and the ending inventory at retail was $52,800, what are the average inventory and the inventory turnover rounded to the nearest tenth?

CHECK YOUR ANSWERS WITH THE SOLUTIONS ON PAGE 563.

RFID—Smart Shopping

Long checkout lines at the grocery store are one of the biggest complaints about the shopping experience. According to howstuffworks.com, soon these lines could disappear when the ubiquitous Universal Product Code (UPC) bar code is replaced by **smart labels**, also called **radio frequency identification** (RFID) tags. RFID tags are intelligent bar codes that can communicate to a networked system to track every product that you put in your shopping cart.

Imagine going to the grocery store, filling up your cart, and walking right out the door. No longer will you have to wait as someone rings up each item in your cart one at a time. Instead, these RFID tags will communicate with an electronic reader that will detect every item in the cart and ring each up almost instantly. The reader will be connected to a large network that will send information on your products to the retailer and product manufacturers. Your bank will then be notified and the amount of the bill will be deducted from your account. No lines, no waiting!

Source: www.howstuffworks.com

16-8 CALCULATING INVENTORY TURNOVER RATE AT COST

Frequently, the inventory turnover rate of a company is expressed in terms of cost dollars rather than selling price or retail dollars. When this is the case, the cost of goods sold is used as the measure of sales volume and becomes the numerator in the formula. The denominator, average inventory, is calculated at cost.

STEPS TO CALCULATE INVENTORY TURNOVER RATE AT COST

STEP 1. Calculate the average inventory at cost.

$$\text{Average inventory}_{\text{at cost}} = \frac{\text{Beginning inventory at cost} + \text{Ending inventory at cost}}{2}$$

STEP 2. Calculate the inventory turnover at cost.

$$\text{Inventory turnover}_{\text{at cost}} = \frac{\text{Cost of goods sold}}{\text{Average inventory at cost}}$$

EXAMPLE8 CALCULATING INVENTORY TURNOVER RATE AT COST

Metro Mechanical, Inc., had cost of goods sold of $416,200 for the year. If the beginning inventory at cost was $95,790 and the ending inventory at cost was $197,100, what are the average inventory at cost and the inventory turnover at cost rounded to the nearest tenth?

SOLUTIONSTRATEGY

Step 1. $\text{Average inventory}_{\text{at cost}} = \dfrac{\text{Beginning inventory at cost} + \text{Ending inventory at cost}}{2}$

$\text{Average inventory}_{\text{at cost}} = \dfrac{95,790 + 197,100}{2} = \dfrac{292,890}{2} = \underline{\$146,445}$

Step 2.
$$\text{Inventory turnover}_{\text{at cost}} = \frac{\text{Cost of goods sold}}{\text{Average inventory at cost}}$$

$$\text{Inventory turnover}_{\text{at cost}} = \frac{416{,}200}{146{,}445} = 2.84 = \underline{2.8 \text{ times}}$$

▶ TRYITEXERCISE 8

E-Z Kwik Grocery Store had cost of goods sold of $756,400 for the year. If the beginning inventory at cost was $43,500 and the ending inventory at cost was $59,300, what are the average inventory at cost and the inventory turnover rounded to the nearest tenth?

CHECK YOUR ANSWERS WITH THE SOLUTIONS ON PAGE 563.

CALCULATING TARGET INVENTORIES BASED ON INDUSTRY STANDARDS

16-9

When inventory turnover is below average for a particular size firm, it may be a signal that the company is carrying too much inventory. Carrying extra inventory can lead to extra expenses such as warehousing costs and insurance. It also ties up money the company could use more efficiently elsewhere. In certain industries, some additional risks of large inventories would be losses due to price declines, obsolescence, or deterioration of the goods.

Trade associations and the federal government publish a wide variety of important industry statistics, ratios, and standards for every size company. When such inventory turnover figures are available, merchandise managers can use the following formulas to calculate the **target average inventory** required by their firm to achieve the published industry standards for a company with similar sales volume.

target average inventory Inventory standards published by trade associations and the federal government for companies of all sizes in all industries. Used by managers as *targets* for the ideal amount of inventory to carry for maximum efficiency.

$$\text{Target average inventory}_{\text{at cost}} = \frac{\text{Cost of goods sold}}{\text{Published inventory turnover at cost}}$$

$$\text{Target average inventory}_{\text{at retail}} = \frac{\text{Net sales}}{\text{Published inventory turnover at retail}}$$

EXAMPLE9 CALCULATING TARGET INVENTORIES BASED ON INDUSTRY STANDARDS

F-Stop Photo, Inc., a wholesale photo supply business, had cost of goods sold of $950,000 for the year. The beginning inventory at cost was $245,000, and the ending inventory at cost amounted to $285,000. According to the noted business research firm Dun & Bradstreet, the inventory turnover rate at cost for a photo business of this size is five times. Calculate the average inventory and actual inventory turnover for F-Stop. If the turnover is less than five times, calculate the target average inventory needed by F-Stop to theoretically come up to industry standards.

IN THE Business World

- When industry figures are published at "cost," target inventory is calculated by using *cost of goods sold*.
- When industry figures are published at "retail," target inventory is calculated by using *net sales*.

▶ SOLUTIONSTRATEGY

Step 1.
$$\text{Average inventory}_{\text{at cost}} = \frac{\text{Beginning inventory at cost} + \text{Ending inventory at cost}}{2}$$

$$\text{Average inventory}_{\text{at cost}} = \frac{245{,}000 + 285{,}000}{2} = \frac{530{,}000}{2} = \underline{\$265{,}000}$$

Step 2.
$$\text{Inventory turnover}_{\text{at cost}} = \frac{\text{Cost of goods sold}}{\text{Average inventory at cost}}$$

$$\text{Inventory turnover}_{\text{at cost}} = \frac{950{,}000}{265{,}000} = 3.58 = \underline{3.6 \text{ times}}$$

Step 3. The actual inventory turnover for F-Stop is *3.6 times* per year compared with the industry standard of five times. This indicates that the company is carrying too much inventory. Let's calculate the target average inventory F-Stop should carry to meet industry standards.

$$\text{Target average inventory}_{\text{at cost}} = \frac{\text{Cost of goods sold}}{\text{Published inventory turnover at cost}}$$

$$\text{Target average inventory}_{\text{at cost}} = \frac{950,000}{5} = \$190,000$$

The actual average inventory carried by F-Stop for the year was $265,000 compared with the target inventory of $190,000. This indicates that at any given time, the inventory for F-Stop averaged about $75,000 higher than that of its competition.

▶TRYITEXERCISE 9

Satellite Communications, Inc., had net sales of $2,650,000 for the year. The beginning inventory at retail was $495,000, and the ending inventory at retail amounted to $380,000. The inventory turnover at retail published as the standard for a business of this size is seven times. Calculate the average inventory and actual inventory turnover for the company. If the turnover is less than seven times, calculate the target average inventory needed to theoretically come up to industry standards.

CHECK YOUR ANSWERS WITH THE SOLUTIONS ON PAGES 563–564.

SECTION III 16 REVIEW EXERCISES

Assuming that all net sales figures are at *retail* and all cost of goods sold figures are at *cost*, calculate the average inventory and inventory turnover for the following. If the actual turnover is less than the published rate, calculate the target average inventory necessary to come up to industry standards. Round inventories to the nearest dollar and inventory turnovers to the nearest tenth.

	Net Sales	Cost of Goods Sold	Beginning Inventory	Ending Inventory	Average Inventory	Inventory Turnover	Published Rate	Target Average Inventory
1.	$500,000		$50,000	$70,000	$60,000	8.3	10.0	$50,000.00
2.		$335,000	$48,000	$56,000	$52,000	6.4	6.0	Above
3.		$1,200,000	$443,000	$530,000			3.5	
4.	$4,570,000		$854,000	$650,300			8.2	
5.		$258,400	$76,300	$43,500			5.2	
6.	$540,000		$133,250	$71,200			4.8	
7.	$1,329,000		$545,800	$387,120			2.6	
8.		$884,500	$224,130	$134,900			5.9	

9. Bubbles Bath Boutique had net sales of $245,300 for the year. The beginning inventory at retail was $62,600, and the ending inventory at retail was $54,200.

   a. What was the average inventory at retail?

   b. What was the inventory turnover rounded to the nearest tenth?

10. A Circle K convenience store had net sales of $1,350,000 for the six months ending June 30. The beginning inventory at retail was $87,300, and the ending inventory at retail was $72,100.

    a. What was the average inventory at retail?

    b. What was the inventory turnover rounded to the nearest tenth?

Circle K has been one of North America's most popular and successful operators of convenience stores for more than 50 years. Today there are more than 3,300 Circle K locations across the United States and over 4,000 Circle K locations across the globe, including Japan, Mexico, China, and Guam.

To become a Circle K franchisee, you must have access to $100,000 in liquid assets and have a net worth of $300,000 as the initial investment. Circle K Stores, Inc., is a subsidiary of Alimentation Couche-Tard, Inc., based in Quebec, Canada. It's the second-largest convenience store operator in North America and the leader in Canada. Alimentation Couche-Tard is French for "food for those who go to bed late."

11. The Gourmet's Delight, a cooking equipment wholesaler, had cost of goods sold of $458,900 for the year. The beginning inventory at cost was $83,600, and the ending inventory at cost was $71,700.

    a. What was the average inventory at cost?

    b. What was the inventory turnover rounded to the nearest tenth?

12. Riverside Industries had cost of goods sold of $359,700 for the year. The beginning inventory at cost was $73,180, and the ending inventory at cost was $79,500.

    a. What was the average inventory at cost?

    b. What was the inventory turnover rounded to the nearest tenth?

13. Summit Supply is an electrical parts wholesaler. Last year its average inventory at cost was $132,500 and its cost of goods sold was $690,400. The inventory turnover rate published for a business of this size is 5.5 times.

    a. Calculate the actual inventory turnover rate at cost for Summit Supply. Round to the nearest tenth.

    b. If the turnover rate is below the industry average of 5.5 times, calculate the target average inventory needed to match the industry standard.

14. Kwik-Mix Concrete Corporation had cost of goods sold of $1,250,000 for the third quarter. The beginning inventory at cost was $135,000, and the ending inventory at cost amounted to $190,900. The inventory turnover rate published as the industry standard for a business of this size is 9.5 times.

    a. Calculate the average inventory and actual inventory turnover rate for the company.

    b. If the turnover rate is less than 9.5 times, calculate the target average inventory needed to theoretically come up to industry standards.

15. Trophy Masters had net sales for the year of $145,000. The beginning inventory at retail was $36,000, and the ending inventory at retail amounted to $40,300. The inventory turnover rate published as the industry standard for a business of this size is 4.9 times.

    a. Calculate the average inventory and actual inventory turnover rate for the company.

    b. If the turnover rate is less than 4.9 times, calculate the target average inventory needed to theoretically come up to industry standards.

BUSINESS DECISION: KEEP YOUR EYE ON THE FEET

16. Another way to look at the concept of inventory turnover is by measuring sales per square foot. Taking the average inventory at retail and dividing it by the number of square feet devoted to a particular product will give you *average sales per square foot*. When you multiply this figure by the inventory turnover rate, you get the *annual sales per square foot*.

    It is important to know the amount of sales per square foot your merchandise is producing, both on average and annually. These figures should be tracked monthly and compared with industry standards for businesses of similar size and type.

    You own Electron Magic, a large multi product electronics store in a regional mall. The store has 10,000 square feet of selling space divided into five departments.

    a. From the table below, calculate the average and annual sales per square foot. Then calculate the annual sales for each department and the total sales for the entire store.

DVD/Blu-ray and Streaming
Streaming of videos is expected to overtake Blu-ray/DVD videos within another couple of years, as home Internet connections continue to get faster.

© Sergey Ash/Shutterstock.com

Electron Magic—2014 Sales

Department	Square Feet	Average Inventory at Retail	Average Sales per Sq. Foot	Inventory Turnover	Annual Sales per Sq. Foot	Departmental Annual Sales
Televisions	3,500	$153,000	_____	5.2	_____	_____
Blu-ray/DVDs	2,800	$141,000	_____	4.6	_____	_____
Digital cameras	2,100	$38,500	_____	4.1	_____	_____
Cell phones	500	$12,700	_____	2.3	_____	_____
Video gaming	1,100	$45,000	_____	4.7	_____	_____
					Total Sales	_____

    b. If industry standards for this size store and type of merchandise is $200 per square foot in annual sales, which departments are below standards? What can be done to improve the situation?

    c. (Optional) Use the Internet to research and share with the class the current "industry standard" sales per square foot and inventory turnover rates for the merchandise categories of your store.

CHAPTER FORMULAS

Inventory Valuation—Average Cost Method

$$\text{Average cost per unit} = \frac{\text{Cost of goods available for sale}}{\text{Total units available for sale}}$$

$$\text{Ending inventory} = \text{Units in ending inventory} \times \text{Average cost per unit}$$

Inventory Estimation—Retail Method

$$\text{Cost ratio} = \frac{\text{Goods available for sale at cost}}{\text{Goods available for sale at retail}}$$

$$\text{Estimated ending inventory at cost} = \text{Ending inventory at retail} \times \text{Cost ratio}$$

Inventory Estimation—Gross Profit Method

$$\text{Estimated cost of goods sold} = \text{Net sales}(100\% - \text{Gross margin \%})$$

Inventory Turnover—Retail

$$\text{Average inventory}_{\text{retail}} = \frac{\text{Beginning inventory at retail} + \text{Ending inventory at retail}}{2}$$

$$\text{Inventory turnover}_{\text{retail}} = \frac{\text{Net sales}}{\text{Average inventory at retail}}$$

Inventory Turnover—Cost

$$\text{Average inventory}_{\text{cost}} = \frac{\text{Beginning inventory at cost} + \text{Ending inventory at cost}}{2}$$

$$\text{Inventory turnover}_{\text{cost}} = \frac{\text{Cost of goods sold}}{\text{Average inventory at cost}}$$

Target Inventory

$$\text{Target average inventory}_{\text{cost}} = \frac{\text{Cost of goods sold}}{\text{Published inventory turnover at cost}}$$

$$\text{Target average inventory}_{\text{retail}} = \frac{\text{Net sales}}{\text{Published inventory turnover at retail}}$$

CHAPTER SUMMARY

Section I: Inventory Valuation

Topic	Important Concepts	Illustrative Examples
Pricing Inventory by Using the First-In, First-Out (FIFO) Method **Performance Objective 16-1, Page 536**	FIFO assumes that the items purchased first are the first items sold. The items in inventory at the end of the year are matched with the cost of items of the same type that were purchased most recently. *Inventory Pricing—FIFO:* 1. List the number of units on hand at the end of the year and their corresponding costs starting with the ending balance and working *backward* through the incoming shipments. 2. Multiply the number of units by the corresponding cost per unit for each purchase. 3. Calculate the value of ending inventory by totaling all the extensions from Step 2.	The following data represent the inventory figures for imported jewelry boxes at The Gift Collection. <table><tr><td>Date</td><td></td><td>Units</td><td>Cost per Unit</td></tr><tr><td>Jan. 1</td><td>Beg. Inv.</td><td>55</td><td>$12.30</td></tr><tr><td>Mar. 9</td><td>Purch.</td><td>60</td><td>13.50</td></tr><tr><td>Aug. 12</td><td>Purch.</td><td>45</td><td>13.90</td></tr><tr><td>Nov. 27</td><td>Purch.</td><td>75</td><td>14.25</td></tr></table> On December 31, physical inventory revealed 130 jewelry boxes in stock. Calculate the value of the ending inventory by using FIFO.

Section I (continued)

Topic	Important Concepts	Illustrative Examples
		With the assumption under FIFO that the inventory cost flow is made up of the most recent costs, the 130 jewelry boxes would be valued as follows:

Date	Units	Cost per Unit	Total
Nov. 27	75	$14.25	$1,068.75
Aug. 12	45	13.90	625.50
Mar. 9	10	13.50	135.00
	130		$1,829.25

Pricing Inventory by Using the Last-In, First-Out (LIFO) Method

Performance Objective 16-2, Page 538

LIFO assumes that the items purchased last are sold or removed from inventory first. The items in inventory at the end of the year are matched with the cost of the same type items purchased earliest.

Inventory Pricing—LIFO:
1. List the number of units on hand at the end of the year and their corresponding costs starting with the beginning inventory and working *forward* through the incoming shipments.
2. Multiply the number of units by the corresponding cost per unit for each purchase.
3. Calculate the value of ending inventory by totaling all the extensions from Step 2.

Using the data on page 559 for The Gift Collection, calculate the value of the 130 jewelry boxes in ending inventory by using LIFO. With the assumption under LIFO that the inventory cost flow is made up of the earliest costs, the 130 jewelry boxes would be valued as follows:

Date	Units	Cost per Unit	Total
Jan. 1	55	$12.30	$ 676.50
Mar. 9	60	13.50	810.00
Aug. 12	15	13.90	208.50
	130		$1,695.00

Pricing Inventory by Using the Average Cost Method

Performance Objective 16-3, Page 540

The average cost method, also known as the weighted average method, assumes that the cost of each unit of inventory is the average cost of all goods available for sale during that accounting period.

1. Calculate the average cost per unit by

$$\text{Average Cost} = \frac{\text{Cost of goods available for sale}}{\text{Total units available for sale}}$$

2. Calculate the value of ending inventory by multiplying the number of units in ending inventory by the average cost per unit.

Using the average cost method of inventory pricing, what is the dollar value of the 130 jewelry boxes in ending inventory for The Gift Collection?

First, we extend and sum each purchase to find the total units available and the total cost of those units available for sale.

Date	Units	Cost per Unit	Total
Jan. 1	55	$12.30	$ 676.50
Mar. 9	60	13.50	810.00
Aug. 12	45	13.90	625.50
Nov. 27	75	14.25	1,068.75
	235		$3,180.75

$$\text{Average cost} = \frac{3,180.75}{235} = \$13.54$$

Ending inventory = 130 × 13.54 = $1,760.20

Pricing Inventory by Using the Lower-of-Cost-or-Market (LCM) Rule

Performance Objective 16-4, Page 541

When the market price or current replacement price of an inventory item declines below the actual price paid for the item, a company is permitted to use the lower-of-cost-or-market rule.

1. Choose the lower of cost or market as the valuation basis.
2. Multiply the number of units by the valuation basis price.
3. Add the extended totals in the Amount column to get the value of ending inventory.

From the following inventory data for small, medium, and large lamps at The Lighting Center, calculate the value of the ending inventory by using the LCM rule.

Units	Unit Price Cost	Market	Valuation Basis	Amount
Small				
34	$40	$43	Cost	$1,360
Medium				
55	70	65	Market	3,575
Large				
47	99	103	Cost	4,653
			Ending inventory =	$9,588

Section II: Inventory Estimation

Topic	Important Concepts	Illustrative Examples
Estimating the Value of Ending Inventory by Using the Retail Method **Performance Objective 16-5, Page 546**	When it is too costly or not feasible to take a physical inventory count, inventory can be estimated. The retail method, as the name implies, is used by retail operations of all sizes. 1. List beginning inventory and purchases at both cost and retail. 2. Add purchases to beginning inventory to determine goods available for sale. 3. Calculate the cost ratio by $$\text{Cost ratio} = \frac{\text{Goods available for sale at cost}}{\text{Goods available for sale at retail}}$$ 4. Calculate ending inventory at retail by subtracting net sales from goods available for sale at retail. 5. Convert ending inventory at retail to ending inventory at cost by multiplying the ending inventory at retail by the cost ratio.	Estimate the value of the ending inventory at cost on July 31 from the following information for Central Distributors, Inc. <table><tr><td></td><td>Cost</td><td>Retail</td></tr><tr><td>Beg. Inv.</td><td>$300,000</td><td>$450,000</td></tr><tr><td>Net Purch.</td><td>100,000</td><td>150,000</td></tr><tr><td colspan=3>Net Sales $366,000</td></tr></table> <table><tr><td></td><td>Cost</td><td>Retail</td></tr><tr><td>Beg. Inv.</td><td>$300,000</td><td>$450,000</td></tr><tr><td>Net Purch.</td><td>+ 100,000</td><td>+ 150,000</td></tr><tr><td>Goods Avail.</td><td>$400,000</td><td>$600,000</td></tr></table> $$\text{Cost ratio} = \frac{400,000}{600,000} = .67$$ Good avail. at retail $600,000 − Net sales − 366,000 Ending inventory at retail $234,000 Ending inventory at cost = 234,000 × .67 = $156,780
Estimating the Value of Ending Inventory by Using the Gross Profit Method **Performance Objective 16-6, Page 548**	The gross profit or gross margin method uses a company's gross margin percent to estimate the ending inventory. This method assumes that a company maintains approximately the same gross margin from year to year. 1. Calculate the goods available for sale. Beginning inventory + Net purchases Goods available for sale 2. Find the estimated cost of goods sold by multiplying net sales by the cost of goods sold percent (complement of gross margin percent). 3. Calculate the estimate of ending inventory by Goods available for sale − Estimated cost of goods sold Estimated ending inventory	The Stereo Connection maintains a gross margin of 60% on all speakers. In June, the beginning inventory was $95,000, net purchases were $350,600, and net sales were $615,000. What is the estimated cost of ending inventory using the gross profit method? Beginning inv. $95,000 + Net purchases + 350,600 Goods available $445,600 Estimated cost of goods sold = Net sales(100% − Gr. margin%) = 615,000(100% − 60%) = $246,000 Goods available $445,600 − Estimated CGS − 246,000 Est. ending inv. $199,600

Section III: Inventory Turnover and Targets

Topic	Important Concepts	Illustrative Examples
Calculating Inventory Turnover Rate at Retail **Performance Objective 16-7, Page 553**	Inventory or stock turnover rate is the number of times during an operating period that the average inventory is sold out or turned over. Average inventory may be expressed at either retail or cost. 1. Calculate the average inventory at retail by $$\text{Average inventory}_{retail} = \frac{\substack{\text{Beginning} \\ \text{inventory} \\ \text{at retail}} + \substack{\text{Ending} \\ \text{inventory} \\ \text{at retail}}}{2}$$ 2. Calculate the inventory turnover at retail by $$\text{Inventory turnover}_{retail} = \frac{\text{Net sales}}{\text{Average inventory at retail}}$$	Tip Top Roofing Supply had net sales of $66,000 for the year. If the beginning inventory at retail was $24,400 and the ending inventory at retail was $19,600, what are the average inventory and the inventory turnover rate? $$\text{Average inventory at retail} = \frac{24,400 + 19,600}{2}$$ $$= \$22,000$$ $$\text{Inventory turnover at retail} = \frac{66,000}{22,000} = 3 \text{ times}$$

Section III (continued)

Topic	Important Concepts	Illustrative Examples
Calculating Inventory Turnover Rate at Cost **Performance Objective 16-8, Page 554**	Inventory turnover may also be calculated at cost by using cost of goods sold and the average inventory at cost. 1. Calculate average inventory at cost by $$\text{Average inventory}_{cost} = \frac{\begin{array}{c}\text{Beginning} \quad \text{Ending}\\ \text{inventory} \; + \; \text{inventory}\\ \text{at cost} \qquad \text{at cost}\end{array}}{2}$$ 2. Calculate the inventory turnover at cost by $$\text{Inventory turnover}_{cost} = \frac{\text{Cost of goods sold}}{\text{Average inventory at cost}}$$	Atlantic Importers had \$426,000 in cost of goods sold on oriental rugs. The beginning inventory at cost was \$75,000, and the ending inventory at cost was \$95,400. What are Atlantic's average inventory at cost and inventory turnover rate? $$\text{Average inventory at cost} = \frac{75,000 + 95,400}{2}$$ $$= \underline{85,200}$$ $$\text{Inventory turnover at cost} = \frac{426,000}{85,200} = \underline{\underline{5 \text{ times}}}$$
Calculating Target Inventories Based on Industry Standards **Performance Objective 16-9, Page 555**	When inventory turnover is below average based on published industry standards, it may be a signal that a company is carrying too much inventory. This can lead to extra expenses such as warehousing and insurance. The following formulas can be used to calculate target average inventories at cost or retail to theoretically achieve the published turnover rate. $$\text{Target inventory at cost} = \frac{\text{Cost of goods sold}}{\text{Published rate at cost}}$$ $$\text{Target inventory at retail} = \frac{\text{Net sales}}{\text{Published rate at retail}}$$	Playtime Toys had cost of goods sold of \$560,000 on stuffed animals for the year. The beginning inventory at cost was \$140,000, and the ending inventory was \$180,000. The published rate for a firm this size is four times. Calculate the average inventory and turnover rate for Playtime. If the rate is less than four times, calculate the target average inventory. Average inventory at cost $$= \frac{140,000 + 180,000}{2} = \$160,000$$ $$\text{Inventory turnover at cost} = \frac{560,000}{160,000}$$ $$= \underline{3.5 \text{ times}}$$ $$\text{Target average inventory} = \frac{560,000}{4}$$ $$= \underline{\$140,000}$$

TRY IT: EXERCISE SOLUTIONS FOR CHAPTER 16

1.

FIFO Inventory Valuation

Units	Cost/Unit	Total
300	\$8.75	\$2,625
80	9.00	720
380		\$3,345

2.

LIFO Inventory Valuation

Units	Cost/Unit	Total
200	\$8.00	\$1,600
100	8.50	850
80	9.00	720
380		\$3,170

3.

Average Cost Method

$$\text{Average cost/unit} = \frac{\text{Cost of goods available}}{\text{Total units available}} = \frac{7,325}{850} = \$8.62$$

Ending inventory = Units in inventory × Average cost per unit

Ending inventory = 380 × 8.62 = $\underline{\$3,275.60}$

4.

		LCM Rule		
		The Personal Touch Gift Shop		
Description	Quantity	Valuation Basis	Price	Amount
Lamps	75	Market	$ 9.20	$ 690.00
Jewelry Boxes	120	Cost	26.30	3,156.00
16" Vases	88	Market	39.70	3,493.60
12" Vases	64	Market	21.40	1,369.60
Fruit Bowls	42	Cost	36.90	1,549.80
			Total Value of Inventory	$10,259.00

5.

	Cost	Retail
Beginning inventory	$600,000	$800,000
+ Net purchases	+ 285,000	+ 380,000
Goods available for sale	$885,000	$1,180,000

$$\text{Cost ratio} = \frac{\text{Goods available for sale at cost}}{\text{Goods available for sale at retail}} = \frac{885,000}{1,180,000} = .75 = 75\%$$

Goods available at retail	1,180,000
− Net sales	− 744,000
Ending inventory at retail	$436,000

Ending inventory at cost = Ending inventory at retail × Cost ratio

Ending inventory at cost = 436,000 × .75 = $327,000

6.

Beginning inventory	$137,000
+ Net purchases	+ 220,000
Goods available for sale	$357,000

Estimated cost of goods sold = Net sales (100% − Gross margin %)

Estimated cost of goods sold = 410,000 (100% − 39%)

Estimated cost of goods sold = 410,000 (.61) = $250,100

Goods available for sale	$357,000
− Estimated cost of goods sold	− 250,100
Estimated ending inventory	$106,900

7. $$\text{Average inventory}_{\text{retail}} = \frac{\text{Beginning inventory at retail} + \text{Ending inventory at retail}}{2}$$

$$\text{Average inventory}_{\text{retail}} = \frac{65,100 + 52,800}{2} = \$58,950$$

$$\text{Inventory turnover}_{\text{retail}} = \frac{\text{Net sales}}{\text{Average inventory at retail}}$$

$$\text{Inventory turnover}_{\text{retail}} = \frac{260,700}{58,950} = 4.4 \text{ times}$$

8. $$\text{Average inventory}_{\text{cost}} = \frac{\text{Beginning inventory at cost} + \text{Ending inventory at cost}}{2}$$

$$\text{Average inventory}_{\text{cost}} = \frac{43,500 + 59,300}{2} = \$51,400$$

$$\text{Inventory turnover}_{\text{cost}} = \frac{\text{Cost of goods sold}}{\text{Average inventory at cost}}$$

$$\text{Inventory turnover}_{\text{cost}} = \frac{756,400}{51,400} = 14.7 \text{ times}$$

9. $$\text{Average inventory} = \frac{\text{Beginning inventory} + \text{Ending inventory}}{2}$$

$$\text{Average inventory} = \frac{495,000 + 380,000}{2} = \$437,500$$

$$\text{Inventory turnover} = \frac{\text{Net sales}}{\text{Average inventory at retail}} = \frac{2,650,000}{437,500} = 6.1 \text{ times}$$

$$\text{Target average inventory} = \frac{\text{Net sales}}{\text{Published turnover}}$$

$$\text{Target average inventory} = \frac{2,650,000}{7} = \$378,571.43$$

CONCEPT REVIEW

1. Goods that a company has in its possession at any given time are known as _____. (16-1)

2. A(n) _____ inventory system is physically counted at least once a year to determine the value of the goods available for sale. (16-1)

3. A(n) _____ inventory system updates goods available for sale on a continuous basis by computer. (16-1)

4. An inventory valuation method in which each item in inventory is matched or coded with its actual cost is known as the specific _____ method. (16-1)

5. An inventory valuation method that assumes the items purchased by a company *first* are the *first* items to be sold is known as the _____ method. Its abbreviation is _____. (16-1)

6. An inventory valuation method that assumes the items purchased by the company *last* are the *first* items to be sold is known as the _____ method. Its abbreviation is _____. (16-2)

7. An inventory valuation method that assumes the cost of each unit of inventory is the *average* cost of all goods available for sale during that accounting period is known as the average cost or _____ average method. (16-3)

8. An inventory valuation method whereby items in inventory are valued at their actual cost or current replacement value, whichever is lower, is known as the _____ rule. Its abbreviation is _____. (16-4)

9. The two generally accepted methods for *estimating* the value of an inventory are the _____ method and the gross _____ method. (16-5, 16-6)

10. The number of times during an operating period that the average dollars invested in inventory was theoretically sold out or turned over is known as the _____ turnover or _____ turnover. (16-7, 16-8)

11. Inventory or stock turnover may be calculated in _____ dollars or in _____ dollars. (16-7, 16-8)

12. Write the formula for average inventory. (16-7, 16-8)

13. The ideal amount of inventory a company should carry for maximum efficiency is known as the _____ average inventory. (16-9)

14. When the target average inventory is calculated at *cost*, the numerator of the formula is the cost of _____ _____; when the target average inventory is calculated *at retail*, the numerator of the formula is net _____. (16-9)

ASSESSMENT TEST

1. Calculate the total number of Maytag Neptune washing machines available for sale and the cost of goods available for sale from the following inventory figures for Southern Distributors, Inc.

Date	Units Purchased	Cost per Unit	Total Cost
Beginning Inventory, March 1	24	$525	_____
Purchase, May 19	12	479	_____
Purchase, August 26	18	540	_____
Purchase, November 27	27	488	_____
Washing Machines Available for Sale	___	**Cost of Goods Available for Sale**	_____

2. When the buyer for Southern Distributors (Exercise 1) took physical inventory on December 31, 48 washing machines remained in inventory.

   a. Calculate the dollar value of the 48 washing machines by using FIFO.

   b. Calculate the dollar value of the 48 washing machines by using LIFO.

   c. Calculate the dollar value of the 48 washing machines by using the average cost method.

3. Calculate the total number of imported silk ties available for sale and the cost of goods available for sale from the following inventory figures for Ritz Fashions, Inc.

Date	Units Purchased	Cost per Unit	Total Cost
Beginning Inventory, January 1	59	$46.10	_____
Purchase, March 29	75	43.50	_____
Purchase, July 14	120	47.75	_____
Purchase, October 12	95	50.00	_____
Purchase, December 8	105	53.25	_____
Total Units Available	‗‗	**Cost of Goods Available for Sale**	‗‗‗‗

4. When the merchandise manager for Ritz Fashions (Exercise 3) took physical inventory on December 31, 128 silk ties remained in inventory.

   a. Calculate the dollar value of the 128 ties by using FIFO.

   $$\begin{array}{rll} 105 & @ \ \ 53.25 = & 5,591.25 \\ \underline{\ 23} & @ \ \ 50.00 = & \underline{1,150.00} \\ 128 & & \end{array}$$

   b. Calculate the dollar value of the 128 ties by using LIFO.

   $$\begin{array}{rll} 59 & @ \ \ 46.10 = & 2,719.90 \\ \underline{\ 69} & @ \ \ 43.50 = & \underline{3,001.50} \\ 128 & & \end{array}$$

   c. Calculate the dollar value of the 128 ties by using the average cost method.

   $$\text{Average cost} = \frac{22,053.65}{454} = \$48.58 \text{ per unit}$$

   $$128 \times 48.58 =$$

5. Determine the value of the following inventory for Iberia Tile by using the lower-of-cost-or-market rule.

Description	Quantity in Square Feet	Unit Price		Valuation Basis	Amount
		Cost	Market		
Terracotta 12"	8,400	$4.55	$5.10	_____	_____
Super Saltillo 16"	7,300	8.75	8.08	_____	_____
Monocottura 10"	4,500	3.11	2.90	_____	_____
Glazed Ceramic	6,200	4.50	5.25	_____	_____
Brick Pavers	12,700	3.25	3.15	_____	_____
			Total Value of Inventory		_____

CHAPTER 16

6. Using the retail method, estimate the value of the ending inventory at cost on May 31 from the following information for Fortune Industries, Inc. Round the cost ratio to the nearest tenth of a percent.

Fortune Industries, Inc.
May 1–May 31

	Cost	Retail
Beginning Inventory, May 1	$145,600	$196,560
Purchases	79,000	106,650
Net Sales $210,800		

7. On July 24, a tornado destroyed Astro Wholesalers' main warehouse and all its contents. Company records indicate that at the time of the tornado, the net sales to date were $535,100 and the purchases were $422,900. The beginning inventory on January 1 was $319,800. For the past three years, the company has maintained a gross margin of 35%. Use the gross profit method to estimate the inventory loss for the insurance claim.

Assuming that all net sales figures are at *retail* and all cost of goods sold figures are at *cost*, calculate the average inventory and inventory turnover for Exercises 8–11. If the actual turnover is below the published rate, calculate the target average inventory necessary to come up to industry standards. Round inventories to the nearest dollar and inventory turnovers to the nearest tenth.

	Net Sales	Cost of Goods Sold	Beginning Inventory	Ending Inventory	Average Inventory	Inventory Turnover	Published Rate	Target Average Inventory
8.	$290,000		$88,000	$94,000	_____	_____	4.4	_____
9.		$760,000	$184,000	$123,000	_____	_____	6.8	_____
10.		$237,550	$24,670	$43,120	_____	_____	5.9	_____
11.	$454,000		$87,900	$75,660	_____	_____	6.2	_____

12. A Foot Locker store had net sales of $435,900 for the year. The beginning inventory at retail was $187,600, and the ending inventory at retail was $158,800.

   a. What is the average inventory at retail?

   b. What is the inventory turnover rounded to the nearest tenth?

   c. If the turnover rate for similar-sized competitors is 3.8 times, calculate the target average inventory needed to theoretically come up to industry standards.

Foot Locker, Inc., is the world's leading retailer of athletic footwear and apparel. Headquartered in New York City, it operates approximately 3,600 athletic retail stores in 21 countries in North America, Europe, and Australia under the brand names Foot Locker, Footaction, Lady Foot Locker, Kids Foot Locker, and Champs Sports.

CHAPTER 16

13. The Fabric Mart had cost of goods sold of $884,000 for the year. The beginning inventory at cost was $305,500, and the ending inventory at cost amounted to $414,200. The inventory turnover rate published as the industry standard for a business of this size is five times.

    a. What is the average inventory at cost?

    b. What is the inventory turnover rounded to the nearest tenth?

    c. What is the target average inventory needed to theoretically come up to the industry standard?

BUSINESS DECISION: INVENTORY VALUATION AND THE BOTTOM LINE

14. You are the chief accountant of Pan American Industries, Inc. In anticipation of the upcoming annual stockholders' meeting, the president of the company asked you to determine the effect of the FIFO, LIFO, and average inventory valuation methods on the company's income statement.

    Beginning inventory, January 1, was 10,000 units at $5 each. Purchases during the year consisted of 15,000 units at $6 on April 15, 20,000 units at $7 on July 19, and 25,000 units at $8 on November 2.

    a. If ending inventory on December 31 was 40,000 units, calculate the value of this inventory by using the three valuation methods.

        FIFO: _____   LIFO: _____   Average Cost: _____

    b. Calculate the income statement items below for each of the inventory valuation methods.

Net sales	30,000 units at $12 each
Operating expenses	$100,000
Income tax rate	30%

Pan American Industries, Inc.

	FIFO	LIFO	Average Cost
Net sales	_____	_____	_____
Beginning inventory	_____	_____	_____
Purchases	_____	_____	_____
Cost of goods available for sale	_____	_____	_____
Ending inventory	_____	_____	_____
Cost of goods sold	_____	_____	_____
Gross profit	_____	_____	_____
Operating expenses	_____	_____	_____
Income before taxes	_____	_____	_____
Income tax	_____	_____	_____
Net income	_____	_____	_____

    c. Which inventory method should be used if the objective is to pay the least amount of taxes?

    d. Which inventory method should be used if the objective is to show the greatest amount of profit in the annual report to the shareholders?

Dollars AND Sense

This Business Decision, "Inventory Valuation and the Bottom Line," clearly illustrates how the various inventory methods can affect a company's profit picture. Note the significant variation in net income among the three methods.

CHAPTER 16

COLLABORATIVE LEARNING ACTIVITY

1. The Counting Game!

As a team, choose two or three competitive retail stores in your area, such as supermarkets, drug stores, hardware stores, shoe stores, or clothing stores. Speak with an accounting and/or merchandise manager for each store to get answers to the following questions.

a. Approximately how many different items are carried in inventory?

b. What method of inventory valuation is being used? Why?

c. What is the store's average inventory?

d. How often is a physical inventory count taken? Who does it?

e. Does the company have a computerized perpetual inventory system? If so, how does it work?

f. What is the inventory turnover ratio? How does this compare with the published industry figures for a company that size? Where did you find the published figures?

g. Which of the companies your team researched has the most efficient inventory system? Why?

2. Radio Frequency Identification, RFID—Today

In teams, use www.rfidjournal.com, www.rfidnews.org, and other sources to find the following information about radio frequency identification (RFID). Present your findings to the class. Use visuals whenever possible.

a. What is radio frequency identification (RFID)?

b. Briefly describe how RFID works, technically.

c. List and describe the applications of RFID and some of the companies using it in these fields:

- Retail
- Manufacturing
- Supply chain management
- Apparel
- Healthcare and hospitals
- Security and privacy
- Logistics
- Other _____

CHAPTER 17 Depreciation

SECTION I

17

TRADITIONAL DEPRECIATION—METHODS USED FOR FINANCIAL STATEMENT REPORTING

long-term or **long-lived assets** Relatively fixed or permanent assets such as land, buildings, tools, equipment, and vehicles that companies acquire in the course of operating a business.

depreciation, or **depreciation expense** The decrease in value from the original cost of a long-term asset over its useful life.

book value The value of an asset at any given time. It is the original cost less the accumulated depreciation to that point.

total cost, or **original basis** The total amount a company pays for an asset, including shipping, handling, and setup charges.

residual, **scrap**, **salvage**, or **trade-in value** The value of an asset at the time it is taken out of service.

useful life The length of time an asset is expected to generate revenue.

In Chapter 15, we learned a firm's assets are divided into three categories: current assets; property, plant, and equipment; and investments and other assets. This chapter deals with the valuation of the **long-term** or **long-lived assets** of the firm: the property, plant, and equipment. Companies acquire these relatively fixed or permanent assets in the course of building and operating a business. Some examples of these assets would be land, buildings, equipment, machinery, vehicles, furniture, fixtures, and tools.

As time goes by, the usefulness or productivity of these assets, except land, decreases. Think of this decrease as a loss of revenue earning power. Accordingly, the cost of these assets is distributed over their useful life to coincide with the revenue earned. This cost write-off is known as **depreciation**. On the income statement, depreciation is listed under operating expenses as **depreciation expense**. On the balance sheet, it is used to determine the current **book value** of an asset, whereby

> **Book value = Original cost − Accumulated depreciation**

Assets depreciate for a number of reasons. They may physically wear out from use and deterioration, or they may depreciate because they have become inadequate and obsolete. Four important factors must be taken into account to determine the amount of depreciation expense of an asset.

1. The **total cost**, or **original basis**, of the asset. This amount includes such items as shipping, handling, and setup charges.
2. The asset's estimated **residual value** at the time it is taken out of service. This is also known as **scrap value**, **salvage value**, and **trade-in value**.
3. An estimate of the **useful life** of the asset, or the length of time it is expected to generate revenue. To be depreciated, an asset must have a life greater than one year.
4. The method of calculating depreciation must match the way in which the asset will depreciate. Some assets depreciate evenly over the years (straight-line depreciation), whereas others depreciate more quickly at first and then slow down in the later years (accelerated depreciation). Regardless of which method a company chooses, at the end of the useful life of an asset, the total amount of depreciation expense write-off will be the same.

This chapter examines the various methods used to depreciate assets. In Section I, we learn to calculate depreciation by the four traditional methods: straight-line, sum-of-the-years' digits, declining-balance, and units-of-production. Any of these methods may be used for financial statement reporting. However, once a method has been implemented, it cannot be changed.

Frequently, the amount of depreciation reported by a company on its financial statements will differ from the amount reported to the IRS for income tax purposes because the IRS allows additional options for calculating depreciation expense. Today the most widely used method for tax purposes is known as the Modified Accelerated Cost Recovery System (MACRS). This method is covered in Section II.

Depreciation is more frequently based on time, how many years an asset is expected to last. Certain assets, however, are depreciated more accurately on the basis of some productivity measure, such as units of output for production machinery or mileage for vehicles, regardless of time. This section deals with both time- and productivity-based depreciation methods.

17-1 CALCULATING DEPRECIATION BY THE STRAIGHT-LINE METHOD

straight-line depreciation A method of depreciation that provides for equal periodic charges to be written off over the estimated useful life of an asset.

Straight-line depreciation is by far the most widely used method in business today. It provides for equal periodic charges to be written off over the estimated useful life of the asset.

Once the annual depreciation has been determined, we can set up a **depreciation schedule**. The depreciation schedule is a chart illustrating the depreciation activity of the asset for each year of its useful life. The chart shows the amount of depreciation each year, the accumulated depreciation to date, and the book value of the asset.

depreciation schedule Chart showing the depreciation activity (depreciation, accumulated depreciation, and book value) of an asset for each year of its useful life.

STEPS TO PREPARE A DEPRECIATION SCHEDULE BY THE STRAIGHT-LINE METHOD

STEP 1. Determine the total cost and salvage value of the asset.

STEP 2. Subtract salvage value from total cost to find the total amount of depreciation.

$$\text{Total depreciation} = \text{Total cost} - \text{Salvage value}$$

STEP 3. Calculate the annual amount of depreciation by dividing the total depreciation by the useful life of the asset.

$$\text{Annual depreciation} = \frac{\text{Total depreciation}}{\text{Estimated useful life (years)}}$$

STEP 4. Set up the depreciation schedule in the form of a chart with the following headings:

End of Year	Annual Depreciation	Accumulated Depreciation	Book Value

Learning Tip

On a depreciation schedule, the starting book value is the *original cost* of the asset and the last book value is the *salvage value* of the asset.

EXAMPLE1 CALCULATING STRAIGHT-LINE DEPRECIATION

Cascade Enterprises purchased a computer system for $9,000. Shipping charges were $125, and setup and programming amounted to $375. The system is expected to last 4 years and has a residual value of $1,500. If Cascade elects to use the straight-line method of depreciation for the computer, calculate the total cost, total depreciation, and annual depreciation. Prepare a depreciation schedule for its useful life.

SOLUTIONSTRATEGY

Step 1. Total cost = Cost + Shipping charges + Setup expenses
Total cost = 9,000 + 125 + 375 = $9,500

Step 2. Total depreciation = Total cost − Salvage value
Total depreciation = 9,500 − 1,500 = $8,000

Step 3. $\text{Annual depreciation} = \dfrac{\text{Total depreciation}}{\text{Estimated useful life (years)}}$

$\text{Annual depreciation} = \dfrac{8,000}{4} = \$2,000$

Step 4.

Cascade Enterprises
Straight-Line Depreciation Schedule
Computer System

End of Year	Annual Depreciation	Accumulated Depreciation	Book Value
			(original cost) $9,500
1	$2,000	$2,000	7,500
2	2,000	4,000	5,500
3	2,000	6,000	3,500
4	2,000	8,000	(salvage value) 1,500

Expensive assets such as this construction equipment are considered long-lived assets, the value of which depreciates over time.

► TRYITEXERCISE 1

Wild Flour Bakery purchased a new bread oven for $125,000. Shipping charges were $1,150, and installation amounted to $750. The oven is expected to last 5 years and has a trade-in value of $5,000. If Wild Flour elects to use the straight-line method, calculate the total cost, total depreciation, and annual depreciation of the oven. Prepare a depreciation schedule for its useful life.

CHECK YOUR ANSWER WITH THE SOLUTION ON PAGE 593.

17-2 CALCULATING DEPRECIATION BY THE SUM-OF-THE-YEARS' DIGITS METHOD

accelerated depreciation Depreciation methods that assume an asset depreciates more in the early years of its useful life than in the later years.

sum-of-the-years' digits A method of accelerated depreciation that allows an asset to depreciate the most during the first year, with decreasing amounts each year thereafter. Total depreciation is based on the total cost of an asset less its salvage value.

The sum-of-the-years' digits and the declining-balance methods of calculating depreciation are the two **accelerated depreciation** methods. These methods assume that an asset depreciates more in the early years of its useful life than in the later years. Under the sum-of-the-years' digits method, the yearly charge for depreciation declines steadily over the estimated useful life of the asset because a successively smaller fraction is applied each year to the total depreciation (total cost − salvage value).

This fraction is known as the **sum-of-the-years' digits** fraction. The denominator of the fraction is the sum of the digits of the estimated life of the asset. This number does not change. The numerator of the fraction is the number of years of useful life remaining. This number changes every year as the asset gets older and older. This sum-of-the-years' digits depreciation rate fraction can be expressed as

$$\text{SYD depreciation rate fraction} = \frac{\text{Years of useful life remaining}}{\text{Sum of the digits of the useful life}}$$

The denominator (the sum of the years' digits) can be calculated by adding all the digits of the years or by using the following formula:

$$\text{SYD} = \frac{n(n+1)}{2}$$

where

$n = $ **the number of years of useful life of the asset**

For example, let's compute the depreciation rate fractions for an asset that has a useful life of 4 years. The denominator, the sum of the digits of 4, is 10. This is calculated by $4 + 3 + 2 + 1 = 10$ or by the SYD formula $4(4 + 1) \div 2 = 10$. Remember, the denominator does not change. The numerator of the fractions will be 4, 3, 2, and 1 for each succeeding year.

Year	Depreciation Rate Fraction	Depreciation Rate Decimal	Depreciation Rate Percent
1	$\frac{4}{10}$	.40	40%
2	$\frac{3}{10}$	.30	30%
3	$\frac{2}{10}$	.20	20%
4	$\frac{1}{10}$	.10	10%

From this chart, we can see that an asset with 4 years of useful life will depreciate $\frac{4}{10}$, or 40%, in the first year; $\frac{3}{10}$, or 30%, in the second year; and so on. The accelerated rate of 40% depreciation write-off in the first year gives the business a reduced tax advantage and therefore an incentive to invest in new equipment.

STEPS TO PREPARE A DEPRECIATION SCHEDULE BY USING THE SUM-OF-THE-YEARS' DIGITS METHOD

STEP 1. Find the total depreciation of the asset by

$$\text{Total depreciation} = \text{Total cost} - \text{Salvage value}$$

STEP 2. Calculate the SYD depreciation rate fraction for each year by

$$\text{SYD depreciation rate fraction} = \frac{\text{Years of useful life remaining}}{\dfrac{n(n+1)}{2}}$$

STEP 3. Calculate the depreciation for each year by multiplying the total depreciation by that year's depreciation rate fraction.

$$\text{Annual depreciation} = \text{Total depreciation} \times \text{Depreciation rate fraction}$$

STEP 4. Set up a depreciation schedule in the form of a chart with the following headings:

End of Year	Total Depreciation	×	Depreciation Rate Fraction	=	Annual Depreciation	Accumulated Depreciation	Book Value

EXAMPLE2 CALCULATING SUM-OF-THE YEARS' DIGITS DEPRECIATION

Spectrum Industries purchased a delivery truck for $35,000. The truck is expected to have a useful life of 5 years and a trade-in value of $5,000. Using the sum-of-the-years' digits method, prepare a depreciation schedule for Spectrum.

SOLUTIONSTRATEGY

The following steps are used to prepare a depreciation schedule by using sum-of-the-years' digits:

Step 1. Total depreciation = Total cost − Salvage value

Total depreciation = 35,000 − 5,000 = $30,000

Step 2. Year 1: SYD depreciation rate fraction = $\dfrac{\text{Years of useful life remaining}}{\dfrac{n(n+1)}{2}}$

SYD depreciation rate fraction = $\dfrac{5}{\dfrac{5(5+1)}{2}} = \dfrac{5}{15}$

The depreciation rate fraction for year 1 is $\frac{5}{15}$. The depreciation fractions for the remaining years will have the same denominator, 15 (the sum of the digits of 5). Only the numerators will change, in descending order. The depreciation fractions for the remaining years are $\frac{4}{15}$, $\frac{3}{15}$, $\frac{2}{15}$, and $\frac{1}{15}$.

Note how accelerated this SYD method is: $\frac{5}{15}$, or $\frac{1}{3}$ (33.3%), of the asset is allowed to be written off in the first year. This is compared with only $\frac{1}{5}$ (20%) per year when using the straight-line method.

Step 3. Annual depreciation = Total depreciation × Depreciation rate fraction

Annual depreciation (year 1) = $30,000 \times \dfrac{5}{15} = \$10,000$

Annual depreciation (year 2) = $30,000 \times \dfrac{4}{15} = \$8,000$

Continue this calculation for each of the remaining 3 years. Then prepare the schedule.

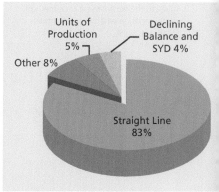

Depreciation Pie According to an Accounting Trends and Techniques survey conducted by the American Institute of Certified Public Accountants (AICPA), the above pie chart shows the breakdown of depreciation methods used by the 600 largest U.S. companies.

Step 4.

Spectrum Industries
SYD Depreciation Schedule
Delivery Truck

End of Year	Total Depreciation	×	Depreciation Rate Fraction	=	Annual Depreciation	Accumulated Depreciation	Book Value
							(new) $35,000
1	$30,000	×	$\dfrac{5}{15}$	=	$10,000	$10,000	25,000
2	30,000	×	$\dfrac{4}{15}$	=	8,000	18,000	17,000
3	30,000	×	$\dfrac{3}{15}$	=	6,000	24,000	11,000
4	30,000	×	$\dfrac{2}{15}$	=	4,000	28,000	7,000
5	30,000	×	$\dfrac{1}{15}$	=	2,000	30,000	5,000

▶ TRYITEXERCISE 2

Bow Valley Kitchens purchased new production-line machinery for a total of $44,500. The company expects this machinery to last 6 years and have a residual value of $2,500. Using the sum-of-the-years' digits method, prepare a depreciation schedule for Bow Valley.

CHECK YOUR ANSWER WITH THE SOLUTION ON PAGE 593.

17-3

CALCULATING DEPRECIATION BY THE DECLINING-BALANCE METHOD

declining-balance A method of accelerated depreciation that uses a multiple (150% or 200%) of the straight-line rate to calculate depreciation.

double-declining balance Name given to the declining-balance method of depreciation when the straight-line multiple is 200%.

The second widely accepted method of accelerated depreciation in business is known as the **declining-balance** method. This method uses a *multiple* of the straight-line rate to calculate depreciation. The most frequently used multiples are 1.5 and 2. When 1.5 is used, it is known as the 150% declining balance. When 2 is the multiple, the method is known as the **double-declining balance**.

To calculate the declining-balance rate, we first determine the straight-line rate by dividing 1 by the number of years of useful life, then multiplying by the appropriate declining-balance multiple. For example, when using the double-declining balance, an asset with a useful life of 4 years would have a straight-line rate of 25% per year ($1 \div 4 = \frac{1}{4} = 25\%$). This rate is then multiplied by the declining-balance multiple, 2, to get 50%, the double-declining rate. The following formula should be used for this calculation:

$$\text{Declining-balance rate} = \frac{1}{\text{Useful life}} \times \text{Multiple}$$

To further accelerate the depreciation, this declining-balance rate is applied to the original total cost of the asset. Salvage value is not considered until the last year of depreciation. When preparing a depreciation schedule by using the declining-balance method, the depreciation stops when the book value of the asset reaches the salvage value. By IRS regulations, the asset cannot be depreciated below the salvage value.

STEPS TO PREPARE A DEPRECIATION SCHEDULE BY USING THE DECLINING-BALANCE METHOD

STEP 1. Calculate the declining-balance rate by the formula

$$\text{Declining-balance rate} = \frac{1}{\text{Useful life}} \times \text{Multiple}$$

STEP 2. Calculate the depreciation for each year by applying the rate to each year's beginning book value, which is the ending book value of the previous year.

$$\text{Depreciation for the year} = \text{Beginning book value} \times \text{Declining-balance rate}$$

STEP 3. Calculate the ending book value for each year by subtracting the depreciation for the year from the beginning book value.

$$\text{Ending book value} = \text{Beginning book value} - \text{Depreciation for the year}$$

STEP 4. When the ending book value equals the salvage value, the depreciation is complete.

STEP 5. Set up a depreciation schedule in the form of a chart with the following headings:

End of Year	Beginning Book Value	Depreciation Rate	Depreciation for the Year	Accumulated Depreciation	Ending Book Value

IN THE Business World

From Chapter 15, "Financial Statements and Ratios," remember that depreciation appears on both the balance sheet and the income statement.

- *Balance sheet*—Used to determine book value of an asset.
- *Income statement*—Listed as an operating expense.

EXAMPLE3 CALCULATING DECLINING BALANCE DEPRECIATION

Allstate Shipping bought a forklift for $20,000. It is expected to have a 5-year useful life and a trade-in value of $2,000. Prepare a depreciation schedule for this asset by using the double-declining balance method.

►SOLUTIONSTRATEGY

Step 1. Declining-balance rate $= \dfrac{1}{\text{Useful life}} \times \text{Multiple}$

Declining-balance rate $= \dfrac{1}{5} \times 2 = .20 \times 2 = .40 = \underline{40\%}$

Step 2. Depreciation for the year = Beginning book value × Declining-balance rate

Depreciation: Year 1 = 20,000 × .40 = $8,000

Step 3. Ending book value = Beginning book value − Depreciation for the year

Ending book value: Year 1 = 20,000 − 8,000 = $12,000

Repeat Steps 2 and 3 for years 2, 3, 4, and 5.

Step 4. In year 5, although the calculated depreciation is $1,036.80 (2,592 × .4), the allowable depreciation is limited to $592 (2,592 − 2,000) because the book value has reached the $2,000 salvage value. At this point, the depreciation is complete.

Step 5.

Allstate Shipping
Double-Declining Balance Depreciation Schedule Forklift

End of Year	Beginning Book Value	Depreciation Rate	Depreciation for the Year	Accumulated Depreciation	Ending Book Value
					(new) $20,000
1	$20,000	40%	$8,000	$8,000	12,000
2	12,000	40%	4,800	12,800	7,200
3	7,200	40%	2,880	15,680	4,320
4	4,320	40%	1,728	17,408	2,592
5	2,592	40%	592*	18,000	2,000

*Maximum allowable to reach salvage value.

▶TRYITEXERCISE 3

Kelowna Air Service bought a small commuter airplane for $386,000. It is expected to have a useful life of 4 years and a trade-in value of $70,000. Prepare a depreciation schedule for the airplane by using the 150% declining-balance method.

CHECK YOUR ANSWER WITH THE SOLUTION ON PAGE 593.

17-4 CALCULATING DEPRECIATION BY THE UNITS-OF-PRODUCTION METHOD

units-of-production Depreciation method based on how much an asset is used, such as miles, hours, or units produced, rather than the passage of time.

When the useful life of an asset is more accurately defined in terms of how much it is used rather than the passage of time, we may use the **units-of-production** method to calculate depreciation. To apply this method, the life of the asset is expressed in productive capacity, such as miles driven, units produced, or hours used. Some examples of assets typically depreciated by using this method would be cars, trucks, airplanes, production-line machinery, engines, pumps, and electronic equipment.

To calculate depreciation by using this method, we begin by determining the depreciation per unit. This number is found by dividing the amount to be depreciated (cost − salvage value) by the estimated units of useful life:

$$\text{Depreciation per unit} = \frac{\text{Cost} - \text{Salvage value}}{\text{Units of useful life}}$$

For example, let's say that a hole-punching machine on a production line had a cost of $35,000 and a salvage value of $5,000. If we estimate that the machine had a useful life of 150,000 units of production, the depreciation per unit would be calculated as follows:

$$\text{Depreciation per unit} = \frac{\text{Cost} - \text{Salvage value}}{\text{Units of useful life}} = \frac{35,000 - 5,000}{150,000} = \frac{30,000}{150,000} = \$.20 \text{ per unit}$$

Once we have determined the depreciation per unit, we can find the annual depreciation by multiplying the depreciation per unit by the number of units produced each year.

$$\text{Annual depreciation} = \text{Depreciation per unit} \times \text{Units produced}$$

In the previous example, if the hole-punching machine produced 30,000 units in a year, the annual depreciation for that year would be as follows:

$$\text{Annual depreciation} = \text{Depreciation per unit} \times \text{Units produced} = .20 \times 30,000 = \$6,000$$

STEPS TO CALCULATE DEPRECIATION BY USING THE UNITS-OF-PRODUCTION METHOD

STEP 1. Determine the depreciation per unit by using

$$\text{Depreciation per unit} = \frac{\text{Cost} - \text{Salvage value}}{\text{Units of useful life}}$$

(Round to the nearest tenth of a cent when necessary.)

STEP 2. Calculate the annual depreciation by using

$$\text{Annual depreciation} = \text{Depreciation per unit} \times \text{Units produced}$$

STEP 3. Set up the depreciation schedule in the form of a chart with the following headings:

End of Year	Depreciation per Unit	Units Produced	Annual Depreciation	Accumulated Depreciation	Book Value

EXAMPLE4 CALCULATING UNITS-OF-PRODUCTION DEPRECIATION

Colorcraft Manufacturing purchased a new metal stamping press for $8,500 with a salvage value of $500. For depreciation purposes, the press is expected to have a useful life of 5,000 hours. From the following estimate of hours of use, prepare a depreciation schedule for the press by using the units-of-production method.

Year	Hours of Use
1	1,500
2	1,200
3	2,000
4	500

►SOLUTIONSTRATEGY

Step 1.
$$\text{Depreciation per unit (hours)} = \frac{\text{Cost} - \text{Salvage value}}{\text{Hours of useful life}}$$

$$\text{Depreciation per unit} = \frac{8,500 - 500}{5,000} = \frac{8,000}{5,000} = \$1.60 \text{ per hour}$$

Step 2.
$$\text{Annual depreciation} = \text{Depreciation per unit} \times \text{Units produced}$$

Annual depreciation (year 1) = 1.60 × 1,500 = $2,400

Annual depreciation (year 2) = 1.60 × 1,200 = $1,920

Continue this procedure for the remaining years.

Step 3.

Colorcraft Manufacturing
Units-of-Production Depreciation Schedule
Metal Stamping Press

End of Year	Depreciation per Hour	Hours Used	Annual Depreciation	Accumulated Depreciation	Book Value
					(new) $8,500
1	$1.60	1,500	$2,400	$2,400	6,100
2	1.60	1,200	1,920	4,320	4,180
3	1.60	2,000	3,200	7,520	980
4	1.60	500	480*	8,000	500

*Maximum allowable to reach salvage value.

TRY IT EXERCISE 4

Prestige Limousine Service purchased a limousine with an expected useful life of 75,000 miles. The cost of the limousine was $54,500, and the residual value was $7,500. If the limousine was driven the following number of miles per year, prepare a depreciation schedule by using the units-of-production method. After finding the depreciation per mile, round this dollar amount to three decimal places for use in calculating your schedule.

Year	Miles Driven
1	12,500
2	18,300
3	15,900
4	19,100
5	12,400

CHECK YOUR ANSWER WITH THE SOLUTION ON PAGE 594.

17 SECTION I REVIEW EXERCISES

Note: Round answers to the nearest cent when necessary.

Calculate the total cost, total depreciation, and annual depreciation for the following assets by using the straight-line method.

	Cost	Shipping Charges	Setup Charges	Total Cost	Salvage Value	Estimated Useful Life (years)	Total Depreciation	Annual Depreciation
1.	$45,000	$150	$500	$45,650	$3,500	10	$42,150	$4,215.00
2.	$88,600	$625	$2,500	_____	$9,000	7	_____	_____
3.	$158,200	0	$1,800	_____	$20,000	5	_____	_____
4.	$900,000	0	$15,500	_____	$100,000	12	_____	_____
5.	$220,000	$400	0	_____	$24,500	10	_____	_____
6.	$76,200	$1,600	$850	_____	$4,500	11	_____	_____
7.	$470,000	0	0	_____	$54,000	8	_____	_____
8.	$34,800	$600	$1,900	_____	$8,100	6	_____	_____

9. The Fluffy Laundromat purchased new washing machines and dryers for $57,000. Shipping charges were $470, and installation amounted to $500. The machines are expected to last 5 years and have a residual value of $2,000. If Fluffy elects to use the straight-line method of depreciation, prepare a depreciation schedule for these machines.

The Fluffy Laundromat
Straight-Line Depreciation Schedule
Laundry Equipment

End of Year	Annual Depreciation	Accumulated Depreciation	Book Value
		(new)	_____
1	_____	_____	_____
2	_____	_____	_____
3	_____	_____	_____
4	_____	_____	_____
5	_____	_____	_____

10. White Mountain Supply Company purchases warehouse shelving for $18,600. Shipping charges were $370, and assembly and setup amounted to $575. The shelves are expected to last for 7 years and have a scrap value of $900. Using the straight-line method of depreciation,

  a. What is the annual depreciation expense of the shelving?

  b. What is the accumulated depreciation after the third year?

  c. What is the book value of the shelving after the fifth year?

Complete Exercises 11–16 as they relate to the sum-of-the-years' digits method of depreciation.

	Useful Life (years)	Sum-of-the- Years' Digits	Depreciation Rate Fraction		
			Year 1	Year 3	Year 5
11.	5	15	$\frac{5}{15}$	$\frac{3}{15}$	$\frac{1}{15}$
12.	7	_____	_____	_____	_____
13.	10	_____	_____	_____	_____
14.	6	_____	_____	_____	_____
15.	15	_____	_____	_____	_____
16.	12	_____	_____	_____	_____

17. Vanguard Manufacturing, Inc., purchased production-line machinery for $445,000. It is expected to last for 6 years and have a trade-in value of $25,000. Using the sum-of-the-years' digits method, prepare a depreciation schedule for Vanguard.

Vanguard Manufacturing, Inc.
SYD Depreciation Schedule
Production-Line Machinery

End of Year	Total Depreciation	Depreciation Rate Fraction	Annual Depreciation	Accumulated Depreciation	Book Value
				(new)	_____
1	_____	_____	_____	_____	_____
2	_____	_____	_____	_____	_____
3	_____	_____	_____	_____	_____
4	_____	_____	_____	_____	_____
5	_____	_____	_____	_____	_____
6	_____	_____	_____	_____	_____

Complete Exercises 18–23 as they relate to the declining-balance method of depreciation. Round to the nearest hundredth of a percent when necessary.

	Useful Life (Years)	Straight-Line Rate (%)	Multiple (%)	Declining-Balance Rate (%)
18.	6	16.67	200	33.34
19.	10	_____	150	_____
20.	4	_____	200	_____
21.	8	_____	150	_____
22.	3	_____	150	_____
23.	20	_____	200	_____

24. A U-Haul franchise bought new trucks for $180,000. The trucks are expected to have an 8-year useful life and a trade-in value of $35,000. Prepare a depreciation schedule by using the 150% declining-balance method for the trucks.

U-Haul
150% Declining-Balance Depreciation Schedule
Truck Fleet

End of Year	Beginning Book Value	Depreciation Rate	Depreciation for the Year	Accumulated Depreciation	Ending Book Value
				(new)	_____
1	_____	_____	_____	_____	_____
2	_____	_____	_____	_____	_____
3	_____	_____	_____	_____	_____
4	_____	_____	_____	_____	_____
5	_____	_____	_____	_____	_____
6	_____	_____	_____	_____	_____
7	_____	_____	_____	_____	_____
8	_____	_____	_____	_____	_____

Since 1945, **U-Haul** has been the first choice of do-it-yourself movers, with a network of more than 15,950 locations in all 50 states in the United States and in 10 Canadian provinces. The U-Haul fleet consists of more than 100,000 trucks, 78,500 trailers, and 31,100 towing devices. U-Haul also offers more than 389,000 rooms and more than 34 million square feet of storage space at more than 1,055 owned and managed facilities throughout North America.

Major competitors include Avis Budget Group, Inc.; Penske Truck Leasing; Public Storage Inc.; Extra Space Storage Inc.; and Sovran Self Storage Inc.

Complete Exercises 25–30 as they relate to the units-of-production method of depreciation. Round to the nearest tenth of a cent when necessary.

	Asset	Cost	Salvage Value	Units of Useful Life	Depreciation per Unit
25.	Pump	$15,000	$2,800	100,000 gallons	$.122
26.	Automobile	$27,400	$3,400	60,000 miles	_____
27.	Assembly robot	$900,000	$20,000	4,000,000 units	_____
28.	Sewing machine	$9,000	$1,800	120,000 garments	_____
29.	Air compressor	$6,500	$700	35,000 hours	_____
30.	Tour bus	$135,000	$10,000	225,000 miles	_____

31. Thunderbird Manufacturing purchased a new stamping machine for $45,000 with a salvage value of $5,000. For depreciation purposes, the machine is expected to have a useful life of 250,000 units of production. Complete the following depreciation schedule by using the units-of-production method:

Thunderbird Manufacturing
Units-of-Production Depreciation Schedule
Stamping Machine

End of Year	Depreciation per Unit	Units Produced	Annual Depreciation	Accumulated Depreciation	Book Value
				(new)	_____
1	_____	50,000	_____	_____	_____
2	_____	70,000	_____	_____	_____
3	_____	45,000	_____	_____	_____
4	_____	66,000	_____	_____	_____
5	_____	30,000	_____	_____	_____

32. You are the accountant for Raleigh Industries, a manufacturer of plastic gears for electric motors. The company's production facility in Pittsburgh has a cost of $3,800,000, an estimated residual value of $400,000, and an estimated useful life of 40 years. You are using the straight-line method of depreciation for this asset.

a. What is the amount of the annual depreciation?

b. What is the book value of the property at the end of the twentieth year of use?

c. If at the start of the twenty-first year you revise your estimate so that the remaining useful life is 15 years and the residual value is $120,000, what should be the depreciation expense for each of the remaining 15 years?

BUSINESS DECISION: REPLACING AN ASSET

33. Supreme Auto Service opened a new service center three decades ago. At the time the center was preparing to open, new equipment was purchased totaling $388,000. Residual value of the equipment was estimated to be $48,000 after 20 years. The company accountant has been using straight-line depreciation on the equipment.

a. How much was the annual depreciation for the original equipment?

b. If the hydraulic lift had originally cost $11,640, what would its residual value be after 20 years?

c. After six years of operation, the original hydraulic lift was replaced with a new model that cost $22,000. Book value was allowed for the old machine as a trade-in. What was the old hydraulic lift's book value when the replacement machine was bought?

d. What was the book value of the equipment inventory at the six-year point, substituting the new hydraulic lift for the original after the new lift had joined the inventory?

David Young-Wolff/Photo Edit

AAMCO has been the recognized leader in the transmission business for over 40 years and has expanded its services into the $200 billion general automotive repair aftermarket. With brand recognition in excess of 90%, AAMCO has almost 900 independently owned and operated shops throughout the United States, Canada, and Puerto Rico.

To purchase an AAMCO franchise requires a down payment of $75,000 and a total capital investment of between $183,000 and $193,000. Twenty-five percent of franchisees own more than one franchise unit.

Section I of this chapter described the depreciation methods used by businesses for the preparation of financial statements. For income tax purposes, the Internal Revenue Service (IRS), through federal tax laws, prescribes how depreciation must be taken.

As part of the Economic Recovery Act of 1981, the IRS introduced a depreciation method known as the accelerated cost recovery system (ACRS), which allowed businesses to depreciate assets more quickly than they could with traditional methods. Faster write-offs encouraged businesses to invest in new equipment and other capital assets more frequently, thereby sparking needed economic growth. Essentially, ACRS discarded the concepts of estimated useful life and residual value. In their place, it required that businesses compute a **cost recovery allowance**.

After the ACRS was modified by the Tax Equity and Fiscal Responsibility Act of 1982 and the Tax Reform Act of 1984, it was significantly overhauled by the Tax Reform Act of 1986. The resulting method was known as the **modified accelerated cost recovery system (MACRS)**. This is the system we will use to calculate depreciation for federal income tax purposes.

cost recovery allowance Term used under MACRS meaning the amount of depreciation of an asset that may be written off for tax purposes in a given year.

modified accelerated cost recovery system (MACRS) A 1986 modification of the property classes and the depreciation rates of the accelerated depreciation method; used for assets put into service after 1986.

17-5 CALCULATING DEPRECIATION BY USING THE MODIFIED ACCELERATED COST RECOVERY SYSTEM (MACRS)

According to the IRS, the modified accelerated cost recovery system (MACRS) is the name given to tax rules for getting back, or recovering, through depreciation deductions the cost of property that is used in a trade or business or to produce income. These rules generally apply to tangible property placed into service *after 1986*.

Before we can calculate the amount of depreciation for a particular asset, we must determine the **basis for depreciation**, or "cost," of that asset for depreciation purposes. Sometimes the basis for depreciation is the original cost of the asset; however, in many cases, the original cost (original basis) is "modified" by various IRS rules, Section 179 deductions, and special depreciation allowances. Once the basis for depreciation has been established, the MACRS depreciation deduction can be calculated for each year and the depreciation schedule can be prepared.

Table 17-1 exhibits the nine main property classes of MACRS and their recovery periods with some examples of assets included in each class. Once the **property class** for the asset has been identified, the amount of depreciation each year can be manually calculated or found by using percentage tables. As a general rule, the 3-, 5-, 7-, and 10-year property class assets are depreciated by using the 200% declining-balance method; the 15- and 20-year classes use the 150% declining-balance method; and the 25-year property, residential rental property, and nonresidential rental property classes use straight-line depreciation.

Because these calculations were already covered in Section I of this chapter, we will focus on using one of the **cost recovery percentage** tables provided by the IRS. Table 17-2 is such a table.

Note that the number of recovery years is one greater than the property class. This is due to a rule known as the **half-year convention**, which assumes that the asset was placed in service in the middle of the first year and therefore begins depreciating at that point. Quarterly tables are listed in IRS Publication 946, How to Depreciate Property, for assets placed in service at other times of the year.

basis for depreciation The cost of an asset for MACRS depreciation purposes. This figure takes into account business usage rules, Section 179 deductions, and special depreciation allowances.

property class One of several time categories to which property is assigned under MACRS that shows how many years are allowed for cost recovery.

cost recovery percentage An IRS-prescribed percentage that is multiplied by the original basis of an asset to determine the depreciation deduction for a given year. Based on property class and year of asset life.

half-year convention IRS rule under MACRS that assumes all property is placed in service or taken out of service at the midpoint of the year regardless of the actual time.

DETERMINING THE ASSET'S BASIS FOR DEPRECIATION

The basis for depreciation of an asset is determined by the percentage of time it is used for business, Section 179 deductions, and special depreciation allowances. To qualify for depreciation, an asset must be used for business a "minimum of 50%" of the time. An asset used for business 100% of the time may be depreciated completely. If, for example, an asset is used only 75% of the time for business, then only 75% of the original cost can be depreciated.

TABLE 17-1 MACRS Property Classes (Recovery Period) General Depreciation System

3-Year Property (3 years)

Over-the-road tractors
Some horses and hogs
Special handling devices for the
  manufacture of food and beverages
Specialty tools used in the manufacture
  of motor vehicles
Specialty tools used in the manufacture
  of finished products made of plastic,
  rubber, glass, and metal

5-Year Property (5 years)

Automobiles and taxis
Buses and trucks
Computers and peripherals
Office machinery
Breeding or dairy cattle, sheep and goats
Airplanes (except those in commercial use)
Trailers and trailer-mounted containers
Assets used in construction
Assets used in the manufacture of knitted
  goods, textile yarns, carpets, medical
  and dental supplies, chemicals, and
  electronic components
Assets used in radio and television
  broadcasting, and CATV

7-Year Property (7 years)

Office furniture and fixtures
Railroad cars and engines
Commercial airplanes
Assets used in the manufacture of wood,
  pulp, and paper products
Assets used in printing and publishing
Assets used in the production of tobacco,
  leather, stone, and steel products
Assets used in the production of sporting
  goods, toys, jewelry, and musical instruments
Assets used in theme and amusement
  parks, theaters, concert halls, and
  miniature golf courses

10-Year Property (10 years)

Vessels, barges, and tugs
Single-purpose agricultural structures
Trees and vines bearing fruits or nuts
Assets used in the production of grain, sugar,
  and vegetable oil products
Assets used in petroleum refining
Assets used in the manufacture and repair of
  ships, boats, and marine drilling rigs

15-Year Property (15 years)

Depreciable improvements made to land,
such as shrubbery, fences, roads, and
bridges
Assets used to manufacture cement
Gas and petroleum utility pipelines
Industrial steam and electric generation and/
  or distribution systems
Water taxis and ferry boats

20-Year Property (20 years)

Farm buildings
Railroad structures and improvements
Communication cable and long-line systems
Water, electric, gas, and steam utility plants and
  equipment

25-Year Property (25 years)

Municipal sewers
Certain water utility property integral to
the
  gathering, treatment, or commercial
  distribution of water

Residential Rental Property (27.5 years)

This is any building or structure, such as a
rental home (including a mobile home), if
80% of its gross rental income for the tax
year is from dwelling units. A dwelling
unit is a house or an apartment used to
provide living accommodations.

Nonresidential Real Property (39 years)

This is property such as an office building,
a store, or a warehouse that is not residential
rental property.

TABLE 17-2 Cost Recovery Percentage Table MACRS

Recovery Year	Depreciation Rate for Property Class					
	3-year	5-year	7-year	10-year	15-year	20-year
1	33.33%	20.00%	14.29%	10.00%	5.00%	3.750%
2	44.45	32.00	24.49	18.00	9.50	7.219
3	14.81	19.20	17.49	14.40	8.55	6.677
4	7.41	11.52	12.49	11.52	7.70	6.177
5		11.52	8.93	9.22	6.93	5.713
6		5.76	8.92	7.37	6.23	5.285
7			8.93	6.55	5.90	4.888
8			4.46	6.55	5.90	4.522
9				6.56	5.91	4.462
10				6.55	5.90	4.461
11				3.28	5.91	4.462
12					5.90	4.461
13					5.91	4.462
14					5.90	4.461
15					5.91	4.462
16					2.95	4.461
17						4.462
18						4.461
19						4.462
20						4.461
21						2.231

Learning Tip

In MACRS, the entire asset is
depreciated. There is no salvage value.
Note that the percents for any given
property class in the Cost Recovery
Percentage Table add up to 100%.

To stimulate business activity, Congress signed into law "The Jobs and Growth Tax Relief Reconciliation Act of 2003" on May 18, 2003. This federal act contains major depreciation rule changes that affect many individual taxpayers and small businesses.

SECTION 179 DEDUCTIONS

As the table below shows, Section 179 deductions have varied widely over the years.

Section 179 deductions are a way for small businesses to write off in one year all or part of certain business assets that are usually depreciated over many years using MACRS. These assets include most business machinery and equipment, furniture, fixtures, storage facilities, and off-the-shelf software. Table 17-3 lists the Section 179 deductions over the past few years.

SPECIAL DEPRECIATION ALLOWANCE

The law provided additional depreciation allowances for qualified MACRS assets with a class life of 20 years or less and acquired and placed into service according to the dates in Table 17-4. This allowance is an additional deduction after the Section 179 deduction and before regular depreciation under MACRS. Certain limits and numerous restrictions apply to these depreciation tax rules. For the latest information, once again refer to IRS Publication 946, How to Depreciate Property, at www.irs.gov.

Dollars AND Sense

You can allocate the Section 179 deduction among qualifying assets in any way you want, thus reducing the basis of each of the assets. It is generally to your advantage to take the deduction on those assets that have the longest life, thus recovering your basis sooner, and use the regular depreciation methods on those assets that have short lives.

TABLE 17-3 Section 179 Deductions

Year Asset Was Placed into Service	Maximum Section 179 Deduction	
1996	$17,500	
1997	$18,000	
1998	$18,500	
1999	$19,000	
2000	$20,000	
2001	$24,000	
2002	$25,000	
2003	$100,000	◄ Jobs and Growth Tax Relief Act
2004–2005	$102,000	
2006	$108,000	
2007	$112,000	
2008–2010	$250,000	◄ The Great Recession
2011–2014	$500,000	

TABLE 17-4 Special Depreciation Allowance

Certain Qualified Asset Placed into Service	Special Allowance
September 11, 2001–May 5, 2003	30%
May 6, 2003–January 1, 2005	50%
December 31, 2007–January 1, 2015	50%

STEPS TO PREPARE A DEPRECIATION SCHEDULE BY USING MACRS

STEP 1. Calculate the basis for depreciation—the **cost** of the particular asset for depreciation purposes.

a. Percent of business use: If an asset is used for business less than 100% of the time, multiply the original cost by the business-use percentage of the asset. (*Note*: The minimum percentage for an asset to qualify for depreciation is 50%.)

Business-use basis = Original cost × Business-use percentage

b. Section 179 deduction: Determine the amount of the Section 179 deduction you choose to take, up to the limit, and subtract that amount from the business-use basis for depreciation.

Tentative basis = Business-use basis − Section 179 deduction

c. Special depreciation allowances: For qualifying assets, apply any special depreciation allowances, as specified in Table 17-4, to the tentative basis for depreciation.

Basis for depreciation =
Tentative basis(100% − Special depreciation allowance percent)

STEP 2. Set up the depreciation schedule in the form of a chart with the following headings:

End of Year	Basis for Depreciation	Cost Recovery Percentage	MACRS Depreciation Deduction	Accumulated Depreciation	Book Value

Use Table 17-1 to determine the property class for the asset and Table 17-2 to find the cost recovery percentages for each year. Calculate the MACRS depreciation deduction for each year by multiplying the basis for depreciation by the cost recovery percentages.

MACRS depreciation deduction =
Basis for depreciation × Cost recovery percentage for that year

---

EXAMPLE5 — PREPARING A MACRS DEPRECIATION SCHEDULE

On July 27, 2013, Utopia Industries purchased and placed into service new office and computer equipment costing $400,000. This equipment is used for business 100% of the time. The accountants have elected to take a $30,000 Section 179 deduction. Prepare a depreciation schedule for the new asset by using MACRS.

►SOLUTIONSTRATEGY

We begin by calculating the basis for depreciation:

Step 1a. Because the equipment is used for business 100% of the time, the business-use basis for depreciation is the same as the original cost of the asset.

Business-use basis = Original cost × Business-use percentage
Business-use basis = $400,000 × 100% = $400,000

Step 1b. We find the tentative basis for depreciation by subtracting the section 179 deduction of $30,000 from the business-use basis.

Tentative basis = Business-use basis − Section 179 deduction
Tentative basis = $400,000 − $30,000 = $370,000

Step 1c. We find the basis for depreciation by applying the special depreciation allowance.

Basis for depreciation = Tentative basis(100% − Special depreciation allowance percent)
Basis for depreciation = $370,000(100% − 50%) = $185,000

Step 2. Let's set up the depreciation schedule. From Table 17-1, we find that office and computer equipment is in the 5-year property class. Table 17-2 provides the cost recovery percentage for each year. Note once again, the extra year is to allow for the assumption that the asset was placed in service at mid-year.

Utopia Industries
MACRS Depreciation Schedule
Office and Computer Equipment

End of Year	Basis for Depreciation	Cost Recovery Percentage	MACRS Depreciation Deduction	Accumulated Depreciation	Book Value
					(new) $185,000
1	$185,000	20.00%	$37,000	$37,000	148,000
2	185,000	32.00	59,200	96,200	88,800
3	185,000	19.20	35,520	131,720	53,280
4	185,000	11.52	21,312	153,032	31,968
5	185,000	11.52	21,312	174,344	10,656
6	185,000	5.76	10,656	185,000	0

▶ **TRYITEXERCISE 5**

Roadway Trucking purchased and placed into service an over-the-road tractor for $135,500 in 2014. The vehicle was used for business 80% of the time. The accountant took a $20,000 Section 179 deduction for the year 2014. Prepare a depreciation schedule for this new asset by using MACRS.

CHECK YOUR ANSWER WITH THE SOLUTION ON PAGE 594.

17-6 CALCULATING THE PERIODIC DEPLETION COST OF NATURAL RESOURCES

Just as depreciation is used to write off the useful life of plant assets such as trucks, equipment, and buildings, depletion is used to account for the consumption of natural resources such as coal, petroleum, timber, natural gas, and minerals. **Depletion** is the proportional allocation of the cost of natural resources to the units used up, or depleted, per accounting period. In accounting, natural resources are also known as **wasting assets** because they are considered to be exhausted, or used up, as they are converted into inventory by mining, pumping, or cutting.

Depletion of natural resources is calculated the same way as the units-of-production method of depreciation for plant assets. To calculate the depletion allocation, we must determine the following:

depletion The proportional allocation or write-off of the cost of natural resources to the units used up, or depleted, per accounting period. Calculated the same way as units-of-production depreciation.

wasting assets An accounting term used to describe natural resources that are exhausted, or used up, as they are converted into inventory by mining, pumping, or cutting.

a. *Total cost of the natural resource package*, including the original purchase price, exploration expenses, and extraction or cutting expenses.
b. *Residual or salvage value* of the property after resources have been exhausted.
c. *Estimated total number of units* (tons, barrels, and board feet) of resource available.

STEPS **TO CALCULATE THE PERIODIC DEPLETION COST OF NATURAL RESOURCES**

STEP 1. Compute the average depletion cost per unit by

$$\text{Average depletion cost per unit} = \frac{\text{Total cost of resource} - \text{Residual value}}{\text{Estimated total units available}}$$

(Round to the nearest tenth of a cent when necessary.)

STEP 2. Calculate the periodic depletion cost by

$$\text{Periodic depletion cost} = \frac{\text{Units produced in}}{\text{current period}} \times \frac{\text{Average depletion}}{\text{cost per unit}}$$

EXAMPLE6   CALCULATE THE PERIODIC DEPLETION COST OF NATURAL RESOURCES

Black Gold Oil, Inc., purchased a parcel of land containing an estimated 1.5 million barrels of crude oil for $16,000,000. Two oil wells were drilled at a cost of $3,400,000. The residual value of the property and equipment is $2,500,000. Calculate the periodic depletion cost for the first year of operation if 325,000 barrels were extracted.

▶SOLUTIONSTRATEGY

Step 1. Average depletion cost per unit $= \dfrac{\text{Total cost of resource} - \text{Residual value}}{\text{Estimated total units available}}$

Average depletion cost barrel $= \dfrac{(16,000,000 + 3,400,000) - 2,500,000}{1,500,000} = \$11.27$ per barrel

Step 2. Periodic depletion cost = Units produced in current period × Average depletion cost per unit

Periodic depletion cost $= 325,000 \times 11.27 = \underline{\$3,662,750}$

▶TRYITEXERCISE 6

The Canmore Mining Company paid $5,330,000 for a parcel of land, including the mining rights. In addition, the company spent $900,000 on labor and equipment to prepare the site for mining operations. After mining is completed, it is estimated that the land and equipment will have a residual value of $400,000. Geologists estimated that the mine contains 185,000 tons of coal. If Canmore mined 15,000 tons of coal in the first year, what is the amount of the depletion cost?

CHECK YOUR ANSWER WITH THE SOLUTION ON PAGE 594.

Natural resources are also known as wasting assets because they are considered to be used up when converted into inventory.

© Smit/Shutterstock.com

REVIEW EXERCISES

17   SECTION II

1. Ink Masters Printing purchased a new printing press for $660,000 on February 9, 2010. The press is used for business 90% of the time. As the accountant for the company, you elected to take a $100,000 Section 179 deduction. The press also qualified for a special depreciation allowance. (See Table 17-4.)

   a. What was the basis for depreciation of the printing press?

   Business-use basis = 660,000 × .9 = $594,000
   Tentative basis = 594,000 − 100,000 = $494,000
   The asset qualifies for a 50% special depreciation allowance (Table 17-4).
   Basis for depreciation = 494,000 (100% − 50%) = $247,000

   b. What was the amount of the third year's depreciation using MACRS?

   Printing presses are in the 7-year property class (Table 17-1).
   Third-year depreciation = 17.49% (Table 17-2)
   247,000 × .1749 = $43,200.30

2. Trident Developers purchased a computer system for $75,000 on April 27, 2014. The computer system is used for business 100% of the time. The accountant for the company elected to take a $10,000 Section 179 deduction, and the asset qualified for a special depreciation allowance. (see Table 17-4)

a. What was the basis for depreciation of the computer system?

b. What was the amount of the first year's depreciation using MACRS?

3. Mid-State Construction built roads and a bridge at Atlantis World in Orlando, Florida, at a cost of $15,000,000. Atlantis World uses MACRS for tax purposes. No Section 179 or special depreciation allowances were taken.

a. What is the second year's depreciation deduction?

b. What is the ninth year's depreciation deduction?

4. Sunnyland Orange Groves planted fruit trees valued at $375,000 on February 12, 2014. The accountant for the company took a $75,000 Section 179 deduction, and the asset is entitled to a special depreciation allowance.

a. What is the basis for depreciation of the fruit trees?

b. What is the property class for this asset under MACRS?

c. What is the percentage for the sixth year of depreciation for this property?

d. What is the amount of the depreciation expense in the final year of write-off?

5. Island Hoppers Airways of Hawaii purchased a new commercial airplane for $2,400,000. The airplane is used for business 100% of the time. No Section 179 or special allowances are available for this asset. As the accountant for the company, prepare a depreciation schedule for the asset by using MACRS.

6. All-That-Glitters Mining Company paid $49,250,000 for a parcel of land, including the gold mining rights. In addition, the company spent $7,462,500 to prepare the site for mining operations. It is estimated that the residual value of the asset will be $5,300,000. Geologists estimate the site contains a total of 225,000 ounces of gold.

a. What is the average depletion cost per ounce?

Total depletion = 49,250,000 + 7,462,500 − 5,300,000 = $51,412,500

$$\text{Average depletion cost per ounce} = \frac{51,412,500}{225,000} = \underline{\underline{\$228.50}}$$

b. If 16,200 ounces were mined in the first year of operation, what is the amount of the depletion cost?

First-year depletion cost = 16,200 × 228.50 = $3,701,700

7. Sequoia Timber Company purchased land containing an estimated 6,500,000 board feet of lumber for $3,700,000. The company invested another $300,000 to construct access roads and a company depot. The residual value of the property and equipment is estimated to be $880,000.

a. What is the average depletion cost per board foot of lumber?

b. If 782,000 board feet were cut in the second year of operation, what is the amount of the depletion cost for that year?

BUSINESS DECISION: INTANGIBLE WRITE-OFFS

8. As you have seen in this chapter, companies depreciate, or write off, the expense of *tangible assets* such as trucks and equipment over a period of their useful lives. Many companies also have *intangible assets* that must be accounted for as an expense over a period of time.

Intangible assets are resources that benefit the company but do not have any physical substance. Some examples are copyrights, franchises, patents, trademarks, and leases. In accounting, intangible assets are written off in a procedure known as asset amortization. This is much like straight-line depreciation, but there is no salvage value.

You are the accountant for Front Line Pharmaceuticals, Inc. In January 2000, the company purchased the patent rights for a new medication from Novae, Inc., for $9,000,000. The patent had 15 years remaining as its useful life. In January 2005, Front Line Pharmaceuticals successfully defended its right to the patent in a lawsuit that cost $550,000 in legal fees.

a. Using the straight-line method, calculate the patent's annual amortization expense for the years before the lawsuit.

b. Calculate the revised annual amortization expense for the remaining years after the lawsuit.

CHAPTER FORMULAS

Straight-Line Method

Total cost = Cost + Shipping charges + Setup expenses

Total depreciation = Total cost − Salvage value

$$\text{Annual depreciation} = \frac{\text{Total depreciation}}{\text{Estimated useful life (years)}}$$

Sum-of-the-Years' Digits Method

$$\text{SYD depreciation rate fraction} = \frac{\text{Years of useful life remaining}}{\dfrac{n(n+1)}{2}}$$

Annual depreciation = Total depreciation × Depreciation rate fraction

Declining-Balance Method

$$\text{Declining-balance rate} = \frac{1}{\text{Useful life}} \times \text{Multiple}$$

Depreciation for the year = Beginning book value × Declining-balance rate

Ending book value = Beginning book value − Depreciation for the year

Units-of-Production Method

$$\text{Depreciation per unit} = \frac{\text{Cost} - \text{Salvage value}}{\text{Units of useful life}}$$

Annual depreciation = Depreciation per unit × Units produced

MACRS Depreciation

Business-use basis = Original cost × Business-use percentage

Tentative basis = Business-use basis − Section 179 deduction

Basis for depreciation = Tentative basis(100% − Special depr. allowance percent)

MACRS depr. deduction = Basis for depr. × Cost recovery percentage for that year

Natural Resource Depletion

$$\text{Average depletion cost per unit} = \frac{\text{Total cost of resource} - \text{Residual value}}{\text{Estimated total units available}}$$

Periodic depl. cost = Units produced in current period × Average depl. cost per unit

CHAPTER SUMMARY

Section I: Traditional Depreciation—Methods Used for Financial Statement Reporting

Topic	Important Concepts	Illustrative Examples
Calculating Depreciation by the Straight-Line Method **Performance Objective 17-1, Page 570**	Straight-line depreciation provides for equal periodic charges to be written off over the estimated useful life of the asset. 1. Determine the total cost and residual value of the asset. 2. Subtract residual value from total cost to find the total amount of depreciation. Total depr. = Total cost − Residual value 3. Calculate the annual depreciation by dividing the total depreciation by the useful life of the asset. $\text{Annual depreciation} = \dfrac{\text{Total depreciation}}{\text{Estimated useful life}}$	Golden National Bank purchased a closed-circuit television system for $45,000. Shipping charges were $325, and installation expenses amounted to $2,540. The system is expected to last 5 years and has a residual value of $3,500. Prepare a depreciation schedule for the system. Total cost = 45,000 + 325 + 2,540 = $47,865 Total depr. = 47,865 − 3,500 = $44,365 Annual depr. = $\dfrac{44,365}{5}$ = $8,873

Section I (continued)

Topic	Important Concepts	Illustrative Examples
	4. Set up a depreciation schedule in the form of a chart.	

End of Year	Annual Depreciation	Accumulated Depreciation	Book Value

End of Year	Annual Depr.	Accum. Depr.	Book Value
			(new) $47,865
1	$8,873	$8,873	38,992
2	8,873	17,746	30,119
3	8,873	26,619	21,246
4	8,873	35,492	12,373
5	8,873	44,365	3,500

Calculating Depreciation by the Sum-of-the-Years' Digits Method

Performance Objective 17-2, Page 572

The sum-of-the-years' digits method is one of the accelerated methods of calculating depreciation.

1. Find the total depreciation of the asset:

$$\text{Total depreciation} = \text{Total cost} - \text{Residual value}$$

2. Calculate the SYD depreciation rate fraction for each year:

$$\text{SYD depr. rate fraction} = \frac{\text{Years of life remaining}}{\dfrac{n(n+1)}{2}}$$

3. Calculate the depreciation for each year:

$$\text{Annual depreciation} = \text{Total depreciation} \times \text{Depreciation rate fraction}$$

Illustrative Examples:

The Gourmet Diner purchased new kitchen equipment for $165,000 with a 4-year useful life and a salvage value of $5,000. Using the sum-of-the-years' digits method, calculate the depreciation expense for year 1 and year 3.

Total depr. $= 165,000 - 5,000 = \underline{160,000}$

$$\text{Rate fraction year 1} = \frac{4}{\dfrac{4(4+1)}{2}} = \frac{4}{10}$$

$$\text{Depr. year 1} = 160,000 \times \frac{4}{10} = \underline{\$64,000}$$

$$\text{Rate fraction year 3} = \frac{2}{\dfrac{4(4+1)}{2}} = \frac{2}{10}$$

$$\text{Depr. year 3} = 160,000 \times \frac{2}{10} = \underline{\underline{\$32,000}}$$

Calculating Depreciation by the Declining-Balance Method

Performance Objective 17-3, Page 574

Declining-balance depreciation, the second accelerated method, uses a multiple of the straight-line rate, such as 150% or 200%. Salvage value is not considered until the last year.

1. Calculate the declining-balance rate:

$$\text{Declining-balance rate} = \frac{1}{\text{Useful life}} \times \text{Multiple}$$

2. Calculate the depreciation for each year by applying the rate to each year's beginning book value.

$$\text{Depreciation for year} = \text{Beginning book value} \times \text{Declining balance rate}$$

3. Calculate the ending book value for each year by subtracting the depreciation for the year from the beginning book value.

$$\text{Ending book value} = \text{Beginning book value} - \text{Depreciation for year}$$

4. The depreciation is complete when the ending book value equals the salvage value.

Illustrative Examples:

The Fitness Factory purchased a treadmill for $5,000. It is expected to last 4 years and have a salvage value of $1,000. Use 150% declining-balance depreciation to calculate the book value after each year. Round your answer to dollars.

$$\text{Declining-balance rate} = \frac{1}{4} \times 1.5 = .375$$

Year 1:
Depr. $= 5,000 \times .375 = 1,875$
Book value $= 5,000 - 1,875 = \underline{\$3,125}$

Year 2:
Depr. $= 3,125 \times .375 = 1,172$
Book value $= 3,125 - 1,172 = \underline{\$1,953}$

Year 3:
Depr. $= 1,953 \times .375 = 732$
Book value $= 1,953 - 732 = \underline{\$1,221}$

Year 4:
Depr. $= 1,221 \times .375 = 458$
Book value $= 1,221 - 221 = \$1,000*$

*In year 4, the calculated depreciation is $458. Because the book value of an asset cannot fall below the salvage value, the allowable depreciation is limited to $\underline{\$221}$ $(1,221 - 1,000 = 221)$.

Section I (continued)

Topic	Important Concepts	Illustrative Examples
Calculating Depreciation by the Units-of-Production Method **Performance Objective 17-4, Page 576**	When the useful life of an asset is more accurately defined in terms of how much it is used, such as miles driven or units produced, we may apply the units-of-production method. 1. Determine the depreciation cost per unit by using $$\text{Depreciation per unit} = \frac{\text{Cost} - \text{Salvage value}}{\text{Units of useful life}}$$ 2. Calculate the depreciation for each year by using Annual depreciation = Depreciation per unit × Units produced	Vita Foods purchased a new canning machine for one of its chicken soup production lines at a cost of \$455,000. The machine has an expected useful life of 1,000,000 cans and a residual value of \$25,000. In the first year, the machine produced 120,000 cans. Calculate the depreciation on the machine for year 1. $$\text{Depreciation per unit} = \frac{455,000 - 25,000}{1,000,000}$$ $$= \$0.43$$ First-year depreciation cost = 120,000 × .43 $$= \$51,600$$

Section II: Asset Cost Recovery Systems—IRS–Prescribed Methods for Income Tax Reporting

Topic	Important Concepts	Illustrative Examples

Calculating Depreciation by Using the Modified Accelerated Cost Recovery System (MACRS)
 	
Performance Objective 17-5, Page 582
	MACRS is used for assets placed in service after 1986. This system uses property classes, Table 17-1, and recovery percentages, Table 17-2. To determine the basis for depreciation, use the Section 179 deductions in Table 17-3 and the special depreciation allowance dates in Table 17-4.
	
	1. Calculate the basis for depreciation.
	  a. Percent of business use (Minimum 50% to qualify):
	
	  Business-use basis =
	    Original cost × Business-use percentage
	
	  b. Section 179 deduction (Table 17-3):
	
	  Tentative basis =
	    Business-use basis − Section 179 deduction
	
	  c. Special Depreciation Allowances (Table 17-4):
	
	  Basis for depreciation = Tentative basis
	  (100% − Special depreciation allowance percent)
	
	2. **MACRS depreciation deduction (Tables 17-1 and 17-2)**
	
	  MACRS depreciation deduction =
	    Basis for depreciation × Cost recovery
	                  percentage for that year
		Harbor Helpers purchased a tugboat for \$650,000. The boat is used for business 100% of the time. No Section 179 or special allowances were available. As the accountant, use MACRS to calculate the depreciation expense for the second and fifth year.
		  Using Table 17-1, we find that tugboats are considered 10-year property.
		
		MACRS Depreciation Expense:
		
		Year 2:
		  650,000 × .18 = \$117,000
		
		Year 5:
		  650,000 × .0922 = \$59,930

Calculating the Periodic Depletion Cost of Natural Resources **Performance Objective 17-6, Page 586**	Depletion is the proportional allocation of natural resources to the units used up, or depleted, per accounting period. Depletion is calculated the same way as the units-of-production method of depreciation. 1. Compute the average depletion cost per unit: $$\text{Average depletion/unit} = \frac{\text{Total cost} - \text{Salvage}}{\text{Total units available}}$$ 2. Calculate the periodic depletion cost: Periodic depletion cost = Current units × Average depletion per unit	The Mother Lode Mining Company purchased a parcel of land containing an estimated 800,000 tons of iron ore. The cost of the asset was \$2,000,000. An additional \$350,000 was spent to prepare the property for mining. The estimated residual value of the asset is \$500,000. If the first year's output was 200,000 tons, what is the amount of the depletion allowance? $$\text{Avg. depl. per unit} = \frac{2,350,000 - 500,000}{800,000}$$ $$= \$2.31 \text{ per ton}$$ First-year depletion cost = 200,000 × 2.31 $$= \$462,000$$

TRY IT: EXERCISE SOLUTIONS FOR CHAPTER 17

1. Total cost = Cost + Shipping charges + Setup expenses

Total cost = 125,000 + 1,150 + 750 = $\underline{\underline{\$126,900}}$

Total depreciation = Total cost − Salvage value

Total depreciation = 126,900 − 5,000 = $\underline{\underline{\$121,900}}$

$$\text{Annual depreciation} = \frac{\text{Total depreciation}}{\text{Estimated useful life}}$$

$$\text{Annual depreciation} = \frac{121,900}{5} = \underline{\underline{\$24,380}}$$

Wild Flour Bakery
Straight-Line Depreciation Schedule
Bread Oven

End of Year	Annual Depreciation	Accumulated Depreciation	Book Value
			(cost) $126,900
1	$24,380	$24,380	102,520
2	24,380	48,760	78,140
3	24,380	73,140	53,760
4	24,380	97,520	29,380
5	24,380	121,900	(salvage value) 5,000

2. Total depreciation = Total cost − Salvage value

Total depreciation = 44,500 − 2,500 = $\underline{\underline{\$42,000}}$

$$\text{SYD depreciation rate fraction} = \frac{\text{Years of useful life remaining}}{\frac{n(n+1)}{2}}$$

$$\text{Rate fraction year 1} = \frac{6}{\frac{6(6+1)}{2}} = \frac{6}{\frac{42}{2}} = \frac{6}{21}$$

Bow Valley Kitchens

End of Year	Total Depreciation	Rate Fraction	Annual Depreciation	Accumulated Depreciation	Book Value
					(new) $44,500
1	$42,000	$\frac{6}{21}$	$12,000	$12,000	32,500
2	42,000	$\frac{5}{21}$	10,000	22,000	22,500
3	42,000	$\frac{4}{21}$	8,000	30,000	14,500
4	42,000	$\frac{3}{21}$	6,000	36,000	8,500
5	42,000	$\frac{2}{21}$	4,000	40,000	4,500
6	42,000	$\frac{1}{21}$	2,000	42,000	2,500

3. $\text{Declining-balance rate} = \dfrac{1}{\text{Useful life}} \times \text{Multiple}$

$\text{Declining-balance rate} = \dfrac{1}{4} \times 1.5 = .375$

Kelowna Air Service

End of Year	Beginning Book Value	Depreciation Rate	Depreciation for Year	Accumulated Depreciation	Ending Book Value
					(new) $386,000.00
1	$386,000.00	37.5%	$144,750.00	$144,750.00	241,250.00
2	241,250.00	37.5%	90,468.75	235,218.75	150,781.25
3	150,781.25	37.5%	56,542.97	291,761.72	94,238.28
4	94,238.28	37.5%	24,238.28*	316,000.00	70,000.00

*Maximum allowable to reach salvage value

4. Depreciation per unit $= \dfrac{\text{Cost} - \text{Salvage value}}{\text{Units of useful life}}$

Depreciation per unit $= \dfrac{54{,}500 - 7{,}500}{75{,}000} = \$0.627/\text{mile}$

Prestige Limousine Service

End of Year	Depreciation per Mile	Miles Used	Annual Depreciation	Accumulated Depreciation	Book Value
					(new) $54,500.00
1	$.627	12,500	$7,837.50	$7,837.50	46,662.50
2	.627	18,300	11,474.10	19,311.60	35,188.40
3	.627	15,900	9,969.30	29,280.90	25,219.10
4	.627	19,100	11,975.70	41,256.60	13,243.40
5	.627	12,400	5,743.40*	47,000.00	7,500.00

*Maximum allowable to reach salvage value.

5. MACRS 3-Year Property

Business-use basis = Original cost × Business-use percentage

Business-use basis = 135,500 × 80% = $108,400

Tentative basis = Business-use basis − Section 179 deductions

Tentative basis = 108,400 − 20,000 = $88,400

There are no special allowances available for this asset.

Basis for depreciation = $88,400

Roadway Trucking
Over-the-Road Tractor

End of Year	Original Basis	Cost Recovery Percentage	Cost Recovery	Accumulated Depreciation	Book Value
					(new) $88,400.00
1	$88,400	33.33	$29,463.72	$29,463.72	58,936.28
2	88,400	44.45	39,293.80	68,757.52	19,642.48
3	88,400	14.81	13,092.04	81,849.56	6,550.44
4	88,400	7.41	6,550.44	88,400.00	0

6. Average depletion cost per unit $= \dfrac{\text{Total cost} - \text{Residual value}}{\text{Estimated total units available}}$

Average depletion cost per unit $= \dfrac{(5{,}330{,}000 + 900{,}000) - 400{,}000}{185{,}000} = \dfrac{5{,}830{,}000}{185{,}000}$

$= 31.513 = \$31.51$

Periodic depletion cost = Units produced × Average depletion cost per unit

Periodic depletion cost (1st year) = 15,000 × 31.51 = $\underline{\$472{,}650}$

CONCEPT REVIEW

1. The decrease in value from the original cost of a long-term asset over its useful life is known as _____. (17-1)

2. The total cost or original _____ is the total amount a company pays for an asset. The _____ value is an asset's value at any given time during its useful life. (17-1)

3. The useful _____ is the length of time an asset is expected to generate revenue. The value of an asset at the time it is taken out of service is known as its _____, scrap, salvage, or trade-in-value. (17-1)

4. _____ depreciation is a method of depreciation that provides for equal periodic charges to be written off over the life of an asset. (17-1)

5. Depreciation methods that assume an asset depreciates more in the early years of its useful life are known as _____ depreciation. (17-2)

6. _____ digits is a method of accelerated depreciation that allows an asset to depreciate the most during the first year of its useful life. (17-2)

7. Write the formula for the sum of the digits of the useful life of an asset, where *n* is the number of years of useful life. (17-2)

8. A method of accelerated depreciation that uses a multiple (150% or 200%) of the straight-line rate is known as the _____ method. (17-3)

9. Write the formula for the declining-balance rate. (17-3)

10. Write the formula for the depreciation per unit in the units-of-production method. (17-4)

11. According to the IRS, the depreciation system for getting back, or recovering, the cost of property used to produce income is known as the _____ system. This system is abbreviated as _____. (17-5)

12. The IRS system named in item 11 lists assets in various time categories known as _____ classes. Once an asset's class has been determined, a table is used to find the cost _____ percentage for the recovery year in question. (17-5)

13. The depreciation of natural resources is known as _____. The accounting term used to describe these natural resources is _____ assets. (17-6)

14. When natural resources are depleted, the average depletion cost per unit is equal to _____. (17-6)

ASSESSMENT TEST

Calculate the total cost, total depreciation, and annual depreciation for the following assets by using the straight-line method.

	Cost	Shipping Charges	Setup Charges	Total Cost	Salvage Value	Estimated Useful Life (years)	Depreciation Total	Depreciation Annual
1.	$5,600	$210	$54	_____	$600	6	_____	_____
2.	$16,900	$310	0	_____	$1,900	4	_____	_____

EXCEL 2

3. Oxford Manufacturing, Inc., purchased new equipment totaling $648,000. Shipping charges were $2,200, and installation amounted to $1,800. The equipment is expected to last 4 years and have a residual value of $33,000. If the company elects to use the straight-line method of depreciation, prepare a depreciation schedule for these assets.

Oxford Manufacturing, Inc.
Straight-Line Depreciation Schedule
Manufacturing Equipment

End of Year	Annual Depreciation	Accumulated Depreciation	Book Value
		(new)	_____
1	_____	_____	_____
2	_____	_____	_____
3	_____	_____	_____
4	_____	_____	_____

Complete the following as they relate to the sum-of-the-years' digits method of depreciation.

	Useful Life (years)	Sum-of-the-Years' Digits	Depreciation Rate Fraction Year 2	Year 4	Year 6
4.	8	_____	_____	_____	_____
5.	9	_____	_____	_____	_____

6. Mr. Fix-It purchased a service truck for $32,400. It has an estimated useful life of 3 years and a trade-in value of $3,100. Using the sum-of-the-years' digits method, prepare a depreciation schedule for the truck.

Mr. Fix-It
SYD Depreciation Schedule
Service Truck

End of Year	Total Depreciation	Depreciation Rate Fraction	Annual Depreciation	Accumulated Depreciation	Book Value
					(new) _____
1	_____	____	_____	_____	_____
2	_____	____	_____	_____	_____
3	_____	____	_____	_____	_____

Complete the following as they relate to the declining-balance method of depreciation. Round to the nearest hundredth if necessary.

	Years	Straight-Line Rate (%)	Multiple (%)	Declining-Balance Rate (%)
7.	9	____	150	____
8.	4	____	200	____

9. Award Makers bought a computerized engraving machine for $33,800. It is expected to have a 5-year useful life and a trade-in value of $2,700. Prepare a depreciation schedule for the *first three years* by using the 150% declining-balance method for the machine.

Award Makers
150% Declining-Balance Depreciation Schedule
Computerized Engraving Machine

End of Year	Beginning Book Value	Depreciation Rate	Depreciation for the Year	Accumulated Depreciation	Ending Book Value
					(new) _____
1	_____	____	_____	_____	_____
2	_____	____	_____	_____	_____
3	_____	____	_____	_____	_____

Complete the following as they relate to the units-of-production method of depreciation. Round answers to the nearest tenth of a cent.

	Asset	Cost	Salvage Value	Units of Useful Life	Depreciation per Unit
10.	Pump	$8,900	$250	500,000 gallons	_____
11.	Copier	3,900	0	160,000 copies	_____

12. Screen Gems Movie Theater purchased a new projector for $155,000 with a salvage value of $2,000. Delivery and installation amounted to $580. The projector is expected to have a useful life of 15,000 hours. Complete the following depreciation schedule for the *first four years* of operation by using the units-of-production method.

EXCEL 3

Screen Gems Movie Theater
Units-of-Production Depreciation Schedule
Projector

End of Year	Depreciation per Hour	Hours	Annual Depreciation	Accumulated Depreciation	Book Value
					(new) _____
1	____	2,300	_____	_____	_____
2	____	1,890	_____	_____	_____
3	____	2,160	_____	_____	_____
4	____	2,530	_____	_____	_____

Websites such as boxoffice.com and boxofficemojo.com track box office revenue for movies playing in theaters in the United States and around the world.

© StockLite/Shutterstock.com

13. Stone Age Concrete, Inc., purchased cement manufacturing equipment valued at $420,000 on March 14, 2014. The equipment is used for business 100% of the time. The firm's accountant elected to take a $100,000 section 179 deduction. You have been asked to review the depreciation figures used for this equipment.

    a. What is the basis for depreciation of this equipment?

    b. Prepare a depreciation schedule for the first five years of operation of this equipment by using MACRS.

Stone Age Concrete, Inc.
MACRS Depreciation Schedule
Cement Manufacturing Equipment

End of Year	Original Basis (cost)	Cost Recovery Percentage	Cost Recovery (depreciation)	Accumulated Depreciation	Book Value
				(new)	_____
1	_____	____	_____	_____	_____
2	_____	____	_____	_____	_____
3	_____	____	_____	_____	_____
4	_____	____	_____	_____	_____
5	_____	____	_____	_____	_____

14. The Platinum Touch Mining Company paid $4,000,000 for a parcel of land, including the mining rights. In addition, the company spent $564,700 to prepare the site for mining operations. When mining is completed, it is estimated that the residual value of the asset will be $800,000. Scientists estimate that the site contains 15,000 ounces of platinum.

    a. What is the average depletion cost per ounce?

    b. If 1,220 ounces were mined in the first year of operation, what is the amount of the depletion cost?

15. In January 2002, Marine Science Corporation was awarded a patent for a new boat hull design. The life of the patent is 20 years. The company estimates the value of the patent over its lifetime is $7,500,000. Marine Science's accountant amortizes the patent using straight-line depreciation to zero value at the end of the 20 years. In January 2010, Marine Science successfully defended its patent in a lawsuit at a legal expense of $486,000.

    a. Using the straight-line method, calculate the patent's annual amortization expense for the years before the lawsuit.

    b. Calculate the revised annual amortization expense for the remaining years after the lawsuit.

CHAPTER
17

Dollars
AND Sense

This Business Decision, "A Dispute with the IRS," clearly illustrates how an IRS-prescribed change in property class under MACRS can affect the bottom line of a company's income statement.

BUSINESS DECISION: A DISPUTE WITH THE IRS

16. You are the accountant for the Millenium Corporation. Last year the company purchased a $2,500,000 corporate jet to be used for executive travel. To help offset the cost of the airplane, your company occasionally rents the jet to the executives of two other corporations when it is not in use by Millenium.

   When the corporate tax return was filed this year, you began depreciating the jet by using MACRS. Today you received a letter from the IRS informing you that because your company occasionally rents the airplane to others, it is considered a commercial aircraft and must be depreciated as such. The corporate lawyers are considering disputing this IRS ruling and have asked you the following questions:

   a. How much depreciation did you claim this year?

   b. Under the new category, how much depreciation would be claimed?

   c. If the company pays 30% income tax, what effect will this change have on the amount of tax owed, assuming the company made a net profit this year?

COLLABORATIVE LEARNING ACTIVITY

Going, Going, Gone!

1. Have each member of your team choose his or her favorite vehicle and determine the price of a new one from a dealership. Then check the classified ads of your local newspaper, a publication of used vehicle prices, or the Internet to determine the price of the same vehicle at one, two, three, four, and five years old.

   a. Prepare a depreciation schedule based on the information found.
   b. Calculate the percent of the vehicle's original value that was lost each year.
   c. Construct a line graph of the five years of depreciation of the vehicle.
   d. Does it seem to be straight-line or accelerated?
   e. Compare the depreciation for each team member's vehicle. Which models depreciated the fastest? The slowest?

2. As a team, choose a local industry. Have each member of the team pick a different company within that industry and speak with an accountant who works there. Identify three major assets that are being depreciated, such as a truck, production-line equipment, a computer system, or office furniture and fixtures. For each asset, determine the following:

   a. Original purchase price
   b. Useful life
   c. Salvage value
   d. Depreciation method used for financial statement reporting
   e. Depreciation method used for income tax purposes

Chapter 2

RICH ABRAHAMSON·FORT COLLINS COLORADOAN

Careful study of this chapter should enable you to:

LO1   Define the accounting elements.

LO2   Construct the accounting equation.

LO3   Analyze business transactions.

LO4   Show the effects of business transactions on the accounting equation.

LO5   Prepare and describe the purposes of a simple income statement, statement of owner's equity, and balance sheet.

LO6   Define the three basic phases of the accounting process.

Analyzing Transactions: The Accounting Equation

At Rob's Bike Courier Service in Fort Collins, Colorado, Rob believes "less is more." His small company doesn't "have a fleet of vehicles, just some pretty cool bicycles." His mission is providing successful bike delivery service, perfect for both traditional business delivery services and residential errands. Since January of 2005, Rob's Bike Courier Service has been the alternative to gas-powered vehicle delivery. Thus, besides great rates and friendly, reliable service, Rob offers earth-friendly service.

Currently, he delivers wholesale bagels from a mid-town baker to several downtown coffee shops. He does the same for another pastry chef. Rob also picks up recycling materials, offers bike towing services, and will go to a customer's home to fix flat bike tires and make repairs.

Though his company is small, Rob still needs an accounting system to maintain records of his business transactions and to prepare financial statements. Currently, he uses Quickbooks®, an accounting program used by many small companies. In Chapters 2 through 6, we learn how to account for a service business like Rob's by using an example of a similar company: Rohan's Campus Delivery.

The entire accounting process is based on one simple equation, called the accounting equation. In this chapter, you will learn how to use this equation to analyze business transactions. You will also learn how to prepare financial statements that report the effect of these transactions on the financial condition of a business.

THE ACCOUNTING ELEMENTS

LO1 Define the accounting elements.

Before the accounting process can begin, the entity to be accounted for must be defined. A business entity is an individual, association, or organization that engages in economic activities and controls specific economic resources. This definition allows the personal and business finances of an owner to be accounted for separately.

Three basic accounting elements exist for every business entity: assets, liabilities, and owner's equity. These elements are defined below.

Assets

Assets are items that are owned by a business and will provide future benefits. Examples of assets include cash, merchandise, furniture, fixtures, machinery, buildings, and land. Businesses may also have an asset called accounts receivable. This asset represents the amount of money owed to the business by its customers as a result of making sales "on account," or "on credit." Making sales on account simply means that the customers have promised to pay sometime in the future.

Liabilities

Liabilities represent something owed to another business entity. The amount owed represents a probable future outflow of assets as a result of a past event or transaction. Liabilities are debts or obligations of the business that can be paid with cash, goods, or services.

The most common liabilities are accounts payable and notes payable. An account payable is an unwritten promise to pay a supplier for assets purchased or services received. Acquiring assets or services by promising to make payments in the future is referred to as making a purchase "on account," or "on credit." Formal written promises to pay suppliers or lenders specified sums of money at definite future times are known as notes payable.

Owner's Equity

Owner's equity is the amount by which the business assets exceed the business liabilities. Other terms used for owner's equity include net worth and capital. If there are no business liabilities, the owner's equity is equal to the total assets.

The owner of a business may have business assets and liabilities as well as nonbusiness assets and liabilities. For example, the business owner probably owns a home, clothing, and a car, and perhaps owes the dentist for dental service. These are personal, nonbusiness assets and liabilities. According to the business entity concept, nonbusiness assets and liabilities are not included in the business entity's accounting records.

If the owner invests money or other assets in the business, the item invested is reclassified from a nonbusiness asset to a business asset. If the owner withdraws money or other assets from the business for personal use, the item withdrawn is reclassified from a business asset to a nonbusiness asset. These distinctions are important and allow the owner to make decisions based on the financial condition and results of the business apart from nonbusiness activities.

LEARNING KEY
Pay close attention to the definitions for the basic accounting elements. A clear understanding of these definitions will help you analyze even the most complex business transactions.

LEARNING KEY
The business entity's assets and liabilities are separate from the owner's nonbusiness assets and liabilities.

Checkpoint ✓

Complete Checkpoint-1 on page 41 to test your basic understanding of LO1.

© CHAMPIOFOTO/SHUTTERSTOCK.COM

A Broader View

Assets and the Cost of Products We Buy

Next time you buy something, think of all the assets a company needs to produce that product. If the product comes from a capital-intensive industry, one that requires heavy investments in assets, the company must price the product high enough to cover the cost of using the assets and replacing them when they wear out. For example, AT&T recently reported that the cost of property, plant, and equipment used for operating purposes came to over $274 billion.

THE ACCOUNTING EQUATION

LO2 Construct the accounting equation.

The relationship between the three basic accounting elements—assets, liabilities, and owner's equity—can be expressed in the form of a simple equation known as the accounting equation.

Assets	=	Liabilities	+	Owner's Equity

This equation reflects the fact that both outsiders and insiders have an interest in the assets of a business.

- Liabilities represent the outside interests of creditors.
- Owner's equity represents the inside interests of owners.

Or, viewed another way,

The left side of the equation shows the assets.   *The right side of the equation shows where the money came from to buy the assets.*

When two elements are known, the third can always be calculated. For example, assume that assets on December 31 total $60,400. On that same day, the business liabilities consist of $5,400 owed for equipment. Owner's equity is calculated by subtracting total liabilities from total assets, $60,400 – $5,400 = $55,000.

LEARNING KEY

If you know two accounting elements, you can calculate the third element.

Total assets	$60,400
Total liabilities	–5,400
Owner's equity	$55,000

Assets	=	Liabilities	+	Owner's Equity
$60,400	=	$5,400	+	$55,000
$60,400	=		**$60,400**	

If during the next accounting period, assets increased by $10,000 and liabilities increased by $3,000, owner's equity must have increased by $7,000 ($10,000 – $3,000) as shown on the next page.

	Assets	=	Liabilities	+	Owner's Equity
BB	$60,400		$5,400		$55,000
	+10,000	=	+3,000	+	+7,000
EB	$70,400	=	$8,400	+	$62,000
	$70,400	=	$70,400		

BB: Beginning balance
EB: Ending balance

Checkpoint ✓

Complete Checkpoint-2 on page 41 to test your basic understanding of LO2.

Note also that after computing the ending balances for assets, liabilities, and owner's equity, the accounting equation remains in balance.

ANALYZING BUSINESS TRANSACTIONS

LO3   Analyze business transactions.

A business transaction is an economic event that has a direct impact on the business. A business transaction almost always requires an exchange between the business and another outside entity. We must be able to measure this exchange in dollars. Examples of business transactions include buying goods and services, selling goods and services, buying and selling assets, making loans, and borrowing money.

All business transactions affect the accounting equation through specific accounts. An account is a separate record used to summarize changes in each asset, liability, and owner's equity of a business. Account titles provide a description of the particular type of asset, liability, or owner's equity affected by a transaction.

Three basic questions must be answered when analyzing the effects of a business transaction on the accounting equation. These questions help address the steps in the accounting process discussed in Chapter 1.

1. **What happened?**
   - Make certain you understand the event that has taken place.

2. **Which accounts are affected?**
   - Identify the accounts that are affected.
   - Classify these accounts as assets, liabilities, or owner's equity.

3. **How is the accounting equation affected?**
   - Determine which accounts have increased or decreased.
   - Make certain that the accounting equation remains in balance after the transaction has been entered.

EFFECT OF TRANSACTIONS ON THE ACCOUNTING EQUATION

LO4   Show the effects of business transactions on the accounting equation.

In Chapters 2 through 6, we will focus on learning how to account for a business similar to Rob's Bike Courier Service, discussed in the chapter opener. In these chapters, we will focus on Rohan's Campus Delivery. By studying Rohan's business transactions and accounting techniques, you will learn about business and accounting. A major advantage of studying accounting is that it helps you learn a great deal about business.

As explained previously, we must first understand the economic substance of events. Then, we must determine how that information is entered into the accounting system. If Rohan does not understand the economic events affecting his delivery business and their impact on the accounting equation, the events will not be correctly entered into the accounting system.

Each transaction affects at least two accounts and one or more of the three basic accounting elements. A transaction increases or decreases specific asset, liability, or owner's equity accounts. Assume that the following transactions occurred during June 20--, the first month of operations for Rohan's Campus Delivery.

Transaction (a): Investment by owner

An Increase in an Asset Offset by an Increase in Owner's Equity. Rohan Macsen opened a bank account with a deposit of $2,000 for his business. The new business now has $2,000 of the asset Cash. Since Rohan contributed the asset, the owner's equity element, Rohan Macsen, Capital, increases by the same amount.

> Remember, capital does not mean cash. The cash is shown in the cash account.

Assets (Items Owned)	=	Liabilities (Amounts Owed)	+	Owner's Equity (Owner's Investment)
Cash	=			Rohan Macsen, Capital
(a) $2,000	=			$2,000

Transaction (b): Purchase of an asset for cash

An Increase in an Asset Offset by a Decrease in Another Asset. Rohan decided that the fastest and easiest way to get around campus and find parking is on a motor scooter. Thus, he bought a motor scooter (delivery equipment) for $1,200 cash. Rohan exchanged one asset, cash, for another, delivery equipment. This transaction reduces Cash and creates a new asset, Delivery Equipment.

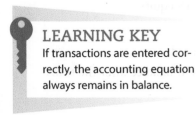

LEARNING KEY
If transactions are entered correctly, the accounting equation always remains in balance.

Assets (Items Owned)		=	Liabilities (Amounts Owed)	+	Owner's Equity (Owner's Investment)
Cash	+ Delivery Equipment	=			Rohan Macsen, Capital
$2,000					$2,000
(b) −1,200	+ $1,200				
$ 800	+ $1,200	=			$2,000
$2,000		=			$2,000

Transaction (c): Purchase of an asset on account

An Increase in an Asset Offset by an Increase in a Liability. Rohan hired a friend to work for him, which meant that a second scooter would be needed. Given Rohan's limited cash, he bought a secondhand model for $900. The seller agreed to allow Rohan to spread the payments over the next three months. This transaction increased an asset, Delivery Equipment, by $900 and increased the liability, Accounts Payable, by an equal amount.

Assets (Items Owned)			=	Liabilities (Amounts Owed)	+	Owner's Equity (Owner's Investment)
Cash	+	Delivery Equipment	=	Accounts Payable	+	Rohan Macsen, Capital
(c) $800 ____ $800	+	$1,200 + 900 $2,100	=	+ $900 $900	+	$2,000 ____ $2,000
		$2,900	=			$2,900

Transaction (d): Payment on a loan

A Decrease in an Asset Offset by a Decrease in a Liability. Rohan paid the first install-ment on the scooter of $300 [see transaction (c)]. This payment decreased the asset, Cash, and the liability, Accounts Payable, by $300.

Assets (Items Owned)			=	Liabilities (Amounts Owed)	+	Owner's Equity (Owner's Investment)
Cash	+	Delivery Equipment	=	Accounts Payable	+	Rohan Macsen, Capital
(d) $800 − 300 $500	+	$2,100 ____ $2,100	=	$900 − 300 $600	+	$2,000 ____ $2,000
		$2,600	=			$2,600

Expanding the Accounting Equation: Revenues, Expenses, and Withdrawals

In the preceding sections, three key accounting elements of every business entity were defined and explained: assets, liabilities, and owner's equity. To complete the explana-tion of the accounting process, three additional elements must be added to the discus-sion: revenues, expenses, and withdrawals.

Revenues

Revenues represent the amount a business charges customers for products sold or services performed. Customers generally pay with cash or a credit card, or they promise to pay at a later date. Most businesses recognize revenues when earned, even if cash has not yet been received. Separate accounts are used to recognize different types of revenue. Examples include Delivery Fees; Consulting Fees; Rent Revenue, if the business rents space to others; Interest Revenue, for interest earned on bank deposits; and Sales, for sales of merchandise. *Revenues increase both assets and owner's equity.*

Expenses

Expenses represent the *decrease* in assets (or *increase* in liabilities) as a result of a com-pany's efforts to produce revenues. Common examples of expenses are rent, salaries, supplies consumed, and taxes. As with revenues, separate accounts are used to keep the accounting records for each different type of expense. Expenses are "incurred" as

- assets are consumed (such as supplies), or
- services are provided (by employees, for example) to the business.

The two main purposes of recognizing an expense are (a) to keep track of the amount and types of expenses incurred and (b) to show the reduction in owner's equity. Again, an expense can cause a reduction in assets or an increase in liabilities. Wages earned by employees is a good example.

- If paid, the expense reduces owner's equity and an asset, Cash.
- If not paid, the expense reduces owner's equity and increases a liability, Wages Payable.

Either way, owner's equity is reduced. If total revenues are greater than total expenses for the period, the excess is the net income, or net profit, for the period. On the other hand, if total expenses are greater than total revenues for the period, the excess is a net loss for the period.

LEARNING KEY
It is important to remember that expenses do not always reduce cash and revenues do not always increase cash right away.

Revenues	$900	Revenues	$ 300
Expenses	500	Expenses	500
Net income	$400	Net loss	$(200)

The owner can determine the time period used in the measurement of net income or net loss. It may be a month, a quarter (three months), a year, or some other time period. The concept that income determination can be made on a periodic basis is known as the accounting period concept. Any accounting period of 12 months is called a fiscal year. The fiscal year frequently coincides with the calendar year.

Withdrawals

Withdrawals, or drawing, reduce owner's equity as a result of the owner taking cash or other assets out of the business for personal use. Since earnings are expected to offset withdrawals, this reduction is viewed as temporary.

The accounting equation is expanded to include revenues, expenses, and withdrawals. Note that revenues increase owner's equity, while expenses and drawing reduce owner's equity.

LEARNING KEY

Owner's Equity	
Decrease	Increase
Expenses	Revenues
Drawing	Owner's Investments

Assets (Items Owned)			=	Liabilities (Amounts Owed)	+	Owner's Equity (Owner's Investment)			+	(Earnings)	
Cash	+	Delivery Equipment	=	Accounts Payable	+	Rohan Macsen, Capital	−	Rohan Macsen, Drawing	+	Revenues − Expenses	
Balance $500	+	$2,100	=	$600	+	$2,000					
	$2,600		=			$2,600					

Effect of Revenue, Expense, and Withdrawal Transactions on the Accounting Equation

To show the effects of revenue, expense, and withdrawal transactions, the example of Rohan's Campus Delivery will be continued. Assume that the following transactions took place in Rohan's business during June 20--.

Transaction (e): Delivery revenues earned in cash

An Increase in an Asset Offset by an Increase in Owner's Equity Resulting from Revenue. Rohan received $500 cash from clients for delivery services. This transaction increased the asset, Cash, and increased owner's equity by $500. The increase in owner's equity is shown by increasing the revenue account, Delivery Fees, by $500.

	Assets (Items Owned)		=	Liabilities (Amounts Owed)	+	Owner's Equity (Owner's Investment)		+	(Earnings)		
	Cash	+ Delivery Equipment	=	Accounts Payable	+	Rohan Macsen, Capital	− Rohan Macsen, Drawing	+	Revenues	− Expenses	Description
	$ 500	$2,100		$600		$2,000					
(e)	+ 500								+ $500		Deliv. Fees
	$1,000	+ $2,100	=	$600	+	$2,000		+	$500		
	$3,100		=			$3,100					

Transaction (f): Paid rent for month

A Decrease in an Asset Offset by a Decrease in Owner's Equity Resulting from an Expense. Rohan rents a small office on campus. He paid $200 for office rent for June. This transaction decreased both Cash and owner's equity by $200. The decrease in owner's equity is shown by increasing an expense called Rent Expense by $200. An increase in an expense decreases owner's equity.

	Assets (Items Owned)		=	Liabilities (Amounts Owed)	+	Owner's Equity (Owner's Investment)		+	(Earnings)		
	Cash	+ Delivery Equipment	=	Accounts Payable	+	Rohan Macsen, Capital	− Rohan Macsen, Drawing	+	Revenues	− Expenses	Description
	$1,000	+ $2,100		$600		$2,000			$500		
(f)	− 200									+ $200	Rent Exp.
	$ 800	+ $2,100	=	$600	+	$2,000		+	$500	− $200	
	$2,900		=			$2,900					

Transaction (g): Paid phone bill

A Decrease in an Asset Offset by a Decrease in Owner's Equity Resulting from an Expense. Rohan paid $50 in cash for phone service. This transaction, like the previous one, decreased both Cash and owner's equity. This decrease in owner's equity is shown by increasing an expense called Phone Expense by $50.

	Assets (Items Owned)		=	Liabilities (Amounts Owed)	+	Owner's Equity (Owner's Investment)		+	(Earnings)		
	Cash	+ Delivery Equipment	=	Accounts Payable	+	Rohan Macsen, Capital	− Rohan Macsen, Drawing	+	Revenues	− Expenses	Description
	$800	$2,100		$600		$2,000			$500	$200	
(g)	− 50									+ 50	Phone Expense
	$750	+ $2,100	=	$600	+	$2,000		+	$500	− $250	
	$2,850		=			$2,850					

Transaction (h): Delivery revenues earned on account

An Increase in an Asset Offset by an Increase in Owner's Equity Resulting from Revenue. Rohan extends credit to regular customers. Often, delivery services are performed for which payment will be received later. Since revenues are recognized when earned, an increase in owner's equity must be reported by increasing the revenue account. Since no cash is received at this time, Cash cannot be increased. Instead, an increase is reported for another asset, Accounts Receivable. *The total of Accounts Receivable at any point in time reflects the amount owed to Rohan by his customers.* Deliveries made on account amounted to $600. Accounts Receivable and Delivery Fees are increased.

	Assets (Items Owned)			=	Liabilities (Amounts Owed)	+	Owner's Equity (Owner's Investment)		+	(Earnings)		
Cash +	Accounts Receivable	+	Delivery Equipment	=	Accounts Payable	+	Rohan Macsen, Capital	– Rohan Macsen, Drawing	+	Revenues	– Expenses	Description
$750			$2,100		$600		$2,000			$ 500	$250	
(h)	+ $600									+ 600		Deliv. Fees
$750 +	$600	+	$2,100	=	$600	+	$2,000		+	$1,100	– $250	
	$3,450			=				$3,450				

Transaction (i): Purchase of supplies

An Increase in an Asset Offset by a Decrease in an Asset. Rohan bought pens, paper, delivery envelopes, and other supplies for $80 cash. These supplies should last for several months. Since they will generate future benefits, the supplies should be recorded as an asset. The accounting equation will show an increase in an asset, Supplies, and a decrease in Cash.

	Assets (Items Owned)				=	Liabilities (Amounts Owed)	+	Owner's Equity (Owner's Investment) +			(Earnings)		
Cash +	Accounts Receivable	+	Supplies +	Delivery Equipment	=	Accounts Payable	+	Rohan Macsen, Capital	– Rohan Macsen, Drawing	+	Revenues	– Expenses	Description
$750	$600			$2,100		$600		$2,000			$1,100	$250	
(i) – 80			+ $80										
$670 +	$600	+	$80 +	$2,100	=	$600	+	$2,000		+	$1,100	– $250	
	$3,450				=				$3,450				

Transaction (j): Payment of insurance premium

An Increase in an Asset Offset by a Decrease in an Asset. Since Rohan plans to graduate and sell the business next January, he paid $200 for an eight-month liability insurance policy. Insurance is paid in advance and will provide future benefits. Thus, it is treated as an asset. We must expand the equation to include another asset, Prepaid Insurance, and show that Cash has been reduced.

Assets (Items Owned)					=	Liabilities (Amounts Owed)	+	Owner's Equity (Owner's Investment)	+	(Earnings)		
Cash +	Accounts Receivable +	Supplies +	Prepaid Insurance +	Delivery Equipment	=	Accounts Payable	+	Rohan Macsen, Capital -	Rohan Macsen, Drawing	+ Revenues -	Expenses	Description
$670	$600	$80		$2,100		$600		$2,000		$1,100	$250	
(j) − 200			+ $200									
$470 +	$600 +	$80 +	$200 +	$2,100	=	$600	+	$2,000		+ $1,100 −	$250	
		$3,450			=			$3,450				

Transaction (k): Cash receipts from prior sales on account

An Increase in an Asset Offset by a Decrease in an Asset. Rohan received $570 in cash for delivery services performed for customers earlier in the month [see transaction (h)]. Receipt of this cash increases the cash account and reduces the amount due from customers reported in the accounts receivable account. *Notice that owner's equity is not affected in this transaction. Owner's equity increased in transaction (h) when revenue was recognized as it was earned, rather than now when cash is received.*

As shown in transactions (i), (j), and (k), transactions do not always affect both sides of the accounting equation.

Assets (Items Owned)					=	Liabilities (Amounts Owed)	+	Owner's Equity (Owner's Investment)	+	(Earnings)		
Cash +	Accounts Receivable +	Supplies +	Prepaid Insurance +	Delivery Equipment	=	Accounts Payable	+	Rohan Macsen, Capital -	Rohan Macsen, Drawing	+ Revenues -	Expenses	Description
$ 470	$600	$80	$200	$2,100		$600		$2,000		$1,100	$250	
(k) + 570	− 570											
$1,040 +	$ 30 +	$80 +	$200 +	$2,100	=	$600	+	$2,000		+ $1,100 −	$250	
		$3,450			=			$3,450				

Transaction (l): Purchase of an asset on account making a partial payment

An Increase in an Asset Offset by a Decrease in an Asset and an Increase in a Liability. With business increasing, Rohan hired a second employee and bought a third motor scooter. The scooter cost $1,500. Rohan paid $300 in cash and will spread the remaining payments over the next four months. The asset Delivery Equipment increases by $1,500, Cash decreases by $300, and the liability Accounts Payable increases by $1,200. *Note that this transaction changes three accounts. Even so, the accounting equation remains in balance.*

Assets (Items Owned)					=	Liabilities (Amounts Owed)	+	Owner's Equity (Owner's Investment)	+	(Earnings)		
Cash +	Accounts Receivable +	Supplies +	Prepaid Insurance +	Delivery Equipment	=	Accounts Payable	+	Rohan Macsen, Capital -	Rohan Macsen, Drawing	+ Revenues -	Expenses	Description
$1,040	$30	$80	$200	$2,100		$ 600		$2,000		$1,100	$250	
(l) − 300				+ 1,500		+ 1,200						
$ 740 +	$30 +	$80 +	$200 +	$3,600	=	$1,800	+	$2,000		+ $1,100 −	$250	
		$4,650			=			$4,650				

Transaction (m): Payment of wages

A Decrease in an Asset Offset by a Decrease in Owner's Equity Resulting from an Expense. Rohan paid his part-time employees $650 in wages. This represents an additional business expense. As with other expenses, Cash is reduced and owner's equity is reduced by increasing an expense.

	Assets (Items Owned)					=	Liabilities (Amounts Owed)	+	Owner's Equity (Owner's Investment) + (Earnings)				
Cash +	Accounts Receivable +	Supplies +	Prepaid Insurance +	Delivery Equipment =			Accounts Payable	+	Rohan Macsen, Capital	− Rohan Macsen, Drawing	+ Revenues −	Expenses	Description
$740	$30	$80	$200	$3,600			$1,800		$2,000		$1,100	$250	
(m) − 650												+ 650	Wages Exp.
$ 90 +	$30 +	$80 +	$200 +	$3,600	=		$1,800	+	$2,000	+	$1,100 −	$900	
	$4,000					=			$4,000				

Transaction (n): Deliveries made for cash and on account

An Increase in Two Assets Offset by an Increase in Owner's Equity. Total delivery fees for the remainder of the month amounted to $1,050: $430 in cash and $620 on account. Since all of these delivery fees have been earned, the revenue account increases by $1,050. Also, Cash increases by $430 and Accounts Receivable increases by $620. Thus, revenues increase assets and owner's equity. Note, once again, that recording these revenues impacts three accounts while the equation remains in balance.

	Assets (Items Owned)					=	Liabilities (Amounts Owed)	+	Owner's Equity (Owner's Investment) + (Earnings)				
Cash +	Accounts Receivable +	Supplies +	Prepaid Insurance +	Delivery Equipment =			Accounts Payable	+	Rohan Macsen, Capital	− Rohan Macsen, Drawing	+ Revenues −	Expenses	Description
$ 90	$ 30	$80	$200	$3,600			$1,800		$2,000		$1,100	$900	
(n) + 430	+ 620										+ 1,050		Deliv. Fees
$520 +	$650 +	$80 +	$200 +	$3,600	=		$1,800	+	$2,000	+	$2,150 −	$900	
	$5,050					=			$5,050				

LEARNING KEY

Withdrawals by the owner are reported in the drawing account. Withdrawals are the opposite of investments by the owner.

Transaction (o): Withdrawal of cash from business

A Decrease in an Asset Offset by a Decrease in Owner's Equity Resulting from a Withdrawal by the Owner. At the end of the month, Rohan took $150 in cash from the business to purchase books for his classes. Since the books are not business related, this is a withdrawal. Withdrawals can be viewed as the opposite of investments by the owner. Both owner's equity and Cash decrease.

	Assets (Items Owned)					=	Liabilities (Amounts Owed)	+	Owner's Equity (Owner's Investment) + (Earnings)				
Cash +	Accounts Receivable +	Supplies +	Prepaid Insurance +	Delivery Equipment =			Accounts Payable	+	Rohan Macsen, Capital	− Rohan Macsen, Drawing	+ Revenues −	Expenses	Description
$520	$650	$80	$200	$3,600			$1,800		$2,000		$2,150	$900	
(o) − 150										+ $150			
$370 +	$650 +	$80 +	$200 +	$3,600	=		$1,800	+	$2,000 −	$150	+ $2,150 −	$900	
	$4,900					=			$4,900				

FIGURE 2-1 Summary of Transactions Illustrated

Trans-action	Cash	+	Accounts Receivable	+	Supplies	+	Prepaid Insurance	+	Delivery Equipment	=	Accounts Payable	+	Rohan Macsen, Capital	–	Rohan Macsen, Drawing	+	Revenues	–	Expenses	Description
	Assets (Items Owned)									**=**	**Liabilities** (Amounts Owed)	**+**	**Owner's Equity** (Owner's Investment) + (Earnings)							
Balance (a)	2,000												2,000							
Balance (b)	2,000 (1,200)								1,200				2,000							
Balance (c)	800								1,200 900		900		2,000							
Balance (d)	800 (300)								2,100		900 (300)		2,000							
Balance (e)	500 500								2,100		600		2,000				500			Deliv. Fees
Balance (f)	1,000 (200)								2,100		600		2,000				500		200	Rent Exp.
Balance (g)	800 (50)								2,100		600		2,000				500		200 50	Phone Exp.
Balance (h)	750		600						2,100		600		2,000				500 600		250	Deliv. Fees
Balance (i)	750 (80)		600		80				2,100		600		2,000				1,100		250	
Balance (j)	670 (200)		600		80		200		2,100		600		2,000				1,100		250	
Balance (k)	470 570		600 (570)		80		200		2,100		600		2,000				1,100		250	
Balance (l)	1,040 (300)		30		80		200		2,100 1,500		600 1,200		2,000				1,100		250	
Balance (m)	740 (650)		30		80		200		3,600		1,800		2,000				1,100		250 650	Wages Exp.
Balance (n)	90 430		30 620		80		200		3,600		1,800		2,000				1,100 1,050		900	Deliv. Fees
Balance (o)	520 (150)		650		80		200		3,600		1,800		2,000		150		2,150		900	
Balance	**370**	**+**	**650**	**+**	**80**	**+**	**200**	**+**	**3,600**	**=**	**1,800**	**+**	**2,000**	**–**	**150**	**+**	**2,150**	**–**	**900**	

Cash	$ 370	Accounts Payable	$1,800
Accounts Receivable	650	Rohan Macsen, Capital	2,000
Supplies	80	Rohan Macsen, Drawing	(150)
Prepaid Insurance	200	Delivery Fees	2,150
Delivery Equipment	3,600	Rent Expense	(200)
Total Assets	**$4,900**	Phone Expense	(50)
		Wages Expense	(650)
		Total Liabilities and Owner's Equity	**$4,900**

Amounts in ( ) are subtracted

As with the running totals in the table, the listing immediately below the table provides proof that the accounting equation is in balance.

Checkpoint ✓

Complete Checkpoint-3 on page 41 to test your basic understanding of LO3/4.

Figure 2-1 shows a summary of the transactions. Use this summary to test your understanding of transaction analysis by describing the economic event represented by each transaction. At the bottom of Figure 2-1, the asset accounts and their totals are compared with the liability and owner's equity accounts and their totals.

FINANCIAL STATEMENTS

LO5   Prepare and describe the purposes of a simple income statement, statement of owner's equity, and balance sheet.

Three financial statements commonly prepared by a business entity are the income statement, statement of owner's equity, and balance sheet. The transaction information gathered and summarized in the accounting equation may be used to prepare these financial statements. Figure 2-2 shows the following:

1. A summary of the specific revenue and expense transactions and the ending totals for the asset, liability, capital, and drawing accounts from the accounting equation.

2. The financial statements and their linkages with the accounting equation and each other.

Note that each of the financial statements in Figure 2-2 has a heading consisting of:

HEADING FOR FINANCIAL STATEMENTS	
1. The name of the company	Rohan's Campus Delivery
2. The title of the statement	Income Statement, Statement of Owner's Equity, or Balance Sheet
3. The time period covered or the date of the statement	For Month Ended June 30, 20--, or June 30, 20--

The income statement and statement of owner's equity provide information concerning events covering a period of time, in this case, *the month ended* June 30, 20--. The balance sheet, on the other hand, offers a picture of the business on *a specific date*, June 30, 20--.

GUIDELINES FOR PREPARING FINANCIAL STATEMENTS
1. Financial statements are prepared primarily for users not associated with the company. To make a good impression and enhance understanding, financial statements must follow a standard form with careful attention to placement, spacing, and indentations.
2. All statements have a heading with the name of the company, name of the statement, and accounting period or date.
3. Single rules (underlines) indicate that the numbers above the line have been added or subtracted. Double rules (double underlines) indicate a total.
4. Dollar signs are used at the top of columns and for the first amount entered in a column beneath a ruling.
5. On the income statement, some companies list expenses from highest to lowest dollar amount, with miscellaneous expense listed last.
6. On the balance sheet, assets are listed from most liquid to least liquid. **Liquidity** measures the ease with which the asset will be converted to cash. Liabilities are listed from most current to least current.

The Income Statement

The income statement, sometimes called the profit and loss statement or operating statement, reports the profitability of business operations for a specific period of time.

FIGURE 2-2   Summary and Financial Statements

Trans-action	Assets (Items Owned)					=	Liabilities (Amounts Owed)	+	Owner's Equity (Owner's Investment) + (Earnings)				
	Cash	+ Accounts Receivable	+ Supplies	+ Prepaid Insurance	+ Delivery Equipment	=	Accounts Payable	+ Rohan Macsen, Capital	− Rohan Macsen, Drawing	+ Revenues	− Expenses	Description	
(e)										500		Deliv. Fees
(f)											200	Rent Exp.
(g)											50	Phone Exp.
(h)										600		Deliv. Fees
(m)											650	Wages Exp.
(n)										1,050		Deliv. Fees
Balance	370	+ 650	+ 80	+ 200	+ 3,600	=	1,800	+ 2,000	− 150	+ 2,150	− 900	

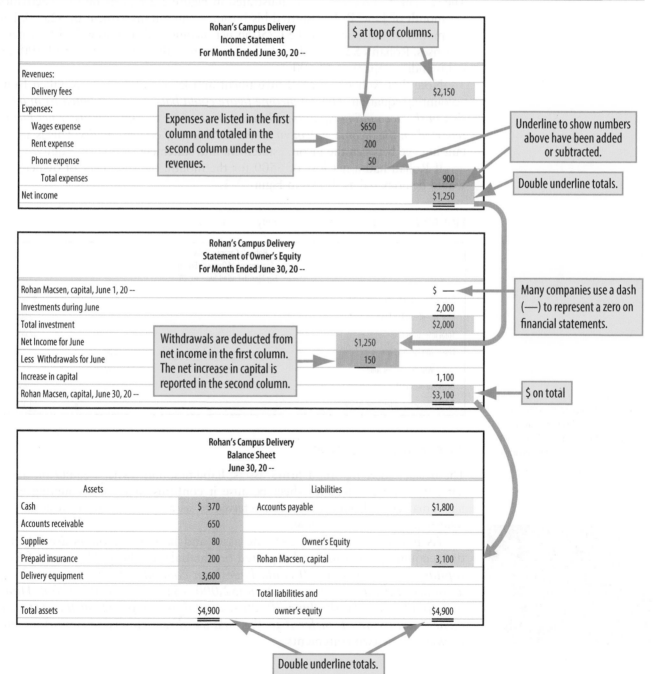

Rohan's Campus Delivery
Income Statement
For Month Ended June 30, 20 --

Revenues:		
Delivery fees		$2,150
Expenses:		
Wages expense	$650	
Rent expense	200	
Phone expense	50	
Total expenses		900
Net income		$1,250

$ at top of columns.

Expenses are listed in the first column and totaled in the second column under the revenues.

Underline to show numbers above have been added or subtracted.

Double underline totals.

Rohan's Campus Delivery
Statement of Owner's Equity
For Month Ended June 30, 20 --

Rohan Macsen, capital, June 1, 20 --		$ —
Investments during June		2,000
Total investment		$2,000
Net Income for June	$1,250	
Less Withdrawals for June	150	
Increase in capital		1,100
Rohan Macsen, capital, June 30, 20 --		$3,100

Many companies use a dash (—) to represent a zero on financial statements.

Withdrawals are deducted from net income in the first column. The net increase in capital is reported in the second column.

$ on total

Rohan's Campus Delivery
Balance Sheet
June 30, 20 --

Assets		Liabilities	
Cash	$ 370	Accounts payable	$1,800
Accounts receivable	650		
Supplies	80	Owner's Equity	
Prepaid insurance	200	Rohan Macsen, capital	3,100
Delivery equipment	3,600		
		Total liabilities and	
Total assets	$4,900	owner's equity	$4,900

Double underline totals.

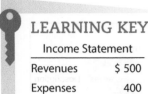
Rohan's income statement shows the revenues earned for the month of June. Next, the expenses incurred as a result of the efforts made to earn these revenues are deducted. If the revenues are greater than the expenses, net income is reported. If the expenses are greater than the revenue, a net loss is reported.

By carefully studying the income statement, it is clear that Rohan earns revenues in only one way: by making deliveries. If other types of services were offered, these revenues would also be identified on the statement. Further, the reader can see the kinds of expenses that were incurred. The reader can make a judgment as to whether these seem reasonable given the amount of revenue earned. Finally, the most important number on the statement is the net income. This is known as the "bottom line."

The Statement of Owner's Equity

The statement of owner's equity illustrated in Figure 2-2 reports on these activities for the month of June. Rohan started his business with an investment of $2,000. During the month of June, he earned $1,250 in net income and withdrew $150 for personal expenses. Rohan's $2,000 original investment, plus the net increase of $1,100, results in his ending capital of $3,100.

Note that Rohan's original investment and later withdrawal are taken from the accounting equation. *The net income figure could have been computed from information in the accounting equation. However, it is easier to simply transfer net income as reported on the income statement to the statement of owner's equity.* This is an important linkage between the income statement and statement of owner's equity.

If Rohan had a net loss of $500 for the month, the statement of owner's equity would be prepared as shown in Figure 2-3.

FIGURE 2-3   Statement of Owner's Equity with Net Loss

Rohan's Campus Delivery			
Statement of Owner's Equity			
For Month Ended June 30, 20 --			
Rohan Macsen, capital, June 1, 20 --			$ —
Investments during June			2,000
Total investment			$2,000
Less: Net loss for June		$500	
Withdrawals for June		150	
Decrease in capital			(650)
Rohan Macsen, capital, June 30, 20 --			$1,350

Most firms also prepare a statement of cash flows. Given the complexity of this statement, we will postpone its discussion until later in this text.

The Balance Sheet

The balance sheet reports a firm's assets, liabilities, and owner's equity on a specific date. It is called a balance sheet because it confirms that the accounting equation has remained in balance. It is also referred to as a statement of financial position or statement of financial condition.

As illustrated in Figure 2-2, the asset and liability accounts are taken from the accounting equation and reported on the balance sheet. *The total of Rohan's capital account on June 30 could have been computed from the owner's equity accounts in the accounting equation ($2,000 – $150 + $2,150 – $900). However, it is simpler to take the June 30, 20--, capital as computed on the statement of owner's equity and transfer it to the balance sheet.* This is an important linkage between these two statements.

Checkpoint ✓

Complete Checkpoint-4 on page 41 to test your basic understanding of LO5.

OVERVIEW OF THE ACCOUNTING PROCESS

LO6 Define the three basic phases of the accounting process.

Figure 2-4 shows the three basic phases of the accounting process in terms of input, processing, and output.

- Input. Business transactions provide the necessary *input*.
- Processing. Recognizing the effect of these transactions on the assets, liabilities, owner's equity, revenues, and expenses of a business is the *processing* function.
- Output. The financial statements are the *output*.

FIGURE 2-4   Input, Processing, and Output

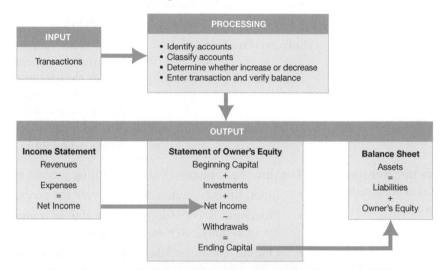

Self-Study

LEARNING OBJECTIVES	Key Points to Remember
LO1 Define the accounting elements.	The three key accounting elements are assets, liabilities, and owner's equity. Owner's equity is expanded in LO4 to include revenues, expenses, and drawing.
LO2 Construct the accounting equation.	The accounting equation is: Assets = Liabilities + Owner's Equity
LO3 Analyze business transactions.	Three questions must be answered in analyzing business transactions: 1. What happened? 2. Which accounts are affected? 3. How is the accounting equation affected?
LO4 Show the effects of business transactions on the accounting equation.	Each transaction affects at least two accounts and one or more of the three basic accounting elements. The transactions described in this chapter can be classified into five groups: 1. Increase in an asset offset by an increase in owner's equity. 2. Increase in an asset offset by a decrease in another asset.

(continued)

LEARNING OBJECTIVES	Key Points to Remember

	3. Increase in an asset offset by an increase in a liability. 4. Decrease in an asset offset by a decrease in a liability. 5. Decrease in an asset offset by a decrease in owner's equity.
LO5 Prepare and describe the purposes of a simple income statement, statement of owner's equity, and balance sheet.	The purposes of the income statement, statement of owner's equity, and balance sheet can be summarized as follows: **STATEMENT** — **PURPOSE** Income statement — Reports net income or loss Revenues – Expenses = Net Income or Loss Statement of owner's equity — Shows changes in the owner's capital account Beginning Capital + Investments + Net Income – Withdrawals = Ending Capital Balance sheet — Verifies balance of accounting equation Assets = Liabilities + Owner's Equity
LO6 Define the three basic phases of the accounting process.	The three basic phases of the accounting process are shown below. • **Input.** Business transactions provide the necessary input. • **Processing.** Recognizing the effect of these transactions on the assets, liabilities, owner's equity, revenues, and expenses of a business is the processing function. • **Output.** The financial statements are the output.

DEMONSTRATION PROBLEM

Kenny Young has started his own business, Home and Away Inspections. He inspects property for buyers and sellers of real estate. Young rents office space and has a part-time assistant to answer the phone and help with inspections. The transactions for the month of September are as follows:

(a) On the first day of the month, Young invested cash by making a deposit in a bank account for the business, $15,000.

(b) Paid rent for September, $300.

(c) Bought a used truck for cash, $8,000.

(d) Purchased tools on account from Crafty Tools, $3,000.

(e) Paid electricity bill, $50.

(f) Paid two-year premium for liability insurance on truck, $600.

(g) Received cash from clients for services performed, $2,000.

(h) Paid part-time assistant (wages) for first half of month, $200.

(i) Performed inspection services for clients on account, $1,000.

(j) Paid phone bill, $35.

(k) Bought office supplies costing $300. Paid $100 cash and will pay the balance next month, $200.

(l) Received cash from clients for inspections performed on account in (i), $300.

(m) Paid part-time assistant (wages) for last half of month, $250.

(n) Made partial payment on tools bought in (d), $1,000.

(o) Earned additional revenues amounting to $2,000: $1,400 in cash and $600 on account.

(p) Young withdrew cash at the end of the month for personal expenses, $500.

REQUIRED

1. Enter the transactions in an accounting equation similar to the one illustrated below.

		Assets (Items Owned)					=	Liabilities + (Amounts Owed)	Owner's Equity (Owner's Investment)+ (Earnings)				
Cash +	Accounts Receivable	+ Supplies +	Prepaid Insurance	+ Tools + Truck =				Accounts Payable	+ Kenny Young, Capital	− Kenny Young, Drawing	+ Revenues	− Expenses	Description

2. Compute the ending balances for all accounts.

3. Prepare an income statement for Home and Away Inspections for the month of September 20--.

4. Prepare a statement of owner's equity for Home and Away Inspections for the month of September 20--.

5. Prepare a balance sheet for Home and Away Inspections as of September 30, 20--.

Solution 1, 2.

	Cash +	Accounts Receivable	+ Supplies +	Prepaid Insurance	+ Tools +	Truck =	Accounts Payable	+ Kenny Young, Capital	− Kenny Young, Drawing	+ Revenues	− Expenses	Description
(a)	15,000							15,000				
(b)	(300)										300	Rent Exp.
(c)	(8,000)				8,000							
(d)					3,000		3,000					
(e)	(50)										50	Utilities Exp.
(f)	(600)		600									
(g)	2,000									2,000		Inspect. Fees
(h)	(200)										200	Wages Exp.
(i)		1,000								1,000		Inspect. Fees
(j)	(35)										35	Phone Exp.
(k)	(100)		300				200					
(l)	300	(300)										
(m)	(250)										250	Wages Exp.
(n)	(1,000)						(1,000)					
(o)	1,400	600								2,000		Inspect. Fees
(p)	(500)								500			
Bal.	**7,665** +	**1,300** +	**300** +	**600**	+ **3,000** +	**8,000** =	**2,200**	+ **15,000** −	**500**	+ **5,000**	− **835**	

3.

Home and Away Inspections Income Statement For Month Ended September 30, 20 --		
Revenues:		
Inspection fees		$ 5,000
Expenses:		
Wages expense	$450	
Rent expense	300	
Utilities expense	50	
Phone expense	35	
Total expenses		835
Net income		$ 4,165

4.

Home and Away Inspections Statement of Owner's Equity For Month Ended September 30, 20 - -		
Kenny Young, capital, September 1, 20 - -		$ ——
Investment during September		15,000
Total investment		$15,000
Net income for September	$4,165	
Less withdrawals for September	500	
Increase in capital		3,665
Kenny Young, capital, September 30, 20 - -		$18,665

5.

Home and Away Inspections Balance Sheet September 30, 20 --			
Assets		**Liabilities**	
Cash	$ 7,665	Accounts payable	$ 2,200
Accounts receivable	1,300		
Supplies	300	**Owner's Equity**	
Prepaid insurance	600	Kenny Young, capital	18,665
Tools	3,000		
Truck	8,000		
		Total liabilities and	
Total assets	$20,865	owner's equity	$20,865

KEY TERMS
....

account (23)   A separate record used to summarize changes in each asset, liability, and owner's equity of a business.

account title (23)   Provides a description of the particular type of asset, liability, owner's equity, revenue, or expense.

accounting equation (22)   The accounting equation consists of the three basic accounting elements: Assets = Liabilities + Owner's Equity.

accounting period concept (26)   The concept that income determination can be made on a periodic basis.

accounts payable (21)   An unwritten promise to pay a supplier for assets purchased or services received.

accounts receivable (21)   An amount owed to a business by its customers as a result of the sale of goods or services.

asset (21)   An item that is owned by a business and will provide future benefits.

balance sheet (34)   Reports assets, liabilities, and owner's equity on a specific date. It is called a balance sheet because it confirms that the accounting equation is in balance.

business entity (21)   An individual, association, or organization that engages in economic activities and controls specific economic resources.

business entity concept (21)   The concept that nonbusiness assets and liabilities are not included in the business entity's accounting records.

business transaction (23)   An economic event that has a direct impact on the business.

capital (21)   Another term for owner's equity, the amount by which the business assets exceed the business liabilities.

drawing (26)   Withdrawals that reduce owner's equity as a result of the owner taking cash or other assets out of the business for personal use.

expenses (25)   The decrease in assets (or increase in liabilities) as a result of efforts to produce revenues.

fiscal year (26)   Any accounting period of 12 months' duration.

income statement (32)   Reports the profitability of business operations for a specific period of time.

input (35)   Business transactions provide the necessary input for the accounting information system.

liability (21)   Something owed to another business entity.

liquidity (32)   A measure of the ease with which an asset will be converted to cash.

net income (26)   The excess of total revenues over total expenses for the period.

net loss (26)   The excess of total expenses over total revenues for the period.

net worth (21)   Another term for owner's equity, the amount by which the business assets exceed the business liabilities.

notes payable (21)   A formal written promise to pay a supplier or lender a specified sum of money at a definite future time.

operating statement (32)   Another name for the income statement, which reports the profitability of business operations for a specific period of time.

output (35)   The financial statements are the output of the accounting information system.

owner's equity (21)   The amount by which the business assets exceed the business liabilities.

processing (35)   Recognizing the effect of transactions on the assets, liabilities, owner's equity, revenues, and expenses of a business.

profit and loss statement (32)   Another name for the income statement, which reports the profitability of business operations for a specific period of time.

revenues (25)   The amount a business charges customers for products sold or services performed.

statement of financial condition (34)   Another name for the balance sheet, which reports assets, liabilities, and owner's equity on a specific date.

statement of financial position (34)   Another name for the balance sheet, which reports assets, liabilities, and owner's equity on a specific date.

statement of owner's equity (34)   Reports beginning capital plus net income less withdrawals to compute ending capital.

withdrawals (26)   Reduce owner's equity as a result of the owner taking cash or other assets out of the business for personal use.

SELF-STUDY TEST QUESTIONS

True/False

1. **LO1**   Assets are items that are owned by the business and are expected to provide future benefits.

2. **LO1**   Accounts Payable is an example of an asset account.

3. **LO1**   According to the business entity concept, nonbusiness assets and liabilities are not included in the business's accounting records.

4. **LO2**   The accounting equation (Assets = Liabilities + Owner's Equity) must always be in balance.

5. **LO2**   When an asset increases, a liability must also increase.

6. **LO3**   Expenses represent outflows of assets or increases in liabilities as a result of efforts to produce revenues.

7. **LO5**   When total revenues exceed total expenses, the difference is called net loss.

Multiple Choice

1. **LO4**   An increase to which of these accounts will increase owner's equity?

   (a) Accounts Payable   (c) Client Fees
   (b) Drawing   (d) Rent Expense

2. **LO4**   When delivery revenue is earned in cash, which accounts increase or decrease?

   (a) Cash increases; Revenue increases.
   (b) Cash decreases; Revenue increases.
   (c) Cash decreases; Revenue decreases.
   (d) Cash does not change; owner's equity increases.

3. **LO4** When delivery revenue is earned on account, which accounts increase or decrease?

(a) Cash increases; Revenue increases.
(b) Accounts Receivable increases; Revenue increases.
(c) Accounts Receivable increases; Revenue decreases.
(d) Accounts Receivable decreases; Revenue decreases.

4. **LO4** When payment is made on an existing debt, which accounts increase or decrease?

(a) Cash increases; Accounts Receivable increases.
(b) Cash decreases; Accounts Payable increases.
(c) Cash increases; Accounts Payable increases.
(d) Cash decreases; Accounts Payable decreases.

5. **LO5** Which of the following accounts does not appear on the income statement?

(a) Delivery Fees   (c) Drawing
(b) Wages Expense   (d) Rent Expense

Checkpoint Exercises

1. **LO1** Label each of the following accounts as an asset (A), a liability (L), or owner's equity (OE), using the following format:

Account	Classification
Accounts Receivable	_____
Accounts Payable	_____
Judy Smith, Capital	_____

2. **LO2** What is missing from the accounting equation below?

_____?_____ = Liabilities + Owner's Equity

3. **LO3/4** What are the effects of the following transactions on the accounting equation? Indicate an increase (+) or decrease (−) under the appropriate asset, liability, and owner's equity headings.

Transaction	Assets	Liabilities	Owner's Equity
a. Purchase of an asset on account.	_____	_____	_____
b. Made payment on account for transaction (a).	_____	_____	_____

4. **LO5** Classify the following accounts as assets (A), liabilities (L), owner's equity (OE), revenue (R), or expense (E). Indicate the financial statement on which the account belongs—income statement (IS), statement of owner's equity (SOE), or balance sheet (BS).

Account	Classification	Financial Statement
Accounts Payable	_____	_____
Peggy Welsch, Drawing	_____	_____
Rent Expense	_____	_____
Sales	_____	_____
Equipment	_____	_____

The answers to the Self-Study Test Questions are at the end of the chapter (page 49).

Applying Your Knowledge

REVIEW QUESTIONS

LO1   1. Why is it necessary to distinguish between business assets and liabilities and nonbusiness assets and liabilities of a single proprietor?

LO1/4   2. Name and define the six major elements of the accounting equation.

LO3   3. List the three basic questions that must be answered when analyzing the effects of a business transaction on the accounting equation.

LO5   4. What is the function of an income statement?

LO5   5. What is the function of a statement of owner's equity?

LO5   6. What is the function of a balance sheet?

LO6   7. What are the three basic phases of the accounting process?

SERIES A EXERCISES

E 2-1A   **(LO1)**   **ACCOUNTING ELEMENTS** Label each of the following accounts as an asset (A), a liability (L), or owner's equity (OE), using the following format:

Item	Account	Classification
Money in bank	Cash	
Office supplies	Supplies	
Money owed	Accounts Payable	
Office chairs	Office Furniture	
Net worth of owner	John Smith, Capital	
Money withdrawn by owner	John Smith, Drawing	
Money owed by customers	Accounts Receivable	

E 2-2A   **(LO2)**   **THE ACCOUNTING EQUATION** Using the accounting equation, compute the missing elements.

Assets	=	Liabilities	+	Owner's Equity
_____	=	$27,000	+	$17,000
$32,000	=	$18,000	+	_____
$27,000	=	_____	+	$20,000

E 2-3A   **(LO3/4)**

✓ Assets following (d): $32,200

SHOW
ME HOW

EFFECTS OF TRANSACTIONS (BALANCE SHEET ACCOUNTS) John Sullivan started a business. During the first month (February 20--), the following transactions occurred. Show the effect of each transaction on the accounting equation: *Assets = Liabilities + Owner's Equity.* After each transaction, show the new totals.

(a) Invested cash in the business, $27,000.

(b) Bought office equipment on account, $7,500.

(c) Bought office equipment for cash, $1,600.

(d) Paid cash on account to supplier in transaction (b), $2,300.

E 2-4A   (LO3/4)

✓ Assets following (k): $31,586

SHOW
ME HOW

EFFECTS OF TRANSACTIONS (REVENUE, EXPENSE, WITHDRAWALS) This exercise is an extension of Exercise 2-3A. Assume John Sullivan completed the following additional transactions during February. Show the effect of each transaction on the basic elements of the expanded accounting equation: *Assets = Liabilities + Owner's Equity (Capital – Drawing + Revenues – Expenses)*. After transaction (k), report the totals for each element. Demonstrate that the accounting equation has remained in balance.

(e) Received cash from a client for professional services, $1,500.

(f) Paid office rent for February, $600.

(g) Paid February phone bill, $64.

(h) Withdrew cash for personal use, $1,000.

(i) Performed services for clients on account, $750.

(j) Paid wages to part-time employee, $1,200.

(k) Received cash for services performed on account in transaction (i), $400.

E 2-5A   (LO1/5)

FINANCIAL STATEMENT ACCOUNTS Label each of the following accounts as an asset (A), liability (L), owner's equity (OE), revenue (R), or expense (E). Indicate the financial statement on which the account belongs—income statement (IS), statement of owner's equity (SOE), or balance sheet (BS)—in a format similar to the following.

Account	Classification	Financial Statement
Cash		
Rent Expense		
Accounts Payable		
Service Fees		
Supplies		
Wages Expense		
Ramon Martinez, Drawing		
Ramon Martinez, Capital		
Prepaid Insurance		
Accounts Receivable		

E 2-6A   (LO5)

✓ Capital, 6/30: $22,000

STATEMENT OF OWNER'S EQUITY REPORTING NET INCOME Betsy Ray started an accounting service on June 1, 20--, by investing $20,000. Her net income for the month was $10,000, and she withdrew $8,000. Prepare a statement of owner's equity for the month of June.

E 2-7A   (LO5)

✓ Capital, 6/30: $9,000

STATEMENT OF OWNER'S EQUITY REPORTING NET LOSS Based on the information provided in Exercise 2-6A, prepare a statement of owner's equity assuming Ray had a net loss of $3,000.

SERIES A PROBLEMS

P 2-8A   (LO1/2)

✓ 3: $32,040 = $12,910 + $19,130

SHOW
ME HOW

THE ACCOUNTING EQUATION Dr. John Salvaggi is a chiropractor. As of December 31, he owned the following property that related to his professional practice.

Cash	$ 3,500
Office Equipment	6,400
X-ray Equipment	10,220
Laboratory Equipment	6,840

He also owes the following business suppliers:

Chateau Gas Company	$ 3,430
Aloe Medical Supply Company	4,120

REQUIRED

1. From the preceding information, compute the accounting elements and enter them in the accounting equation shown as follows.

Assets	=	Liabilities	+	Owner's Equity
_____	=	_____	+	_____

2. During January, the assets increase by $8,540, and the liabilities increase by $3,360. Compute the resulting accounting equation.

3. During February, the assets decrease by $3,460, and the liabilities increase by $2,000. Compute the resulting accounting equation.

P 2-9A   (LO3/4)

✓ Total cash following (g): $12,950

EFFECT OF TRANSACTIONS ON ACCOUNTING EQUATION Jay Pembroke started a business. During the first month (April 20--), the following transactions occurred.

(a) Invested cash in business, $18,000.

(b) Bought office supplies for $4,600: $2,000 in cash and $2,600 on account.

(c) Paid one-year insurance premium, $1,200.

(d) Earned revenues totaling $3,300: $1,300 in cash and $2,000 on account.

(e) Paid cash on account to the company that supplied the office supplies in transaction (b), $2,300.

(f) Paid office rent for the month, $750.

(g) Withdrew cash for personal use, $100.

REQUIRED

Show the effect of each transaction on the individual accounts of the expanded accounting equation: *Assets = Liabilities + Owner's Equity (Capital – Drawing + Revenues – Expenses)*. After transaction (g), report the totals for each element. Demonstrate that the accounting equation has remained in balance.

P 2-10A   (LO5)

✓ Net income: $2,550

SHOW
ME HOW

INCOME STATEMENT Based on Problem 2-9A, prepare an income statement for Jay Pembroke for the month of April 20--.

P 2-11A   (LO5)

✓ Capital, 4/30: $20,450

SHOW
ME HOW

P 2-12A   (LO5)

✓ Total assets, 4/30: $20,750

SHOW
ME HOW

STATEMENT OF OWNER'S EQUITY Based on Problem 2-9A, prepare a statement of owner's equity for Jay Pembroke for the month of April 20--.

BALANCE SHEET Based on Problem 2-9A, prepare a balance sheet for Jay Pembroke as of April 30, 20--.

SERIES B EXERCISES

E 2-1B   (LO1)

ACCOUNTING ELEMENTS Label each of the following accounts as an asset (A), liability (L), or owner's equity (OE) using the following format.

Account	Classification
Cash	
Accounts Payable	
Supplies	
Bill Jones, Drawing	
Prepaid Insurance	
Accounts Receivable	
Bill Jones, Capital	

E 2-2B   (LO2)

THE ACCOUNTING EQUATION Using the accounting equation, compute the missing elements.

Assets	=	Liabilities	+	Owner's Equity
_____	=	$20,000	+	$ 5,000
$30,000	=	$15,000	+	_____
$20,000	=	_____	+	$10,000

E 2-3B   (LO3/4)

✓ Assets following (d): $32,500

SHOW
ME HOW

EFFECTS OF TRANSACTIONS (BALANCE SHEET ACCOUNTS) Jon Wallace started a business. During the first month (March 20--), the following transactions occurred. Show the effect of each transaction on the accounting equation: *Assets = Liabilities + Owner's Equity*. After each transaction, show the new account totals.

(a) Invested cash in the business, $30,000.

(b) Bought office equipment on account, $4,500.

(c) Bought office equipment for cash, $1,600.

(d) Paid cash on account to supplier in transaction (b), $2,000.

E 2-4B   (LO3/4)

✓ Assets following (k): $34,032

SHOW
ME HOW

EFFECTS OF TRANSACTIONS (REVENUE, EXPENSE, WITHDRAWALS) This exercise is an extension of Exercise 2-3B. Assume Jon Wallace completed the following additional transactions during March. Show the effect of each transaction on the basic elements of the expanded accounting equation: *Assets = Liabilities + Owner's Equity (Capital – Drawing + Revenues – Expenses)*. After transaction (k), report the totals for each element. Demonstrate that the accounting equation has remained in balance.

(e) Performed services and received cash, $3,000.

(f) Paid rent for March, $1,000.

(g) Paid March phone bill, $68.

(h) Jon Wallace withdrew cash for personal use, $800.

(continued)

(i) Performed services for clients on account, $900.

(j) Paid wages to part-time employee, $500.

(k) Received cash for services performed on account in transaction (i), $500.

E 2-5B   (LO1/5)

FINANCIAL STATEMENT ACCOUNTS Label each of the following accounts as an asset (A), liability (L), owner's equity (OE), revenue (R), or expense (E). Indicate the financial statement on which the account belongs—income statement (IS), statement of owner's equity (SOE), or balance sheet (BS)—in a format similar to the following.

Account	Classification	Financial Statement
Cash		
Rent Expense		
Accounts Payable		
Service Fees		
Supplies		
Wages Expense		
Amanda Wong, Drawing		
Amanda Wong, Capital		
Prepaid Insurance		
Accounts Receivable		

E 2-6B   (LO5)
✓ Capital, 6/30: $14,000

STATEMENT OF OWNER'S EQUITY REPORTING NET INCOME Efran Lopez started a financial consulting service on June 1, 20--, by investing $15,000. His net income for the month was $6,000, and he withdrew $7,000 for personal use. Prepare a statement of owner's equity for the month of June.

E 2-7B   (LO5)
✓ Capital, 6/30: $6,000

STATEMENT OF OWNER'S EQUITY REPORTING NET LOSS Based on the information provided in Exercise 2-6B, prepare a statement of owner's equity assuming Lopez had a net loss of $2,000.

SERIES B PROBLEMS

P 2-8B   (LO1/2)
✓ 3: $25,235 = $10,165 + $15,070

SHOW
ME HOW

THE ACCOUNTING EQUATION Dr. Patricia Parsons is a dentist. As of January 31, Parsons owned the following property that related to her professional practice:

Cash	$3,560
Office Equipment	4,600
X-ray Equipment	8,760
Laboratory Equipment	5,940

She also owes the following business suppliers:

Cupples Gas Company	$1,815
Swan Dental Lab	2,790

REQUIRED

1. From the preceding information, compute the accounting elements and enter them in the accounting equation as shown below.

Assets	=	Liabilities	+	Owner's Equity
_____	=	_____	+	_____

2. During February, the assets increase by $4,565, and the liabilities increase by $3,910. Compute the resulting accounting equation.

3. During March, the assets decrease by $2,190, and the liabilities increase by $1,650. Compute the resulting accounting equation.

P 2-9B   (LO3/4)
✓ Total cash following (g): $11,300

EFFECT OF TRANSACTIONS ON ACCOUNTING EQUATION David Segal started a business. During the first month (October 20--), the following transactions occurred.

(a) Invested cash in the business, $15,000.

(b) Bought office supplies for $3,800: $1,800 in cash and $2,000 on account.

(c) Paid one-year insurance premium, $1,000.

(d) Earned revenues amounting to $2,700: $1,700 in cash and $1,000 on account.

(e) Paid cash on account to the company that supplied the office supplies in transaction (b), $1,800.

(f) Paid office rent for the month, $650.

(g) Withdrew cash for personal use, $150.

REQUIRED

Show the effect of each transaction on the individual accounts of the expanded accounting equation: *Assets = Liabilities + Owner's Equity (Capital – Drawing + Revenues – Expenses)*. After transaction (g), report the totals for each element. Demonstrate that the accounting equation has remained in balance.

P 2-10B   (LO5)
✓ Net income: $2,050

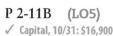

SHOW ME HOW

INCOME STATEMENT Based on Problem 2-9B, prepare an income statement for David Segal for the month of October 20--.

P 2-11B   (LO5)
✓ Capital, 10/31: $16,900

SHOW ME HOW

STATEMENT OF OWNER'S EQUITY Based on Problem 2-9B, prepare a statement of owner's equity for David Segal for the month of October 20--.

P 2-12B   (LO5)
✓ Total assets, 10/31: $17,100

SHOW ME HOW

BALANCE SHEET Based on Problem 2-9B, prepare a balance sheet for David Segal as of October 31, 20--.

Check List
☑ Check List
☐ Managing
☐ Planning
☐ Drafting
☐ Break
☐ Revising
☐ Managing

MANAGING YOUR WRITING

Write a brief memo that explains the differences and similarities between expenses and withdrawals.

MASTERY PROBLEM

Lisa Vozniak started her own business, We Do Windows. She offers interior and exterior window cleaning for local area residents. Lisa rents a garage to store her tools and cleaning supplies and has a part-time assistant to answer the phone and handle third-story work. (Lisa is afraid of heights.) The transactions for the month of July are as follows:

(a) On the first day of the month, Vozniak invested cash by making a deposit in a bank account for the business, $8,000.

(b) Paid rent for July, $150.

(c) Purchased a used van for cash, $5,000.

(d) Purchased tools on account from Clean Tools, $600.

(e) Purchased cleaning supplies that cost $300. Paid $200 cash and will pay the balance next month, $100.

(f) Paid part-time assistant (wages) for first half of month, $100.

(g) Paid for advertising, $75.

(h) Paid two-year premium for liability insurance on van, $480.

(i) Received cash from clients for services performed, $800.

(j) Performed cleaning services for clients on account, $500.

(k) Paid phone bill, $40.

(l) Received cash from clients for window cleaning performed on account in transaction (j), $200.

(m) Paid part-time assistant (wages) for last half of month, $150.

(n) Made partial payment on tools purchased in transaction (d), $200.

(o) Earned additional revenues amounting to $800: $600 in cash and $200 on account.

(p) Vozniak withdrew cash at the end of the month for personal expenses, $100.

REQUIRED

1. Enter the above transactions in an accounting equation similar to the one illustrated below.

Assets (Items Owned)						=	Liabilities (Amounts Owed)	+	Owner's Equity					
									(Owner's Investment) +		(Earnings)			
Cash +	Accounts Receivable +	Supplies +	Prepaid Insurance +	Tools + Van		=	Accounts Payable	+	Lisa Vozniak, Capital –	Lisa Vozniak, Drawing	+ Revenues	– Expenses	Description

2. After transaction (p), compute the balance of each account.

3. Prepare an income statement for We Do Windows for the month of July 20--.

4. Prepare a statement of owner's equity for We Do Windows for the month of July 20--.

5. Prepare a balance sheet for We Do Windows as of July 31, 20--.

CHALLENGE PROBLEM

In this chapter, you learned about three important financial statements: the income statement, statement of owner's equity, and balance sheet. As mentioned in the margin note on page 34, most firms also prepare a statement of cash flows. Part of this statement reports the **cash received** from customers and **cash paid** for goods and services.

REQUIRED

Take another look at the Demonstration Problem for Kenny Young's "Home and Away Inspections." Note that when revenues are measured based on the amount earned, and expenses are measured based on the amount incurred, net income for the period was $4,165. Now, compute the difference between cash received from customers and cash paid to suppliers of goods and services by completing the form provided below. Are these measures different? Which provides a better measure of profitability?

Cash from customers _____
Cash paid for wages _____
Cash paid for rent _____
Cash paid for utilities _____
Cash paid for insurance _____
Cash paid for supplies _____
Cash paid for phone _____
Total cash paid for operating items _____

Difference between cash received from
customers and cash paid for
goods and services _____

Answers to Self-Study Test Questions

True/False

1. T

2. F (Accounts Payable is a liability.)

3. T

4. T

5. F (Other changes could occur: capital could increase, revenue could increase, etc.)

6. T

7. F (net income)

Multiple Choice

1. c   2. a   3. b   4. d   5. c

Checkpoint Exercises

1.
Account	Classification
Accounts Receivable	A
Accounts Payable	L
Judy Smith, Capital	OE

2. Assets = Liabilities + Owner's Equity

3.
Transaction	Assets	Liabilities	Owner's Equity
a. Purchase of an asset on account.	+	+	_____
b. Made payment on account for transaction (a).	–	–	_____

4.
Account	Classification	Financial Statement
Accounts Payable	L	BS
Peggy Welsch, Drawing	OE	SOE
Rent Expense	E	IS
Sales	R	IS
Equipment	A	BS

Chapter 3

The Double-Entry Framework

Tired of receiving spam e-mail messages? Or, are you worried about your computer picking up a virus? Businesses have the same concerns. Computer viruses can cause serious financial damage to a business. In response to demand for e-mail and Web security, AppRiver was founded in April of 2002 to provide simple, yet powerful protection from Internet-based threats to businesses of any size. The company is based in Gulf Breeze, Florida, and maintains multiple data centers at secure locations in the United States, Europe, and Asia. AppRiver's 200 employees protect more than 47,000 companies around the world from spam, viruses, and Internet pollution.

Just as Internet security is important to you in your personal life and to businesses, the same can be said about accounting. A solid understanding of financial accounting will help you manage your personal finances and help you understand business transactions in your professional life. In this chapter, you will learn about the double-entry framework used by businesses to enter transactions into an accounting system. You could use the same concepts for your personal transactions or for a business you might start.

The terms asset, liability, owner's equity, revenue, and expense were explained in Chapter 2. Examples showed how individual business transactions change one or more of these basic accounting elements. Each transaction had a dual effect. An increase or decrease in any asset, liability, owner's equity, revenue, or expense was *always* accompanied by an offsetting change within the basic accounting elements. The fact that each transaction has a dual effect upon the accounting elements provides the basis for what is called **double-entry accounting**. To understand double-entry accounting, it is important to learn how T accounts work and the role of debits and credits in accounting.

THE T ACCOUNT

LO1 Define the parts of a T account.

The assets of a business may consist of a number of items, such as cash, accounts receivable, equipment, buildings, and land. The liabilities may consist of one or more items, such as accounts payable and notes payable. Similarly, owner's equity may consist of the owner's investments and various revenue and expense items. A separate account is used to record the increases and decreases in each type of asset, liability, owner's equity, revenue, and expense.

The T account gets its name from the fact that it resembles the letter T. The three major parts of an account are as follows:

1. the title,
2. the debit, or left side, and
3. the credit, or right side.

Title	
Debit = Left	Credit = Right

The debit side is always on the left, and the credit side is always on the right. This is true for all types of asset, liability, owner's equity, revenue, and expense accounts.

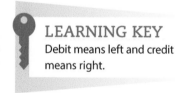

LEARNING KEY
Debit means left and credit means right.

Sometimes new accounting students think that a debit is bad because it sounds like "debt." Similarly, credit sounds like a good thing, especially when the bank says they will credit your account. Please clear your mind of these thoughts. *In accounting, debit simply means left and credit means right.*

BALANCING A T ACCOUNT

LO2 Foot and balance a T account

To determine the balance of a T account at any time, simply total the dollar amounts on the debit and credit sides. These totals are known as footings. The difference between the footings is called the balance of the account. This amount is then written on the side with the larger footing.

In Chapter 2, the accounting equation was used to analyze business transactions. This required columns in which to record the increases and decreases in various accounts. Let's compare this approach with the use of a T account for the transactions affecting cash. When a T account is used, increases in cash are recorded on the debit side and decreases are recorded on the credit side. Transactions for Rohan's Campus Delivery are shown in Figure 3-1.

FIGURE 3-1 Cash T Account

COLUMNAR SUMMARY (From Chapter 2, page 31)		T ACCOUNT FORM			
Transaction	**Cash**	**Cash**			
(a)	2,000	(a)	2,000	(b)	1,200
(b)	(1,200)	(e)	500	(d)	300
(d)	(300)	(k)	570	(f)	200
(e)	500	(n)	430	(g)	50
(f)	(200) footing →		**3,500**	(i)	80
(g)	(50)			(j)	200
(i)	(80)			(l)	300
(j)	(200)			(m)	650
(k)	570			(o)	150
(l)	(300) Balance →		370		**3,130** ← footing
(m)	(650)				
(n)	430				
(o)	(150)				
Balance	370				

Checkpoint ✓

Complete Checkpoint-1 on page 74 to test your basic understanding of LO2.

DEBITS AND CREDITS

LO3 **Describe the effects of debits and credits on specific types of accounts.**

To debit an account means to enter an amount on the left or debit side of the account. To credit an account means to enter an amount on the right or credit side of the account. *Debits may increase or decrease the balances of specific accounts. This is also true for credits. To learn how to use debits and credits, it is best to focus on the accounting equation.*

Abbreviations: Often debit and credit are abbreviated as: Dr. = Debit, Cr. = Credit (based on the Latin terms "debere" and "credere")

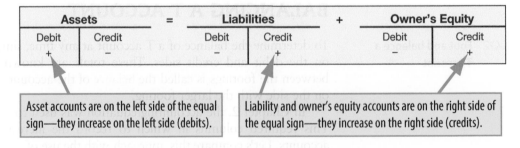

Assets		=	Liabilities		+	Owner's Equity	
Debit +	Credit –		Debit –	Credit +		Debit –	Credit +

Asset accounts are on the left side of the equal sign—they increase on the left side (debits).

Liability and owner's equity accounts are on the right side of the equal sign—they increase on the right side (credits).

ASSETS

Assets are on the left side of the accounting equation. Therefore, increases are entered on the left (debit) side of an asset account, and decreases are entered on the right (credit) side.

Liabilities and Owner's Equity

Liabilities and owner's equity are on the right side of the equation. Therefore, increases are entered on the right (credit) side, and decreases are entered on the left (debit) side.

The Owner's Equity Umbrella

Owner's equity includes four types of accounts: Owner's Capital, Revenues, Expenses, and Drawing. Expanding the accounting equation helps illustrate the use of debits and credits. Since these accounts affect owner's equity, they are shown under the "umbrella" of owner's equity in the accounting equation in Figure 3-2. It is helpful to think of the Owner's Capital account as hovering over the revenue, expense, and drawing accounts like an umbrella. Since revenues increase Owner's Capital, the revenue account is shown under the credit side of Owner's Capital. Since expenses and drawing reduce Owner's Capital, they are shown under the debit side of Owner's Capital.

FIGURE 3-2   The Accounting Equation and the Owner's Equity Umbrella

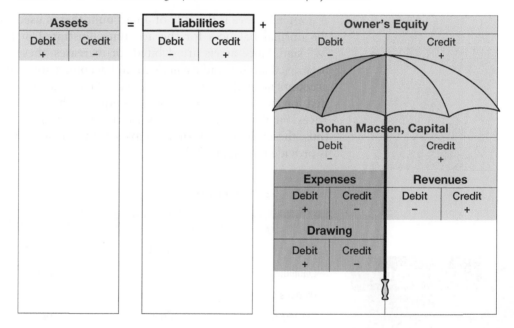

Owner's Capital

The owner's capital account, Rohan Macsen, Capital, in Figure 3-2 reports the amount the owner has invested in the business. These investments increase the owner's equity and are credited to the owner's capital account.

Revenues

Revenues increase owner's equity. Revenues could be recorded directly on the credit side of the owner's capital account. However, readers of financial statements are interested in the specific types of revenues earned. Therefore, specific revenue accounts, like Delivery Fees, Sales, and Service Fees, are used. These specific accounts are credited when revenue is earned.

Remember: An increase in an expense decreases owner's equity.

Expenses

Expenses decrease owner's equity. Expenses could be recorded on the debit side of the owner's capital account. However, readers of financial statements want to see the types of expenses incurred during the accounting period. Thus, specific expense accounts are maintained for items like rent, wages, advertising, and utilities. These specific accounts are debited as expenses are incurred.

Drawing

Withdrawals of cash and other assets by the owner for personal reasons decrease owner's equity. Withdrawals could be debited directly to the owner's capital account. However, readers of financial statements want to know the amount of withdrawals for the accounting period. Thus, as shown in Figure 3-2, withdrawals are debited to a separate account, Drawing.

Normal Balances

A normal balance is the side of an account that is used to increase the account. Thus, the normal balances for the accounts illustrated in Figure 3-2 are shown with a "+" sign. Since assets are debited for increases, these accounts normally have debit balances. Liability and owner's capital accounts are credited for increases; thus, these accounts normally have credit balances. Since expense and drawing accounts are debited for increases (reducing owner's equity), these accounts normally have debit balances. Finally, revenue accounts are credited for increases (increasing owner's equity); thus, these accounts normally have credit balances. A summary of normal balances is provided in Figure 3-3.

FIGURE 3-3 Normal Balances

ACCOUNT	INCREASE	DECREASE	NORMAL BALANCE
Assets	Debit	Credit	Debit
Liabilities	Credit	Debit	Credit
Owner's Capital	Credit	Debit	Credit
Revenues	Credit	Debit	Credit
Expenses	Debit	Credit	Debit
Drawing	Debit	Credit	Debit

Checkpoint ✓

Complete Checkpoint-2 on page 74 to test your basic understanding of LO3.

LO4 Use T accounts to analyze transactions.

LEARNING KEY

Since the accounting equation must stay in balance, there must be at least one debit and at least one credit for each transaction.

TRANSACTION ANALYSIS

In Chapter 2, you learned how to analyze transactions by using the accounting equation. Here, we continue to use the accounting equation, but add debits and credits by using T accounts. As shown in Figure 3-4, the three basic questions that must be answered when analyzing a transaction are essentially the same but are expanded slightly to address the use of the owner's equity umbrella and T accounts. You must determine the location of the account within the accounting equation and/or the owner's equity umbrella. You must also determine whether the accounts should be debited or credited.

FIGURE 3-4   Steps in Transaction Analysis

1. **What happened?**
   Be sure you understand the event that has taken place.

2. **Which accounts are affected?**
   Once you understand what happened, you must:

   - Identify the accounts that are affected.
   - Classify these accounts as assets, liabilities, owner's equity, revenues, or expenses.
   - Identify the location of the accounts in the accounting equation and/or the owner's equity umbrella—left or right.

3. **How is the accounting equation affected?**

   - Determine whether the accounts have increased or decreased.
   - Determine whether the accounts should be debited or credited.
   - Make certain the accounting equation remains in balance after the transaction has been entered.
     (1) Assets = Liabilities + Owner's Equity.
     (2) Debits = Credits for every transaction.

Debits and Credits: Asset, Liability, and Owner's Equity Accounts

Transactions (a) through (d) from Rohan's Campus Delivery (Chapter 2) demonstrate the double-entry process for transactions affecting asset, liability, and owner's equity accounts.

As you study each transaction, answer the three questions: (1) What happened? (2) Which accounts are affected? and (3) How is the accounting equation affected? The transaction statement tells you what happened. The analysis tells which accounts are affected. The illustration shows you how the accounting equation is affected.

Transaction (a): Investment by owner

Rohan Macsen, opened a bank account with a deposit of $2,000 for his business (Figure 3-5).

Analysis. As a result of this transaction, the business acquired an asset, Cash. In exchange for the asset, the business gave Rohan Macsen, owner's equity. The owner's equity account is called Rohan Macsen, Capital. The transaction is entered as an increase in an asset and an increase in owner's equity. Debit Cash and credit Rohan Macsen, Capital for $2,000.

FIGURE 3-5   Transaction (a): Investment by Owner

Assets		=	Liabilities		+	Owner's Equity	
Debit +	Credit −		Debit −	Credit +		Debit −	Credit +
Cash						**Rohan Macsen, Capital**	
(a) 2,000							(a) 2,000
$2,000		=	$0		+	$2,000	
$2,000		=		$2,000			

Transaction (b): Purchase of an asset for cash

Rohan bought a motor scooter (delivery equipment) for $1,200 cash (Figure 3-6).

Analysis. Rohan exchanged one asset, Cash, for another, Delivery Equipment. Debit Delivery Equipment and credit Cash for $1,200. Notice that the total assets are still $2,000 as they were following transaction (a). Transaction (b) shifted assets from cash to delivery equipment, but total assets remained the same.

FIGURE 3-6   Transaction (b): Purchase of an Asset for Cash

Assets		=	Liabilities		+	Owner's Equity	
Debit +	Credit −		Debit −	Credit +		Debit −	Credit +
Cash						Rohan Macsen, Capital	
Bal. 2,000							Bal. 2,000
	(b) 1,200						
Bal. 800							
Delivery Equipment							
(b) 1,200							
$2,000		=	$0		+	$2,000	
$2,000		=			$2,000		

Transaction (c): Purchase of an asset on account

Rohan bought a second motor scooter on account for $900 (Figure 3-7). Recall from Chapter 2 that "on account" means Rohan will pay for the asset later.

Analysis. The asset, Delivery Equipment, increases by $900 and the liability, Accounts Payable, increases by the same amount. Thus, debit Delivery Equipment and credit Accounts Payable for $900.

FIGURE 3-7   Transaction (c): Purchase of an Asset on Account

Assets		=	Liabilities		+	Owner's Equity	
Debit +	Credit −		Debit −	Credit +		Debit −	Credit +
Cash			Accounts Payable			Rohan Macsen, Capital	
Bal. 800				(c) 900			Bal. 2,000
Delivery Equipment							
Bal. 1,200							
(c) 900							
Bal. 2,100							
$2,900		=	$900		+	$2,000	
$2,900		=			$2,900		

Transaction (d): Payment on account

Rohan made the first $300 payment on the scooter purchased in transaction (c) (Figure 3-8).

Analysis. This payment decreases the asset, Cash, and decreases the liability, Accounts Payable. Debit Accounts Payable and credit Cash for $300.

FIGURE 3-8   Transaction (d): Payment on Account

Assets		=	Liabilities		+	Owner's Equity	
Debit +	Credit −	=	Debit −	Credit +	+	Debit −	Credit +
Cash			**Accounts Payable**			**Rohan Macsen, Capital**	
Bal. 800	(d) 300		(d) 300	Bal. 900			Bal. 2,000
Bal. 500				Bal. 600			
Delivery Equipment							
Bal. 2,100							
$2,600		=	$600		+	$2,000	
$2,600		=			$2,600		

Notice that for transactions (a) through (d), the debits equal credits and the accounting equation is in balance. Review transactions (a) through (d). Again, identify the accounts that were affected and how they were classified (assets, liabilities, or owner's equity). Finally, note each account's location within the accounting equation.

Debits and Credits: Including Revenues, Expenses, and Drawing

Transactions (a) through (d) involved only assets, liabilities, and the owner's capital account. To complete the illustration of Rohan's Campus Delivery, the equation is expanded to include revenues, expenses, and drawing. Remember, revenues increase owner's equity and are shown under the credit side of the capital account. Expenses and drawing decrease owner's equity and are shown under the debit side of the capital account. The expanded equation is shown in Figure 3-9.

> **LEARNING KEY**
> Credits increase the capital account. Revenues increase capital. Thus, revenues are shown under the credit side of the capital account. Debits decrease the capital account. Expenses and drawing reduce owner's equity. Thus, they are shown under the debit side of the capital account.

FIGURE 3-9   The Expanded Accounting Equation

Assets		=	Liabilities		+	Owner's Equity					
Debit +	Credit −	=	Debit −	Credit +	+	Debit −				Credit +	
						Drawing		**Expenses**		**Revenues**	
						Debit +	Credit −	Debit +	Credit −	Debit −	Credit +

Transaction (e): Delivery revenues earned in cash

Rohan made deliveries and received $500 cash from clients (Figure 3-10).

Analysis. The asset, Cash, and the revenue, Delivery Fees, increase. Debit Cash and credit Delivery Fees for $500.

FIGURE 3-10 Transaction (e): Delivery Revenues Earned in Cash

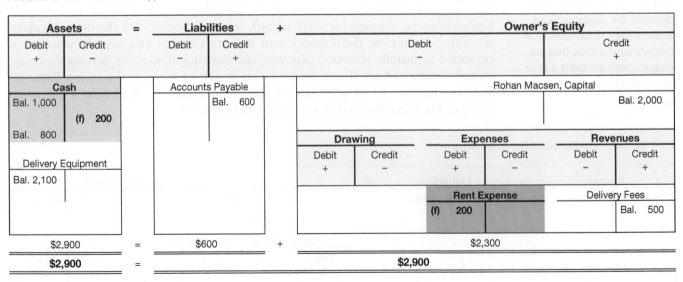

Assets		=	Liabilities		+	Owner's Equity	
Debit +	Credit −		Debit −	Credit +		Debit	Credit +

Cash	
Bal. 500	
(e) 500	
Bal. 1,000	

Accounts Payable	
	Bal. 600

Rohan Macsen, Capital	
	Bal. 2,000

Delivery Equipment	
Bal. 2,100	

Drawing		Expenses		Revenues	
Debit +	Credit −	Debit +	Credit −	Debit −	Credit +

	Delivery Fees	
	(e) 500

$3,100	=	$600	+	$2,500
$3,100	=			$3,100

Transaction (f): Paid rent for month

Rohan paid $200 for office rent for June (Figure 3-11).

Analysis. Rent Expense increases and Cash decreases. Debit Rent Expense and credit Cash for $200.

A debit to an expense account *increases* that expense and *decreases* owner's equity. Notice that the placement of the plus and minus signs for expenses is opposite the placement of the signs for owner's equity. Note also that expenses are located on the left (debit) side of the owner's equity umbrella.

FIGURE 3-11 Transaction (f): Paid Rent for Month

Assets		=	Liabilities		+	Owner's Equity	
Debit +	Credit −		Debit −	Credit +		Debit	Credit +

Cash	
Bal. 1,000	
	(f) 200
Bal. 800	

Accounts Payable	
	Bal. 600

Rohan Macsen, Capital	
	Bal. 2,000

Delivery Equipment	
Bal. 2,100	

Drawing		Expenses		Revenues	
Debit +	Credit −	Debit +	Credit −	Debit −	Credit +

Rent Expense		Delivery Fees	
(f) 200			Bal. 500

$2,900	=	$600	+	$2,300
$2,900	=			$2,900

Transaction (g): Paid phone bill

Rohan paid for phone service, $50 (Figure 3-12).

Analysis. This transaction, like the previous one, increases an expense and decreases an asset. Debit Phone Expense and credit Cash for $50.

FIGURE 3-12   Transaction (g): Paid Phone Bill

Assets		=	Liabilities		+	Owner's Equity	
Debit +	Credit −		Debit −	Credit +		Debit −	Credit +

Cash			Accounts Payable			Rohan Macsen, Capital	
Bal. 800				Bal. 600			Bal. 2,000
	(g) 50						
Bal. 750							

Delivery Equipment	
Bal. 2,100	

		Drawing		Expenses		Revenues	
		Debit +	Credit −	Debit +	Credit −	Debit −	Credit +

Rent Expense		Delivery Fees	
Bal. 200			Bal. 500

Phone Expense	
(g) 50	

$2,850	=	$600	+	$2,250
$2,850	=			**$2,850**

Transaction (h): Delivery revenues earned on account

Rohan made deliveries on account for $600 (Figure 3-13).

Analysis. As discussed in Chapter 2, delivery services are performed for which payment will be received later. This is called offering services "on account" or "on credit." Instead of receiving cash, Rohan receives a promise that his customers will pay cash in the future. Therefore, the asset, Accounts Receivable, increases. Since revenues are recognized when earned, the revenue account, Delivery Fees, also increases. Debit Accounts Receivable and credit Delivery Fees for $600.

FIGURE 3-13   Transaction (h): Delivery Revenues Earned on Account

Assets		=	Liabilities		+	Owner's Equity	
Debit +	Credit −		Debit −	Credit +		Debit −	Credit +

Cash			Accounts Payable			Rohan Macsen, Capital	
Bal. 750				Bal. 600			Bal. 2,000

Accounts Receivable	
(h) 600	

Delivery Equipment	
Bal. 2,100	

		Drawing		Expenses		Revenues	
		Debit +	Credit −	Debit +	Credit −	Debit −	Credit +

Rent Expense		Delivery Fees	
Bal. 200			Bal. 500
			(h) 600
			Bal. 1,100

Phone Expense	
Bal. 50	

$3,450	=	$600	+	$2,850
$3,450	=			**$3,450**

Review transactions (e) through (h). Note the following:

- Expense and revenue transactions do not always affect cash.
- The debits equal credits, and the accounting equation is in balance after each transaction.

Upcoming transactions (i) and (j) both involve an exchange of cash for another asset. As you analyze these two transactions, you may wonder why prepaid insurance and supplies are assets while the rent and phone bill in transactions (f) and (g) are expenses. Prepaid insurance and supplies are assets because they will provide benefits for more than one month. Rohan pays his rent and his phone bill each month so they are classified as expenses. If Rohan paid his rent only once every three months, he would need to set up an asset account called Prepaid Rent. He would debit this account when he paid the rent.

Transaction (i): Purchase of supplies

Rohan bought pens, paper, delivery envelopes, and other supplies for $80 cash (Figure 3-14).

Analysis. These supplies will last for several months. Since they will generate future benefits, the supplies should be recorded as an asset. An asset, Supplies, increases, and an asset, Cash, decreases. Debit Supplies and credit Cash for $80.

FIGURE 3-14 Transaction (i): Purchase of Supplies

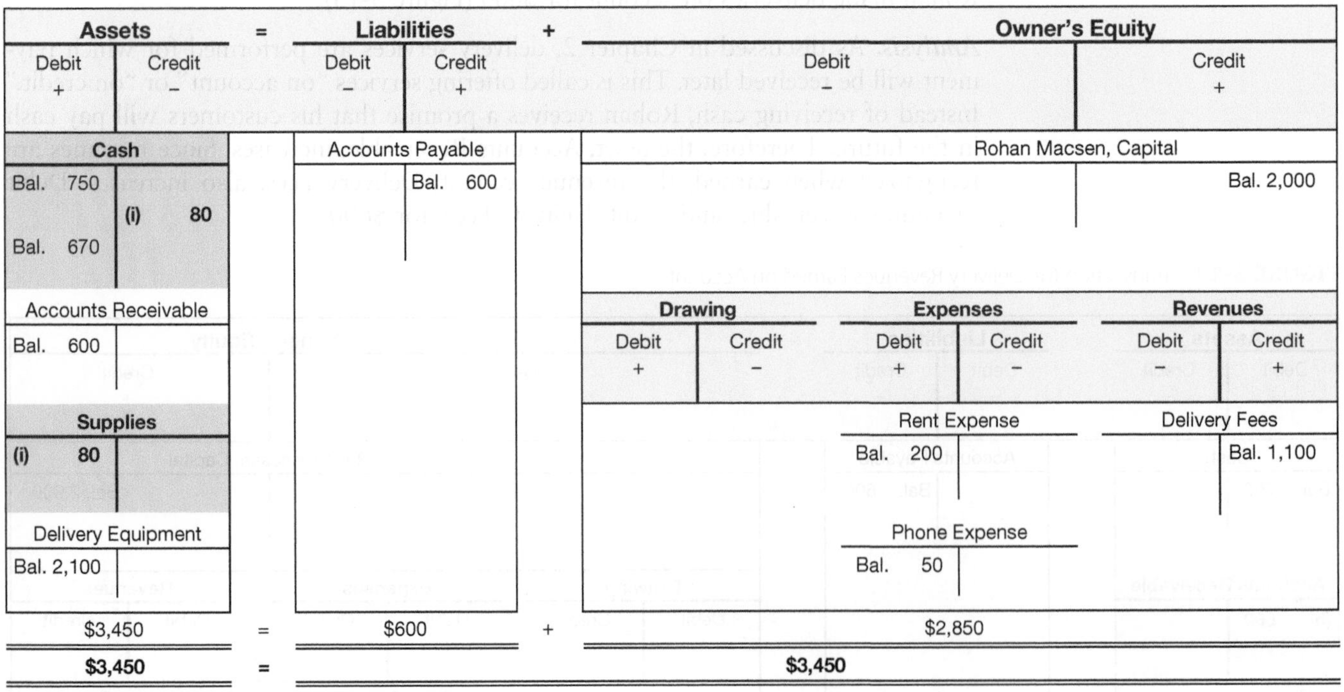

A Broader View

Supplies—Asset or Expense?

When businesses buy office supplies from Staples or other suppliers, the supplies are initially recorded as assets. This is done because the supplies will provide future benefits. Those still remaining in inventory at the end of the accounting period are reported on the balance sheet as assets. Supplies actually used during the period are recognized as an expense on the income statement. We will discuss how to account for the expense in Chapter 5.

CONVERY FLOWERS/ALAMY

Transaction (j): Payment of insurance premium

Rohan paid $200 for an eight-month liability insurance policy (Figure 3-15).

Analysis. Since insurance is paid in advance and will provide future benefits, it is treated as an asset. Therefore, one asset, Prepaid Insurance, increases and another, Cash, decreases. Debit Prepaid Insurance and credit Cash for $200.

FIGURE 3-15   Transaction (j): Payment of Insurance Premium

Assets		=	Liabilities		+	Owner's Equity	
Debit +	Credit −		Debit −	Credit +		Debit −	Credit +

Cash			Accounts Payable			Rohan Macsen, Capital	
Bal. 670				Bal. 600			Bal. 2,000
	(j) 200						
Bal. 470							

Accounts Receivable				Drawing		Expenses		Revenues	
Bal. 600				Debit +	Credit −	Debit +	Credit −	Debit −	Credit +

Supplies					Rent Expense		Delivery Fees	
Bal. 80					Bal. 200			Bal. 1,100

Prepaid Insurance					Phone Expense	
(j) 200					Bal. 50	

Delivery Equipment	
Bal. 2,100	

$3,450	=	$600	+	$2,850
$3,450	=			$3,450

Transaction (k): Cash receipts from prior sales on account

Rohan received $570 in cash for delivery services performed for customers earlier in the month [see transaction (h)] (Figure 3-16).

Analysis. This transaction increases Cash and reduces the amount due from customers reported in Accounts Receivable. Debit Cash and credit Accounts Receivable $570.

As you analyze transaction (k), notice which accounts are affected and the location of these accounts in the accounting equation. Rohan received cash, but this transaction did not affect revenue. The revenue was recorded in transaction (h). Transaction (k) is an exchange of one asset (Accounts Receivable) for another asset (Cash).

FIGURE 3-16   Transaction (k): Cash Receipts from Prior Sales on Account

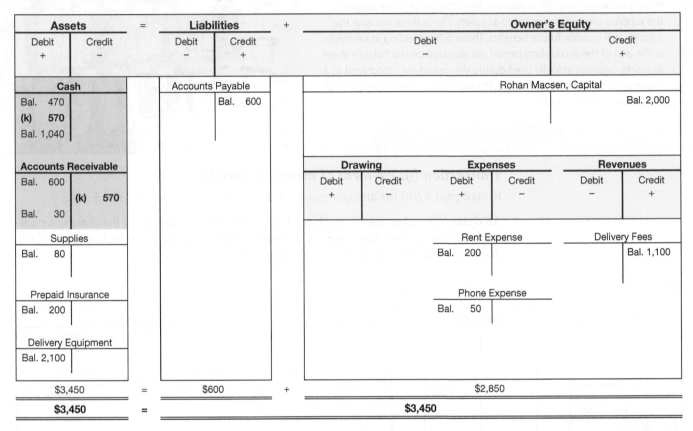

As you analyze transactions (l) through (o), make certain that you understand what has happened in each transaction. Identify the accounts that are affected and the locations of these accounts within the accounting equation. Notice that the accounting equation remains in balance after every transaction and debits equal credits for each transaction.

Transaction (l): Purchase of an asset on credit making a partial payment

Rohan bought a third motor scooter for $1,500. Rohan made a down payment of $300 and spread the remaining payments over the next four months (Figure 3-17).

Analysis. The asset, Delivery Equipment, increases by $1,500, Cash decreases by $300, and the liability, Accounts Payable, increases by $1,200. Thus, debit Delivery Equipment for $1,500, credit Cash for $300, and credit Accounts Payable for $1,200. This transaction requires one debit and two credits. Even so, total debits ($1,500) equal the total credits ($1,200 + $300) and the accounting equation remains in balance.

Transaction (m): Payment of wages

Rohan paid his part-time employees $650 in wages (Figure 3-18).

Analysis. This is an additional business expense. Wages Expense increases and Cash decreases. Debit Wages Expense and credit Cash for $650.

FIGURE 3-17   Transaction (l): Purchase of an Asset on Credit Making a Partial Payment

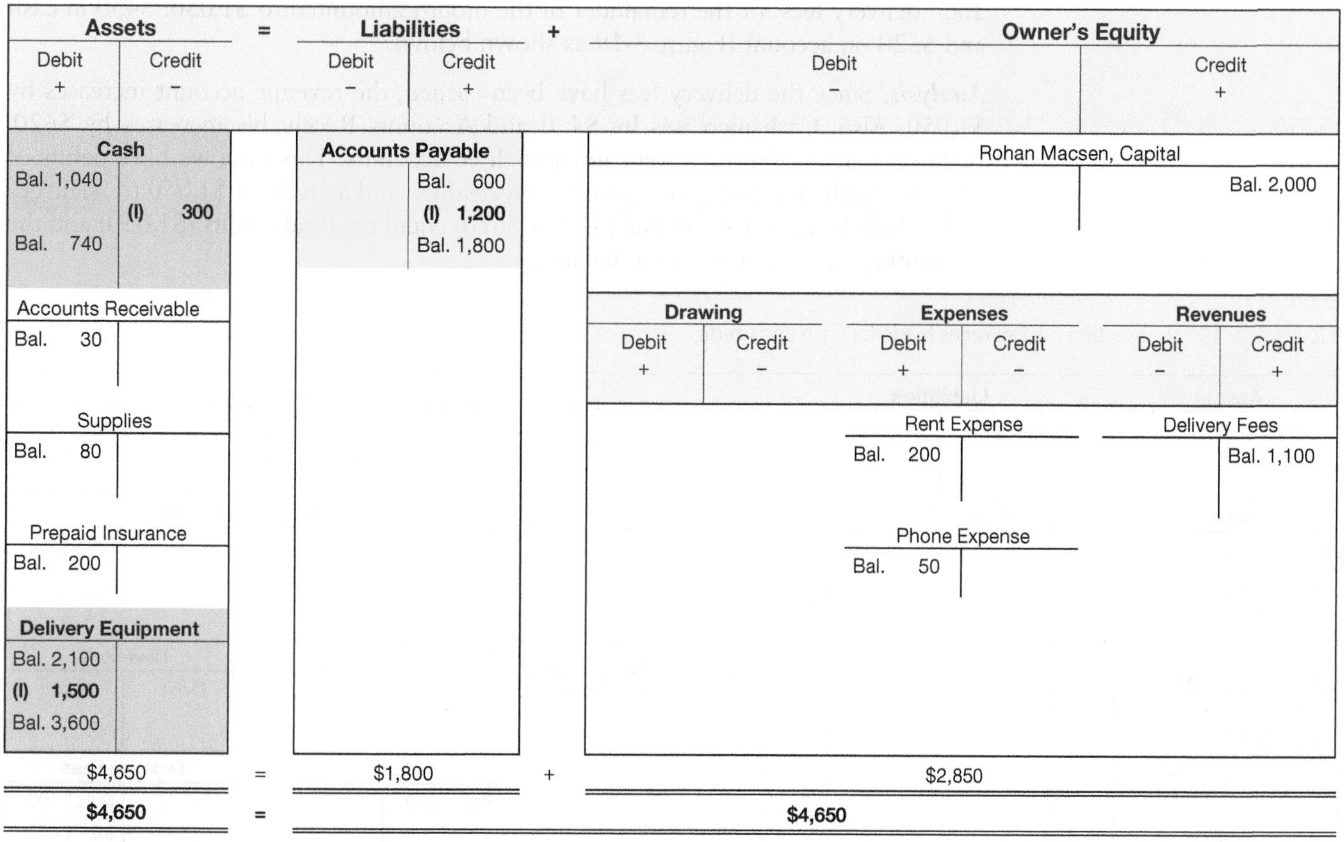

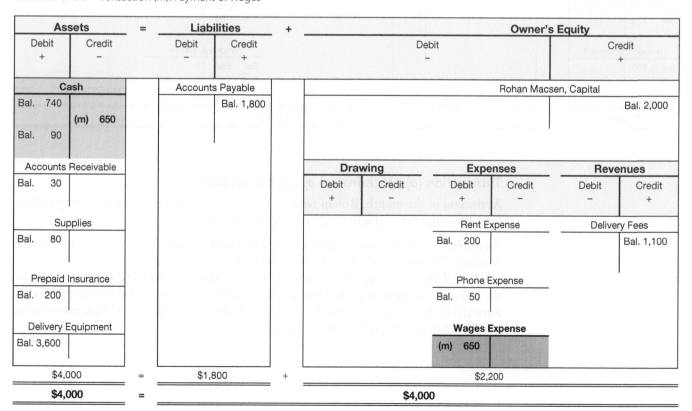

FIGURE 3-18   Transaction (m): Payment of Wages

Transaction (n): Deliveries made for cash and credit

Total delivery fees for the remainder of the month amounted to $1,050: $430 in cash and $620 on account (Figure 3-19 as shown below).

Analysis. Since the delivery fees have been earned, the revenue account increases by $1,050. Also, Cash increases by $430 and Accounts Receivable increases by $620. Note once again that one event impacts three accounts. This time we have debits of $430 to Cash and $620 to Accounts Receivable, and a credit of $1,050 to Delivery Fees. As before, the total debits ($430 + $620) equal the total credits ($1,050) and the accounting equation remains in balance.

FIGURE 3-19   Transaction (n): Deliveries Made for Cash and Credit

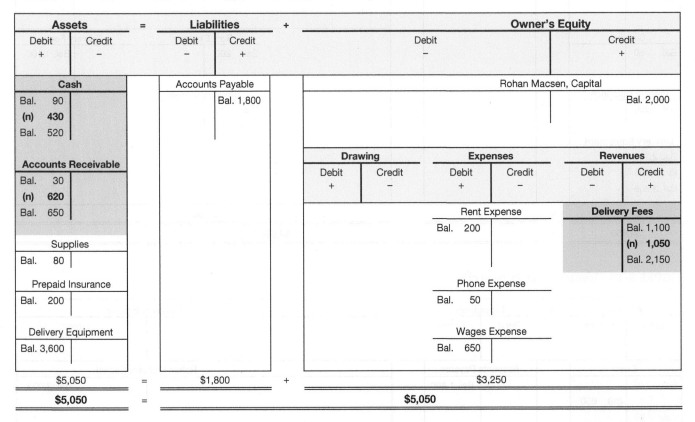

Transaction (o): Withdrawal of cash from business

At the end of the month, Rohan withdrew $150 in cash from the business to purchase books for his classes (Figure 3-20 on the next page).

Analysis. Cash withdrawals decrease owner's equity and decrease cash. Debit Rohan Macsen, Drawing and credit Cash for $150.

Withdrawals are reported in the drawing account. Withdrawals by an owner are the opposite of an investment. You could debit the owner's capital account for withdrawals. However, using a specific account tells the user of the accounting information how much was withdrawn for the period.

FIGURE 3-20 Transaction (o): Withdrawal of Cash from Business

Assets			=	Liabilities			+	Owner's Equity		
Debit +	Credit −			Debit −	Credit +			Debit −		Credit +

Cash			Accounts Payable			Rohan Macsen, Capital	
Bal. 520	(o) 150			Bal. 1,800			Bal. 2,000
Bal. 370							

Accounts Receivable	
Bal. 650	

Drawing			Expenses			Revenues	
Debit +	Credit −		Debit +	Credit −		Debit −	Credit +

Supplies	
Bal. 80	

Rohan Macsen, Drawing			Rent Expense			Delivery Fees	
(o) 150			Bal. 200				Bal. 2,150

Prepaid Insurance	
Bal. 200	

Phone Expense	
Bal. 50	

Delivery Equipment	
Bal. 3,600	

Wages Expense	
Bal. 650	

$4,900	=	$1,800	+	$3,100
$4,900	=			**$4,900**

Summary of Transactions

In illustrating transactions (a) through (o), each T account for Rohan's Campus Delivery shows a balance before and after each transaction. To focus your attention on the transaction being explained, only a single entry was shown. In practice, this is not done. Instead, each account gathers all transactions for a period. Rohan's accounts, with all transactions listed, are shown in Figure 3-21. Note the following four items:

Checkpoint ✓

Complete Checkpoint-3 on page 74 to test your basic understanding of LO4.

1. The footings are directly under the debit (left) and credit (right) sides of the T account for those accounts with more than one debit or credit.

2. The balance is shown on the side with the larger footing.

3. The footing serves as the balance for accounts with entries on only one side of the account.

4. If an account has only a single entry, it is not necessary to enter a footing or balance.

FIGURE 3-21   Summary of Transactions (a) Through (o)

Assets		=	Liabilities		+	Owner's Equity	
Debit +	Credit –		Debit –	Credit +		Debit –	Credit +

Assets

Cash

(a)	2,000	(b)	1,200
(e)	500	(d)	300
(k)	570	(f)	200
(n)	430	(g)	50
	3,500	(i)	80
		(j)	200
		(l)	300
		(m)	650
		(o)	150
			3,130
Bal.	370		

Accounts Receivable

(h)	600	(k)	570
(n)	620		
	1,220		
Bal.	650		

Supplies

(i)	80	

Prepaid Insurance

(j)	200	

Delivery Equipment

(b)	1,200	
(c)	900	
(l)	1,500	
Bal.	3,600	

Liabilities

Accounts Payable

(d)	300	(c)	900
		(l)	1,200
			2,100
		Bal.	1,800

Owner's Equity

Rohan Macsen, Capital

		(a)	2,000

Drawing			Expenses			Revenues	
Debit +	Credit –		Debit +	Credit –		Debit –	Credit +

Rohan Macsen, Drawing

(o)	150	

Rent Expense

(f)	200	

Phone Expense

(g)	50	

Wages Expense

(m)	650	

Delivery Fees

		(e)	500
		(h)	600
		(n)	1,050
		Bal.	2,150

$4,900	=	$1,800	+	$3,100
$4,900	=			**$4,900**

THE TRIAL BALANCE

LO5 Prepare a trial balance and explain its purposes and linkages with the financial statements.

Recall the following two very important rules in double-entry accounting:

1. The sum of the debits must equal the sum of the credits.

   At least two accounts are affected by each transaction. This rule is so important that many computer accounting programs will not permit a transaction to be entered into the accounting system unless the debits equal the credits.

2. The accounting equation must remain in balance.

   In illustrating the transactions for Rohan's Campus Delivery, the equality of the accounting equation was verified after each transaction. Because of the large number of transactions entered each day, this is not done in practice. Instead, a trial balance is prepared periodically to determine the equality of the debits and credits. A trial balance is a list of all accounts showing the title and balance of each account. By totaling the debits and credits, their equality can be tested.

A trial balance of Rohan's accounts, taken on June 30, 20--, is shown in Figure 3-22. This date is shown on the third line of the heading. The trial balance shows that the debit and credit totals are equal in amount. This is proof that (1) in entering transactions (a) through (o), the total of the debits was equal to the total of the credits, and (2) the accounting equation has remained in balance.

A trial balance is not a formal statement or report. Normally, only the accountant sees it. As shown in Figure 3-23, a trial balance can be used as an aid in preparing the financial statements.

FIGURE 3-22 Trial Balance

ACCOUNT TITLE	DEBIT BALANCE	CREDIT BALANCE
Cash	3 7 0 00	
Accounts Receivable	6 5 0 00	
Supplies	8 0 00	
Prepaid Insurance	2 0 0 00	
Delivery Equipment	3 6 0 0 00	
Accounts Payable		1 8 0 0 00
Rohan Macsen, Capital		2 0 0 0 00
Rohan Macsen, Drawing	1 5 0 00	
Delivery Fees		2 1 5 0 00
Rent Expense	2 0 0 00	
Phone Expense	5 0 00	
Wages Expense	6 5 0 00	
	5 9 5 0 00	5 9 5 0 00

Rohan's Campus Delivery
Trial Balance
June 30, 20 --

FIGURE 3-23 Linkages Between the Trial Balance and Financial Statements

Rohan's Campus Delivery
Trial Balance
June 30, 20 --

ACCOUNT TITLE	DEBIT BALANCE	CREDIT BALANCE
Cash	3 7 0 00	
Accounts Receivable	6 5 0 00	
Supplies	8 0 00	
Prepaid Insurance	2 0 0 00	
Delivery Equipment	3 6 0 0 00	
Accounts Payable		1 8 0 0 00
Rohan Macsen, Capital		2 0 0 0 00
Rohan Macsen, Drawing	1 5 0 00	
Delivery Fees		2 1 5 0 00
Rent Expense	2 0 0 00	
Phone Expense	5 0 00	
Wages Expense	6 5 0 00	
	5 9 5 0 00	5 9 5 0 00

(continued)

FIGURE 3-23   Linkages Between the Trial Balance and Financial Statements (*concluded*)

If the beginning capital balance was $2,000 and Rohan made no additional investments, the statement would be prepared as follows:

Rohan's Campus Delivery
Statement of Owner's Equity
For Month Ended June 30, 20 --

Rohan Macsen, capital, June 1, 20 --	$2,000
Net income for June	$1,250
Less withdrawals for June	150
Increase in capital	1,100
Rohan Macsen, Capital, June 30, 20 --	$3,100

Rohan's Campus Delivery
Income Statement
For Month Ended June 30, 20 --

Revenue:		
Delivery fees		$2,150
Expenses:		
Wages expense	$650	
Rent expense	200	
Phone expense	50	
Total expenses		900
Net income		$1,250

Rohan's Campus Delivery
Statement of Owner's Equity
For Month Ended June 30, 20 --

Rohan Macsen, capital, June 1, 20 --		$ —
Investments during June		2,000
Total investment		$2,000
Net income for June	$1,250	
Less withdrawals for June	150	
Increase in capital		1,100
Rohan Macsen, capital, June 30, 20 --		$3,100

Checkpoint ✓

Complete Checkpoint-4 on page 74 to test your basic understanding of LO5.

Rohan's Campus Delivery
Balance Sheet
June 30, 20 --

Assets		Liabilities	
Cash	$ 370	Accounts payable	$1,800
Accounts receivable	650		
Supplies	80	Owner's Equity	
Prepaid insurance	200	Rohan Macsen, capital	3,100
Delivery equipment	3,600		
Total assets	$4,900	Total liabilities and owner's equity	$4,900

Self-Study

LEARNING OBJECTIVES	Key Points to Remember
LO1 **Define the parts of a T account.**	The parts of a T account are: 1. the title, 2. the debit or left side, and 3. the credit or right side. **Title** Debit = Left | Credit = Right

LEARNING OBJECTIVES	Key Points to Remember

LO2 Foot and balance a T account.

Rules for footing and balancing T accounts are:

1. The footings are directly under the debit (left) and credit (right) sides of the T account for those accounts with more than one debit or credit.
2. The balance is shown on the side with the larger footing.
3. The footing serves as the balance for accounts with entries on only one side of the account.
4. If an account has only a single entry, it is not necessary to enter a footing or balance.

LO3 Describe the effects of debits and credits on specific types of accounts.

Rules for debits and credits. (See illustration below.)

1. Assets are on the left side of the accounting equation. Therefore, increases are entered on the left (debit) side of an asset account and decreases are entered on the right (credit) side.
2. Liabilities and owner's equity are on the right side of the accounting equation. Therefore, increases are entered on the right (credit) side and decreases are entered on the left (debit) side.
3. Revenues increase owner's equity. Therefore, increases are entered on the right (credit) side and decreases are entered on the left (debit) side.
4. Expenses and drawing decrease owner's equity. Therefore, increases are entered on the left (debit) side and decreases are entered on the right (credit) side.

Accounting Equation with Owner's Equity Umbrella

LO4 Use T accounts to analyze transactions.

Picture the accounting equation in your mind as you analyze transactions. When entering transactions in T accounts:

1. The sum of the debits must equal the sum of the credits.
2. At least two accounts are affected by each transaction.
3. When finished, the accounting equation must remain in balance.

LO5 Prepare a trial balance and explain its purposes and linkages with the financial statements.

A trial balance shows that the debit and credit totals are equal. A trial balance also can be used in preparing the financial statements.

DEMONSTRATION PROBLEM

CLGL

Celia Pints opened We-Buy, You-Pay Shopping Services. For a fee that is based on the amount of research and shopping time required, Pints and her associates will shop for almost anything from groceries to home furnishings. Business is particularly heavy around Christmas and in early summer. The business operates from a rented store front. The associates receive a commission based on the revenues they produce and a mileage reimbursement for the use of their personal automobiles for shopping trips. Pints decided to use the following accounts to record transactions.

Assets	Owner's Equity
Cash	Celia Pints, Capital
Accounts Receivable	Celia Pints, Drawing
Office Equipment	Revenue
Computer Equipment	Shopping Fees
Liabilities	Expenses
Accounts Payable	Rent Expense
Notes Payable	Phone Expense
	Commissions Expense
	Utilities Expense
	Travel Expense

The following transactions are for the month of December 20--.

(a) Pints invested cash in the business, $30,000.

(b) Bought office equipment for $10,000. Paid $2,000 in cash and promised to pay the balance over the next four months.

(c) Paid rent for December, $500.

(d) Provided shopping services for customers on account, $5,200.

(e) Paid phone bill, $90.

(f) Borrowed cash from the bank by signing a note payable, $5,000.

(g) Bought a computer and printer, $4,800.

(h) Collected cash from customers for services performed on account, $4,000.

(i) Paid commissions to associates for revenues generated during the first half of the month, $3,500.

(j) Paid utility bill, $600.

(k) Paid cash on account for the office equipment purchased in transaction (b), $2,000.

(l) Earned shopping fees of $13,200: $6,000 in cash and $7,200 on account.

(m) Paid commissions to associates for last half of month, $7,000.

(n) Paid mileage reimbursements for the month, $1,500.

(o) Paid cash on note payable to bank, $1,000.

(p) Pints withdrew cash for personal use, $2,000.

REQUIRED

1. Enter the transactions for December in T accounts. Use the accounting equation as a guide for setting up the T accounts.

2. Foot the T accounts and determine their balances as necessary.

3. Prepare a trial balance of the accounts as of December 31 of the current year.

4. Prepare an income statement for the month ended December 31 of the current year.

5. Prepare a statement of owner's equity for the month ended December 31 of the current year.

6. Prepare a balance sheet as of December 31 of the current year.

Solution 1, 2.

Assets		=	Liabilities		+	Owner's Equity	
Debit +	Credit −		Debit −	Credit +		Debit −	Credit +

Cash

(a) 30,000	(b) 2,000		
(f) 5,000	(c) 500		
(h) 4,000	(e) 90		
(l) 6,000	(g) 4,800		
45,000	(i) 3,500		
	(j) 600		
	(k) 2,000		
	(m) 7,000		
	(n) 1,500		
	(o) 1,000		
	(p) 2,000		
	24,990		

Bal. 20,010

Accounts Receivable

(d) 5,200	(h) 4,000
(l) 7,200	
12,400	

Bal. 8,400

Office Equipment

(b) 10,000	

Computer Equipment

(g) 4,800	

Accounts Payable

(k) 2,000	(b) 8,000
	Bal. 6,000

Notes Payable

(o) 1,000	(f) 5,000
	Bal. 4,000

Celia Pints, Capital

	(a) 30,000

Drawing		Expenses		Revenues	
Debit +	Credit −	Debit +	Credit −	Debit −	Credit +

Celia Pints, Drawing

(p) 2,000	

Rent Expense

(c) 500	

Shopping Fees

	(d) 5,200
	(l) 13,200
	Bal. 18,400

Phone Expense

(e) 90	

Commissions Expense

(i) 3,500	
(m) 7,000	
Bal. 10,500	

Utilities Expense

(j) 600	

Travel Expense

(n) 1,500	

$43,210	=	$10,000	+	$33,210
$43,210	=		**$43,210**	

3.

We-Buy, You-Pay Shopping Services Trial Balance December 31, 20 --										
ACCOUNT TITLE	DEBIT BALANCE					CREDIT BALANCE				
Cash	20	0	1	0	00					
Accounts Receivable	8	4	0	0	00					
Office Equipment	10	0	0	0	00					
Computer Equipment	4	8	0	0	00					
Accounts Payable						6	0	0	0	00
Notes Payable						4	0	0	0	00
Celia Pints, Capital						30	0	0	0	00
Celia Pints, Drawing	2	0	0	0	00					
Shopping Fees						18	4	0	0	00
Rent Expense		5	0	0	00					
Phone Expense			9	0	00					
Commissions Expense	10	5	0	0	00					
Utilities Expense		6	0	0	00					
Travel Expense	1	5	0	0	00					
	58	4	0	0	00	58	4	0	0	00

4.

We-Buy, You-Pay Shopping Services Income Statement For Month Ended December 31, 20 --		
Revenue:		
Shopping fees		$18,400
Expenses:		
Commissions expense	$10,500	
Travel expense	1,500	
Utilities expense	600	
Rent expense	500	
Phone expense	90	
Total expenses		13,190
Net income		$ 5,210

5.

We-Buy, You-Pay Shopping Services Statement of Owner's Equity For Month Ended December 31, 20 - -		
Celia Pints, capital, December 1, 20 --		$ —
Investments during December		30,000
Total investment		$30,000
Net income for December	$5,210	
Less withdrawals for December	2,000	
Increase in capital		3,210
Celia Pints, capital, December 31, 20 --		$33,210

6.

We-Buy, You-Pay Shopping Services Balance Sheet December 31, 20 - -			
Assets		**Liabilities**	
Cash	$20,010	Accounts payable	$ 6,000
Accounts receivable	8,400	Notes payable	4,000
Office equipment	10,000	Total liabilities	$10,000
Computer equipment	4,800		
		Owner's Equity	
		Celia Pints, capital	33,210
Total assets	$43,210	Total liabilities and owner's equity	$43,210

KEY TERMS

balance (51) The difference between the footings of an account.

credit (52) To enter an amount on the right side of an account.

credit balance (54) The normal balance of liability, owner's equity, and revenue accounts.

debit (52) To enter an amount on the left side of an account.

debit balance (54) The normal balance of asset, expense, and drawing accounts.

double-entry accounting (51)   A system in which each transaction has a dual effect on the accounting elements.

footings (51)   The total dollar amounts on the debit and credit sides of an account.

normal balance (54)   The side of an account that is increased.

trial balance (66)   A list of all accounts, showing the title and balance of each account, used to prove that the sum of the debits equals the sum of the credits.

SELF-STUDY TEST QUESTIONS

True/False

1. **LO3**   To debit an account is to enter an amount on the left side of the account.

2. **LO3**   Liability accounts normally have debit balances.

3. **LO3**   Increases in owner's equity are entered as credits.

4. **LO3**   Revenue accounts normally have debit balances.

5. **LO3**   To credit an account is to enter an amount on the right side of the account.

6. **LO3**   A debit to an asset account will decrease it.

Multiple Choice

1. **LO3**   A common example of an asset is

   (a) Professional Fees.
   (b) Rent Expense.
   (c) Accounts Receivable.
   (d) Accounts Payable.

2. **LO3**   The accounting equation may be expressed as

   (a) Assets = Liabilities − Owner's Equity.
   (b) Assets = Liabilities + Owner's Equity.
   (c) Liabilities = Owner's Equity − Assets.
   (d) all of the above.

3. **LO3**   Liability, owner's equity, and revenue accounts normally have

   (a) debit balances.
   (b) large balances.
   (c) negative balances.
   (d) credit balances.

4. **LO4**   To record the payment of rent expense, an accountant would

   (a) debit Cash; credit Rent Expense.
   (b) debit Rent Expense; debit Cash.
   (c) debit Rent Expense; credit Cash.
   (d) credit Rent Expense; credit Cash.

5. **LO4**   An investment of cash by the owner will

   (a) increase assets and owner's equity.
   (b) increase assets and liabilities.
   (c) increase liabilities and owner's equity.
   (d) increase owner's equity and decrease liabilities.

Checkpoint Exercises

1. **LO2** Foot and balance the accounts receivable T account shown below.

Accounts Receivable	
100	50
200	30

2. **LO3** Complete the following questions using either "debit" or "credit":
   (a) The asset account Supplies is increased with a _____.
   (b) The owner's capital account is increased with a _____.
   (c) The rent expense account is increased with a _____.

3. **LO4** Analyze the following transaction using the T accounts provided below. Robb Todd purchased equipment for $300 cash.

Cash		Equipment	

4. **LO5** The following accounts have normal balances. Prepare a trial balance. Accounts Payable, $20; Accounts Receivable, $90; Capital, $40; Sales, $200; Cash, $100; Rent Expense, $70.

The answers to the Self-Study Test Questions are at the end of the chapter (page 84).

Applying Your Knowledge

REVIEW QUESTIONS

LO1	1. What are the three major parts of a T account?
LO1	2. What is the left side of the T account called? the right side?
LO2	3. What is a footing?
LO3	4. What is the relationship between the revenue and expense accounts and the owner's equity account?
LO5	5. What is the function of the trial balance?

SERIES A EXERCISES

E 3-1A   (LO2)

✓ Cash bal.: $1,200 (Dr.)

FOOT AND BALANCE A T ACCOUNT Foot and balance the cash T account shown below.

Cash	
500	100
400	200
600	

E 3-2A (LO3)

DEBIT AND CREDIT ANALYSIS Complete the following statements using either "debit" or "credit":

(a) The cash account is increased with a _____.

(b) The owner's capital account is increased with a _____.

(c) The delivery equipment account is increased with a _____.

(d) The cash account is decreased with a _____.

(e) The liability account Accounts Payable is increased with a _____.

(f) The revenue account Delivery Fees is increased with a _____.

(g) The asset account Accounts Receivable is increased with a _____.

(h) The rent expense account is increased with a _____.

(i) The owner's drawing account is increased with a _____.

E 3-3A (LO2/3/4)

✓ Cash bal. after (c): $3,100 (Dr.)

SHOW
ME HOW

ANALYSIS OF T ACCOUNTS Richard Gibbs began a business called Richard's Shoe Repair.

1. Create T accounts for Cash; Supplies; Richard Gibbs, Capital; and Utilities Expense. Identify the following transactions by letter and place them on the proper side of the T accounts:

   (a) Invested cash in the business, $6,500.

   (b) Purchased supplies for cash, $700.

   (c) Paid utility bill, $2,700.

2. Foot the T account for cash and enter the ending balance.

E 3-4A (LO3)

NORMAL BALANCE OF ACCOUNT Indicate the normal balance (debit or credit) for each of the following accounts:

1. Cash
2. Wages Expense
3. Accounts Payable
4. Owner's Drawing
5. Supplies
6. Owner's Capital
7. Equipment

E 3-5A (LO4)

TRANSACTION ANALYSIS Linda Kipp started a business on May 1, 20--. Analyze the following transactions for the first month of business using T accounts. Label each T account with the title of the account affected and then place the transaction letter and the dollar amount on the debit or credit side.

(a) Invested cash in the business, $5,000.

(b) Bought equipment for cash, $700.

(c) Bought equipment on account, $600.

(d) Paid cash on account for equipment purchased in transaction (c), $400.

(e) Withdrew cash for personal use, $900.

E 3-6A (LO2)

✓ Cash bal. after (e): $3,000 (Dr.)

FOOT AND BALANCE T ACCOUNTS Foot and balance the T accounts prepared in Exercise 3-5A if necessary.

E 3-7A (LO2/4)

✓ Cash bal. after (k):
$24,400 (Dr.)

SHOW
ME HOW

ANALYSIS OF TRANSACTIONS Charles Chadwick opened a business called Charlie's Detective Service in January 20--. Set up T accounts for the following accounts: Cash; Accounts Receivable; Office Supplies; Computer Equipment; Office Furniture; Accounts Payable; Charles Chadwick, Capital; Charles Chadwick, Drawing; Professional Fees; Rent Expense; and Utilities Expense.

The following transactions occurred during the first month of business. Record these transactions in T accounts. After all transactions are recorded, foot and balance the accounts if necessary.

(a) Invested cash in the business, $30,000.

(b) Bought office supplies for cash, $300.

(c) Bought office furniture for cash, $5,000.

(d) Purchased computer and printer on account, $8,000.

(e) Received cash from clients for services, $3,000.

(f) Paid cash on account for computer and printer purchased in transaction (d), $4,000.

(g) Earned professional fees on account during the month, $9,000.

(h) Paid cash for office rent for January, $1,500.

(i) Paid utility bills for the month, $800.

(j) Received cash from clients billed in transaction (g), $6,000.

(k) Withdrew cash for personal use, $3,000.

E 3-8A   (LO5)

✓ Trial bal. total debits: $46,000

SHOW ME HOW

TRIAL BALANCE Based on the transactions recorded in Exercise 3-7A, prepare a trial balance for Charlie's Detective Service as of January 31, 20--.

E 3-9A   (LO5)

✓ Trial bal. total debits: $42,800

TRIAL BALANCE The following accounts have normal balances. Prepare a trial balance for Kenny's Lawn Service as of September 30, 20--.

Cash	$10,000
Accounts Receivable	6,000
Supplies	1,600
Prepaid Insurance	1,200
Delivery Equipment	16,000
Accounts Payable	4,000
Kenny Young, Capital	20,000
Kenny Young, Drawing	2,000
Delivery Fees	18,800
Wages Expense	4,200
Rent Expense	1,800

E 3-10A, E 3-11A, E 3-12A

Provided below is a trial balance for Juanita's Delivery Service. **Use this trial balance for Exercises 3-10A, 3-11A, and 3-12A.**

Juanita's Delivery Service
Trial Balance
September 30, 20 --

ACCOUNT TITLE	DEBIT BALANCE	CREDIT BALANCE
Cash	5 0 0 0 00	
Accounts Receivable	3 0 0 0 00	
Supplies	8 0 0 00	
Prepaid Insurance	6 0 0 00	
Delivery Equipment	8 0 0 0 00	
Accounts Payable		2 0 0 0 00
Juanita Raye, Capital		10 0 0 0 00
Juanita Raye, Drawing	1 0 0 0 00	
Delivery Fees		9 4 0 0 00
Wages Expense	2 1 0 0 00	
Rent Expense	9 0 0 00	
	21 4 0 0 00	21 4 0 0 00

E 3-10A   (LO5)
✓ Net income: $6,400

SHOW
ME HOW

INCOME STATEMENT From the information in the trial balance presented above, prepare an income statement for Juanita's Delivery Service for the month ended September 30, 20--.

E 3-11A   (LO5)
✓ Capital, 9/30: $15,400

SHOW
ME HOW

STATEMENT OF OWNER'S EQUITY From the information in the trial balance presented above, prepare a statement of owner's equity for Juanita's Delivery Service for the month ended September 30, 20--.

E 3-12A   (LO5)
✓ Total assets, 9/30: $17,400

SHOW
ME HOW

BALANCE SHEET From the information in the trial balance presented for Juanita's Delivery Service on page 76, prepare a balance sheet for Juanita's Delivery Service as of September 30, 20--.

SERIES A PROBLEMS

P 3-13A   (LO2/4/5)
✓ Cash bal. after (p): $21,805 (Dr.)
✓ Trial bal. total debits: $44,900

SHOW
ME HOW

T ACCOUNTS AND TRIAL BALANCE Wilhelm Kohl started a business in May 20-- called Kohl's Home Repair. Kohl hired a part-time college student as an assistant. Kohl has decided to use the following accounts for recording transactions:

Assets	Owner's Equity
Cash	Wilhelm Kohl, Capital
Accounts Receivable	Wilhelm Kohl, Drawing
Office Supplies	Revenue
Prepaid Insurance	Service Fees
Equipment	Expenses
Van	Rent Expense
Liabilities	Wages Expense
Accounts Payable	Phone Expense
	Gas and Oil Expense

The following transactions occurred during May:

(a) Invested cash in the business, $25,000.
(b) Purchased a used van for cash, $6,000.
(c) Purchased equipment on account, $4,000.
(d) Received cash for services rendered, $7,500.
(e) Paid cash on account owed from transaction (c), $2,300.
(f) Paid rent for the month, $850.
(g) Paid phone bill, $230.
(h) Earned revenue on account, $4,500.
(i) Purchased office supplies for cash, $160.
(j) Paid wages to an assistant, $800.
(k) Purchased a one-year insurance policy, $1,100.
(l) Received cash from services performed in transaction (h), $3,400.
(m) Paid cash for gas and oil expense on the van, $155.
(n) Purchased additional equipment for $4,200, paying $1,500 cash and spreading the remaining payments over the next 10 months.
(o) Earned service fees for the remainder of the month of $3,500: $1,900 in cash and $1,600 on account.
(p) Withdrew cash at the end of the month, $2,900.

1. Enter the transactions in T accounts, identifying each transaction with its corresponding letter.

2. Foot and balance the accounts where necessary.

3. Prepare a trial balance as of May 31, 20--.

P 3-14A (LO5)

✓ Net income: $13,465

✓ Owner's equity, 5/31: $35,565

✓ Total assets, 5/31: $39,965

NET INCOME AND CHANGE IN OWNER'S EQUITY Refer to the trial balance of Kohl's Home Repair in Problem 3-13A to determine the following information. Use the format provided below.

1. a. Total revenue for the month _____

   b. Total expenses for the month _____

   c. Net income for the month _____

2. a. Wilhelm Kohl's original investment

   in the business _____

       + Net income for the month _____

       − Owner's drawing _____

   Increase (decrease) in capital _____

       = Ending owner's equity _____

   b. End of month accounting equation:

Assets	=	Liabilities	+	Owner's Equity
_____	=	_____	+	_____

P 3-15A (LO5)

✓ NI: $13,465

✓ Capital, 5/31/20--: $35,565

✓ Total assets 5/31/20--: $39,965

FINANCIAL STATEMENTS Refer to the trial balance in Problem 3-13A and to the analysis of the change in owner's equity in Problem 3-14A.

1. Prepare an income statement for Kohl's Home Repair for the month ended May 31, 20--.

2. Prepare a statement of owner's equity for Kohl's Home Repair for the month ended May 31, 20--.

3. Prepare a balance sheet for Kohl's Home Repair as of May 31, 20--.

SERIES B EXERCISES

E 3-1B (LO2)

✓ Accts. Pay: $400 (Cr.)

FOOT AND BALANCE A T ACCOUNT Foot and balance the accounts payable T account shown below.

Accounts Payable	
300	450
250	350
	150

E 3-2B (LO3)

DEBIT AND CREDIT ANALYSIS Complete the following statements using either "debit" or "credit":

(a) The asset account Prepaid Insurance is increased with a _____.

(b) The owner's drawing account is increased with a _____.

(c) The asset account Accounts Receivable is decreased with a _____.

(d) The liability account Accounts Payable is decreased with a _____.

(e) The owner's capital account is increased with a _____.

(f) The revenue account Professional Fees is increased with a _____.

(g) The expense account Repair Expense is increased with a _____.

(h) The asset account Cash is decreased with a _____.

(i) The asset account Delivery Equipment is decreased with a _____.

E 3-3B   (LO2/3/4)

✓ Cash bal. after (c): $3,900 (Dr.)

SHOW
ME HOW

ANALYSIS OF T ACCOUNTS Roberto Alvarez began a business called Roberto's Fix-It Shop.

1. Create T accounts for Cash; Supplies; Roberto Alvarez, Capital; and Utilities Expense. Identify the following transactions by letter and place them on the proper side of the T accounts:

    (a) Invested cash in the business, $6,000.

    (b) Purchased supplies for cash, $1,200.

    (c) Paid utility bill, $900.

2. Foot the T account for cash and enter the ending balance.

E 3-4B   (LO3)

NORMAL BALANCE OF ACCOUNT Indicate the normal balance (debit or credit) for each of the following accounts:

1. Cash

2. Rent Expense

3. Notes Payable

4. Owner's Drawing

5. Accounts Receivable

6. Owner's Capital

7. Tools

E 3-5B   (LO4)

TRANSACTION ANALYSIS George Atlas started a business on June 1, 20--. Analyze the following transactions for the first month of business using T accounts. Label each T account with the title of the account affected and then place the transaction letter and the dollar amount on the debit or credit side.

(a) Invested cash in the business, $7,000.

(b) Purchased equipment for cash, $900.

(c) Purchased equipment on account, $1,500.

(d) Paid cash on account for equipment purchased in transaction (c), $800.

(e) Withdrew cash for personal use, $1,100.

E 3-6B   (LO2)

✓ Cash bal. after (e): $4,200 (Dr.)

FOOT AND BALANCE T ACCOUNTS Foot and balance the T accounts prepared in Exercise 3-5B if necessary.

E 3-7B   (LO2/4)

✓ Cash bal. after (k): $9,000 (Dr.)

SHOW
ME HOW

ANALYSIS OF TRANSACTIONS Nicole Lawrence opened a business called Nickie's Neat Ideas in January 20--. Set up T accounts for the following accounts: Cash; Accounts Receivable; Office Supplies; Computer Equipment; Office Furniture; Accounts Payable; Nicole Lawrence, Capital; Nicole Lawrence, Drawing; Professional Fees; Rent Expense; and Utilities Expense.

The following transactions occurred during the first month of business. Record these transactions in T accounts. After all transactions have been recorded, foot and balance the accounts if necessary.

(a) Invested cash in the business, $18,000.

(b) Purchased office supplies for cash, $500.

(c) Purchased office furniture for cash, $8,000.

(d) Purchased computer and printer on account, $5,000.

(e) Received cash from clients for services, $4,000.

(f) Paid cash on account for computer and printer purchased in transaction (d), $2,000.

(g) Earned professional fees on account during the month, $7,000.

(h) Paid office rent for January, $900.

(i) Paid utility bills for the month, $600.

(j) Received cash from clients that were billed previously in transaction (g), $3,000.

(k) Withdrew cash for personal use, $4,000.

E 3-8B   (LO5)

✓ Trial bal. total debits: $32,000

SHOW ME HOW

TRIAL BALANCE Based on the transactions recorded in Exercise 3-7B, prepare a trial balance for Nickie's Neat Ideas as of January 31, 20--.

E 3-9B   (LO5)

✓ Trial bal. total debits: $55,000

TRIAL BALANCE The following accounts have normal balances. Prepare a trial balance for Betty's Cleaning Service as of September 30, 20--.

Cash	$14,000	Betty Par, Capital	$24,000
Accounts Receivable	8,000	Betty Par, Drawing	4,000
Supplies	1,200	Delivery Fees	25,000
Prepaid Insurance	1,800	Wages Expense	6,000
Delivery Equipment	18,000	Rent Expense	2,000
Accounts Payable	6,000		

E 3-10B, E 3-11B, E 3-12B

Provided below is a trial balance for Bill's Delivery Service. **Use this trial balance for Exercises 3-10B, 3-11B, and 3-12B.**

Bill's Delivery Service
Trial Balance
September 30, 20 --

ACCOUNT TITLE	DEBIT BALANCE	CREDIT BALANCE
Cash	7 0 0 0 00	
Accounts Receivable	4 0 0 0 00	
Supplies	6 0 0 00	
Prepaid Insurance	9 0 0 00	
Delivery Equipment	9 0 0 0 00	
Accounts Payable		3 0 0 0 00
Bill Swift, Capital		12 0 0 0 00
Bill Swift, Drawing	2 0 0 0 00	
Delivery Fees		12 5 0 0 00
Wages Expense	3 0 0 0 00	
Rent Expense	1 0 0 0 00	
	27 5 0 0 00	27 5 0 0 00

CHALLENGE PROBLEM

This problem challenges you to apply your cumulative accounting knowledge to move a step beyond the material in the chapter.

✓ Capital, 8/31/20--: $600

Your friend Chris Stevick started a part-time business in June and has been keeping her own accounting records. She has been preparing monthly financial statements. At the end of August, she stopped by to show you her performance for the most recent month. She prepared the following income statement and balance sheet:

Income Statement		Balance Sheet	End of Month	Beginning of Month
Revenues	$500	Cash	$600	$400
Expenses	200	Capital	600	400
Net income	$300			

Chris has also heard that there is a statement of owner's equity, but she is not familiar with that statement. She asks if you can help her prepare one. After confirming that she has no assets other than cash, no liabilities, and made no additional investments in the business in August, you agree.

REQUIRED

1. Prepare the statement of owner's equity for your friend's most recent month.
2. What suggestions might you give to Chris that would make her income statement more useful?

Answers to Self-Study Test Questions

True/False

1. T
2. F (Liability accounts normally have credit balances.)
3. T
4. F (credit balances)
5. T
6. F (increase)

Multiple Choice

1. c   2. b   3. d   4. c   5. a

Checkpoint Exercises

1.
Accounts Receivable	
100	50
200	30
300	**80**
Bal. 220	

2. (a) The asset account Supplies is increased with a <u>debit</u>.
   (b) The owner's capital account is increased with a <u>credit</u>.
   (c) The rent expense account is increased with a <u>debit</u>.

3.
Cash		Equipment	
300		300	

4.
Trial Balance		
Cash	100	
Accounts Receivable	90	
Accounts Payable		20
Capital		40
Sales		200
Rent Expense	70	
	260	260

E 3-10B   (LO5)
✓ Net income: $8,500
SHOW ME HOW

INCOME STATEMENT From the information in the trial balance presented above, prepare an income statement for Bill's Delivery Service for the month ended September 30, 20--.

E 3-11B   (LO5)
✓ Capital, 9/30: $18,500
SHOW ME HOW

STATEMENT OF OWNER'S EQUITY From the information in the trial balance presented above, prepare a statement of owner's equity for Bill's Delivery Service for the month ended September 30, 20--.

E 3-12B   (LO5)
✓ Total assets, 9/30: $21,500

SHOW ME HOW

BALANCE SHEET From the information in the trial balance presented for Bill's Delivery Service on page 80, prepare a balance sheet for Bill's Delivery Service as of September 30, 20--.

SERIES B PROBLEMS

P 3-13B   (LO2/4/5)
✓ Cash bal. after (p): $20,200 (Dr.)
✓ Trial bal. total debits: $44,300

SHOW ME HOW

T ACCOUNTS AND TRIAL BALANCE Sue Jantz started a business in August 20-- called Jantz Plumbing Service. Jantz hired a part-time college student as an administrative assistant. Jantz has decided to use the following accounts:

Assets	Owner's Equity
Cash	Sue Jantz, Capital
Accounts Receivable	Sue Jantz, Drawing
Office Supplies	Revenue
Prepaid Insurance	Service Fees
Plumbing Equipment	Expenses
Van	Rent Expense
Liabilities	Wages Expense
Accounts Payable	Phone Expense
	Advertising Expense

The following transactions occurred during August:

(a) Invested cash in the business, $30,000.
(b) Purchased a used van for cash, $8,000.
(c) Purchased plumbing equipment on account, $4,000.
(d) Received cash for services rendered, $3,000.
(e) Paid cash on account owed from transaction (c), $1,000.
(f) Paid rent for the month, $700.
(g) Paid phone bill, $100.
(h) Earned revenue on account, $4,000.
(i) Purchased office supplies for cash, $300.
(j) Paid wages to student, $500.
(k) Purchased a one-year insurance policy, $800.
(l) Received cash from services performed in transaction (h), $3,000.
(m) Paid cash for advertising expense, $2,000.
(n) Purchased additional plumbing equipment for $2,000, paying $500 cash and spreading the remaining payments over the next six months.
(o) Earned revenue from services for the remainder of the month of $2,800: $1,100 in cash and $1,700 on account.
(p) Withdrew cash at the end of the month, $3,000.

1. Enter the transactions in T accounts, identifying each transaction with its corresponding letter.

2. Foot and balance the accounts where necessary.

3. Prepare a trial balance as of August 31, 20--.

P 3-14B   (LO5)

✓ Net income: $6,500

✓ Owner's equity, 8/31: $33,500

✓ Total assets, 8/31: $38,000

NET INCOME AND CHANGE IN OWNER'S EQUITY Refer to the trial balance of Jantz Plumbing Service in Problem 3-13B to determine the following information. Use the format provided below.

1. a. Total revenue for the month   _____

    b. Total expenses for the month   _____

    c. Net income for the month   _____

2. a. Sue Jantz's original investment in the business   _____

        + Net income for the month   _____

        – Owner's drawing   _____

        Increase (decrease) in capital   _____

        = Ending owner's equity   _____

    b. End of month accounting equation:

Assets	=	Liabilities	+	Owner's Equity
_____	=	_____	+	_____

P 3-15B   (LO5)

✓ NI: $6,500

✓ Capital, 8/31/20--: $33,500

✓ Total assets, 8/31/20--: $38,000

FINANCIAL STATEMENTS Refer to the trial balance in Problem 3-13B and to the analysis of the change in owner's equity in Problem 3-14B.

1. Prepare an income statement for Jantz Plumbing Service for the month ended August 31, 20--.

2. Prepare a statement of owner's equity for Jantz Plumbing Service for the month ended August 31, 20--.

3. Prepare a balance sheet for Jantz Plumbing Service as of August 31, 20--.

☑ Check List
- ☐ Managing
- ☐ Planning
- ☐ Drafting
- ☐ Break
- ☐ Revising
- ☐ Managing

MANAGING YOUR WRITING

Write a one-page memo to your instructor explaining how you could use the double-entry system to maintain records of your personal finances. What types of accounts would you use for the accounting elements?

MASTERY PROBLEM

✓ Cash bal. after (p): $1,980 (Dr.)

✓ Trial bal. debit total: $5,840

✓ Net income: $500

✓ Total assets: $4,300

Craig Fisher started a lawn service called Craig's Quick Cut to earn money over the summer months. Fisher has decided to use the following accounts for recording transactions:

(continued)

Assets	Revenue
Cash	Lawn Fees
Accounts Receivable	Expenses
Mowing Equipment	Rent Expense
Lawn Tools	Wages Expense
Liabilities	Phone Expense
Accounts Payable	Gas and Oil Expense
Notes Payable	Transportation Expense
Owner's Equity	
Craig Fisher, Capital	
Craig Fisher, Drawing	

Transactions for the month of June are listed below.

(a) Invested cash in the business, $3,000.

(b) Bought mowing equipment for $1,000: paid $200 in cash and promised to pay the balance over the next four months.

(c) Paid garage rent for June, $50.

(d) Provided lawn services for customers on account, $520.

(e) Paid phone bill, $30.

(f) Borrowed cash from the bank by signing a note payable, $500.

(g) Bought lawn tools, $480.

(h) Collected cash from customers for services performed on account in transaction (d), $400.

(i) Paid associates for lawn work done during the first half of the month, $350.

(j) Paid for gas and oil for the equipment, $60.

(k) Paid cash on account for the mowing equipment purchased in transaction (b), $200.

(l) Earned lawn fees of $1,320: $600 in cash and $720 on account.

(m) Paid associates for last half of month, $700.

(n) Reimbursed associates for costs incurred using their own vehicles for transportation, $150.

(o) Paid on note payable to bank, $100.

(p) Withdrew cash for personal use, $200.

1. Enter the transactions for June in T accounts. Use the accounting equation as a guide for setting up the T accounts.

2. Foot and balance the T accounts where necessary.

3. Prepare a trial balance of the accounts as of June 30, 20--.

4. Prepare an income statement for the month ended June 30, 20--.

5. Prepare a statement of owner's equity for the month ended June 30, 20--.

6. Prepare a balance sheet as of June 30, 20--.